# A*b*normal
# PSYCHOLOGY
## Clinical and Scientific Perspectives

### Fifth Edition

**Charles A. Lyons**     **Barclay Martin**

# BVT Publishing

**Better textbooks, better prices**

www.BVTPublishing.com

Publisher and Marketing Manager: Richard Schofield

Managing Editor: Joyce Bianchini

Permissions Coordinator, Project Research and Development: Jenefier Winchell

Production and Fulfillment Manager: Janai Bryand

Cover and Interior Design: Esther Scannell

Typesetting Manager: Rhonda Minnema

Proofreader: Annie Schofield

Pre-production Coordinator and Photo Researcher: Tommi Morgenthal

Photo Credits: Cover and Title page image Getty Image; page xi image, Dreamstime.

Softcover ISBN: 978-1-61882-637-4

Looseleaf ISBN: 978-1-61882-638-1

TEXTBOOK-Plus Bundle ISBN: 978-1-61882-634-3

# About the Authors

Charles A. Lyons is Professor of Psychology at Eastern Oregon University, where he teaches courses in abnormal psychology, clinical interventions, behavior analysis, psychological assessment, human sexuality, and evolution & behavior.

He earned his PhD from Utah State University with a specialization in the Analysis of Behavior. As a licensed clinical psychologist, he worked for several years with inpatient populations at a large state psychiatric facility where he provided treatment, assessment, and forensic evaluations.

As a researcher, he has published articles on animal behavior, basic learning processes, language, and addictive behaviors. His most recent interests include social and compulsive gambling.

Barclay Martin received his PhD in Psychology from Stanford University in 1953. He taught at the University of Wisconsin at Madison before joining the faculty at the University of North Carolina at Chapel Hill in 1971. The author of numerous articles and books, he retired in 1990.

# Brief Contents

# Contents

**CHAPTER 1**

## Introduction..... 3

**CHAPTER 2**

## Historical Perspectives..... 23

**CHAPTER 3**

## Contemporary Frameworks..... 49

**CHAPTER 4**

## Classification, Diagnosis, and Assessment . . . . . . . 87

**CHAPTER 5**

## Stress and Trauma-Related Disorders . . . . . . . . . 113

**CHAPTER 6**

## Anxiety and Obsessive-Compulsive Disorders . . . . . . . 139

**CHAPTER 7**

## Somatic Symptom and Dissociative Disorders . . . . . . . 165

## CHAPTER 8
# Personality Disorders ....... 189

## CHAPTER 9
# Sexual and Gender Disorders ....... 217

## CHAPTER 10
# Schizophrenia and Psychotic Disorders ....... 247

## CHAPTER 11
## Mood Disorders and Suicide . . . . . 285

## CHAPTER 12
## Substance-Related and Addictive Disorders . . . . . . . 319

**CHAPTER 13**

# Neurodevelopmental and Disruptive Disorders........... 355

**CHAPTER 14**

# Eating, Sleep, and Elimination Disorders........... 389

**CHAPTER 15**

# Neurocognitive Disorders ....... 415

**CHAPTER 16**

# Legal, Ethical, and Professional Issues in Abnormal Psychology

# Preface

The previous edition of *Abnormal Psychology: Clinical and Scientific Perspectives* was prepared with the goal of producing a useful, inexpensive reference resource that could serve as a primary text for students in undergraduate abnormal psychology courses. This new (5th) edition continues that intent, with the additional goal of clarifying the extensive changes made in the official system for classifying mental disorders, the *Diagnostic and Statistical Manual of Mental Disorders,* Fifth Edition (*DSM-5*). Besides helping readers to understand the *DSM-5* and to recognize the variety of treatments available, I hope to also encourage critical thinking and appreciation of the value of evidence.

This edition incorporates several improvements, including:

- Thorough description of *DSM-5* classification, with frequent examples of diagnostic criteria and highlighted changes from the *DSM-IV*

- Extensive attention to diagnostic reliability and validity

- Coverage of continued controversies within psychiatry and psychology

- Many new and updated references from the professional literature

- Expanded Glossary

- Improved Subject and Author Index

- New "Questions For Study" at the end of each chapter

- Updated student study materials including practice quizzes, instructor's test banks, and PowerPoint™ slides at www.BVTLab.com

- Available in a variety of formats ranging from eBook to bound textbook

The original framework of Barclay Martin's *Abnormal Psychology: Clinical and Scientific Perspectives* reflected the substantial changes taking place in clinical psychology and psychiatry in the early 1980s. At that time, a new diagnostic system for psychopathology (the *DSM-III*) had appeared and Martin recognized the implications of the shift from a more subjective and analytic era in abnormal psychology to the less theory-dependent, more objective *DSM-III* model. The value of a science of clinical psychology was becoming apparent and issues such as diagnostic reliability, validity, and empirical outcome data began to drive the classification and treatment of mental disorders.

The present text reflects the extensive subsequent developments in research and practice since the *DSM-III*: In the past 33 years, the *DSM* has undergone four revisions; new diagnostic categories have been added, others have been proposed, and still others modified or removed. Thousands of research studies have been published exploring the biological, genetic, social, cognitive, and behavioral foundations of psychopathology; the effectiveness of various psychological and biological interventions; the incidence of disorders among populations; and the usefulness of different classifications. A strongly biomedical model of abnormal behavior became dominant within psychiatry, enabling the proliferation of pharmacological interventions for nearly every *DSM*-identified condition. Still, many of the questions about etiology and treatment considered in Martin's text remain unanswered. In nearly all cases of mental disorder, there are no biological markers or laboratory tests that can identify or confirm any *DSM* diagnosis. Many contributory factors have been identified, but any necessary or sufficient causes of mental disorders remain elusive. Medications can offer some symptom relief; but, as of yet, they provide no cures, nor do they correct any presumed underlying biological abnormalities. Indeed, for many conditions, psychological interventions have been developed that are at least as effective as medication, with fewer side-effects and lower risk of relapse.

The history of abnormal psychology contains many conceptual blind alleys and mistaken assumptions. Adopting a scientific perspective does not prevent such errors, but it does allow us to eventually recognize them. The current state of the science reminds us that we have often been too quick to oversimplify and too slow to think skeptically about both causes and treatments. Inevitably, mental disorders are defined within a social and cultural context, diagnosed within an interpersonal behavioral exchange, and treated within a biological-environmental interaction; they are bio-psycho-social developments. Therefore, I have endeavored to avoid the use of the common terms "mental illness" or "mental disease"—which may imply that we know more than we actually do—and instead refer to these conditions more accurately as "mental disorders." It should be noted that this informed skepticism does not discount the very real distress and disability associated with many *DSM* conditions, nor the importance of prompt and effective treatment.

There is always a danger in such an environment that pseudoscience can masquerade as an acceptable alternative. There are dozens, if not hundreds, of competing therapies for common disorders such as depression and anxiety. The high level of nonspecific (or placebo) response in treatment increases the risk of promoting ineffective therapies and fosters conceptual confusion. Fortunately, such problems are ultimately solved by the scientific method itself through careful comparisons, empirical testing, and evaluation of outcomes. I have highlighted research involving direct treatment comparisons or the use of randomized controlled trials that provides empirical support for any particular therapeutic intervention over others.

Because the *DSM* model is so widely accepted, I have provided a careful description of the current diagnostic system (the *DSM-5*), tracing the evolution of diagnosis and treatment within various categories of mental disorders while also providing data on the reliability and validity of these diagnoses whenever possible. The professional literature on psychopathology is enormous and continually expanding. I have given preference to reviewing the more empirical and evaluative publications and, as a result, articles from neuroscience, behavioral psychology, and cognitive psychology are over-represented in the bibliography. I readily admit to a bias in favor of the scientific method over all other approaches in the field. However, I also accept that outcomes and consequences drive the selective process, and I realize that what may appear to be today's truth may be tomorrow's folly. We can expect continued revision of the content and structure of our diagnostic system, as well as our treatments. I hope to have correctly reported the current state of affairs within this fascinating subject, without minimizing the many disputes, controversies, and unresolved issues that exist.

Charles A. Lyons
August, 2013
La Grande, Oregon

# Supplements & Resources

## Instructor Supplements

A complete teaching package is available for instructors who adopt this book. This package includes an **online lab**, **instructor's manual**, **test bank**, **course management software**, and **PowerPoint slides**.

| | |
|---|---|
| **BVT*Lab*** | An online lab is available for this textbook at www.BVTLab.com, as described in the BVT*Lab* section below. |
| **Test Bank** | An extensive test bank is available to instructors in both hard copy and electronic form. Each chapter has 120 to 150 multiple choice questions ranked by difficulty and style, as well as 20 written-answer questions. Each question is referenced to the appropriate section of the text to make test creation quick and easy. |
| **Course Management Software** | BVT's course management software, Respondus, allows for the creation of tests and quizzes that can be downloaded directly into a wide variety of course management environments such as Blackboard, Web CT, Desire2Learn, ANGEL, E-Learning, eCollege, Canvas, Moodle, and others. |
| **PowerPoint Slides** | A set of PowerPoint slides includes about 30 slides per chapter, comprising a chapter overview, learning objectives, slides covering all key topics, key figures and charts, as well as summary and conclusion slides. |

## Student Resources

Student resources are available for this textbook at www.BVTLab.com. These resources are geared toward students needing additional assistance as well as those seeking complete mastery of the content. The following resources are available:

| | |
|---|---|
| **Practice Questions** | Students can work through hundreds of practice questions online. Questions are multiple choice or true/false in format and are graded instantly for immediate feedback. |
| **Flashcards** | BVT*Lab* includes sets of flashcards for each chapter that reinforce the key terms and concepts from the textbook. |
| **Chapter Summaries** | A convenient and concise chapter summary is available as a study aid for each chapter. |
| **PowerPoint Slides** | All instructor PowerPoints are available for convenient lecture preparation and for students to view online for a study recap. |

## BVT*Lab*

BVT*Lab* is an affordable online lab for instructors and their students. It includes an online classroom with grade book and chat room, a homework grading system, extensive test banks for quizzes and exams, and a host of student study resources.

| | |
|---|---|
| **Course Setup** | BVT*Lab* has an easy-to-use, intuitive interface that allows instructors to quickly set up their courses and grade books, and to replicate them from section to section and semester to semester. |
| **Grade Book** | Using an assigned passcode, students register themselves into the grade book; and all homework, quizzes, and tests are automatically graded and recorded. |
| **Chat Room** | Instructors can post discussion threads to a class forum and then monitor and moderate student replies. |
| **Student Resources** | All student resources for this textbook are available in BVT*Lab* in digital form. |
| **eBook** | A web-based eBook is available within the lab for easy reference during online classes, homework, and study sessions. |

Even if a class is not taught in the lab, students can still utilize the many student resources described above

## *Customization*

BVT's Custom Publishing Division can help you modify this book's content to satisfy your specific instructional needs. The following are examples of customization:

- Rearrangement of chapters to follow the order of your syllabus
- Deletion of chapters not covered in your course
- Addition of paragraphs, sections, or chapters you or your colleagues have written for this course
- Editing of the existing content, down to the word level
- Customization of the accompanying student resources and online lab
- Addition of handouts, lecture notes, syllabus, etc.
- Incorporation of student worksheets into the textbook

All of these customizations will be professionally typeset to produce a seamless textbook of the highest quality, with an updated table of contents and index to reflect the customized content.

# CHAPTER OVERVIEW

# CHAPTER OPENER QUESTIONS

What does the term "abnormal behavior" mean?

What is a "psychological disability"?

Is there a sharp dividing line between
  normal and abnormal?

How can we study abnormal behavior scientifically?

(Shutterstock)

# chapter 1

# Introduction

Humans engage in a vast range of activities, emotions, beliefs, perceptions, and memories. These types of behaviors (both overt and covert) can be viewed as adaptations to the world around us and to the requirements of life, and different people find very different ways of expressing them. All humans share many similarities; but even within the boundaries of our biology, our culture, and our experience, great variety exists in what people do.

Societies differ to some extent over which variations of behavior are acceptable, but they also share the tendency to identify certain patterns as something other than "normal." Sometimes, people act and feel in ways that we could call *maladjusted* or *disturbed*: their behaviors cause distress or harm to themselves or to others. They may act in ways that other people would consider unusual and objectionable. How have strange and puzzling behaviors been explained in different cultures, in different historical periods, and by different theorists? What techniques can be used to help individuals overcome such difficulties? This book will address those important questions. First, however, a more fundamental issue is at hand: What is abnormal behavior?

## 1.1 What Is Abnormal Behavior?

The term "**abnormal behavior**" implies behavior that is different, unusual, or deviant. Distinctiveness alone, of course, is not sufficient to imply abnormality. Olympic athletes,

> **What does the term "abnormal behavior" mean?**

Nobel Laureates, gifted musicians, and investors who make a killing on the stock market—all deviate considerably from the norm. Yet we are not inclined to consider them abnormal as the term is generally used. Although abnormal behavior does, for the most part, deviate from cultural norms, only certain kinds of deviant behaviors are likely to be called abnormal—namely, behavior that is culturally inappropriate, is accompanied by subjective distress, and involves a psychological impairment (inability to cope with life's demands).

## 1.1a Cultural Inappropriateness

The key concept here is that the behavior seems at odds with cultural expectations of appropriateness and propriety: The behavior is something that others find disturbing, puzzling, or irrational.

Ordinarily, a specific behavior is not judged strange in itself, only in the context of a particular situation. When sports "fans" (a term, incidentally, derived from the word *fanatic*) shout and shake their fists at a football game, there will be few lifted eyebrows; doing the same thing in church or in the public library, however, may be seen as unusual and troubling by others who witness these acts. Similarly, those who smear their faces in fake blood, dress up as dead people, and go door-to-door asking for treats would be viewed as very strange indeed—except in the United States, on October 31.

Anthropologists have convincingly made the point that judgment of another person's normality will depend on the values and traditions of the culture in which he or she lives. For example, hearing voices and going into a trance are likely to be labeled abnormal in our society; and yet, among the Plains Indians of North America, such behaviors were highly valued as evidence of special talent for communication with the spirit world. Prestige and

**Abnormal behavior**

Behavior that is culturally inappropriate, is accompanied by subjective distress, and involves a psychological impairment (inability to cope with life's demands)

status would often accrue to the person having these experiences. What, however, would be the response today if a young woman from New Jersey announced that she heard divine voices instructing her to take over the position of Chairman of the Joint Chiefs of Staff of the U.S. Armed Forces in order to protect this country from foreign dangers? No doubt she would find a few followers, but it is unlikely that she would be as successful as Joan of Arc in accomplishing her mission. Even in Joan's case not everyone bought her story.

When sport "fans" (a term, incidentally, derived from the word fanatic) shout and shake their fist at a football game, there will be few lifted eyebrows, but doing the same thing in church or in the public library may be seen as strange. (AP Wide World Photo)

When Ruth Benedict (1934) made her study of the Melanesian culture of the Dobu, she found the society was characterized by a degree of suspicion and mistrust that would be labeled **paranoia** in American culture. There was universal preoccupation with poisoning. No woman left her cooking pot untended for a moment; and because all others' food was considered to be deadly poison, community stores were out of the question. Their polite phrase at the acceptance of a gift was, "And if you now poison me, how shall I repay you for this present?" There was one man in this Dobu society who had a sunny, kindly disposition and liked to be helpful. Others laughed at him and thought him silly, simple, and a little crazy. Prevailing cultural beliefs, then, will influence how strange or inappropriate a given behavior is perceived to be.

*Prevailing cultural beliefs influence how strange or inappropriate a given behavior, such as that of a shaman, is perceived to be.*
(Wikimedia Commons)

Anthropologists ( for example, Kiev [1969] and Murphy [1964]), however, point out that we must not take too simple a view of the **cultural relativity** of abnormal behavior. For example, the trance states of shamans (priest-doctors such as voodoo priests and medicine men) show some similarities to psychopathological reactions in our society, but there are also important differences. Primarily, the shaman appears to be more in control of the trance state, deciding on which occasions to enter it and, most important, appears to be behaving according to cultural expectations while in it. A person who goes into trance states at inappropriate times and behaves in unpredictable ways might well be considered strange or "crazy" by the community. Marvin Harris (1989) notes that all known societies identify individuals (like shamans) who "have a special aptitude for obtaining help from the spirit world" (p. 411). Social rules probably dictate the "normal" methods for appealing for spiritual help in all of them.

**Paranoia**

Unfounded, irrational, or exaggerated suspicion or mistrust of others

**Cultural relativity**

The perspective that different cultures may utilize different standards in the definition of abnormality

The question still remains: Can abnormality be defined largely in terms of cultural inappropriateness? There are some problems with such an approach. Take, for example, an individual in Nazi Germany who might, in belief and action, have differed from the prevailing anti-Semitic views and other aspects of the Nazi philosophy. Such a person would clearly have been deviating from acceptable cultural views and by this definition would have been considered abnormal. In the late twentieth century, some dissidents in the Soviet Union were labeled mentally ill and placed in institutions because they voiced opposition to the Soviet dictatorship. Even now, women in some Islamic countries are considered deviant because of their wish to complete an education. Do we want to label this kind of behavior abnormal? On the contrary, it might be argued that standing up in this way against prevailing viewpoints takes considerable psychological strength.

There are other problems with cultural inappropriateness as the major criterion of abnormality. Many individuals in our society conform almost slavishly to the customs and laws of the community and yet experience inhibitions, anxieties, and great personal unhappiness. Although their overt behavior is not culturally inappropriate, their reactions may be considered, in some sense, abnormal. Other individuals (for example, professional criminals) defy societal laws but otherwise function quite well as spouses, parents, colleagues, and friends. Their behavior might more accurately be defined as criminal rather than abnormal. Cultural inappropriateness, although a characteristic of most abnormal behavior in all societies, is not entirely satisfying as the sole criterion of abnormality.

## 1.1b Subjective Distress

**Subjective distress** refers to internal emotions or experiences that are real to the person but cannot be observed directly by other people. Unhappiness, fear, apathy, terrifying visual and auditory experiences, and physical aches and pains are examples. Reports of subjective distress commonly accompany abnormal reactions and may include a variety of unpleasant emotions such as guilt, nervous tension, depression, and the pain of migraine headaches.

The individual's distress is an important dimension of abnormality that should be included as one aspect of an overall definition. Once again, however, there are exceptions. Some individuals, especially those with *manic disorders*, may deny any subjective distress and maintain that they feel wonderful. Individuals labeled *sociopathic* experience little remorse or distress associated with their antisocial behavior. In these cases, reports about the degree of subjective distress would not be an accurate indication of the presence of abnormality.

Jeff Hall is a Neo-Nazi supporter. Hall has helped lead demonstrations in Riverside and Los Angeles, where white supremacists waved swastika flags, chanted "white power" and gave stiff-armed Nazi salutes surrounded by hundreds of counterprotesters. (AP Wide World Photo)

## 1.1c Psychological Disability

When persons are unable to function adequately in their roles as students, workers, parents, spouses, or friends, they can be considered to have a psychological disability, impairment, or dysfunction. They are unable to cope adequately with life's stresses and demands. Sometimes they are not able to function effectively as a parent. When depressed or having a migraine headache, they are hardly able to get through the day and may frequently take to bed. Their interpersonal relationships are hampered by an inability to assert themselves appropriately.

One way of viewing the concept of psychological disability or dysfunction is to say that individuals with such handicaps have fewer alternative ways of behaving and thinking open to them. In this sense, psychological impairments are analogous to physical impairments; indeed, many of the terms used interchangeably with abnormality (such as *psychopathology*, *behavior pathology*, *behavior disorder*, *mental illness*, and *mental disease*) imply a parallel with physical disease. For example, persons with a broken leg or pneumonia are handicapped by those conditions and cannot do things they normally could. Although some writers, such as Szasz (1960), have severely criticized the idea that mental illness is similar to physical illness, the disease metaphor is widely employed today in psychiatry and psychology. As we shall see in later chapters, disease models of mental disorders have both strengths and weaknesses; and there are alternative perspectives that propose that many mental disorders may be acquired by individuals on the basis of life experiences. The concept of psychological disability or impairment, however, need not imply any particular theory of how abnormality develops.

What is a "psychological disability"?

**Subjective distress**

Emotion or internal experience that is distressing to the individual, but cannot be directly observed by others

It is important to note that the person with a psychological impairment is *unable* to do certain things, as opposed to the person who simply does not do them because of personal values, lack of interest, or similar reasons. One cannot always tell from the behavior itself whether or not it stems from a psychological impairment and has, instead, to make a judgment as to whether the person is able to do otherwise. A succession of short-lived marriages does not in itself indicate a handicap; however, when a person wants a lasting marriage, and is physically healthy—yet seems to be involved in one disastrous marriage after another—a psychological disability would be suspected.

In sum, then, most but not all forms of abnormal behavior are likely to be culturally inappropriate and accompanied by subjective distress. In addition, all forms of abnormality might be conceived as reflecting a psychological impairment: a restriction in response alternatives that makes it difficult to cope with life's demands and stresses. These considerations form the basis for current definitions of the mental disorders that will be addressed in this book.

## 1.2  Abnormality Is a Continuum

The conception of abnormality may be clarified further by viewing it as a continuum, with extreme abnormality at one end and positive mental health at the other. In extreme forms of abnormal behavior the person is severely handicapped, suffers much subjective distress, and is so culturally inappropriate as to evoke intense fear or revulsion in others. From these extreme instances, in which most observers would agree that something is wrong, we move by imperceptible steps to the range of behaviors that we call normal.

Milder forms of psychological impairments include the boy who is too timid to ask a girl for a date, the homemaker who feels vaguely dissatisfied and unfulfilled, the alienated student who finds nothing of interest in the world of the establishment, or the young person who feels acutely irritated whenever confronted by anyone in authority. Mild impairments are experienced from time to time by the vast majority of people in the middle range of this hypothetical continuum. Who among us does not have some occasional reaction that impairs work efficiency,

> **Is there a sharp dividing line between normal and abnormal?**

disrupts interpersonal relationships, or otherwise hampers our ability to meet life's demands? Some of us feel anxious about speaking before an audience, some have minor irrational fears, and some get a little disorganized under the pressure of a course examination.

There is, then, no single point at which one can draw a line separating normal from abnormal, only varying degrees of psychological disability, subjective distress, and cultural inappropriateness (Figure 1-1). Let us consider for a moment what is meant by the other end of the continuum, the psychologically healthy person.

## 1.3  What Is Mental Health?

Psychologically healthy persons do not necessarily escape the stresses and strains of life. From time to time they wrestle with conflicting impulses, encounter crises in interpersonal relationships, and experience unpleasant emotions such as grief, anger, or fear. In general, however, they are able to function effectively and to find satisfaction in life. They can have lasting and emotionally gratifying relations with friends, spouses, parents, and children; they can work effectively and productively; and they can laugh, play, relax, and have fun. They are likely to make a

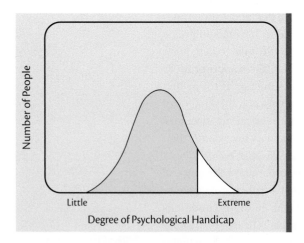

**Figure 1-1**   *Psychological Disability Seen as a Continuum Along Which People Vary*

Most of us fall in the middle range with only mild-to-moderate handicaps. Any exact border between normal and abnormal, such as the line separating the unshaded area above, is arbitrary.

realistic appraisal of their own talents and shortcomings, or at least they do not resort to extreme forms of denial or distortion of those aspects of themselves they wish were different. Basically, they view themselves as worthy members of the human race.

This idealized description of mental health in no way implies that such persons have to be conformists, adjusting passively to the demands of their culture. In the present definition of mental health, freedom from psychological disability is emphasized. Mentally healthy persons are able to pursue with effectiveness and satisfaction any number of life goals. They have weighed the value and desirability of the specific uses to which they put their psychological energies. A salesperson who enjoys selling, has mutually satisfying relationships with others, plays golf on Saturday, and drinks beer while watching the Sunday afternoon pro football game on TV would, by most criteria, be leading a conventional, middle-class life—and by our definition, be enjoying mental health. A member of a rural commune who likewise has satisfying interpersonal relationships, enjoys organic farming, and relaxes by playing the guitar has an equal degree of mental health. Persons who try to reform society, such as political or religious leaders, may create a much more stressful life situation for themselves than either of the other two examples; yet to the extent that they successfully cope with these stresses, they also enjoy mental health. An individual with the necessary abilities and relative freedom from psychological handicaps should be able to choose among these and other life-styles. Good mental health leaves a person open to many alternative ways of behaving. It is not some idealized and unattainable state but is, instead, that end of the dimension where individuals have relatively few psychological disabilities.

## 1.3a By What Name Shall We Call It?

Many terms have been used to refer to abnormal behavior, including *psychopathology*, *mental illness*, *behavior disorder*, and *emotional disturbance*. While some use of labels is inescapable, it is reasonable to ask about the value in applying such general labels to people. Such terms refer to a broad and complex range of phenomena, which, as previously suggested, can be seen as a continuum on which there is no sharp dividing line. The causes of these phenomena may be very complex and interconnected to biology, genetics, culture, and individual life history. It is easy to fall into the **naming fallacy** where, by giving something a name or label, we assume we have in some sense explained it. Regardless of how we name a disorder, we must also be able to describe objectively what the abnormal behaviors are, understand how they develop (and perhaps how they could be prevented), and consider how they might be modified to help restore a person to a more healthy state. As we shall see, mental disorders are easier to label than to explain and understand.

Furthermore, there is a tendency for any term used in referring to these phenomena to acquire a derogatory meaning, and that fact deserves some comment. Most people feel frightened or repelled by individuals who behave abnormally. These reactions account, in part, for the fact that abnormally behaving people have historically been the object of ridicule and abuse. Any term used to refer to such individuals seems to acquire, in time, a negative connotation. To say that a person is "mentally ill" or "sick" is likely to evoke negative reactions in many listeners, yet use of the term *mental illness* was initially promoted

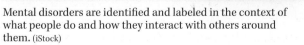

Mental disorders are identified and labeled in the context of what people do and how they interact with others around them. (iStock)

**Naming fallacy**

The incorrect assumption that by applying a label or name to something, we have in some sense explained it

by enlightened physicians seeking to reduce some of the negative attitudes associated with terms such as lunacy and notions such as demonic possession. To minimize the negative connotations of labeling, the *Diagnostic and Statistical Manual of Mental Disorders, Fourth Edition* (or more simply, the *DSM-IV*), published by the American Psychiatric Association (2000), noted that it is preferable to refer to someone we might call a "schizophrenic" as "a person with schizophrenia." While helping prevent the application of inevitably pejorative labels to individual people, this solution may also have the unfortunate effect of separating the behavioral disability from the person, and giving it an existence of its own (rather like a virus) apart from the individual. We should not forget, however, that we can only identify and label these disorders in the context of what people do and how they interact with others around them.

| *DSM-5* | **Definition of a Mental Disorder** |
| --- | --- |
| A mental disorder is a clinically significant syndrome reflecting a dysfunction in psychological, biological, or developmental processes, usually involving:<br>A. Disturbance in cognition, emotion regulation, or behavior<br>B. Significant personal distress or<br>C. Disability in social, occupational, or other important activities | **Excluded from the definition:**<br><br>A. Expected or culturally approved responses to common stressors or loss, such as death of a loved one<br>B. Deviant political, religious, or sexual behavior<br>C. Conflicts that are primarily between the individual and society |

Source: Reprinted with permission from the *Diagnostic and Statistical Manual of Mental Disorders,* Fifth Edition, (Copyright 2013). American Psychiatric Association.

## What Is a Mental Disorder?

According to the current version of the *DSM* series, the *DSM-5*, a mental disorder is a "syndrome characterized by clinically significant disturbance in an individual's cognition, emotion regulation, or behavior that reflects a dysfunction in the psychological, biological, or developmental processes underlying mental function" (American Psychiatric Association, 2013, p. 20). The disturbance usually involves significant personal distress or disruption in important activities in a person's life, such as occupational or social functions (see *DSM-5* Definition of a Mental Disorder). To be "clinically significant," the behavioral or psychological syndrome would be considered important and serious enough to presume that the individual is usually not able to manage the condition alone—although the manual notes that a diagnosis is not equivalent to the need for treatment.

Certain types of significant syndromes or patterns of behavior are excluded from the definition of a mental disorder in the *DSM-5*, as well. Culturally-appropriate and acceptable reactions to important events, like the death of a loved one, usually include strong responses such as grief, depression, sleep disturbance, loss of appetite, and social withdrawal. Within each culture, members expect and accept those reactions as normal events; in fact, it may appear abnormal if these reactions *don't* occur. Even though grief ( for example) involves present distress and impairment in functioning for the bereaved, it is not a mental disorder within the limits of cultural expectations. Among current cultures, the sorts of sanctioned responses to the death of a loved one can vary widely. In some Native American cultures in the Pacific Northwest, for example, it is not unusual to wear certain types of clothing or to continue setting a place at the table for the lost loved one for a year after the loss. In the larger society, most Americans would not consider it unusual if the mourner's social and occupational involvements were disrupted for weeks, or even a few months. At some point, however, cultures expect grief to subside and the intense reactions to lessen. If that does not happen, then a diagnosis of mental disorder becomes possible.

**BVT** *Lab*

Flashcards are available for this chapter at www.BVTLab.com.

Other potentially distressing and harmful patterns or syndromes are also excluded from the definition. We tolerate a very large range of religious beliefs and practices. Political goals, motives, and means can take many forms. There is great diversity in our sexual desires and practices. Although these patterns of behavior may at times seem very much out of the norm, they are not—by that virtue alone—considered mental disorders. Similarly, some persons find themselves in conflict with their culture or their government. Some people instigate rebellions, protest the actions of businesses, governments and religions, or violate the laws of a nation or a community. Some people engage in terrorist acts to intentionally create fear and havoc, and to kill or maim unsuspecting victims. These syndromes can be called subversive or criminal, but they are not mental disorders for those reasons alone.

It may seem obvious that there will be instances in which professionals might disagree as to whether a person is suffering from a mental disorder or not. Thus, the **diagnostic reliability** of mental disorders is a very important issue for the *DSM* system, as we shall consider later. Complicating the matter further, some people diagnosed with mental disorders also commit deviant political, religious, sexual, or criminal activities. The extent to which the mental disorder accounts for those acts may be unclear.

# 1.4 The Prevalence of Abnormality

The looseness of definition should not in any way obscure the existence of abnormal behavior—which is both real and pervasive, as a number of studies have shown. In an early study, Leo Srole and his associates (1962) interviewed and administered a questionnaire to a random sample of 1,660 individuals living on Manhattan's East Side. Symptoms indicative of mental disorder were measured, and the percentage of individuals falling into six categories representing degree of impairment was as follows:

| | |
|---|---|
| Well | 18.5% |
| Mild | 36.3% |
| Moderate | 21.8% |
| Marked | 13.2% |
| Severe | 7.5% |
| Incapacitated | 2.7% |

If the last three categories are combined, 23.4% of the sample was considered to have at least a marked degree of psychological handicap. Similar results were obtained in studies involving rural as well as urban populations (Warheit, Holzer, & Arey, 1975). An interview of a random sample of adults in an area of New Haven, Connecticut concluded that 15% were experiencing a psychiatric disorder and that 18% of the people interviewed had experienced a depressive disorder of at least a moderate degree sometime during the past year (Weissman & Myers, 1978).

More recently, Kessler and his colleagues (2005) estimated the prevalence of some of the more common mental disorders among the U.S. population, in terms of whether a disorder had been experienced in the previous year (12-month prevalence) or had ever been experienced by a person (lifetime prevalence). The most common mental disorders were anxiety disorders with a 12-month prevalence of 18.1% of the population, and a lifetime prevalence of 28.8% of the population (see Figure 1-2). Following anxiety disorders were mood disorders (such as depression), impulse-control disorders, and substance disorders. If all disorders are combined, about 26.6% of Americans experienced a defined disorder in the past 12 months. Over the course of our lifetimes, nearly half (46.4%) of us will experience at least one of the disorders.

**Diagnostic reliability**
Consistency and agreement between clinicians in use of a diagnostic label

*Figure 1-2*   **Prevalence of Mental Disorders**

Prevalence of mental disorders within the population, during the previous 12-month period and over the course of a person's lifetime.

Source: Kessler, R. C., Burglund, P., Demler, O., Jin, R., Merikangas, K. R., & Walters, E. E. (2005, June). Lifetime prevalence and age-of-onset distributions of *DSM-IV* disorders in the National Comorbidity Survey Replication. *Archives of General Psychiatry, 62*(6), 593–602. & Kessler, R. C., Chiu, W. T., Demler, O., Merikangas, K. R., & Walters E. E. (2005, June). Prevalence, severity, and comorbidity survey replication. *Archives of General Psychiatry.* 62(6), 617–627

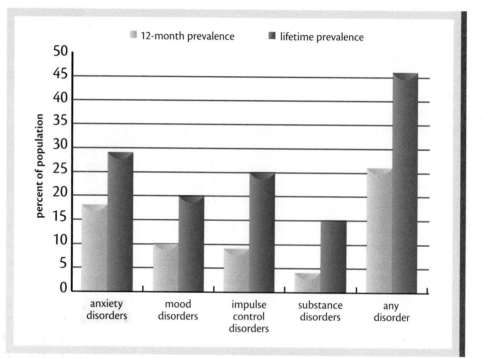

## 1.5  The Scientific Study of Abnormal Behavior

Only recently have we attempted to study ourselves with the same objectivity that we have used in trying to understand the inanimate world and other living organisms. Abnormal behavior, especially, has lent itself to beliefs and superstitions that have yielded only slowly to the advance of scientific understanding. The history of changing conceptions of abnormality will be traced in subsequent chapters. First, consideration of common methodologies used in the scientific study of abnormal behavior and the advantages and disadvantages associated with them is warranted.

### 1.5a  The Case Study

Carefully documented **case studies** of individuals have played an important role historically in the study of abnormal behavior. Typically, the investigator derives information from talking with a person who displays abnormal behavior (or those who know the person) and describing, in narrative form, the behavior of interest, related environmental circumstances, and past events that might make the present behavior intelligible. The intensive study of individuals and the changes in symptoms that occur during therapy has been a rich source of ideas about the nature and causation of abnormal behavior.

> How can we study abnormal behavior scientifically?

**Case study**

The study of an individual clinical case

> " *... there is really no scientific or other method by which men can steer safely between the opposite dangers of believing too little or of believing too much. To face such dangers is apparently our duty, and to hit the right channel between them is the measure of our wisdom as men.* "
>
> William James (1897)

Although case studies are useful in illustrating different forms of abnormal behavior and in generating theories, they are not proper scientific methods; and they cannot be used to "prove" a theory. For one thing, there is a tendency to select, as evidence, cases that support one's theory while ignoring those cases that are embarrassingly inconsistent with it. Furthermore, the information used in a case report is highly selective, and one rarely has any way of knowing how much information was omitted or never sought in the first place. By simply tracking the changes that take place in a person's condition, we cannot distinguish causal influences from simple coincidence. Finally, even when the findings for a given case are accurate, they cannot be generalized to anyone other than the person being studied unless, as discussed in the following section, similar information was obtained from a sample of individuals. We should be careful, then, not to be led into believing that a general proposition has been demonstrated by a case study, no matter how persuasive and sensible the material seems to be.

## 1.5b Epidemiological Research

It can be useful to have certain descriptive information about abnormal behavior—for example, the frequency of different forms of psychopathology among different socioeconomic classes, genders, ethnic groups, age groups, and so forth. Research aimed at getting this kind of information is called normative or **epidemiological research.** The study of the prevalence of depression in the New Haven area, cited earlier, is an example of this kind of research, as is the more current work of Kessler and his colleagues (2005). Epidemiology often involves the study of the incidence of a disorder in a population (that is, the number of new cases within a specific period) or the prevalence of a disorder (that is, the number of people who show the disorder at any one time). The data produced by epidemiological research can provide important information about public health trends and risks across different elements of the population. Basic requirements for good epidemiological research, as well as other kinds of research, are **random sampling**, and **reliability** and **validity** of measurement. Let us look at what is meant by these terms.

## 1.5c Sampling and Generalization

Weissman and Myers (1978), in their epidemiological study of depression, randomly sampled 1 out of every 14 households in the New Haven area and then randomly selected one adult from each household. Such an approach ensures that, within a certain range of chance variation, estimates of the incidence of depression will fairly accurately reflect the actual incidence in the larger population. Kessler and his colleagues (2005) calculated 12-month and lifetime prevalence rates of different disorders from information collected in structured face-to-face interviews with a nationally representative sample of households, including over 9,200 persons. If these investigators had instead relied on statistics based on individuals who had sought treatment for mental disorders, their results would be incomplete because of the omission of untreated cases of depression.

The nature of the population randomly sampled is important in determining to what groups of people a given finding can be generalized. Thus generalizations about the incidence of disorders can be safely made only to those populations that resemble the selected

**Epidemiological research**

Often involves the study of the incidence of a disorder in a population

**Random sampling**

Selecting subjects by chance from some larger population

**Reliability**

The extent to which a measure consistently yields the same results on repeated trials

**Validity**

The extent to which a measure assesses what it is purported to assess

sample in terms of ethnic, socioeconomic, and other factors. Most research on psychopathology is not aimed at estimating rates of incidence in the general population but aimed, rather, at understanding something about the nature or treatment of a given disorder. In this case, too, it is important to know to what populations the results can be generalized. Thus, Mosher and Menn (1978) assessed the effectiveness of a special treatment facility with schizophrenic patients. The patients used in this study were young, had not had more than one brief hospitalization previously, and were unmarried. Paul and Lentz (1977) evaluated the effectiveness of another approach to rehabilitating schizophrenic patients. Their patients averaged 45 years of age, had been hospitalized for an average of 17 years, and had recently been found unacceptable for transfer to an extended-care facility outside the hospital. Clearly, one cannot assume that results obtained in one of these studies can be generalized to the population of individuals sampled in the other study.

## 1.5d   Reliability and Validity of Measurement

**BVT** *Lab*

Visit **www.BVTLab.com** to explore the student resources available for this chapter.

Reliability of measurement refers to the extent to which a measure consistently yields the same result on repeated trials. In physical measurements reliability tends to be quite high. If several people measured the width of a table with a yardstick, their measurements would differ only by small amounts, perhaps one-sixteenth of an inch. Such a measure is highly reliable for most purposes, although for some endeavors such as fine machine tool work it would not be. Psychological measurement is never as precise as physical measurement. One reason for this imprecision is that when physical attributes (such as height, or weight) are measured, we assess the entire domain of the attribute in question: We measure all of a person's height or all of a person's weight. The same is never true when we measure behavior; we can only sample a small part of the domain of how a person acts, or thinks, or feels. In order to determine whether a person is depressed, for example, we must rely on reports of how that person feels most of the time, under most circumstances. All of us show variations in our psychological states, so the application of a diagnostic label is a judgment call. Therefore, diagnostic reliability is an important problem to consider in the measurement of abnormality.

One type of reliability that is particularly important in psychological research is **interobserver reliability**: the extent to which different observers (or raters) agree on the way they categorize or in some way quantify a given observation. Suppose, for example, that an investigator wished to measure aggressive behavior of mental patients. One method would be to count the instances of aggressive behavior among the patients. For this information to be useful, however, the investigator must demonstrate that two or more independent observers agree on their ratings or counts of aggression. Thus it is usually necessary for observers to undergo preliminary training in which they practice making ratings until they can agree on which behaviors they are going to label a certain way—in this case as aggressive. The careful researcher will always report in some fashion the degree of agreement between independent observers. Similarly, clinicians interviewing clients have been trained in the application of a diagnostic label; inter-observer reliability is shown when the same patient receives a consistent diagnosis from two or more different clinicians.

A measure is valid if it measures what it purports to measure. When measuring certain clearly defined behaviors, such as the number of times a person talks to or hits another person, there is little problem of validity. The problem arises when one must, in order to obtain a measurement, make an inference about a psychological trait or process that is itself not directly definable in terms of specific, observable behaviors. If, for example, raters are asked to judge the degree of aggressiveness shown by a person, we want to know if the resulting score really measures aggression—or something else. This is not always an easy issue to resolve. Ordinarily the best procedure is to provide a detailed description of what observable behaviors were used to make an inference about aggression (such as hitting and verbal insults) and let the reader decide whether the inference is reasonable.

**Interobserver reliability**

The extent to which different observers (or raters) agree on the way they categorize or in some way quantify a given observation

The problem of validity becomes especially acute when certain behaviors are considered "signs" of some underlying and unobservable process. For example, fear of small enclosed places might be interpreted as a fear of death, or excessive consumption of alcohol as a sign of fixation at the oral stage of development (see Chapter 3). Unobservable states or characteristics—such as oral fixations or dispositions to be hostile, fearful, and so on—are frequently referred to as **constructs**; and the term **construct validity** is used to refer to the validity of some specific way of measuring the hypothetical construct.

High reliability does not guarantee high validity. Two observers might agree that one person punching another lightly in the ribs indicated aggression, when in fact the behavior was meant in a friendly way. Similarly, clinicians might agree that a person's report of visual and auditory hallucinations points to a diagnosis of schizophrenia, but their agreement does not necessarily make it so. (Perhaps the person has recently ingested a drug, such as LSD, that produces hallucinations.) Construct validity is usually determined by the way that a given measure relates to other measures and conditions. If a given measure of the construct "disposition to be aggressive" predicts aggressive behavior in other situations, and if subjects high on this measure show more aggression than those low on it, we would conclude that there is some positive evidence for the construct validity of the measure.

Some psychologists have proposed that hypothetical constructs like 'fixation at the oral stage' may help account for excessive drinking. (Shutterstock)

## 1.5e  Correlational Research

Another method used to obtain knowledge about abnormal behavior is **correlational research**. In a correlational study the investigator attempts to demonstrate an association or correlation between two or more measures. For example, people's height and weight tend to be correlated. If we measure these characteristics in 100 people, we would find, in general, that taller people are heavier. The correlation would not be perfect; some tall people would weigh less than some short people, but the general association would be positive. A descriptive statistic called the **correlation coefficient**, which varies between –1.00 and +1.00, is one way of quantifying how strong the relationship is. As the correlation coefficient moves closer to a perfect +1.00, the two measures move up or down together in a very predictable way. For example, as the weight of a vehicle increases, its fuel consumption increases as well. There is a strong positive correlation between weight and fuel use. A correlation coefficient approaching a perfect -1.00 indicates as one measure increases, the other decreases in a very predictable way. For example, increasing income is negatively correlated with financial aid: As income goes up, aid goes down. A zero correlation indicates that two measures are not related in any predictable way; no association is apparent. The correlation between two measures can be graphically portrayed by a *scatter plot*.

Correlation can tell researchers something about the strength and direction of a relationship, but correlations do not demonstrate causation. Several years ago, medical scientists began to find a correlation between cigarette smoking and lung cancer. Studies showed that the more cigarettes people smoked per day, the more likely they were to have lung cancer. The tobacco companies, their scientific zeal perhaps enhanced by the prospect of decreased profits, were quick to point out that such correlations did not prove that cigarette smoking caused lung cancer. It was quite possible that lung cancer and cigarette smoking were both influenced by some unknown third factor. For example, a person with certain physiological characteristics might be predisposed to both tobacco smoking and lung cancer. In such a case, it would not matter whether the person smoked or not since the occurrence of lung cancer would depend on the unknown physiological variable and not on smoking. Another possibility considered was that people experiencing chronic nervous tension were more likely to smoke and develop lung cancer and that lung cancer was caused by nervous tension,

**Constructs**

Hypothetical or theoretical concepts that cannot be measured directly

**Construct validity**

Refers to the validity of some specific way of measuring the hypothetical construct

**Correlational research**

When the investigator attempts to demonstrate an association or correlation between two or more measurements

**Correlation coefficient**

A measure of the direction and strength of the relationship between variables

***Figure 1-3*** ***Examples of Scatterplots Showing Correlations of Different Magnitudes between Two Variables, X and Y***

Each person is represented by a point that reflects scores on the two dimensions. The correlation of +.57, for example, could be the relationship between height and weight for a sample of 11 individuals.

Source: Adapted from Runyon & Haber, 1971

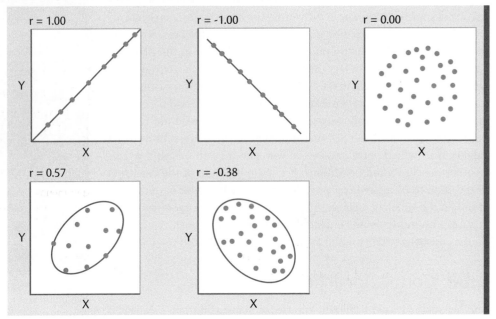

not smoking. As is frequently the case with correlational findings, one can go on at some length thinking up alternative explanations. In Figure 1-3, for example, we see examples of correlations of different magnitudes between two variables, X and Y.

Correlational research, however, should not be discarded too lightly. It does make a difference whether one finds a strong positive correlation or no correlation, since a positive finding is consistent with the *possibility* of a causative relationship. No relationship, causative or otherwise, is likely to be associated with a zero correlation. It is possible, also, to rule out certain factors as the complete explanation (or cause) by controlling these factors. Thus, to return to the smoking example, we could divide our sample of cigarette smokers into a number of subgroups in which the individuals all show about the same amount of nervous tension—individuals very high in nervous tension would be in one group, those with moderate nervous tension would be in another group, and so on. If one still found a correlation between smoking and lung cancer within each group of people who have the same degree of nervous tension, then it would be difficult to explain the correlation by this particular variable. The problem is that there can be an unknown number of other variables that might be contributing to the observed relationship. As for lung cancer and smoking, subsequent correlational research that controlled for a number of other variables and experimental research with animals has demonstrated that smoking, indeed, is a leading cause of lung cancer, as well as other serious diseases. The correlation research was valuable in leading to later, confirmatory experimental research that produced important information of great significance for public health.

Although preliminary studies did show a correlation between lung cancer and the number of cigarettes smoked per day, the correlation alone did not prove causation. (Shutterstock)

Much of the subject matter of abnormal psychology must be studied by correlational methods for practical and ethical reasons. For example, we cannot ethically manipulate brain neurochemistry or family environments in an effort to produce schizophrenic offspring. If we are aware of and can avoid the interpretive pitfalls associated with correlational research, a great deal of understanding can be achieved by this method.

## 1.5f Experimental Research

The most powerful way of shedding light on factors that affect human behavior is the **experimental method**. The essence of the psychological experiment is that the people to be studied are randomly assigned to two or more groups, in the simplest case to an **experimental group** and a **control group**. The experimental group experiences some special condition (a manipulation or treatment) while the control group does not. The logic of this approach is that if the experimental group shows effects not shown by the control group, then these effects can be considered to be caused by the experimental manipulation or treatment. Since the subjects are randomly assigned to the two groups, it is assumed that the groups

Confirmatory experimental research with animals produces important information of great significance for matters affecting public health. (iStock)

are alike in every respect except for the experience of the particular treatment. Suppose, for example, that mental patients are randomly assigned to two groups, one of which is given tranquilizing pills while the other is not. We could say then that any consequent difference in symptoms between these two groups is attributable to the administration of the tranquilizing pills.

How large does the difference in symptoms between the experimental and control groups have to be before you can conclude that it is not just a chance difference that could occur between any two random samples? Statistical techniques are available for helping to make this kind of decision. These techniques permit the prediction of how often a difference of a certain magnitude would be expected if the research were repeated many times with different random samples. Thus, one can predict that a given difference would occur by chance once in every 20 times that the study was repeated, or once in every 100 or once in every 4. The greater the number of studies that demonstrate difference of a certain magnitude, the less likely it is that the obtained difference is due to chance. Somewhat arbitrarily, psychologists usually accept a probability of 5 in 100 times ($p = .05$) as a **significant difference**—that is, a difference unlikely to have occurred by chance and therefore reflecting a real effect.

Unfortunately, interpreting the results of an experiment is not always simple. For example, in the experiment just described, we concluded that a significantly greater reduction in symptoms among subjects in the experimental group could be attributed to the administration of the tranquilizing pills. However, administering pills involves a number of factors in addition to what the pill does after it dissolves in the stomach of the recipient. Perhaps the patients who were given the pills were also given the expectation of improvement, since we expect medicine to alleviate symptoms of illness. When an expectation of improvement communicated by the doctors and nurses is sufficient to cause improvement, it is called a **placebo effect**. Perhaps the doctors and nurses, knowing who got the pills and who did not, unconsciously spent more time with those patients who received the medication. Perhaps the observers who rated the patients on their symptomatic behaviors were aware of who got the pills and who did not, and unconsciously distorted their ratings to produce the obtained effect.

The experimental method by itself does not automatically lead to unambiguous results, but experiments can be designed to rule out many of these alternative interpretations. Thus the proper control group in our illustration might be one in which the patients are

**Experimental method**
Research method in which conditions are manipulated in order to test the effects of manipulations on various measures

**Experimental group**
Group on which manipulation of interest is performed in an experimental design

**Control group**
Group that is treated similarly to the experimental group, except that no manipulation is performed

**Significant difference**
A difference unlikely to have occurred by chance and therefore reflecting a real effect

**Placebo effect**
When an expectation of improvements is sufficient to cause improvement

given a sugar pill (placebo), and the doctors and nurses administering the pills are kept ignorant of which pill is which. This type of experimental design, in which both subjects and personnel are kept blind with respect to whether a subject is in the experimental or the control group, is called the **double-blind design**. Properly used, the experimental method can be an incisive way of answering questions about the nature, genesis and development, and modification of abnormal behavior.

There are also experimental methods that do not rely on groups of people, but rather on individual subjects. These **single-subject experimental designs** have been widely employed in some research areas (such as applied behavior analysis) to systematically study an individual's behavior under a variety of experimental conditions, with the goal of understanding the functional relationships between the conditions imposed and the resulting behavior of interest. Unlike case studies, in which observations are not made under systematic controlled conditions, single-subject experiments employ techniques, such as repeatedly alternating baseline and experimental conditions or systematically introducing interventions across successive settings, to control for confounding variables and to provide replicable objective evidence that the experimental variables are influencing the behavior. These techniques have some strengths and some weaknesses when compared to experimental group studies, but they do provide a scientific method for intensively studying the causes of the behavior of individuals.

This brief introduction to some of the more fundamental aspects of scientific inquiry is by no means exhaustive of the methodological issues involved in research in this area. Later, in the context of specific investigations, the various methods of research discussed above will be illustrated with examples from the research literature. As these examples will show, a scientific analysis of abnormal behavior has been very fruitful in uncovering many of the causes of psychopathology, as well as in identifying effective ways to prevent and treat many of the mental disorders. At the same time, the methods of science can reveal the limitations of our techniques and our understanding. That, too, is a valuable and important outcome.

A placebo pill is used to negate effects from treatment that do not depend on the treatment itself. Placebos commonly accompany the actual medicine in prescription packets of birth control pills. The placebos allow the user to remain in the daily habit of taking the pill. (Shutterstock)

---

**BVT** *Lab*

Improve your test scores. Practice quizzes are available at **www.BVTLab.com**.

**Double-blind design**

Type of experimental design in which both subjects and personnel are kept blind with respect to whether a subject is in the experimental or control group

**Single-subject experimental design**

Experimental methods that do not rely on groups of people, but rather on repeated measures from individual subjects

# Chapter Review

## TO SUM UP ...

- Three characteristics are commonly considered in defining abnormal behavior: cultural inappropriateness, subjective distress, and psychological impairment. In general, abnormality does not lend itself to precise definition. The emphasis in this book will be on understanding the current diagnostic system for identifying mental disorders, which includes identifying the behavior of interest, the factors that have led to its development, and the ways in which the behavior might be changed.

- Abnormality can be seen as residing in an interpersonal system, such as a family or larger social group, as well as being a characteristic of an individual.

- It makes sense to view abnormality as a continuum in which incapacitation and distress are extreme at one end and minimal at the other end. Most of us fall in the middle, with some mild inhibitions or anxieties that do not seriously handicap us.

- Despite some looseness in definition, psychological disorders are identifiable syndromes and they affect a substantial proportion of our population.

- The study of abnormal behavior can be approached in a scientific manner. To do so, we need to be familiar with such concepts as sampling and generalization, reliability and validity of measurement, normative research, correlational research, and experimental research.

## KEY TERMS

Abnormal behavior   3

Case study   10

Constructs   13

Construct validity   13

Control group   15

Correlational research   13

Correlation coefficient   13

Cultural relativity   4

Diagnostic reliability   9

Double-blind design   16

Epidemiological research   11

Experimental group   15

Experimental method   15

Interobserver reliability   12

Naming fallacy   7

Paranoia   4

Placebo effect   15

Random sampling   11

Reliability   11

Significant difference   15

Single-subject experimental design   16

Subjective distress   5

Validity   11

# QUESTIONS FOR STUDY

- What is the role of cultural context in the determination of abnormal behavior? Provide two examples of behaviors that, depending on cultural context, could be considered either normal or abnormal.

- What are the strengths and limitations of the different methods for investigating abnormal behavior?

- Give several examples of positive or negative correlations between two variables that reflect a causative relationship between the variables, and several other examples that do not reflect a causative relationship between the variables.

# POP QUIZ

1. _____ would **not** be one of the text's criteria for abnormal behavior.
   A. Subjective distress
   B. Psychological impairment
   C. Cultural inappropriateness
   D. Distinctiveness

2. A behavior that seems abnormal in one cultural context may very well be perfectly acceptable in a different culture or society. This is called _____.
   A. cultural relativity
   B. cultural bias
   C. behavior specificity
   D. epidemiological reaction

3. If an individual's behavior deviates widely from the culturally accepted norm, would that behavior be abnormal according to your text?
   A. Yes, any behavior that is not culturally sanctioned is considered abnormal.
   B. Yes, cultural relativity points out that abnormal behavior is defined across cultures in the same manner.
   C. No, the behavior would have to be accompanied by subjective distress and psychological impairment to be abnormal
   D. No, deviant behavior is always criminal behavior, not abnormal behavior

4. Jake's behavior has been deemed a psychological impairment. What does this mean?
   A. Jake is quite distressed by the behavior.
   B. The behavior is not common in Jake's culture.
   C. The behavior is not appropriate in Jake's culture.
   D. Jake's behavior interferes with his ability to function in his roles.

5. Which of the following is emphasized in the present definition of mental health provided in the text?
   A. freedom from psychological disability
   B. absence of the stresses and strains of life
   C. lack of conflicting impulses or crises in interpersonal relationships
   D. conformity to cultural demands

6. The line separating normal from abnormal behavior is difficult to establish because abnormality is on a _____.
   A. fine line
   B. narrow range
   C. trimodal distribution
   D. continuum

7. Mental disorders are easier to _____ than to _____.
   A. define; describe
   B. explain; define
   C. label; explain
   D. describe; label

8. Dr. Miller and Dr. Thomas agree that specific behaviors are characteristic of Major Depressive Disorder. Both consistently apply the Major Depressive Disorder label when these specific behaviors are apparent. The agreement between Dr. Miller and Dr. Thomas in terms of the use of the Major Depressive Disorder label indicates _____.
   A. content validity
   B. diagnostic reliability
   C. construct validity
   D. test-retest reliability

9. _____ have a lifetime prevalence rate of about 30% in the U.S. population.
   A. Mood disorders
   B. Psychotic disorders
   C. Substance disorders
   D. Anxiety disorders

10. Why would a researcher choose to conduct a case study for an individual with a rare and unusual mental disorder?
    A. The findings could be used to "prove" the researcher's theory.
    B. The research could be a rich source of ideas about the nature of the abnormal behavior.
    C. Causal influences could be differentiated from simple coincidence.
    D. The findings can be accurately generalized to others.

11. Which of the following is true in epidemiological research?
    A. Its measures consistently yield the same result on repeated trials.
    B. The frequency of behaviors among different groups is calculated.
    C. Relationships between two variables are plotted on a scatter plot.
    D. One variable is manipulated to determine its effect on another variable.

12. Requirements for good epidemiological research studies include which of the following?

    A. case studies, correlations, and experiments

    B. correlation coefficients and placebo effects

    C. experimental and control groups

    D. random sampling, reliability, and validity

13. Generalizations can only be made to populations that share the characteristics of the original study's participants. Thus, generalization of findings is closely related to _____.

    A. random sampling

    B. reliability

    C. constructs

    D. validity

14. In a double-blind study, which of the following is true?

    A. The participants do not know whether or not they received the manipulated variable.

    B. The researchers do not know whether or not the participants received the manipulated variable.

    C. Both the researchers and the participants do not know whether or not the participants received the manipulated variable.

    D. Both the researchers and the participants do not know of the study's outcomes.

15. Which of the following methods is best able to reveal cause-and-effect relationships between variables?

    A. correlational research

    B. epidemiological research

    C. the case study

    D. the experiment

Additional study resources are available at **www.BVTLab.com**

## CHAPTER OVERVIEW

## CHAPTER OPENER QUESTIONS

Is abnormal behavior caused by invading demons?

How have ideas about abnormal behavior changed over time?

Do diseased brains cause abnormal behavior?

Do ideas, emotional conflicts, and upsetting experiences cause abnormal behavior?

(Shutterstock)

# Historical Perspectives

# chapter 2

## The Witch Trials of Salem

In the summer and early fall of 1693, 17 women and two men were taken by cart to Gallows Hill near Salem, Massachusetts, and hanged as witches. The principal accusers of these alleged witches were a group of young girls. Betty, the youngest at age 9, and her cousin Abigail, age 11, were the first to show the symptoms of a strange malady that led to this tragic end. These two girls had listened secretly to the stories of a slave woman from the West Indies, Tituba, and later other girls in the village participated in these exciting yet forbidden sessions. Betty, always sensitive and subject to fits of weeping, began to act strangely. Sometimes her mother would find her sitting motionless staring fixedly at some invisible object. If called by her mother, Betty would startle violently, scream, and be unable to give an explanation for her behavior other than meaningless babbling. This reaction was especially likely to come on during prayer. Her father, the minister for Salem Village, learned to leave her alone because if he reproved her, she remained as rigid as ever but worked her mouth and gave off hoarse choking sounds, something like the barking of a dog.

Abigail caught the affliction as if by contagion, but went beyond Betty in the imaginativeness of her display. She got down on hands and knees and ran about, barking and braying, and sometimes went into convulsions where she would writhe and scream as though suffering the torments of the damned. Within a short time the affliction spread to other young girls in the village.

At another time or place such a phenomenon might have run its course and soon been forgotten. In the religious context of the time, however, notions of devil-possession and witchcraft were widespread; and soon the local physicians and ministers began to suspect that these innocent children were being possessed and tormented by witches. When the authorities first asked them to name the people (witches) who were afflicting them, they were unable to do so. No one afflicted them; it just happened. The minister and townspeople began to ask leading questions; names of suspects were suggested to the girls, and their reactions sharply studied. Eventually Betty cried out, "Tituba ... oh Tituba," and the other girls followed suit. Ignorant and confused, Tituba "confessed" to being a witch, and unfortunately in the process referred vaguely to nine other witches.

As the witch trials proceeded, they developed a common pattern. One of the girls in her fits and convulsions would claim to see the spectral form of a village member tormenting her, and this so-called "spectral evidence" was enough for the judges to render a verdict of guilty. Rebecca Nurse, 71-year-old matriarch of the Nurse family, was deeply pious, steeped in scripture, and had reared her children in loving devotion to both their spiritual and temporal welfare. Nor did her family ever desert her in the ordeal she underwent. Accused of witchcraft by several of the girls, she was brought to court and asked by one of the judges if she was a witch. Her answer was unheard by the audience at the hearing because, almost as if on signal, the girls fell into convulsions and set up a "hideous screitch and noise" that could be heard some distance away. "Oh, Lord, help me!" cried poor Rebecca as she spread her hands helplessly. The girls immediately spread their hands in like manner; and thereafter whatever move Rebecca made, they duplicated. Before the very eyes of the court she demonstrated her witchcraft; she made these innocent children follow her every motion (Starkey, 1961).

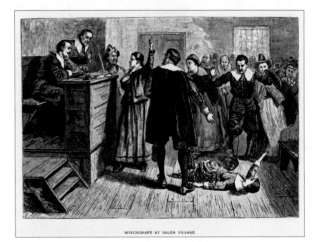

WITCHCRAFT AT SALEM VILLAGE

(Getty Images)

From the perspective of the twenty-first century, these young girls might be seen as showing a form of disturbed behavior called conversion disorder (formerly labeled "hysteria"); and more prosaic causes than possession by the devil might be sought. Initially, Betty provided the other girls with a model of strange behavior. Soon the townspeople began to take notice, and the girls became the object of concern and interest. Starkey (1961) suggests that growing up in puritan Salem was at best a drab and no-nonsense business. Any inclinations toward fun, frivolity, and occasional mischief were dourly inhibited. Under the cloak of an acceptable reason, these girls were having the time of their lives. They gave vent to uninhibited physical and verbal expressions and were given more attention than if "they had married the king and all his court."

## 2.1 Models and Metaphors

In trying to understand any new phenomena, we tend to apply ideas that were useful in some more familiar domain. Thus in ancient times the world was sometimes conceived as a flat surface supported by a giant animal such as a turtle or an elephant—based presumably on the everyday experience that the earth looks flat and the knowledge that objects would fall unless supported. Later this metaphor was replaced by a model of a universe in which the sun, moon, and stars moved in perfect circles around the earth (the geocentric model). That model was in turn replaced by a view of a solar system in which planets, including the earth, revolved around the sun (the heliocentric model). After this notion became commonplace and familiar, it was used as a way of conceiving the atom—that is, as a nucleus encircled by planetary electrons. What an atom actually looks like has been much more difficult to determine than was the appearance of the solar system; and although this model has been useful to a degree, it has not been found to fit empirical data in a number of respects. In fact, many features of modern physics have been difficult to visualize by any familiar conceptions taken from everyday reality.

As a science like physics progresses, it moves through a series of models—called paradigms—concerning how its subject matter should be viewed (Kuhn, 1970). A **paradigm** provides a framework with which to view a phenomenon, the vocabulary to use in discussing the subject, and a "recipe" for how to conduct research on the topic. The value of a paradigm is in the organization it gives to the masses of data collected by those who investigate a scientific puzzle. A paradigm helps researchers make sense of their results, and it is retained as long as it serves that purpose better than another model does. Occasionally, data are collected that are not easily accounted for by the leading paradigm. If enough of these anomalies accumulate, the paradigm (such as the geocentric model of the universe) is eventually abandoned in favor of a newer one (the heliocentric model) that is better at explaining and predicting observations. According to Kuhn, that change is not a slow and gradual one but instead something like a social revolution which leads to a change in worldview. "What were ducks in the scientist's world before the revolution are rabbits afterwards" (p. 111) as Figure 2-1 illustrates.

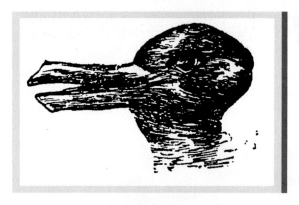

*Figure 2-1*   **Is It a Rabbit, or a Duck?**

Source: From *Mindsights: Original Visual Illusions, Ambiguities and Other Anomalies, with a Commentary on the Play of Mind in Perception and Art* by Roger N. Shepard, ©1990 by Roger N. Shepard.

Mature sciences, like physics, have moved through a series of paradigms, each one more powerful than the one before. Kuhn notes, for example, that early in the history of electrical research, one competing school of thought believed electricity was something like a fluid. Researchers employing that metaphor attempted to conduct electricity through metal tubes and to bottle it. (This work actually led to the invention of the Leyden jar, an early type of

**Paradigm**

A model or framework from which to view a phenomenon

storage battery). It was Benjamin Franklin's experiments with lightning that helped overthrow the fluid model and led to the development of the modern view of electricity.

The status of psychology is somewhat different. It is a relatively new science in which no single ruling paradigm has yet emerged. Instead, a series of competing viewpoints still exist, each offering a different model or metaphor to explain observations and predict events. It is important to recognize that one consequence of accepting a certain metaphor of abnormal behavior is that it largely determines how we talk about and interpret these behaviors, what we look for in terms of causes, and how we construe treatment.

As we have seen, the strange behavior of the young girls of Salem might be interpreted from a different perspective than that of possession by witches. To take another example, if we apply an *illness* or *disease* metaphor to abnormal behavior, then the observed disturbances in behavior tend to be seen as *symptoms* that are caused by some underlying physical or biochemical pathology. Working within this paradigm it makes sense to conclude that modifying (that is, in some way getting rid of) the symptoms without treating the underlying cause will be futile and perhaps produce even more severely disturbed behavior. It also naturally follows that treatment would usually include biological interventions such as surgery or medications. However, from a behavioral perspective many abnormal behaviors are viewed as responses that have been shaped and modified by their consequences, rather than viewed as symptoms. Their causes would thus be found in a person's experiences and prior personal history. As such, these responses should be capable of being changed or corrected, provided the basic principles of human learning are properly applied. In this view no assumptions are made about hypothetical disease processes, and it would seem to follow that treatment should be directly focused on the abnormal behaviors. These and other alternative models or metaphors will be considered in more detail later in the context of their explanations for specific mental disorders, but it might be mentioned here that neither of these particular metaphors may turn out to be wholly adequate in capturing the reality of disordered behaviors. Ultimately, their value will be found in the degree to which they account for the observations we make and the effectiveness of the treatments they provide.

A witch trial in Salem, Massachusetts. Did the tragedy of the Salem witch trials result, in part, from the actions of psychologically disturbed girls? (Getty Images)

## 2.2 Demon Possession versus Naturalistic Explanations

Abnormal behavior has apparently been a part of the human condition in all times and in all cultures. We can recognize in ancient writings descriptions of the convulsive fits that we now

> Is abnormal behavior caused by invading demons?

call *epilepsy* or perhaps *hysteria*; excited, hyperactive states that we now call *mania*; melancholic, dejected reactions that we now label *depression*; severe disturbances in rational thinking that we now call *schizophrenia*; and irrational fears now known as *phobias*. Quite independently, it would seem, people in diverse lands and cultures developed a remarkably similar "theory" or metaphor to explain these aberrations—possession by some god, spirit, or demon.

## 2.2a Early Demonology

Theories of demon possession may have existed even in prehistoric times, as suggested by skulls showing **trephining**. Tools, probably of stone, were used in this procedure to make a sizable hole in the skull, possibly with the intent of permitting entrapped demons to escape. Some specimens show evidence of healing around the holes, indicating that those persons survived the operation. Other explanations besides **demonology** are possible; however, based on our understanding of early cultures, trephination appears to be quite consistent with a procedure derived from a theory of demon possession.

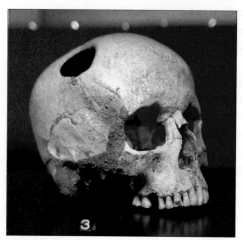

Trepanated skull, Iron Age. The perimeter of the hole in the skull is rounded off by ingrowth of new bony tissue, indicating that the patient survived. (Wikimedia Commons)

The Bible and other early literature are full of variations on the theme of spirit possession, and even today our language betrays how deeply we have been influenced by demonological conceptions. We still say, "Whatever *possessed* you?" or "What's gotten into him?" The expression "She was beside herself with anger" originally meant that the person's spirit left the body while the demon took over.

## 2.2b Hippocrates

Even in the ancient world, however, not everyone subscribed to the prevailing belief in spirit possession. Many Greek and Roman physicians and philosophers held points of view that were essentially modern in their denial of supernatural explanations for both physical and mental disorders. The Greek physician Hippocrates (460–377 BC) was one of the first to advocate naturalistic explanations for disturbed behaviors. In speaking about epilepsy, referred to in those days as the sacred disease because of the belief that it reflected possession by a god, Hippocrates says, "It thus appears to me to be in no way more divine, nor more sacred than other diseases, but has a natural cause from which it originates like other affections." And again, "If you cut open the head, you will find the brain humid, full of sweat and smelling badly. And in this way you may see that it is not a god which injures the body, but disease" (*Sacred Disease* by Hippocrates, as quoted in Zilboorg & Henry, 1941, pp. 43–44). Hippocrates was a careful clinical observer; and his own classification of mental diseases included phobias, epilepsy, mania, melancholia, and paranoia (more like mental deterioration than what we currently call paranoia).

If psychological abnormalities are caused by spirit possession, then treatment would likely involve ways of ridding the body of the invading spirit, whether by opening a hole in the skull or by **exorcism** techniques such as uttering religious incantations, whipping, starvation,

**Trephining**

Tools, probably of stone, were used to make a sizable hole in a skull, possibly with the intent of permitting entrapped demons to escape

**Demonolgy**

The belief that possession by demons or spirits explains abnormal behavior

**Exorcism**

The practice of expelling demons from a body that they possess

The four important bodily fluids, yellow bile, black bile, blood, and phlegm, make up the Four Humors, each symbolizing a different temperament: Yellow bile ("choleric"); black bile ("melancholic"); blood ("sanguine"); phlegm ("phlegmatic"). (Wikimedia Commons)

or other efforts to make the body an uncomfortable vessel for the demon. In contrast, the naturalistic approach of the Greeks (as illustrated by Galen, who was strongly influenced by the earlier work of Hippocrates) proposed that psychological abnormalities were caused by imbalances of important bodily fluids called the four humors: yellow bile, black bile, blood, and phlegm. An excess of yellow bile would lead a person to be easily angered and with a hot temper ("choleric"), whereas if black bile dominated, the patient would sleep poorly and be depressed ("melancholic"). Too much blood caused amorative and hopeful behavior ("sanguine"), and too much phlegm suppressed emotions and produced calm ("phlegmatic").

Hippocrates, operating from the metaphor that behavioral abnormalities were sicknesses in the same sense as physical disorders, advocated "medical" approaches to treatment, such as moderate exercise and physical tranquility. To correct the imbalance of fluids, techniques such as bleeding and purging were practiced. His theories of bodily functioning were crude and frequently inaccurate by today's standards; yet in looking to natural causes and eschewing demonology, his general viewpoint and attitude is essentially modern. Greek and Roman physicians such as Galen, Asclepiades and Aretaeus carried on this tradition. With the fall of Rome, however, much of the collected science was lost to European culture. As Pronko (1989) notes, naturalism was stunted by a developing religious view that held the Bible was the source of all knowledge. Therefore, "research" involved careful study of the holy word, rather than observation and dissection. For most of Europe, scientific approaches were curtailed for centuries. Fortunately, many of the works of Greek scientists and scholars were preserved in Islamic countries, where humane and enlightened approaches to treatment emerged at this time—in stark contrast to the harsh demonology that characterized the European world during these "dark ages."

## 2.2c  Dance Manias in the Middle Ages

A curious phenomenon developed near the end of the Middle Ages and appeared on and off for several hundred years—the **dance manias**. Peter Herental describes one such episode that occurred in 1374:

> Both men and women were abused by the devil to such a degree that they danced in their homes, in the churches and in the streets, holding each other's hands and leaping in the air. While they danced, they called out the names of demons, such as Friskes and others; but they were neither aware of this nor did they pay attention to modesty even though people watched them. At the end of the dance, they felt such pains in the chest, that if their friends did not tie linen clothes tightly around their waists, they cried out like madmen that they were dying. In Liège they were freed of their demons by means of exorcisms such as those employed before baptism (Rosen, 1968, pp. 196–197).

Similar dancing manias were called *tarantism* in Italy because they were believed to be caused by the bite of a tarantula, and in other parts of Europe they were known as *St. Vitus' dance* (after a 1518 episode in which dancers were sent to a chapel of St. Vitus). The dancers, mostly from the lower socioeconomic classes, sometimes set wreaths on their heads, bound themselves around with cloths or towels, or went half-naked. They would work themselves into a kind of ecstasy, suddenly throwing themselves on the ground with convulsive and twitching movements, sometimes losing consciousness and foaming at the mouth. In some areas the dance mania became institutionalized as an annual ritual. One group of women, for example, made an annual pilgrimage to a chapel of St. Vitus, where they would dance

An exorcism of an evil spirit in the streets of Akra, India.
(Shutterstock)

**Dance manias**

Episodes of apparent mass madness in which groups of people danced in the streets ecstatically until they collapsed from exhaustion. For several weeks before the pilgrimage they suffered from feelings of restlessness and a feeling of painful heaviness, but after the dance they were freed of these attacks and could anticipate a year of wellbeing (Rosen, 1968).

## 2.2d Demonology Triumphant: Witchcraft

During most of the Middle Ages, physicians confronted with various forms of psychopathology put together, as best they could, some of the traditional, and by then somewhat garbled, views of the ancient Greeks and Romans and the astrology, alchemy, demonology, and simple prayers of their own day. Exorcising demons was not necessarily a brutal affair. Laying on of hands, the utterance of certain prayers, or the ingestion of unsavory potions were common procedures. Beginning near the end of the fifteenth century and continuing for some two hundred years, a more virulent form of demonology led to a widespread preoccupation with witches and their identification and destruction. Several historical conditions may have contributed to this phenomenon: A church whose doctrines were being severely challenged by the Reformation (protestants, however, soon started their own witch-hunts) and general unrest caused by wars, economic depressions, and the Black Plagues increased people's readiness to blame their woes on handy scapegoats.

The lengths to which physicians and clergymen would go to drive out invading devils became more and more extreme. Flogging, starving, immersion in hot water, and more refined forms of torture were employed. Initially, a distinction existed between individuals who had been unwittingly seized by a devil and those who had intentionally signed a pact to do the devil's work. Only the latter were known as witches. The distinction, however, became blurred. If persons suspected of being a witch did not confess, they were likely to be tortured until they did. Following the biblical injunction,

> *"Thou shalt not suffer a witch to live"*
>
> (Exodus 22:18)

(iStock)

convicted witches were put to death, frequently by burning at the stake. To individuals like Boguet, a French judge, the world seemed infested with witches:

> I believe that the sorcerers could form an army equal to that of Xerxes, who had one million, eight hundred thousand men.
>
> As to myself, I have no doubt, since a mere glance at our neighbors will convince us that the land is infested with this unfortunate and damnable vermin. Germany cannot do anything but raise fires against them; Switzerland is compelled to do likewise, thus depopulating many of its villages …
>
> No, no, the sorcerers reach everywhere by the thousands; they multiply on the earth like the caterpillars in our gardens … I want them to know that if the results were to correspond to my wishes, the earth would be quickly purged, because I wish they could all be united in one body so that all could be burned on one fire. (Zilboorg & Henry, 1941, pp. 162–163)

The witchcraft phenomenon is relevant to the study of abnormal behavior because some individuals suffering from mental disorders were probably convicted as witches and may even have, in some cases, believed themselves to be witches. Most convicted witches, however, were probably relatively normal people who simply had the ill fortune at the wrong time in history to get into an argument with a neighbor a few weeks before the neighbor's child got sick or the neighbor's cow died. However, individuals with behavior disorders played other roles in this affair. Recall how the children of Salem successfully accused others of witchcraft while in the throes of hysterical reactions.

## 2.2e  Voices of Reason

To draw too sharp a line between medieval and modern views of mental disorders would be inaccurate. Throughout the Dark Ages and medieval times, some individuals maintained the more scientific and humane attitudes of the ancient Greek and Roman physicians. In Arabian civilization, especially, these views prevailed. For example, a mental hospital, where humane care for the mentally disturbed was provided, was established as early as 792 AD in Baghdad.

At the height of the European obsession with witches lived Johann Weyer (1515–1588), a man whose views on mental disorders were far ahead of his time. His ability to see natural causes of deviant human behavior without becoming caught up in the prevailing theological explanations is illustrated by the case of Barbara Kremers. This 10-year-old girl had become a celebrity; miraculously she never ate, urinated, or moved her bowels, but was in good health. This "miracle" had followed a severe illness. For 6 months following the illness, Barbara had remained mute; after that time she had ceased to eat. Learned men came to see her and marvel, and the City Council awarded her a certificate testifying to the truth of this wonder. Weyer became interested in the girl and arranged to have her and her sister come to live at the estate where he lived (as personal physician to a Duke). It was soon discovered that Barbara and her sister had engaged in a clever swindle in which her sister had secretly supplied her with food. Weyer treated Barbara with kindness, and in less than a week's time she was eating regular meals at Weyer's table. She had also been partially lame and walked on crutches and suffered, in addition, from a twist in her arms. Weyer cured her lameness merely by rubbing bland oil on her back, and shortly thereafter the twist in her arms also disappeared. Weyer's clinical writings are full of examples of this kind in which a combination of astute clinical observation, uncluttered by demonological speculations, and a kindly respect for the person foreshadow modern psychiatry.

Weyer believed that many witches were mentally disturbed individuals who needed care and treatment, not torturing and burning. He made a careful study of witchcraft and published a book on the subject in which he deplored the senseless torturing and killing of innocent people. It was not until long after Weyer's death that the common sense appeal of his book began to be accepted by medical authorities. The reaction of Church authorities at the time is summed up by the statement of Father Spina:

> "*Recently Satan went to a Sabbath (a witches' gathering) attired as a great prince, and told the assembled witches that they need not worry since, thanks to Weyer and his followers, the affairs of the Devil were brilliantly progressing*"
>
> (Castiglioni, 1946, p. 253).

Eventually, in the face of growing attacks, demonology gave ground. In England, Reginald Scott (1538–1599) exposed the fallacies of witchcraft and demonology in a book called *The Discovery of Witchcraft*, published in 1584. He especially denied the role of demons in producing mental disorders. St. Vincent de Paul (1576–1660), likewise at the risk of his own life, argued that mental diseases were similar in kind to bodily disease.

**BVT** *Lab*

Flashcards are available for this chapter at **www.BVTLab.com**.

# 2.3 Demonology Today: Alive and Well in the USA?

In most abnormal psychology textbooks, demon possession is discussed as a curious and interesting belief of ancient and medieval times that has given way to modern, scientific approaches to the understanding of human behavior. Although hardly in the mainstream of the scientific study of abnormal psychology, theories of demon possession still have their adherents. In fact, Rice (2003) reported that over half of the respondents in a random telephone survey of Southern states believed that people are sometimes possessed by the devil.

Belief in occult phenomena—witchcraft, astrology, and so on—enjoyed a revival that began in the second half of the twentieth century. Movies such as *Rosemary's Baby* and *The Exorcist* dealt explicitly and seriously with demon possession, and they became immensely popular and successful. Hollywood and the press continued to feed the public's interest in all things supernatural, so tales of the living being tormented by the dead, or of battles between unseen forces for the control of the physical world, have become commonplace in American popular media. A resurgent fundamentalist influence also helped re-establish and legitimize religious possession metaphors for mental disorders. By the 1990s, some members of the medical and psychological communities were proposing that a particular type of a rare condition, formerly called multiple personality disorder but now termed **dissociative identity disorder**, was caused by satanic ritualistic abuse. Allegedly, adults and children as young as infants were initiated into satanic cults by secret ritual practices that included killing and eating babies, torture, human and animal sacrifice, and sexual abuse, often while in a trance-like state induced by devil worshippers. Initiates were then supposedly "brain-washed" and "programmed" to kill others, without having any conscious awareness of the cult influence. These unseen and unrecognized influences later allegedly manifested themselves in terms of several different personalities co-existing within the same person. Although the outward symptoms among the afflicted often involved anxiety, depression, and other rather common psychological problems, proponents of these claims used questionable techniques involving hypnosis and/or drugs to "recover the repressed memories" of their clients and to bring out the many personalities so that they could be "integrated."

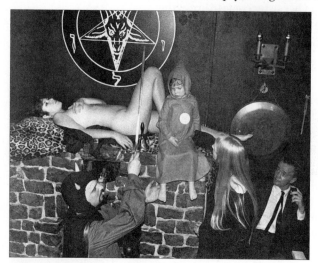

High priest of the Church of Satan, Anton LaVey, performs a satanic baptism of his three-year-old daughter in 1967 with the assistance of his wife Diane (right). The nude woman who serves as a living altar is priestess Isabel Bolotov. (AP Wide World)

**Dissociative identity disorder**

Rare dissociative reaction in which relatively separate and distinctive personalities develop within the same person

Ritualistic abuse by Satan worshipers became a popular (and exciting) explanation for multiple personality disorder featured in many television programs and magazines. "Experts" in the field developed expensive, long-term inpatient programs that kept some clients hospitalized for years. Speakers delivered workshops and seminars to train others in how to diagnose and reprogram those who had been initiated into the secret cults. Finally, as public interest continued to grow, the FBI conducted an investigation into the allegations of sexual abuse, torture, killings, and cannibalism supposedly occurring across the nation and involving thousands of victims. After an extensive review of facts, the 1992 FBI report concluded as follows:

> *"Until hard evidence is obtained and corroborated, the public should not be frightened into believing that babies are being bred and eaten, that 50,000 missing children are being murdered in human sacrifices, or that satanists are taking over America's day care centers or institutions. No one can prove with absolute certainty that such activity has NOT occurred. The burden of proof, however, as it would be in a criminal prosecution, is on those who claim that it has occurred. The explanation that the satanists are too organized and law enforcement is too incompetent only goes so far in explaining the lack of evidence. For at least eight years American law enforcement has been aggressively investigating the allegations of victims of ritual abuse. There is little or no evidence for the portion of their allegations that deals with large-scale baby breeding, human sacrifice, and organized satanic conspiracies. Now it is up to mental health professionals, not law enforcement, to explain why victims are alleging things that don't seem to have happened"*
>
> (Lanning, 1992).

Satanic ritualistic abuse, then, seems to be an unlikely explanation for multiple personality disorder. Instead, it appears to be another example of an idea that spreads quickly because of its entertaining social (and financial) consequences rather than its paradigmatic value and that is accepted at face value by suggestible people, much as the Salem witchcraft possession cases illustrated hundreds of years earlier. Although we should reject no explanations out of hand, a reasonable approach to such ideas is skepticism and insistence on supporting evidence. That sort of scientific reasoning will, slowly over time, lead us to increasingly more powerful models of abnormal behavior, and away from those that simply catch the public's eye.

> **How have ideas about abnormal behavior changed over time?**

## 2.4 Humanitarian Reforms

### 2.4a The Early Asylums

In medieval times the fate of the mentally disturbed was varied. Some were simply allowed to wander the streets and the countryside, begging or stealing, making out as best they could. Some more troublesome individuals wound up in prisons or dungeons alongside common criminals; or if they were lucky, they found a place in the occasional monastery that provided assistance for these unfortunates. The first institutions devoted entirely to the care of the mentally impaired, called asylums, frequently had their start in monasteries. Although asylums usually began as havens where the mentally disturbed could find food, shelter, and some kindly attention, as time went by they tended to become overcrowded, noisy, unsanitary repositories. Patients were frequently chained, and no concern was shown for whether these conditions were helpful in restoring mental equilibrium. The living conditions at Bethlehem Hospital, a London asylum opened in 1547, became so noisy and chaotic that the word *bedlam* was derived from its name. Passersby could observe the more violent patients for a penny a look, and the more harmless individuals were

The octagon tower of the former New York Insane Asylum on New York's Roosevelt Island (formerly Welfare Island and Blackwell's Island), which opened in 1839 (Library of Congress)

forced to beg on the streets of London. In Vienna, the so-called Lunatics Tower was constructed in 1784. Patients were confined between inner rooms and the outer curved wall, where in some cases they could be observed by the local citizenry.

## 2.4b  Treating Mental Patients Like Human Beings

In the eighteenth and nineteenth centuries, several reformers began improving the care of the mentally disturbed. One of the most famous promoters of humanitarian approaches was Philippe Pinel. In the midst of the French Revolution in 1792, Pinel was placed in charge of a hospital for the insane, La Bicêtre in Paris. Although the leaders of the Revolution loudly proclaimed their ideals of liberty, equality, and fraternity, they were less than enthusiastic about Pinel's proposal to remove the chains from the insane and treat them with kindness and dignity. After considerable pleading, Pinel was granted permission to try his experiment. Patients chained for as long as 40 years were cut free and permitted to see the sun and breathe fresh air once more. Many of these patients, after experiencing the freer and more humane conditions created by Pinel, were eventually able to leave the hospital (incidentally, Pinel benefited as well: he was saved from the hands of an unruly mob of revolutionaries by a former inmate who recognized him).

Dr. Philippe Pinel at the Salpêtrière, 1795 by Tony Robert-Fleury. Pinel ordering the removal of chains from patients at the Paris Asylum for insane women (Wikimedia Commons)

In other ways Pinel's reforms were forerunners of the modern psychiatric hospital. He interviewed and studied the patients carefully, making notes of what they said and of any other information relevant to their difficulties. In short, he introduced the keeping of systematic records on patients, an essential step if knowledge about the nature of these disorders was to progress.

Similar reforms were begun in England where the Quaker, William Tuke, founded the York Retreat in the English countryside where patients were permitted to rest and work in an accepting religious environment. However, these reforms begun by specific individuals did not immediately spread to all institutions. The history of mental hospital care has been and continues to be one of cyclical rediscovery of dehumanizing treatment and the advocacy of reforms. In mid-nineteenth century America, a New England schoolteacher named Dorothea Dix (1802–1887) launched a campaign against the inhumane conditions in asylums. In 1848 she sent a report of what she had seen to the Congress of the United States:

> … more than 90 idiots, epileptics and insane in the United States, destitute of appropriate care and protection … bound with galling chains, bowed beneath fetters and heavy iron balls attached to drag chains, lacerated with ropes, scourged with rods and terrified beneath storms of execration and cruel blows; now subject to jibes and scorn and torturing tricks; now abandoned to the most outrageous violations. (Zilboorg & Henry, 1941, pp. 583–584)

During the 40 years of her endeavors, Dix was instrumental in founding or enlarging more than 30 state institutions for the proper custody and treatment of mental patients.

Modern reformers still note the dehumanizing psychological impact of the institutional environment. Although there is still a need—at some level—for the asylum, the modern mental health system endorses the value of deinstitutionalization and the creation of more residential treatment facilities in home-like settings in the community.

**BVT** *Lab*

Visit **www.BVTLab.com** to explore the student resources available for this chapter.

# 2.5  The Organic View

The **organic view**—based on the belief that mental disorders have their origin in some biological malfunction transmitted through heredity or caused by a disease, injury, lesion, or more subtle biochemical disturbance in the brain—is as old as Hippocrates. The theory and the methods of study have become more refined in recent years, but the basic idea remains the same—mental disturbances are diseases of the central nervous system.

> **Do diseased brains cause abnormal behavior?**

As we have seen, in the Middle Ages there was a retreat from scientific approaches to mental disorders, including the organic view. In the sixteenth and seventeenth centuries, however, a resurgence of scientific thinking in Europe led to a series of great discoveries and inventions for the study of the world around us. An influential perspective, formalized by the philosopher René Descartes (1596–1650), proposed that humans and animals worked much as machines did—arms and legs moved through mechanisms of the body that were not so different from ropes and pulleys. Descartes thought that the behavior of animals was therefore mindless, automatic, and reflexive. Humans were different, according to Descartes, because in addition to this machinery, they have a soul and could act voluntarily. This notion of the separation of mind and body (**dualism**) has presented some impediments to more modern scientific perspectives of behavior, but one of its earliest ramifications was positive for the developing field of medicine. Since the body was only the physical housing for the soul, the Catholic Church allowed dissection of the human body by physicians. (Although the physical realm of the body was conceded to medicine, the Church retained imminence in the study of the mind, or soul.) By the middle of the nineteenth century the notion that disordered behavior was related in some way to disordered brains had regained considerable prominence. A German psychiatrist, Wilhelm Griesinger (1817–1868), contended that classification of mental disorders should be based on underlying brain lesions; and a French psychiatrist, Morel (1809–1873), proposed that mental illness resulted from brain deterioration, itself the consequence of a hereditary neural weakness.

## 2.5a  An Influential Classification System: Emil Kraepelin

The monumental work of Emil Kraepelin (1855–1926) further solidified the organic view and provided us with a classification system that has continued to influence psychiatric thinking to this day. Following a strategy that was paying off in the study of physical diseases, Kraepelin looked for individuals with patterns of symptoms, or "symptom-complexes," that showed a similar onset, course, and outcome. He then combined symptom patterns previously considered as separate categories into two major syntheses: *manic-depressive psychosis* and *dementia praecox* (roughly comparable to *schizophrenia* in current terminology). Mania (excited, elated reactions) was linked with depression or melancholia to form the manic-depressive category because the psychiatric records showed that (1) these symptoms sometimes alternated with each other in the same person, (2) both mania and melancholia showed an abrupt onset and a periodic course in which the person tended to show spontaneous recovery but a high likelihood of future recurrences, and (3) in neither case was there progressive mental deterioration or physical symptoms such as paralysis. Dementia praecox represented an amalgam of an even greater variety of symptoms that had in common two characteristics: an early onset, usually in adolescence or young adulthood (thus praecox or precocious), and a progressive downhill course toward an incurable *dementia* (mental

Emil Kraepelin (Wikimedia Commons)

**Organic view**

Belief that abnormal behavior is caused primarily by biological factors

**Dualism**

The belief that mind and body are separate and follow different laws incompetence). While irreversible, however, the outcome was not death but rather stabilization at a very reduced level of mental and social capacity. Kraepelin also included a third category, paranoia, which occurred less frequently than the other two symptom patterns and consisted of one symptom, a highly systematized delusional belief of a persecutory nature.

Kraepelin's two major classifications accounted for about two-thirds of all the patients in mental hospitals at that time. The importance of his work lay in the possibility that investigation of the cause and cure of these disorders could proceed more rationally if, indeed, these categories reflected distinct disease processes. Kraepelin himself thought that the manic-depressive psychosis was the result of some disturbance in metabolic function (probably inherited since this disorder seemed to run in families), while dementia praecox was caused by some abnormality in the sex glands. The framework by which mental disorders are classified has changed significantly since that time, but the current system still shows Kraepelin's contribution.

## 2.5b  The Search for Physical Causes and Cures

With almost no knowledge of heredity or neurology, most authorities on mental disorders in the eighteenth and nineteenth centuries looked toward seemingly naturalistic factors, such as fluid imbalances, or astrological influences to explain abnormality—much as did Hippocrates before them. Bleeding was a common treatment for many diverse disorders, both physical and mental. There was widespread acceptance that the position of the stars and planets influenced behavior and personality; **lunatics** were those whose mental problems were traceable to the phases of the moon. One of the most serious of the purported causes of insanity (as well as epilepsy, poor eyesight, stupidity, and a host of other afflictions) was masturbation, or "self-abuse." Convinced that the act was a dangerous threat to health, doctors lectured on the importance of purity and prescribed various devices invented to help wayward individuals resist the dangerous temptation to self-pleasure—such as genital cages, anti-erection rings, caustic chemicals, and restraints.

In the United States, Benjamin Rush (1745–1813) founded American psychiatry and wrote its first textbook, *Medical Inquiries and Observations upon the Diseases of the Mind* in 1812. A signer of the Declaration of Independence, he promoted humane treatment for patients and believed that with the right treatment mental disease could be cured. Although he was in some ways a visionary who helped introduce modern concepts to psychiatry, his approach reflected a combination of scientific, astrological, and superstitious thinking. Influenced by Tissot, a Swiss physician, Rush believed that "bodily energy" must be kept in proper balance to avoid disease. Masturbation disturbed the balance of energy and resulted in serious disorders. Some of the treatments he employed were bloodletting, purgatives, and spinning patients on wooden boards (or in special "tranquilizing chairs") to make blood rush to the brain.

## 2.5c  An Example of Organic Causation: General Paresis

The discovery of the nature of a mental disorder called **general paresis**, one of the great achievements of medical science, gave strong impetus to the development of organic theories of abnormal behavior. General paresis involved a symptom-complex consisting of delusions of grandeur, dementia, and progressive paralysis. The paralysis and mental deterioration progressed rapidly to a fatal outcome. Although many contemporary physicians had thought that paralysis might be a secondary accompaniment of many forms of madness, in 1826 Bayle presented even more precise descriptions of both the mental and physical symptoms of general paresis and argued strongly that they represented a single form of mental illness that could be distinguished from other disorders.

Progress was slow for several decades. Then around 1860, it became possible to demonstrate, with the use of improved microscopes, that the brains of patients who died from general

(iStock)

**Lunatics**

Those whose mental problems were traceable to the phases of the moon

**General paresis**

Severe disorder characterized by various mental symptoms as well as bodily paralyses and caused by a syphilitic infection of the brain paresis revealed widespread destruction of nervous tissue. In 1884, Fournier provided highly suggestive evidence that the symptoms of general paresis were related to and perhaps part of the sexually transmitted disease, syphilis. He found that 65% of patients with general paresis had a history of syphilis, compared with only 10% of patients with other mental disorders. Sixty-five percent was still short of 1%; and it remained for Krafft-Ebing, in 1897, to perform a convincing if ethically questionable study. He inoculated nine paretic patients, who had denied having a prior syphilitic infection, with matter from syphilitic sores. None of these patients developed symptoms of syphilis, indicating that immunity had resulted from a previous or continuing infection. The specific infectious agent for syphilis, a spirochete called *Treponema pallidum*, was identified in 1905 by Schaudinn; and in 1913 Noguchi and Moore found this organism in the brain tissue of paretic patients.

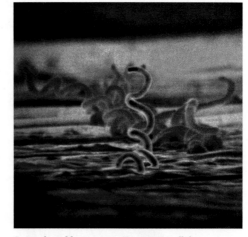

Spirochetal bacterium *Treponema pallidum* (Syphilis). In 1884 Fournier provided highly suggestive evidence that the symptoms of general paresis were related to and perhaps part of the sexually transmitted disease, syphilis. (Wikimedia Commons)

Once the cause of general paresis—untreated syphilis—was identified, the discovery of an effective treatment remained. Initial success came in 1917, with the development of **malarial fever therapy**. Wagner-Juaregg in Vienna used blood from a soldier with malaria to infect patients who had general paresis. The resulting infection caused a high fever, which in turn killed off the syphilis spirochete. The patient then worked to recover from the malaria itself. A much more effective and palatable therapy was developed decades later with the discovery of penicillin, but the malarial fever technique was a paradigmatic success.

Thus one identifiable pattern of mental disorder was found to have a clearly specified onset, course, and outcome, and most importantly, to be caused by an infectious agent in the same manner as pneumonia or diphtheria. It is no wonder that medical scientists were encouraged to expect other forms of mental disorders to reveal in time their own brand of organic causation. In some instances, this hope has been fulfilled; but after a century of organically oriented research, the foundation of the disease model today remains surprisingly incomplete. With very few exceptions, there are no laboratory tests that can be conducted to detect the presence (or absence) of a mental disorder, or even any biochemical findings that are specific to particular disorders. In fact, a precise physical cause has never been found for most *DSM-5* diagnoses. However, there have been great developments in understanding the genetic and neurochemical bases of brain functioning and in the use of pharmacological agents that can provide significant symptom alleviation. These are very active areas of research, to be considered in greater detail in the next chapter. In no sense, however, has an organic "cure" like that for general paresis been formulated for the vast majority of mental disorders.

## 2.6  The Psychological View

The view that psychological events—such as our personal experiences, beliefs, emotions, and ideas—might cause abnormal behavior developed along two very different lines of work. One arose largely through the study of *hysteria* and *hypnosis*, while the other emerged from the study of animal learning.

**Do ideas, emotional conflicts, and upsetting experiences, cause abnormal behavior?**

### 2.6a  Healing by Suggestion: Anton Mesmer

**Hysteria** includes not only the popularly recognized "hysterical attack," involving uncontrolled emotional outbursts of weeping, laughter, or other inappropriate behaviors, but also certain altered states of consciousness and a host of changeable bodily symptoms (such as paralyses, muscular contractions, and defects in hearing and vision) that have no identifiable organic basis. The term itself, derived from the Greek word for uterus, *hystera*, reflects a belief

**Malarial fever therapy**

A treatment for general paresis that involved infecting the patient with malaria to cause a high fever

**Hysteria**

A condition that includes emotional arousal and physical symptoms that seem to have no organic basis

Anton. Mesmer (Shutterstock)

A. MESMER

common in the ancient world that these disorders occurred in women only and resulted from a wandering or displaced uterus, for which Hippocrates might have prescribed marriage (to allow the uterus to produce a child).

In the late eighteenth century, the rise of a psychological metaphor for understanding these disorders began with the flamboyant career of Anton Mesmer (1734–1815). Trained as a physician, Mesmer was influenced by the astrological and pseudoscientific beliefs of his time. He believed that all human behavior was under the influence of the stars and that this influence was accomplished through a constant flow of a magnetic fluid that fills the universe. Physical symptoms developed when the distribution of the magnetic fluid became unbalanced within a person. Healing was produced by permitting a flow of the magnetic fluid into or from the person by the "magnetizer" or healer. Expelled from the Viennese medical profession for his unorthodox approaches to treatment, Mesmer went to Paris where he soon established a flourishing practice.

A typical session in Mesmer's clinic was highly theatrical. The patients gathered around a *bacquet* (a tub) whose floor was covered with powdered glass and iron filings and from which protruded iron rods that were applied to the afflicted areas of the body. As Zweig (1932) described the session, Mesmer, wearing a blue robe and playing music, would enter the room, draw near to the patients, and stroke them with his magnetic wand while gazing intently at them. "Usually no great time elapsed before one or the other of the company would begin to tremble. Then the limbs would start to twitch convulsively, and the patient would break out in perspiration, would scream, or groan. No sooner had such tokens manifested themselves in one member of the chain, than the others, too, would feel the onset of the famous crisis which was to bring relief. All would begin to twitch, a mass psychosis [sic] would arise, a second and a third patient would be seized with convulsions. ... Some would fall to the ground and go into convulsions, others would laugh shrilly, others would scream, and choke and groan, and dance like dervishes, others would appear to faint ..." (pp. 55–56).

MESMER'S TUB;

Austrian hypnotist Anton Mesmer and his tub in 1784 (iStock)

Under these dramatic conditions, many patients experienced relief from various aches, pains, and other symptoms. The medical profession, however, was not impressed; and in 1784 a committee of prominent men (including Benjamin Franklin, Joseph-Ignace Guillotin, and Antoine-Laurent de Lavoisier, the discoverer of oxygen) was appointed to investigate Mesmer and his therapeutic techniques. The committee concluded that Mesmer was a fraud and a charlatan. Magnetism, they said, could not be weighed, observed, or measured. Conducting some small experiments of their own, the committee concluded, "that imagination without magnetism produces convulsions and that magnetism without imagination produces nothing." Anticipating the importance that psychologists currently give to observational learning or imitation, they said, "The spectacle of the crises is equally dangerous because of that imitation of which nature, it seems to us, made a law; consequently any public treatment cannot but have at length very harmful results" (Semalaigne, as quoted in Zilboorg & Henry, 1941, pp. 345–346). Mesmer was discredited and forced to leave Paris.

Although Mesmer himself faded into obscurity, his techniques provoked continuing interest and controversy. **Mesmerism** became a popular term for procedures used to induce trances and other altered states of consciousness. In time these phenomena came to be subsumed under the general heading of **hypnosis**, and most of the trappings and

**Hypnosis**

A trancelike state induced through suggestion in cooperative subjects

**Mesmerism**

Closely related to the phenomenon of hypnosis; derived from the techniques of Anton Mesmer

associated theory used by Mesmer were dropped. The central features of most hypnotic procedures, then as now, included some way of narrowing the field of attention to some specific stimulus ( for example, the hypnotist's voice, a swinging pendulum, or a shining light), an atmosphere of expectation that an unusual state would indeed be forthcoming, and a willing, cooperative subject.

## 2.6b  The Scientific Study of Hysteria: Jean-Martin Charcot

In the nineteenth century, the prevailing medical view of hysterical symptoms was that either they resulted from an organic brain disorder or they were displays by flighty women seeking attention and sympathy, not to be taken seriously. Hypnotism continued to be associated with the occult, strange theories of "magnetic fluids," and charlatanism, or was considered mere suggestion by the medical establishment. Although by no means the first person to study the relationship between hypnosis and hysteria, Jean-Martin Charcot, a distinguished French neurologist, was largely responsible for making both topics respectable objects of scientific investigation.

A puzzling but significant fact about hysteria was the almost unlimited variety of symptoms it encompassed. In Charcot's day, one symptom was the *grande hysterie*, in which the person lost consciousness, fell, showed muscular contractions similar to those in epileptic attacks, and proceeded to various other "gymnastics" such as a tetanus-like posture in which the body was bent in an arc resting only on head and heels. Following these physical contortions, the patient might express various emotions (such as pleasure, pain, fear, or hatred) that, in some cases, related clearly to a disturbing incident in the patient's life. After recovering from such an attack, the patient would be amnesic, that is, remember nothing about it.

Disturbances in sensory perception were frequent in hysterical patients. Most common of all was **anesthesia**, a lack of ordinary sensation in the skin where the body surface becomes insensitive to touch, pain, or heat. In some cases the whole body would be affected; more usually the lack of sensation would only occur on some part of the body. In **hemianesthesia** the whole of one side of the body became insensitive. In other cases, a hand, an arm, or some patch of skin lost the sense of touch. Other senses were sometimes affected. Hysterical blindness or deafness occurred but was rare; lesser impairments in vision and hearing were more frequent. In some individuals, for example, the field of vision was restricted so that they looked at the world as through a tunnel.

Hysterical pains were innumerable, especially in the head, abdomen, ovarian region, back, and joints. Various reflexes could become involved, causing persistent coughing, sneezing, yawning, or hiccoughing. A host of afflictions occurred in the musculature: **tics** (mild spasms, usually of the facial muscles), muscular tremors, muscular contractions, and paralysis. In the contractions, a hand might be permanently bent at the knuckles or at the wrist, a knee drawn up, or one leg crossed over the other. Paralysis could affect any muscle group: legs, arms, or speech muscles, as in mutism. A particularly puzzling paralysis was **abasia**, the inability to walk. Patients with this symptom were frequently young and in good health. When examined in bed, they could execute all normal movements and there seemed to be no detectable physical

French neurologist Jean-Martin Charcot was largely responsible for making hypnosis and hysteria respectable objects of scientific investigation. (Wikimedia Commons)

**Anesthesia**

A lack of ordinary sensation in which the body surface becomes insensitive to touch, pain, or heat

**Hemianesthesia**

The condition of the whole of one side of the body becoming insensitive

**Tics**

Involuntary muscular twitching, usually in the facial muscles

**Abasis**

The inability to walk

problem. Yet they were absolutely incapable of walking. If made to get out of bed, they fell to the floor. Other selective defects frequently seemed related to occupations: a dressmaker who could no longer sew or a pianist who could not play the piano, even though in neither case was there a paralysis of the hand.

Charcot realized that some patients exaggerated or simulated certain symptoms with conscious intent, but in most instances the symptoms seemed to be as mysterious and unexplainable to the patient as to the physician. He also observed a number of ways in which hysterical symptoms tended to differ from similar symptoms arising from known organic causes. For example, patients having real epileptic seizures are likely to fall and hurt themselves; by contrast the hysterical seizure patients have an uncanny knack of falling so that no harm results and may engage in the more spectacular display previously described. Several features seemed unlike physical paralyses: general lack of atrophy of the affected limb, disappearance of the affliction under chloroform (but not in ordinary sleep), normal reflexes, sudden onset, and occasionally sudden disappearance. Additionally, hysterical anesthesias were especially striking in that they frequently involved effects on the body that no known organic lesion or disease process could produce. In so-called **glove or sleeve anesthesias**, the insensitive area of the hand or arm corresponded with that which would be covered by a glove or sleeve, an outcome that could not result from any combination of injuries to the three sensory nerve tracts going to the arm and hand. Many hysterical patients, instead of being worried or depressed about their physical symptoms, appeared calm and indeed quite cheerful in some cases—a characteristic that Charcot christened **la belle indifférence**.

Because Charcot was a neurologist, consistent with the prevailing climate of medical opinion he was strongly disposed to explain bodily symptoms, including the hysterical variety, in terms of central nervous system pathology. The various ways in which hysterical symptoms were found to differ from known organic diseases were enough to arouse his suspicion and lead him to consider a different explanation. Charcot, clearly impressed with the power of psychological events to produce hysterical symptoms, wondered if hysterical symptoms could be produced through **autosuggestion** in a process something like self-hypnosis. He soon found he could put hysterical patients under hypnosis, produce new symptoms at will, and relieve the existing symptoms of at least some patients—depending on how chronic the conditions were.

Charcot's hypnotic demonstrations were largely limited to hysterical patients, but other investigators ( for example, Liebault and Bernheim) were reporting that hysterical symptoms could be induced in subjects with no previous history of hysteria.

The view that psychological factors played an important role in the causation of hysterical symptoms gained momentum toward the end of the nineteenth century. Many young physicians came to study with Charcot in Paris and were influenced by his teachings and demonstrations. A young man from Vienna, Sigmund Freud, spent the year 1885–1886 at Charcot's hospital. In later years, Freud recognized the importance of this experience in his own career:

> What impressed me most of all while I was with Charcot were his latest investigations on hysteria, some of which were carried out under my own eyes. He proved for instance the genuineness of hysterical phenomena and their conformity to laws ... the frequent occurrence of hysteria in men, the production of hysterical paralysis and contractures by hypnotic suggestion and the fact that such artificial products showed, down to their smallest detail, the same features as spontaneous attacks which were often brought on traumatically. (Freud, 1948, p. 22)

The stage was set for the more dynamic theories of Freud, to be considered in the next chapter.

## 2.6c  The Scientific Study of Learning and Behavior

The second path of investigation lending insight into the psychological causes of abnormal behavior derived from animal experiments on how behavior was affected by experience.

**BVT** *Lab*

Improve your test scores. Practice quizzes are available at **www.BVTLab.com**.

**Glove or sleeve anesthesias**

When the insensitive area of the hand or arm corresponded with that which would be covered by a glove or sleeve

**La belle indifférence**

The condition of hysterical patients appearing calm and indeed quite cheerful, instead of being worried or depressed about their physical symptoms

**Autosuggestion**

A process that is similar to self-hypnosis

After Charles Darwin wrote his paradigm-shifting work *On the Origin of Species* in 1857, humans came to be seen as members of the family of animals on the great "Tree of Life." Perhaps, then, some knowledge about human physiology and behavior could be gained by research with other species.

Already, studies on frogs had revealed important information about how nerves worked and how reflexes could be triggered and modified. Sherrington organized the laws of the reflex, describing rules about the relationships of the stimulus that triggered the reflex and the response it produced. Ivan Pavlov in Russia was working on digestion—efforts that would later win him a Nobel Prize in physiology—by measuring the salivary reflex in dogs, as a response to the stimulus of powdered meat placed into their mouths. Pavlov controlled events in a laboratory setting, which allowed a high level of scientific precision in his procedures and his measurements. A cannula was implanted into the dog's cheek to collect saliva and channel it to a beaker where the quantity could be measured and a record could be made of its timing within the session (see Figure 2-2). In this way, the precise amount of salivation and its temporal relationship to other events (such as the introduction of meat powder) could be recorded.

Salivation was clearly related to digestion, and the salivary reflex was readily understood in that context. However, Pavlov noted that the dogs soon came to salivate *before* meat powder was delivered into the mouth, apparently at just the sight of the laboratory workers engaged in the study. He undertook a series of experiments to understand the nature of this "psychic" reflex. From Aristotle's time, it was known that if two sensations were combined, one later would evoke or trigger the memory of the other.

After Charles Darwin published *On the Origin of Species* in 1857, scientists began to use animal studies to gain insight into human physiology and behavior.
(Wikimedia Commons)

## Figure 2-2  *Pavlov's Conditioning Apparatus*

An apparatus similar to that used by Pavlov to study classical conditioning in dogs.

Source: Illustration adapted from *An Introduction to Psychology*, by Ralph Norman Haber and Aharon H. Fried, 1975. Copyright© by Holt, Rinehart, and Winston.

The British associationists expanded that framework to the philosophical exploration of how ideas are formed. Pavlov's work gave scientific definition to how association worked, both mentally and physically.

Pavlov (1928) discovered that if a stimulus such as a tone, bell, or light that previously had no capacity to produce salivation was paired with the presentation of meat powder on a number of occasions, this stimulus would in time elicit salivation—even when no meat powder was provided. In other words, the dog had learned something new—to salivate to a bell. Pavlov called this learning process *conditioning*, and he developed a terminology for the component features. The meat powder was called the **unconditioned stimulus** (or *US*). Salivation produced by the meat powder was called the **unconditioned response** (or *UR*). The neutral stimulus (such as a bell or light) was called the **conditioned stimulus** (or *CS*); and the response of salivation to the conditioned stimulus was called the **conditioned response** (or *CR*).

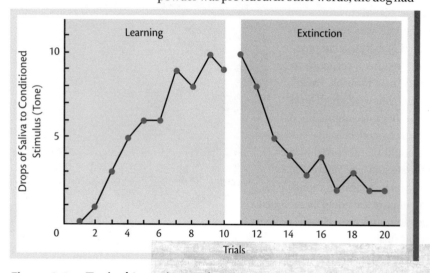

**Figure 2-3    *Typical Learning and Extinction Curve in a Conditioning Experiment***

Quantitative studies showed that conditioning followed a regular pattern. For example, if one plotted the amount that a dog salivated in response to the bell, the curve would look like that in Figure 2-3. Furthermore, if the experimenter stopped giving meat powder in association with the bell signal, the dog would gradually stop salivating until after a while the bell would no longer elicit salivation. The procedure of withholding the unconditioned stimulus was called **extinction**. If the conditioned stimulus were occasionally presented after extinction had occurred, often the conditioned response would briefly reappear before again vanishing. This brief reappearance was called **spontaneous recovery**. Two other processes were evident as a result of conditioning. In **generalization**, stimuli that were increasingly similar to the CS also exerted some control over the CR. With continued conditioning, **discrimination** occurs, narrowing the range of controlling stimuli to those closest to the CS.

It soon became obvious that stimuli other than bells could serve as conditioned stimuli and that reflexes other than salivation could become conditioned responses. Subsequent research has shown that almost any stimulus that an organism can detect can become a CS, whether it is an auditory, visual, or tactile stimulus, a taste, or a smell. It also appears that not only glandular reflexes such as salivation can be conditioned but also muscular, sexual, immunological, and emotional reflexes as well. There are important exceptions and qualifications regarding the rules of Pavlovian conditioning—some pairings work much better than others—but conditioning appears to play a very broad role in animal, and human, functioning.

Pavlov believed that most, if not all, human behavior could be analyzed and explained in terms of innate and acquired (conditioned) reflexes. An interesting experiment that perhaps suggests a Pavlovian analysis of abnormal behavior is related in Rachlin (1991). One of Pavlov's students, Shenger-Krestovnikova, had trained dogs to salivate when presented with a circle drawn on a card. She then found that the dogs also salivated if an ellipse, rather than a circle, was shown on the card (generalization). She trained the dogs to discriminate the circle from the ellipse by pairing food only with the circle and then refined the discrimination to more similar stimuli (Figure 2-4). When faced with the discrimination of (a) and (d), Pavlov reported that one animal's behavior shifted dramatically:

**Unconditioned stimulus**

Stimulus that is naturally capable of eliciting the unconditioned response

**Unconditioned response**

Response that occurs naturally or innately to an unconditional stimulus

**Conditioned stimulus**

An originally neutral stimulus that becomes capable of eliciting a conditioned response after repeated pairing with an unconditioned response

**Conditioned response**

A response that is elicited by a conditioned stimulus after repeated pairing with an unconditioned stimulus

## Figure 2-4    *Discrimination of (A) from (D) Produced "Neurosis"*

Source: From Rachland, 1991

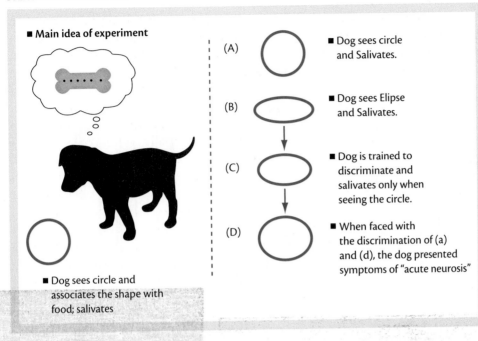

The hitherto quiet dog began to squeal in its stand, kept wriggling about, tore off the apparatus with its teeth for mechanical stimulation of the skin, and bit through the tubes connecting the animal's room with the observer, a behavior which never happened before. On being taken into the experimental room the dog now barked violently, which was also contrary to its usual custom; in short, it presented all the symptoms of acute neurosis. On testing the cruder differentiations, she also found them to be destroyed (Pavlov, 1927, quoted in Rachlin, 1991, p. 78).

Pavlov was not the only scientist exploring learning. In the late 1890s, E. L. Thorndike began studying the process whereby animals learned to escape from a "puzzle box" (Figure 2-5). Hungry cats, for example, when placed in the box learned by trial and error to operate a latch that opened a door through which they could escape to get food. The cats slowly became more adept at the required response, taking less and less time to get out of the puzzle box on succeeding trials (see Figure 2-6).

On the basis of additional research of this kind, Thorndike (1911) formulated the "law of effect": When a behavior is followed by a satisfying consequence, it is more likely to be repeated; when followed by a punishing or annoying consequence, it is less likely to recur. In other words, whether a given behavior is strengthened or weakened depends upon its consequences or effects.

Although Pavlov's work focused on the stimuli that preceded the response, the learning process studied by Thorndike (often called instrumental learning or **operant conditioning** to distinguish it from classical or **Pavlovian conditioning**) emphasized the stimuli that followed the response. Further research showed that many of the same events that are found in Pavlovian conditioning—such as extinction, generalization, discrimination, and spontaneous recovery—also occur in operant conditioning.

Thorndike viewed the law of effect as a process of *selection*: that is, the environment "selected" effective responses by the positive outcomes those responses produced. In other words, cats engaged in many different activities inside the puzzle box, but only those that opened the door were selected and strengthened by the situation. Those responses that did not produce pleasant outcomes became less frequent and eventually disappeared. Thorndike saw the similarity between Darwin's concept of natural selection of physical attributes and

**Extinction**

Repeated presentation of the conditioned stimulus without the unconditioned stimulus with the frequency and strength of conditioned responses tending to decrease, eventually to zero

**Spontaneous recovery**

The brief reappearance of the conditioned response with occasional presentation of the condition stimulus

**Generalization**

Responding similarly to similar stimuli

**Discrimination**

Narrowing the range of controlling stimuli for a response

**Operant conditioning**

Type of learning in which the consequences of a response control the response's future probability

**Pavlovian conditioning**

Learning process whereby a formerly neutral stimulus comes to elicit a response as a result of pairing with an unconditioned stimulus

*Figure 2-5 Thorndike's "Puzzle Box"*

Source: From Thorndike, 2011

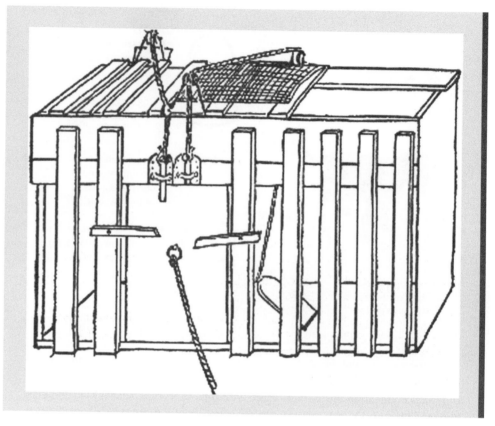

his view of learning as environmental selection of behavior. He also considered that as consequences changed behavior, neural connections in the brain were also changed (Donahoe, 1999). His views thus anticipated those of modern behavioral neuroscientists in these respects and influenced the behavioral theories of B. F. Skinner, who combined these two different types of learning into a model of behavior that will be discussed in Chapter 3.

**Figure 2-6**
**Time (in seconds) to Escape from a Puzzle Box for One Cat**

Thorndike found that cats become more effective in exiting the puzzle box with successive trials, as reinforcement selected and strengthened rapid escape skills.

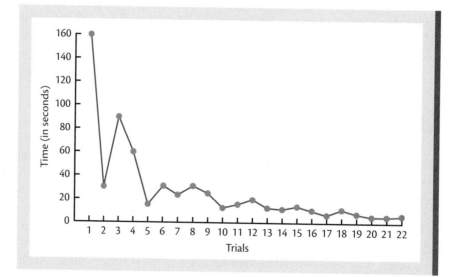

# Chapter Review

## TO SUM UP ...

- Attempts to explain strange phenomena are usually couched in familiar metaphors, and this has been true for explanations of abnormal behavior.

- Demon possession has been a popular but scientifically unsupportable explanation for abnormal behavior in many times and places.

- Some ancient Greeks and Romans, such as Hippocrates and Galen, proposed more naturalistic explanations, including the idea that fluid imbalances or disordered brains caused disordered behavior.

- In the late Middle Ages and afterward, many individuals, some of whom were probably suffering from mental disorders, were convicted and put to death as witches.

- Some courageous individuals, including Johann Weyer and Reginald Scott, spoke against the prevailing beliefs and argued that mental illnesses resulted from natural causes, not from demon possession.

- Humanitarian reforms in the treatment of the mentally ill have waxed and waned throughout history. Especially important landmarks were the reforms instituted by Philippe Pinel in Paris in 1792 and by Dorothea Dix in the United States in the mid-nineteenth century.

- The organic view of abnormal behavior experienced a revival in the nineteenth century, especially in the work and writings of men such as Wilhelm Greisinger and Emil Kraepelin. Kraepelin's development of two major categories of severe mental disorders, manic-depressive and dementia praecox, was a milestone in psychiatric diagnosis.

- The discovery that a syphilitic infection produced the symptom pattern known as general paresis was particularly important in strengthening the organic view.

- One psychological view of abnormal behavior arose largely from the study of hysteria, developing from the prescientific views of Anton Mesmer to the carefully documented work of Jean-Martin Charcot. Clinical observations strongly suggested that many hysterical symptoms did not result from organic disease but from strong emotional conflicts and the social context in which the person lived.

- A second psychological perspective of abnormal behavior developed from laboratory studies on animal conditioning and learning. The work of Ivan Pavlov and Edward Thorndike set the stage for behavioral theories of how both normal and abnormal behavior can be acquired and modified through learning processes.

## KEY TERMS

## QUESTIONS FOR STUDY

- Explanations for phenomena rely on the use of familiar metaphors. What does this mean? How do metaphors guide our understanding of abnormal behavior?

- Compare demonology, the organic view, and the psychological view in their assumptions about the causes of hysteria.

# POP QUIZ

1. Shifting from a demonology model to a naturalistic model is an example of
   _____.
   A. Mesmerism
   B. the organic view
   C. dualism
   D. a paradigm change

2. Who was among the first to advocate naturalistic explanations for disturbed behaviors?
   A. Anton Mesmer
   B. Philippe Pinel
   C. Hippocrates
   D. Dorothea Dix

3. The first asylums devoted entirely to the care of the mentally impaired frequently were started by _____.
   A. governmental officials
   B. the medical community
   C. monasteries
   D. local dignitaries

4. Who was instrumental in founding or enlarging more than 30 state institutions for the proper custody and treatment of mental patients?
   A. Philippe Pinel
   B. William Tuke
   C. Dorothea Dix
   D. Sigmund Freud

5. _____ is credited with the philosophical belief of the separation of the mind and the body.
   A. Philippe Pinel
   B. Ivan Pavlov
   C. Sigmund Freud
   D. René Descartes

6. Kraepelin's third category, paranoia, occurred less frequently than his other two symptom patterns and consisted of _____ symptom(s).
   A. one
   B. two
   C. three
   D. four

7. Benjamin Rush advocated all **except** which of the following as effective treatments of abnormal behavior?
   A. spinning patients on boards
   B. laying on of hands
   C. bloodletting
   D. tranquilizing chairs

8. Which of the following is true of general paresis?
   A. It is characterized by delusions of grandeur, dementia, and progressive paralysis, caused by a sexually transmitted spirochete.
   B. It is a bizarre treatment for hysteria, from the early-1900s, in which individuals were exposed to blood infected with malaria.
   C. It is a symptom of multiple personality disorder, caused by severe psychological anguish stemming from ritual abuse.
   D. It is an interesting side effect of hypnosis therapy, in which the hand or arm loses sensation and motor control while in the trance state.

9. _____ was a popular term in the late 1700s for procedures used to induce trances and other altered states of consciousness.
   A. Conditioning
   B. Mesmerism
   C. Autosuggestion
   D. Abasia

10. In hemianesthesia, the whole of one side of the body becomes _____.
   A. extremely cold
   B. overheated
   C. insensitive
   D. sensitive

11. Instead of being worried or depressed about their physical symptoms, many hysterical patients appear calm and indeed quite cheerful in some cases, which is known as _____.
   A. a characteristic of multiple personality disorder
   B. hemianesthesia
   C. la belle indifférence
   D. dualism

12. _____ is a learning process whereby a formerly neutral stimulus comes to elicit a response as a result of having been paired with another stimulus that already causes that response.
   A. Generalization
   B. Operant conditioning
   C. Pavlovian conditioning
   D. General conditioning

13. Loud noises, such as his clock's alarm, cause Alvaro to startle into a state of high awareness. Just before the alarm goes off, the clock makes a light clicking noise, which initially Alvaro didn't even notice. Now that he has had the clock for some time, Alvaro has found that he startles into wakefulness when the clock makes the clicking noise, before the alarm even goes off. In this example, the unconditioned response is _____.
   A. the alarm
   B. the clicking noise
   C. being startled into a state of high awareness
   D. turning the alarm off

14. _____ occurs when the frequency and strength of the conditioned response tends to decrease, eventually to zero, after repeated presentations of the conditioned stimulus without the unconditioned stimulus.
    A. Generalization
    B. Discrimination
    C. Spontaneous recovery
    D. Extinction

15. Pavlovian conditioning focuses on the stimuli that _____ the response; operant conditioning emphasizes the stimuli that _____ the response.
    A. follow; follow
    B. precede; precede
    C. precede; follow
    D. follow; precede

Additional study resources are available at **www.BVTLab.com**

# CHAPTER OVERVIEW

# CHAPTER OPENER QUESTIONS

How does psychodynamic theory explain and treat psychological problems?

What treatments have developed from the behavioral model?

What is the biological perspective of abnormality?

How does the humanistic approach differ from other perspectives?

Can assessment of treatment outcomes contribute to a more unified framework?

(Wikimedia Commons)

# Contemporary Frameworks

The last chapter traced the historical development of different models or paradigms of abnormal behavior. In this chapter, the current general models or frameworks of psychopathology are presented. We begin with the framework developed from Sigmund Freud's perspective of the mind, which became the first comprehensive model of psychology and psychiatry: the psychodynamic approach. The cardinal feature of the psychodynamic view is this: To comprehend abnormal behavior, one must understand the dynamic interplay of those intrapsychic events—motives, drives, emotions, fantasies, and conflicts—that underlie the surface manifestations of symptoms. Thus, psychological symptoms are seen as analogous to physical symptoms, such as fever, which can only be understood and effectively treated if the underlying disease process causing the symptom, such as an infection, is identified. Such a view clearly represents a variant of the illness metaphor. In this case, the underlying disease is not some physical lesion or infection but rather a pathological condition existing among the intrapsychic processes of the mind—in short, a mental disease.

## 3.1 Freud's Psychoanalytic Theory

A central idea in Freud's theory of psychological symptoms is that emotionally distressing past experiences may be put out of one's mind or *repressed*, but they can continue in some manner to find expression, such as through bodily symptoms and altered states of consciousness. Freud came to view the mind as consisting of different "levels" of activity with most of the action occurring outside of conscious awareness. According to his *Depth Hypothesis*, the largest part of the mind is the **unconscious**, of which we are unaware and from which material is normally unavailable. A much smaller part involves our conscious awareness and our psychological contact with the things around us. According to his *Structural Hypothesis*, the mind can also be divided into three parts: the id, which is concerned with basic instinctive drives of the unconscious; the ego, which serves to mediate the expressions of the id in the real world; and the *superego*, containing our internalized values and corresponding to something like a "conscience." The relationship between these levels and structures of the mind can be illustrated by an iceberg metaphor: Only a small amount is easy to observe while most exists submerged and unseen (Figure 3-1).

## 3.1a Basic Features of Freud's Early Theory

### Unconscious Motivation

In the course of working with many patients, Freud elaborated on the basic theme of unacceptable impulses struggling for and finding expression in various disguises, and thus he evolved the concept of unconscious motivation. He used this concept to explain not only hysterical and other symptoms but also all manner of irrational human behavior. There is, in fact, nothing incomprehensible about any human behavior (according to Freud) once we understand the underlying unconscious motivation. All behavior is completely determined. A slip of the tongue, for example, is not a chance mistake but quite precisely reflects some unconscious conflict.

**Unconscious**

In psychoanalytic theory, that part of the mind outside of conscious awareness, containing hidden instincts, impulses, and memories

*Figure 3-1*   *The Iceberg Metaphor of the Mind*

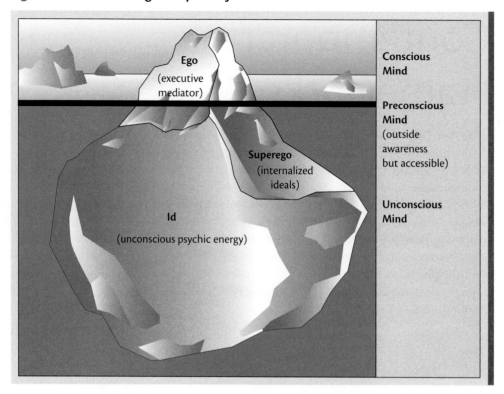

Dreams, likewise, are not nonsensical collections of images and feelings; they are determined to the last detail by experiences of the recent and remote past, by unconscious motivations and conflicts, and by defensive strategies designed to keep the dreamer unaware of the dream's "true" meaning. According to Freud most, perhaps all, dreams include elements of wish fulfillment.

Sigmund Freud was an Austrian neurologist who is best known for his theories of the unconscious mind, defense mechanism of repression, and for creating a clinical practice of psychoanalysis through dialogue between a patient and trained therapist. (Wikimedia Commons)

## The Sexual Basis of Psychological Symptoms

As Freud helped patients explore further and further into the hidden and disguised bases of their symptoms, it seemed that inevitably the trail led eventually to a sexual conflict. At first he thought that many, perhaps all, of his patients had actually experienced in childhood some kind of sexual attack or seduction by an adult, which had caused the sexual conflict and its associated anxiety. Freud soon abandoned this theory and proposed instead that the patient as a young child had *imagined* that such events had taken place and in retrospect was unable to distinguish clearly between what had been wish and fear and what had, in fact, happened.

The sexual basis of symptom-producing conflicts remained a cornerstone of Freud's theory and was the feature that provoked the strongest critical reactions, not only from the public at large, but from his professional colleagues as well. To Freud's mind, the intensity and the irrationality of the attacks on him and his theory seemed to prove further the validity of his position. Why would people resist the idea so strongly if the idea were not tapping their own unconscious sexual conflicts?

## The Oedipal Conflict

It was not just any sexual conflict that seemed to be at the root of hysterical and other symptoms, however; the sexual problem seemed to take a rather special form—the **Oedipal conflict**. In essence, the Oedipal conflict involves a sexual attraction to the opposite-sex parent, accompanied by feelings of competition and antagonism toward the same-sex parent, as in the Greek myth of Oedipus who, unaware of their true identity, slew his father and married his mother. The Oedipal conflict (usually reaching its peak around 4 to 5 years of age) has no easy solution for the young child since the child cannot, in reality, affect a sexual liaison with the opposite-sex parent nor vanquish the competitor, the same-sex parent.

The conflict is further fueled by fantasied elaborations. A boy, for example, may harbor death wishes against his father and begin, in turn, to imagine that his father will do bodily harm to him as a punishment for his (the boy's) own impulses and feelings. The imagined harm at the hands of his father is likely to take the form of castration since it is sexual pleasure associated with his penis that is causing all the trouble. Thus castration anxiety becomes a driving force behind the Oedipal conflict and its eventual resolution. The young girl, discovering that she has no penis, assumes she has already been castrated. As a result she experiences "penis envy," which leads her to seek a man as a possessor of a penis. In her sexual desire for her father, her mother is her rival.

The young child of either sex copes with this seemingly insoluble problem by pushing the whole thing—erotic interest in the opposite-sex parent, hostile wishes toward the same-sex parent, and fears of retaliation—out of his or her mind, in short, by repression. Normally, their sexual urges are later redirected to others, and they may in the end marry someone like mom or dad. If children have had to deal with an especially intense Oedipal conflict, they are vulnerable in adolescence and young adulthood, when the sexual drive becomes increasingly intense, to re-arousals of the conflict and ineffective repressive defenses. The result, according to Freud, can be symptoms of psychological disorders.

Albert Greiner as Oedipus in an 1896 theatrical production of Oedipus Rex. In the Greek tragedy, Oedipus murdered his father and married his mother. (Wikimedia Commons)

## 3.1b Anxiety and the Mechanisms of Defense

In Freud's thinking, the motivation to avoid awareness and overt expression of unacceptable impulses came to center around the concept of anxiety, a powerful and unpleasant emotion thought by Freud to have its primitive beginnings in the infant's experience of being overwhelmed by uncontrollable stimulation. As the child grows older, anxiety also begins to serve as a signal that warns of some impending danger. The danger may be internal in the form of some disturbing instinctual impulse that threatens to break into awareness and possibly be expressed in overt behavior, or external such as a perceived threat of loss of love or physical injury from significant people in the child's life. The child then learns various strategies, **defense mechanisms**, to prevent anxiety-arousing impulses from entering awareness or being overtly expressed in ways that might evoke retaliation. **Repression** was the primary defense mechanism in Freud's early writing; it is the unconscious but intentional forgetting of memories associated with anxiety-arousing impulses and conflicts. In time Freud expanded the concept of defense to include several other mechanisms in addition to the more basic one of repression.

**Reaction formation** represents an extension of the basic repressive strategy. In this defense, people take the additional step of believing and acting as though they were motivated to do just the opposite of the unacceptable impulse: A man behaves in a kindly, considerate fashion when in fact he has an impulse to be mean, sadistic, or cruel; a woman is excessively neat, clean, and orderly when underneath she wants to be messy and dirty; a person conducts a crusade against pornography to control (and indirectly to gratify) unconscious sexual interests. Reaction formations of this kind are likely to become long-standing character traits that color the whole personality.

**Oedipal conflict**

In Freudian theory, the erotic attachment to the opposite-sex parent, involving feelings of competition and hostility toward the same-sex parent, and fears of retaliation (castration anxiety in boys) from the same-sex parent

**Defense mechanisms**

In Freudian theory, strategies whereby a person avoids anxiety-arousing experiences

**Repression**

Defense mechanism in which the anxiety-arousing memory or impulse is prevented from becoming conscious

**Reaction formation**

Defense mechanism in which a person behaves in a way directly opposite from some underlying impulse

### Figure 3-2   *The Purpose of Defense Mechanism*

Defense mechanisms serve to shield the ego from the harsh aspects of reality

Source: Figure of "The Purpose of the Defense Mechanism" from *Adjustment and Growth* by F. J. Bruno. Copyright © 1983 By F. J. Bruno. Reprinted by permission of John Wiley and Sons, Inc.

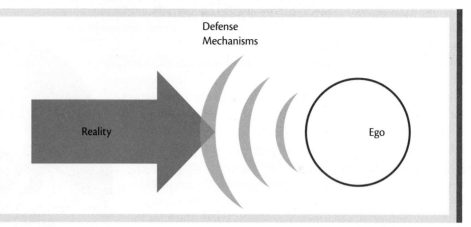

**Isolation**

Defense mechanism in which a person separates emotional from intellectual content, or otherwise separates experiences that would be anxiety arousing if permitted to occur together

**Displacement**

Defense mechanism in which the person shifts a reaction from original target person or situation to some other person or situation (e.g., anger displacement from boss to family)

**Projection**

Defense mechanism in which the person disowns some impulse and attributes it to another person

**Intrapsychic**

Refers to unobservable mental events such as ideas, wishes, and unconscious conflicts

**Id**

In Freudian theory, that part of the mind from which instinctual impulses originate

**Ego**

In Freudian theory, that part of the mind that mediates between id impulses and external reality

**Superego**

In Freudian theory, the internalized representative of parental or cultural values

**Isolation** refers to isolating a memory or impulse in such a way that it no longer creates anxiety. The most common form this defense takes is the separation of an idea from its associated distressing emotions. The person may become able to think of this idea—but in a cold, emotionless way. An incest wish, for example, may be experienced as an abstract, intellectual idea, bereft of both the attracting and repelling emotions previously associated with it. In **displacement**, a disturbing emotion or conflict is transferred from its original source to some less threatening object or situation. A fear of castration might be displaced to a fear of dogs, for example. In **projection**, the person disowns some impulse or attitude and projects it onto another person. "It's not I who am, filled with a murderous rage against you; it's you who have it in for me." "It's not I who have a homosexual attraction for you; it's you who are making homosexual passes at me." The defensive aim of such a mechanism is clear.

This list of defense mechanisms is not complete. In fact, there is no one standard list. Different psychoanalytic authors put together various combinations of ways that people defend against unacceptable impulses. What is agreed is that it is normal, even healthy, for people to make use of defenses, up to a point. However, excessive use of defenses interferes with more healthy methods of coping and functioning in the face of life's demands.

## 3.1c  A Theory of the Mind: The Higher-Order Abstractions

Psychoanalytic theory is not so much concerned with overt behavior (what people do) as with what they think and feel. The basic inquiry of psychoanalysis: What are the mental events, the **intrapsychic** processes, that help us understand other mental events such as dreams and anxieties? As Freud's theory developed further, some aspects became quite abstract and complex.

### The Structure of the Mind

As noted earlier, Freud proposed that the mind could be conceptualized as consisting of three primary parts: the **id**, which is the source of basic instinctual drives seeking immediate gratification; the **ego**, which attempts to mediate between the urgings of the id and the demands of external reality; and the **superego**, an internalized and partially irrational representation of parental or cultural values (see Table 3-1). The ego, according to Freud, governs such processes as perception, learning, and thinking, whereby the person regulates the commerce between the id's impulses and reality; it also includes those mechanisms of defense already described. The superego was thought to develop primarily in the course of the resolution of the Oedipal conflict when children incorporate or internalize their

*Table 3-1*   Mental Structure According to Freud

| Structure | Consciousness | Contents and Functions |
|---|---|---|
| **Id** | Unconscious | Basic impulses (sex and aggression); seeks immediate gratification regardless of consequences; impervious to reason and logic; immediate, irrational, impulsive. |
| **Ego** | Predominantly conscious | Executive mediating between id impulses and superego inhibitions; tests reality; seeks safety and survival; rational, logical, takes account of space and time. |
| **Superego** | Both conscious and unconscious | Ideals and morals; strives for perfection; observes, dictates, criticizes, and prohibits; imposes limitations on satisfactions; becomes the conscience of the individual. |

irrational perception of the same-sex parent. This internalization is another kind of defense mechanism in which the child identifies with the same-sex parent and thereby avoids his or her displeasure—a strategy of "If you can't beat 'em, join 'em." Thereafter, this internalized parental representation becomes a source of praise or condemnation; it becomes, in other words, one's conscience.

## The Libido

One of Freud's most radical notions was that all motivation, other than a few simple physiological drives such as hunger and thirst, arises from the sexual instinct, the **libido**. Many forms of behavior that on the surface seem to have nothing to do with sex he considered *sublimated* expressions of the libidinal instinct. Thus a scientist's curiosity about the workings of nature might be considered to reflect a sexual curiosity that has been redirected to a more socially acceptable and rewarding area of investigation. The motive is "desexualized," changed so that it is no longer recognized as sexual. Sublimation is considered a psychologically healthy mechanism since it allows relatively full expression of the underlying instinctual energy.

Later Freud recognized the death instinct as a second major motivational system, accounting for all destructive behavior, whether people directed it against themselves or others. Not all of Freud's colleagues, however, were willing to accept the existence of an independent death instinct.

## Stages of Psychosexual Development

According to the psychoanalytic theory of personality development, the individual progresses through certain biologically determined stages of psychosexual development in which the basic sexual instinct or libido seeks gratification via *oral, anal,* and finally *genital zones* of the body (see Table 3-2). The *genital stage* can be further subdivided into the phallic stage, corresponding to the Oedipal period from ages 4 to 6; the latency period, starting with the repression of all sexuality as a way of coping with Oedipal conflict and lasting until adolescence; and then eventually the *adult genital stage*, in which the libido finds expression in a mature heterosexual relationship.

**Fixations** at, and **regressions** to, these various stages of development influence later personality traits, including features of abnormal symptomatology. Fixation refers to an undue investment of the sexual instincts at one of these stages of development; for example, oral fixation would tend to involve a continuing interest in oral activities such as the ingestion of liquids and sucking or chewing on objects. An anal fixation might involve excessive interest in messy, dirty activities (because of their symbolic relation to the process of defecation) or in "bathroom" humor. Fixations are thought to occur because the person has been either overindulged or unduly deprived of gratification at a particular stage. If persons are later frustrated or otherwise experience stress at a more "mature" level of psychosexual development, they are likely to regress to the stage at which they had previously become partially fixated. In the face of difficult life circumstances, for example, a person orally

**BVT Lab**

Flashcards are available for this chapter at www.BVTLab.com.

**Libido**

Psychoanalytic concept referring to sexual instincts

**Fixations**

In Freudian theory, refers to an unusual investment of libidinal energy at a certain psychosexual stage

**Regression**

In Freudian theory, refers to a return to some earlier state of psychosexual development in the face of some current frustration

*Table 3-2* Freud's Stages of Psychosocial Development

| Stage | Time Span | Focus of Sexual Gratification |
|---|---|---|
| **Oral** | Birth though first 12 to 18 months | Lips and mouth |
| **Anal** | 12 to 18 months to age three | Anal area |
| **Phallic** | Age three to age five or six | Genitals |
| **Latency** | Age five or six to puberty | No focus—sexual drives unexpressed |
| **Genital** | From puberty on | Sexual relations with people outside the family |

According to Freud's theory, a habit of anxious nail-biting could be considered a form of oral regression. (Shutterstock)

fixated might regress to oral sources of satisfaction and eat or drink excessively. The anal character is commonly thought to show stinginess (related to anal retentiveness), stubbornness (related to opposition to bowel training), and compulsive orderliness and pedantry (reaction formations against urges to be messy and sloppy).

## 3.1d An Illustration

An example of Freudian analysis in the case of anxiety is Little Hans. Hans was a 5-year-old boy who had developed a **phobia** (that is, a fear) of going out in the street because a horse might bite him. Freud described his analysis of the cause of the phobia in his paper, "Analysis of a phobia in a five-year-old boy" (Freud, 1909/1908). Most of Freud's information came not from Hans but from the boy's father, who sent detailed correspondence weekly to Freud about the situation and its background. Freud's report on the case ran to 140 pages; it will be only briefly described here.

Tracing the origin of the phobia required a complete history from Hans's father about the boy's developing sexual interest. At age 3, Hans began showing interest in his penis (which he called his "widdler"). On one occasion Hans was discovered touching his widdler by his mother, who responded by telling Hans that if he did not stop playing with it, he might be sent to a doctor to "have it removed." Still, Hans' interest in his genital area continued. He admitted to playing with his widdler in bed at night before going to sleep. He noticed that his sister did not have a widdler, and this was puzzling to him. At age 4, after a bath, Hans' mother was drying him and powdering him, carefully avoiding touching his penis when Hans said, "Why don't you put your finger here?" His mother responded that "it wouldn't be proper," to which Hans replied with a laugh, "but it would be great fun!"

Talking with his father, Hans sought to learn more about widdlers. He noted that animals had widdlers, and large animals had large ones. He assumed that his father had a large widdler, too. In fact, Hans told his father about a horse he had seen that had a large widdler. Horses were familiar objects on the Vienna streets at the time, and Hans saw them frequently. Recently Hans had been warned by his nursemaid to be careful around a large white horse because it might bite his finger. As the phobia deepened, Hans was afraid that a horse might come into his room and bite him.

In addition to tracing the developments of the situation through the father's letters, Freud interviewed Hans in his office. Asked what it was about horses that frightened him, Hans said he was afraid of what horses wore around their eyes and the black thing around their mouths. He also recalled an accident involving a horse that had fallen to the ground, kicking; Hans was afraid the horse was dead.

Freud's analysis of Hans' fear followed directly from his views on the Oedipal conflict. Hans' fear of horses was symbolic of his unconscious fear of his father. His seductive episode

**Phobia**

Strong, irrational fear of some specific object, animal, or situation

after his bath revealed his sexual desire for his mother, whose remark about having his widdler removed only heightened his castration anxiety and fear of his father, whose widdler was larger. The things that horses wore around their eyes and mouth, which Hans found so frightening, symbolized his father's eyeglasses and moustache. Freud's conclusion was that the phobia had developed as Hans repressed these unacceptable feelings about his father and displaced them onto horses instead. Once the true nature of his fear was revealed to Hans, Freud reported he became less anxious and developed into a "cheerful, good-natured" boy.

## 3.1e  Childhood Origins of Neurotic Symptoms

Neurotic (that is, anxiety-driven) symptoms, according to Freud, result from the interplay between instinctual impulses striving for expression and defensive strategies. The key to understanding the strength of the forces involved lies in an appreciation of their early childhood origin, as the case of Little Hans illustrates. The conflict underlying hysteria, for example, is not between some *adult* sexual urge and some *adult* view of ethics and morality. While this may indeed be a source of conflict and stress, it does not result in the severe incapacitation of neurotic symptoms. Some temptation, rejection, or other stress in the current life situation usually does precipitate the disorder; however, its crucial feature is a re-arousal of urges, fantasies, and fears from early childhood, a time when loss of parental love or threats of punishment were experienced as catastrophic events. The defenses used to cope with these reawakened emotions are likewise not adult modes of handling psychological problems but those used by the young child in a desperate attempt to cope with what, from a child's view, are matters of emotional life or death.

Freud believed the key to understanding neuroses was to determine their early childhood origin. (Shutterstock)

## 3.1f  Psychodynamic Treatment

The psychoanalytic techniques that Freud introduced have been modified over the years, but are still utilized in their general form by various psychodynamically oriented therapists.

> **How does psychodynamic theory explain and treat psychological problems?**

The goal of psychoanalysis essentially remains the same: to make the unconscious conscious, as a way to facilitate greater understanding and insight into the self. Through the relationship between therapist and patient, conflicts can be revealed, emotions can be experienced, and the patient can be changed, through new insights, in positive ways.

Although Freud originally used hypnosis as a tool to connect with the patient's unconscious, he soon found that inducing a trance state was not necessary. He instead developed his method of **free association** in which the patient is instructed to express whatever comes to mind, no matter how seemingly irrelevant, trivial, or embarrassing. Rather than actively organizing thoughts, the patient is encouraged to adopt a passive attitude— reporting the ideas, feelings, and images that come into awareness as though they were scenes observed from a train window. Freud did not expect the patient to be able to comply fully with this instruction; sooner or later the patient drew a blank, began to make well-planned speeches, got into disputes with the therapist, or in many other ways resisted the basic rule of free association. **Resistance**, as this is called, became a primary focus of attention for the therapist, who then attempted to help the patient through such resistances by *interpretation*. Since the way a patient resists is likely to reflect styles of ego defenses used in other situations, insight about these resistances is considered an important therapeutic benefit.

**Free association**

Basic procedure in psychoanalysis in which the patient is asked to say, without censorship, whatever comes to mind

**Resistance**

In psychoanalysis the phenomenon in which patients unconsciously resist gaining insight into unconscious motives and conflicts

Dreams were also viewed as windows to the unconscious. Freud eagerly sought reports of patients' dreams for interpretation of symbols since ego defenses disguised unacceptable impulses symbolically before allowing them to enter consciousness by way of the dream state. The content of dreams, therefore, seemed to provide much valuable information about the sources of conflicts and anxiety hidden deep within the patient's mind.

Within the intimacy of the therapeutic relationship, the patient often begins to interact with the therapist in ways similar to how the patient reacted to important persons from childhood or later life. **Transference** involves the projection of thoughts and feelings from these other relationships to the therapist; in essence, the therapist becomes, in some ways, the mother, father, son, lover, or judgmental authority for whom the patient harbors strong feelings and impulses. Psychodynamic therapists do not try to avoid transference; on the contrary, they expect and welcome it as an opportunity to help a patient work through relationships with an absent significant figure. Transference and counter-transference (that is, the therapist's reaction to the patient's projections) become important tools for insight therapy.

## 3.1g  Variations in Psychodynamic Approaches

As with any movement—whether intellectual, political, or religious—in which individuals propound points of view radically different from the prevailing beliefs, a band of followers developed around Freud devoted to protecting the embryonic psychoanalytic movement from the attacks of the establishment. Just as inevitably, there emerged splinter groups and individuals who disagreed with the developing orthodoxy of psychoanalytic theory. The universal role of sexual conflict in the causation of neurotic disorders was the point on which a number of early adherents began to disagree. Since this proposition was based on interpretations of memories, dreams, and so on provided by patients in the course of treatment, it could not be proved or disproved with any finality. Other analysts began to believe that the symptoms produced by their patients could be interpreted differently.

Alfred Adler, for example, came to believe that it was not sexual conflict that lay behind neurotic symptoms but conflicts revolving around needs to dominate or triumph over others. The free associations of his patients seemed always to lead to a central problem in which they were striving to be superior as a way of compensating for underlying feelings of inferiority. Carl G. Jung also doubted that all human motivation could be traced to sexual urges, and he questioned whether all significant personality characteristics were essentially molded in the first five years of life. Jung went on to emphasize the unconscious as an energy source from which positive, creative acts arose as well as lusts and meanness. He also had a strong mystical bent, reflected for example in his theory of the *collective* or *racial unconscious*, the idea that all humanity shares certain racial memories. These common racial memories, according to Jung, are expressed symbolically in the mythologies of all present and past cultures. Both Adler and Jung broke with Freud and developed their own movements, known respectively as *individual psychology* and *analytical psychology*.

Other individuals developed their own brands of neo-Freudian theories, most rejecting Freud's exclusively sexual interpretation of human motivation and his overly restrictive view of biologically determined stages of psychosexual development. Neo-Freudians—such as Harry Stack Sullivan, Karen Horney, and Erich Fromm—put more emphasis on the social environment as a determinant of personality development. Sullivan, for example, became known for his *interpersonal theory of psychological disorders*, supplementing the Freudian

Carl Jung doubted that all human motivation could be traced to sexual urges, and he questioned whether all significant personality characteristics were essentially molded in the first 5 years of life.
(Wikimedia Commons)

**Transference**

Irrational emotional reaction of a patient to the therapist (usually in psychoanalysis) in which early attitudes toward parents are "transferred" to the therapist

preoccupation with intrapsychic dynamics with an equal concern about who is doing what to whom in the external world of social interaction. Karen Horney believed that most neurotic disorders could be traced back to a *basic anxiety* that has its origins in early childhood. She argued that all children develop aggressive or hostile impulses toward their parents because of the inevitable frustrations that even the best-intentioned parents impose. This hostility can produce strong basic anxiety over the possibility that children may alienate their parents by some hostile or antagonistic expression and thus find themselves deprived of love, their only source of acceptance and nurturance. Growing children, and later adults, engage in all manner of protective maneuvers to ensure that this does not happen. For example, they become overly dependent, submissive, placating, achieving, or competitive to guard against this loss.

More recent extensions of psychoanalytic thought include *object-relations theory*, which analyzes psychological problems in terms of how features of a person's present life symbolize the early social bonds formed by the developing child. These early relationships are internalized; and, in future relations, the person projects the internalized object—for example, the good mother, the demanding teacher, the loving child—onto the situation, effectively reliving the object-relations of childhood in the present. The therapist-patient relationship is seen as a symbolic expression of what is pathological in the patient's life and, therefore, the avenue to produce change.

Karen Horney believed that most neurotic disorders could be traced back to a basic anxiety that has its origins in early childhood. (Shutterstock)

Although psychoanalysis is not as dominant in the treatment of abnormal behavior as it once was, it and its derivatives retain a significant following. The impact of its concepts has historically been stronger in psychiatry than in psychology, presumably because Freud trained as a physician. In fact, for most of the twentieth century advanced psychoanalytic training was available only to students admitted to medical schools—a situation that was not finally resolved until the 1980s, when the American Psychological Association won a lawsuit opening psychoanalytic institutes to psychology students as well. Because its terms do not easily lend themselves to precise definition, objective measurement, or scientific evaluation, it has not compiled a strong research base of support. Its influence, however, can still be widely felt in psychology; and its rich and complex symbolism continues to fascinate philosophers, artists, and writers.

## 3.2 Behavioral Approaches

The work of Pavlov in Russia began to attract the attention of American psychologists in the early twentieth century. At the time, the common approaches used by psychologists in research and therapy—introspection and psychoanalysis—were under attack by some researchers as too unreliable and subjective. One of these critics in particular, John Watson, claimed that psychology would never achieve scientific status by using these techniques. Watson, the leading psychologist in America at the time, knew of Pavlov's conditioning studies; and he saw the value in applying this consistently objective, measurable scientific methodology to the study of behavior. He outlined such an approach, which he called **behaviorism**, and promoted it extensively as the only scientific path open to psychologists, proclaiming

> Psychology as the behaviorist views it is a purely objective experimental branch of natural science. Its theoretical goal is the prediction and control of behavior. Introspection forms no essential part of its methods, nor is the scientific value of its data dependent upon the readiness with which they lend themselves to interpretation in terms of consciousness (Watson, 1913, p. 158).

**Behaviorism**

An approach to understanding behavior that emphasizes the relation between observable behavior and specifiable environmental events (or stimuli)

Watson's view was that the principles of conditioning could explain all behavior, both normal and abnormal. The powerful laws of learning seemed to him a much more reasonable foundation for the developing science of psychology than the subjective and untestable concepts proposed by Freud. He set out to demonstrate this in experiments, including a famous example involving the development of anxiety of a young boy, Little Albert (Watson & Rayer, 1920).

Albert was reportedly a normal, 11-month-old boy with no unusual characteristics or behaviors. In the experiment conducted by Watson and his graduate student Rosalie Rayner, the boy was shown an array of objects, most of them furry, such as a white rat, a rabbit, a dog, and cotton. Albert showed no signs of fear in their presence. To induce fear, the investigators used an unexpected loud noise produced by striking a steel bar with a hammer closely behind the infant. In the first session, the bar was struck on two occasions when Albert reached out to touch a white rat. The loud noise startled Albert and caused him to jump and whimper. A week later, five more paired presentations of rat and noise were given. On the eighth trial the rat alone was presented, and Albert immediately began to cry and to crawl away rapidly. In conditioning terms, the loud noise was the unconditioned stimulus, and the startle reaction was the unconditioned response. After being paired with the loud noise, the rat became the conditioned stimulus, eliciting the conditioned response of fear.

Five days later Albert was tested for generalization of the fear response. He played as usual with wooden blocks, showing no signs of fear. When the rabbit was put in front of him, he responded at once—leaning as far away from the animal as possible, whimpering, and finally bursting into tears. Albert showed similar, though not as strong reactions, to the dog, cotton, and other furry objects, such as a Santa Claus mask. Albert had acquired a phobia of white rats and related furry objects by a simple process of classical conditioning. Subsequent research using different methods also supported a conditioning model for the acquisition of phobias. For example, in a much later experiment, Campbell, Sanderson, and Laverty (1964) used drug-induced respiratory paralysis with voluntary subjects. They found that with just one pairing of this horrific experience with a tone, indications of fear such as palms sweating and change in heart rate became conditioned to the tone and showed no signs of extinguishing over a 3-week period and 100 presentations of the tone by itself.

There is much indirect and anecdotal evidence to suggest that fear responses do, indeed, become associated with previously neutral stimuli on the basis of a few fear-arousing experiences. Some young children's reactions to the white-coated doctor from whom they have received shots on previous occasions are well known to many parents. Individuals who develop intense fear about riding on trains, cars, or motorcycles after having experienced one accident are other examples. It seems likely, then, that some fears can be learned by classical conditioning. In fact, Wolpe and Rachman (1960) reanalyzed Freud's case of Little Hans and suggested that this celebrated example of a phobia could also be explained by a simple conditioning account.

Clearly, Watson's approach to the study of anxiety was very different than that of Freud. The version of behaviorism promoted by Watson was incomplete because he relied solely on classical conditioning as an explanatory mechanism and because he downplayed biological contributions to behavior, largely as a reaction to their overstated role proposed by instinct theorists of the time. Still, his attempt to promote a rigorous and objective approach to the study of behavior was groundbreaking, and it provided an enticing and parsimonious alternative to psychodynamic theory.

## 3.2a  Operant Conditioning

The behavioral model was expanded and significantly strengthened by another American psychologist, B. F. Skinner. In his book, *The Behavior of Organisms* (1938), Skinner recognized two basic and distinct learning processes: classical conditioning which concerned reflexive or elicited behaviors and operant conditioning which involved "voluntary" or emitted behaviors. The latter derived from Thorndike's "Law of Effect," which was restated to eliminate subjective experience, so that *satisfiers* and *annoyers* became *reinforcers* and *punishers*—that is, defined by their effect on behavior.

Skinner created a laboratory environment (still called a "Skinner box") to initially focus his approach, which he termed "the experimental analysis of behavior," on simple activities such as lever pressing by rats and key pecking by pigeons under controlled environmental situations. The animal subjects were placed inside of the apparatus, which automatically recorded the target responses and provided access to food or water contingent on responses occurring at certain times, such as when a light was illuminated. By systematically manipulating different components of the experimental procedure, he was able to describe lawful relationships between behavior and its consequences and to produce and control patterns of responding.

B. F. Skinner (1904–1990), founder of behavior analysis.
(AP Wide World)

Although Skinner began his work on the simple, observable responses of animals, he made it clear that he intended to expand his analysis of behavior to complex human activities, including language, and to internal or private events such as feeling and thinking. He considered the barrier of the skin to be unimportant in terms of the law of effect and viewed thoughts and beliefs not as causes of behavior but rather as behaviors themselves, evoked by the environmental context and shaped (that is, influenced and directed) by their consequences.

The essence of operant conditioning is that the organism learns to make a response that operates on the environment so as to produce some consequence favorable to the organism. Skinner and others have used the term **reinforcement** to refer to a consequence that strengthens or increases the likelihood that a response will be repeated. Some consequences are almost universally reinforcing: water when thirsty, food when hungry, sleep when tired, and sexual activity after deprivation. These biologically important consequences are called **primary reinforcers**, and humans share similar sensitivities to these types of consequences. Other reinforcers, however, such as money, praise, and social status, are called secondary or **conditioned reinforcers**. These secondary or conditioned reinforcers are established by their association with other reinforcers. Different types of consequences weaken or suppress the behaviors that produce them, and these are called **punishers**. Punishers can also be primary or secondary. A primary punisher (or aversive stimulus) is electric shock, for example, while a secondary punisher might be criticism or disapproval.

There is no sure way of knowing whether a given consequence will, in fact, be reinforcing or punishing for a given individual, but this does not matter for the behavioral approach. Reinforcement simply involves a consequence that increases behavior, and punishment involves a consequence that decreases behavior. Because they have had different learning histories, people differ in the sorts of secondary reinforcers and punishers that affect them. The value of a reinforcer also changes due to satiation and deprivation

Careful balancing of your bank account is negatively reinforced, because overdraft fees are avoided. (Shutterstock)

**Reinforcement**

Consequence that strengthens the future probability of a response that produces it

**Primary reinforcers**

Events, usually biological in nature, which almost always provide reinforcement, such as eating when hungry (Primary reinforcers do not acquire their reinforcing properties through learning.)

**Conditioned reinforcers**

Consequences that have gained their reinforcing value by being paired with other reinforcers

**Punishers**

Types of consequences that weaken or suppress the behaviors that produce them

*Table 3-3* Basic Contingencies of Operant Conditioning

| | Consequence Involves Presentation of Stimulus | Consequences Involves Removal of Stimulus |
|---|---|---|
| **Stimulus is pleasant** | Positive reinforcement | Punishment |
| **Stimulus is aversive** | Punishment | Negative reinforcement |

conditions, its delay in time, and the momentary context of other available reinforcers. In addition, internal events can serve as reinforcers and punishers.. For example, feelings of envy, a fond recollection, a sense of accomplishment, or relief from pain could weaken or strengthen the activities that produced them.

We can further organize the effect of consequences by considering whether the behavioral **contingency** involves the presentation of something or the removal of something. When behavior increases because of the presentation of a positive result (such as winning a jackpot after placing a bet), it is **positive reinforcement**. We become more likely to gamble again in the future. When behavior increases because of the removal of something unpleasant, the result is called **negative reinforcement**. For example, if taking aspirin relieves a headache, we become more likely to use aspirin again in the future. On the other hand, after receiving a painful burn from a hot stove, we are much less likely to touch it again; the presentation of pain is a punisher for that response. A final type of punishment involves the loss of something positive. For instance, a traffic fine for speeding entails the removal of money; and having paid the fine, we are less likely to commit the same offense in a similar setting in the future. These relationships are illustrated in Table 3-3.

Another important concept in the operant learning model is the **discriminative stimulus.** What the organism learns is not just to make a response but also to make it only under certain circumstances. For example, people learn to tell humorous off-color jokes, but not in church, where such activity often earns disapproval. Similarly, touching a hot stove is punished unless we are using a protective hot-pad or mitten so that a burn would not occur. The settings or situations signaling that responses are likely to produce reinforcing outcomes are called discriminative stimuli, and they serve to guide our actions.

Although we quickly learn to discriminate (that is, to distinguish) the particular setting in which a response will produce reinforcement from the setting in which it will not, we can also generalize our operant responses to similar situations which we've never encountered before. So, based on only a few experiences, we may learn how to operate any type of automobile, or not to trust any stranger. As generalization proceeds, our responses may become topographically varied while remaining functionally similar; they may form *generalized response classes* (such as "making excuses" or "telling jokes") which include many different specific activities that achieve similar reinforcing functions.

## Three Levels of Selection

Thorndike had originally assumed that the type of learning he studied in the puzzle box was the result of selection by the environment. That is, behavioral variability was present, and environmental consequences selected the effective actions and eliminated ineffective ones. In a classic paper (1981), Skinner further developed this idea. Specifically, he proposed that operant conditioning and natural selection were actually the same process, operating over different time spans and on different aspects of the organism. He called that process selection by consequences.

In natural selection, many variations exist between organisms within a species. Some are larger, heavier, faster, or more sensitive to light; some have different markings or colors. If any variation provided an advantage, however slight, to an organism in terms of succeeding at reproduction, that advantage could be passed on to offspring. Over time, the advantageous trait would become more common in the population, and eventually the species would

**Contingency**

The specified dependency between a behavior and its antecedents and consequences

**Positive reinforcement**

The contingent presentation of a pleasant result, which strengthens subsequent responding

**Negative reinforcement**

The contingent removal of an unpleasant stimulus, which strengthens subsequent responding

**Discriminative stimulus**

A stimulus that serves as a signal that a certain response will lead to a reinforcer

become different from their ancestors. Said another way, the consequence in natural selection is reproduction, and the effect is that organisms are slowly modified in ways that make reproduction more likely. The unit of this level of selection is the gene; given enough time (perhaps hundreds or thousands of generations), the result is evolution, or a change in species.

In the case of operant conditioning, variations also exist within the behavioral repertoire of an individual organism. If any behavioral variation provides an advantage in acquiring reinforcement or avoiding punishment in a particular situation, that behavior will become more likely the next time a similar circumstance occurs and other competing actions will become less likely. In time, the overall pattern of behavior is altered by the result. The consequence of operant conditioning is reinforcement, and the reinforcing environment modifies an organism's actions to make certain behavior more likely. The unit of this level of selection is individual behavior; and on this time scale (moments), the result is a change in the repertoire of activities the organism displays.

A third level of selection is cultural selection. Variations exist within the practices of a culture or social group, such as in language, religion, business, politics, scientific research, or the practice of medicine. If a cultural practice provides an advantage to the group in terms of maintaining its survival or stability in the face of challenges, that variation tends to be maintained. Cultures that provide effective educational practices, for example, are more likely to continue than those that do not. The consequences of selection at this level include the strengthening of the cultural practice. On this time scale (decades or centuries), the result of selection is the emergence and evolution of cultures.

According to Skinner, the mechanism for these three levels of selection is the same: selection by consequences. On the shortest time span, individual behavior is modified. On a longer time span, cultures are modified; and given enough time, species are modified— all by the consequences that variations have produced. Since humans have been on this planet for many thousands of years, Skinner proposed that any complete explanation of human behavior, and human problems, always involved an appeal to all three levels. As one example, consider the problem of overconsumption of calories and the resultant obesity that we see in America at this time. At the species level, humans have inherited genetic attributes that make us susceptible to sweet and high-fat foods and that provide ways to store excess calories in the body in the form of fat. Presumably this is adaptive because our ancestors had to endure times of limited food availability or famine. At the individual level, we have learned particular food preferences and how to accumulate tasty foods for quick consumption or easy preparation, to modify their flavors with condiments and dressings, and perhaps to follow the meal with delicious, high-calorie desserts such as ice cream. We have also learned to eat while doing other things and to snack—both to satisfy hunger and as a way to pass the time or perhaps to enhance an activity such as viewing a movie. At the cultural level, we are exposed to constant promotions for fast food and sugary treats and find opportunities to consume large portions of high-calorie, high-fat foods on every highway and in every shopping mall in every town in the country. Fast foods are easy to consume because the culture keeps them inexpensive, convenient, and readily available; so it is much easier to order a Big Mac and fries than it is to cook a healthy meal. The result of selection on these three levels is a dramatic increase in the percentage of the American population that is obese. Similar analyses could be made for alcoholism, pornography, and aggression.

At the cultural level, we are exposed to constant promotions for fast food, sugary treats and alcohol. The result is a dramatic increase in the percent of people that are obese or drink frequently. (Shutterstock)

To Skinner, then, the origin of behavior is the same as the origin of species: variation and selection. However, we are not yet able to intervene effectively in the selective process at the genetic level. In the case of obesity, we cannot change the genome of obese persons.

Intervention at the cultural level is possible, but much time and effort is required to alter our fast-food culture; and economically powerful institutions, such as the food industry, would likely resist the effort. Only at the individual level can we quickly and effectively intervene by shaping different eating habits and food choices. Thus, operant conditioning provides the most effective way to change behavior.

## 3.2b Operant Learning and Abnormal Behavior

**Reversal design**

This experimental design is one in which new reinforcement contingencies are instated for a period of time, followed by reinstatement of the old reinforcement contingencies, and finally the installment of the original, new contingencies. Sometimes a fourth reversal is included, the purpose of which is to show that the new contingencies are causing any observed changes in behavior.

Skinner himself did not work in the area of abnormal behavior, but many other investigators have used the operant model as a way of understanding the development of abnormal reactions and as a basis for devising treatment procedures. Their basic assumption is that abnormal behavior is shaped because it produces reinforcing consequences in some way; thus, it should be subject to unlearning if the setting conditions and consequences are appropriately changed. From this point of view, children may develop strong and recurrent temper tantrums because such behavior is reinforced by parental attention or by giving in to the child's demands. A depressed person who expresses feelings of worthlessness and preoccupation with physical complaints may be reinforced because his family comforts him at these times. An alcoholic may escape from stressors in life, achieve a temporary sense of enjoyment, and avoid unpleasant withdrawal symptoms by continuing to drink.

The most impressive demonstrations of the power of external consequences to influence our behavior are experimental studies in which the investigator changes the consequences in such a way that old behavior is eliminated and new behavior is instituted. In a **reversal design**, the experimenter subsequently reinstates the original consequences and observes whether or not the former behavior returns. Then the new consequences are put into effect a second time to see whether the new behavior again replaces the old behavior. It is hard to argue with data of this kind; different external consequences clearly have led to different behavior. A reversal design is illustrated in the following clinical report.

## Ann's Shyness Is Modified by Changing Consequences

Ann was a four-year-old girl who had become more and more isolated from the other children in her preschool, showing an increasing preference for interaction with the adult teachers. As time went by, she spent an even greater proportion of her time simply standing and looking. Mild, tic-like behaviors such as picking her lower lip, pulling a strand of hair, or fingering her cheek also developed. Careful observation of Ann's behavior indicated that she was using many techniques for gaining and prolonging the attention of adults, and that most adult attention was contingent upon (was a consequence of) behaviors that were incompatible with playing with peers.

An intervention program was instituted in which Ann received adult attention as a consequence of play with another child. This attention, of course, had to be given in such a way that it did not draw her away from her interaction with the other children. No adult attention was given for isolate behavior or in response to bids for interaction with adults. Almost immediately after these new consequences were introduced, Ann's play with other children increased dramatically and her interactions with adults decreased (see Figure 3-3).

After five days of the new consequences, the procedure was reversed. The teachers responded as they had originally, giving attention when Ann was showing isolate behavior or interacting with adults. Ann's peer interaction quickly dropped to its previous level. After five more days the new consequences were once more provided, again with immediate effects on Ann's behavior.

*Figure 3-3*

Percent of time Ann spent in social interaction with adults and with peers during approximately two hours of each morning session.

Source: Adapted from Allen, Hart, Buell, Harris, and Wolf, 1965. Originally published in *Child Development*, 1964, 35, 511–518. Copyright 1964 by the Society for Research in Child Development.

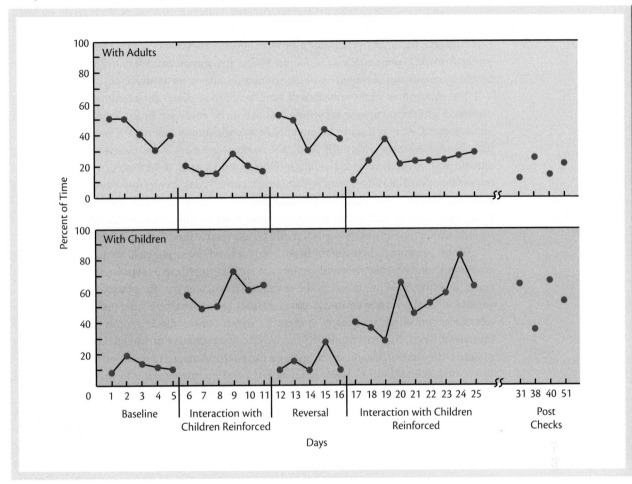

During the last days of the second reversal period, the teachers gave increasingly intermittent (nonsystematic) attention for interaction with other children. Many laboratory studies have shown that such intermittent or partial reinforcement increases the resistance to extinction of newly learned responses. No systematic attempt was made to maintain the program after the twenty-fifth day. On days 31, 38, 40, and 51 checks of Ann's behavior indicated that her new rate of interaction with peers was holding up moderately well. Perhaps enjoyable play with other children had come to serve increasingly as reinforcement in its own right for social interaction with peers.

## 3.2c Behavioral Treatment

**What treatments have developed from the behavioral model?**

A variety of treatment interventions have been developed within the behavioral model. Typically, when building new behaviors, a contingency management technique like that illustrated in Ann's case is attempted. The baseline level of the target behavior is assessed, and then a contingency is implemented such that engaging in the target behavior produces a reinforcing consequence. At first, these are artificial arrangements; however, once the behavior is established, an attempt is made to fade into more natural consequences that will maintain the improvement after the contingency management program ends. In Ann's case, adult attention initially was the reinforcer, but later the natural consequences of peer play came to maintain the social interactions. Sometimes, these sorts of contingency arrangements can be made between couples in marriage counseling; at other times, behavioral contacting might be used to outline the contingencies in a self-control program.

Because peers can hold strong influence over a client's behavior, **modeling** is an important intervention. If a model performs the appropriate behavior, it is more likely to be imitated by other members of the peer group. This is especially true if the model receives positive consequences for his or her actions. A variety of positive behaviors, such as social interactions, problem solving, persistence at academic tasks, and important safety behaviors have been taught by employing peer models who demonstrate successful approaches to problems.

There are times when punishment programs are applied—for example, when seriously disturbed children engage in self-destructive acts such as head banging. Unpleasant consequences, such as a squirt of lemon juice into the mouth or a mist of water onto the face, have been used quite effectively as punishers in stopping self-destructive activities among autistic and mentally-retarded children (Dorsey, Iwata, Ong, & McSween, 1980). Because of important ethical considerations, punishment is usually a last-resort intervention, applied only when the behavior is seriously harmful and needs to be stopped quickly. More often, extinction techniques are used to decrease an unwanted behavior. In either case, the treatment would also include reinforcement components to build an alternative (and more appropriate) behavior.

Other behavioral treatments have been derived from classical conditioning. Strong emotional reactions like fear and anxiety are similar to reflexive responses in that they can come to be triggered by stimuli in the environment such as specific places, social situations, sounds, or images. In **systematic desensitization**, patients are first trained in a muscle relaxation procedure to achieve a state in which most muscle groups of the body are un-tensed. Then, they are exposed, gradually, to more anxiety-provoking stimuli while they maintain the state of relaxation. Because we cannot feel anxious and relaxed at the same time, this "counterconditioning" approach makes it possible to encounter former fear-producing stimuli (such as airplanes, a dogs, or social situations) without triggering a phobic response,

Some classical conditioning techniques are designed to increase, rather than decrease, the unpleasant arousal that a stimulus can produce. A smoker, for example, may have an easier time quitting if the sight or smell of a cigarette produced unpleasant reactions in the body. Through techniques of aversive counterconditioning, attempts are made to create an aversion to an unwanted activity that had been reinforcing in order to make the behavior less likely. For example, aversive conditioning has been used to make alcoholics become nauseous at the smell or taste of alcohol by pairing the flavor of alcohol with a drug that produces stomach upset. One type of aversive conditioning, **covert sensitization**, involves the use of imagery, rather than actual aversive consequences (Cautela & Kearney, 1993). Patients can be instructed to vividly imagine engaging in the problem activity and then experiencing very negative consequences such as illness, embarrassment, and shame. They practice imagining resisting the problem behavior and feeling great relief. Such approaches have been used to help deter smokers, overeaters, and sex offenders from their problem activities.

## 3.2d Variations in Behavioral Approaches

Increasingly, behavioral techniques have been combined with other approaches to produce hybrids. Some psychologists disagreed with the emphasis on observable behavior and argued that internal events such as expectancies and thoughts are appropriately considered causes of behavior. Cognitive psychologists such as Aaron Beck have focused on how humans process and store information and how attitudes, beliefs, and thought processes participate in normal and abnormal psychological states. The cognitive perspective on depression, for example, assumes that depression is caused by certain types of irrational thought processes and negative expectations about the person, the world, and the future (Clark, Beck, & Alford, 1999). Essentially, a depressed person expects failure, overlooks evidence of improvement,

**Modeling**

Teaching a behavior by performing the behavior and having the learner imitate it

**Systematic desensitization**

A counterconditioning procedure in which subjects are exposed to gradually stronger anxiety-producing stimuli while maintaining a state of relaxation

**Covert sensitization**

Form of behavior therapy in which the person is asked to imagine an upsetting scene in order to produce a form of aversion conditioning

and selectively remembers bad events more readily than good ones. When combined with behavioral techniques that produce changes in physical activity and social involvement, cognitive-behavioral therapies challenge these depressive cognitions and can be very useful treatments. In fact, cognitive-behavioral therapies are among the most effective psychological interventions for a variety of psychological disorders, as we shall see in later chapters. Their goal is to change the way a patient talks and thinks about the problem, as well as changing the problem activity itself.

A more recent development in therapy is Acceptance and Commitment Therapy, or ACT, (Hayes, 2004), which developed more directly from the behavioral perspective. In ACT, patients are taught to recognize the presence of certain bothersome emotions (such as depression or anxiety) in the present, to observe them as if from a distance, and to accept their occurrence. This stance is often termed *mindfulness*. In fact, since they are generally reflexive, these feelings are not necessarily within our control. In that circumstance, attempting to suppress the unpleasant emotion can make it worse. Patients are taught that the feelings can be experienced without becoming overwhelmed or disabled by them. At the same time, patients make a commitment to engage in the important behaviors of normal life while "just noticing" the emotional difficulty in the background. As they do so, the natural contingencies of those important behaviors come to maintain them.

Behavioral techniques have also been combined with biological models (to be discussed next) in the growing field of behavioral neuroscience. The effects of learning on the brain, and the effects of brain changes on learning, can be studied in animal models in the laboratory using the powerful techniques of behavior analysis and brain science. The Skinner box is widely employed in research to define the behavioral effects of drugs and to develop new drugs, by carefully examining how ongoing operant behavior is affected by pharmacological agents. These studies are producing important information on how the brain is involved in conditions such as drug addiction, fear, anxiety, and pain.

## 3.3  Biological Approaches

Biological science has made great progress in understanding the physical bases for behavior. Research into the anatomy and neurochemistry of the brain is providing insights into their role in emotions and emotional disorders and into avenues for treatment. In an astonishingly short time, the human genome has been decoded, unlocking a treasure of data to be mined for years to come, with the hope of identifying genetic signatures for physical and mental disorders and of developing medications that can influence the way in which the genome is expressed.

Of course, behavior is not possible without biology. As living organisms, our biology is necessarily involved with everything we do. Any movement we execute, any stimulus we sense, and probably any thought that we think—all involve neurochemical activity and biological variation among tissues. It is less clear whether a particular biological state results in any specific behavior.

The biological or disease model, which proposes that mental disorders have their fundamental causes in physiological conditions in the brain, has expanded significantly since the discovery that syphilis can cause general paresis. Strong evidence has been collected about the biology and genetics of mental disorders and about medications that are available for treating the symptoms of nearly every disorder. We begin our overview of the biological model with heredity.

## 3.4  Heredity

One of the most important developments in the history of biology at the beginning of the twenty-first century was the decoding (sequencing) of the human genome. The human genetic code can be found in the nucleus of any cell in the trillions of cells in the body.

**BVT** *Lab*

Improve your test scores. Practice quizzes are available at www.BVTLab.com.

# **3.4a** Chromosomes and Genes

Each human body cell contains 23 pairs of **chromosomes**, each containing many **genes**. Information about inherited characteristics is carried in the genes by a large molecule called *deoxyribonucleic acid* (DNA). The male sperm cell and the female egg cell (ovum) have only 23 single chromosomes; however, as a result of sexual mating these two cells combine to form a new cell with 23 pairs of chromosomes (see Figure 3-4). The genetic information in this cell is passed on to every cell in the growing fetus and directs its subsequent development. The particular set of genes in a given individual is referred to as the **genotype**.

Genes are sections of DNA base pairs located on chromosomes (see Figure 3-5) that code for the production of specific amino acids and proteins which, in turn, govern the anatomical and biochemical features of the growing organism. It is through these mechanisms that genes affect physical function and behavior. There are four chemical nucleobases (A or adenine, T or thymine, C or cytosine, G or guanine) that form the "rungs" of the twisted "ladder" that the DNA molecule resembles. Also, there are rules about how they can combine: C only pairs with G, and A only pairs with T. Those rules allow the DNA molecule to replicate during cell division (see Figure 3-6).

Genes come in alternative forms or *alleles*, one of which is inherited from the father and the other from the mother. These alleles may be dominant or recessive. Dominant forms of a gene are usually associated with adaptive or healthy traits, and these genes typically express their influence through protein production. Recessive alleles do not typically express themselves unless they are combined with another recessive gene. There are about three billion base pairs in the human genome, and there are about 20,000–25,000 human genes. Although some individual traits may be controlled largely by a single gene, more often many different genes combine their effects in the expression of a single trait. It is also possible for

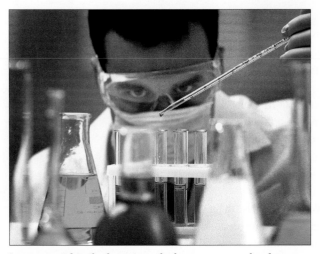

In an astonishingly short time, the human genome has been decoded; unlocking a treasure of data to be mined for years to come. This discovery may lead to identifying genetic signatures for physical and mental disorders and development of medications. (Shutterstock)

**Chromosomes**

Elongated bodies in cells that carry genetic information; there are 23 pairs of chromosomes in human cells

**Genes**

Units of hereditary information carried in a chromosome by DNA

**Genotype**

Total set of inherited characteristics determined by a person's genetic makeup

*Figure 3-4*

The chromosome complement of a normal person consists of 22 matched pairs of chromosomes, plus 2 sex chromosomes (2 X chromosomes for females, and an X and a Y for males). The chromosomes shown below are those of a male. These chromosomes are shown with color added to distinguish pairs. (Source: Wikimedia Commons)

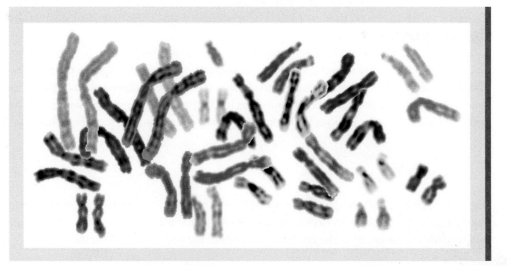

Figure 3-5    *Chromosomes Consist of Strands of DNA*

Source: Illustration courtesy of Genome Management Information Systems, U.S. Department of Energy Genome Programs at http://genomics.energy.gov

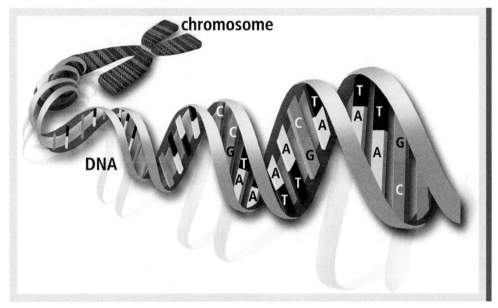

Figure 3-6

Source: Illustration courtesy of Genome Management Information Systems, U.S. Department of Energy Genome Programs at http://genomics.energy.gov.

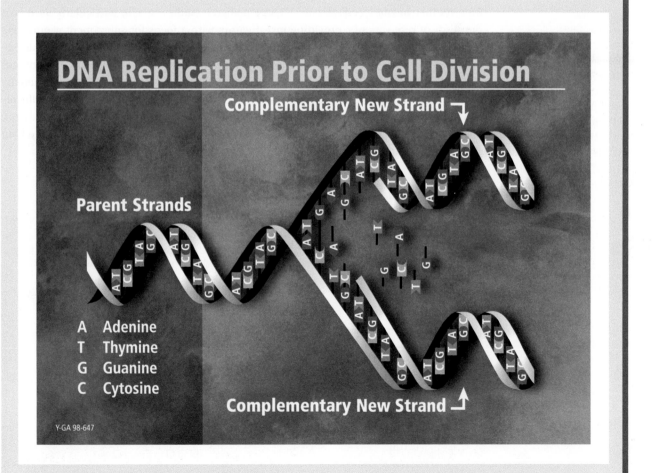

a single gene to have an impact on many different characteristics. To further add complexity and variety to the genetic picture, some genes are constantly active (or almost constantly silent) while other genes activate for a relatively brief period (such as puberty) and then shut off. Much of what is known about the influence of genes is based on inferences from observed characteristics, physical or behavioral. These observable characteristics are referred to as **phenotypes**. Phenotypes are not inherited but are, instead, the result of a given genotype interacting with given environmental circumstances to produce traits.

With increasingly sophisticated abilities in genetic screening, more complex relationships between genotypes and phenotypes have emerged. For example, a recent study found that rather than a single genotype for schizophrenia, most schizophrenics may have their own, unique genetic alterations (Walsh, et al., 2008). It now appears that some genes don't directly code for traits, but rather they serve as "switches" that activate or inactivate other genes. The growing field of epigenetics proposes that these gene switches can be "flipped" by particular environmental conditions and life experiences—making the gene-environment interaction much more complicated than suspected.

## 3.4b  Research Methods for Studying Hereditary Influences

Mental disorders are not inherited in a direct manner from parents, but there is evidence that heredity plays an important role in psychopathology. Ethical as well as practical considerations place experimental "breeding" research beyond the pale of acceptable procedures for studying hereditary transmission of abnormal behaviors in humans. By collecting information about family members who have mental disorders, the distribution of the disorder in the family pedigree can provide information about the genetic involvement in the disorder. Linkage studies can suggest modes of inheritance by examining whether the disorder appears in certain patterns—for example, on one side of a family or in a line from mother-to-son (see Figure 3-7). Large pedigree studies remain particularly useful for the study of rare variants, providing investigators with a focus for subsequent sequencing (Wisman, 2012). With the decoding of the human genome, a much broader approach to linkage is now possible. Recently, Smoller and his colleagues (2013) compared the genomes of 33, 332 patients diagnosed with autism spectrum disorder, attention deficit-hyperactivity disorder, bipolar disorder, major depressive disorder, or schizophrenia with 27,888 controls and found that the five disorders shared statistical variations at several specific genetic sites. Two other research methods are also used in the study of hereditary influences: the twin study method and the adoption method.

**Phenotypes**

Observed characteristics that result from interaction between genotype and environmental influences

### Figure 3-7  *Example of a Family Pedigree of Alzheimer's Disease*

Alzheimer's disease within a family: Blackened symbols are positive cases. Symbols with strike-through were decreased at the time of tracking, and circles designate females.

Source: Pedigree of family with Alzheimer's disease. (After P. H. St. George-Hyslop, R. E. Tanzi, R. J. Polinsky, J. L. Haines, L. Nee, et al. (1987). The genetic defect causing familial Alzheimer's disease maps on chromosome 21. *Science, 235,* 885–892. Copyright © 1987 by the AAAs.

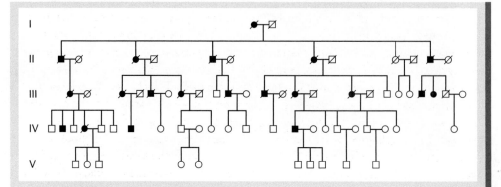

## The Twin Study Method

Fortunately, nature has helped us in our study of heredity by providing us with two types of twins: **identical or monozygotic (MZ) twins** that result from the splitting of a single fertilized ovum and **fraternal or dizygotic (DZ) twins** that result from the simultaneous fertilization of two separate ova. Identical twins have the same genetic endowments; fraternal twins, on the average, are no more alike genetically than any two non-twin siblings born to the same parents. Since genetic sex is determined by whether a Y chromosome is contributed by the father, identical twins are always of the same sex, whereas fraternal twins are no more likely to be of the same sex than other non-twin sibling pairs.

The logic of the twin method might be summarized as follows: Differences in degree of behavioral similarity between identical and fraternal twins will be largely due to the greater genetic similarity of the identical twins, if it is assumed that both MZ and DZ twins share roughly equal environments. Should there be no hereditary influence in the development of a given form of abnormality, then there should be no difference in the degree of similarity in a trait (or **concordance**) shown in the two kinds of twins for this particular abnormality. If there are significant hereditary influences, then MZ twins should be more alike than DZ twins on the behavior being observed.

This conclusion must be qualified, however, if it can be shown that people respond with greater similarity to identical twins than to fraternal twins or if twins don't share the same environments. In other words, twin methods must presume that the environmental variable is relatively controlled in order to see the genetic component. One way that behavior geneticists hope to accomplish this is to find cases in which identical twins are separated shortly

The adoption method compares a child's behavior with his or her biological and adoptive parents in an attempt to assess the degree of genetic and environmental influence. (Shutterstock)

after birth and reared in completely different environments. Any similarities between the separated MZ twins are inferred to reflect genetic influences, whereas differences between the separated twins are assumed to reflect environmental influences. However, it is possible that environmental as well as genetic influences may be operating to produce any greater concordance found in identical twins. For example, it is known that identical twins are more likely to share a placenta in the prenatal environment than are fraternal twins, suggesting the possibility that important environmental effects are overlooked even when MZ twins reared apart share similarities (Phelps, Davis, & Schartz, 1997).

## The Adoption Study Method

Another method of assessing genetic influence is to compare two other kinds of children who have been removed from their biological parents at or shortly after birth and adopted or raised by foster parents: (1) Children in which one or both biological parents showed a form of behavior disorder, and (2) children whose biological parents did not show the disorder. If the environments provided by the adoptive or foster parents do not differ on the average for the two types of children, and the children whose parents were abnormal subsequently develop the same disorder, then we might infer that genetic factors were largely responsible. An advantage of this method over the twin study approach is that it avoids completely the question of whether identical twins experience a more similar environment than do fraternal twins. However, because "the environment" cannot be readily measured or quantified, the assumption of fundamental environmental similarity remains only an assumption. (Even an assumption that siblings raised in the same home share the same environment may be incorrect. Susan has a sister named Sally—but Sally has a sister named Susan.) Still, to the

**Identical or monozygotic (MZ) twins**

Twins resulting from the splitting of a single fertilized ovum who have exactly the same genetic makeup

**Fraternal or dizygotic (DZ) twins**

Twins that result from the simultaneous fertilization of two separate ova with such a pair having the same degree of genetic similarity as any two non-twin siblings born to the same parents

**Concordance**

In genetic research, the degree to which related individuals share a similar trait

extent that an adoptee is more like the adopting parents than the biological parents, we might infer environmental influences, whereas to the extent that the adoptee is more like the biological parent than the adoptive parents, we might infer genetic influences.

## 3.4c  Estimates of Genetic Influences

There is indeed evidence that identical twins tend to be more alike on measures of heart rate, blood pressure, and palmar sweating than are fraternal twins (Hume, 1973; Lader & Wing, 1966; Zahn, 1977). Several studies have also reported that identical twins are more alike on various psychological measures (such as intelligence, extroversion, and openness to experience) than are fraternal twins, as one might expect if psychological traits are strongly influenced by genetics (Bourchard, Lykken, McGue, Segal, & Tellegan, 1990). However, substantial rates of non-concordance for a trait (that is, lack of agreement between twins) suggest that non-genetic factors must also play a role in psychological characteristics. The general finding from twin and adoption studies is that, for most behavioral traits, genes may account for about half of the variability between people, whereas environmental factors account for the other half. Genetic influence appears to be stronger for some mental disorders (such as bipolar mood disorders) than for other disorders (like schizophrenia) that are, nonetheless, assumed to have a strong biological substrate. We must be careful in drawing conclusions from these estimates because calculations of heritability do not tell us to what extent either genetics or environment "causes" a psychological trait, nor whether any individual will develop the trait. Even biological traits in simple animals are influenced by both genetic and environmental factors (Moore, 2001).

Eye color is not actually determined at conception but develops from the interactions of many genes and many environmental factors.
(iStock)

Some physical characteristics such as eye color, blood type, and fingerprint configurations may seem, at first glance, to be determined almost entirely by the genotype and altered little, if at all, by environmental influences. Some behavioral characteristics, as well, can appear to be almost wholly the result of genetics. For example, one rare form of intellectual disability is caused by, **phenylketonuria (PKU)**, a recessive condition involving the lack of a specific gene required for the metabolization of an important dietary ingredient, phenylalanine (because its metabolism is blocked, phenylalanine builds up in the brain, preventing normal brain development). Although it is tempting to try to parcel out the contribution of genetics and environment to the expression of a phenotype, it is not possible to do so because all traits necessarily include both genetic and environmental influences—and these influences do not simply combine additively. The internal biochemical environment interacts with genes to produce proteins. Those proteins then interact with the internal environment to produce physiological systems; and physiological systems then interact with the external environment to produce behavior (see Figure 3-8). Finally, behavioral events and their consequences feedback to influence the both the external and internal environments. As a result, traits are more complex than they first appear. For example, eye color is not actually determined at conception but develops from the interactions of many genes and many environmental factors. Similarly, the intellectual disability associated with PKU will not develop if certain dietary restrictions are followed. The genetic/environmental interactions involved in most behavioral characteristics are more complicated than these examples, so that conclusions about relative influences of genes and environment depend largely upon which factor is held constant. The situation may be analogous to trying to decide whether the temperature or the humidity is more important in predicting snow (Moore, 2001).

**Phenylketonuria (PKU)**

Rare single-gene recessive metabolic disorder that results in intellectual disability

**Figure 3-8**    *Process Involved in Producing Behavior*

Behavior is the result of a set of processes involving genes, proteins, and physiological systems interacting with the environment at each step.

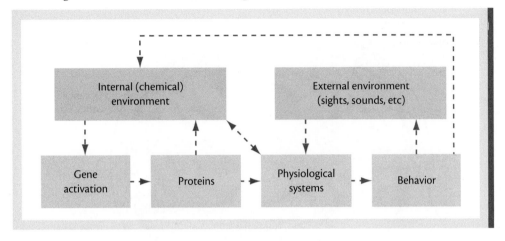

## 3.5 The Human Brain

It is obvious that mental disorders could be affected by genes that, through the proteins they direct, influence the development and functioning of every aspect of the physiology and chemistry of an organism, including the brain and nervous system. The human brain is a complex organ weighing about three pounds, composed of about 86 billion nerve cells and an equal number of non-nerve cells (Azevedo, et al., 2009). The brain is connected to the top of the spinal column, and together they compromise the central nervous system.

In an evolutionary sense, the older parts of the human brain (the hindbrain) are deeper inside the organ; and they control basic physical functioning such as heartbeat, respiration, blood pressure, and balance. The midbrain controls sleep and waking and many basic reflexes, while the more recent forebrain includes sections nearer to the surface where much motor function, sensation, and emotion are innervated. Perhaps the most highly developed structure in the human brain is the cerebral cortex. It has two halves, or hemispheres, which are connected by fibers in the corpus callosum. The left side of the brain, generally, is connected to the right optic pathway and the right side of the body, while the right hemisphere is innervated to the left side.

The cerebral cortex maximizes its surface area by way of many convolutions throughout its several lobes, which are involved with seeing, hearing and other sensations, fine motor control, speech and language, learning, and other higher functions (Figure 3-9). Nearly 20% of the nerve cells in the central nervous system are found in the cerebral cortex (Azevedo, et al., 2009).

## 3.5a Neurotransmission

As noted above, the human brain contains many billions of tiny nerve cells, called **neurons** (see Figure 3-10). Nerve impulses are collected from other neurons and passed along, as a moving electrical charge, from the branching **dendrites**, through the cell body, and down to the neuron's **axon**. In normal resting state, the neuron carries a slight negative electrical charge (–70 millivolts). As an impulse moves across a neuron, the cell membrane depolarizes and allows positively charged sodium ions to enter the cell, briefly altering its electrical potential to a positive state (+50 millivolts). Then positive ions are expelled, and the neuron resets to its negative resting potential. Through this cycle, which can be completed within 3 milliseconds, the electrical impulse (the *action potential*) is propagated as a moving depolarization that travels down the length of the neuron. Transmission between neurons, however, is not electrical; it is chemical.

**Neurons**

Individual nerve cells

**Dendrites**

Branching fibers of a neuron that receive input from other neurons

**Axon**

Part of the neuron that carries neural impulses to other cells

*Figure 3-9*   ***Localization of Cortical Functions in the Brain***

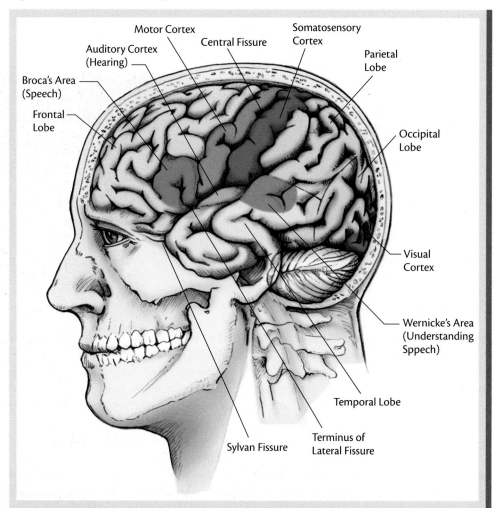

Neurons do not interact with each other through direct physical contact. Instead, they meet at the **synapse**. A tiny gap, called the synaptic cleft, separates the pre-synaptic neuron's axon from the post-synaptic neuron's membranes. To transverse this gap, the electrical nerve impulse triggers a release of molecules of specialized chemicals called **neurotransmitters**, which are stored in the synaptic vesicles near the end of the axon. Once released, the neurotransmitter diffuses across the synaptic cleft and lodges into receptor sites in the membrane of the post-synaptic neuron. If enough neurotransmitter substance binds to enough receptor sites, the post-synaptic neuron begins to depolarize and an action potential moves across its surface to the next connecting nerve cells in the circuit. There are complex arrays of interconnections, with some neurons receiving input from thousands of others, resulting in trillions of possible synaptic connections in the brain.

More than 100 neurotransmitter chemicals are known. Among the most common neurotransmitters are acetylcholine (ACh), the catecholamines such as adrenaline or epinephrine (E), noradrenaline or norepinephrine (NE), dopamine (DA), and the indolamine serotonin (5-HT). Other neurotransmitters are amino acids, including gamma-aminobutyric acid (GABA), glysine, and glutamate. However, each neuron releases only one type of chemical neurotransmitter into the synaptic cleft. At some synapses, the effect on the post-synaptic cell is excitatory, meaning that their actions sum together to make the post-synaptic neuron more likely to fire. Other synapses produce effects that are inhibitory and make the post-synaptic neuron less likely to fire. A single neuron can receive both excitatory and inhibitory influences at the same time, and these are integrated or summed together in determining the firing state of a neuron.

**Figure 3-10** *Neuronal Communication*

Neurons communicate with each other at the synapse.

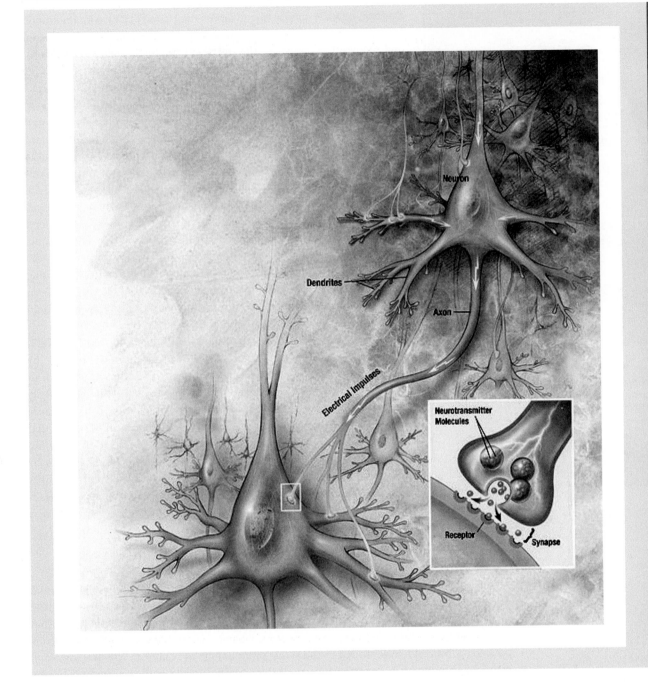

# 3.5b Biological Treatments

Treatments derived from the biological perspective of
mental disorders have included convulsive therapies,
psychosurgery, and psychotropic medications.

**What is the biological
perspective of abnormality?**

## Convulsive Therapies

Early in the 1900s, observations were noted that mentally disturbed people showed improvement
in their symptoms after recovering from a convulsive seizure. That led some neurosurgeons to
suggest that, perhaps, seizure disorders (like epilepsy) were incompatible with schizophrenia.

By 1934, von Meduna was deliberately inducing convulsions by injecting camphor into mental patients. Cerletti and Bini improved the technique in 1938 by using electric current, passed through the brain, to induce seizures. The application of **electroconvulsive therapy**, or **ECT**, quickly spread across the United States, with thousands of applications per year employed to treat schizophrenia, depression, and many other disorders. The treatment produced violent convulsions, as well as broken bones and significant residual memory loss. Over time, improvements were implemented. Tranquilizing and muscle-relaxing drugs were added, so that the seizure produced very little outward movement. Also, current was passed through only one hemisphere of the brain rather than both. This unilateral ECT, especially if applied to the non-dominant hemisphere, resulted in less impairment in memory. In recent decades, the use of ECT has been restricted almost entirely to serious mood disorders, for which it appears to be more effective than either placebo (sham) ECT or antidepressant medications over the short term (Pagnin, de Queiroz, Pini, & Cassano, 2008). Typically, patients are treated 3 times per week for a total of from six to twelve applications. However, its long-term effectiveness has not been established; and rate of relapse is high, with perhaps 85% of patients who do not receive other maintenance therapies relapsing within six months. The exact mechanisms of action of ECT have not been determined although it is known to modify neurotransmitter release and receptor sensitivity, among many other brain effects (Lisanby, 2007).

The application of electroconvulsive therapy, or ECT, was employed to treat schizophrenia, depression, and many other disorders. Actress Carrie Fisher, who played the famous Princess Leia in the renowned *Star Wars* Trilogy, was treated with ECT for manic-depression.
(AP Wide World)

Newer types of somatic treatments have been derived from ECT. *Magnetic seizure therapy* involves stimulation of brain regions by magnetic fields, rather than electrical current, at sufficient strength to result in convulsions. Results of this experimental therapy for temporarily reducing depressive symptoms appear promising thus far. In a procedure known as repetitive transcranial magnetic stimulation (rTMS), repeated magnetic pulses at subseizure levels of intensity are used to stimulate areas of the cortex, which appears to alter neurotransmission. Results for rTMS are also promising, but its effectiveness has not reached ECT levels. Finally, the FDA has approved *vagus nerve stimulation*, using implanted electrodes placed in specific brain areas, for use with treatment-resistant depression. Again, this newer development seems promising but as yet cannot match ECT for size of effect or speed of effect (Lisanby, 2007).

## Psychosurgery

At the same time convulsive therapies were appearing, a Portuguese physician named Antonio Moniz began performing surgery on the brain to treat mental disorders. In 1935, he demonstrated a procedure called a frontal lobotomy to separate the frontal lobes from the deeper parts of the brain as a treatment for violent, agitated, depressed, or dangerous patients. A burr-hole was drilled in the skull, and a hollow needle from which a wire loop could be extended was inserted into the brain. As the needle (called a *leucotome*) was rotated, the loop could cut small circular areas in brain tissue. Although the results were not impressive (about one-third of his subjects improved), Moniz was awarded the Nobel Prize in Medicine in 1949 for developing the procedure. Ironically, he was later shot in the leg by a patient and spent the rest of his life in a wheelchair. During the 1940s and 1950s, tens of thousands of lobotomies were performed; however, evidence of their effectiveness was limited, and the irreversible changes wrought in the brain often produced permanent disability and functional impairment. In recent decades much more limited and anatomically focused procedures have been explored, usually employing microsurgery with instruments inserted through the nose or eye socket rather than through the cranium, for specialized groups of patients such as those with particularly severe obsessive-compulsive disorders. However, **psychosurgery** remains an experimental practice and is not a part of standard biological treatment at the present.

**Electroconvulsive therapy, or ECT**

Therapeutic induction of convulsive seizures by applying electrical current to the head; found to have some effectiveness with severe depressions

**Psychosurgery**

Procedure that attempts to treat abnormal behavior by surgical intervention on the brain

## Pharmacology

The biggest revolution in the biological approach to treatment has involved the development of drugs that impact neurotransmission in the brain. These psychotropic compounds represent the main thrust of treatment within the model; and their wide application has produced a multi-billion dollar industry, with over 11% of American adults receiving psychotropic medications in 2002 (Paulose-Ram, Safran, Jonas, Gu, & Orwig, 2007). Medications are now available to relieve some of the symptoms of nearly every defined mental disorder although they also carry with them several undesirable side effects. None of them appear to arrest, or cure, the disorders they treat.

Even before 1900, drugs such as alcohol, heroin, cocaine, and various other sedative/hypnotic and stimulant substances had been used as treatments for mental disorders. By 1950, benzedrine had been used for hyperactivity and lithium salts had been used to treat mania (Willerman & Cohen, 1990). Other new treatments were discovered, accidentally, while researchers were working on different problems. Antihistamines, for example, produced sedation and later were noted to calm psychiatric patients. The first antipsychotic medication, chlorpromazine, was derived from antihistamines for its sedative effects; its antipsychotic effects were discovered subsequently. Marketed as Thorazine, it dramatically changed the treatment of hospitalized schizophrenic patients in a very short time. It worked by blocking dopamine receptor sites at the synapse, and for many patients the result was to reduce the severity of active symptoms such as hallucinations and delusions. Soon, there were many other phenothiazine drugs on the market for the treatment of schizophrenia. Within a few decades, the population of patients being treated inside of mental institutions dropped by two-thirds.

In a similarly indirect way, antidepressant drugs were accidentally discovered during investigations for treating tuberculosis. A medication that had antibacterial effects against the agent that caused tuberculosis also "energized" the patients and by 1957 had been employed specifically as an antidepressant (Wilson, Nathan, O'Leary, & Clark, 1996). The drug appeared to increase levels of neurotransmitters, like norepinephrine, by delaying their oxidation and reuptake after their release into the synaptic cleft. This effectively allowed the neurotransmitter to remain longer in the synapse (it was a *monoamine oxidase inhibitor*, or MAO-I). Other agents were quickly developed, affecting both NE and serotonin: the *tricyclic antidepressants*—the *selective serotonin reuptake inhibitors*, or SSRIs, widely used at present for the treatment of depression and other disorders, and the *selective serotonin and norepinephrine reuptake inhibitors*, or SNRIs, which are used for both depression and anxiety.

The revolutionary development of antipsychotic and antidepressant medications also led to the development of biological theories of the disorders they treat. As the mechanisms of their actions at the synapse became understood, neurotransmitter theories about the causes of schizophrenia and depression were developed. In their earliest forms, the **dopamine hypothesis of schizophrenia** proposed that the disorder was caused by excessive dopamine activity in the brain (hence, DA-blocking drugs like Thorazine were useful); and the **catecholamine hypothesis of depression** proposed that the mood disorder resulted from a relative depletion of NE in the brain (hence, MAO-I drugs were useful because they enhanced NE activity). As newer medications with more specific transmitter effects have been researched and developed, these theories have been refined and modified as well. They will be discussed in later chapters on specific disorders.

Effective anti-anxiety and anti-mania drugs have also been developed. Together with stimulants and sedative/hypnotics, they comprise the formulary of psychotropic medications that are widely prescribed by psychiatrists, family physicians, and nurse practitioners (see Table 3-4).

The drug revolution has resulted in symptom relief, but none of the medications correct or resolve the biological condition presumed to underlie the symptoms. Instead, their general effect is to inhibit, or to disinhibit, the transmission of nerve impulses. There are also significant concerns about medication side effects to consider. The older antipsychotic medications could

**Dopamine hypothesis of schizophrenia**

Proposed that the disorder was caused by excessive dopamine activity in the brain (Hence, DA-blocking drugs like Thorazine were useful)

**Catecholamine hypothesis of depression**

Proposed that the mood disorders resulted from a relative depletion of NE in the brain (Hence, MAO-I drugs were useful because they enhanced NE activity)

*Table 3-4*    Examples of Frequently Used Medications for Mental Disorders

| Purpose | Drug Class | Generic Name | Trade Name |
|---|---|---|---|
| Antipsychotic (Schizophrenia, psychosis) | Phenothiazines<br>Butyrophenones<br>Dibenzodiazepines<br>Dibenzoxazepines | Chlorpromaize<br>Thiordazine<br>Fluphenazine<br>Haloperidol<br>Clozapine<br>Lozapine | Thorazine<br>Mellaril<br>Prolixin<br>Haldol<br>Clozaril<br>Loxitan |
| Selective Serotonin and Norepinephrine Reuptake Inhibitors (SNRIs) | MAO inhibitors<br>Tricyclics (TAC)<br>Selective serotonin reuptake inhibitors (SSRI)<br>Atypical antidepressants | Phenelzine<br>Imipramin<br>Amitripyline<br>Sertraline<br>Fluoxetine<br>Buporpoin<br>Venlafaxine<br>Duloxetin<br>Respiridone<br>Aripiprazole | Nardil<br>Tofranil<br>Elavil<br>Zoloft<br>Prozac<br>Wellbutrin<br>Effexor<br>Cymbalta<br>Resperdal<br>Abilify |
| Anxiety (Anxiety disorders, panic) | Benzodiazapines<br>Azapirone | Diazepam<br>Alprazolam<br>Buspirone | Valium<br>Xanax<br>Buspar |
| Antimanic (Bipolar Disorder, mood swings) | | Lithium carbonate<br>Carbamazepine<br>Valproate | Eskalith<br>Tegretol<br>Depakene |
| Stimulant (Attention deficit, narcolepsy) | | Methylphenidate<br>Pemoline | Ritalin<br>Cylert |

produce increased pulse rates, sweating, dry mouth, disturbed sexual function, movement problems, shuffling gait, grimacing, tongue spasms, and fine motor tremors. Involuntary tongue darting and chewing motions reflected an incurable problem called **tardive dyskinesia** that resulted directly from prolonged use. Newer antipsychotic medications have reduced many of these side effects but also carry their own potential problems, including a potentially fatal blood disease called *agranulocytosis*. The antidepressants, as well, triggered troubling side effects that included dry mouth, blurry vision, sexual problems, constipation, dizziness, sleep disturbance, and hypotension. In addition, the early antidepressants carried a significant risk of fatal overdose, especially important for depressed patients. Many antianxiety drugs have a strong risk of dependence and addiction, becoming very dangerous when mixed with alcohol; the common antimanic drug, lithium, must be carefully monitored so that toxic levels in the bloodstream are not reached. Frequently, additional medications are prescribed to help patients control the side effects of psychotropic medications, and relapse is high once the medications are discontinued. As a result, some patients often must continue drug therapy for years. Many of these medications are also associated with weight gain. All of these factors must be considered when weighing the risks of drug therapy to the symptomatic benefits of treatment. Still, prescription of psychotropic medication is routine within the biological model for most mental disorders at this time.

**Tardive dyskinesia**

Occasional long-term side effect of phenothiazine treatment of schizophrenia and involves rhythmical, stereotyped movements and lip smacking

## 3.6 Humanistic-Experiential Approaches

The frameworks discussed above differ from each other in many ways, but they share at least one common characteristic: They are deterministic models, meaning that they consider abnormal behavior to have specific causes in the childhood, learning history, or biology of the individual. Some writers, psychotherapists for the most part, have reacted strongly against the implications of deterministic models. These individuals (Frankl, 1969; Mahrer, 1978; May, 1967; Rogers, 1961) have variously called their point of view *humanistic, existential, phenomenological,* and *experiential.* Although by no means totally in accord, these writers tend to agree on a number of points. All, for example, tend to emphasize an experiential or phenomenological approach, terms that refer to the person's subjective "experiencings." To understand another

> **How does the humanistic approach differ from other perspectives?**

person, they say, we need to know what that person perceives, feels, or thinks. To analyze that person— whether in terms of id impulses and ego defense mechanisms, behavioral and cognitive influences, or biological state—inevitably forces these subjective experiencings into a mold that does not fit. The only way we can truly understand why persons behave as they do is to see and feel the world from the other's vantage point.

To some extent the **humanistic approach** is antitheoretical, even anti-intellectual; it implies that Western civilization, in fostering abstract, theoretical thinking, has cut us off from direct experience. A related idea is that it is not necessary to reconstruct past history in order to understand a person. Such a reconstruction would inevitably be theoretical in nature and take us away from the immediate here-and-now experiencings of the individual. Although to look at a human being in the same detached, analytical manner that we view atoms, molecules, or the functioning of the cardiovascular system may be scientific, in a certain sense that neglects, they say, the uniquely human quality of the person. The phenomenologically experienced self cannot be broken down into smaller units and analyzed—the proper unit is the self.

The concept of free will or free choice plays a central role in the humanistic approach. The psychoanalytic, biological, and behavioral/cognitive approaches assume that behavior has specific and discoverable causes, although they disagree on the determining forces. The experientially oriented therapist believes that accepting responsibility for making one's "existential" choices is a key factor in therapy. This emphasis on choice dates back to European philosophers such as Kierkegaard. Kierkegaard maintained that personality is determined by the series of choices each person makes. The crucial decisions are between *inauthentic* and *authentic existence.* In inauthentic choices, persons permit themselves to be shaped by the demands and expectations of others; in authentic choices they assume full responsibility for their own fate and existence. Existential anxiety occurs when persons face the prospect of taking responsibility for their own destiny; failure in this endeavor can lead to an existential neurosis according to the proponents of this point of view. A humanistic view then, sees persons as valued human beings, struggling with the problems of their existence, and free to make their own choices—not as subjects for psychoanalysis, behavior modification, or drug therapy.

One point on which there is some disagreement among humanistic writers is the question of whether people are basically good, or bad, or neither. Freud's theory suggests that underneath the veneer of civilized behavior humans harbor strong aggressive, lustful, greedy, and selfish urges that have to be controlled and regulated by the society's internalized representative, the ego. Some humanistic writers such as Abraham Maslow and Carl Rogers argue that people are basically motivated toward self-fulfillment and constructive personality growth. Unfortunate life experiences can, however, warp or sidetrack this fundamental impulse. Other humanistic or existential writers ( for example, (Binswagner, 1999; May, 1967) conceptualize human nature as neither good nor bad. Mahrer (1978), espousing a humanistic theory of personality and therapy, takes the latter position. He proposes that each of us has experiential potentials, of which some are conscious and rather directly control our behavior and others exist on a deeper, unconscious level. Some of these experiential *potentials* may be viewed as good and some as bad from ethical or societal standards; however, there is no *one* basic potential that represents either a striving for "good," constructive personality growth or a striving for evil or destructive ends.

**Humanistic approach**

Emphasis on viewing people as whole human beings rather than analyzing them in an impersonal fashion

What exactly are the metaphors used to explain abnormal behavior in the humanistic framework? One such metaphor deriving from existential philosophy and mentioned previously is that symptoms of mental disorder occur when individuals make too many inauthentic choices and fail to confront the existential anxiety associated with taking responsibility for their own lives. Another, perhaps more common, metaphor is that symptoms occur when persons cut themselves off from their own experiencings. This metaphor is quite similar to the psychodynamic metaphor and perhaps differs primarily in avoiding theorizing about such constructs as id, superego, ego, fixations, and so on. It is useful to be reminded that our subjective experiences are rich, varied, and—in many respects—likely to be unique for each of us; any theoretical formulation will probably not capture all the nuances of these experiencings. There is also an ethical quality of humaneness that pervades this approach. Adherents of other approaches can be, and frequently are, just as humane; but the humanistic writers have most insistently reminded us that abnormally behaving people are persons, not cases to be considered only as interesting examples of psychopathology. On the other hand, the humanistic approach has not generated much research that has illuminated the nature of abnormal behavior. This is not surprising in view of the negative views of its adherents toward categorizing, quantifying, and experimenting with human behavior. Although humanistic writers sometimes imply that we are on the verge of some new methodology for studying subjective experience, how can they or anyone ever directly study somebody else's subjective experience—short of some kind of extrasensory, telepathic communication?

The experientially oriented therapist believes that accepting responsibility for making one's "existential" choices is a key factor in therapy. Kierkegaard maintained that personality is determined by the series of choices each person makes. (iStock)

## 3.7 Approaching an Integrated Model

There are, of course, many other psychological perspectives that have not been covered here although most could be viewed, to some extent, within these four basic frameworks. It is also true that the models presented above are not as distinct as they seem. Psychodynamic and biological frameworks have long coexisted within the practice of psychiatry while the behavioral, cognitive, and biological models combined within the neurosciences; and some merging between humanistic concerns and behavioral methodologies is evident in the emergence of "positive psychology" approaches that emphasize empirically-based interventions to increase personal happiness (Seligman, Steen, Park, & Peterson, 2005). Practicing psychotherapists commonly draw from humanistic, behavioral, and cognitive models while interacting with clients. At the same time, our understanding of psychopathology remains very incomplete, and many questions remain unanswered. An eclectic approach, many would agree, is the best one for the current state of affairs.

> Can assessment of treatment outcomes contribute to a more unified framework?

Research is progressing rapidly, nonetheless, on many fronts; and it seems very likely that a more unified or integrated model will be the result. The activity of science opens many new doors, and also closes old ones. Psychotropic medications are subjected to controlled demonstrations of their effectiveness and risks, and the established formulary contains those that have been approved for specific uses (see Table 3-4). In a similar way, a greater reliance on empirical assessment of outcomes of psychotherapies has already resulted in initial compilations of "empirically validated" or "demonstrably effective" therapy techniques such as

*Table 3-5*    Treatments for Selected Disorders

Well-established and probably efficacious psychotherapies for selected disorders

| Disorder | Well-Established Treatments | Probably Efficacious Treatments |
|---|---|---|
| Anxiety | Cognitive behavior therapy for panic disorder<br>Cognitive behavior therapy for generalized anxiety disorder<br>Exposure treatment for agoraphobia<br>Exposure and response prevention for obsessive-compulsive disorder | Applied relaxation for panic disorder<br>Applied relaxation for generalized anxiety disorder<br>Cognitive behavior therapy for social phobia<br>Cognitive therapy for obsessive-compulsive disorder<br>Exposure treatment for post-traumatic stress disorder<br>Eye movement desensitization and reprogramming for post-traumatic stress disorder<br>Systematic desensitization for social anxiety |
| Depression | Behavior therapy for depression<br>Cognitive therapy for depression<br>Interpersonal therapy for depression | Brief dynamic therapy for depression<br>Cognitive therapy for geriatric depression<br>Self-control therapy for depression |
| Health problems | Behavior therapy for headache<br>Cognitive behavior therapy for bulimia<br>Cognitive behavior therapy for rheumatic pain<br>Cognitive behavior therapy with relapse prevention for smoking cessation | Behavior therapy for childhood obesity<br>Cognitive behavior therapy for binge-eating disorder<br>Cognitive behavior therapy for chronic pain<br>EMG Biofeedback for chronic pain |
| Childhood problems | Behavior modification for enuresis<br>Parent training for children with oppositional disorder | Behavior modification for encopresis<br>Exposer therapy for simple phobia<br>Cognitive behavior therapy for anxiety |
| Marital problems | Behavioral marital therapy | Emotionally focused couples therapy<br>Insight-oriented marital therapy |
| Other problems | | Behavior therapy for cocaine abuse<br>Cognitive therapy for opiate dependence<br>Brief dynamic therapy for opiate dependence<br>Community Reinforcement Approach for alcohol dependence<br>Masters and Johnson's sex therapy for female orgasmic dysfunction<br>Behavior modification for sex offenders<br>Dialectical behavior therapy for borderline personality disorder<br>Social skills training for social adjustment of schizophrenic patients |

Source: Adapted from Chambless et al., 1998

those in Table 3-5. The interventions listed as "well-established treatments" have been shown to be effective in two well-designed group experiments or a large series of well-designed single-subject experiments, compared to either placebo or alternative therapies, while those listed as "probably efficacious treatments" have been shown to be superior to control groups or equivalent to established treatments in fewer controlled studies (Chambless, et al., 1998). Although there is much disagreement among psychologists about the value of such lists, there is every reason to expect that outcome research will persist in this endeavor.

As these empirical efforts to define "effective" treatments continue, the very significant financial (and political) power of the health care business enters into the equation. Insurance companies and the managed-care industry are interested in paying only for effective treatments, of course. As outcome research continues, it will not be surprising to find more limitations on the types of interventions that health care agencies will cover. Such a contingency hopefully adds to, rather than conflicts with, the general tendency of science to continually refine its approach toward a paradigm. So long as the scientific expectations outweigh the financial ones, we may eventually learn the form of an integrated perspective on both normal, and abnormal, psychology.

# Chapter Review

## TO SUM UP ...

- The psychodynamic framework explains psychological symptoms in terms of intrapsychic events such as motives, fantasies, and conflicts. Freud held that conflicts about sexuality play an important role in all neurotic disorders. He proposed that discovering the underlying psychic conflict and bringing it to conscious awareness through psychoanalysis was critical to treatment.

- Other investigators differed with Freud and proposed psychodynamic theories of their own, renouncing the idea that sexual conflicts lay behind all neurotic disorders. They suggested other factors, such as strivings for superiority and basic anxiety arising from a conflict between needs for affection and hostility, should be the targets of therapy.

- The behavioral framework explains psychological symptoms as the result of personal experiences and learning histories, interacting with the current set of prevailing contingencies of reinforcement and punishment. It proposes that symptoms are treated by providing new learning experiences and altering contingencies to favor the development of more adaptive behaviors.

- The cognitive approach modifies the behavioral perspective to include beliefs, expectations, attitudes, and thought patterns as sources of problems and targets to modify.

- The biological approach explains psychological symptoms as the result of underlying biological or chemical abnormalities. It proposes that symptoms are treated medically, usually with psychotropic medication.

- Humanistic-experiential approaches explain psychological symptoms as the existential anxiety produced by blockage of growth or the results of inauthentic subjective experiences. Treatment involves the freely-chosen acceptance of responsibility for one's own life experience

- Increased reliance on outcome assessment has resulted in efforts to empirically identify effective treatments. That trend may combine with the tendency within science to refine a paradigm, moving the study of psychopathology toward a more unified model.

# KEY TERMS

Axon   71

Behaviorism   57

Catecholamine hypothesis of
   depression   75

Chromosomes   66

Concordance   69

Conditioned reinforcers   59

Contingency   60

Covert sensitization   64

Defense mechanism   51

Dendrites   71

Discriminative stimulus   60

Displacement   52

Dopamine hypothesis of
   schizophrenia   75

Ego   52

Electroconvulsive therapy, or
   ECT   74

Fixations   53

Fraternal or dizygotic (DZ) twins   69

Free association   55

Genes   66

Genotype   66

Humanistic approach   77

Id   52

Identical or monozygotic (MZ)
   twins   69

Intrapsychic   52

Isolation   52

Libido   53

Modeling   64

Negative reinforcement   60

Neurons   71

Neurotransmitters   72

Oedipal conflict   51

Phenotypes   68

Phenylketonuria (PKU)   70

Phobia   54

Positive reinforcement   60

Primary reinforcer   59

Projection   52

Psychosurgery   74

Punishers   59

Reaction formation   51

Regressions   53

Reinforcement   59

Repression   51

Resistance   55

Reversal design   62

Superego   52

Synapse   72

Systematic desensitization   64

Tardive dyskinesia   76

Transference   56

Unconscious   49

## QUESTIONS FOR STUDY

- Describe a healthy use of defense mechanisms, distinguishing it from an unhealthy use of defenses mechanisms.

- How might selection by consequences at the biological, individual, and cultural levels account for drug abuse?

- Describe two methods of studying hereditary influences.

## POP QUIZ

1.  According to Freud, the mind can be divided into three parts: _____, _____, _____.
    A. oral, anal, and phallic
    B. brain stem, limbic system, and cortex
    C. genetic, neural, and biological
    D. id, ego, and superego

2.  The ___ is concerned with basic instinctive drives in the unconscious.
    A. id
    B. ego
    C. unconscious
    D. superego

3.  The ___ contains our internalizing values and is something like a "conscience".
    A. id
    B. ego
    C. unconscious
    D. superego

4.  The driving force behind the Oedipal conflict for a young boy is _____.
    A. transference
    B. castration anxiety
    C. thantos
    D. penis envy

5.  _____ is a defense mechanism in which a person behaves in a way directly opposite from some underlying impulse.
    A. reaction formation
    B. projection
    C. isolation
    D. displacement

6. Chuck had a really bad day at work. In particular, he is very angry that his boss presented Chuck's ideas for marketing a new product to the marketing team without giving Chuck credit for the idea. Of course, Chuck cannot express his anger to his boss, as that might lead to him getting fired. When Chuck gets home, he angrily picks a fight with his wife. This is most likely an example of _____.
   A. projection
   B. isolation
   C. reaction formation
   D. displacement

7. The _____ is the predominantly conscious part of the mind.
   A. id
   B. ego
   C. superego
   D. unconscious

8. In Watson's attempt to create a phobia in Little Albert, what was the unconditioned stimulus?
   A. the rat
   B. the loud noise
   C. fear
   D. the startle reaction

9. What is the difference between positive and negative reinforcement?
   A. In positive reinforcement, something is presented; in negative reinforcement, something is taken away.
   B. In positive reinforcement behavior is strengthened, in negative reinforcement behavior is weakened.
   C. Positive reinforcement shapes positive behaviors; negative reinforcement shapes negative behaviors.
   D. Positive reinforcement is reward; negative reinforcement is punishment.

10. Training in deep muscle relaxation is usually the first step for which intervention procedure?
    A. negative reinforcement
    B. systematic desensitization
    C. covert sensitization
    D. ACT

11. According to Skinner, operant conditioning is a form of _____.
    A. representation
    B. association
    C. selection
    D. extinction

12. Twins resulting from the splitting of a single fertilized ovum are _____ twins.
    A. monozygotic
    B. multizygotic
    C. dizygotic
    D. zygotic

13. All **except** which one of the following is a neurotransmitter?
    A. dopamine
    B. phenylalanine
    C. serotonin
    D. GABA

14. Which procedure involves stimulation of brain regions by magnetic fields?
    A. rTMS
    B. vagus nerve stimulation
    C. ECT
    D. unilateral ECT

15. The emphasis on the immediate here-and-now experiencing of the individual is the _____ approach.
    A. behavioral
    B. biological
    C. humanistic
    D. psychoanalytic

Additional study resources are available at **www.BVTLab.com**

# CHAPTER OVERVIEW

# CHAPTER OPENER QUESTIONS

What are the problems in classifying behavior disorders?

Is a categorical approach the best one for diagnosing mental disorders?

How well can different clinicians independently arrive at the same diagnosis?

What are some common diagnostic procedures and tests?

(Shutterstock)

# chapter 4

# Classification, Diagnosis, and Assessment

People differ from one another on nearly every measure we can select. In physical attributes, we vary in height, weight, hair color and texture, eye color, skin color, fingerprint ridges, and shoe size, to name but a few. We also differ in physical and sensory capabilities, in the flexibility of our spines, and in our individual body odors. Even wider variety characterizes human behavior. How we act, how we feel, and how well we remember our lives are only some behavioral characteristics that distinguish us from one another. By any comprehensive measure, no two people are exactly alike. The particular physical arrangement of our parts makes each of us recognizable as a unique human, while the patterns of our actions, feelings, and capabilities make us each a unique *person*. How then can we distinguish the borders of "normal" and "abnormal?"

## 4.1 Classification

In the beginning stages of most sciences, investigators try to make sense of nature's complexities by classifying observations. The early chemists sorted compounds with certain properties into a group they called acids while other compounds with different properties were classified as bases. This categorization was useful because once chemists found that a compound had certain properties of an acid, for example, they would know automatically that it also had a number of other predictable properties. Once acids and bases had been separated into useful classes, investigators could look deeper into the basic nature of these compounds and make subtler distinctions. Classification, then, can be the start of a process that leads to a more fundamental understanding of basic principles rather than just a labeling process that is an end in itself.

The attempt to develop a classification system for abnormal behavior was based in large part on the example of the value of classification in the area of physical disease. People with a certain syndrome (pattern of symptoms) that showed a typical course and outcome without treatment—the symptoms of malaria, for example—were classified as having the same disease. Once a **syndrome** had been identified, research in many instances proceeded to identify the physical causes of the disease and to develop effective treatments or even preventive measures.

The attempt to develop a classification system for abnormal behavior was based in large part on the example of the value of classification in the area of physical disease. (Shutterstock)

Investigators in the field of psychopathology have reaped similar benefits in several notable ways. As we saw in Chapter 2, the first step in the long process of fully understanding the mental disorder known as general paresis was the identification of a pattern of symptoms with an associated course and outcome. If physicians had not been interested in classification, it is hard to see how progress could have been made in separating out this particular disorder from the mass of mental disorders and discovering its highly specific cause—a syphilitic infection.

**Syndrome**

Pattern of symptoms that tend to occur together in a particular disease or condition

Thus a major aim of psychopathologists in developing classificatory systems is to discover to what extent there are distinctive patterns of abnormal behaviors with their own causative histories. The realization of this aim allows them not only to seek out causative influences but also to devise rational treatment and to detect individuals in the early stages of certain disorders before the disorders become more serious. This chapter will outline the classification scheme most widely used for abnormal behavior and consider some of the problems that classification systems encounter.

## 4.1a Development of a System of Classification

As noted earlier, different types of abnormal behavior have been identified since the Greek period. Melancholia was recognized as a different condition than hysteria, for example. Freud differentiated neuroses from psychoses, such as schizophrenia, and treated a range of neurotic disorders through psychoanalysis. However, a classification model had not yet been developed for general application. During World War I, for example, the U.S. Navy had a system by which all mentally disturbed sailors were assigned to one of two categories: "insane, restraint" or "insane, other." Clearly, mental health professionals needed a more sophisticated classification system.

In 1949, the World Health Organization included a section for the classification of psychiatric or mental disorders in its *International Classification of Diseases and Related Health Problems, Sixth Edition* (*ICD-6*). It had little impact and was rarely employed by the mental health field. In the United States, the American Psychiatric Association set up a model to replace the *ICD-6* section that was called the *Diagnostic and Statistical Manual of Mental Disorders* (*DSM-I*), first published in 1952. This new model was strongly influenced by the theories of Freud and Adolf Meyer. Many of the disorders that were listed in the *DSM-I* were considered, under Meyer's influence, to be reactions of the personality to important psychological or biological events. For example, a schizophrenic reaction could be contrasted to a depressive reaction. The manual was revised in 1968 into the *DSM-II*; and, in the process, the number of mental disorders listed was increased by 50%. Although the term "reaction" was generally removed from the names of disorders, it remained strongly influenced by Freud's concepts of neurosis and psychosis. Thus, the *depressive reaction* of *DSM-I* became *depressive neurosis* in *DSM-II* and given a code number in line with the newer *ICD-8*.

> What are the problems in classifying behavioral disorders?

### A Critical Challenge

Clearly, there were concerns about the accuracy and consistency with which the *DSM-II* labels could be applied; agreement among clinicians on the use of a label often was no better than chance. A researcher at Stanford University, David Rosenhan, believed that the diagnosis of psychiatric problems was unlike medical diagnoses because the latter could be verified or validated in some physical way whereas psychiatric labels were maintained by consensus alone. For example, homosexuality was listed as a mental disorder under the *DSM-II*, but it was subsequently removed from the list of disorders. That decision was the result of a vote by members of the American Psychiatric Association—a process that presumably would not be used in determining the validity of an actual medical diagnosis. Rosenhan (1973) set out to demonstrate that the context of the diagnostic situation was more important in applying a psychiatric label than was any objective examination of the patient. Eight normal people (confederates in the study) appeared at 12 psychiatric hospitals in five different states on both the east and west coasts of the United States, presenting the same complaint of hearing voices. In response to questions from the hospital's admission staff, the pseudopatients stated that often the voices were unclear, but seemed to say the words "empty," "hollow," or

**BVT** *Lab*

Flashcards are available for this chapter at www.BVTLab.com.

"thud." Apart from giving false personal information (name and employment, for example), the pseudopatients reported no other symptoms or psychiatric history.

All of the pseudopatients were admitted to the hospitals and in all but one case were given the diagnosis of schizophrenia. (The other case was labeled manic depressive psychosis.) Once in the hospital, all pseudopatients acted as normal as possible, given the setting. They remained hospitalized from 7 to 52 days before being discharged with a diagnosis of "schizophrenia, in remission." None of the pseudopatients were detected by hospital staff as "fakes" although nearly a third of actual patients in the admissions wards expressed their suspicions about them (e.g., "You're not crazy. You're a journalist or professor checking up on the hospital."). Apparently, the professional staff was unable to distinguish actual schizophrenics from imposters who presented only a single, initial, verbal symptom.

In response to criticism from a teaching hospital which had heard of these results, Rosenhan conducted a second experiment (Rosenhan, 1973). He informed the hospital that at some time in the next 3 months, one or more pseudopatients would seek admission there. Hospital staff members were asked to rate patients during that time period on the likelihood that they were pseudopatients. Although no pseudopatients were ever sent to the hospital, 19 actual patients were identified by at least one psychiatrist and one other staff member as being probable fakes. Rosenhan concluded that the "sane" could not be differentiated from the "insane" under the prevailing diagnostic model. Of course, as some critics pointed out, it may be an unfair test of a diagnostic process to send in people who pretended to be disturbed and presented false symptoms. Since the goal of the hospital staff was to help those in need, it is not surprising that they would accept the feigned symptoms as real. It is also true that many medical diagnoses have reliability problems, and an imposter coming to a medical hospital complaining of a bleeding ulcer would probably also be admitted. However, there are physical examinations and laboratory tests that would eventually confirm or disconfirm the presence of an ulcer. As Rosenhan noted, there were no similar sources for verification of the diagnosis of schizophrenia, once it is given.

## Multiaxial Diagnosis

In light of such definitional problems, a major overhaul of the diagnostic system was needed; and it came with the publication of the third edition of the *DSM* in 1980 (*DSM-III*). *DSM-III* represented a marked improvement from the two earlier systems in several ways. The criteria used to make a diagnosis were described in more objective, behavioral terms and less tied to theoretical assumptions about intrapsychic causes. In the case of schizophrenia, for example, the criteria specified active psychotic symptoms, a required duration of the disturbance, and a decline in function compared to earlier periods. It is safe to say that under the *DSM-III* Rosenhan's pseudopatients would not have received the diagnosis for the single symptom they presented. Some categories of doubtful utility were dropped while the total number of diagnostic categories more than doubled. Perhaps the largest structural change involved the introduction of five separate domains (or axes) on which individuals could be evaluated, in order to give a more complete clinical picture of a person. This multiaxial approach was continued through the next three revisions of the *DSM*.

The *DSM-III* was well received. However, several inconsistencies and unclear criteria sets became apparent after its implementation, and it underwent another major refitting in 1987 with the *DSM-III-R* ("R" for "Revision"). Its multiaxial structure was retained, but the axes were restructured and over one third of the diagnostic categories were modified in some way. The *DSM-III-R* gave way to the next revision in the sequence, the *DSM-IV*, in 1994. Its terms were adjusted to be consistent with the *ICD-9*. Some relatively minor modifications were made in 2000, intended to update supporting information without altering criteria sets, in the *DSM-IV-TR* (TR for "Text Revision").

Throughout these editions, the multiaxial diagnostic framework of the *DSM* was generally as follows:

Axis I    Clinical disorders and/or other conditions that may be a focus of clinical attention

Axis II   Personality disorders and mental retardation

Axis III  General medical conditions potentially relevant to Axis I and II listings

Axis IV   Psychosocial and environmental problems

Axis V    Global assessment of functioning

Each axis of the *DSM* system was intended to capture a different component or "layer" of the total picture of disturbance. Axes I and II represented the basic classificatory system of mental disorders. It was thought that separating these two axes made it less likely that the clinician would overlook long-term personality styles that might be missed when attention is directed to a current episode of disturbance. Another distinction between these two axes involved onset of the disorders. Usually, those disorders on Axis I were more florid and had a point of onset—that is, a time when the presence of the disorder was noted as a different state for the person. The Axis I disorders (for example, major depressive disorder) also generally had an offset as the disorder remitted and the person recovered. Axis II disorders, by contrast, seemed to be characteristic of the long-standing functioning of the person, evident in some respects in nearly all situations and traceable back to adolescence or childhood.

Like medical diagnoses in general, both of these axes were categorical in nature. In other words, disturbed behavior patterns were organized into diagnostic "boxes" or categories if the symptoms were of sufficient intensity and duration to reach criterion level for use of the particular diagnostic label. Some psychologists raised objections to applying a categorical system for diagnosing psychological and behavioral disorders on the grounds that disturbances exist not as discreet entities but rather along a continuum or dimension. It is true that one cannot be a "little bit pregnant," for example, but perhaps one could be a little bit depressed or a little bit anxious. Nonetheless, the categorical model of diagnosing mental disorders was central to the *DSM* series at this time.

> **Is a categorical approach the best one for diagnosing mental disorders?**

Still, there were lingering concerns about the *DSM-IV*. One long-standing problem was that the overlap between some categories could be problematic. For example, mood disorders and anxiety disorders often coexisted, leading to questions about whether the boundaries between these categories can be accurately delineated (Brown, Di Nardo, Lehman, & Campbell, 2001; van Pragg, 2005). Diagnostic overlap resulted in a proliferation of diagnoses using the NOS descriptor ("not otherwise specified," meaning that the condition did not entirely meet the criteria for a disorder), which indicated a need for greater specificity in diagnostic criteria (American Psychiatric Association, 2012). Additionally, psychometric research into personality traits had increasingly favored a dimensional five-factor model, the "Big Five," that did not correspond well with the personality categories in the *DSM-IV* (Ryder, Costa, & Bagby, 2007). The American Psychiatric Association appointed a task force to work on the *DSM-5* (the APA opted to discontinue the Roman numeral indicator of edition), and draft criteria of the new system were produced in 2008. Following extensive research and field work, the final version of the *DSM-5* was approved and released in 2013.

The process was not without controversy. During the period allowed for open public comments on the draft versions, many professional organizations expressed strong reservations about the early proposals. The American Counseling Association, among many others, was concerned that normal bereavement would be pathologized if it was no longer excluded from a diagnosis of major depression, as it had been under the *DSM-IV*. The organization also worried that the number of personality disorders would expand. The Society for Humanistic Psychology launched an on-line "Open Letter to the *DSM-5*" expressing similar sentiments and recommending against lowering the thresholds for attention-deficit hyperactivity disorder, already suspected of being over-diagnosed. It also criticized as unwarranted *DSM-5*'s implied assumption that all mental disorders reflect an underlying biological dysfunction. The letter eventually garnered more than 14,500 signatures. The British Psychological Society objected to *DSM-5*'s categorical rather than dimensional framework, and several divisions of the American Psychological Association also joined the critics. Subsequent draft revisions of the *DSM-5* addressed some of these issues; yet the final draft left the British Psychological Society, and many other groups, "concerned" (Lane, 2012). Some of the strongest criticism of the *DSM-5* came from those who worked on earlier editions. For example, Allen Frances, the chair of the *DSM-IV* task force, has warned that "*DSM-5* is a travesty of careless suggestions that will likely turn our current diagnostic inflation into hyperinflation. Let the buyer beware" (Frances, 2013).

Much was altered with the *DSM-5*. First, the multiaxial structure of the earlier system was abandoned, and disorders formerly distinguished as Axis I, II, or III were compressed into a single list, in part to more closely accord with the *ICD-10* and to harmonize with the coming *ICD-11*. Although it includes approximately the same number of disorders as did the *DSM-IV-TR*, several categories have been reorganized and redefined; and the notion of a *spectrum* of disorders is now applied to some categories that had similar "relatives." For example, autistic disorder and Asperger's disorder in the *DSM-IV-TR* became autism spectrum disorders in the *DSM-5*. The organization of diagnoses in the *DSM-5* can be seen in Table 4-1.

*Table 4-1*    Categorical Organization of the DSM-5

| *DSM-5* **Category** | **Specific Examples** |
|---|---|
| Neurodevelopmental disorders | Intellectual disability, communication disorders, autism spectrum disorder, attention-deficit hyperactivity disorder |
| Schizophrenia spectrum and other psychotic disorders | Schizophrenia, delusional disorder |
| Bipolar and related disorders | Bipolar I disorder, cyclothymic disorder |
| Depressive disorders | Major depressive disorder, dysthymic disorder |
| Anxiety disorders | Panic disorder, social phobia |
| Obsessive-compulsive and related disorders | Obsessive-compulsive disorder, kleptomania |
| Trauma- and stressor-related disorders | Post-traumatic stress disorder, adjustment disorder |
| Dissociative disorders | Dissociative amnesia, dissociative identity disorder |
| Somatic symptom and related disorders | Conversion disorder, illness anxiety disorder |
| Feeding and eating disorders | Pica, bulimia nervosa |
| Elimination disorders | Encopresis |
| Sleep-wake disorders | Narcolepsy, obstructive sleep apnea |
| Sexual dysfunctions | Erectile dysfunction, hypoactive sexual desire |
| Gender dysphoria | Gender identity disorder |
| Disruptive, impulse-control, and conduct disorders | Intermittent explosive disorder, conduct disorder |
| Substance related and addictive disorders | Alcohol use disorder |
| Neurocognitive disorders | Dementia of the Alzheimer's type |
| Personality disorders | Antisocial personality disorder, histrionic personality disorder |
| Paraphilic disorders | Exhibitionism, pedophilia |
| Other mental disorders | Gambling disorder |
| Medication-induced movement disorders and other adverse effects of medication | Tardive dyskinesia |
| Other conditions that may be a focus of clinical attention | Grief, parent-child relational problem |

Source: Reprinted with permission from the *Diagnostic and Statistical Manual of Mental Disorders*, Fifth Edition, (Copyright 2013). American Psychiatric Association.

*Table 4-2*    Some Conditions Listed for Further Study in the *DSM-5*

| Proposed Disorder | Description of Symptoms |
| --- | --- |
| Attenuated Psychosis Syndrome | Some psychotic symptoms (such as delusions, hallucinations, or disorganized speech) at least weekly for the past month, but not of sufficient intensity or duration to meet the definition of any particular psychotic disorder |
| Persistent Complex Bereavement Disorder | After the death of a close friend or relative, persistent impairment, distress, and/or preoccupation with the death after 12 months (6 months for children), beyond that of cultural or religious norms |
| Caffeine Use Disorder | Inability (over the past 12 months) to cut down on caffeine use in spite of physical, psychological, social, or domestic problems that result, often accompanied by craving, tolerance, or withdrawal |
| Internet Gaming Disorder | For the past 12 months, persistent preoccupation with internet gaming that interferes with normal interpersonal, occupational, educational, and/or career functions or opportunities |
| Suicidal Behavior Disorder | At least one suicidal attempt in the past 24 months, not due to religious or political motivation or during a period of confusion or delirium |
| Nonsuicidal self-injury | Intentional self-inflicted body injury or damage, on five or more days during the past 12 months, that functioned to induce a positive feeling or reduce a negative feeling, without the intention of serious bodily harm |

Source: Reprinted with permission from the *Diagnostic and Statistical Manual of Mental Disorders,* Fifth Edition, (Copyright 2013). American Psychiatric Association.

Note that Table 4-1 contains not only the primary clinical syndromes or disorders but also movement problems or tremors that can result from use of medications prescribed as treatments for other conditions, as well as "other conditions that may be a focus of clinical attention." These "other conditions" are not mental disorders in themselves but rather present problems for which a person might seek treatment, or for which the patient's reaction is a relatively normal one. For example, the grief that follows the death of a loved one may result in significant distress, leading one to consult a clinician for assistance. However, grieving is not considered evidence of a mental disorder, unless it became particularly severe or long-lasting. Similarly, other sub-clinical problems could lead a person to seek assistance, such as a parent-child relationship problem, an episode of abuse, an acculturation issue, or difficulties at work or at school.

Like its predecessors, the *DSM-5* also includes a listing (in Section III of the manual) of conditions that have not yet been accepted as mental disorders but that are being considered for membership. Some of those potential future diagnoses are listed in Table 4-2. Generally, adequate information about the usefulness of these potential diagnoses has not yet been gathered; the research that exists to date does not support their status as distinctive mental disorders. They are included in the manual to generate research that could lead to their future inclusion or exclusion.

Although *DSM-5* remains a categorical rather than dimensional diagnostic system, it includes specific dimensional assessments for some conditions to quantify degree of symptom severity or to measure personality traits. Some of these assessments are completed by the patient, others by the clinician. A Level 1 assessment involves a brief survey of 12 or 13 symptom domains (such as depression, anxiety, psychosis, physical complaints, and anxiety) rated on a five-point severity scale (none, slight, mild, moderate, or severe). A rating of mild or higher on an issue would trigger a more in-depth Level 2 assessment involving various additional checklists and rating scales that are more specific to the issue. For personality disorders, a self-rated personality inventory for the *DSM-5* is included to measure the presence of five personality trait domains (Negative Affectivity, Detachment, Antagonism, Disinhibition, and Psychoticism) similar to, but different from, the Big Five model of personality currently favored by personality psychologists. These Level 1 and Level 2 assessments are intended to help guide clinical decision-making, and to provide a way to track response to treatment, but not to be used as the sole basis for diagnosis.

It is illustrative to compare various editions of the *DSM* series in the way they have defined and diagnosed a single disorder over the years. Recall that both Freud and Watson used their work on animal-phobic children to demonstrate the strength of their theories. Phobias are among the more common disorders, involving strong fear or anxiety when confronted by a specific object or circumstance. Table 4-3 shows the *DSM* guidelines for the diagnosis of phobia, from *DSM-I* to *DSM-5*. Note the appearance of coding numbers from the *ICD-8* with the *DSM-II* diagnosis; the *DSM-5* includes codes for both the *ICD-9* and the *ICD-10* (in parentheses; these numbers will be used beginning October 1, 2014).

# 4.2 Problems Associated with Classification Systems

Two important questions should be asked of any classification system: (1) How reliably can the categories be judged? (2) How valid are the categories in the sense of discriminating among disorders that have distinctive etiologies and possibly require different treatments? In order for a diagnosis to be reliable, different clinicians should come to the same diagnostic conclusion after independently examining the same patient. Their agreement on a diagnosis suggests that the label can be applied in a consistent way. **Diagnostic reliability** is not itself adequate for any classification system because it is possible for a diagnosis to be reliable but at the same time to be invalid. For example, two clinicians may agree that a person suffers from schizophrenia when, in fact, the person's hallucinations and delusions are actually the result of ongoing use of psychoactive drugs. **Diagnostic validity** concerns whether the diagnosis measures what it claims to measure. The refinements in the *DSM* classification system have been largely driven by the need to improve reliability and validity.

> **How well can different clinicians independently arrive at the same diagnosis?**

**Diagnostic reliability**

Consistency and agreement between clinicians in use of a diagnostic label

**Diagnostic validity**

The extent to which a diagnosis measures what it purports to measure

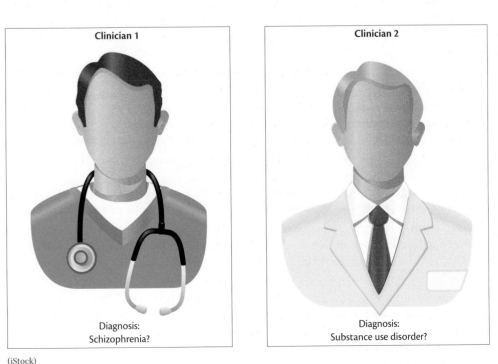

Clinician 1

Diagnosis: Schizophrenia?

Clinician 2

Diagnosis: Substance use disorder?

(iStock)

*Table 4-3*    Comparison of Diagnostic Criteria for Phobia, *DSM-I* Through *DSM-5*

| Edition | Diagnostic Criteria |
|---|---|
| *DSM-I* (American Psychiatric Association, 1952) | **000-x04 Phobic Reaction**<br><br>The anxiety of these patients becomes detached from a specific idea, object, or situation in the daily life and is displaced to some symbolic idea or situation in the form of a specific neurotic fear. The commonly observed forms of phobic reaction include fear of syphilis, dirt, closed places, high places, open places, animals, etc. The patient attempts to control his anxiety by avoiding the phobic object or situation.<br><br>In recording this diagnosis the manifestations will be indicated. The term is synonymous with the former term "phobia" and includes some of the cases formerly classified as "anxiety hysteria." |
| *DSM-II* (American Psychiatric Association, 1968) | **300.2 Phobic Neurosis**<br><br>This condition is characterized by intense fear of an object or situation which the patient consciously recognizes as no real danger to him. His apprehension may be experienced as faintness, fatigue, palpitations, perspiration, nausea, tremor, and even panic. Phobias are generally attributed to fears displaced to the phobic object or situation from some other object of which the patient is unaware. A wide range of phobias has been described. |
| *DSM-III* (American Psychiatric Association, 1980) | **300.29 Simple Phobia**<br><br>A. A persistent, irrational fear of, and compelling desire to avoid an object or situation, other than being alone or in public places away from home (Agoraphobia), or of humiliation or embarrassment in certain social situations (Social Phobia). Phobic objects are often animals, and phobic situations frequently involve heights or closed spaces.<br>B. Significant distress from the disturbance and recognition by the individual that his or her fear is excessive or unreasonable.<br>C. Not due to another mental disorder, such as Schizophrenia or Obsessive Compulsive Disorder. |
| *DSM-IV* (American Psychiatric Association, 1994) | **300.29 Specific Phobia**<br><br>A. Marked and persistent fear that is extensive or unusual, cued by the presence or anticipation of a specific object or situation (e.g., flying, heights, animals, receiving and injection, seeing blood).<br>B. Exposure to the phobic stimulus almost invariably provokes an immediate anxiety response, which may take the form of a situationally bound or situationally predisposed panic attack. *Note*: In children, the anxiety may be expressed by crying, tantrums, freezing, or clinging.<br>C. The person recognizes that the fear is excessive or unreasonable. *Note*: In children, this feature may be absent.<br>D. The phobic situation(s) is avoided or else is endured with intense anxiety or distress.<br>E. The avoidance, anxious anticipation, or distress in the feared situation interferes significantly with the person's normal routine, occupational (or academic) functioning, or social activities or relationships, or there is marked distress about having the phobia.<br>F. In individuals under age 18 years, the duration is at least 6 months.<br>G. The anxiety, Panic Attacks, or phobic avoidance associated with the specific object or situation are not better accounted for by another mental disorder, such as Obsessive-Compulsive Disorder (e.g., fear of dirt in someone with an obsession about contamination), Posttraumatic Stress Disorder (e.g., avoidance of stimuli associated with a severe stressor), Separation Anxiety Disorder (e.g., avoidance of school), Social Phobia (e.g., avoidance of social situations because of fear of embarrassment), Panic Disorder With Agoraphobia, or Agoraphobia Without History of Panic Disorder.<br><br>*Specify* type:<br>Animal Type    Natural Environment Type    Blood-Injection-Injury Type    Situational Type    Other Type |
| *DSM-5* (American Psychiatric Association, 2013) | **Specific Phobia**<br><br>A. Marked fear or anxiety about a specific object or situation (e.g., flying, heights, animals, receiving an injection, seeing blood). Note: In children, the fear or anxiety may be expressed by crying, tantrums, freezing, or clinging.<br>B. The phobic object or situation almost always provokes immediate fear or anxiety.<br>C. The phobic object or situation is actively avoided or endured with intense fear or anxiety.<br>D. The fear or anxiety is out of proportion to the actual danger posed by the specific object or situation and to the sociocultural context.<br>E. The fear, anxiety, or avoidance is persistent, typically lasting 6 months or more.<br>F. The fear, anxiety, or avoidance causes clinically significant distress or impairment in social, occupational, or other important areas of functioning.<br>G. The disturbance is not better accounted for by the symptoms of another mental disorder, including fear, anxiety, and avoidance of situations associated with panic-like symptoms or other incapacitating symptoms (as in agoraphobia); objects or situations related to obsessions (as in obsessive-compulsive disorder); reminders of traumatic events (as in posttraumatic stress disorder); separation from home or attachment figures (as in separation anxiety disorder); or social situations (as in social anxiety disorder).<br><br>*Specify* if:<br>Code based on phobic stimulus:<br>300.29 (F40.218) Animal    300.29 (F40.228) Natural environment    300.29 (F40.23x) Blood-injection-injury<br>Coding note: Select specific ICD-10-CM code as follows: F40.230 fear of blood; F40.231 fear of injections and transfusions; F40.232 fear of other medical care; or F40.233 fear of injury<br>300.29 (F40.248) Situational    300.29 (F40.298) Other |

Source: *Diagnostic and Statistical Manual of Mental Disorders*, American Psychiatric Association.

# 4.2a  The Reliability of Categories

In the early versions of the *DSM* series, diagnostic reliability was largely ignored. Independent psychiatrists agreed on a schizophrenic diagnosis in 53% of the cases in one study (Beck, Ward, Mendelson, Mock, & Erbaugh, 1962). Agreement on subcategories within the broader categories was even less. An important component of the *DSM-III* involved the use of extensive field trials to evaluate reliability by having pairs of clinicians make independent diagnoses on several hundred patients. During the development of the *DSM-III*, two phases of the field trials were conducted with the *DSM-III* draft criteria employed in Phase One and revised criteria employed in Phase Two. Inter-rater reliability was measured using the kappa statistic, which considers the possibility of chance agreement in its calculation (like correlations, kappa values of 1.0 mean perfect agreement). In the *DSM-III*, a reliability estimate of 0.70 or higher was said to indicate good agreement in the use of the diagnosis.

The results of the *DSM-III* field trials were included in the manual as an appendix, allowing users to compare the relative reliabilities of different diagnostic categories. Some general results of the *DSM-III* field trials for adult patients are displayed in Table 4-4. The most reliable diagnostic categories (those with kappa values of 0.70 and above) included mental retardation, mood disorders, substance use disorders, and schizophrenia. Less reliable diagnoses included somatoform disorders, factitious disorders, and personality disorders. Overall, the results showed that reliability had improved compared to the *DSM-II*, but it was still disappointing in several areas.

As the *DSM-IV* was prepared, the task force assigned to the revision conducted extensive field trials to again evaluate improvements in diagnostic reliability. Unfortunately, the results of these reliability trials were not included with the publication of either the *DSM-IV* or *DSM-IV-TR*, nor have they been widely disseminated in the professional literature. Some reliability figures for the *DSM-IV* are found in the published reports of the task force teams that reviewed specific disorders. Among the few examples, Keller and his colleagues (1995) reported that the mood disorders field trials found "fair" to "good" inter-rater, inter-site reliabilities for major depression (.52) and dysthymia (.59). In a later, independent study of *DSM-IV* criteria for anxiety and mood disorders conducted on 362 patients in New York and Boston (Brown, Di Nardo, Lehman, & Campbell, 2001), reliabilities above .70 were found for all principal anxiety

*Table 4-4*   Diagnostic Reliabilities for Selected *DSM-III* Adult Disorders

| *DSM-III* Diagnostic Class | Reliability Range (Phase 1 – Phase 2) |
|---|---|
| Mental Retardation | 0.80–0.83 |
| Dementias (senile and pre-senile) | 0.85–0.91 |
| Substance Use Disorders | 0.86–0.80 |
| Schizophrenic Disorder | 0.81–0.81 |
| Affective (mood) Disorder | 0.69–0.83 |
| Anxiety Disorder | 0.63–0.72 |
| Somatoform Disorder | 0.54–0.42 |
| Dissociative Disorder | 0.80– –0.003 |
| Psychosexual Disorders | 0.92–0.75 |
| Factitious Disorders | 0.66– –0.005 |
| Adjustment Disorders | 0.67–0.68 |
| Personality Disorders | 0.56–0.65 |
| Overall kappa of Axis I | 0.68–0.72 |
| Overall kappa of Axis II | 0.56–0.64 |

Source: Adapted from the *Diagnostic and Statistical Manual of Mental Disorders,* Third Edition, (Copyright 1980). American Psychiatric Association.

and mood diagnoses except for major depression (.68) and dysthymia (.22). Compared to the *DSM-III*, reliability was significantly improved for the anxiety disorder subtypes of generalized anxiety disorder and panic disorder. Data collected during the development of *ICD-10* (to which the *DSM-IV* was coordinated) during global field trials in 39 countries involving 100 sites showed good category reliabilities for schizophrenic disorders (.82), substance use disorders (.80), mood disorders (.77), and anxiety disorders (.74), but much poorer reliability (.47) for personality disorders (Sartorius, et al., 1993). However, subtype-level agreement was weaker: schizophrenia catatonic type (.39) and histrionic personality disorder (.12) demonstrated poor reliability. Generally, these studies indicate that *DSM-IV* diagnoses were at least as reliable as their *DSM-III* counterparts, although the need for improvement remained.

As the *DSM-5* field trials were underway, the American Psychiatric Association, perhaps stung by the disappointing results for the *DSM-IV*, appeared to be lowering expectations about improved reliability. In a commentary in the organization's main journal, Kraemer and his colleagues (2012) stated that "to see a $k_I$ [kappa] for a *DSM-5* diagnosis above 0.8 would be almost miraculous; to see $k_I$ between 0.6 and 0.8 would be cause for celebration. A realistic goal is $k_I$ between 0.4 and 0.6, while $k_I$ between 0.2 and 0.4 would be acceptable" (p. 14), implying that the earlier expectations for *DSM* reliability were unreasonably high. In fact, preliminary results of *DSM-5* field trials, involving 665 children and adolescent patients and 1,593 adult patients, have been mixed (see Table 4-5). Some categories, such as major neurocognitive disorder and post-traumatic stress disorder, showed test-retest reliabilities near or above 0.70; others such as bipolar disorder and oppositional defiant disorder showed kappa values between 0.40 and 0.60, whereas major depressive disorder and generalized anxiety disorder reliabilities were both below 0.35; mixed anxiety/depressive disorder and antisocial personality disorder were unreliable, showing kappa values below 0.06 (Regier, et al., 2012). Spectrum diagnoses tended to show better reliability. The kappa values for several categories were below those measured for the *DSM-III*, although it should be noted that differences in methodology (e.g., random sampling in the *DSM-III* field trials vs. stratified sampling in the *DSM-5* field trials) make direct comparisons problematic.

## 4.2b The Validity of Categories

It is important to remember that a reliable classification is not necessarily a valid one. A valid classification measures what it claims to measure. Consistency of use can be achieved for categories without that fact constituting validation of the disorder itself, as demonstrated in the case of homosexuality, which was a mental disorder under the *DSM-II* but is not a disorder currently. If diagnoses show *construct validity*, then the separations between

*Table 4-5*   Diagnostic Reliabilities for Selected *DSM-5* Disorders

| *DSM-5* Diagnosis | Kappa Reliability (95% confidence interval) | *DSM-5* Interpretation of Reliability |
|---|---|---|
| Posttraumatic stress disorder | 0.69 (0.59–0.78) | Very good |
| Alcohol use disorder | 0.40 (0.27–0.54) | Good |
| Major depressive disorder | 0.25 (0.13–0.36) | Questionable |
| Mild traumatic brain injury | 0.36 (0.13–0.55) | Questionable |
| Borderline personality disorder | 0.34 (0.18–0.51) | Questionable |
| Schizophrenia | 0.46 (0.34–0.59) | Good |
| Bipolar I disorder | 0.56 (0.45–0.67) | Good |
| Mixed anxiety-depressive disorder | -0.004 (-0.10–0.09) | Unacceptable |
| Binge eating disorder | 0.56 (0.32–0.77) | Good |
| Major neurocognitive disorder | 0.78 (0.68–0.88) | Very good |

Source: Regier et al., 2012

different categories should be discernible. Evidence should be available to support what belongs inside the category (*convergent validity*) as well as what does not (*divergent validity*). If a diagnosis has *predictive validity*, we should be able to say something about what to expect in terms of outcome or course.

**BVT** *Lab*

Visit **www.BVTLab.com** to explore the student resources available for this chapter.

One reason to subject the *DSM* to continuous evaluation and revision is to assess whether or not the diagnoses are valuable as separate types of disorders. Sometimes, diagnoses have been relocated in the scheme of classifications to better reflect assumptions about the disorder. For example, pervasive developmental disorders such as autism, and specific developmental disorders such as reading or arithmetic learning disorders and speech disorders, were placed on Axis II in the *DSM-III* series but moved to Axis I in the *DSM-IV*. In other cases, some diagnoses found to be of questionable value have been moved out of the main system into provisional status, as in the case of passive aggressive personality disorder, which was an Axis II classification in *DSM-III* and *DSM-III-R* but retracted for further study in the *DSM-IV*. Some proposals under further study may indeed become diagnostic categories in the next *DSM* edition: Premenstrual dysphoric disorder and binge-eating disorder were elevated to mental disorder status in the *DSM-5*. Other candidates were later abandoned as *DSM* revisions proceeded, including "rapism" (because rape is best accounted for as criminal behavior) and "self-defeating personality disorder" (because the proposed characteristics are already included under existing classifications). There is general agreement that *DSM-5* criteria, though far from perfect, make some valid distinctions between different symptom presentations; and those distinctions can be meaningful in selecting treatment and in projecting the course of many disorders. For example, a diagnosis of schizophrenia implies the disorder would follow a different course, and would lead to different treatments, than would a diagnosis of depression. However, validity presupposes reliability; the validity of any *DSM-5* diagnostic category is limited by the reliability of that diagnosis.

It is important to recognize that the *DSM* series is a product of the medical profession and consequently reflects the perspective that psychological disorders should be classified and treated in the same way as physical diseases. The fact that abnormal behaviors can be described, given a name, and diagnosed with fair reliability using *DSM-5* criteria does not mean that the disease model or metaphor is a valid one. As some critics of the medical model have noted, diagnoses are not diseases (Mindham, Scadding, & Cawley, 1992; Szasz, 1991) and there remain many challenges to the adequacy of disease conceptualizations of *DSM* disorders (Larkin, Wood, & Criffiths, 2006; Peele, 2007). Because nearly all of the diagnostic criteria are behavioral, evidence of status as an illness or disease requires verification apart from the behaviors used to define the disorder in the first place. Research into the genetic bases of mental disorders is very active, and a great many chromosome loci are being evaluated for candidate genes contributing to various diagnoses. The recent report of small but significant genetic overlap between five major disorders (autism, ADHD, bipolar disorder, major depression and schizophrenia) highlights both the possibility of shared genetic influences and the problem of diagnostic validity (Smoller, et al., 2013). At present, there are no medical or biological tests that can confirm or verify the vast proportion of specific *DSM-5* diagnoses. Until an underlying genetic or biological abnormality specific to and diagnostic of a disorder can be identified, its status as a medical disease remains an assumption. At the same time, the pharmacological industry continues to develop and promote symptomatic interventions for virtually every category of disorder in the *DSM-5*, furthering the financial investment in a disease perspective. In spite of obvious limitations, it is probable that the disease metaphor will remain a dominant influence in the *DSM* system for the foreseeable future.

## 4.3  The Diagnostic Process

Although some clinicians, especially those from the humanistic-experiential, have resisted attempts at diagnostic assessment, preferring to move immediately into treatment, in most clinical settings (and probably all settings in which insurance payments are involved) an attempt to provide a *DSM-5* diagnosis will be made. In addition to determining how to categorize the person's problem, the clinician may be expected to answer a number of other specific questions on the basis of the diagnostic process: Is organic brain pathology present? Are the person's symptoms partly a reaction to drugs?

> What are some common diagnostic procedures and tests?

Is the person reacting to some acute situational crisis or is it a long-term problem? How severe is the disturbance? Is hospitalization indicated? Is suicide a risk? Is the person motivated for treatment? Is the person intellectually disabled? In some cases a thorough physical and neurological examination is called for, perhaps including specialized measures

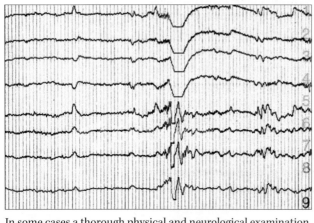

In some cases a thorough physical and neurological examination is called for, perhaps including specialized measures such as an electroencephalogram (EEG; measure of brainwave patterns).
(iStock)

such as an **electroencephalogram (EEG)**, which measures brainwave patterns, or blood tests. There are some specific techniques for imaging the brain and its functions (to be described later), and at times these assist in the diagnostic process. However, the primary methods for obtaining and evaluating diagnostic information for most mental disorders are *interviews*, *observations*, and *psychological tests*.

## 4.3a  The Interview

The interview is the basic, and often the only, instrument of assessment because the diagnostic criteria of the *DSM-5* are based largely on a person's self-report of symptoms. Ordinarily a diagnostic interview (sometimes called an *intake interview*) is given when a person is first seen at a clinic or institution. It involves an interaction between the patient or client and the clinician or interviewer, who usually formulates an initial diagnostic impression, supplemented by information from the medical and social history.

The nature of the diagnostic interview may vary as a function of the theoretical orientation of the interviewer and the setting in which the interview is conducted. Clinicians employing different models will tend to view different types of information as more enlightening as they seek to understand the person's dysfunction. As for setting, the diagnostic problems seen in a college counseling center are likely to be quite different from those typical of a large mental hospital or a child guidance clinic. However, the general goals of the diagnostic interview include establishing rapport with the client, decreasing the client's anxiety about the process, and collecting some basic details about the problem. Certain types of information are needed to work toward a reasonable preliminary classification and treatment plan.

Typically, the interviewer will need to know about the presenting problem. How severe are the symptoms? How long do they last, and how do they impact the client's daily social, occupational, and educational functioning? Have there been previous episodes, and if so, how were they resolved? In addition to these sorts of questions, the interviewer commonly asks about family background (including any mental disorders or problems evident in other members of the family), social relationships and the degree of social support available to the client, work history, educational background, medical history, substance use patterns, legal history, and any prevailing stressors that might be influencing symptoms.

Formal, structured clinical interviews have recently been playing a larger role in diagnosis, especially in research situations. These standardized interviews lead the diagnostician to ask specific questions tied to *DSM* categorization. For example, the Structured Clinical Interview for *DSM* Disorders (SCID) was created to collect the information necessary for *DSM-III-R* diagnoses (Spitzer, Williams, Gibbson, & First, 1990). It has since been updated and expanded as the *DSM* has been revised. Like other similar structured interviews, it allows

**Electroencephalo-gram (EEG)**

A record of electrical activity of the brain in terms of brain frequencies, measured from the scalp

The interview is the basic instrument of diagnostic assessment. (Shutterstock)

focused evaluation of patient symptoms in relationship to *DSM* criteria, focusing the interview process to produce more reliable use of a diagnostic label.

The interview as a source of diagnostic information is not without its problems. One is that the interviewer relies heavily on the accuracy of the person's self-report. Various circumstances can affect what a patient tells an interviewer: the skill of the interviewer in helping the patient feel at ease and in facilitating open and honest expression, personal characteristics of the patient (such as articulateness and defensiveness), and the immediate circumstances and purposes of the interview. The situational factors can be extremely important. Have persons sought outpatient help on their own initiative? Are they being interviewed at a mental hospital after being brought there against their will? Have they been referred by a judge with the understanding that psychological treatment is an alternative to jail? Have children been taken to a clinic because their teachers or parents want the clinic to "do something about their disruptive behavior"? Experienced clinicians are aware of these possible influences and take them into account as best they can.

It is essential to attend to cultural factors that can influence the interview (and consequently, the diagnostic) process. When the interviewer and the client are of different ages, genders, and/or ethnic origins, bias and misinterpretation of self-report are common outcomes (Okazaki & Sue, 1995). A lack of eye contact or a very soft speaking voice may reflect different communication styles rather than indications of social dysfunction or mood disturbance. There is also considerable variation between cultures in how psychological distress is described, and there are forms of psychological problems that are highly specific to certain cultural groups. A variety of culture-bound syndromes are noted in the *DSM-5*, including Dhat syndrome (a folk term in South Asia referring to anxiety involving negative health consequences that result from the discharge of semen), the related *koro* (a sudden and intense anxiety, usually reported in south and east Asia, that the penis will recede into the body and cause death), and *mal de ojo* (or "evil eye," a concept common among Mediterranean cultures that other peoples' feelings of envy or hatred can cause physical and psychological problems for the targeted individual). Often, these syndromes can be related to *DSM-5* categories such as major depressive disorder, somatic symptom disorder, or delusional disorder (American Psychiatric Association, 2013). The cultural interpretation of such symptoms or complaints is an important consideration during the diagnostic interview and in the application of a *DSM* label.

## 4.3b Observation

The psychological interview cannot answer adequately all diagnostic questions. Further information may be

Mal de ojo, or "evil eye," a concept common among Mediterranean cultures that is believed to cause crying, vomiting, and a fever in children (iStock)

obtained by observational procedures, which are concerned with what persons do rather than what they say they do. Some observational information is usually obtained as part of the interview. Often, observations made during the interview, together with a person's responses to certain types of questions, comprise a **mental status examination**, providing a current picture of the person's level of functioning. Almost immediately, the interviewer makes note of the general appearance of the client. Characteristics such as posture, cleanliness, and use of gestures can provide valuable information to supplement the clinical overview. Someone who has not bathed in some time, whose nails and teeth have been neglected, and whose clothes are improperly worn may be experiencing a more global level of impairment than one who attends to appearance, dress, and personal hygiene. Level of activity can reveal clues about high- or low-levels of energy. Degree of eye contact and tone and volume of the voice may reveal something about general emotional intensity.

Characteristics such as posture, cleanliness, attire, and use of gestures can provide useful information in the clinical interview. (Shutterstock)

Observations of the person's use of language may provide reasons to suspect lower intelligence, delusional thinking, mood disorders, substance use, or neurological impairment. For example, digressive or incomprehensible speech, or use of many unusual words, can suggest psychotic conditions, whereas rapid or pressured speech may lead a clinician to consider a manic mood state. Sometimes, clients are asked to repeat certain statements or to say the alphabet as a means to assess degree of verbal control. Other common speech tasks within a mental status exam serve to screen for memory problems ("What did you eat for breakfast this morning?" or "Who is the president of the United States?"), orientation difficulties ("Do you know where you are? What day of the week is this?"), ability to concentrate ("Say the days of the week in reverse order, starting with Sunday") and to estimate intellectual functioning ("What do we mean when we say 'The grass is always greener on the other side of the fence'?").

As the interview progresses, an experienced clinician can formulate some hypotheses about the person's levels of attention and concentration, general intelligence, emotional state, memory ability, and presence of psychotic symptoms. These impressions from observation and interview might then indicate a need to further refine the diagnostic process through a more formal procedure: psychological testing.

## 4.3c  Psychological Tests

**Psychological tests** are another source of diagnostic information. Briefly, a psychological test is a highly standardized procedure for obtaining a sample of behavior from which inferences can be made about the person's general psychological functioning. Tests are usually constructed so that a person's responses can be quantified and compared with norms obtained from a large sample of other individuals. In general, tests seek to reduce some of the uncontrolled influences that operate in the interview and to provide more standardized information. Psychologists have access to hundreds of current tests for different diagnostic purposes.

Intelligence tests, such as the Stanford-Binet and Wechsler's intelligence scales for adults and children, are especially useful when there is a question of intellectual disability or when for some other reason an estimate of the person's general level of intellectual ability is required. *The Wechsler Adult Intelligence Scale, Fourth Edition* (*WAIS-4*) was published in 2008 for use with people age 16 and above. The carefully constructed scales provide a reliable measure of intellectual functioning in areas of verbal comprehension, short-term memory, perceptual organization, and processing speed, expressed in terms of a standardized index score (an intelligence quotient, or IQ) that allows comparison of the person's abilities with that of same-aged peers across the nation. These intelligence index scores are normalized

**Mental status examination**

Brief interview and observation method to provide an overview of a person's general level of psychological functioning

**Psychological tests**

Highly standardized procedures for obtaining samples of behavior

Psychological tests are another source of diagnostic information. Briefly, a psychological test is a highly standardized procedure for obtaining a sample of behavior from which inferences can be made about the person's general psychological functioning. (iStock)

with a mean score of 100 and a standard deviation of 15, meaning that someone who achieved a score of 115 does as well as or better than 84% of the same-aged population while a person scoring 85 does as well or better than only 16% of the population. Similar measurements can be acquired for younger people on the Wechsler intelligence scales for children ages 6–16, and preschool children ages 2–7. The *Stanford-Binet Fifth Edition* intelligence test provides similar standard normalized measures for examinees ages 2 to 89. Many other reliable intelligence tests are available, including some that are adapted specifically to measure nonverbal intelligence. These tests have value apart from their obvious use of detecting intellectual disability or exceptional abilities: an individual's pattern of strengths and weaknesses across various parts of the tests can provide evidence of specific types of learning disorders, developmental disabilities, neurological impairments, and memory problems.

Another major class of psychological testing involves personality tests—such as characteristic motives, defenses, conflicts, self-image, and thought processes—used primarily by clinicians to assess various aspects of personality. The two most common types of personality tests are projective tests (or *techniques*, as some clinicians prefer to call them) and personality inventories. Let us look more closely at them.

## 4.3d  Projective Tests

In **projective tests**, the person is asked to respond to ambiguous stimulus materials. Thus for the Rorschach Test, created in 1911, the person is shown cards depicting inkblots and asked to describe what they look like. The clinician scores and interprets the perceptual responses. The *Thematic Apperception Test (TAT)*, created in 1935, consists of pictures of varying degrees of ambiguity about which the person is asked to make up stories. The themes and imagery in the stories can then be used to make inferences about the person's motives, self-concept, emotions, and conflicts. Some other types of projective tests involve filling in the blanks of incomplete sentences, creating the dialogue between people in a cartoon, or drawing a picture of a person.

The basic assumption in all projective techniques, derived from the psychodynamic perspective, is that people *project* their own internal dispositions into their responses, whether into what they "see" in an inkblot or what they tell in a story. The content of the following story, told by a patient who was diagnosed as paranoid schizophrenic, supports other information suggesting a long-term resentment of his mother's attempt to dominate

**Projective tests**

Tests in which the person is presented with ambiguous stimulus materials and asked to respond in some way, based on the assumption that persons project characteristics of their own intrapsychic processes onto their responses

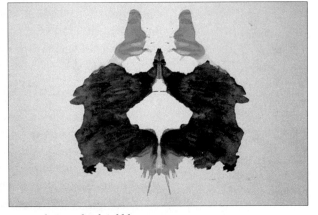

A sample Rorschach inkblot (Wikimedia Commons)

and control him. The patient was shown TAT Card I, a picture of a young boy sitting at a table contemplating a violin, and told to make up a story about it.

The Thematic Apperception Test (TAT) is composed of pictures like this one. Stories told about the pictures are thought to reflect important motives, emotions, and conflicts of the storyteller. (Wikimedia Commons)

There's a young boy...a young boy looking at a violin, wondering whether he should take the violin or not. He doesn't want to. He doesn't like it in the least. He doesn't like the idea. But his mother has told him to take the violin. Therefore he must take it. And he doesn't see any way to get out of it. So he's sitting there thinking about chopping the violin to pieces if he can get away with it, or destroying it, or perhaps thinking whether he should go to his mother and tell her, "I refuse to take the violin," but he knows he can't do that so he'll just think about it, and he'll look at the violin and hate it. (How will the story end?) He'll probably take the violin until he gets to a point where he's old enough to do what he pleases. (Shneidman, 1955, p. 111)

Projective techniques, once the most common form of psychological assessment, are now employed less often than other forms of personality tests. The reliability, validity, and usefulness of projective tests continue to be topics of disagreement. As the illustration of the TAT response above illustrates, the scoring and interpretation of projective tests is a complicated task that requires much clinical experience. In fact, even experienced clinicians who frequently use projective techniques may disagree on the specific interpretation of a TAT response. It is unlikely that they could have diagnosed the storyteller above with paranoid schizophrenia, or any other disorder, based on this story, if his diagnostic status was unknown beforehand. Of course, valuable information might be contained in the results of projective testing, but without a reliable scoring method an interpretation might be just as likely to be incorrect.

Earlier research did not provide consistent support for the validity of the Rorschach and the TAT (Zubin, Eron, & Schumer, 1965), and attempts to standardize scoring systems for projective tests were made. For example, Exner (1993) proposed a comprehensive system for scoring the Rorschach involving computer-assisted interpretation, but many critics have remained unconvinced (Wood, Nezworski, Garb, & Lilienfeld, 2001). A major problem with the psychometric quality of the projective techniques involves an aspect that many clinicians consider their asset: the open-ended, unstructured responses that the tests evoke. With continued improvements in test construction, more objective methods of assessing personality that show better evidence of reliability and validity have gradually become dominant in personality testing. These newer techniques are often empirically keyed, standardized, and normalized; and their structures are often derived from complex mathematical techniques such as factor analysis. Projective techniques such as the Rorschach and the TAT, however, will probably continue to be used mainly in an intuitive and clinical fashion by more psychodynamically-oriented therapists.

## 4.3e Personality Inventories

**Personality inventory**

A self-report questionnaire in which brief responses to a collection of test items are used to assess personal characteristics or behaviors across various personality dimensions

**Personality inventories** consist of a large number of statements to which the person is asked to respond in terms of fixed categories such as Yes, No, or Cannot Say. The important contrasts with the projective techniques are that the stimulus materials are not so ambiguous and that the person is not permitted the same freedom of response. The inventories are usually divided into various subscales to measure different aspects of the personality.

*The Minnesota Multiphasic Personality Inventory* (*MMPI*) is perhaps the most widely used personality inventory in the field of abnormal psychology. This test developed by Hathaway and

McKinley (1943) and revised as the *MMPI-2* in 1989, consists of over 550 items covering a wide range of topics, including physical health, religious attitudes, moods, beliefs, fears, and social interests. When the test was being developed the items were administered to eight groups of psychiatric patients with known diagnoses (such as hysteria, depression, and schizophrenia) and a control group of normals. Subscales were then constructed from clusters of test items that distinguished each group, so that a person scoring high on a scale is essentially answering certain groups of questions in the same way as people with certain diagnoses.

Several validity scales of the *MMPI-2*—including the Lie Scale (L), F Scale, and Correction Scale (K)—reflect different ways in which a subject's style of responding might affect the validity of the other scales. The L scale is composed of a number of items that are mildly derogatory but probably true for most of us (such as "I get angry sometimes"). A person who denies many of these items may be trying to "look good." F detects the tendency to over-report psychopathology, or simple confusion in taking the test. K is a general measure of defensiveness, somewhat more subtle than L; a high score indicates that the person is rather guarded and not inclined to disclose things that would seem unfavorable. See Table 4-6 for a summary of personality characteristics associated with elevations on some of the different *MMPI* scales.

*Table 4-6*    Personality Characteristics Associated with Elevations of the Basic *MMPI-2*

| Scale | Characteristics |
|---|---|
| L.  Lie Scale | A validity scale that indicates the tendency to present oneself in an overly favorable or virtuous light. |
| F.  Scale | A validity scale composed of highly infrequent items. A high score suggests carelessness, confusion, or exaggeration of symptoms. |
| K.  Subtle Defensiveness | A validity scale that measures defensiveness of a subtle nature. |
| 1.  (HS), Hypochondriasis | High scorers report somatic complaints or concern about physical symptoms. |
| 2.  (D), Depression | High scorers report moody, pessimistic, shy, and despondent symptoms. |
| 3.  (Hy), Hysteria | High scorers tend to have multiple physical concerns and express psychological conflict through vague and unbiased physical complaints. |
| 4.  (Pd), Psychopathic Deviate | High scorers endorse items relating to impulsive, rebellious, and antisocial tendencies. They often have difficulty in marital or family relationships and trouble with the law or authority in general. |
| 5.  (MF), Masculinity-Femininity | High-scoring males are described as sensitive, aesthetic, passive, or feminine. High-scoring females are described as aggressive, rebellious, and unrealistic. |
| 6.  (Pa), Paranoia | Elevations on this scale are often associated with being suspicious, aloof, shrewd, guarded, worrisome, and overly sensitive. |
| 7.  (Pt), Psychasthenia | High scores report feeling tense, anxious, ruminative, preoccupied, obsessional, phobic, and rigid. They frequently are self-condemning and feel inferior and inadequate. |
| 8.  (Sc), Schizophrenia | High scores answer like those who are often withdrawn, shy, unusual, or strange and have peculiar thoughts or ideas. They may have poor reality contact and in severe cases bizarre sensory experiences—delusions and hallucinations. |
| 9.  (Ma), Mania | High scorers endorse items like those who are called sociable, outgoing, impulsive, overly energetic, optimistic, and in some cases amoral, flighty, confused, or disoriented. |
| 10. (Si), Social Introversion-Extroversion | High scorers (introverts) tend to be modest, shy, private, withdrawn, and inhibited. Low scorers (extroverts) tend to be outgoing, spontaneous, sociable, and confident. |

Psychologists have conducted voluminous research on the *MMPI* and *MMPI-2*, much of it suggesting that this test does have some value as an aid to diagnosis (Dahlstrom, Welsh, & Dahlstrom, 1975; Butcher, 2006). Others question its usefulness and suggest that it rests on an outdated model of diagnosis (Helmes & Reddon, 1993). In practice, it has become nearly a standard component of personality assessment and of psychological evaluations relating to such legal issues as child custody, likelihood to reoffend, competency to stand trial, and insanity. The interpretation of the *MMPI-2* is more structured than interpretation of projective techniques, but it remains a complex activity with room for disagreement. A high score on Sc (Schizophrenia), for example, does not mean that a person is behaving in a clearly schizophrenic fashion, and a high score on Hy (Hysteria) does not mean that a person is showing clear-cut hysterical symptoms. It is the configuration of several scale scores that is most useful diagnostically, not the score on a single scale. Many clinicians, in fact, tend to use the *MMPI* in a rather loose fashion, drawing upon their past experience and clinical intuition to make inferences about personality dynamics and psychopathology from a particular profile. However, as actuarial data have accumulated, interpretative manuals containing empirically derived descriptors of many possible *MMPI* profiles have become available, along with computer-based administration and interpretation packages. These typically provide a variety of possible behavioral and diagnostic hypotheses that the psychologist can consider in the evaluative process. An example of an *MMPI-2* profile is shown in Figure 4-1. This hypothetical client is acknowledging some distress; and the profile is consistent with depression, anxiety, and substance abuse.

## Other Self-Report Inventories

Many other carefully constructed self-report devices are available for use, including other personality inventories (such as the *Personality Assessment Inventory*, or *PAI*) that can provide psychologists with ways to quantify the degree of a person's distress or psychological impairment. The *PAI* has found broad use among psychologists, in part because it measures more specific aspects of disorder categories such as anxiety and depression than does the *MMPI-2*. However, the *MMPI-2* seems to be better at detecting people who fake their responses in order to feign disorders such as depression or PTSD (Lange, Sullivan, & Scott, 2010) and people who tend to provide random answers to the questions (Clark, Gironda, & Young, 2003). Other tests seek to assess a more specific range of symptoms, such as the 1961 Beck Depression Inventory (BDI), revised as the BDI-II in 1996. The scale consists of a series of questions in which the examinee can select statements reflecting the severity of symptoms like "hopelessness" and "sadness" as in this example:

0. I do not feel sad.

1. I feel sad.

2. I am sad all the time and I can't snap out of it.

3. I am so sad or unhappy that I can't stand it.

Total scores are calculated across 21 questions, with cutoff scores over 20 suggesting moderate depression and over 29 suggesting severe depression. Like other self-report rating scales, such as the *Hamilton Depression Rating Scale*, the BDI-II can be useful in diagnosis but cannot alone provide or confirm a *DSM* diagnosis. Similar self-report scales exist for assessing anxiety, fear, obsessive-compulsive disorder, substance abuse, and pathological gambling, and many other disorders.

## 4.3f Neuropsychological Assessment

In addition to various psychological tests, other techniques designed to provide information about brain functioning can offer valuable information to the diagnostic process. Some of these assess behavioral abilities to infer neurological integrity, while others involve imaging of the physical brain and its metabolic functioning.

## Figure 4-1   *Example of a Profile of MMPI-2 Scale Scores*

Scale scores were devised so that the original standardization sample of normal individuals had a mean of 50 and a standard deviation of 10, the so-called T-scores shown on the ordinate. Thus a score of 70 on a scale indicated that the person scored higher than 97% of the normal sample, two standard deviations above the mean.

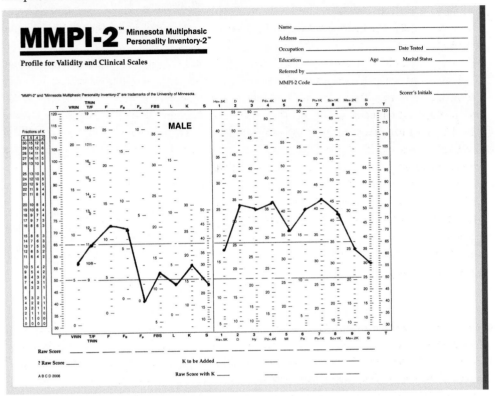

## Neuropsychological Testing

Measuring a person's capacities in memory, attention, expressive and receptive language, and eye-hand coordination can indicate whether neurological difficulties should be suspected as the source of a person's dysfunction. Some tests involve showing the examinee a geometric design and having that person reproduce it on paper, either directly or from memory. Others involve recalling the contents of a short story after a time delay, saying a list of numbers in backwards order, or tapping the index finger on each hand as quickly as possible. More complete test packages, such as the *Halstead-Reitan Neurological Battery*, consist of a variety of tasks involving verbal, auditory, and tactile assessments that can give an Impairment Index score indicating comparison of test results to that of normal, unimpaired people. Many of these tests have become increasingly sophisticated and correlate well with later confirmation of brain damage. They have become important components of psychological evaluations for dementia and other degenerative neurological conditions and amnesic syndromes. However, they require several hours of time to administer, and their results are considered suggestive but not definitive of physical brain impairment.

## Brain Imaging

A rapidly advancing technology in brain imaging techniques is providing vast improvement in our abilities to observe the structures of the living brain and its function. Earlier computer technology made the **computerized axial tomography (CAT or CT)** scans possible. CAT scans involved taking a series of X rays of the brain, organized by computers as slices or layers that allow progressive scanning for tumors or other structural abnormalities. These types of images showed that the fluid-filled ventricles of the brain are enlarged in many (but not all) schizophrenics, raising hopes that imaging may provide a direct method of psychiatric

**Computerized axial tomography (CAT or CT)**

Computer-guided X-ray technique to image 3-dimensional representations of the brain and other organs

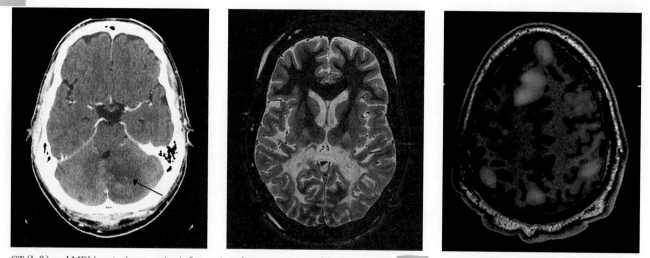

CT (left) and MRI (center) scans give information about structures of the brain, while fMRI (right) tracks brain activity. (Wikimedia Commons)

diagnosis. However, enlarged ventricles also occur in other conditions including alcoholism; they are not specific to a diagnosis of schizophrenia. A more recent technique, called **magnetic resonance imaging (MRI)**, makes images produced by the energy of vibrating hydrogen molecules in the brain via a strong magnetic field. The MRI provides a much clearer picture of structure than does a CT-scan, although one drawback is that it requires patients to remain motionless in a small, confined area for long periods.

Other imaging techniques emphasize the activity of the brain rather than its structure. **Positron emission tomography (or PET)** scanning involves observation of the uptake and use of glucose (the brain's main source of energy) that has been radioactively labeled and injected. Active and inactive areas of brain, as indicated by rates of metabolism, can then be mapped. A newer method is the **functional MRI (fMRI)** that essentially allows tracking of blood flow in the brain in real time. Such scans give important information about how people utilize specific sections of their brains during different activities. The brain imaging technology can reveal differences between the activity levels of the brains of normal persons, compared to those with certain diagnoses such as dementia of the Alzheimer's type and obsessive-compulsive disorder.

While the progress in brain imaging technology holds great promise, brain imaging is not currently useful for diagnosing an individual with a disorder, or for verifying a diagnosis, for several reasons. There is much variability in brain activity patterns between people, and not everyone who carries a particular diagnosis will demonstrate the same patterns of brain functioning. There are no clearly identified norms for brain functioning in any diagnostic categories. Perhaps most importantly, emotions and other psychological states are not as strictly localized in specific brain areas as once thought, but instead appear to involve cascading activity in many diverse areas of the brain stem and the cortex. As a result, the physiological and psychological meanings of blood flow differences revealed in brain image studies are not yet well understood (Kagan, 2007). To add to the uncertainty, a recent meta-analysis of brain volume studies found that there has been a significant bias in the professional literature in terms of reporting volume differences in people with various mental disorders, with publication disproportionately favoring positive rather than negative findings—to the extent that "such bias threatens the validity of the overall literature on brain volume abnormalities" (Ioannidis, 2011, p. 778).

For the time being, the diagnostic process in abnormal psychology remains a largely verbal, interactive exchange between a clinician and a client, consisting of matching sets of behavioral symptoms and self-reported emotional states to a list of established criteria that define the boundaries of diagnostic classes. Psychological testing, physiological examination, neurological assessment, and brain imaging—all can provide important supportive data but cannot, in themselves, verify the existence of a mental disorder. That remains a matter of clinical judgment and consensus.

**Magnetic resonance imaging (MRI)**

Imaging technique using variations in magnetic fields to produce 3-dimensional images of the brain and other organs with better resolution than the CT scans

**Positron emission tomography (PET)**

Imaging technique that measures metabolic activity (such as glucose utilization) as an indication of the functioning of the brain or other organs

**Functional MRI (fMRI)**

Imaging technique that uses magnetic fields to detect changes in blood flow, producing a measure of brain activity

# Chapter Review

## TO SUM UP ...

- Classification is helpful in the first stages of most sciences. In the study of abnormal behavior, a primary purpose in developing classificatory systems is to discover to what extent distinctive patterns of symptoms and their causes can be isolated.

- *The Diagnostic and Statistical Manual of Mental Disorders, Fifth Edition* (*DSM-5*) provides the classification scheme for abnormal behaviors currently used in this country.

- The *DSM-5* is a categorical system of classification, strongly influenced by the medical perspective. It discontinued the multiaxial framework that had been used for the previous 33 years, and reorganized categories in an attempt to reduce overlapping diagnoses and to improve diagnostic reliability.

- Diagnostic reliability involves the consistency with which a diagnosis can be given. Reliability is good for some classifications in the *DSM* system and fair to poor for other classifications.

- The *DSM-5* makes valid distinctions between many categories of disorders and provides useful information about the differential course of various disorders. However, the status of the disease or illness metaphor remains controversial. Definable physical, biological, or genetic bases unique to specific disorders have yet to be consistently identified; and there are no biological or medical tests that can verify a mental disorder apart from the behaviors used to diagnose it.

- The process of diagnosing a mental disorder relies heavily on the diagnostic interview. Observational procedures, psychological tests, and physical assessments can provide valuable information to be used in the diagnostic process.

- Psychological tests are standardized procedures for obtaining a sample of behavior from which inferences can be made about the person's general psychological functioning. Tests have been useful in the assessment of both intellectual and personality characteristics. Personality tests tend to be of two basic types, projective tests and inventories.

- In projective tests, the person is asked to respond to ambiguous stimuli—for example, to report what inkblots look like or to tell a story about a picture. These responses are then used as a basis for psychological interpretation on the assumption that the person has projected inner mental processes into the stimulus materials. Although these tests perhaps are useful to the individual clinician, research has not provided strong support for their reliability or their validity.

- The stimulus materials and responses called for on the personality inventories are more structured than on the projective tests. Usually, the person is asked to respond to a number of statements with either Yes, No, or Cannot Say. The *MMPI-2*, the most widely used test of this kind, has been shown to have moderate validity as an aid to diagnosis.

- Important advances in imaging the physical brain and its metabolic activity have allowed for some observations of functional and structural differences between normal and affected individuals. As yet, brain imaging is not useful for diagnosing specific mental disorders in individual patients.

## KEY TERMS

Computerized axial tomography (CAT or CT)   105

Diagnostic reliability   93

Diagnostic validity   93

Electroencephalogram (EEG)   98

Functional MRI (*f* MRI)   106

Magnetic resonance imaging (MRI)   106

Mental status examination   100

Personality inventory   102

Positron emission tomography (PET)   106

Projective tests   101

Psychological tests   100

Syndrome   87

## QUESTIONS FOR STUDY

- Describe some of the changes that have occurred over the last five *DSM* editions in the way mental disorders are diagnosed.

- Describe the distinction between diagnostic reliability and diagnostic validity. Can a diagnosis be reliable, but invalid? Can a diagnosis be valid, but unreliable?

- Discuss the strengths and limitations of the disease perspective that currently guides diagnosis of abnormal behavior.

- Contrast and compare different ways to assess a client for the presence of depression.

# POP QUIZ

1. A pattern of symptoms that tend to occur together in a particular disease is known as a(n) _____.
   A. specified disorder
   B. syndrome
   C. diagnosis
   D. axial structure

2. When the *DSM* was revised in _____ into the *DSM-II*, the number of mental disorders listed was increased by 50%.
   A. 1946
   B. 1952
   C. 1962
   D. 1968

3. The *DSM-III-R* was published in _____.
   A. 1952
   B. 1968
   C. 1987
   D. 1994

4. In the *DSM III* through *DSM-IV*, personality disorders and mental retardation were listed on _____.
   A. Axis I
   B. Axis II
   C. Axis III
   D. Axis IV

5. Which of the following is one concern about the *DSM-IV* that prompted the drive to revise the manual?
   A. There were too many categories of disorders.
   B. There were too few categories of disorders.
   C. Categories were too distinct from each other.
   D. Categories overlapped too often.

6. While the *DSM-III* used a kappa reliability level of 0.70 to indicate good diagnostic reliability, the American Psychiatric Association may accept levels of _____ to indicate "acceptable" reliability for the *DSM-5*.
   A. above .80
   B. between .60 and .80
   C. between .40 and .60
   D. between .20 and .40

7. Which of the following is **not** a *DSM-5* category?
   A. Brain damage disorders
   B. Anxiety disorders
   C. Depressive disorders
   D. Trauma and stressor-related disorders

8. Which of the following is listed as potential future diagnoses in Section II of the *DSM-5*?
   A. Hebopedophiliac disorder
   B. Internet pornography disorder
   C. Shopping addiction disorder
   D. Caffeine use disorder

9. A mental status exam includes all of the following **except** assessment of _____.
   A. blood chemistry
   B. hygiene
   C. memory impairment
   D. speech characteristics

10. _____ are highly standardized procedures for obtaining a sample of behavior, and have been normed through the use of representative samples.
    A. Diagnostic interviews
    B. Neuropsychological batteries
    C. Observational procedures
    D. Psychological tests

11. The Rorschach is an example of a _____.
    A. neurological battery
    B. intelligence scale
    C. projective test
    D. personality inventory

12. Subjects are asked to make up stories about pictures of varying degrees of ambiguity on the _____.
    A. *MMPI-2*
    B. Rorschach Test
    C. Halstead-Reitan Battery
    D. Thematic Apperception Test

13. The _____ on the *MMPI-2* is composed of a number of items that are mildly derogatory but probably true for most of us.
    A. L-scale
    B. K-scale
    C. F-scale
    D. G-scale

14. The _____ consists of a series of questions in which the examinee can select statements reflecting the severity of symptoms like sadness and hopelessness.
    A. *MMPI*
    B. Rorschach Test
    C. Beck Depression Inventory
    D. Hamilton Depression Scale

15. The _____ is a newer method of brain imaging that essentially allows the tracking of blood flow in the brain in real time.
    A. EEG
    B. CAT
    C. fMRI
    D. MRI

Additional study resources are available at **www.BVTLab.com**

# CHAPTER OVERVIEW

## CHAPTER OPENER QUESTIONS

How does stress affect the body?

Do the effects of some terrifying experiences never go
   away?

Can psychological circumstances affect physical health?

How can stress impair immune function?

What types of stressors produce the greatest effect?

(Shutterstock/iStock)

# chapter 5

# Stress and Trauma-Related Disorders

All living things face challenges in the course of their existence, and their adaptations to those challenges define life. Their survival depends on successfully balancing the demands of the world around them and the conditions of the world inside of them. Here we consider the types of physical and psychological demands people face, the factors that can make those challenges seem either manageable or overwhelming, and the effects that stress can have on our health and our behavior.

## 5.1 Defining Stress

Psychologists have studied the effects of various events, challenges, and adaptive demands on physiology and behavior for many years. As research expanded, it became clear that stress could have very significant impacts on present and future functioning. Canadian physiologist Hans Selye developed a model of stress in 1936 called the **general adaptation syndrome (GAS)**. The GAS consists of three stages: the alarm stage, in which physical resources are mobilized following the recognition of the stress event; the resistance stage, involving coping responses to the ongoing challenge; and if the stress challenges persists long enough, the exhaustion phase, in which coping resources are depleted and the body suffers permanent damage or death. Selye (1956) also distinguished "negative" stress (or *distress*) from "positive" stress (or *eustress*); both weddings and funerals are challenges that require adjustment. Over time, the terminology used to describe these challenges and the reactions they provoke became somewhat inconsistent. The term stress was used to refer to both the challenge to the organism and to the resulting physical and behavioral events triggered by the challenge. Gradually, the term **stressor** has been employed to refer to the challenge and demand, and the effects it produces are referred to as the **stress response**.

## 5.2 The Stress Response

In the course of evolution, human beings have developed biological systems for coping with stressful experiences: physical injuries, extremes of heat and cold, situations calling

> **How does stress affect the body?**

for physical exertion, dangerous animals, and so on. Emotional responses play an important role in most people's reactions to stressors, but these responses have been difficult to study because they are largely subjective in nature and cannot be directly measured. Investigators usually infer emotions from three sources: verbal report ("I'm angry"); behavior (hitting another person); or physiological responses (increased blood pressure). Despite imperfections in measurement, emotions—joy, excitement, fear, anger, grief, shame, disgust, and so on—are obviously real. Before we consider some psychological forms of emotional response, let us take a look at one of the body's physiological systems that is involved in almost all emotional responses, the *autonomic nervous system*.

**General adaptation syndrome (GAS)**
A generalized model of physical stress response that includes the alarm stage, the resistance stage, and (if stress continues) the exhaustion stage

**Stressor**
A challenge or demand requiring adjustment by an organism

**Stress response**
The physical, behavioral, and/or psychological effects of a stressor

## 5.2a The Autonomic Nervous System

**Autonomic nervous system**

Portion of the nervous system that controls the functioning of many internal bodily processes such as heart rate, digestive processes, and so on

The **autonomic nervous system** primarily regulates the internal environment of the organism by facilitating or inhibiting digestive and eliminative processes, distributing blood flow toward or away from the heart and skeletal muscles, increasing or decreasing oxygen intake, and so on. Broadly speaking, it controls responses that, on the one hand, prepare a person to meet stressful environmental demands or, on the other hand, aid in the conservation and restoration of bodily resources. The former function is generally accomplished by the **sympathetic nervous system** and the latter by the **parasympathetic nervous system** (see Figure 5-1).

### Figure 5-1 The Autonomic Nervous System and Some of the Organs that It Innervates

Many organs are served by both sympathetic and parasympathetic nerves, each functioning in opposition to the other.

Source: Adapted from Lyle E. Bourne, Jr. and Bruce R. Ekstrand, *Psychology: Its Principles and Meanings*, 3rd Edition, 1979. Copyright 1979 by Holt, Rinehart, and Winston. Reproduced by permission of Holt, Rinehart, and Winston.

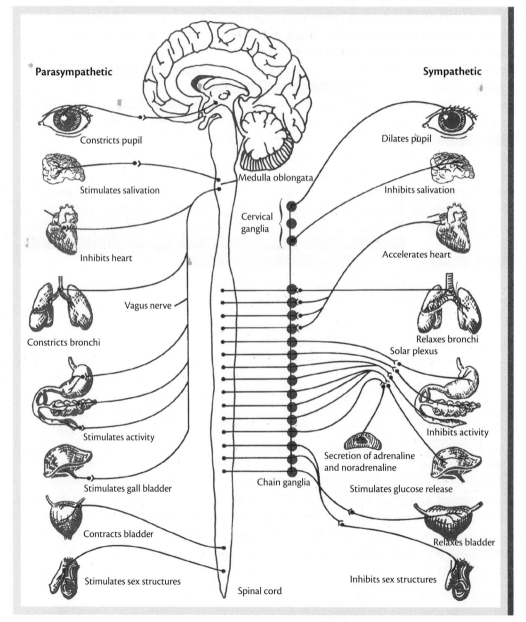

## Sympathetic Division

Arousal of the sympathetic division of the autonomic nervous system helps the organism cope with an emergency by fighting, running away, or some other form of physical exertion. The biological significance of most sympathetic reactions (see Table 5-1) is reasonably clear. The rate and force of contraction of the heart increase; and blood vessels to the viscera (stomach, intestines, and colon) and skin constrict so that the blood supply to the organs needed for emergency action, primarily the heart and the skeletal muscles, is increased. The combination of increased cardiac output and constriction of visceral and skin blood vessels results in an increase in blood pressure. Salivation in the mouth, muscular contractions in the stomach and intestines, and gastric secretions are inhibited. Bronchial passages in the lungs are dilated to permit greater oxygen intake to meet higher rates of body metabolism. The pupils dilate to increase visual sensitivity, and sweating occurs on the palmar surfaces of the hands and feet.

The adrenal medulla gland is stimulated to secrete epinephrine (adrenaline) and norepinephrine (noradrenaline) into the bloodstream while the adrenal cortex secretes cortisol. Epinephrine tends to sustain many of the sympathetic reactions initiated directly by sympathetic nerves. For example, it acts directly on the heart to increase the force of contraction and causes the liver to convert glycogen to glucose (blood sugar) to provide additional metabolic fuel. Circulating norepinephrine produces constriction of the blood vessels in the skin and viscera. In addition to being secreted by the adrenal medulla, norepinephrine plays a part in the chemical transmission of nerve impulses in the brain and from the end of sympathetic nerves to the smooth muscles of the viscera and blood vessels. The stress hormone cortisol prepares the organism for emergency responding, in part, by temporarily inhibiting the immune system's response to injury and giving priority to immediate physical actions, such as fighting and escape, over the later reactions of inflammation and healing.

## Parasympathetic Division

The parasympathetic division functions to conserve and restore, rather than expend, bodily resources. Thus activation results in slower heartbeat and dilation of skin and visceral blood vessels. The accompanying drop in blood pressure tends to decrease the utilization of fuels throughout the body. Parasympathetic stimulation promotes digestive processes, increasing muscle activity and dilation of blood vessels in the stomach and intestinal tracts and the

**Sympathetic nervous system**

Division of the autonomic nervous system primarily involved in stress or emergency reactions that, for example, produces an increase in heart rate and blood pressure

**Parasympathetic nervous system**

Division on the autonomic nervous system primarily involved in conservation of energy, such as increasing digestive processes

*Table 5-1*  Sympathetic and Parasympathetic Responses of the Autonomic Nervous System

| Organ | Sympathetic Response | Parasympathetic Response |
|---|---|---|
| Heart | Rate increases<br>Force of contraction increases | Rate decreases |
| Lungs | Air passages dilate | Air passages constrict |
| Blood vessels, from heart to skeletal muscles and viscera (stomach, intestines, colon) | Dilate, blood flow increases<br>Constrict, blood flow decreases | Constrict, blood flow decreases<br>Dilate, blood flow decreases |
| Stomach | Inhibits secretion of acid and pepsin | Secretes acid and pepsin |
| Salivary glands | Inhibited | Secrete saliva |
| Liver | Releases sugar | None |
| Colon | Inhibited | Tone increases |
| Rectum | Inhibited | Releases feces |
| Genitals | Ejaculation (males)<br>Blood vessel constriction (females) | Erection (males)<br>Blood vessel dilation (females) |
| Eyes | Pupils dilates | Pupils constricts |
| Sweat glands and palmar surfaces | Secrete sweat | None |
| Adrenal medulla glands | Secrete epinephrine (adrenaline) and norepinephrine (noradrenaline) | None |

secretion of gastric juices in the stomach. Eliminative processes are also facilitated, and the pupil is constricted to reduce external stimulation. As can be seen, in many cases the two divisions of the autonomic nervous system affect the same organ in opposite ways.

### Regulation of the Autonomic Nervous System

The autonomic nervous system is regulated largely by the hypothalamus, the posterior part being associated with sympathetic activation and the anterior part with parasympathetic activation. At the beginning of a predominantly sympathetic reaction, the anterior part of the hypothalamus is inhibited to reduce parasympathetic activation and vice versa for the start of parasympathetic arousal. This process, called *reciprocal inhibition*, amplifies the effects of the system being aroused since so many organs are affected in opposite ways by the two systems. The hypothalamus is in direct connection with the master gland, the *pituitary*, which secretes a hormone (called adrenocorticotrophic hormone, or ACTH) that induces the adrenal gland to produce the cortisol. These interacting components comprise the *hypothalamic-pituitary-adrenocortical*, or HPA, axis of the stress response. Elevated levels of cortisol, in turn, provide feedback to the hypothalamus, which begins to shut down sympathetic activity.

### Homeostatic Mechanisms

Homeostatic mechanisms in the autonomic nervous system also serve to restore equilibrium after imbalances have occurred. (**Homeostasis** is a general term referring to equilibrium in a dynamic system.) After sympathetic activation has resulted in increased blood pressure, pressure-sensitive receptors in the aorta and other arteries send neural impulses to certain brain centers that, in turn, cause blood vessel dilation and heart rate decrease. The result is a drop in blood pressure. Homeostasis is achieved through systems of this kind in which forces are set in operation by the original response that tend to dampen or reverse that response. This cycle is called a *negative feedback loop*. The homeostatic principle can also be seen in the working of a thermostat that regulates the temperature level of a house. Reciprocal inhibition, on the other hand, works in an opposite fashion; the original response sets in motion forces that tend to further increase or amplify the response (sometimes called a positive feedback loop). Such a system, if allowed to go unchecked, would destroy equilibrium or homeostasis. In the well-functioning autonomic system, the initial amplifying effects of reciprocal inhibition are eventually reversed by homeostatic controls. However, the system can lose its regulatory stability if it is subjected to chronic challenges; over time, increased levels of cortisol may damage cells in the hypothalamus and impair its ability to control the stress response.

Homeostasis, in terms of the living body, is the regulation of its internal environment in order to maintain a stable, constant condition. (Shutterstock)

## 5.2b The Nature of Stressors and Their Severity

Selye's work on the GAS stimulated further efforts to describe and measure the impact of stressful events on the nervous system, on learning, and on psychopathology. For example, Holmes and Rahe (1967) proposed that stressful life events could be assigned "life change unit" values indicating their severity: The death of a spouse was assigned a value of 100 units—compared to 73 for divorce, 40 for pregnancy, 23 for trouble with the boss, and 12 for Christmas. Across more than 40 rated life events, point values could be summed to determine the health risk a person faced from a combination of recent stressors. A total score of 300 predicted greater than two-thirds likelihood of major illness within the next two years. There are several problems with assigning stress values, however. Individuals may vary widely in their reactions to life

**Homeostasis**

State of equilibrium or balance in a dynamic system

events and may find divorce less stressful than continuing in an unhappy marriage, depending on circumstances. Instead of the stressor itself, the temporal and psychological contexts of its presentation appear to be the more important factors in the degree of the stress response.

> **Do the effects of some terrifying experiences never go away?**

The impact of stressors on physical and behavioral function is, in part, a function of the intensity of the stressor and the pattern of its delivery. Stressors may be brief, time-limited, or sustained; they may be discrete or continuous; they may be part of an acute or chronic pattern. Chronic stressors generally produce more damaging effects on mood, health, and behavior, especially in older or health-compromised persons (Schneiderman, Ironson, & Siegal, 2005). Chronic stressors (such as unemployment, incarceration, homelessness, or those imposed by a physical or behavioral limitation) can affect many components of an individual's life; and since it is not clear when or if they will ever subside, they generally have more severe or long-lasting effects than more acute stressors (such as a pending surgery or a legal proceeding). However, intensity is an important factor in the magnitude of the stress response. Very intense acute events, especially those involving serious threat to life or physical safety (**traumas**), can promote the most destabilizing effects on mood and behavior—even if these events are witnessed, rather than directly experienced.

Some stressors may be sustained; they may be discrete or continuous such as a stressful occupation; chronic stressors generally produce more damaging effects on mood, health, and behavior. (Shutterstock)

The psychological context concerns the influence of an individual's prior history, current psychological functioning, and subjective interpretation on stressor severity. The degree to which stressors are experienced as predictable or controllable plays a large role in the reaction both to the current stressor and to future ones. One research method for assessing the relative importance of the predictability of stressors is the *triadic design* (see Figure 5-2). In studies using this approach, three groups of subjects are typically compared: experimental or "master" subjects (who receive some warning signal or information predicting the delivery of the stressor); yoked subjects (who receive exactly the same intensity, frequency, and duration of the stressor as the experimental subjects, but who do not have any prior warning); and control subjects (who are present in the experimental setting but do not experience the specific stressor). After a series of trials involving stressor presentation, comparisons can be made on a variety of behavioral and physical measurements. If yoked subjects experience more severe outcomes than experimental subjects, the difference can be attributed to the unpredictable nature of stressor delivery—rather than its intensity, frequency, or duration.

**Trauma**

Intense stressor involving threat of death, serious injury, or violence to self or others

## *Figure 5-2* *The Triadic Design*

Comparisons between the three groups allow assessment of the effects of stressor predictability and/or controllability on stress response.

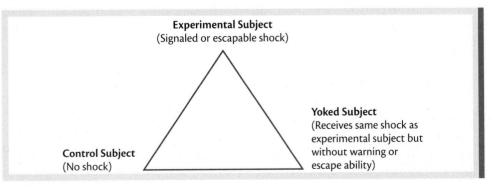

The arrangement is similar for the examination of controllable or uncontrollable stressors. In an animal study of stress, for example, the experimental group can postpone or turn off a shock by pressing a lever. Members of the yoked group are placed into an identical apparatus whose shock grids are connected to the grids of the experimental animals. Whenever an experimental animal receives a shock, so does the yoked animal; but the yoked group's levers are disconnected—so there is no escape or avoidance response possible. Differences in stressor impact between the experimental and yoked groups can then be attributed to controllability of the event.

Several animal studies have demonstrated that unpredictable electric shock produces greater fear and arousal (including higher plasma corticosterone levels, greater weight loss, and more stomach ulceration) than shocks of equal intensity that were preceded by a warning stimulus (Seligman, Chronic fear produced by unpredictable electric shock, 1968; Weiss, Somatic effects of predictable and unpredictable shock, 1970). Similarly, uncontrollable shock produces larger effects on fear, corticosterone levels, and ulceration than does shock of equal intensity and frequency, delivered during an escape or avoidance procedure in which the subject can emit responses that affect shock delivery. In addition, losing control over a previously effective avoidance response produced even stronger ulceration and hormonal effects than simple uncontrolled shock (Weiss, 1971). Exposure to uncontrollable or inescapable stressors can also impair future learning (Overmier & Seligman, 1967), an effect that together with the impact on emotion and mood led Seligman (1975) to propose that uncontrollable events are the basis for depressive disorders (as discussed in Chapter 11, Mood Disorders).

## 5.2c Stress and Cardiovascular Health

Much research on stress-related health effects broadly involves the impact of psychological and behavioral factors on physical health, as illustrated by the long-term interest in the relation between behavior styles and health problems such as heart disease and stomach ulcers. A variety of large-scale studies have indicated that the "**Type A personality**"—a pattern of behavior that involves competitiveness, aggressiveness, hostility, and time urgency—is associated with a greater risk of coronary heart disease (CHD) than the more relaxed, less-hurried "**Type B personality**" behavior style. Typically, classification of participants as Type A or Type B is based on an interview or questionnaire. The Framingham Heart Study included more than 1,600 men and women, followed for eight years

> Can psychological circumstances affect physical health?

after being identified as Type A or B. Among white-collar workers, 3 times as many Type A participants developed CHD as Type B (Haynes, Feinleib, & Kannel, 1980). These results are similar to other large scale studies in the United States, Belgium, and Finland.

There have been inconsistent findings, however; some researchers have not found a clear link between Type A and CHD (e.g., Hollis, Connett, Stevens, & Greenlick, 1990). Other work indicated that not all aspects of Type A behavior patterns were equally damaging to heart health; indeed, some could be protective in certain situations, such as in survival after a first heart attack (Ragland & Brand, 1988). Rather, particular components of the Type A pattern—especially anger and hostility—appear to be more directly related to CHD. Hostility and impatience have also been linked to a doubling in the risk for hypertension, which is a major risk factor for heart disease (Yan, Liu, Matthews, Daviglus, Ferguson, & Kiefe, 2003).

The stress response has also been linked to cardiovascular health, hypertension, and coronary heart disease more generally. Monkeys who were subjected to stressful social conditions (by changing cagemates regularly) developed greater accumulation of plaques in the arteries (artherosclerosis) than did monkeys with stable cagemates (Kaplan, Adam, Clarkson, Manuck, & Shively, 1991); artherosclerosis is known to be a cause of heart disease. In humans, heart attacks have been observed to increase under threatening conditions, such as the 1992 Los Angeles earthquake (Leor, Poole, & Kloner, 1996).

**Type A personality**

A personal behavior pattern characterized by competitiveness, hostility, and time urgency

**Type B personality**

A personal behavior pattern that is more relaxed, less competitive, and less hurried

In spite of some remaining controversies and inconsistencies, many of which appear to be linked to methodological problems of trying to separate subjects into two distinct personality "types" when much overlap undoubtedly occurs, it is reasonable to conclude that psychological factors impact coronary health. To the extent that anger and hostility are associated with stress, there is general support that stress-related behavior patterns are connected with CHD. Consistent with these findings, activities that reduce risk of CHD, such as increased activity level, also reduce stress.

Prolonged or chronic stress can have direct impact on immune function, since one effect of the stress hormone cortisol is to suppress immune response. Stress can lead to depletion of resources necessary for adequate immunological function, (Shutterstock)

## 5.2d  Stress and Immune Functioning

Prolonged or chronic stress can have direct impact on immune function since one effect of the stress hormone cortisol is to suppress immune response. It is also likely that prolonged stress leads to a physical depletion, characterized by Selye's exhaustion stage, of resources and energies necessary for adequate immunological function. Certainly, these outcomes would be expected based on the physical and temporal characteristics of a stressor, but immune impairment is also the result of the psychological context of a stressor's delivery and individual learning histories associated with it.

An important development in our understanding of the relationship between stress and disease came with the landmark demonstration by Ader and Cohen (1975) that the immune function could be directly conditioned by Pavlovian procedures. The authors were initially working on a study of **conditioned taste aversion**, which typically involves the pairing of a novel flavor (in this case, saccharin) with a substance that produces stomach upset. Even though there may be

> **How can stress impair immune function?**

no direct temporal or causal link between the flavor and the stomach discomfort—there is often a long delay between the two—subjects usually form an aversion to the novel flavor and will avoid it in the future after only a single pairing of flavor and illness. (Many humans have experienced the same thing—sometimes called the "sauce béarnaise syndrome"—when they have eaten a novel food at the same time they were coming down with the stomach flu. In many cases, they will consistently avoid that food in the future even though it did not cause their stomach upset.) Taste aversion studies with rats frequently employ substances such as lithium or exposure to radiation to produce gastric upset; this defines the unconditioned reflex in Pavlovian arrangements (i.e., the US is lithium and the UR is stomach upset). The novel flavor (saccharin) precedes the lithium; it becomes the CS for the CR of nausea. Taste aversion is then indicated by a drop in consumption of water that contains the novel flavor. In the Ader and Cohen research, a different substance, cyclophosphamide (CY), was used to produce stomach upset. Rats were first given water flavored with saccharin (SACC), followed by an injection of CY, and then were returned to their home cages. The authors were later surprised to discover that some of the experimental animals had died, with highest mortality among those who received the strongest saccharin flavor. Their attempts to discover the reason for the animal mortality led them into a different direction in their research.

Ader and Cohen realized that cyclophosphamide had unconditioned effects apart from stomach upset. CY is an immunosuppressant drug used in transplant patients to prevent the immune system from rejecting the newly transplanted organ. It appeared that the SACC flavor had taken on immunosuppressive properties, and this effect was responsible for the increased mortality in animals that received the SACC-CY pairing. They conducted a controlled experiment to examine this possibility. Rats in the conditioned group received water flavored with SACC and 30 minutes later were injected with CY. Non-conditioned

**Conditioned taste aversion**

Aversion to a novel flavor, produced by pairing of that flavor with nausea or illness

animals received plain, unflavored water followed by CY. The placebo group received plain water followed an inactive injection (saline). Then, three days later, all animals were injected with a small amount of sheep red blood cells (SRBC), as an antigen to stimulate immune response. In the next six days, subgroups received either water or additional SACC followed by saline or CY injections. Antibody titers in the blood, measuring how much antibody the rats produced, were used as an index of the strength of immune response. The results are shown in Figure 5-3.

During a study of *conditioned taste aversion*, rats were given a novel flavor, saccharin, preceding being dosed with lithium, which caused stomach upset. Taste aversion is then indicated by a drop in consumption of water flavored with saccharin due to the connection made between saccharin and experiencing upset stomach. (Shutterstock)

The effect of two injections of CY can be seen in the US group results, indicating that CY as an unconditioned stimulus strongly inhibited antibody immune response to SRBC. Full immune response to SRBC can be seen in the placebo group's results. The CS groups clearly show that exposure to SACC on subsequent days resulted in a weakened antibody response with two additional SACC exposures producing the greatest immunosuppression. In terms of Pavlovian conditioning, the flavor of SACC (the CS) had taken on some of the immunosuppressive properties of CY (the US).

The Ader and Cohen (1975) results have been replicated in other work (e.g., Rogers, Reich, Strom, & Carpenter, 1976) and have been shown to be reliable. Subsequent studies have demonstrated that additional re-exposure to the CS does produce greater suppression of immune response and may have longer-lasting effects (Ader, Cohen, & Bovbjerg, 1982; Vogle, Castro, Solar, & Soto, 2007); and similar results can be demonstrated using other immunosuppressive drugs (e.g., cyclosporin) as the unconditioned stimulus. Research continues into the particular neural mechanisms mediating the conditioning effects of behaviorally conditioned immunosuppression (e.g., Exton, et al., 2002). However, the fact that previously neutral stimuli can acquire immunosuppressive properties strongly implies that individual learning history and environmental context can play a significant role in the effects of stress on

## Figure 5-3 *Conditioned Immunosuppression Results from Ader and Cohen (1975)*

Placebo = $H_2O$ followed by saline. NC = $H_2O$ followed by CY, then SACC. CS groups = SACC followed by CY, then SACC once or twice again. US = $H_2O$ followed by CY, then repeated.

Source: Data from Ader, R., and Cohen, N. (1975). Behaviorally conditioned immunosuppression. *Psychosomatic Medicine, 37,* 333–340.

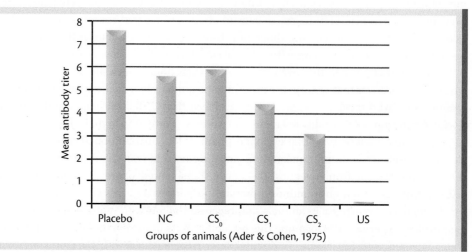

physical health. (Such findings also have obvious relevance to understanding the placebo effect.) These and additional studies of immunosuppression have defined a specialty area of research called **psychoneuroimmunology**, the study of the neural effects of psychological events on the immune system—a field that clearly has much to contribute to our understanding of the effects of stressors as well.

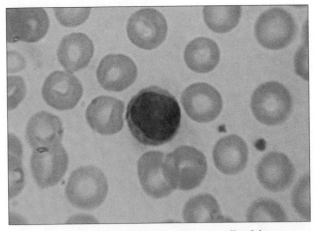

White blood cells (WBCs), or leukocytes, are cells of the immune system involved in defending the body against both infectious disease and foreign material. (Wikimedia Commons)

Other research on the role of psychological events in compromising immune function reveals that unpredictable or uncontrollable stressors generally have a greater impact on immune function than do stressors of equal intensity that are predictable or delivered under one's control. This relationship is illustrated in a study by Visintainer, Volpicelli, and Seligman (1982). Using a triadic design, the impact of escapable and inescapable shock on rejection of cancerous skin tumors was investigated. A dose of tumor cells of sufficient strength to induce tumors in 50% of unshocked animals was injected subcutaneously into 93 rats. The next day, the animals were divided into three groups. The escapable group (N = 30) received 60 trials in which floor grid shock was delivered at random intervals but could be terminated by pressing the response lever. The yoked animals (N = 30) received the same amount of shock simultaneously but bar pressing was ineffective. The control group (N = 33) was never shocked. Rats were then observed over the next 30 days for tumor growth. The results are displayed in Figure 5-4. In the control group, 54% of the animals rejected the tumor, as might be expected by the dosage strength. Sixty-three percent of the escapable group, but only 27% of the inescapable (yoked) group, rejected the tumor. Yoked animals were thus only half as likely to reject the tumor, and twice as likely to die, as animals receiving no shock or escapable shock. Presumably, inescapable (but not escapable) shock impaired immunological function in the animals that received it.

Additional work has explored the connection between stressors and immune function more directly. Mormede, Dantzer, Michaud, Kelley, and Le Moal (1988) used triadic design procedures to compare the effects of unpredictable and uncontrollable shock on immune

**Psychoneuro-immunology**

The study of the neural effects of psychological events on the immune system

*Figure 5-4* ***Tumor Rejection After Escapable and Inescapable Shock***

Animals in the escapable and inescapable groups received identical shock but differed in the availability of an escape response.

Source: Data from Visinatier, M. A., Volpicelli, J. R., & Seligman, M. E. P. (1982). Tumor rejection in rats after inescapable or escapable shock. *Science, 216,* 437–349.

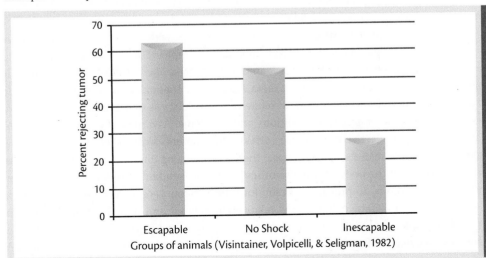

response. Three groups of rats were exposed either to unsignalled foot shock at random intervals, identical shock preceded by ten seconds of a warning tone, or no shock. Animals were then sacrificed, and spleens were removed and stimulated by three different mitogens to assess immunoactive response. Although measures of plasma corticosterone were high in both shocked groups, the mitogenic response was reduced by up to 34% among unsignalled shock animals when compared to those who received the warning signals.

Most often, the word stress is interpreted with a negative connotation. *Eustress* is a healthy, motivational type of stress that gives one a feeling of fulfillment or other positive feelings. Eustress is a process of exploring potential gains. (iStock)

The animal data, then, strongly support the role of stressful psychological events, or of stimuli paired with illness, in suppressing normal function of the immune system. Research with humans has been less clear, in part because of methodological limitations since circumstances cannot be as tightly controlled for human subjects as in the animal laboratory. Nonetheless, the human findings appear consistent with the animal work. For example, decreased natural killer cell immunological activity has been produced in humans exposed to uncontrollable, but not controllable, noise (Sieber, et al., 1992) and other studies have demonstrated a connection between the intensity and timing of a stressor and inflammatory immune disease (Jessop, Richards, & Harbuz, 2004). There are still many questions concerning the specific relationships between various stressful events and immune dysfunction in humans, however. In a recent review of over 300 empirical research studies concerning stress and human immune function conducted over the past 30 years, Segerstrom and Miller (2004) found that acute stressors, lasting minutes, appear to be associated with an unregulation of some types of immune responses and a down regulation of others, while chronic stressors are associated with decreased immune function in general. They concluded "stressful events reliably associate with changes in the immune system and that characteristics of those events are important in determining the kind of change that occurs" (p. 617).

## 5.2e Other Stress-Health Relationships

To date, many studies have indicated that stressful circumstances may contribute to or worsen other physical conditions. For example, recurrence of genital herpes appears to be related to the level of stressors that an individual has recently experienced, and stress-reduction techniques can be effective in reducing the frequency and duration of outbreaks (Burnette, Koehn, Kenyon-Jump, Hutton, & Stark, 1991). Stressful life experiences also appear to influence susceptibility to the common cold (Cohen, Doyle, & Skoner, 1999), and symptom severity in asthma (Chen & Miller, 2007).

If stressors can impact health, then effective ways to cope with stressors may be valuable in healthcare. The behavioral health field can offer many examples. For one, stress-management techniques have been associated with less emotional distress and better immune function in HIV-positive gay men (Antoni, Cruess, Cruess, Lutgendorf, Kumar, & Ironson, 2000) and with higher cancer survival rates (Williams & Schneiderman, 2002), as well as decreased symptom severity in many other physical conditions and problems. A variety of coping techniques have been used effectively, including stress-management skills such as **progressive relaxation**, which involves the systematic training of tensing and relaxing specific muscle groups throughout the body, and **stress inoculation**, the gradual introduction of a stressor in manageable "doses" to prepare a person for future encounters with the stressor. Indeed, "coping techniques" may include many relatively unrelated and undefined practices such as meditation, learned optimism, guided imagery, prayer, and physical exercise. While the general effectiveness of stress-reduction techniques implicates the involvement of the HPA

**Progressive relaxation**

The systematic tensing and relaxing of specific muscle groups

**Stress inoculation**

The gradual introduction of a stressor in manageable doses, to prepare for future encounters with that stressor

axis in mediating many areas of physical health, there is as yet no clear understanding of exactly how psychosocial factors influence such serious physical disorders as cancer although there are many possible physical mechanisms that may be involved (Antoni &Lutgendorf, 2007). Clearly, much careful work is needed to carefully define the relations between stressors, psychological factors, and health.

Stressor influence is mediated by biological and genetic variables as well as psychological ones. It is not surprising that individuals differ in stress reactions for genetic and physiological reasons, as well as for psychological ones, considering the central role played by the nervous system in stress response. The heritability of the stress response is demonstrated by the fact that selective breeding can

(iStock)

produce strains of rats that differ in HPA response to stressors (Anisman, Prakash, Merali, & Poulter, 2007). In humans, men and women differ in their HPA axis response to various stressors and stressor patterns (Renard, Suarez, Levin, & Rivarola, 2005). Genetic factors are also among those that influence susceptibility to acute stressors and coping responses (Frank, et al., 2006).

Recently, some research looking more closely at stress-gene interactions has suggested that stressors can even produce *trans-generational* effects. Radtke and his colleagues (2011) examined a group of 25 women and their children, ages 10–19, for the methylation status of their glucocorticoid receptor (GR) gene, according to whether the mothers had been exposed to intimate partner violence (IPV) before, during, or after their pregnancies. (The GR gene helps regulate the activity of the HPA axis; methylation is a process that essentially turns the gene off.) Blood samples collected and sequenced for GR status showed no association between the mothers' methylation status and their own exposure to IPV, or between mother and child GR status when IPV had either never been experienced or occurred before or after pregnancy. However, children of mothers who experienced IPV during their pregnancy showed significantly increased GR methylation, more than a decade after their birth. This demonstration of epigenetic influence indicates that maternal stress can be "transmitted" in utero to the offspring by inhibiting gene expression and so HPA function in the child. Similar results were reported earlier in mice: uncontrollable stress (maternal separation) at a young age (1–14 days) produced depressive-like behavior, not only in mice, but in their offspring as well (Franklin, et al., 2010).

The ways in which psychological and physical factors interact in the stress response will continue to be an important area of research. One obvious source of imprecision is the almost global use of the term "stress." Clearly, many factors play into how each individual defines and responds to stressors. In addition to genetic influences, the psychological contexts in which stressors are experienced, including conditioning history and prior experience with unpredictable or uncontrollable events, are presumably different for each person; these contexts mediate the degree of the stress response at the neurobiological, emotional, and behavioral levels. Different paradigms have provided different explanations of why events for one person might be much more stressful than for others and how stress may contribute to mental disorders. Genetic and biological variations are, of course, important considerations. Events in the environment can also take on different meanings for different people due to individual object relations processes (within psychodynamic accounts), different attributional explanatory styles (within cognitive accounts), and particular, derived relational responding histories (within behavioral accounts). None of these perspectives propose that all individuals react the same way to what seems to be the same stressor. As interactive organisms, however, we are aroused by, changed by, and sometimes damaged by the types of events that we experience. When stressors are sufficiently severe, a range of mental disorders described by the *DSM-5* can occur.

## 5.2f An Illustration of the Range of Trauma- and Stressor-Related Disorders

One widely cited model of mental disorder is the **diathesis-stress model,** which proposes that stressful circumstances trigger the onset of a disorder in those who carry a predisposition (diathesis) for that disorder. The predisposition may be biological, genetic, or psychological in origin; the stressor serves as the "straw that broke the camel's back." In that view, stressors may be involved in the expression of nearly every *DSM-5* disorder, and this point will be considered in future chapters. There are some disorders, however, that are so directly linked to stressor involvement that the presence of an identifiable precipitating event is a requirement of the diagnostic criteria. The trauma- and stressor-related disorders of the *DSM-5* are shown in Table 5-2. Consider the following examples that illustrate the trauma- and stressor-related disorders in the *DSM-5* (see Case Studies).

Susan's experience is one recognized in the *DSM-5* not as a mental disorder but as one of the "Other Conditions That May Be a Focus of Clinical Attention," a category that includes several reactions and disturbances that can develop in the absence of any disorder. The most likely label for Susan's stress-related condition is uncomplicated bereavement.

**Bereavement** is a normal stress reaction, considering the definition of "normal" for Susan in terms of her psychological, social, and cultural background. Grief, sadness, loss of appetite, and sleep disturbance are common parts of a typical grief response—so normal that we might consider the absence of such reactions after the unexpected loss of a loved

**Diathesis-stress model**

A model of mental disorders that proposes disorders develop when an individual with a diathesis (predisposition) experiences significant psychological stress

**Bereavement**

A normal reaction of grief and sadness in response to the death of a loved one

## Case Study 1

**Susan B.** recently lost her dearest and closest friend, Pat. When she heard that Pat had died suddenly of a stroke, Susan initially refused to accept it as true. Then, she remembered that Pat recently told her about having high cholesterol and taking cholesterol-reducing drugs. Still, the news was unexpected, and Susan was overcome with grief. She could not report for work the day she heard the news or the next day or even the next. She spent much time wondering how she could continue without her friend. Her life seemed disrupted and empty, she had no appetite, and she slept poorly. At times, she awakened from a brief slumber thinking that she was talking with Pat but then realized it was only a dream. Slowly, she came to the realization that Pat was gone and forced herself to begin her life again.

*Table 5-2*   *DSM-5* Trauma and Stressor-Related Disorders

| Disorder | Key Symptoms | Minimum Duration for Diagnosis | Sex Ratio |
|---|---|---|---|
| Reactive attachment disorder | In a child, inhibited and emotionally withdrawn behavior toward adult caregivers, with social and emotional disturbances relating to neglect or insufficient care | None, but onset before age 5 | Equal |
| Disinhibited social engagement disorder | In a child, approaching and interacting with unfamiliar adults in an overfamiliar and disinhibited manner, related to neglect or insufficient care | None | Equal |
| Posttraumatic stress disorder | After exposure to intense trauma, recurrent recollection and distress related to the trauma with marked arousal | 1 month | More common in females |
| Acute stress disorder | After exposure to intense trauma, recurrent recollection and distress related to the trauma with marked arousal | 3 days | More common in females |
| Adjustment disorders | Development of behavioral or emotional symptoms within 3 months of the onset of a stressor | None | Equal |

one as abnormal. Still, there is wide latitude in how we define the normal response to grief. After some length of time, or beyond some level of intensity of symptoms, the reaction moves beyond "normal" for the culture and is then considered a mental disorder. If Susan remains consumed by grief several months after Pat's death, or if the symptoms become more severe than "normal" sadness, major depression would be considered as a diagnosis. There are other diagnostic criteria involved in giving a label of major depression, but departure from the normal response to the loss of a loved one could be a factor, discussed in more detail in Chapter 11 (Mood Disorder and Suicide).

## Case Study 2

**Don W.** thought he had a stable job, good income, and secure retirement until the large company where he had worked for 20 years went bankrupt. He suddenly found himself without a job or a pension account and unable to make the payments on a recent home purchase. In his specialized field of work, there were very few job opportunities; and his savings were quickly being spent. Feelings of desperation and panic began to grow whenever he thought about his home mortgage or medical insurance. Don soon spent much of his time worrying about his future, angry about the financial fraud that he believed was involved, and depressed and helpless about his prospects. After 6 months of unemployment, he saw his situation as so hopeless that he seriously considered suicide. Eventually, a family member found a way for Don to resume employment, and he began working at a lower-paying job, resolved to make the best he could of his circumstance.

Although anyone would be greatly troubled by such a loss of security, Don's response to financial loss included some symptoms of both anxiety (such as desperate worry and panic) and depression (such as hopelessness and suicidal thoughts), and their severity warrants a diagnosis of adjustment disorder.

Adjustment disorders require an identifiable stressor that produces a maladaptive reaction within 3 months of stressor onset (see *DSM-5* Diagnostic Criteria for Adjustment Disorders). However, bereavement is explicitly excluded from consideration within the diagnosis. Common stressors that can produce such reactions include divorce, loss of job, health problems, arrest, or other major changes in life circumstances. Among children, moving to a new town or transferring to a different school may be common triggers. Adjustment disorders are by definition time-limited, such that the impairment or maladaptive reaction to the stressor is expected to remit within 6 months if the stressor is removed. (Of course, the stressor may be long-lasting, in which case the disturbance continues.) Only reactions that are in excess of "normal" reactions qualify for the diagnosis; and the dysfunction may manifest as depressed mood, anxiety, disturbance of conduct, or a combination of these symptoms. In Don's case, "adjustment disorder with mixed anxiety and depressed mood" would be a reasonable label.

Adjustment disorders appear to be relatively common with prevalence rates between 5% and 20% in mental health outpatients, and up to 50% in hospital psychiatric consultation settings (American Psychiatric Association, 2013). Some reviews have found adjustment disorders to be prevalent among children and adolescents, causing notable impairment and poor outcomes (Newcorn & Strain, 1992). Among adults, suicide is a significant risk. Of 119 patients at the University of Virginia Hospital who carried a diagnosis of adjustment disorder, over 60% had made suicide attempts (Kryzhanovskaya & Canterbury, 2001).

Given the prevalence and potential seriousness of adjustment disorders, it is interesting that the clinical literature does not contain more information on it. There may be several reasons for this apparent neglect. Because the *DSM-IV-TR* considered adjustment disorders a "residual category," clinicians were cautioned to consider whether an exacerbation of another

| DSM-5 | **Diagnostic Criteria for Adjustment Disorders** |

### Adjustment Disorders

A. The development of emotional or behavioral symptoms in response to an identifiable stressor(s) occurring within 3 months of the stressor(s).

B. These symptoms or behaviors are clinically significant, as evidenced by one or both of the following:

1. Marked distress that is out of proportion with the severity or intensity of the stressor, taking into account the external context and the cultural factors that might influence symptom severity and presentation.

2. Significant impairment in social, occupational, or other important areas of functioning.

C. The stress-related disturbance does not meet the criteria for another mental disorder and is not merely an exacerbation of a preexisting mental disorder.

D. The symptoms do not represent normal bereavement.

E. Once the stressor or its consequences have terminated, the symptoms do not persist for more than an additional 6 months.

Specify whether:

309.0 (F43.21) With depressed mood
309.24 (F43.22) With anxiety
309.28 (F43.23) With mixed anxiety and depressed mood
309.3 (F42.24) With disturbance of conduct
309.4 (F43.25) With mixed disturbance of emotions and conduct
309.9 (F43.20) Unspecified
[**Note:** ICD-9-CM code (ICD-10-CM Code)]

Source: Reprinted with permission from the *Diagnostic and Statistical Manual of Mental Disorders*, Fifth Edition, (Copyright 2013). American Psychiatric Association.

disorder (such as an existing mood or personality disorder) could account for the reaction before resorting to the diagnosis. The *DSM-5* no longer holds this position, in the sense that it conceptualizes adjustment disorders as heterogeneous stress response syndromes in their own right. It is also possible that what appears to be an adjustment disorder is actually an early phase, or mild form, of an emerging major disorder (Strain & Newcorn, 2004). The possible overlap and mixing of symptoms within the category, and the similarity of symptoms with other categories (such as mood and anxiety disorders), may lower diagnostic reliability. Still, clinicians use the diagnosis often when treating clients involved in family, occupational, or marriage conflicts; many people without other mental disorders can find themselves overwhelmed by events—a not unexpected occurrence, given the pervasiveness of stressful circumstances in life.

# Case Study 3

**Tom S.** taught his son to drive safely; and although he was himself a very good driver, Tom felt most secure when his son was behind the wheel. For that reason, the accident that took his son's life and nearly killed Tom seemed especially unfair. The driver at fault was speeding the wrong way down the highway in an attempt to elude police. In the split second before the accident as Tom saw the collision developing, it seemed to him that the other driver had hit them intentionally. The impact was so violent that twisted metal nearly decapitated his son; and Tom was left gasping for breath and unable to move, crushed between debris and seeing only his dead family member beside him for nearly an hour before he could be extricated from the wreck. Although his physical injuries were healing, Tom could not escape the searing memories of the moment—the look of surprise on the dead son's face, the smells and sounds of the highway emergency. He often awakens in panic from nightmares about the moments before the accident and the near suffocation that followed. For the past 3 months, Tom has been unable to ride in a car without feelings of terror, and he has been reluctant to leave home where he spends much of his time trying not to think about that fateful day. He no longer makes any plans for the future. Friends who stop to see him think he is detached from them, and he seems little comforted by their company.

Such extreme stressors, and the intense psychological reactions they can produce, comprise posttraumatic stress disorder (PTSD). The stressors that lead to posttraumatic stress disorder are so intense that they could presumably cause maladaptive reactions in anyone (refer to *DSM-5* Diagnostic Criteria for Posttraumatic Stress Disorder). They involve a threat to life or physical integrity and to which the reaction is intense fear, helplessness, or horror. These stressors may include natural events such as tornadoes, floods, and earthquakes; accidental human disasters such as fires, airplane crashes, or automobile collisions; and intentional human traumas such as war, rape, torture, or terrorist acts. PTSD involves not only the intense reaction to the trauma but also the reliving of the event through intrusive and recurrent thoughts, images, and dreams; sometimes, hallucinations occur. Reactions can be re-triggered by stimuli such as fireworks, dark passages, the smell of diesel fuel, or other potent and salient reminders of the event. Often, in cases involving loss of life, victims harbor guilt feelings for surviving when many others did not.

The criteria given in *DSM-5* Diagnostic Criteria for Posttraumatic Stress Disorder apply to adults, adolescents, and children over age 6. Below that age, the *DSM-5* provides modified criteria for PTSD, noting that younger children may appear socially withdrawn and may display intrusive recollections or enact flashbacks of the event during play reenactment, sometimes without apparent distress. Impairment for this age group is seen in school behavior and in relationships with parents, siblings, peers, or caregivers. Posttraumatic stress disorder can begin any time after 1 year of age; lifetime risk by age 75 is 8.7% (American Psychiatric Association, 2013).

The *DSM-5* provides similar diagnostic criteria for the related diagnosis of acute stress disorder (ASD), except that symptoms are less than one month in duration. If the disturbance persists longer than that, the ASD diagnosis is changed to PTSD. Thus, nearly all cases of PTSD begin as ASD. The exceptions involve a particular qualifier of PTSD, "with delayed expression." That means that PTSD can be diagnosed, in some situations, when the symptoms do not appear soon after the trauma but much later—months or even years later. In contrast, symptoms in ASD must persist at least three days, but no longer than a month after the trauma.

The concept of PTSD developed from effects of combat on soldiers. Few human experiences can compare with the horrors of battle; in every war, a certain proportion of military personnel develop incapacitating psychological symptoms—called *shell shock* in World War I and *war neuroses, combat fatigue,* or *combat exhaustion* in subsequent wars. These reactions usually start with increasing irritability, difficulty in sleeping, and a tendency to react with startle to minor noises. The reaction may then proceed to intense distress, extreme terror and incapacitation. Notably, impairment can remain long after the war has ended.

> **What types of stressors produce the greatest effect?**

Some early studies by psychologists indicated that disturbances produced by severe stress could last for many years and, in some cases, increase in severity with the passage of time. For example, in 1957 the gasoline tanker Mission San Francisco collided with Elna II, a freighter, on the Delaware River. An intense explosion occurred in which 10 men were killed. Many of the survivors of this traumatic experience were given a psychiatric examination at the time and again about four years later (Leopold & Dillon, 1963). Most of the survivors reported symptoms of one kind or another: nervousness, tension, general upset, sleep disturbances, and gastrointestinal symptoms. In general, there was a tendency for the number of disturbances to *increase* over the 4-year period. Many men were unable to return to sea on a regular basis,

Conditions such as the civil war in Ethiopia or genocide in Darfur can lead to PTSD. For someone suffering from PTSD, reactions to everyday stressors may involve intense fear, helplessness, or horror. (Corbis)

| *DSM-5* | **Diagnostic Criteria for Posttraumatic Stress Disorder** |

308.81 (F43.10) Posttraumatic Stress Disorder

**Note:** The following criteria apply to adults, adolescents, and children older than 6 years old.

A. Exposure to actual or threatened death, serious injury, or sexual violence in one (or more) of the following ways:

   1. Directly experiencing the traumatic event(s).

   2. Witnessing, in person, the event(s) as it occurred to others.

   3. Learning that the traumatic event(s) occurred to a close family member or a close friend. In cases of actual or threatened death of a family member or friend, the event(s) must have been violent or accidental.

   4. Experiencing repeated or extreme exposure to aversive details of the traumatic event(s) (e.g., first responders collecting human remains; police officers repeatedly exposed to details of child abuse).

**Note:** Criterion 4 does not apply to exposure through electronic media, television, movies, or pictures, unless this exposure is work related.

B. Presence of one (or more) of the following intrusion symptoms associated with the traumatic event(s), beginning after the traumatic event(s) occurred:

   1. Recurrent, involuntary, and intrusive distressing memories of the traumatic event(s).

**Note:** In children older than 6 years, repetitive play may occur in which themes or aspects of the traumatic event(s) are expressed.

   2. Recurrent distressing dreams in which the content and/or affect of the dream are related to the traumatic event(s).

**Note:** In children, there may be frightening dreams without recognizable content.

   3. Dissociative reactions (e.g., flashbacks) in which the individual feels or acts as if the traumatic event(s) were recurring. (Such reactions may occur on a continuum, with the most extreme expression being a complete loss of awareness of present surroundings.)

**Note:** In children, trauma-specific reenactment may occur in play.

   4. Intense or prolonged psychological distress at exposure to internal or external cues that symbolize or resemble an aspect of the traumatic event(s).

   5. Marked physiological reactions to internal or external cues that symbolize or resemble an aspect of the traumatic event(s).

C. Persistent avoidance of stimuli associated with the traumatic event(s), beginning after the traumatic event(s) occurred, as evidenced by one or both of the following:

   1. Avoidance of or efforts to avoid distressing memories, thoughts, or feelings about or closely associated with the traumatic event(s).

   2. Avoidance of or efforts to avoid external reminders (people, places, conversations, activities, objects, situations) that arouse distressing memories, thoughts, or feelings about or closely associated with the traumatic event(s).

D. Negative alterations in cognitions and mood associated with the traumatic event(s), beginning or worsening after the traumatic event(s) occurred, as evidenced by two (or more) of the following:

   1. Inability to remember an important aspect of the traumatic event(s) (typically due to dissociative amnesia and not to other factors such as head injury, alcohol, or drugs).

   2. Persistent and exaggerated negative beliefs or expectations about oneself, others, or the world (e.g., "I am bad," "No one can be trusted," "The world is completely dangerous," "My whole nervous system is completely ruined").

   3. Persistent, distorted cognitions about the cause or consequences of the traumatic event(s) that lead the individual to blame himself/herself or others.

   4. Persistent negative emotional state (e.g., fear, horror, anger, guilt, or shame).

   5. Markedly diminished interest or participation in significant activities.

   6. Feelings of detachment or estrangement from others.

   7. Persistent inability to experience positive emotions (e.g., inability to experience happiness, satisfaction, or loving feelings).

E. Marked alterations in arousal and reactivity associated with the traumatic event(s), beginning or worsening after the traumatic event(s) occurred, as evidenced by two (or more) of the following:

   1. Irritable behavior and angry outbursts (with little or no provocation) typically expressed as verbal or physical aggression toward people or objects.

   2. Reckless or self-destructive behavior.

   3. Hypervigilance.

   4. Exaggerated startle response.

   5. Problems with concentration.

   6. Sleep disturbance (e.g., difficulty falling or staying asleep or restless sleep).

F. Duration of the disturbance (Criteria B, C, D, and E) is more than 1 month.

G. The disturbance causes clinically significant distress or impairment in social, occupational, or other important areas of functioning.

H. The disturbance is not attributable to the physiological effects of a substance (e.g., medication, alcohol) or other medical condition.

Specify whether:

With dissociative symptoms: The individual's symptoms meet the criteria for posttraumatic stress disorder, and in addition, in response to the stressor, the individual experiences persistent or recurrent experiences of either of the following:

1. Depersonalization: Persistent or recurrent experiences of feeling detached from, and as if one were an outside observer of, one's mental processes or body (e.g., feeling as though one were in a dream; feeling a sense of unreality of self or body or of time moving slowly).

2. Derealization: Persistent or recurrent experiences of unreality of surroundings (e.g., the world around the individual is experienced as unreal, dreamlike, distant, or distorted.

Note: To use this subtype, the dissociative symptoms must not be attributable to the physiological effects of a substance (e.g., blackouts, behavior during alcohol intoxication) or another medical condition (e.g., complex partial seizures).

Specify if:

With delayed expression: If the full diagnostic criteria are not met until at least 6 months after the event (although the onset and expression of some symptoms may be immediate).

Source: Reprinted with permission from the *Diagnostic and Statistical Manual of Mental Disorders*, Fifth Edition, (Copyright 2013). American Psychiatric Association.

and most of those that did indicated that they were tense and fearful aboard ship although going to sea was a matter of occupational necessity.

Similar persisting effects were found for survivors of Nazi concentration camps (Chodoff, 1963) and for soldiers suffering from combat fatigue (Archibald & Tuddenham, 1965). In the latter study, 62 veterans who had experienced combat fatigue 20 years previously in World War II were compared with a control group of combat veterans who had not shown combat fatigue. The combat fatigue veterans reported more depression, restlessness, irritability, jumpiness, fatigue, difficulty in concentration, sweaty hands, headaches, sleeplessness, yawning, and other signs of persisting anxiety. Later, the long-lasting but often delayed problems experienced by many Vietnam-era soldiers brought increased attention to these reactions, first listed in 1980 in the *DSM-III* along with the recognition that PTSD was a predictable, serious, and relatively frequent outcome among combat veterans, as well as civilians in the path of war. Recent reports from the U.S. Army indicate that about 10% of American forces completing one tour of duty in the wars in Iraq and Afghanistan meet diagnostic criteria for PTSD, and the risk increases by half again for those serving an additional tour (Tyson, 2006).

PTSD is now more widely conceptualized than the original military focus, and a great many people are exposed to conditions that can produce PTSD. In the past decade, the terrorist attacks on the World Trade Center, the devastation of Hurricane Katrina along the U.S. Gulf Coast, the earthquake and tidal waves in Indonesia, the wars in the Middle East, and the genocide in Darfur have left millions of people at risk. Sexual abuse and rape are also disturbingly prevalent throughout the world. Amnesty International (2004) reported that globally one in three women has been beaten, abused, or forced to have sex during their lifetimes; a woman is raped in the United States every six minutes. Such figures are especially noteworthy for PTSD risk because *DSM-5* reports that the dysfunction may be especially severe and long-lasting if the precipitating stressor is intentional and interpersonal (American Psychiatric Association, 2013).

Incidence rates for PTSD approaching one-third to one-half of victims are found among rape survivors, military captives, political prisoners, and targets of genocide (American Psychiatric Association, 2013). Not everyone exposed to severe stressors develops ASD or PTSD. Gender plays one role: the diagnosis is given about twice as often to females as to males (Kessler, Sonnega, Bromet, Hughes, & Nelson, 1995). Variations in susceptibility to PTSD could also be influenced by genetics, by previous stressor experience, situational differences, and ethnic background.

Sexual abuse and rape are also disturbingly prevalent throughout the world. PTSD symptoms are common among rape survivors, military captives, political prisoners, and targets of genocide such as the women and children of Darfur. (iStock)

About one-half of victims recover completely within 3 months (American Psychiatric Association, 2013). There is also much variability in course. La Greca, Silverman, Vernberg, and Prinstein (1996) found that of almost 30% of children who developed PTSD after Hurricane Andrew, less than 13% continued to show the same level of disturbance after 10 months; but Kessler and his colleagues (2008) found an increase in PTSD, suicidal activity, and other serious mental disorders one year after Hurricane Katrina, compared to measures taken 5–8 months after the storm. Differences such as these probably stem in part from different levels of available assistance and support at the time of the trauma and in the months that follow.

Hurricane Andrew off the coast of Florida, 2009. La Greca et al., (1996) found that of almost 30% of children who developed PTSD after Hurricane Andrew, less than 13% continued to show the disturbance after 10 months. (Wikimedia Commons)

The uniquely damaging characteristic of the stressor and the sufferer's extreme fear response to stimuli that are associated with the trauma suggest that one way to conceptualize PTSD is as a strongly conditioned fear response. Foa, Zinbarg, and Rothbaum (1992) reviewed research on uncontrollable and unpredictable stress in animals and proposed a model of PTSD in which symptoms of persistent arousal, re-experience of the event, numbing, and avoidance can be conceptualized as the direct effects of stressors that are not only life-threatening but also, in particular, are experienced as uncontrollable and unpredictable. As we have seen in the review of stress effects on health, these are the most damaging kind of stressors.

## 5.2g  Treatment for Severe Stress Reactions

It might seem obvious that quick emergency assistance in trauma situations is necessary to blunt or avoid serious psychological reactions. Crisis intervention and critical incident stress debriefing involve supportive and integrative interventions within hours or days of the crisis, often provided by therapists brought into the situation to help decrease the likelihood that the acute reactions will develop into more serious PTSD. However, it has been difficult to document the value of this type of early intervention, with little or no support for its effectiveness in controlled studies. After the terrorist attacks on New York in 2001, for example, some 9,000 counselors descended on the city to provide rapid mental health assistance, even though there was no evidence that typical psychological debriefing interventions would be effective. In fact, there was some indication that those services could *impede* recovery (e.g., McNally, Bryant, & Ehlers, 2003), perhaps by encouraging emotional expression too quickly. Reviews of two randomized controlled trials of critical incident stress debriefing actually found harmful long-term effects of treatment among burn victims and victims of automobile accidents, compared to assessment-only controls (Lilienfeld, 2007). It seems reasonable to expect that some sorts of assistance shortly after the trauma might be valuable, but the important components of such assistance remain undefined. Clearly, careful outcome research is needed to develop evidence-based practices for early intervention in trauma.

Fortunately, there are effective treatments for PTSD and other stress reactions. The psychological interventions that appear to be most effective are cognitive-behavioral therapies (CBT) that involve a combination of stress management and re-exposure to the stressor. Stress management may include systematic desensitization techniques, in which the patient is first taught a method for relaxation and then is confronted with gradually increasing exposure to the stressor while maintaining a relaxed state. Re-exposure is often done in massed trials, in which the patient confronts either actual or imagined scenes containing the most terrifying aspects of the trauma for prolonged periods. (In the behavioral literature, this technique is sometimes called **flooding**.) Such exposure leads to **habituation** of autonomic responding and a decatastrophizing of the event itself. For example, Jaycox, Zoellner, and Foa (2002) describe a CBT intervention for rape survivors that involves (1) establishing a trusting therapeutic relationship, (2) breathing and relaxation training and practice, (3) prolonged exposure by vividly and repeatedly retelling the story of the trauma in detail for 45–60 minutes each session, and (4) examining and challenging dysfunctional thoughts about the trauma (**cognitive restructuring**).

Another intervention for PTSD, eye movement desensitization and reprocessing (EMDR), is more controversial but appears to be as effective as CBT in some comparisons. According to its developer, Francine Shapiro (1995), back-and-forth eye movements play a role in reducing disturbing thoughts—perhaps related to their value in REM sleep. She proposed that patients track a moving object (such as the therapist's finger) with their eyes while recalling the most distressing and intense images of the trauma. Sets of eye movements under these conditions are repeated until the patient notes a reduction in the distressing value of the image during the therapeutic session. Several published reports have attested to the technique's effectiveness even though Davidson and Parker's (2001) review of the EMDR literature concluded that equivalent results were possible without the eye movements at all—indicating that EMDR might owe its effectiveness to prolonged exposure.

From the biological perspective, there are pharmacological interventions that can be effective in relieving symptoms of PTSD. Minor tranquilizers, such as benzodiazepines that can impact sympathetic arousal, are not particularly effective as PTSD treatments. However, the tricyclic antidepressants and the selective serotonin reuptake inhibitors or SSRIs (such as Zoloft and Paxil) have received stronger support, with the latter being the medications of choice (Ballanger, Davidson, Lecrubier, & Nutt, 2000) for both ASD and PTSD at this time. Recent studies indicate that SSRIs may provide broader and more global improvements in symptoms than do other drug options (Yehaud, Marshall, Penkower, & Wong, 2002). Due to associated side effects, however, discontinuation rates for most pharmacological treatments are higher than those for CBT. Recently, there have been some experimental tests of the recreational drug MDMA (also known as ecstasy) in the treatment of PTSD, with initially promising results. For example, a small, randomized control study involving treatment-refractory patients with PTSD showed an 83% response rate for MDMA compared to 25% for placebo, with no evidence of serious adverse drug effects (Mithoefer, Wagner, Mithoefer, Jerome, & Doblin, 2010). There are plans to further investigate MDMA and MDMA-assisted psychotherapy as treatment options for PTSD victims.

## 5.2h  Other Stress-Related Disorders

Two additional trauma- and stressor-related disorders result, not from intense trauma or discrete stressors, but rather a history of neglect and substandard care of children. Reactive attachment disorder was listed in the *DSM-IV* under a category known as "Disorders usually first diagnosed in infancy, childhood, or adolescence," but relocated to the stress-related disorders in the *DSM-5* and expanded to include a second condition, disinhibited social engagement disorder. Although the symptom presentations differ, both disorders are functionally related to parental neglect.

Reactive attachment disorder involves social and emotional disturbance and withdrawal toward adult caregivers following a history of inadequate care (see *DSM-5* Diagnostic Criteria for Reactive Attachment Disorder). The disturbance begins before age 5 in a child with a developmental age of at least 9 months. Essentially, these children do not form normal attachments to adults or others, although the capacity is assumed to be present. They are not easily comforted (or resist comforting) when distressed and show little positive emotion in most interactions with caregivers. In the *DSM-IV* parlance, this symptom presentation was considered the "inhibited" subtype of the reactive attachment disorder.

**Flooding**

Therapeutic technique in which the person is made to confront the stimuli that arouse anxiety until the anxiety extinguishes

**Habituation**

Lessening of a response as a function of repeated presentations of the eliciting stimulus

**Cognitive restructuring**

Therapeutic technique in which dysfunctional thoughts and beliefs are examined and challenged

| *DSM-5* | **Diagnostic Criteria for Reactive Attachment Disorder** |

313.89 (F94.1) Reactive Attachment Disorder

A. A consistent pattern of inhibited, emotionally withdrawn behavior toward adult caregivers, manifested by both of the following:
   1. The child rarely or minimally seeks comfort when distressed.
   2. The child rarely or minimally responds to comfort when distressed.

B. A persistent social and emotional disturbance characterized by at least two of the following:
   1. Minimal social and emotional responsiveness to others.
   2. Limited positive affect.
   3. Episodes of unexplained irritability, sadness, or fearfulness that are evident even during nonthreatening interactions with adult caregivers.

C. The child has experienced a pattern of extremes of insufficient care as evidenced by at least one of the following:
   1. Social neglect or deprivation in the form of persistent lack of having basic emotional needs for comfort, stimulation, and affection met by caregiving adults.
   2. Repeated changes of primary caregivers that limit opportunities to form stable attachments (e.g., frequent changes in foster care).
   3. Rearing in unusual settings that severely limit opportunities to form selective attachments (e.g., institutions with high child-to-caregiver ratios).

D. The care in Criterion C is presumed to be responsible for the disturbed behavior in Criterion A (e.g., the disturbances in Criterion A begin following a lack of adequate care in Criterion C).

E. The criteria are not met for autism spectrum disorder.

F. The disturbance is evident before age 5 years.

G. The child has a developmental age of at least 9 months.

Specify if:

Persistent: The disorder has been present for more than 12 months.

Specify current severity:

Reactive attachment disorder is specified as severe when a child exhibits all symptoms of the disorder, with each symptom manifesting at relatively high levels.

Source: Reprinted with permission from the *Diagnostic and Statistical Manual of Mental Disorders,* Fifth Edition, (Copyright 2013). American Psychiatric Association.

Reactive attachment disorder can be associated with developmental delays, but it is not accounted for by intellectual disability or another developmental disorder. It appears to be a rare condition, but its prevalence in the general population is not known—and even in severely neglected children it appears uncommon (less than 10%). Malnutrition and other physical conditions associated with extreme neglect and child abuse and comorbid language delays and depression may also occur (American Psychiatric Association, 2013).

Some therapists have promoted "holding therapy" as a treatment for reactive attachment disorder. In this approach, an individual is held via physically or psychologically enforced restraint, which may include grabbing or physically lying on top of the child's body. Restraint and enforced eye contact are meant to encourage anger and rage, in the belief that anger due to past abandonment or mistreatment has been suppressed, and the emotional release will thus have cathartic value (Pignotti & Mercer, 2007). However, its coercive nature is controversial and dangerous: at least three deaths have been associated with the intervention, and whatever empirical support exists is thin (Zilberstein, 2006).

Although disinhibited social engagement disorder stems from the same sort of substandard care and neglect, it involves disinhibited or externalizing symptoms such as overly familiar behavior with relative strangers that violates the normal social boundaries of the culture (see *DSM-5* Diagnostic Criteria for Disinhibited Social Engagement Disorder). These children are inadequately cautious in approaching unknown adults, showing indiscriminate sociability or a lack of selectivity in choice of attachment figures. In the *DSM-IV*, this pattern was listed as the "disinhibited type" of reactive attachment disorder.

| *DSM-5* | **Diagnostic Criteria for Disinhibited Social Engagement Disorder** |
| --- | --- |

313.89 (F94.2) Disinhibited Social Engagement Disorder

A. A pattern of behavior in which a child actively approaches and interacts with unfamiliar adults and exhibits at least two of the following:

    1. Reduced or absent reticence in approaching and interacting with unfamiliar adults.

    2. Overly familiar verbal or physical behavior (that is not consistent with culturally sanctioned and with age-appropriate social boundaries).

    3. Diminished or absent checking back with adult caregiver after venturing away, even in unfamiliar settings.

    4. Willingness to go off with an unfamiliar adult with minimal or no hesitation.

B. The behaviors in Criterion A are not limited to impulsivity (as in attention-deficit/hyperactivity disorder) but include socially disinhibited behavior.

C. The child has experienced a pattern of extremes of insufficient care as evidenced by at least one of the following:

    1. Social neglect or deprivation in the form of persistent lack of having basic emotional needs for comfort, stimulation, and affection met by caregiving adults.

    2. Repeated changes of primary caregivers that limit the opportunities to form stable attachments (e.g., frequent changes in foster care).

    3. Rearing in unusual settings that severely limit opportunities to form selective attachments (e.g., institutions with high child-to-caregiver ratios).

D. The care in Criterion C is presumed to be responsible for the disturbed behavior in Criterion A (e.g., the disturbances in Criterion A began following the pathogenic care in Criterion C).

E. The child has a developmental age of at least 9 months.

Specify if:

Persistent: The disorder has been present for more than 12 months.

Specify current severity:

Disinhibited social engagement disorder is specified as severe when the child exhibits all symptoms of the disorder, with each symptom manifesting at relatively high levels.

Source: Reprinted with permission from the *Diagnostic and Statistical Manual of Mental Disorders,* Fifth Edition, (Copyright 2013). American Psychiatric Association.

As preschoolers, children with disinhibited social engagement disorder may continue to show indiscriminate familiarity with adults and with peers, who often find their expression of emotions as shallow and inauthentic. Some later receive comorbid diagnoses of attention deficit/hyperactivity disorder, as well as cognitive and language delays (American Psychiatric Association, 2013).

There are additional conditions in this category, listed as "Other specified trauma- and stressor-related disorders," that do not meet the full criteria for the disorders listed thus far. For example, adjustment-like disorders may appear more than 3 months following a stressor, or may persist more than 6 months after the stressor remits. A few cultural syndromes (see Chapter 4) relate to stressors and may be included here. A proposed Section III disorder, persistent complex bereavement disorder, involves prolonged grief and disruption for more than 12 months after the death of a loved one, and as currently proposed could result from either normal or traumatic death exposures. Finally, the category also allows for "Unspecified trauma- and stressor-related disorder" for those related conditions that either do not meet any of the criteria above or for which there is insufficient information for a more specific label.

BVT *Lab*

Improve your test scores. Practice quizzes are available at www.BVTLab.com.

# Chapter Review

## TO SUM UP ...

- Strong emotions play a central role in many psychological disorders. Responses of the autonomic nervous system are especially important physiological accompaniments of these emotions.

- Stressors that are prolonged or intense can have damaging effects to health. Stressors that are experienced as unpredictable or uncontrollable appear to have the most harmful health effects.

- Stressors can also impair the functioning of the immune system. Through Pavlovian conditioning, neutral stimuli such as novel flavors can take on some of the immunosuppressive properties of drugs with which they have been paired. In stress studies, unpredictable or uncontrollable stressors appear to produce greater reduction in immune functioning.

- Stress- and trauma-related diagnoses in the *DSM-5* range from normal response patterns (bereavement) to time-limited impairment (adjustment disorders) to severe, long-lasting, or delayed impairments (posttraumatic stress disorders).

- Posttraumatic stress disorders may be conceptualized as intense, conditioned fear responses produced by unpredictable and uncontrollable traumatic events.

- Effective treatments for stress-related disorders include stress management, exposure techniques such as systematic desensitization and cognitive-behavioral therapy, and some antidepressant medications such as SSRIs.

## KEY TERMS

Autonomic nervous system   114

Bereavement   124

Cognitive restructuring   131

Conditioned taste aversion   119

Diathesis-stress model   124

Flooding   131

General adaptation syndrome (GAS)   113

Habituation   131

Homeostasis   116

Parasympathetic nervous system   115

Progressive relaxation   122

Psychoneuroimmunology   121

Stress inoculation   122

Stressor   113

Stress response   113

Sympathetic nervous system   115

Trauma   117

Type A personality   118

Type B personality   118

# QUESTIONS FOR STUDY

- Discuss the actions of the autonomic nervous system. Which part of the system is active during stressful situations? How does the arousal abate?

- Explain how the triadic design can be useful in exploring the stress response.

- Describe two ways that psychological stress can affect physical health.

# POP QUIZ

1. In 1936, which of the following models of stress did Hans Selye develop?
   A. the Posttraumatic Stress Disorder syndrome
   B. the general adaptation syndrome
   C. the hypothalamic-pituitary-adrenocortical pathway
   D. life change unit value system

2. During the _____ stage of the GAS, coping responses to the ongoing challenge are depleted.
   A. alarm
   B. resistance
   C. exhaustion
   D. transition

3. If you hear strange noises in the middle of the night, and believe there is a burglar in your home, this is the division of the autonomic nervous system that would activate the _____.
   A. sympathetic nervous system
   B. central nervous system
   C. somatic nervous system
   D. parasympathetic nervous system

4. The _____ is the division of the autonomic nervous system which functions to conserve and restore, rather than expend energy.
   A. sympathetic nervous system
   B. central nervous system
   C. somatic nervous system
   D. parasympathetic nervous system

5. The _____ is often referred to as the master gland.
   A. adrenal
   B. pituitary
   C. medulla
   D. pineal

6. Maintaining _____ is a general term referring to equilibrium in a dynamic system.
   A. adrenocortical response
   B. reciprocity
   C. homeostasis
   D. homeastasis

7. According to Holmes and Rahe, the death of a spouse was assigned a value of _____ units.
   A. 100
   B. 73
   C. 40
   D. 23

8. _____ is not one of the chronic stressors cited in your text.
   A. Unemployment
   B. Incarceration
   C. Pending surgery
   D. Homelessness

9. Exposure to uncontrollable or inescapable stressors can impair future learning, an effect that led _____ (1975) to propose that uncontrollable events are the basis for depressive disorders.
   A. Beck
   B. Freud
   C. Seligman
   D. Foa

10. One effect of the stress hormone _____ is to suppress immune response.
    A. norepinephrine
    B. cortisol
    C. serotonin
    D. insulin

11. Ader and Cohen's (1975) study of conditioned immunosuppression showed which of the following?
    A. Drugs may influence illness.
    B. Illness may be influenced by learning history.
    C. Illness may influence mental functioning.
    D. Drug effects may be influenced by learning history.

12. In the _____ of mental disorders, the predisposition for a particular disorder is considered to be biological, genetic, or psychological in origin.
    A. cognitive model
    B. diathesis-dynamic model
    C. diathesis-stress model
    D. diathesis-eustress model

13. The stressors that lead to _____ are so intense that they could presumably cause maladaptive reactions in anyone.
    A. PTSD
    B. GAD
    C. OCD
    D. SAD

14. PTSD was first listed as a mental disorder in the *DSM-III* in _____.
    A. 1980
    B. 1987
    C. 1994
    D. 1996

15. What does EMDR stand for?
    A. eye movement desensitization and reprocessing
    B. eye movement desensitization and reprogramming
    C. eye movement disinhibition and restructuring
    D. eye movement discipline and repetition

Additional study resources are available at **www.BVTLab.com**

# CHAPTER OVERVIEW

# CHAPTER OPENER QUESTIONS

What are the most common mental disorders in the United States?

How do different paradigms attempt to explain the development of anxiety disorders?

How important are specific traumatic experiences in the development of phobias?

Which treatments are effective for anxiety disorders?

What are obsessions and compulsions?

How effective are treatments for obsessive-compulsive and related disorders?

(Shutterstock)

# Anxiety and Obsessive-Compulsive Disorders

In the last chapter we saw that severe stress can precipitate psychological and physiological disturbances, some of which clear up when the stress is removed and some of which do not. Among the emotional consequences of stressors are fear and anxiety, although stress-related reactions may involve other emotional states as well. In this chapter we review the *DSM-5* disorders in which fear and anxiety are central to the diagnosis. One danger in following a system such as the *DSM* too uncritically is that it can leave the impression that we are dealing with a series of discrete and separate disorders. This is not always the case. People can, and do, often show mixtures of anxiety symptom patterns, which also overlap with the mood disorders. Still, anxiety symptoms are quite frequent in the United States. Based on epidemiological studies (e.g., Kessler, Burgland, Demler, Jin, Merikangas, & Walters, 2005), the category of anxiety disorders comprises the most common of the *DSM-5* diagnoses, with lifetime prevalence rates of over 28% of the population.

## 6.1 Fear and Anxiety

Charles Darwin's description of fear, written over a century ago, remains an excellent portrayal of this emotion:

> What are the most common mental disorders in the United States?

> Fear is often preceded by astonishment, and is so far akin to it, that both lead to the senses of sight and hearing being instantly aroused. In both cases the eyes and mouth are widely opened and the eyebrows raised. The frightened man at first stands like a statue motionless and breathless, or crouches down as if instinctively to escape observation.
>
> The heart beats quickly and violently, so that it palpitates or knocks against the ribs; but it is very doubtful whether it then works more efficiently than usual, so as to send a greater supply of blood to all parts of the body; for the skin instantly becomes pale, as during incipient faintness ... In connection with the disturbed action of the heart, the breathing is hurried. The salivary glands act imperfectly; the mouth becomes dry and is often opened and shut. I have also noticed that under slight fear there is a strong tendency to yawn. One of the best-marked symptoms is the trembling of all the muscles of the body; and this is often first seen in the lips. From this cause, and from dryness of the mouth, the voice becomes husky or indistinct, or may altogether fail ... (Darwin, 1873, pp. 290–291).

(Wikimedia Commons)

Humans, as well as most mammalian species, are born with the innate capacity to experience fear. Although there are neurophysiological systems in the brain associated with this emotion, we ordinarily infer its existence more indirectly from three kinds of data: (1) reports of subjective experiences of apprehension—such as dread, fright, tension, inability to concentrate, the desire to

139

flee a particular situation, and physical sensations such as a pounding heart or sinking feeling in the pit of the stomach (reports of this kind are, of course, limited to individuals who have the capacity to verbalize these experiences); (2) behavioral manifestations—such as flight, disorganization of speech, motor incoordination, impairment of performance on complex problem-solving tasks, or sometimes immobilization as in being "paralyzed by fear"; and (3) measurable physiological responses—such as rapid and irregular heartbeat and breathing, palmar sweating, dry mouth, dilated pupils, and muscular trembling. The physiological responses largely reflect activation of the sympathetic nervous system; however, some responses, such as diarrhea and increased frequency of urination, are produced by parasympathetic arousal. It is, perhaps, more accurate to say that the autonomic nervous system is thrown out of balance with both subdivisions showing wide swings in activation.

A variation that may occur in acute fear is **fainting**. The physiological component in the fainting response, in contrast to the mixed sympathetic-parasympathetic pattern just described, is largely parasympathetic, involving abrupt dilation of the blood vessels in the viscera, slowing of the heartbeat, a drop in blood pressure, and loss of muscle tone. These effects result in a sharp decrease in the blood supply to the brain and produce loss of consciousness. The parasympathetic-dominated fainting response is likely to occur only in strong, acute fear states.

Most of us have a pretty good idea of what an extreme fear response is like either from our own experience or from observing others. Anyone who has seen the terror expressed by a frightened young child who has not yet been taught by society to conceal fear can appreciate the reality and potential intensity of this emotion. In humans the fear response, regardless of whatever unlearned tendencies exist for certain stimuli to elicit fear, is a highly learnable response that can become associated with almost any situation or stimulus (external or internal) that happens to be present when the fear occurs. It is, also, likely to be powerfully influenced by observational learning.

A distinction is usually made between the responses of fear and anxiety. Perhaps Darwin would agree with the notion that **fear** is an adaptive state for dealing with a real threat or danger, while **anxiety** is a chronic fear sensation that is not clearly associated with any specific stimulus.

Anyone who has seen terror expressed by a frightened young child who has not yet been taught by society to conceal fear can appreciate the reality and potential intensity of this fear.
(Shutterstock)

**Fainting**

Loss of consciousness, slowing of heart rate, and drop in blood pressure often associated with acute fear states

**Fear**

A sense of dread, terror, or fright

**Anxiety**

A sense of worry, concern, or apprehension

**Panic attack**

Rapidly developing sense of intense fear and anxiety

# 6.2 Diagnosis of Anxiety Disorders

## 6.2a Characteristic Symptoms

The *DSM-5* classifies the different anxiety disorders, in part, based on the occurrence of certain components of the anxiety symptom complex. One of these is the **panic attack**, involving a rapid onset of at least four of the symptoms in *DSM-5* Symptoms of a Panic Attack—such as pounding heart, sensations of choking or suffocation, trembling, and fear of losing control—which progress to a peak within 10 minutes. People undergoing a panic attack feel intense discomfort; some think during the first such experience that they are dying. (Frequently, the experience is described either as a "nervous breakdown" or as "losing one's mind" by the sufferer.) Until children reach puberty, it is relatively rare that they experience panic attacks; attacks are much more common among adults in the general population, where the 12-month prevalence is nearly 1 in 9 (American Psychiatric Association, 2013).

Panic attacks are not, themselves, a diagnosable disorder; however, they play a role in several anxiety disorders, depending on how they are experienced. Sometimes panic attacks

| DSM-5 | **Symptoms of a Panic Attack** |
|---|---|

Heart palpitations or accelerated heart rate

Trembling or shaking

Sweating

Chest pain

Shortness of breath or sensation of suffocating

Feelings of choking

Dizziness

Numbness or tingling sensations

Chills or heat sensations

Nausea

Derealization or depersonalization

Fear of losing control

Fear of dying

Source: Reprinted with permission from the *Diagnostic and Statistical Manual of Mental Disorders,* Fifth Edition, (Copyright 2013). American Psychiatric Association.

are expected—that is, cued by or attached to situations—and a recurrence of the trigger (or its anticipation) can produce another attack. For example, specific phobias and social phobias may involve panic attacks associated with particular stimuli, such as blood or public attention. In other disorders (e.g., panic disorder), the attack is unexpected and seems to occur without a cue, or "out of the blue." People who experience panic attacks, especially unexpected episodes, live in fear of having another panic attack. Many of the anxiety disorders in the *DSM-5* can involve panic attacks, but all involve intensely uncomfortable fear or anxiety as the main presenting symptom. As in the case with all *DSM* conditions, the disorders cause interference with or impairment of normal functioning.

The reliability of anxiety disorder diagnoses improved under the *DSM-IV*, with "good" reliability noted for both panic disorder and generalized anxiety disorder (Brown, Di Nardo, Lehman, & Campbell, 2001). However, the *DSM-5* field trials produced a disappointing kappa of only 0.20 for generalized anxiety disorder; other anxiety disorders were not assessed (Regier, et al., 2012). An overview of the main anxiety disorders in the *DSM-5* is listed in Table 6-1.

**BVT** *Lab*

Flashcards are available for this chapter at www.BVTLab.com.

*Table 6-1*  DSM-5 Anxiety Disorders

| Disorder | Key Symptoms | Minimum Duration Required for Diagnosis | Sex Ratio |
|---|---|---|---|
| Separation anxiety disorder | Excessive anxiety concerning separation from home or caregiver | 4 weeks for children/adolescents, 6 months for adults | More common in females |
| Selective mutism | Consistent failure to speak in certain situations but not in others | 1 month | Equal |
| Specific phobia | Marked fear or anxiety cued by specific objects or situations | 6 months | More common in females |
| Social anxiety disorder (Social phobia) | Marked fear or anxiety cued by social or performance situations | 6 months | More common in females |
| Panic disorder | Recurrent unexpected panic attacks | 1 month | More common in females |
| Agoraphobia | Marked fear or anxiety of being in situations from which escape would be difficult if incapacitating or embarrassing symptoms occur. | 6 months | More common in females |
| Generalized anxiety disorder | Excessive anxiety and worry about a number of events or activities | 6 months | More common in females |

Source: Reprinted with permission from the *Diagnostic and Statistical Manual of Mental Disorders,* Fifth Edition, (Copyright 2013). American Psychiatric Association.

### Gender Differences in Anxiety Diagnoses

As can been seen in Table 6-1, anxiety disorders are generally much more common among females than males. In the case of some subtypes (for example, panic disorder), the female-to-male ratio may be as high as 2:1 (American Psychiatric Association, 2013). Although biased application of the diagnostic label is possible, it is unlikely that this would explain persistent differences in prevalence of this magnitude, or of similar gender differences in mood disorders. (Males have much higher prevalence rates of some disorders, such as those involving violent behavior and the sexual paraphilias.) It is possible that females with anxiety disorders come to the attention of therapists more often than males do or that males under-report the incidence of anxiety. Another possible explanation for the gender differences is that females are differentially subjected to more frequent traumas such as rape or sexual abuse that could provoke anxiety-related conditions. However, precipitating traumatic events do not form the basis of diagnosis for most of the anxiety disorders. Weich, Sloggett, and Glyn (1998) did not find support for the proposal that gender differences in prevalence could be explained by the type of social roles (such as traditional caring and domestic ones) that females rather than males tend to occupy. It is, of course, possible that biological differences between males and females in terms of HPA reactivity confer different levels of stress and anxiety or that hormonal distinctions related to reproductive physiology are responsible for higher female prevalence in anxiety disorders (Howell, Castle, & Yonkers, 2006).

An interesting evolutionary speculation for gender differences in anxiety disorders comes from Anne Campbell (1999). Along with other evolutionary theorists, she notes that many male-female behavior differences may be related to differential parental investment during reproduction. Although the male contribution to reproduction can be as little as a few minutes, females must carry a pregnancy, nurse the child, and usually invest years into the raising of offspring. Campbell notes that in tribal societies similar to early human groups, the death of either parent increased the risk of death to offspring, but the death of the mother resulted in a much greater risk of infant mortality than the death of the father. For that reason, natural selection would more strongly favor females who avoid dangerous or harmful situations or direct conflict since their children would be more likely to survive. One result, she suggests, is that women would be more prone than men to experience fear and anxiety, emotions that would tend to remove them from harmful and dangerous situations. Males, on the other hand, benefit reproductively from multiple partners and from successful battles over resources and access to females. These tendencies might lead to male overrepresentation among disorders related to sexual behavior, dangerous activities, and physical aggression.

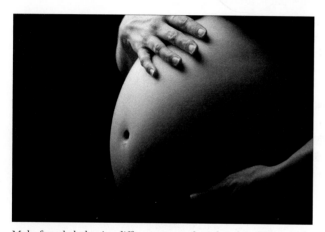

Male-female behavior differences may be related to differential parental investment. Natural selection favors females who avoid dangerous situations. Therefore, Anne Campbell suggests, females would be more prone than men to experience emotions that would remove them from harmful and dangerous situations. (iStock)

Whatever the reasons for gender differences in prevalence of mental disorders, they have been consistently reported since the *DSM-III* and will be noted as each mental disorder is described in the coming chapters. For now, we turn to a closer examination of the anxiety disorders.

## 6.2b Panic Disorder

Panic disorder is characterized by recurrent, spontaneous and unexpected panic attacks (see *DSM-5* Symptoms of a Panic Attack) with anxiety about future attacks and their consequences, including having a heart attack, losing control, or "going crazy." The panic attacks are not due to another medical condition or the effects of a substance; and they have been followed by 1 month or more of persistent concern that the attacks will recur, or of significant changes in behavior related to avoiding another attack. These behavioral changes might include avoiding certain activities (such as physical exertion) and responsibilities (such as going to work), hoping to reduce the chance of an attack. In some cases, the sufferer is anxious about being in places from which escape would be difficult, should the next panic attack begin (see agoraphobia). Up to one-third of sufferers experience nocturnal panic attacks, in which they wake from sleep in a panic state (American Psychiatric Association, 2013).

Not uncommonly, those with panic disorder overreact to mild physical symptoms, expecting them to develop into serious or catastrophic events such as a stroke. Worry and apprehension about health can extend to comorbid problems including depression, generalized anxiety, and illness anxiety disorder. They may view their situation as the result of personal failure or weakness. Onset is typically between adolescence and the mid-30s, and the course is highly variable. Although almost any pattern of attacks is possible, the most common appears to be a chronic one of waxing and waning symptoms (American Psychiatric Association, 2013).

Panic disorder appears to be fairly common, affecting up to 5% of the population at some point in life (Roy-Burne, Craske, & Stein, 2006). As noted above, panic disorder is more common in women by a factor of about 2:1. Especially in men, incidence appears to be much higher among homosexuals and bisexuals than among heterosexuals (Cochran, Sullivan, & Mays, 2003). The *DSM-5* cites a smaller incidence of 2–3%, with higher rates among non-Latino whites than most other ethnic groups. Prevalence appears to peak in adulthood and decline thereafter (American Psychiatric Association, 2013).

## Causal Factors

Several biological factors may increase the risk of developing panic disorder. It is known to run in families, with first-degree relatives of panic disorder victims up to 8 times more likely to also show the disorder (American Psychological Association, 2000). Twin studies also support a modest genetic component, although any genetic mechanism remains unknown (Roy-Burne, Craske, & Stein, 2006). Panic attacks involve intense activity in parts of the brain involved in fear and emotional arousal such as the amygdala. Thus a possible biological hypothesis involves an oversensitivity of the fear network in the brain in those who are most susceptible to the disorder, although the evidence for this as a causal factor is indirect. Another possible factor involves the inhibitory neurotransmitter GABA, which inhibits anxiety. GABA activity is low in some parts of the cortex among those with panic disorder (Goddard, Mason, Rothman, Behar, Petroff, & Krystal, 2004). Panic attacks can be triggered in panic disorder individuals more easily than in normal individuals by infusion of sodium lactate (resembling the lactate that is produced by the body during muscular exertion), by ingestion of stimulants such as caffeine, or by inhaling carbon dioxide (Barlow, 2002). These "physical challenge" data have been used to argue for a biological foundation for panic disorder. Increased risk of panic disorder also exists for smokers and for those with respiratory disturbances such as asthma (American Psychiatric Association, 2013).

Cognitive models (e.g., Beck & Emery, 1985) propose that panic disorder stems from a tendency to make catastrophic misinterpretations of physiological sensations. The susceptible individual may become aware of increased heart rate, which he or she then misinterprets negatively as the early signs of an onset of a panic attack. Engaging in these catastrophic thoughts and expectations then serves to generate the full-blown panic attack, in turn justifying the original catastrophic interpretation.

Bouton, Mineka, and Barlow (2001) propose that, although catastrophic thinking may occur, a conditioning model of panic disorder more readily accounts for both the challenge study outcomes and the cognitive misinterpretations. Early panic attacks are preceded by internal physiological (**interoceptive**) cues, as well as **exteroceptive** cues in the environment. The anxiety associated with the attack becomes conditioned to those early cues, especially in people with an associative history of uncontrollable or unpredictable negative events. The conditioned anxiety elicited by the early interoceptive and exteroceptive cues serves to both predict and to potentiate the developing panic symptoms. Anxiety then

**Interoceptive**

Relating to internal, physiological stimuli

**Exteroceptive**

Relating to external, environmental stimuli

becomes a conditioned stimulus predicting of the next panic attack, which further increases anxiety, spiraling into panic disorder.

Psychodynamic models of panic disorder emphasize internal conflicts rather than biological predispositions or learning history as critical to the development of panic disorder, as they do with all of the anxiety disorders. Freud's original focus was on the sexual and aggressive impulses that produced anxiety in the ego. Ego defenses normally contain the anxiety through defense mechanisms, but these are overwhelmed if the unconscious conflict is too threatening. Because functions involving the unconscious are difficult to test empirically, little research exists to support a psychodynamic model of panic disorder.

> How do different paradigms attempt to explain the development of anxiety disorders?

### Treatment for Panic Disorder

From the biological perspective, treatments for panic disorder have included minor tranquilizers such as the benzodiazepines, which are GABA enhancers and reduce anxiety and panic symptoms. However, medications such as diazepam (Valium) and alprazolam (Xanax) may produce **dependence**, and most patients experience a **relapse** when the medications are discontinued. Sometimes a "rebound effect" occurs (Chouinard, 2004), in which the relapse following drug discontinuation can involve anxiety more severe than that at the time treatment began. Antidepressant medications, especially the SSRIs, have been used effectively in treating panic disorder without the risk of dependence of the benzodiazepines. However, they do not work as quickly, requiring a few weeks before benefits are experienced. Side effects and relapse after discontinuation remain as problems.

Behavioral and cognitive-behavioral therapies typically involve exposure to feared interoceptive or exteroceptive stimuli (including bodily sensations that have predicted panic attacks), sometimes through intentional hyperventilation, exercise, or holding one's breath, with the goal of extinction of the anxiety response and the catastrophic expectations that accompany it. Controlled breathing exercises and relaxation techniques are often included, as well as various other stress-reduction, education, and self-control skills. These treatments have been quite successful, and they appear to be more effective and less subject to relapse than pharmacological methods (Barlow, 2002). Combination of CBT and medication produces mixed results. Adding the antidepressant imipramine to CBT provided some limited additional benefit but also increased relapse rate (Barlow, Gorman, & Sjear, 2000).

## 6.2c Agoraphobia

A second anxiety disorder is agoraphobia (see *DSM-5* Diagnostic Criteria for Agoraphobia). Literally from the Greek for "fear of the marketplace," it involves not fear of open places but rather anxiety about being in places or situations from which escape would be difficult, embarrassing, or impossible in the event of having a panic attack or panic-like symptoms. Individuals might fear getting on a bus or airplane or traveling in the car, because something very embarrassing (such as a bout of diarrhea) or a full-blown panic attack could occur. The fear can cause people to be reluctant to leave home (or another place where they are safe from such possibilities) or to be afraid of being at home alone when help might be needed. Obviously, agoraphobia could interfere with normal occupational, academic, and social activities and functions.

In the *DSM-IV*, agoraphobia was not a separate diagnosis, but rather a specifier that could be linked to other anxiety conditions such as panic disorder. The *DSM-5* elevated it to a free-standing diagnosis in part because of the recognition that many people with agoraphobia did not experience panic. In those cases where both sets of symptoms occur, both diagnoses (agoraphobia and panic disorder) are now given.

The 12-month prevalence rates for agoraphobia are approximately 1.7% for adolescents and adults, and 0.4% for those older than 65. Childhood onset is rare. Stressful events may

**Dependence**

A persistent pattern of drug use involving either tolerance, withdrawal, or inability to cut down dosage

**Relapse**

Re-occurrence of symptoms after a period of improvement

| *DSM-5* | **Diagnostic Criteria for Agoraphobia** |

300.22 (F40.00) Agoraphobia

A. Marked fear or anxiety about two (or more) of the following five situations:

1. Using public transportation (e.g., automobiles, buses, trains, ships, planes).
2. Being in open spaces (e.g., parking lots, marketplaces, bridges).
3. Being in enclosed places (e.g., shops, theaters, cinemas).
4. Standing in line or being in a crowd.
5. Being outside of the home alone.

B. The individual fears or avoids these situations because of thoughts that escape might be difficult or help might not be available in the event of developing panic-like symptoms or other incapacitating or embarrassing symptoms (e.g., fear of falling in the elderly; fear of incontinence).

C. The agoraphobic situations almost always provoke fear or anxiety.

D. The agoraphobic situations are actively avoided, require the presence of a companion, or are endured with intense fear or anxiety.

E. The fear or anxiety is out of proportion to the actual danger posed by the agoraphobic situations and to the sociocultural context.

F. The fear, anxiety, or avoidance is persistent, typically lasting for 6 months or more.

G. The fear, anxiety, or avoidance causes significant distress or impairment in social, occupational, or other important areas of functioning.

H. If another medical condition (e.g., inflammatory bowel disease, Parkinson's disease) is present, the fear, anxiety, or avoidance is clearly excessive.

I. The fear, anxiety, or avoidance is not better explained by the symptoms of another mental disorder—for example, the symptoms are not confined to specific phobia, situational type; do not involve only social situations (as in social anxiety disorder); and are not related exclusively to obsessions (as in obsessive-compulsive disorder), perceived defects or flaws in physical appearance (as in body dysmorphic disorder), reminders or traumatic events (as in posttraumatic stress disorder), or fear of separation (as in separation anxiety disorder).

**Note:** Agoraphobia is diagnosed irrespective of the presence of panic disorder. If an individual's presentation meets criteria for panic disorder and agoraphobia, both diagnoses should be assigned.

Source: Reprinted with permission from the *Diagnostic and Statistical Manual of Mental Disorders,* Fifth Edition, (Copyright 2013). American Psychiatric Association.

be associated with the onset of agoraphobia, but there is also a relatively strong genetic link to phobias. It is often associated with depression and other anxiety disorders, and is more commonly diagnosed among females than among males, who tend to show higher comorbid rates of substance use (American Psychiatric Association, 2013).

Treatment for agoraphobia has most often been studied in patients with accompanying panic disorder, due to the historical linkage between diagnoses. Promising results have been reported for behavioral and cognitive-behavioral interventions that involve controlled exposure to agoraphobic situations, in an effort to promote habituation of the resulting anxiety. For example, Gloster and his colleagues (2011) employed two variants of exposure-based CBT for agoraphobia in a large sample (N = 369): one in which the exposure was discussed, planned, and experienced (the therapist accompanied the patient into the situation), and the other with similar interventions but without the therapist guiding the exposure. Compared to wait-list controls, both groups showed reduction in agoraphobic avoidance, with the greatest improvement in the therapist-guided group. Additional research has indicated that virtual reality exposure therapy alone may be as effective as exposure with CBT for agoraphobia (Malbos, Rapee, & Kavakli, 2013). Pharmacological treatment for agoraphobia usually involves SSRI antidepressants, with outcomes similar to that of CBT. For example, patients aged 60 and older were randomly assigned to receive either paroxetine (an SSRI), CBT, or a wait list control in a small study (N = 49). Both treatments were effective, although CBT showed somewhat better results for those with later onset of the condition (Hendriks, Keijsers, Kampman, Hoogduin, & Oude Voshaar, 2012).

# 6.2d Specific Phobia

Specific phobia involves intense and persistent fear triggered by specific objects or situations (refer to the diagnostic criteria for specific phobia in Chapter 4). The fear reaction is excessive, resulting either from the presentation or anticipation of the triggering stimulus. The onset of anxiety after exposure to the feared stimulus is usually immediate, includes many panic-like symptoms, and may meet the criteria for a cued panic attack. Because the fear is so distressing, individuals avoid or escape from the feared stimulus, which negatively reinforces the avoidance behavior and maintains the phobic response. Often, individuals with phobias realize that their reactions are excessive or unreasonable, but this realization does not reduce the phobic response, in part because they also overestimate the danger in their feared situations. Although many people have intense fears involving certain stimuli (such as snakes or spiders), specific phobia is not diagnosed unless it lasts at least 6 months and interferes significantly with a person's life or is associated with marked distress.

Phobic anxiety can become associated with a variety of objects or situations. Following are some common examples:

Heights: cliffs, roofs, high windows, ladders

Enclosed places: small rooms, closets, elevators, subways

Open places: halls, wide streets, squares, parks, beaches

Animals: dogs, cats, snakes, horses, spiders

Weapons—guns, knives, axes

Public gatherings: crowds, meetings, churches, theaters, stadiums

Vehicles: airplanes, trains, automobiles, buses

Natural dangers: storms, wind, lightning, darkness

The *DSM-5* provides for including subtype indicators in the diagnosis of specific phobia: Animal Type; Natural Environment Type; Blood-Injection-Injury Type (e.g., fear of blood, mutilation, or medical procedures); Situational Type (e.g., fear of flying, closed spaces, or bridges); and Other Types (such as fear of choking, clowns, or noises). The specific phobia diagnosis appears to be one of the most reliable in the anxiety disorder category; Brown and his colleagues (2001) reported a kappa value of 0.86 when it was the principal *DSM-IV* diagnosis. Its reliability was not assessed in the *DSM-5* field trials, however.

Phobias are relatively common disorders, with lifetime prevalence rates of over 12% of the population (Kessler, Chiu, Demler, Merikangas, & Walters, 2005). Women are diagnosed with phobias twice as often as men. First symptoms of phobias tend to appear in childhood or early adolescence; prevalence declines among the elderly (American Psychiatric Association, 2013). There are many different variations of phobias, as Table 6-2 illustrates. Certain phobias may be more easily acquired at different

Phobic anxiety can become associated with a variety of objects or situations. A common example is heights, such as cliffs, roofs, high windows, and ladders. (iStock)

ages and may involve some differences in fear response patterns. For example, fear of heights and driving phobias appear to be associated with later age of onset, and blood/injection phobias may be more likely to involve fainting, relative to other phobias (Anthony, Brown, & Barlow, 1997).

## Causal Factors

Specific phobias are more common in families in which other members have phobias, and monozygotic twins show higher concordance rates than dizygotic twins (Kendler, Neale, Kessler, Heath, & Eaves, 1992), with both points supporting a modest genetic risk factor. As noted before, differences in HPA activity can have a genetic basis, so it is reasonable to

*Table 6-2*    Some Variations of Specific Phobias

| Name | Object(s) Feared | Name | Object(s) Feared |
|---|---|---|---|
| Acrophobia | High places | Monophobia | Being alone |
| Agoraphobia | Open places | Mysophobia | Contamination |
| Ailurophobia | Cats | Nyctophobia | Darkness |
| Algophobia | Pain | Ocholophobia | Crowds |
| Anthropophobia | Men | Pathophobia | Disease |
| Aquaphobia | Water | Phyrophobia | Fire |
| Astraphobia | Storms, thunder, lightning | Syphilophobia | Syphilis |
| Claustrophobia | Closed places | Thanatophobia | Death |
| Cynophobia | Dogs | Xenophobia | Stangers |
| Hematophobia | Blood | Zoophobia | Animals or a single animal |

Source: Table of "Some Varieties of Phobias" From *Abnormal Psychology: A New Look* by Marshall Duke and Stephen Nowicki, Copyright © 1986 by Marshall Duke and Stephen Nowicki. Reprinted by permission of the authors. From, "Family Study of Agoraphobia," by E. L. Harris, R. Noyes, R. R. Crowe, and D. Charudry, from *General Psychiatry*, 40, pp. 1061–1069

expect some differences in phobic response are heritable. Still, there is wide latitude for environmental effects in the formation of phobias.

The behavioral model has proposed conditioning in the etiology of phobias since Watson's demonstration with Little Albert (see Chapter 3). Essentially, the phobia results through classical conditioning when an object or situation is paired with a traumatic event or a strong sensation of fear. For example, some children are "taught" to swim by parents who throw them into the water so that they learn "naturally." A phobia of deep water might easily develop after such an episode: struggling to keep one's head above water (the US) can produce gasping and intense fear (the UR); because of pairing, any water in which the bottom cannot be seen (CS) comes to elicit terror and a sensation of drowning (CR). Once the phobia is established through Pavlovian conditioning, future exposure to the phobic stimulus produces avoidance behavior, which is then operatively reinforced by the reduction in fear that it produces. This negative reinforcement makes future phobic avoidance more likely, thus maintaining the phobia. This model is often referred to as the **two-factor theory** of phobias (Mowrer, 1950) reflecting the involvement of both Pavlovian and operant influences.

> **How important are specific traumatic experiences in the development of phobias?**

Rachman (1977) criticized the conditioning theory as being incomplete. In early classical conditioning theory, any stimulus (object, sound, odor, and so on) might serve equally well as a CS, as long as it has been paired with the unconditioned stimulus; however, various sources of evidence suggest that this is not the case. For example, if all stimuli can serve equally well as CS, why are human phobias most commonly associated with a rather limited set of stimuli—fear of leaving home, specific animals and insects, heights, the dark, situations related to bodily injury or mutilation, and so on? Only rarely do we have phobias of pajamas, electrical outlets, or hammers; yet all of these can be associated with trauma. Pajamas, for example, are present when young children experience fears of the dark or have nightmares, but children rarely develop a pajama phobia.

Severe storms like Hurricane Sandy, which devastated parts of the United States Eastern Seaboard, can produce phobic reactions. (Shutterstock)

**Two-factor theory**

Theory that both Pavlovian and operant influences maintain phobic behavior

Rachman also pointed out that people may undergo repeated fear-arousing experiences and not develop phobias to surrounding stimuli. Thus, despite repeated exposure to fearsome air raids during World War II, only a very small proportion of adults or children developed phobias as a result. Rachman considered these findings as being supportive of a theory previously proposed by Seligman and Hager (1972) to the effect that humans, as well as other animals, could learn to be fearful of some stimuli more readily than they can of other stimuli. There is an innate **preparedness** to become fearful of certain stimuli because in our evolutionary past these were associated with real dangers—animals, the dark, heights, mutilated bodies. This theory of a preparedness to become fearful of some stimuli and not others may help explain why Bregman (1934) was unable to replicate Watson and Rayner's (1920) demonstration of fear conditioning in Little Albert. Bregman attempted to condition fear in 15 infants but used biologically irrelevant objects such as geometrically shaped wooden blocks and cloth curtains, whereas Watson and Rayner used a furry rat. Bandura (1977) agreed that phobias develop more readily to some stimuli than others but argued that this can be explained by differences in the present nature of the stimuli rather than innate tendencies. Thus snakes and various animals are especially likely to become phobic stimuli because they can appear at unpredictable times and places, show great mobility, and inflict injury despite self-protective efforts.

There is considerable laboratory and real-world evidence that both animal and human subjects can learn emotional reactions, including fear, by observing other subjects model these reactions (Bandura, 1977). For example, several people were treated for anxiety reactions after watching the film *The Exorcist* (Bozzuto, 1975); and monkeys raised in laboratory environments do not initially fear snakes, until observing the fearful response of other monkeys (Mineka, Davidson, Cook, & Keir, 1984). Various cognitive processes may also play a role in the learning and maintenance of fear. A child's interpretation of events or expectation about what is going to happen can be important in this respect. The child who hears parents, siblings, or others warn of certain dangers can begin to tell himself about these same anxiety-arousing situations. The child's potential for imaginative elaboration can multiply and maintain the stimuli.

Certainly, large individual differences would be expected in the phobic responses of people exposed to (or observing) particular traumatic events, as well as variations in prior familiarity with the stimulus, history of uncontrollable events, and prior coping experiences. These facts, as well as the issues raised by Rachman and Seligman, have been incorporated into a comprehensive contemporary learning model by Mineka and her colleagues (e.g., Mineka & Sutton, 2006; Minek & Zinbarg, 2006), which combines early learning experiences, **vicarious conditioning**, contextual variables, genetic/temperamental influences, and basic learning principles to account for the development and maintenance of phobias. It arguably remains the most validated and plausible perspective on the etiology of phobias at this time.

The psychodynamic model is illustrated by Freud's analysis of Little Hans, described in Chapter 3. Recall that Hans had developed an animal phobia (of horses), which Freud interpreted as displaced fear of Hans' father, related to an Oedipal castration anxiety. More generally, the psychoanalytic theory of phobia formation would emphasize some initial repression of an anxiety-arousing conflict, the projection of the conflict onto the external world (Little Hans, for example, was said to have projected his wish to attack his father, and thus he believed his father wished to attack him), and then *displacement* of the anxiety onto some other target (horses, in the case of Hans).

## Treatments for Specific Phobias

From the biological perspective, acute fear reactions can be moderated with medications such as benzodiazepines, which act more rapidly than the SSRIs or other antidepressants. However, in the case of specific phobia, no pharmacological intervention has been shown to be effective (Roy-Burne & Cowley, 2002).

**Preparedness**

Biologically-based tendency to form associations between certain stimuli more readily than others

**Vicarious conditioning**

Conditioning based on observing the responses of other people

Nearly all empirically supported therapies for specific phobia involve exposure to the feared stimulus, as initially demonstrated by Mary Cover Jones with Little Peter (1924) and subsequently developed into systematic desensitization by Wolpe (1985; 1973). The many variations of exposure therapy for phobias involve extended exposure, either in vivo or in imagination, with the goal of reducing the fear response through extinction. Systematic desensitization involves maintaining a relaxed state while increasingly fear-provoking phobic stimuli are gradually presented. Participant modeling, in which the therapist first models a calm, non-phobic interaction with the feared stimulus, has been effective as well. Overall, the professional literature provides the strongest empirical support for therapies involving actual rather than imagined exposure, and a consensus has developed that **in vivo exposure** is the treatment of choice for specific phobias (Barlow, Raffa, & Cohen, 2002).

## 6.2e Social Anxiety Disorder (Social Phobia)

Social anxiety disorder (also called social phobia) is similar to specific phobia except that the symptoms are connected to situations in which the person is exposed to unfamiliar people or to the scrutiny of others, and fears acting in a way that might prove embarrassing or humiliating. For example, sufferers may fear appearing stupid, incompetent, or weak, or that others in the social setting will notice their trembling hands during eating or writing or their quivering voice. Exposure to these situations almost immediately triggers distressing fear symptoms, which at times may escalate into panic attacks. As a result, the person tends if possible to avoid social or performance situations to the extent that the phobia interferes with normal daily life. People with social phobia may experience fear far in advance (perhaps every day for several weeks) of an anticipated social activity.

Nearly everyone has felt some anxiety about or embarrassment in some social situations, and these occurrences do not warrant the diagnosis. For example, students may find themselves unprepared for a question from the teacher, and most people unaccustomed to public speaking would be anxious anticipating delivering an address to a large group of people. Social anxiety disorder involves shyness and social anxiety that is severe enough to interfere with normal life in terms of occupational, academic, or interpersonal functioning for at least 6 months. The diagnosis can be sub-typed as "performance only" if the fear is limited to performing or speaking in public.

Incidence estimates vary widely, but the National Comorbidity Survey Replication suggested a 12.1% lifetime prevalence (Kessler, Chiu, Demler, Merikangas, & Walters, 2005) of social phobia, making it one of the most common anxiety disorders, along with specific phobia. The *DSM-5* gives the 12-month prevalence rate at 7% in the U.S., noting much lower prevalence (0.5% to 2.3%) in the rest of the world. Age of onset for the disorder is between 8 and 15 years in 75% of cases (American Psychiatric Association, 2013). Although it is more commonly diagnosed among women, men are represented equally in treatment settings (American Psychological Association, 2000), suggesting they may be more likely to seek treatment for the condition.

As a result of suffering from social anxiety disorder (social phobia), the person tends if possible to avoid social or performance situations to the extent that the phobia interferes with normal daily life. (iStock)

### Causal Factors

As in the other anxiety disorders, social anxiety disorder runs in families, supporting a modest genetic factor: first degree relatives of sufferers have 2–6 times greater risk of developing the condition (American Psychiatric Association, 2013). Some neuro-imaging data suggests that the amygdala responds differently to novel faces rather than to familiar faces in people with social phobia (Cottraux, 2005), although that may be an effect rather than a cause of the disorder.

**In vivo exposure**

Exposure to the actual feared stimulus, rather than an imagined or symbolic stimulus

Learning models assume social phobia develops in similar ways as other phobias, involving a conditioned association between social cues and unpleasant or embarrassing events or social defeats. In retrospective studies, most social phobics recall such conditioning experiences as relevant to the beginning of their symptoms (Ost & Hugdahl, 1981) although retrospective recall may not be a reliable source of information. According to the *DSM-5*, there is no information that establishes any causal relation between social anxiety disorder and childhood maltreatment or other childhood adversity (American Psychiatric Association, 2013). Psychodynamic models tend to emphasize internal conflicts that produce anxiety (as in the other phobias) as the probable cause of social phobia.

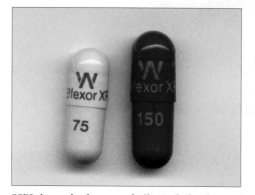

SSRIs have also been used effectively for short-term relief for social anxiety (Roy-Burne and Cowley, 2002). Recent work supports the SNRI venlafaxine (Effexor). (Wikimedia Commons)

## Treatments for Social Phobias

Pharmacologically, benzodiazepines appear to be effective in short-term relief for social anxiety (Davidson, 2004). SSRIs have also been used effectively (Roy-Burne & Cowley, 2002). Recent work supports the SNRI venlafaxine (Effexor) and the anticonvulsant drug pregabalin as promising although long-term studies are still needed (Cottraux, 2005).

Cognitive-behavioral therapies have also been effective in treating social phobia. These techniques typically involve systematic exposure to feared social situations, often combined with relaxation training or desensitization. Newer CBT applications, including virtual reality technologies that provide computer-generated scenarios of public speaking situations, also appear promising for treating social anxiety (Cottraux, 2005), as well as for other anxiety disorders.

## 6.2f  Generalized Anxiety Disorder

Generalized anxiety disorder (GAD) is characterized by a nearly constant state of worry and apprehension about a wide variety of events or activities, on most days, over a 6-month period. Several symptoms of autonomic arousal are present, including disturbed sleep and concentration, muscle tension, irritability, and fatigue, to the extent that they interfere with daily life. Although people with GAD find their worries difficult to control, distressing, and physically troublesome, they do not progress into panic attacks.

People with GAD seem to be always "on edge" and worry about minor events as often as major ones. Children may worry about school, deadlines, or world events—often requiring reassurance about their performance. Adults may worry excessively about finances, health, work, and household duties. Major events, such as nuclear war or other possible catastrophes, are sources of elevated concern as well. Rarely are there periods in which all worry is absent. Comorbidity of GAD with additional diagnoses, such as depression and other anxiety disorders (including panic disorder), is fairly common. GAD is diagnosed among females twice as often as men, and 12-month prevalence is around 2.9% in U.S. adults (American Psychiatric Association, 2013). As noted earlier, the *DSM-5* diagnosis is not very reliable, with a kappa of 0.20, falling in the "questionable" range (Regier, et al., 2012).

### Causal Factors

Biological involvement in generalized anxiety includes several brain pathways that are also active in other anxiety disorders, including the amygdala, the limbic system, and the prefrontal cortex. It is assumed that inhibition of these pathways, mediated by the neurotransmitter GABA, is deficient in GAD sufferers, although there is some indication of serotonin involvement as well. Genetic evidence is mixed; its modest heritability (accounting for about one-third of the risk) may be somewhat smaller than that for other anxiety disorders (American Psychiatric Association, 2013). Overlap of symptoms with mood disorders, and some indications of common biological/genetic involvement between GAD and mood disorders, may indicate that these are related rather than independent clusters of disorders (Tyrer & Baldwin, 2006).

A cognitive-behavioral model of GAD would be similar to that for panic disorder: interoceptive and exteroceptive stimuli become predictive of worry and apprehension, to the point that widespread anxiety occurs as a conditioned response. This would be most likely to occur in people who have a history of uncontrollable and unpredictable events and who would also be less likely to identify periods of safety from threat, resulting in hypervigilance. This would also result in a cognitive tendency to over-appraise and attend to threatening interoceptive and exteroceptive cues, and such an interpretive bias can increase vulnerability to anxiety disorders (Wilson, MacLeod, Mathews, & Rutherford, 2006). In psychodynamic terms, anxiety is created by unconscious conflict, which overwhelms the ego defenses with unacceptable impulses and produces a widespread overt anxiety reaction.

### Treatments for Generalized Anxiety Disorder

Interventions, both medical and psychological, can be helpful for GAD but rarely result in total symptom remission (Tyrer & Baldwin, 2006). Effective medications include GABA stimulants such as the benzodiazepines and buspirone (which has little dependence or abuse potential) for short-term treatments. Antidepressants, especially the SSRIs, may be more helpful both in the longer term and with concomitant depression (Davidson, 2004; Gorman, 2003).

Psychotherapy for GAD can be helpful as well, and appears to be at least as effective as pharmacological treatment. Reviews of the effectiveness of various treatments in controlled clinical trials report that active therapies are superior to nondirective therapies, without clear superiority for any one (Barlow, Raffa, & Cohen, 2002). In a treatment comparison between

> **Which treatments are effective for anxiety disorders?**

cognitive behavioral therapy and a benzodiazepine (diazepam), CBT produced better results 6 months after therapy, while diazepam was no more effective than placebo (Power, Simpson, Swanson, & Wallace, 1990). Some literature reviews (e.g., Westin & Morrison, 2001) found that while CBT is helpful in the short-term for GAD, evidence of sustained improvement is lacking; and, overall, CBT is less effective for GAD than for panic disorder. On the other hand, Borkovec and Ruscio (2001) reviewed 13 well-controlled studies and concluded that CBT is consistently shown to be clinically effective for both anxiety and depression, with low dropout rates and long-term maintenance of improvement.

## 6.2g  Separation Anxiety Disorder

In separation anxiety disorder, a person experiences developmentally inappropriate and excessive fear or anxiety associated with separation from home or from primary caregivers. The distress may include anxiety about getting lost or losing connection to the attachment figure, concern that the attachment figure may be harmed, or fear of being taken away or kidnapped. Associated with these fears, the person with separation anxiety disorder may experience nightmares or physical symptoms and may refuse to attend school or other activities requiring absence from home or the attachment figure. The person may refuse or resist sleeping unless the attachment figure is nearby. The disturbance must last at least 4 weeks in children, and 6 months or more in adults.

Children with this disorder often come from close-knit families. They may fear specific objects or animals that could pose danger of harm, or events such as travel that may result in separation. Anxiety disorders commonly co-occur, and the condition may precede the onset of panic disorder with agoraphobia. Prevalence may be 4% of children, and it appears to be more common among females (American Psychiatric Association, 2013).

Separation anxiety disorder is a strong predictor of subsequent mental disorders, especially panic disorder and major depressive disorder (Lewinsohn, Holm-Denoma, Small, Seeley, & Joiner, 2008). Cognitive-behavioral therapy appears to be effective for separation anxiety disorder in children (Chambless, et al., 1998), and CBT with or without added family therapy was associated with long-term improvement more than 6 years after therapy (Barrett, Duffy, Dadds, & Rapee, 2001).

## 6.2h Selective Mutism

**BVT** *Lab*

Visit www.BVTLab.com to explore the student resources available for this chapter.

The central component of selective mutism is persistent failure to speak in situations where speaking is expected, such as social and school settings. The individual does speak in other situations, however. Because a person may be shy in new situations, the diagnosis is not based on the first month in a new school or other social setting. After the first month, selective mutism can be diagnosed if the failure to speak persists 1 month and is not due to lack of knowledge about the language, comfort with the spoken language, embarrassment about speaking connected to a communication disorder such as stuttering, or a pervasive developmental disorder or psychotic disorder. Sometimes, children with selective mutism will communicate through hand signals or gestures. Onset is usually before age 5, and more females than males are affected. The causes are unknown, although there is some overlap with social anxiety disorder. The incidence is less than 1% of the population (American Psychiatric Association, 2013).

Some have approached the treatment of selective mutism similar to anxiety disorders; case reports suggest antidepressants may be useful. A review of the treatment literature by Pionek, Stone, Kratochwill, Sladezcek, and Serlin (2002) concluded that behavioral interventions including reinforcement, shaping and stimulus control of speech, perhaps combined with modeling, appear to be the treatments of choice for the condition.

## 6.2i Other Anxiety Disorders

Anxiety disorder symptoms may also stem from general medical conditions, such as cardiovascular, respiratory, or neurological conditions, or as a result of substance use. The *DSM-5* provides diagnostic categories for these conditions when they cause significant distress or impairment in important areas of functioning:

*Substance/medication-induced anxiety disorder* involves panic attacks or anxiety, developing soon after intoxication, withdrawal, or exposure to a substance that is capable of producing the anxiety. A variety of substances can provoke anxiety or panic, including alcohol, caffeine, cannabis, cocaine, amphetamines, opioids, inhalants, and hallucinogens. The diagnosis can be coded for each and the anxiety onset specified as during intoxication, withdrawal, or after medication use. Other possible sources of the anxiety (such as an independent anxiety disorder, or a delirium) must be ruled out as well.

*Anxiety disorder* due to another medical condition involves panic or anxiety that can be traced to the direct pathophysiological consequence of another medical condition such as hyperthyroidism, arthritis, congestive heart failure, hypertension, or asthma. Other potential sources of anxiety, including other mental disorders, must be ruled out as well.

*Other specified anxiety disorder* applies to conditions of anxiety and fear that do not meet the full criteria for another anxiety disorder. For example, an individual may experience panic attacks but with fewer than four panic symptoms, or experience generalized anxiety less than 4 days per week. Finally, the remaining presentations of significant anxiety or fear that are not covered by any other category may be labeled as *unspecified anxiety disorder*.

## 6.3 Obsessive-Compulsive and Related Disorders

**Obsessions**

Intrusive thoughts that are difficult to stop or control

**Compulsions**

Actions that one feels compelled to perform

**Obsessions** are thoughts that intrude repeatedly into awareness and are experienced as irrational, unwanted, and difficult to control or stop. **Compulsions** are actions that one is compelled to perform; they are also experienced as irrational and difficult to control. Mild forms of obsessive-compulsive experience—like mild forms of phobic reactions—are not uncommon in normal individuals. The song that intrudes recurrently into the moment or a compulsion to return home to make sure that the door is locked or the stove turned off are all common examples.

**What are obsessions and compulsions?**

There can be preoccupations with certain objects or activities within many different mental disorders, as we shall see. Those basic commonalities led some researchers (e.g., Hollander & Wong, 1995) to propose that a concept of an *obsessive-compulsive spectrum* could include conditions as apparently diverse as pathological gambling, tic disorders, antisocial personality, and autism. The *DSM-5* restructured the classification of obsessive-compulsive disorder, which had been under the anxiety disorder category in both the *DSM-III* and *DSM-IV*, into a new category, the obsessive-compulsive and related disorders (see Table 6-3). Although many different types of obsessions and compulsions can be included in the spectrum, the *DSM-5* excludes certain apparently obsessive-compulsive activities that occur as part of other disorders. For example, an alcohol-dependent person may experience urges and obsessions about drinking and may appear to drink compulsively, but that pre-occupation is already accounted for within a substance use diagnosis. Similarly, those obsessions or compulsions associated with eating disorders, impulse control disorders, certain sexual disorders, or depressed persons with obsessive guilt would be excluded from the current spectrum. On this point, the *DSM-5* distinguishes between the compulsive activities of obsessive-compulsive and related disorders and those of substance dependence (for example) on the basis that the latter individuals derive pleasure from the activity, while those with obsessive-compulsive conditions do not. The diagnoses in this category can be used with specifiers—such as "with poor insight," "absent insight/delusional beliefs," and "tic-related"—to allow for more specificity in their use.

## 6.3a  Obsessive-Compulsive Disorder

In obsessive-compulsive disorder (OCD), obsessions and compulsions reach a handicapping degree of severity, occupying a significant amount of time and interfering

As the obsessions continue to generate increasing anxiety, the person often engages in compulsive acts to neutralize the obsession and reduce anxiety; for example, washing, cleaning excessive orderliness and neatness. (Shutterstock)

**Table 6-3**  DSM-5 Obsessive-Compulsive and Related Disorders

| Disorder | Key Symptoms | Minimum Duration Required for Diagnosis | Sex Ratio |
|---|---|---|---|
| Obsessive-compulsive disorder | Recurrent obsessions or compulsions that cause distress | None | Slightly more common in females |
| Body dysmorphic disorder | Preoccupation with imagined or minor physical defect in appearance | None | Slightly more common in females |
| Hoarding disorder | Persistent difficulty discarding possessions, resulting in excessive clutter | None | More common in males |
| Trichotillomania (hair-pulling) disorder | Recurrent pulling out of hair | None | More common in females |
| Excoriation (skin-picking) disorder | Recurrent picking of skin | None | More common in females |

Source: Reprinted with permission from the *Diagnostic and Statistical Manual of Mental Disorders*, Fifth Edition, (Copyright 2013). American Psychiatric Association.

with normal social, occupational, or academic activities (see *DSM-5* Diagnostic Criteria for Obsessive-Compulsive Disorder). Unwanted, distressing obsessions and thoughts, sometimes aggressive or sexual in nature, may alternate with thoughts or actions that counteract or inhibit them. The most common sorts of obsessions involve thoughts about contamination or repeated doubts, such as whether a necessary act has been performed; "forbidden" urges such as the idea of stabbing, choking, poisoning, shooting, or otherwise injuring one's child, parent, spouse, sibling, or oneself; the idea of shouting obscene words at home, work, or church; the wish that someone were dead; the thought or image of a forbidden sexual adventure, perhaps involving "perverted" sex acts; the thought of committing suicide by jumping out of a window or into the path of a truck; and the thought of contracting some disease from touching doorknobs, banisters, toilets, or other objects in public places.

| DSM-5 | Diagnostic Criteria for Obsessive-Compulsive Disorder |
|---|---|

300.3 (F42) Obsessive-Compulsive Disorder

A. Presence of obsessions, compulsions, or both:

Obsessions are defined by (1) and (2):

1. Recurrent and persistent thoughts, urges, or images that are experienced, at some time during the disturbance, as intrusive and unwanted, and that in most individuals cause marked anxiety or distress.

2. The individual attempts to ignore or suppress such thoughts, urges, or images, or to neutralize them with some other thought or action (i.e., by performing a compulsion).

Compulsions are defined by (1) and (2):

1. Repetitive behaviors (e.g., hand washing, ordering, checking) or mental acts (e.g., praying, counting, repeating words silently) that the individual feels driven to perform in response to an obsession or according to rules that must be applied rigidly.

2. The behaviors or mental acts are aimed at preventing or reducing anxiety or distress, or preventing some dreaded event or situation; however, these behaviors or mental acts are not connected in a realistic way with what they are designed to neutralize or prevent, or are clearly excessive.

**Note:** Young children may not be able to articulate the aims of these behaviors or mental acts.

B. The obsessions or compulsions are time-consuming (e.g., take more than 1 hour per day) or cause clinically significant distress or impairment in social, occupational, or other important areas of functioning.

C. The obsessive-compulsive symptoms are not attributable to the physiological effects of a substance (e.g., a drug of abuse or medication) or another medical condition.

D. The disturbance is not better explained by the symptoms of another mental disorder (e.g., excessive worries, as in generalized anxiety disorder; preoccupation with appearance, as in body dysmorphic disorder; difficulty discarding or parting with possessions, as in hoarding disorder; hair pulling, as in trichotillomania [hair-pulling] disorder; skin picking, as in excoriation disorder [skin-picking] disorder; stereotypies, as in stereotypic movement disorder; ritualized eating behavior, as in eating disorders; preoccupation with substances or gambling, as in substance-related and addictive disorders; preoccupation with having an illness, as in illness anxiety disorder; sexual urges or fantasies, as in paraphilic disorders; impulses, as in disruptive, impulse-control, and conduct disorders; guilty ruminations, as in major depressive disorder; thought insertion or delusional preoccupations, as in schizophrenia spectrum disorders; or repetitive patterns of behavior, as in autism spectrum disorder).

Specify if:

With good or fair insight: The individual recognizes that obsessive-compulsive disorder beliefs are definitely or probably not true or that they may or may not be true.

With poor insight: The individual thinks that obsessive-compulsive disorder beliefs are probably true.

With absent insight/delusional beliefs: The individual is completely convinced that obsessive-compulsive beliefs are true.

Specify if:

Tic-related: The individual has a current or past history of tic disorder.

At first the individual with obsessions usually attempts to ignore or suppress them. As the obsessions continue to generate increasing anxiety, the person often engages in compulsive acts to neutralize the obsession and reduce anxiety. Examples of thoughts or actions designed to counteract forbidden or distressing thoughts are almost any kind of ritual—such as washing or cleaning, counting to oneself, memorizing license plate numbers, reciting certain words or phrases to oneself, or more elaborate verbal rituals that have a scientific, philosophical, or religious basis; excessive politeness; excessive orderliness and neatness; and inordinate attempts to schedule one's activities on a precise timetable.

The obsessions and compulsions are time-consuming, occupying at least 1 hour per day or frequently much longer periods. Individuals may become incapacitated by endless compulsive rituals and the immobilization associated with obsessive indecision and doubting. Sufferers differ in the degree to which they are aware that the obsessions or compulsions are excessive or unreasonable; those who recognize that their obsessive-compulsive beliefs are not true receive the specification "with good insight." About 30% of those with OCD also have a tic disorder (American Psychiatric Association, 2013).

Obsessive-compulsive disorder may have a lifetime prevalence of about 2.5% of the population (12-month prevalence in the U.S. is 1.2%); the rate is slightly higher for females in adult onset, while childhood onset is perhaps more common among boys than girls. Onset is usually gradual with earlier appearance of symptoms in males. If untreated, the disorder usually follows a chronic course with symptoms worsening during periods of stress (American Psychiatric Association, 2013).

## Causal Factors

As with the other anxiety disorders, twin studies and familial patterns suggest a moderate genetic contribution to OCD. Some brain studies utilizing PET scans have reported higher levels of activity in the orbital frontal cortex of the left hemisphere for those with OCD as compared to normals (e.g., Blier, Szabo, Haddjeri, & Dong, 2000). Whether this increased activity is a possible cause of, or a result of, OCD is not yet clear. The risk of OCD is also increased in children who have been subject to traumatic events, including physical and sexual abuse (American Psychiatric Association, 2013).

Behavioral models tend to employ versions of two-factor theory in the analysis of obsessive-compulsive behavior—which according to Williams (2001) "follows the pattern predicted by two factor theory in remarkable detail" (p. 362). In the case of a hand-washing compulsion, for example, it is assumed that stimuli that trigger obsession gained their anxiety-provoking power though a pairing with strong emotions of fear or anxiety in an individual's learning history. Subsequent exposure to an anxiety-producing conditioned stimulus (such as a medical scene or a newspaper article on disease) generates anxiety that persists until it is relieved by giving in to the compulsion to wash the hands. The compulsive act is, thereby, negatively reinforced and strengthened.

In psychoanalytic terminology, obsessive persons may be said to use several defense mechanisms. They *isolate* feelings from intellectual content so that their obsessive thoughts and endless verbosity become detached from their emotional roots; an over-intellectualized pattern of life results. Reaction formations are likewise common. For example, obsessive concern with cleanliness may be a defense against underlying urges to be dirty or sexy (sex may be perceived as dirty or aggressive). Thus compulsive orderliness protects the person from the fear of unleashed aggression, of smashing everything in sight; excessive politeness and formality protect from urges to be cruel and sadistic. *Undoing* refers to many features of compulsive

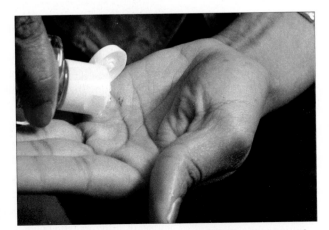

According to psychoanalytic theory compulsive concerns with cleanliness and orderliness represent reaction formations against anal impulses to be dirty and smelly. (iStock)

rituals in which the person attempts to "undo" the harm, real or imagined, that could result from an unacceptable impulse. Engaging in a certain mannerism (such as blinking the eyes, or touching or straightening an object) helps the person to feel that the dangerous impulse is canceled out. Reaction formations are similar to undoing except that they are expressed in broad personality styles rather than in highly specific rituals. From a psychosexual developmental point of view, the obsessive-compulsive person has regressed, in the face of an intense Oedipal conflict, to the anal stage. Compulsive concerns with cleanliness and orderliness represent reaction formations against anal impulses to be dirty and smelly, while compulsive tendencies to inhibit emotion or to be formal or excessively good reflect reaction formations against anal-sadistic impulses, originating in the child's defiance of parental efforts to force compliance with toilet training.

## Treatments for Obsessive-Compulsive Disorder

The most common medical treatment for OCD involves antidepressant medications, especially the SSRIs, some of which are effective in substantially reducing OCD symptoms (Abramowitz, 1997; Dougherty, Rauch, & Jenike, 2002). In particularly unresponsive cases, a form of psychosurgery—a **cingulotomy**, in which a small bundle of nerve fibers connecting the anterior cingulate cortex to the frontal lobes are severed—has produced improvement in some cases, including 8 of 17 patients treated by Jung and his colleagues (2006).

> How effective are treatments for obsessive-compulsive and related disorders?

Psychodynamic therapists have employed interpersonal group therapies (Wells, Glickauf-Hughes, & Buzzell, 1990) as well as individual therapies with mixed results. However, the treatment of choice among psychotherapies is **exposure and response prevention (ERP)**, which is the most effective intervention, producing substantial clinical improvement (Abramowitz, Foa, & Franklin, 2003). ERP requires prolonged and repeated exposure to the obsession, while the compulsive act is prevented. For example, Piacentini and Langley (2004) describe the treatment of a 12-year-old boy obsessed with germs and contamination and compelled to frequently wash his hands. The ERP component of treatment required him to touch trashcans, doorknobs, and public tables, and to play basketball without washing his hands for increasing periods of time. Other components of the program involved education about OCD and cognitive restructuring, common in many CBT approaches to OCD. CBT is effective for OCD whether or not medication is added (Franklin, Abramowitz, Bux, Zoellner, & Feeney, 2002), although ERP is effective with or without CBT added. In one comparison study, both treatments produced significant improvement, but ERP showed stronger effects 3 months after treatment ended (McLean, et al., 2001).

**Cingulotomy**

Psychosurgical technique that severs fibers connecting the anterior cingulate cortex to the frontal lobes

**Exposure and response prevention (ERP)**

Prolonged exposure to fear- or anxiety-producing stimulus or situation while escape, or the compulsive act, is prevented

## 6.3b Body Dysmorphic Disorder

People with body dysmorphic disorder (BDD) are preoccupied with what they consider a defect in their appearance, and they engage in repetitive acts or thoughts related to this preoccupation. The defect is either imaginary or so slight that the preoccupation is clearly excessive. The preoccupation causes significant distress or impairment in normal functioning, and it is not better accounted for by another disorder (for example, anorexia nervosa). Frequently, the preoccupations in BDD involve wrinkles, complexion, facial proportions, the size or shape of lips, nose, eyebrows, cheeks, or ears, or thinning hair—areas of the head and face. However, the disorder can involve any area of the body, showing as excessive concern over the size or shape of hands, feet, buttocks, breasts, genitals, body size, or overall build. A specifier "with muscle dysmorphia" has been added in the *DSM-5* to capture a particular subset of sufferers who believe that their body build is too small or insufficiently muscular.

People with BDD can spend several hours each day checking the imagined defect or finding ways to cover up or hide it. They may alternate between almost constantly looking into mirrors and avoiding them altogether due to the distress associated with viewing themselves. Their concern may lead them to isolate themselves from others or to avoid job interviews, meetings, classes, or dating. Depression, obsessive-compulsive disorder, and social phobia may co-occur, and suicidal ideation may be present. Not uncommonly, sufferers seek surgery or medical intervention, and may even resort to self-surgery, although these interventions do not reduce the concern and may make the problem worse (American Psychiatric Association, 2013).

Based on a recent survey of U.S. households, the point prevalence of body dysmorphic disorder was estimated at 2.4% of the adult population (Koran, Abujaoude, Large, & Serpe, 2008). The prevalence may be higher in mental health settings and up to 15% of patients in dermatological settings. It appears to be equally likely in males and females, begins by adolescence, and tends to have a chronic course. Muscle dysmorphia occurs almost exclusively in males; females are more likely to have co-morbid eating disorders (American Psychiatric Association, 2013).

People with body dysmorphic disorder may spend several hours per day checking for imagined defects. (Shutterstock)

## Causal Factors

Comorbidity with certain other disorders, notably obsessive-compulsive disorder, might suggest a common causal component; there is higher prevalence of body dysmorphic disorder in those who have first-degree relatives with OCD. Childhood neglect and abuse are also risk factors for the condition (American Psychiatric Association, 2013). The current social and cultural emphasis on physical appearance likely plays a role in its development. Neziroglu, Roberts, and Yaryura-Tobias (2004) proposed a behavior model of BDD that suggests children might receive greater attention and reinforcement for their appearance than their behavior.

## Treatments for Body Dysmorphic Disorder

Reportedly, some BDD patients respond well to serotonin reuptake inhibitor medications (Fallon, 2004). Several recent studies have demonstrated that SSRIs work better than other pharmacological interventions for BDD, especially at higher doses and longer intervals of treatment (e.g., Hadley, Kim, Priday, & Hollander, 2006). Typical cognitive-behavioral techniques employ education, relaxation, and systematic desensitization involving graduated exposure to the parts of the body that evoke distress. Response prevention to avoid checking may be included, combined with attention training (to redirect self-observation), self-monitoring, cognitive challenging of automatic dysfunctional thinking, and developing alternative views about personal appearance. These CBT techniques have been shown effective in randomized controlled studies (Looper & Kirmayer, 2002). In fact, CBT may be as effective on BDD as it is on OCD (Cororve & Gleaves, 2001). Currently, both SSRIs and CBT are considered "first-line" treatments for body dysmorphic disorder (Phillips & Hollander, 2008), although one meta-analysis comparing their relative effectiveness concluded that CBT was more useful (Williams, Hadjistavropoulos, & Sharpe, 2006).

# 6.3c Hoarding Disorder

Hoarding was listed among symptoms of OCD and obsessive-compulsive personality disorder in the *DSM-IV*, but received independent status as a standing diagnosis in the *DSM-5*. Historically, it was seen as a dimension of personality and received little professional attention until 1996, when studies examining the condition began to appear more frequently (Mataix-Cols, et al., 2010). Recently, its prevalence in the population was estimated at 5.8%

(Timpano, et al., 2011). Compulsive hoarders collect items that they are later unable to discard. In fact, they have persistent difficulty in parting with personal possessions regardless of their actual value. A review of 20 cases determined that magazines, newspapers, old clothes, junk mail, notes or lists, and old receipts were the most commonly hoarded items, motivated primarily by the fear of discarding something that may be useful now or in the future (Winsberg, Cassic, & Koran, 1999). The hoarding causes clinically significant distress or impairment, and compromises living areas (which are typically cluttered and congested unless someone else intervenes). In addition to insight specifiers, the diagnosis can be specified "with excessive acquisition" when items continue to be collected beyond available space to store them. Hoarding disorder is 3 times more prevalent in older adults than younger adults, showing increasing severity with each decade of life. It tends to run in families: 50% of hoarders have a relative who also hoards (American Psychiatric Association, 2013).

There is little information on pharmacotherapy for hoarding. A multi-component cognitive-behavioral intervention, utilizing a version of ERP (that is, gradually exposing hoarders to discarding and non-acquiring situations), together with training in organizing and decision-making skills and cognitive therapy for dysfunctional beliefs, was effective in a controlled trial of 23 hoarders, compared to the same number of waitlisted subjects (Steketee, Frost, Tolin, Rasmussen, & Brown, 2010). After 26 sessions, the majority of both patients (80%) and therapists (70%) rated the condition as "improved."

## 6.3d  Trichotillomania (Hair-Pulling Disorder)

People with trichotillomania pull out their hair and show noticeable hair loss as a result. Episodes of hair pulling—which can be centered on any area of the body but most often episodes involve the scalp, eyebrows, or eyelashes—occur in bouts that may be brief or may extend for hours. The likelihood of hair pulling often is higher when an individual is under stress, but also occurs in circumstances when the person is relaxed or distracted, such as watching television. Increasing tension (or urge to resist) precedes the act, which itself is associated with pleasure, gratification, or relief. To qualify for the diagnosis, trichotillomania must cause significant distress or impairment and not be associated with a medical condition, such as skin inflammation or another mental disorder that would better account for the activity.

Hair loss is widely variable across cases, ranging from thinning to areas of baldness. Individuals often deny their hair pulling and attempt to hide the effects; they may avoid social situations due to embarrassment. The condition is associated with mood disorders, anxiety disorders, and various obsessive-compulsive spectrum conditions, as well as personality disorders and intellectual disability. In adults, it is much more likely to be diagnosed in females. Twelve-month prevalence estimates in the U.S. are 1%–2%, with females showing a ratio of 10:1 over males. The course is variable and the condition may come and go, remit, or persist into adulthood. (American Psychiatric Association, 2013).

### Causal Factors

The causes of trichotillomania are not well understood. It appears to aggregate in families, and some preliminary data indicate multiple-gene involvement (Chamberlain, Menzies, Sahakian, & Fineberg, 2007). Its similarity to obsessive-compulsive disorder may suggest similar casual factors, but it may differ from that condition in several ways as well, especially in the absence of obsessions.

### Treatments for Trichotillomania

Although some reviewers (e.g., Grant, Odlaung, & Potenza, 2007) conclude that no medication has been shown to be consistently effective in treatment, others (e.g., Bloch, et al., 2007; Chamberlain, Menzies, Sahakian, & Fineberg, 2007) report that clomipramine, a tricyclic antidepressant, is more effective than placebo in reducing symptoms. However, SSRI antidepressants do not appear to be helpful; fluoxetine (Prozac) does not differ from placebo. The most effective treatment for trichotillomania appears to be **habit reversal therapy (HRT)**, a behavioral intervention that combines self-monitoring of hair pulling, training in awareness of high-risk situations that trigger hair pulling, stimulus control techniques to interfere with or prevent hair pulling, and alternate response interventions to require engagement in a substitute or incompatible activity when the temptation or urge to pull is present. The competing or incompatible response may include ( for example) clenching a fist for 1 minute. Several reviews of treatment outcome in controlled studies have shown HRT to be superior to clomipramine, SSRIs, and placebo in reducing hair pulling and maintenance of gains during follow-up (Bloch, et al., 2007; Chamberlain, Menzies, Sahakian, & Fineberg, 2007; Dell'Osso, Altamura, Allen, Marazziti, & Hollander, 2006).

# 6.3e  Excoriation (Skin-Picking) Disorder

People with excoriation (skin-picking) disorder recurrently pick at their skin, causing bleeding, scarring, and infections. The condition tends to first appear in adolescence, often in association with acne; and although it can occur anywhere on the body, it most commonly involves the head and face. Significant amounts of time, sometimes several hours per day, are spent in the activity, in spite of repeated attempt to decrease or stop skin picking. Sufferers experience embarrassment and shame as a result of the picking, and the condition is commonly associated with co-morbid anxiety and depression; its incidence may be as high as 5% in clinical samples (Stein, et al., 2010). Among the general population, the lifetime prevalence in adults is 1.4%, with females showing a 3:1 ratio in prevalence over males. Excoriation disorder tends to run in families and is more common in those with OCD (American Psychiatric Association, 2013).

## *Treatments for Skin-Picking Disorder*

There have been few studies of interventions for skin picking. Some have indicated that SSRI medications may provide a degree of relief (Bloch, Elliott, Thompson, & Koran, 2001), although other case studies have not found medication to be very useful (Christensen, 2004). Because of its similarity to trichotillomania, interventions based on competing response training or HRT have been employed in behavioral therapies. For example, Lane, Thompson, Reske, Gable, and Barton-Arwood (2006) found that occupying the hands with maleable balls of different textures was effective in reducing skin picking in a 9-year-old boy with co-morbid ADHD and learning disability.

# 6.3f  Other Obsessive-Compulsive Related Disorders

*Substance/medication-induced obsessive-compulsive and related disorder* can involve obsessions, compulsions, skin picking, hair pulling, or other repetitive body-focused behaviors that result from intoxication, withdrawal, or exposure to a medication. Most often these are associated with amphetamine or cocaine use, although other substances may be capable of producing the symptoms as well. There are only limited data about the condition, which appears to be very rare in the general population (American Psychiatric Association, 2013).

*Obsessive-compulsive and related disorder due to another medical condition* involves obsessive-compulsive symptoms that can be etiologically related to the presence of another medical condition such as cerebral infarction. Its course usually follows that of the associated condition. *Other specified obsessive-compulsive and related disorder* includes conditions which do not meet the full criteria for the disorders described earlier, such as body dysmorphic disorder symptoms in a person with actual physical flaws, or without repetitive behaviors in response to concerns about appearance. Finally, additional conditions, including those without sufficient information for a more specific diagnosis, could be listed as *unspecified obsessive-compulsive and related disorders* within this category.

**Habit reversal therapy (HRT)**

Therapy that involves awareness training and engagement in a response that is incompatible with the compulsion

# Chapter Review

## TO SUM UP ...

- Anxiety disorders are among the most common *DSM-5* diagnoses, affecting over 28% of the population at some point in their lives. Generally, anxiety disorders are more common among females than males.

- Anxiety includes the subjective feelings of fear, apprehension, dread, worry, and panic. Many of the anxiety disorders can include either panic attacks or agoraphobia in their symptom presentation.

- Panic attacks may be cued or situation-bound (as in phobias or PTSD) or uncued (as in panic disorder). Agoraphobia involves anxiety about being in situations from which escape would be difficult if a panic attack occurred.

- There appears to be a moderate genetic factor in the development of anxiety disorders. However, life experiences, including exposure to unpredictable or uncontrollable events, play a substantial role in their development as well. Etiological models based on biological perspectives emphasize overactivity of fear circuits in the brain and deficiencies in anxiety inhibition systems. Etiological models based on learning propose that anxiety becomes a conditioned response resulting from association between predictive internal and external stimuli and subsequent fear or panic, especially in those with a history of exposure to unpredictable or uncontrollable stressors. Psychoanalytic models presume that ego defenses are overwhelmed by anxiety from internal conflicts, which is then often displaced onto other objects or situations.

- Medications such as benzodiazepines are helpful for short-term relief of symptoms, while SSRIs are effective in treating many of the anxiety disorders for longer terms. There are no particular medications that are effective for specific phobias, however.

- Several psychotherapies are available for anxiety disorders, and the most effective ones involve exposure techniques, systematic desensitization, and cognitive-behavioral interventions. For several disorders—including specific phobias, obsessive-compulsive disorder, and generalized anxiety disorder—these psychotherapies may be more effective than medication, and carry a lower rate of relapse after the end of therapy.

- The obsessive-compulsive spectrum of disorders include conditions in which obsessions, sensed as nearly uncontrollable, produce increasing anxiety until a compulsive act relieves it. Effective psychological treatments include exposure and response prevention, and habit reversal therapy. The most common pharmacotherapy includes the SSRI antidepressants.

# KEY TERMS

Anxiety   140

Cingulotomy   156

Compulsions   152

Dependence   144

Exposure and response prevention
(ERP)   156

Exteroceptive   143

Fainting   140

Fear   140

Habit reversal therapy (HRT)   159

Interoceptive   143

In vivo exposure   149

Obsessions   152

Panic attack   140

Preparedness   148

Relapse   144

Two-factor theory   147

Vicarious conditioning   148

# QUESTIONS FOR STUDY

- Describe the differences between fear and anxiety. Are there any symptoms that are unique to either one?

- Show how panic attacks are involved in various specific anxiety diagnoses.

- What are the most commonly applied treatments for anxiety disorders? Of these treatments, which are the most effective? Support your answer with research findings.

- Distinguish obsessions from compulsions. What are the most effective therapies for obsessive-compulsive disorders?

# POP QUIZ

1. Anxiety disorders affect about _____ of the population at some point in their lives.
   A. 3%
   B. 11%
   C. 28%
   D. 46%

2. _____ is a chronic sensation without being clearly associated with any specific stimulus.
   A. Fear
   B. Anxiety
   C. Specific phobia
   D. Astonishment

3. A panic attack progresses to a peak within _____.
   A. 10 minutes
   B. 30 minutes
   C. 1 hour
   D. 6 hours

4. As part of the criteria for panic disorder, at least one of the panic attacks has been followed by _____ of persistent concern about having additional attacks and a significant change in behavior related to the attacks.
   A. 1 month
   B. 3 months
   C. 6 months
   D. 12 months

5. Panic disorder affects up to ___ of the population at some point in life.
   A. 35%
   B. 20%
   C. 15%
   D. 5%

6. The term _____ is defined as relating to internal, physiological stimuli, while the term _____ is defined as relating to external, environmental stimuli.
   A. interoceptive, exteroceptive
   B. interoceptive, exteraceptive
   C. exteroceptive, interoceptive
   D. exteroceptive, interaceptive

7. As treatment for panic disorder, _____ may produce dependence; and most patients experience a relapse when medications are discontinued.
   A. antidepressants
   B. benzodiazepines
   C. phenothiazines
   D. beta blockers

8. _____ therapies for panic disorder appear to be more effective and less subject to relapse.
   A. Pharmacological
   B. Psychodynamic
   C. Psychosurgical
   D. Cognitive-behavioral

9. Fear of strangers is known as _____.
   A. monophobia
   B. acrophobia
   C. xenophobia
   D. zoophobia

10. A nearly constant state of worry and concern characterizes _____.
    A. agoraphobia
    B. social anxiety disorder
    C. specific phobia
    D. generalized anxiety disorder

11. Grace checks her appearance in the mirror over 40 times a day to make sure no hairs are out of place, her make-up is flawless, and her earrings have not moved. She brushes her hair for exactly 10 minutes on each side and has to count while brushing. If she loses count, she must start all over again. Grace probably suffers from _____ .
    A. social phobia
    B. specific phobia
    C. body dysmorphic disorder
    D. obsessive-compulsive disorder

12. The most effective intervention for obsessive-compulsive disorder appears to be _____.
    A. exposure and response prevention
    B. relaxation training
    C. interpersonal group therapy
    D. habit reversal therapy

13. Obsessive-compulsive disorder, if untreated, usually follows a(n) _____ course with symptoms _____ during periods of stress.
    A. acute; worsening
    B. acute; maintaining the same degree
    C. chronic; worsening
    D. chronic; maintaining the same degree

14. Excoriation disorder involves _____.
    A. hair pulling
    B. skin picking
    C. hoarding
    D. none of the above

15. Habit reversal therapy involves all **except** which of the following?
    A. systematic desensitization
    B. self-monitoring
    C. awareness of high-risk situations
    D. engagement in incompatible activities

Additional study resources are available at **www.BVTLab.com**

# CHAPTER OVERVIEW

# CHAPTER OPENER QUESTIONS

Why would anyone present false symptoms?

Can people learn to be deaf? To not see? To have a paralyzed arm?

What do hypnotism and conversion symptoms have in common?

Can therapists inadvertently create false memories or alternate personalities in their clients?

Do some people really switch from one personality to another without remembering?

(Shutterstock)

# Somatic Symptom and Dissociative Disorders

This chapter concerns bodily symptoms that become preoccupations and certain disruptions of consciousness, memory, and identity. The bodily symptoms are referred to as *somatic symptom disorders* and the disruptions of consciousness as *dissociative disorders*. The symptoms included in both of these categories have been labeled hysteria in the past, and ideas about their causes and treatments were important to the founding, and development of, psychoanalytic thinking. They form a set of unusual and sometimes controversial conditions, illustrating the interplay between psychological and physical functioning and the trauma-related breakdown of the integration of memory and identity.

## 7.1 Malingering

Because the disorders discussed here involve symptoms that can appear strange and sometimes unbelievable, there is always the question of whether the presentation of

> **Why would anyone present false symptoms?**

symptoms is honest. Recall that the Rosenhan (1973) study demonstrated how easily a mental disorder (schizophrenia) could be simulated and how readily a diagnostic label would be given when only a few symptoms are described to hospital doctors. Why would anyone report false symptoms or pretend to have a mental disorder? As it turns out, there are circumstances in which a fraudulent presentation might be beneficial. Sometimes, imaginary or exaggerated symptoms bring social attention that might not otherwise be available, allow one to avoid an unpleasant obligation, or perhaps create a situation that frightens other unwanted people away. Not uncommonly, people facing legal charges may attempt to portray themselves in a way that minimizes their personal legal responsibility. There can be financial benefits from federal agencies or insurance companies that are contingent on a diagnosis as well. When false symptoms are presented with the goal of some personal external benefit, the behavior does not comprise a mental disorder (although it may meet the definition for criminal fraud). Instead, is included in the *DSM-5* under "Other conditions that may be a focus of clinical attention" under the subset "Nonadherence to medical treatment," labeled **malingering**.

Malingering involves "the intentional production of false, or grossly exaggerated, physical or psychological symptoms, motivated by external incentives such as avoiding military duty, avoiding work, obtaining financial compensation, evading criminal prosecution, or obtaining drugs" (American Psychiatric Association, 2013, p. 726). There are several situations in which malingering should be suspected. Some examples include (a) if a person is undergoing an evaluation for legal purposes, (b) if a person's report of disability or distress is inconsistent with objective findings, (c) if a person is uncooperative in the diagnostic evaluation, or (d) if antisocial personality disorder is present (which, as will be described later, often involves lying or "conning" for personal gain). Obviously, the possibility of malingering always exists, but it becomes more likely under the sorts of situations described above. For instance, among a group of criminal defendants undergoing evaluation by experienced forensic psychologists, the incidence of malingering was 8% (Cornell & Hawk, 1989). Malingering can

**Malingering**

The intentional faking of a physical or psychological symptom be difficult to detect, and it may be over-represented among certain conditions such as PTSD (in which case, a clearly identifiable trauma links to a potential outcome such as avoiding combat or receiving financial compensation) and mild head injuries, where the incidence of malingering appears to be at least 7.5%, based on indications of invalid presentations of neuropsychological symptoms (Trueblood & Schmidt, 1993). Somatic symptom disorders and dissociative disorders, in which unusual symptoms cannot be confirmed apart from self-report, may also be particularly difficult to distinguish from malingering; however, nearly all of the *DSM-5* categories are susceptible to malingering, because laboratory testing cannot independently validate their diagnoses.

## 7.1a Factitious Disorder and Factitious Disorder Imposed on Another

Sometimes, individuals may present symptoms that are intentionally produced, but there is no apparent or obvious motive—other than to assume the sick role. This type of

Jennifer, 8, shown with her mother in 1996, underwent 40 operations and over 200 hospitalizations, and was determined to be a victim of Factitious Disorder by Proxy. (iStock)

apparently unmotivated simulation is maladaptive enough to qualify as a mental disorder, called factitious disorder. (Prior to the advent of the *DSM-III,* this condition was called "**Munchausen syndrome**.") Unlike malingerers, people with factitious disorder invent or exaggerate their symptoms for no obvious incentive or apparent reason apart from playing sick. Their fabrication is not the result of another condition such as a psychotic or delusional disorder. *DSM-5* specifiers for factitious disorder include "single episode," and "recurrent episode"; usually, the episodes are intermittent.

Factitious disorder symptoms vary widely. They can include reporting seizures that did not occur, exaggerating symptoms of an existing condition, tainting a urine test by deliberately adding blood, grieving over the death of a non-existent child, or altering a medical record. Sometimes, injuries or infections are intentionally induced, for example by injection of fecal material; in other instances, drugs may be used to alter laboratory results (American Psychiatric Association, 2013). When physical or mental disorders are simulated, the symptoms may not easily correspond to an established diagnosis. Like malingering, the degree of accuracy in the feigned presentation is likely a function of the level of sophistication of the person's understanding of the disorder. Typically, the symptoms worsen when an individual is aware of being observed.

The *DSM-5* prevalence estimate of 1% among hospitalized patients is not very useful because feigning is probably not detected with great accuracy, and a person's ability to make the symptoms appear authentic may improve as interactions with medical professionals increase. Freyberger and Schneider (1994) criticized both the reliability and validity of the diagnostic criteria, which in the *DSM-III* field trials ranged from 0.66 to –0.005 across the two phases. The condition was not among those assessed in the *DSM-5* reliability field trials.

Factitious disorder can involve any symptom presentation and may be related to histories of stress or abuse, although relevant research is limited to case studies. For example, Mileno and his colleagues (2001) relate a series of four cases within a 2-year period in which women requested medical treatment of HIV infection. All claimed to be HIV-positive; and their feigned symptoms included profuse night sweating, weight loss, fever, and chills, and giving false histories of cancer, surgery, and use of anti-viral medications. Upon physical exam and HIV testing, all patients were found to be HIV-negative with normal CD4 cell counts. The four patients responded either with anger or surprise when they were informed of their normal health status. A common factor in all four cases was a background of prolonged sexual or physical abuse. In three of the four cases the women subsequently presented themselves at other clinics seeking HIV treatment.

**Munchausen syndrome**

Earlier terminology for the mental disorder in which symptoms are intentionally feigned, for no apparent reason

The associated diagnosis, factitious disorder imposed on another, involves falsely presenting symptoms in another person. (In the *DSM-IV*, this condition was called "factitious disorder by proxy.") In this type of simulation, the false symptoms are produced on behalf of someone else, who is typically under the individual's care. For example, the caregiver might induce vomiting, diarrhea, fever, seizures, or other physical conditions and then bring the victim in for medical care without acknowledging a role in the cause of symptoms. Most often, the victim of factitious disorder imposed on another is a preschool child, and the perpetrator is the mother. Like factitious disorder, external incentives for the deception are absent. A caregiver who induces injuries in a child in order to collect a financial settlement would not receive the diagnosis (American Psychiatric Association, 2013), but would be guilty of criminal assault.

# 7.2 Somatic Symptom and Related Disorders

The somatic symptom and related disorders (which include the factitious disorders) involve prominent and distressing somatic (bodily) symptoms that produce abnormal thoughts, feelings, or behaviors. These somatic symptoms may or may not be medically explained; in the *DSM-5*, there is no longer the requirement (as in the *DSM-IV*) that supporting physical evidence be absent. Importantly, the symptoms that are expressed in most somatic symptom disorders are not intentionally produced or faked, as in the case of malingering and factitious disorder. Instead, individuals are genuinely distressed by their symptoms, which produce excessive and abnormal responses. The various somatic symptom and related disorders are outlined in Table 7-1.

Historically, these disorders tended to have lower diagnostic reliability than the anxiety disorders described in Chapter 6; the *DSM-III* kappa values from the reliability field trials of the somatoform disorders (as these conditions were previously named) ranged only from 0.54 to 0.43 (American Psychological Association, 1980.) This stemmed in part from limitations in the ability of medical workups to verify or to rule out some medical conditions. It has also been the case that several of these conditions frequently co-occur with anxiety and depression (Lieb, Meinlschmidt, & Araya, 2007). In fact, a review of 206 patients who presented multiple medically unexplained symptoms (Smith, et al., 2005) found that for the majority of the patients, depression and anxiety diagnoses were more accurate characterizations of their conditions than somatoform diagnoses. Reviewers pointed out the conceptual difficulties of relying on "medically unexplained" conclusions and on questionable recollection of past symptoms in the diagnostic process (Reif & Rojas, 2007). The ongoing controversies and debates about reliability and validity, together with theoretical and practical limitations of

*Table 7-1*    DSM-5 Somatic Symptom and Related Disorder

| Disorder | Key Symptoms | Minimum Duration Required for Diagnosis | Sex Ratio |
| --- | --- | --- | --- |
| Somatic symptom disorder | Somatic symptoms causing disproportionate distress and disruption | None | More common among females |
| Illness anxiety disorder | Excessive preoccupation with serious illness | 6 months | Equal |
| Conversion disorder (Functional neurological symptom disorder | Unexplained deficits or symptoms in motor or sensory functions | None | More common among females |
| Psychological factors affecting other medical conditions | Psychological or behavioral factors that adversely affect a medical condition | None | Unclear |
| Factitious disorder | Falsification of physical or psychological symptoms without obvious incentive | None | Unclear |

Source: Reprinted with permission from the *Diagnostic and Statistical Manual of Mental Disorders,* Fifth Edition, (Copyright 2013). American Psychiatric Association.

the diagnoses themselves, led some writers (e.g., Janca, 2005) to conclude that the entire somatoform category was in need of reconceptualization.

In organizing the somatic symptom disorders, the *DSM-5* extensively modified *DSM-IV*'s somatoform categories. Body dysmorphic disorder was moved to the obsessive-compulsive and related disorders, as we have seen. Several conditions (hypochondriasis, somatization disorder, pain disorder, and undifferentiated somatoform disorder) were removed; and the symptoms they classified were redistributed to new syndromes that are less concerned with unexplained medical symptoms and more concerned with the thoughts, feelings, and behaviors the sufferers experience. Initial indications are that the changes may lead to improved reliability: in the *DSM-5* field trials, complex somatic symptom disorder scored a kappa of 0.61, earning it a "very good" reliability classification (Regier, et al., 2013).

## 7.2a  Somatic Symptom Disorder

Somatic symptom disorder typically involves multiple physical complaints that disrupt daily life (see *DSM-5* Diagnostic Criteria for Somatic Symptom Disorder). It can be specified as mild, moderate, or severe, depending on the number of symptoms expressed. There may or may not be an underlying medical condition. Those with the disorder tend to worry about illness a great deal, and interpret their symptoms as overly serious or threatening, in spite of evidence to the contrary. For example, an occasional cough might be misconstrued as lung cancer or imminent respiratory failure; the sensations of the heartbeat may be seen as indications of cardiac disease. The preoccupation continues even after a medical examination has ruled the condition out and a physician has given reassurance that the condition is not present. The disease concerns—which cause distress but do not reach delusional intensity—typically have lasted at least 6 months. Sufferers seek frequent medical attention, often from several physicians at the same time, and their frequent use of medications may lead to substance dependence problems. Within the "persistent" specifier, over the years of the chronic course of the disorder, individuals have received numerous examinations, hospitalizations, and surgeries. The "with predominant pain" specifier incorporates those people who would have

| *DSM-5* | **Diagnostic Criteria for Somatic Symptom Disorder** |
|---|---|

300.82 (F45.1) Somatic symptom disorder

A. One or more somatic symptoms that are distressing or result in significant disruption of daily life.

B. Excessive thoughts, feelings, or behaviors related to the somatic symptoms or associated health concerns as manifested by at least one of the following:
1. Disproportionate and persistent thoughts about the seriousness of one's symptoms.
2. Persistently high level of anxiety about health or symptoms.
3. Excessive time and energy devoted to these symptoms or health concerns.

C. Although any one somatic symptom may not be continuously present, the state of being symptomatic is persistent (typically more than 6 months).

Specify if:

With predominant pain (previously pain disorder). This specifier is for individuals whose somatic symptoms predominantly involve pain.

Specify if:

Persistent: A persistent course is characterized by severe symptoms, marked impairment, and long duration (more than 6 months).

Specify current severity:

Mild: Only one of the symptoms specified in Criterion B is fulfilled.

Moderate: Two or more of the symptoms specified in Criterion B are fulfilled.

Severe: Two or more of the symptoms specified in Criterion B are fulfilled, plus there are multiple somatic complaints (or one very severe somatic symptom).

Source: Reprinted with permission from the *Diagnostic and Statistical Manual of Mental Disorders*, Fifth Edition, (Copyright 2013). American Psychiatric Association.

been diagnosed with pain disorder in the *DSM-IV*. The condition appears to be more common in females than males (American Psychiatric Association, 2013).

It is difficult to get an accurate estimate of incidence of the disorder, but the *DSM-5* suggests incidence may be between 5% and 7% of the population. However, there are some estimates of the frequency with which **psychogenic** (or psychologically-caused) individual symptoms are presented in treatment settings. For example, psychogenic non-epileptic seizures were reported in between 10% and 20% of patients who were referred to epilepsy centers in Britain (Benbadis & Allen Hauser, 2000). A representative community survey estimated the incidence of people experiencing six or more symptoms from two or more bodily sites at about 1.8% of the population (Ladwig, Marten-Mittag, Erazo, & Gundel, 2001).

## Causal Factors

There is a broad set of environmental factors associated with the risk of somatic symptom disorder. It is more frequent in those who have experienced recent stressful life events, those who have low socioeconomic status, and those with fewer years of education. Somatic symptoms occur more commonly among the unemployed, and those with a history of sexual abuse (American Psychiatric Association, 2013), which may contribute to the higher prevalence in females. In a recent group comparison, sexual abuse was 9 times more likely in the background of somatization disorder patients than in matched patients with major depressive disorder (Spitzer, Barnow, Gau, Freyberger, & Grabe, 2008). The matter of causality is complicated, however, by the frequent presence of coexisting disorders, such as anxiety and depression, which themselves are associated with somatic complaints. Generally, behavioral perspectives would focus on the consequences that somatic symptoms might present to the sufferer, while cognitive viewpoints would involve the unduly harsh and catastrophic appraisals that sufferers make of their symptoms. Psychoanalytic perspectives tend to view the medical symptoms as evidence of anxiety produced by unconscious conflicts, often involving sexual themes.

Those with somatic symptom disorder seek frequent medical attention, often from several physicians at the same time, and their constant use of medications may lead to substance dependence problems. Often, individuals have received numerous examinations, hospitalizations, and surgeries. (iStock)

## Treatment for Somatic Symptom Disorder

By its multi-symptom nature, somatic symptom disorder is difficult to treat and rarely remits completely. Individuals tend to seek medical care, which rarely helps relieve their concerns; and they are often shocked by the suggestion that mental health intervention may be helpful (American Psychiatric Association, 2013). Because of the significant overlap with anxiety and depression, therapies for these disorders have provided relief and some symptom reduction. The effectiveness of SSRIs for somatization disorder was less well documented than for some of the other somatoform disorders (Fallon, 2004). One controlled study did report a significant response to St. John's Wort, with 45% of patients showing improvement compared to 21% of those on placebo (Müller, Mannel, Murck, & Rahlf, 2004). Reviews of controlled trials and comparisons between various treatments have shown cognitive behavior therapy (CBT) to be the favored treatment, with stronger evidence of its effectiveness than is found for other approaches (Kroenke, 2007; Sumathipala, 2007). A common component of treatment involves improvement in the doctor-patient relationship, which is frequently frayed by the disorder. Looper and Kirmayer (2002) describe interventions that begin with focusing all medical attention through a single physician (who receives a consultation letter providing information about somatic symptom disorder), followed by group CBT approaches that include problem

**Psychogenic**

Originating from psychological factors

solving, emotional expression, coping skills, and assertiveness. In their review of controlled studies, Kroenke and Swindle (2000) found general support for such interventions, even when therapy was brief. For example, CBT techniques were effective in treating unexplained medical symptoms during a one-session course of treatment (Martin, Rauh, Fichter, & Rief, 2007).

Some research has indicated that St. Johns Wort may be effective in treating somatic symptom disorder. (iStock)

For those who receive the specifier "with predominant pain," treatments can involve pharmacological agents to block pain, or efforts treat any underlying condition which may cause it. Dysfunctional pain processing has been proposed as a possible cause of chronic pain, based on MRI scans that show different levels of cortical brain activity in a group of women with pain disorder, compared to controls, in response to a heat stimulus (Gündel, et al., 2008). It is not clear whether such differences are causal to, or simply descriptive of, pain disorder. Obviously, pain medications are widely consumed and may be associated with risk of dependency. Some antidepressant medications have produced pain relief, especially the SSRIs, in somatic pain patients (Fallon, 2004; Fishbain, Culter, Rosomoff, Rosomoff, & Steele, 1998).

Psychological interventions may attempt to lessen the grip that pain has on the sufferer. Pain is a subjective experience, influenced by its consequences. For example, pain tolerance can be shaped and is modified by social context (Hayes & Wolf, 1984). Cognitive-behavior therapy has been widely employed for pain management, stress reduction, and activity enhancement; and randomized trial studies support its effectiveness (Simon, 2002). A newer development is acceptance and commitment therapy (ACT), which changes one's perspective on chronic pain by focusing not on pain control but on accepting its presence and valuing pain tolerance. Acceptance-based rationales have been shown experimentally to produce higher pain tolerance than control-based rationales (Hayes, et al., 1999). In a recent study, pain acceptance appeared to be superior to a pain control protocol in terms of ability to work through a pain task (Páez-Blarrina, et al., 2008). The value of acceptance and commitment therapy in treating pain has also been demonstrated among children and adolescents (ages 10 to 16) with chronic pain in a randomized control trial (Wicksell, Melin, Lekander, & Olsson, 2009). Children receiving a 10-week ACT intervention showed significantly greater improvements in function and quality of life, and less pain intensity and discomfort, when compared to children receiving standard multidisciplinary treatment involving pain medication.

## 7.2b Conversion Disorder (Functional Neurological Symptom Disorder)

The term **conversion** derives from the psychoanalytic theory that psychic energy is "converted" into a physical symptom. Freud's case study of Anna O. remains a classic demonstration of psychoanalytic technique in the treatment of a woman with multiple unfounded somatic problems, including partial paralysis. In modern usage, conversion disorder refers to symptoms or deficits in voluntary motor or sensory function, such as those described in Table 7-2. The *DSM-5* diagnosis requires the presence of one or more of these sorts of symptoms to the extent that it causes clinically significant distress or impairment

**Can people learn to be deaf? To not see? To have a paralyzed arm?**

**Conversion**

The notion that psychic energy or stress may be converted into physical symptoms

or warrants medical evaluation and is not accounted for by another condition. There must be evidence, from clinical findings, that the symptoms are incompatible with the person's neurological or medical condition—that is, they are not explained by neurological disease.

*Table 7-2* Varieties of Conversion Symptoms

**I. Motor Functions of the Skeletal Musculature**

A. Partial or complete paralysis of the arms, legs, or other body parts

B. Selective loss of function, such as writer's cramp, in which the person cannot write but can use the same muscles for other purposes

C. Contractions involving rigid flection of fingers, toes, knees, elbows, or other body parts

D. Astasia-Abasia (the ability to move legs when lying or sitting but not to stand or walk)

E. Speech disturbances: mutism (total inability to speak) and aphonia (ability to speak only in a whisper)

F. Convulsions similar to epileptic seizures

G. Tics (muscular twitching), usually around eyes or mouth

**II. Sensory Functions**

A. Disturbances in vision: total or partial blindness, tunnel vision, blurred vision, double vision, or night blindness

B. Disturbances in hearing, involving total or partial deafness

C. Anesthesia (general loss of sensitivity to stimulation of skin)

D. Analgesia (insensitivity to superficial pain stimuli applied to skin)

E. Paresthesia (false sensations, such as tingling feelings in skin)

**III. Other Somatic Symptoms**

A. "Lump in the throat"

B. Coughing spells

C. Persistent belching or sneezing

Conversion disorder can be specified by type (e.g., with weakness or paralysis, with anesthesia or sensory loss, with abnormal movement), by duration (acute or persistent), and according to whether a psychosocial stressor has been involved. It appears to be very rare in the general population (less than 0.001%), but may be involved in 5% of referrals to neurology clinics (American Psychiatric Association, 2013).

Of course, a diagnosis of conversion disorder would not be given until an extensive medical examination and work-up has failed to identify any physical explanations for the impairment in sensory or motor functions. There are some clues that suggest conversion disorder. Often, the symptoms presented by the patient do not correspond to known anatomical pathways, as in glove anesthesia. In some patients, **la belle indifférence**, or an obvious lack of concern about the symptoms, is evident. Another clue involves the inconsistency of symptoms—a person with **aphonia** (inability to make speech sounds) may speak only in a whisper but can cough in a normal manner, or a person with "writer's cramp" can use the same muscles to shuffle a deck of cards with dexterity. Seizures do not produce a typical EEG record. Sometimes, movement in an affected paralyzed limb can be briefly observed during routine activities when the patient's attention is directed elsewhere. Movement of paralyzed limbs may also be noted when the patient is asleep. Laurema (1993), for example, observed a 43-year-old woman with conversion paralysis for 5 nights and found she performed 191 movements that were not possible when she was awake. The symptoms of conversion disorder are not intentionally produced, yet the accuracy of the symptom presentation is directly related to the medical sophistication of the patient. The disorder occurs 2 times more often in women than men (American Psychiatric Association, 2013).

> What do hypnotism and conversion symptoms have in common?

**La belle indifférence**

The condition of hysterical patients appearing calm and indeed quite cheerful, instead of being worried or depressed about their physical symptoms

**Aphonia**

Inability to make speech sounds, without apparent physical basis

## Causal Factors

Since the work of Bernheim and Charcot, a close relationship between hypnotically induced bodily symptoms and conversion symptoms has been recognized. Conversion disorder was essentially considered a form of **autosuggestion**, or self-hypnosis, to express and relieve conflict (according to Freud, the *primary gain* of the symptom). Psychoanalytic theory posits that some current situation reawakens an unsatisfactorily resolved Oedipal problem. The unacceptable impulses threaten to break through, creating anxiety that is then controlled by the development of the conversion symptom. (The conversion symptom could also produce *secondary gain* by allowing the sufferer to avoid responsibilities or undesired situations, such as military combat or emotional arguments). Freudian perspectives viewed the particular conversion symptom as the product of unconscious psychosexual conflict. One psychoanalytic authority (Fenichel, 1945) argued that the afflicted body part is determined, in part, by unconscious sexual fantasies whereas another (Bond, 1952) suggested that the erogenous nature of the testicles is often displaced to the eyes, resulting in castration fears. Little empirical evidence of the hypnosis-conversion connection has been found. However, Roelofs and his colleagues (2002) reported that patients with conversion disorder were significantly more susceptible to hypnotic suggestions than a matched control group with mood disorder.

In genetic studies, Slater (1961) found no difference between MZ and DZ twins, indicating little genetic involvement. Ziegler and Schlemmer (1994) reported a case of familial conversion blindness in a father and two of his adult children. Behavioral perspectives generally presume that it is the secondary gain that maintains conversion disorder. Specific stressful experiences are present, either currently or in the recent past, in almost all cases of conversion disorders. In many cases, the immediate motive for developing a bodily symptom may be to escape from some emotionally unbearable situation. Additionally, Mucha and Reinhardt (1970) provide indirect evidence consistent with a modeling effect—among a group of 56 student aviators with conversion symptoms, 70% of their parents had suffered an illness involving the same organ system. An interesting recent speculation appeals to **mirror neurons** to account for the social "contagion" of hysterical symptoms that may occur within families, and even grow into the large-group "dance manias" of the middle ages mentioned in Chapter 2. Lee and Tsai (2010) hypothesize that an inhibitory component of the mirror neuron system, which normally prevents us from imitating everything that we observe, may be faulty in certain subjects, leading them to copy the hysterical actions of others. They also note that mirror neurons are more active in women than in men, possibly explaining the higher female incidence of conversion disorder.

Conversion disorder is frequently co-morbid with panic disorder, as well as other anxiety disorders, depression, and somatic symptom disorder—but not with psychotic or alcohol use disorders (American Psychiatric Association, 2013).

## Treatment for Conversion Disorder

Psychoanalytic approaches, since Freud, have involved therapy aimed at providing recognition of, and insight into, the underlying conflicts presumed to be causing the conversion process. Unfortunately, demonstrations of the effectiveness of these approaches are limited to case studies (as are other treatments for conversion disorder). Sometimes, simply telling the patient that the symptoms will disappear, or showing the patient that test results from the examination are normal, can be followed by improvement. Letonoff, Williams, and Sidhu (2002) reported on three cases in which patients with complete loss of lower extremity function spontaneously recovered and walked out of the hospital after test results were presented to them. Because conversion disorder patients are particularly suggestible (Roelofs, et al., 2002), hypnotic interventions may seem reasonable. A randomized clinical trial of hypnosis compared to waiting list controls indicated that patients in the hypnosis condition showed significant improvement in conversion symptoms that was maintained at a 6-month follow-up (Moene, Spinhoven, Hoogduin, & Dyck, 2003).

Some early behavioral efforts, based on the assumption that the conversion symptoms were learned, attempted to re-shape normal functioning incrementally. An example of this approach is the case study reported by Parry-Jones, Santer-Westrate, and Crawley (1970), who essentially used auditory feedback to reinforce visual discrimination. The patient was a

**Autosuggestion**

Influencing one's own attitudes or behavior; self-hypnosis

**Mirror neurons**

Neurons in primate brains that discharge when a movement is executed, as well as when the movement is observed in others

47-year-old woman who had been totally blind for two and a half years. She had undergone a brain operation for an aneurysm several years before the onset of her blindness, and at first it was thought that the blindness was a delayed result of either the aneurysm or the operation. Further neurological and psychological observations led the clinicians to suspect a hysterical basis, possibly related to a recent break-up of her marriage. Daily treatment sessions of about 15-minute duration were begun. In the first eight sessions she was told simply to push a button every 20 seconds. If she pushed the button within 18 to 21 seconds after the last button press, a buzzer would sound indicating that she had made a correct response. In sessions 9 to 16, without informing the patient, a light bulb was placed in front of her and was turned on as a cue to help her identify the correct time for the next button-press—assuming, of course, that she could see the cue. Her performance improved considerably over these sessions (see Figure 7-1). Before starting session 17 she was told that there was a light bulb that would light up when it was time to press the button, and she was encouraged to look for it and concentrate very hard. In session 19 she suddenly stopped and sat motionless for about 30 seconds. When asked what was the matter, she became tearful and excited and said she could see the light, intermittently, as a dim double image. After this she began to rely on the light altogether; by session 27 she was making 100% correct responses. Her renewed vision was limited, however, to seeing only the light bulb.

The authors then embarked on a systematic attempt to expand her visual capacities to other visual stimuli and to situations outside of the treatment room. For example, she was given practice in seeing and describing large letters and pictures in magazines and encouraged to continue practice outside the treatment room. After 127 of these brief sessions, she had regained normal vision in her everyday life. Two years after the completion of her treatment, her vision remained normal.

Other early behavioral approaches attempted to remove the reinforcement for the conversion symptom so that extinction of the symptom would occur. A good example is the case study from Goldblatt and Munitz (1976). An Israeli soldier had developed complete paralysis of both legs without physical reason. While awake, he was apparently insensitive to pins stuck into the legs although during sleep his legs were observed to move. Among possible incentives for his paralysis were significant benefits for Israeli veterans who were injured in the armed forces, including a pension and exemption from vehicle taxes (which at the time in Israel were twice the cost of the automobile). A "broad-spectrum" extinction

*Figure 7-1*

Percent correct responses in pressing a button to a light stimulus as a function of various therapeutic interventions for a person with hysterical blindness.

Source: Adapted from Parry-Jones, Santer-Westrate, & Crawley, 1970. Copyright 1970 by Pergamon Press and used with permission.

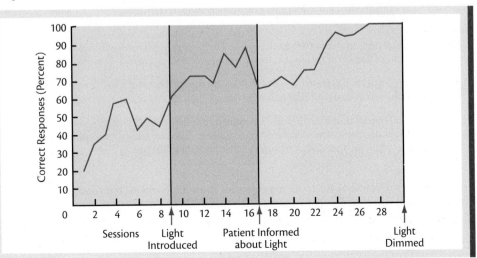

approach was instituted. First, the soldier was told that his disability would not qualify for pension benefits or the waiver of vehicle taxes. He was also informed that his treatment would require him to remain in his room after 8 p.m., meaning he could not socialize and play cards with other patients as he enjoyed doing in the evenings. He was then presented with a noxious-smelling substance, which was described as a "miracle drug" that should be inhaled twice daily (but was actually an inert placebo). On the second day of the program, 1 hour after the first drug administration, the patient was able to move his toes. He was able to walk with crutches by the fourth day of treatment and was walking normally, kicking a soccer ball, and doing cartwheels after 6 days.

Contemporary cognitive-behavioral approaches for conversion disorder build on this framework by removing the reinforcing consequences of the conversion symptom while also working to weaken the traumatic reaction to the initiating event. Comprehensive programs that combine CBT-like procedures with other insight-oriented and expression-oriented approaches have seen positive results as well. Interestingly, the addition of hypnosis did not contribute to improvement nor was "hypnotizability" related to treatment outcome in one such assessment involving 45 patients (Moene, Spinhoven, Hoogduin, & Duck, 2002).

## 7.2c Illness Anxiety Disorder

Illness anxiety disorder (see *DSM-5* Diagnostic Criteria for Illness Anxiety Disorder) involves a preoccupation with the fear that one has, or will acquire a serious disease although somatic symptoms, if present, are mild and frequently transient or normal physiological functions, such as belching. Reaction to these mild symptoms, or to existing medical conditions, is clearly excessive and disproportionate to their actual severity. Individuals have significant anxiety about their health status and are easily alarmed, for example by hearing a news story about a health issue; and their worries are not soothed by a medical evaluation that finds no presence of disease or by reassurances from physicians.

People with illness anxiety disorder are often in conflict with their doctors. They may succeed in getting a series of medical interventions and procedures through their insistence

| *DSM-5* | **Diagnostic Criteria for Illness Anxiety Disorder** |

300.7 (F45.21) Illness Anxiety Disorder

A. Preoccupation with having or acquiring a serious illness.

B. Somatic symptoms are not present, or if present, are only mild in intensity. If another medical condition is present or there is a high risk for developing a medical condition (e.g., strong family history is present), the preoccupation is clearly excessive or disproportionate.

C. There is a high level of anxiety about health, and the individual is easily alarmed about personal health status.

D. The individual performs excessive health-related behaviors (e.g., repeatedly checks his or her body for signs of illness) or exhibits maladaptive avoidance (e.g., avoids doctors and hospitals).

E. Illness preoccupation has been present for at least 6 months, but the specific illness that is feared may have changed over that period of time.

F. The illness preoccupation is not better explained by another mental disorder, such as somatic symptom disorder, panic disorder, generalized anxiety disorder, body dysmorphic disorder, obsessive-compulsive disorder, or delusional disorder, somatic type.

Specify whether:

Care-seeking type: Medical care, including physician visits or undergoing tests and procedures, is frequently used.

Care-avoidant type: Medical care is rarely used.

Source: Reprinted with permission from the *Diagnostic and Statistical Manual of Mental Disorders,* Fifth Edition, (Copyright 2013). American Psychiatric Association.

on a disease that they claim is not receiving proper care. The presence of the feared disease becomes central to self-image and can disrupt family, social, and occupational relationships. No clear gender differences in incidence of the disorder have emerged. Based on earlier estimates for the forerunning *DSM-IV* disorder, hypochondriasis, illness anxiety disorder may affect between 1.3% and 10% of community samples. Up to one-half of cases are of a transient type, whereas for others the course is usually chronic (American Psychiatric Association, 2013).

### Causal Factors

At this point, data about anxiety illness disorder tend to be limited to studies of hypochondriasis. For that condition, no genetic influence was evident. Family studies have not found increased risk of hypochondriasis among first generation relatives of persons diagnosed with the disorder (e.g., Noyes, Holt, Happel, Kathol, & Yagla, 1997). Illness anxiety disorder can co-occur with several conditions, including anxiety and depressive disorder, and other somatic symptom conditions. Some psychodynamic clinicians have assumed that patients defend against poor self-opinion by displacing attention onto physical sensations and symptoms (Ford, 1983). Since misinterpretation of bodily symptoms is common in the presentation, cognitive and learning influences are presumed to be important in the development of the disorder. Sufferers tend to make dysfunctional assumptions about, and over-attend to, physical symptoms. For example, when asked to classify common symptoms as "healthy" or "not healthy," hypochondriac patients were more likely to view symptoms as indicative of disease than were other patients in the same medical setting (Bansky, Coeyfaux, Samie, & Cleary, 1993). Accordingly, a history of previous serious childhood illness is associated with increased risk of the disorder, as is childhood abuse (American Psychiatric Association, 2013).

### Treatment for Illness Anxiety Disorder

Pharmacological approaches employing SSRIs have produced positive results in treating hypochondriasis (Fallon, 2004). Much current effective treatment follows CBT formats, involving stress management, desensitization to anxiety-provoking situations, and reduced attention to troubling physical symptoms. Controlled trials show CBT to be superior to no treatment (Simon, 2002). Even relatively brief CBT is effective in reducing symptom severity and associated depression and anxiety (Looper & Kirmayer, 2002).

## 7.2d Psychological Factors Affecting Other Medical Conditions

For some people with existing medical conditions or symptoms, behavioral or psychological factors can negatively impact the condition, increasing the risk of death or disability. For example, people with cardiac conditions may refuse to seek treatment when experiencing chest pain; occupational stress may exacerbate hypertension. When the evidence is clear that a psychological factor is interfering with treatment or having significant influences on medical outcome, the *DSM-5* provides the category *psychological factors affecting other medical conditions* for diagnostic use. To apply, the interfering psychological or behavioral factors are not better explained by another disorder and should occur in close temporal relationship with the worsening of the existing medical condition. The condition can be specified as mild (increases medical risk), moderate (aggravates underlying condition), severe (necessitates hospitalization or emergency room care), or extreme (results in threat to life).

The diagnosis should distinguish between those factors that increase existing conditions and those factors that may be produced by the health impairment, as in adjustment disorder. Hence, the temporal relationship of the behavior to the exacerbation of the condition is important. The prevalence of psychological factors affecting other medical conditions is

**BVT** *Lab*

Visit **www.BVTLab.com** to explore the student resources available for this chapter.

unclear, although it may be more common than other somatic symptom disorders (American Psychiatric Association, 2013).

## 7.2e   Other Somatic Symptom Disorders

Other specified somatic symptom and related disorder is included in the somatic symptom category to allow coding of conditions that involve somatic symptoms but do not meet the criteria for specific disorders. Perhaps a physical complaint, such as fatigue, or a preoccupation with a serious disease has not lasted the required 6 months, or illness anxiety does not include excessive health related behaviors. In these cases, other somatic symptom disorder would be appropriate. One particular set of somatic symptoms that might be included here is **pseudocyesis.** In that condition, which has been known since the time of Hippocrates, a woman presents with false but medically unexplained symptoms of pregnancy. For example, Ouj (2009) reviewed cases of pseudocyesis in a rural Nigerian hospital over a 4-year period. Eleven of 3787 expectant mothers were confirmed with pseudocyesis during that time. All experienced amenorrhea, and most (eight) showed increase in abdominal girth. Over half reported feeling fetal movement. Ultrasound confirmed that none were pregnant. However, as in all somatic symptom disorders, care is needed to distinguish the proper cataloging of unusual or unconventional symptom sets. For instance, some preoccupations about infection might be better diagnosed as obsessive-compulsive disorder than as illness anxiety disorder. Such distinctions can be difficult to make reliably. Consider the case of psychogenic urinary retention (**paruresis**), characterized by an inability to urinate in a public restroom. Rarely discussed or described in the literature, this condition appears to affect 2.8% of the male population, based on a representative sample (Hammelstein, Pietrowsky, Merbach, & Brahler, 2005). However, paruresis probably would not be coded as a somatic symptom disorder, but rather as a specific form of social phobia.

# 7.3   Dissociative Disorders

*Dissociative disorders* involve certain altered states of consciousness and disruptions of memory and identity. They are generally rare conditions, typically associated with stressful or traumatic experiences; they may include, however, symptoms that could be acceptable within some cultural or religious contexts. It is, therefore, important to consider cross-cultural factors when diagnosing these disorders. An overview of the dissociative disorders is given in Table 7-3.

Compared to many other disorders, the dissociative disorder category has been plagued by problems with diagnostic reliability. In the *DSM-III* field trials, reliability ranged from a solid 0.80 to a dismal –0.003 across the two phases. The reliability of dissociative disorders was not assessed in the *DSM-5* field trials. Although these or similar disorders have been recognized since the time of Freud, much controversy remains about their diagnosis and treatment. All of the symptoms of dissociative disorders can be easily feigned, and they are perhaps over-represented in situations in which malingering should be carefully considered. No controlled studies of these disorders have yet appeared, perhaps because they are so rarely encountered and because they are so difficult to detect. Instead, the professional literature largely consists of case studies, which do not allow authoritative conclusions about causality or effective treatments. Dissociative symptoms can be components of many other conditions, including depressive disorders, anxiety disorders, and schizophrenic disorders.

## 7.3a   Dissociative Amnesia

One type of dissociative disorder, dissociative amnesia (see *DSM-5* Diagnostic Criteria for Dissociative Amnesia), involves a loss of memory for a certain period of time that is too extensive to be explained by ordinary forgetfulness. This is not the type of memory loss

**Pseudocyesis**

False belief of being pregnant, accompanied by reported pregnancy symptoms as well as some objective signs of pregnancy

**Paruresis**

Inability to urinate in a public restroom

*Table 7-3*  DSM-5 Dissociative Disorders

| Disorder | Key Symptoms | Minimum Duration Required for Diagnosis | Sex Ratio |
|----------|--------------|------------------------------------------|-----------|
| Dissociative amnesia | Unexplained inability to recall important personal information | None | More common among females |
| Dissociative identity disorder | Two or more distinct personality states, with inability to recall important personal information | None | More common among females |
| Depersonalization/ derealization disorder | Persistent feelings of being detached or outside of one's self | None | Equal |

Source: Reprinted with permission from the *Diagnostic and Statistical Manual of Mental Disorders,* Fifth Edition, (Copyright 2013). American Psychiatric Association.

that results from a blow to the head or a drug-induced coma; physiological causes must be ruled out before the diagnosis of dissociative amnesia can be given. Instead, the memory loss is usually associated with a traumatic event such as an automobile accident, sexual assault, or war experience. The memory impairment appears as gaps or a series of gaps in one's life history and is most often either **localized amnesia** (failure to recall events that happened during a circumscribed period of time) or **selective amnesia**, in which a person can recall some but not all events during a particular period. Sometimes the amnesia is limited to episodes of violence, self-mutilation, or suicidal behavior, or to the first few hours following a traumatizing event. **Generalized amnesia** is rarer. It involves a complete loss of memory for one's life history and perhaps one's identity, and tends to be more characteristic among those who have experienced combat, sexual assault, or extreme stress. It is also more likely to involve dissociative fugue (see below). Amnesic patients often are not fully aware of the extent of their memory loss and may minimize it, or resist addressing it, when the amnesia is localized (American Psychiatric Association, 2013). Unlike the amnesic syndromes caused by neurological events, the capacity to learn new information usually remains intact (Maldonado, Butler, & Spiegel,

> Can therapists inadvertently create false memories or alternate personalities in their clients?

**Localized amnesia**

Failure to recall events during a circumscribed period of time

**Selective amnesia**

Loss of memory for some but not all events during a particular period of time

**Generalized amnesia**

Complete loss of memory for one's life history

---

**DSM-5**  **Diagnostic Criteria for Dissociative Amnesia**

300.12 (F44.0) Dissociative Amnesia

A. An inability to recall important autobiographical information, usually of a traumatic or stressful nature, that is inconsistent with ordinary forgetting.

**Note:** Dissociative amnesia most often consists of localized or selective amnesia for a specific event or events; or generalized amnesia for identity and life history.

B. The symptoms cause clinically significant distress or impairment in social, occupational, or other important areas of functioning.

C. The disturbance is not attributable to the physiological effects of a substance (e.g., alcohol or other drug of abuse, a medication) or a neurological or other medical condition (e.g., partial complex seizures, transient global amnesia, sequelae of a closed head injury/traumatic brain injury, other neurological condition).

D. The disturbance is not better explained by dissociative identity disorder, posttraumatic stress disorder, acute stress disorder, somatic symptom disorder, or major or mild neurocognitive disorder.

Specify if:

300.13 (F44.1) With dissociative fugue: Apparently purposeful travel or bewildered wandering that is associated with amnesia for identity or for other autobiographical information.

Source: Reprinted with permission from the *Diagnostic and Statistical Manual of Mental Disorders,* Fifth Edition, (Copyright 2013). American Psychiatric Association.

2002). Suicide risk is elevated in amnestic patients, especially as the condition remits and memory returns. Common co-occurring disorders include conversion disorder, depressive disorders, PTSD, and personality disorders (American Psychiatric Association, 2013).

Typically, the onset of dissociative amnesia is sudden, although it may be delayed from the precipitating stressor. The course of dissociative amnesia is variable with most patients spontaneously recovering while others develop a more chronic amnesia. Chronic cases may persist for decades, and tend to develop more gradually. One review of 25 such patients found that the most common presentation was a selective, chronic loss of memory that did not have a sudden onset (Coons & Milstein, 1992). The incidence in the population is unknown, although reported cases of dissociative amnesia relating to previously forgotten childhood traumas increased through the 1990s (American Psychological Association, 2000). It is not clear whether the increase can be ascribed to better identification of cases or to over-diagnosis among highly suggestible individuals. The *DSM-5* notes that a small community study found an incidence of 1.8% (American Psychiatric Association, 2013).

The "with dissociative fugue" specifier for dissociative amnesia stipulates both memory impairment and sudden travel away from home or regular surroundings. At the same time, there is disruption of personal identity, so the person is uncertain about important personal information (including name, residence, or profession). An individual with dissociative fugue may wander for periods of time ranging from brief journeys (of a few hours or days) to several months over thousands of miles. Most often, the person in the fugue state does not form a new identity; when that does occur, it appears to include more outgoing and uninhibited traits than the original one (American Psychological Association, 2000). Sometimes, however, new identities can be quite extensive, including assumption of a different name, a new residence, and involvement in new, complex social activities and functions. Amnesia associated with dissociative fugue can remain after the fugue state remits. Severe stressors or overwhelming life events are typically related to onset; offset is often hastened by removal from the stressful situation (American Psychiatric Association, 2013).

## Causal Factors

There is no clear evidence of genetic or biological influences in the development of the disorder. Most case reports and reviews have suggested that severe stressors or traumas trigger dissociative amnesia. Coons and Milstein (1992) found multiple stressful precipitants among the cases they reviewed. Among precipitating stressors for fugue, the most common appear to be marital discord, financial and occupational problems, and war-related events (Maldonado, Butler, & Spiegel, 2002). The psychoanalytic perspective presumes that the memory loss is the result of unconscious repression (rather than suppression) of the memory due to its threatening or unacceptable content, thus "dissociating" the memory from the person. The behavioral perspective assumes (similarly) that the amnesia is in some way negatively reinforced, as an avoidance or escape response.

## Treatment for Dissociative Amnesia

For years, the typical approaches to treating dissociative amnesia involved hypnosis or the drug sodium amytal, together with free association, to uncover unconscious memories and bring them to the surface. Supportive therapy takes place in a safe environment, working to facilitate recall and provide "reintegration" of the dissociated memories. No careful studies of the effectiveness of these treatments for dissociative amnesia exist, however (Maldonado, Butler, & Spiegel, 2002).

Because people with dissociative disorders are quite suggestible, there is a risk that the memories "recovered" during therapy may be produced through **iatrogenesis**. In other words, a false or altered memory could be created, inadvertently, during the therapy process as the client and therapist interact. There have been several experimental demonstrations of induced false memories in both children and adults, showing that it is possible to get people

**Iatrogenesis**

The inadvertent and avoidable induction of a condition or disorder by a therapist during the treatment process

to remember events that never happened (Loftus, 1997). Simply having people read a set of short articles that describe witnessing the "possession" of someone else caused subjects to rate this implausible event as more plausible and rendered them less certain that they had not experienced the event in childhood (Mazzoni, Loftus, & Kirsch, 2001). Results such as these suggest that iatrogenic false memories for clinically significant phenomena could be created rather easily. Indeed, there have now been legal cases involving clients who have accused their therapists of implanting false memories for the purpose of financial gain. One lawsuit involves a 41-year-old woman who claimed her therapist used hypnosis to implant false memories of rape, involvement in satanic cult rituals, and multiple personalities, after she sought treatment originally for an eating disorder. Other women at the same treatment center have made similar allegations (Caron, 2011). At the same time, there is strong criticism about the validity of the concept of *repressed memory*, which some consider illusionary (Bonanno, 2006). The heated debate, which in part is an argument about the foundations of psychoanalytic theory, continues to be very active, with

Dissociative amnesia is a memory disorder characterized by extreme memory loss that is caused by extensive psychological stress, rather than physical causes. (Shutterstock)

defenders of the notion insisting that repression is a valid concept and others claiming that the empirical evidence shows that trauma, in general, *enhances* memory (Rofé, 2008).

## 7.3b Dissociative Identity Disorder

Dissociative identity disorder (DID), formerly called multiple personality disorder, is perhaps the most unusual of the dissociative disorders. Perhaps because its symptoms are so strange (see *DSM-5* Diagnostic Criteria for Dissociative Identity Disorder), it has also received the most attention in

Do some people really switch from one personality to another without remembering?

| DSM-5 | **Diagnostic Criteria for Dissociative Identity Disorder** |
|---|---|

300.14 (F44.81) Dissociative Identity Disorder

A. Disruption of identity characterized by two or more distinct personality states, which may be described in some cultures as an experience of possession. The disruption in identity involves marked discontinuity in sense of self and sense of agency, accompanied by related alterations in affect, behavior, consciousness, memory, perception, cognition, and/or sensory-motor functioning. These signs and symptoms may be observed by others or reported by the individual.

B. Recurrent gaps in the recall of everyday events, important personal information, and/or traumatic events that are inconsistent with ordinary forgetting.

C. The symptoms cause clinically significant distress or impairment in social, occupational, or other important areas of functioning.

D. The disturbance is not a normal part of a broadly accepted cultural or religious practice.
**Note:** In children, the symptoms are not better explained by imaginary playmates or other fantasy play.

E. The symptoms are not attributable to the physiological effects of a substance (e.g., blackouts or chaotic behavior during alcohol intoxication) or another medical condition (complex partial seizures).

Source: Reprinted with permission from the *Diagnostic and Statistical Manual of Mental Disorders*, Fifth Edition, (Copyright 2013). American Psychiatric Association.

the literature and remains the most controversial. The diagnosis requires the presence of two or more distinct personalities disrupting one's personal identity and sense of personal control (which may also be experienced as being possessed by another person). For example, sufferers may have a sense of observing strong emotions, actions, or speech taking place without their control. Amnesia for some personal information that is usually asymmetrical (that is, some "alters" apparently remember more than others) is typical. It may also include lapses in memory for well-learned skills such as driving or reading. In addition, dissociative fugue is common, and individuals might suddenly find themselves in a place with no recollection of travelling there. Most with the condition also develop PTSD; and many other mental disorders (e.g., depression, somatic symptom disorders, substance-related disorders) are comorbid. Suicide risk is significantly elevated as well (American Psychiatric Association, 2013). Switching between personalities may be triggered by stressors and can occur in a matter of seconds or minutes. As personalities switch, the sufferer may take on a different tone of voice, a change in demeanor, or a different facial expression. The number of personalities may range from 2 to more than 100, but in half of the cases the individual has 10 or fewer identities (American Psychological Association, 2000). Importantly, certain dissociative experiences would not be included in the diagnosis. For example, children may commonly engage in fantasy activities with imaginary playmates, and this would not be considered an indication of DID. Similarly, some cultures practice spiritual or religious rites that result in possession states among participants. Interestingly, according to the *DSM-5*, "the majority of possession states around the world are normal" (American Psychiatric Association, 2013, p. 293), largely because they are not unwanted or involuntary.

In dissociative identity disorder, several years typically lapse between onset of first symptoms and diagnosis. The course tends to be fluctuating and chronic. A review of 50 cases of multiple personality disorder by Coons, Bowman, and Milstein (1988) found that most were women who displayed depression, had made suicide attempts, and carried a history of sexual abuse. Other co-occurring symptoms included headaches and conversion symptoms.

Dissociative identity disorder is a condition in which a person displays multiple distinct identities or personalities (known as alter egos or alters). The diagnosis requires at least two personalities that routinely take control of the individual's behavior with an associated memory loss, and symptoms cannot be due to effects of drug use or a medical condition. (iStock)

According to the *DSM-IV*, DID is much more commonly diagnosed in women than men, by a factor of 9 times or more. Women also tend to display more personalities than males (American Psychological Association, 2000). In contrast, the *DSM-5* is more cautious about sex ratios, noting that although females with DID do predominate in adult clinical settings, males are less likely to acknowledge a background of trauma and may thus be under-diagnosed (American Psychiatric Association, 2013). A recent estimate of prevalence in a city in central Turkey indicated it affects 1.1% of the female population (Sar, Akyuz, & Dooan, 2007). There has been a sharp rise in incidence over the past few decades, increasing from a few hundred cases worldwide to over 30,000 in North America alone; this explosive increase corresponds to increased public interest in popular portrayals of the condition in books and films such as *The Three Faces of Eve and Sybil* (Lilienfeld, et al., 1999). There is much controversy about whether the increase is due to improved diagnostic practice or to over-diagnosis of suggestible people.

Although the extreme dissociation characteristic of this disorder is unusual, the basic tendency to have two or more conflicting "selves" is familiar to most of us. One may be quite a different person at a beer party, at church, and at a political demonstration. Many of us have experienced in the process of growing up a conflict between the conforming, restrained, "good" self on the one hand and the nonconforming, rebellious, "acting out" self on the other hand. This particular kind of split is fairly common in multiple personalities: one may be more passive, while others are more hostile and controlling. Most often, it is the "host" personality that presents for treatment.

There have been reports that the various personalities in DID show physiological variations consistent with being "different" people. For example, handedness may change; some alters may need eyeglasses while others do not, and some manifest different EEG profiles in neurological assessments. However, the diagnostic value of these observations is unclear. For example, Putnam (1984) found that EEG differences in DID patients during personality switching were greater than those produced by stimulating subjects. In contrast, Coons, Milstein, and Marley (1982) found that a person who was role-playing multiple personality disorder was able to produce EEG differences across roles larger than those produced by two DID patients, leading to the conclusion that the EEG data reflect intensity of concentration and mood changes rather than any inherent brain differences. The ability to effectively simulate DID, even to produce different EEG profiles as a result, underlines the difficulty of accurate diagnosis.

Symptoms of DID can also be evoked by common interview and therapy techniques. Spanos, Weekes, and Bertrand (1985) reported they were able to create different personality presentations among college students by using the prevailing methods for DID treatment. Following brief hypnotic induction, the students were then given an interview that was almost identical to the one used to interview the "Hillside Strangler," Kenneth Bianchi, after his arrest for murder (Bianchi attempted to claim DID in his defense). Subjects in the experimental group displayed several symptoms of DID, including personalities with different behaviors and opposite tastes.

## Causal Factors

Very little information about DID comes from sources other than self-report, and there have been no controlled studies on etiology. Twin studies have not produced evidence of heritability although there have been reports that DID runs in families (American Psychological Association, 2000). Any genetic mechanism is unclear. Coons and his colleagues (1988) found no significant neurological or EEG abnormalities among 50 DID patients, suggesting there was no evidence of underlying brain etiology. Co-occurring disorders may influence the development of dissociative symptoms. DID is known to associate with substance abuse and with borderline personality disorder (Dell, 1998).

People with dissociative identity disorder frequently report histories of childhood physical and sexual abuse, and these events are generally considered central to the etiology of the disorder, as well as responsible for the gender differences in incidence. Abuse histories are reported in 70%–97% of DID patients, with incest cited most commonly

Sally Field (left) starred in the 1967 film, *Sybil*, based on a book by Folr Rheta Schreiber. The movie dramatizes the life of a shy young graduate student, Sybil Dorssett (in real life, Shirley Ardell Mason), suffering from dissociative identity disorder as a result of the psychological trauma she suffered as a child. (AP Wide World)

(Maldonado, Butler, & Spiegel, 2002). Similarities between DID and posttraumatic stress disorder have been noted by many, leading to a view that DID is a particular subtype of PTSD caused by severe abuse (e.g., Dell, 1998). Presumably, the individual emotionally escapes the abusive situation by dissociating. This perspective is perhaps the most widely held view on DID at present.

The ability of normal people to produce apparently different personality characteristics as a result of hypnosis or suggestion, together with the malleability of memory and the controversies of recovered memories, led Spanos (1994) to propose a sociocognitive model of dissociation and multiple personality. Within this view, multiplicity is an expectancy-guided and rule-governed display that develops iatrogenically when a suggestible person learns to adapt and enact multiple roles that are inadvertently suggested by therapists and clinicians. As a rule-governed social construction, traumatic experiences are not necessary for the occurrence of multiple personalities, which are established, shaped, legitimized, and maintained through social interaction between patient and therapist. This model would suggest that symptoms of multiple personality tend to develop after (rather than before) contact with therapists and that DID would increase in incidence as a function of the extent to which therapists become familiar with the diagnosis. Both of these arguments receive support in a careful reanalysis of the Spanos model by Lilienfeld and his colleagues (1999), who conclude that an iatrogenic model of DID is consistent with most currently available information on the disorder.

### Treatment for Dissociative Identity Disorder

The process of treatment in DID involves a therapeutic relationship of trust and cooperation, an understanding of the network of alters, treatment for the trauma, and work toward reintegrating the different personalities (often a type of conflict resolution between the different alters). Hypnosis is common, as is social support and involvement in social networks (Maldonado, Butler, & Spiegel, 2002). Many different techniques have been employed, including individual and group psychotherapies, marital therapies, family therapies, medications (including antidepressants, anti-psychotics, tranquilizers, and anticonvulsants), and electroconvulsive therapy. However, no well-controlled efficacy studies are available for DID treatment, either with pharmacotherapy or psychotherapy.

## 7.3c Depersonalization/Derealization Disorder

Depersonalization/derealization disorder involves the feelings of detachment or separation from one's self, or of feeling as though objects and individuals in the surrounding environment were unreal. Sometimes, this is experienced as if in a dream-like state, or as if floating above or observing one's self from the outside. These feelings are relatively common; and many people have experienced them transiently, perhaps in times of fatigue or as an aspect of religious or meditative practices. In fact, the *DSM-5* estimates that half of all adults have experienced the sensation (American Psychiatric Association, 2013). In depersonalization/derealization disorder, such feelings are persistent or recurrent, cause marked distress, and are associated with impairment in daily functioning. Affected people may feel as if they are automatons or as if they are living in a movie. Nonetheless, they do not lose contact with reality by concluding such sensations are literally true.

Transient depersonalization symptoms occur in many people exposed to life-threatening situations and can be associated with several other conditions such as PTSD and panic attacks. Lifetime prevalence of depersonalization is about 2% (American Psychiatric Association, 2013). Average age of onset appears to be around age 16, and onset is rare after age 25. The episodes may be very brief or last for years. Most often, symptoms are described as surroundings seeming unreal, as though looking through a fog or having the body detached from the person (Simeon, Knutelska, Nelson, & Guralnik, 2003). Sufferers sometimes interpret their symptoms as evidence of "going crazy." The course tends to be chronic and worsens under stressful situations. Although the *DSM-IV* reported that it was diagnosed twice as often among females as among males (APA, 2000), the *DSM-5* claims that the male-to-female ratio is 1:1 (American Psychiatric Association, 2013).

## Causal Factors

The cause or causes of depersonalization disorder are unknown, although theories have ranged from the completely physiological to the completely psychological (Maldonado, Butler, & Spiegel, 2002). There are no data on familial or genetic influences at this time. Simeon and his colleagues (2003) report that immediate precipitants among 117 reviewed cases of depersonalization disorder included severe stress, panic, depression, and drug use. According to Maldonado and his colleagues (2002), "exposure to traumatic experiences seems to be the common etiological factor in this disorder" (p. 471). The *DSM-5* notes that there is a clear connection between the disorder and childhood interpersonal trauma for most individuals, although sexual abuse is less reliably associated than in the case of DID (American Psychiatric Association, 2013).

## Treatment of Depersonalization Disorder

No controlled studies have addressed the treatment of depersonalization disorder. SSRIs do not appear to be more effective than placebos in treating depersonalization disorder although in a small, uncontrolled trial the opiate receptor site blocker naltrexone was associated with

a 30% improvement in symptoms (Simeon & Knutelska, 2005). Hypnosis and variety of psychotherapies have been employed in individual cases, but as yet no solid data on relative effectiveness of these treatments are available (Maldonado, Butler, & Spiegel, 2002).

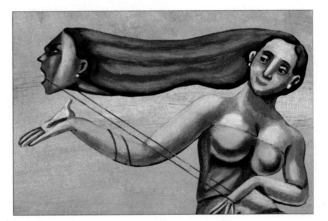
(Corbis)

The remaining dissociative disorder categories are *other specified dissociative disorder* and *unspecified dissociative disorder*. They are used for sub-threshold dissociative conditions in which symptoms may be milder or more acute, or for which the dissociative conditions have not been described elsewhere. For example, "identity disturbance due to prolonged and intense coercive persuasion" may describe conditions in which people change or question their identity as a result of torture, indoctrination, or brainwashing. Another example is dissociative trance, involving profound unresponsiveness and loss of awareness of the immediate surroundings. In this state, individuals seem insensitive to environmental stimuli and may temporarily seem paralyzed or unconscious. Religious or cultural practices that produce trance states would not be considered symptoms (American Psychiatric Association, 2013).

# 7.4 A Concluding Comment

The somatic symptom disorders and dissociative disorders attempt to classify a diverse set of troubling conditions that are particularly difficult to distinguish from malingering and factitious disorder, and that overlap frequently with other types of mental disorders. Many people have combinations of anxiety, depressive, somatoform, and dissociative concerns; and their conditions may not be easily classified among the disorders considered here. At the same time, the very unusual and interesting nature of these disorders guarantees continued clinical interest into their development and their treatment. The changes in these areas wrought by the *DSM-5* will be tested in broad practice application and clinical research, in the coming years, to see if both reliability and validity of these diagnoses have improved in real terms.

# Chapter Review

## TO SUM UP ...

- Somatic symptom disorders involve the development of bodily symptoms that cause excessive distress or impairment.

- Dissociative disorders are disturbances of consciousness, memory, and identity.

- Both the somatic symptom disorders and dissociative classifications suffered, historically, from low diagnostic reliability. In addition, they may be difficult to distinguish from symptoms that are intentionally produced. *DSM-5* revisions in these categories were significant.

- There is limited evidence for a hereditary contribution to somatic symptom disorders and dissociative disorders.

- Specific stressful experiences are present, either currently or in the recent past, in many cases of somatic symptom disorders and dissociative disorders. Co-existing anxiety and depressive disorders are frequently present as well.

- Very few controlled evaluations have been conducted regarding the effectiveness of different treatments for these disorders. Available evidence indicates that selective serotonin reuptake inhibitors and cognitive-behavior therapy are more useful for somatic symptom disorders than for dissociative disorders.

## KEY TERMS

Aphonia   171

Autosuggestion   172

Conversion   170

Generalized amnesia   177

Iatrogenesis   178

La belle indifférence   171

Localized amnesia   177

Malingering   165

Mirror neurons   172

Munchausen syndrome   166

Paruresis   176

Pseudocyesis   176

Psychogenic   169

Selective amnesia   177

# QUESTIONS FOR STUDY

- Describe the differences between malingering, factitious disorder, and conversion disorder. Support your discussion with examples of each type of classification.

- Discuss the rationale behind two treatment approaches for conversion disorder.

- Dissociative identity disorder is particularly fascinating and controversial. Identify two possible explanations for the development of this disorder and the empirical evidence for each explanation.

- Discuss the association between PTSD and the dissociative disorders.

# POP QUIZ

1. Luke was facing 20 years to life for his latest armed robbery. Although he never suffered from a psychiatric disorder in his life, he told the psychiatrist that he was hearing voices which told him to rob other people. This would best be described as _____.

   A. a conversion disorder
   B. factitious disorder
   C. malingering
   D. iatrogenic disorder

2. Laura has a tendency to invent or exaggerate her symptoms for no obvious motive or reason, apart from playing sick. She would be diagnosed with _____.

   A. conversion disorder
   B. factitious disorder
   C. dissociative identity disorder
   D. malingering

3. All **except** which of the following are categorized as *DSM-5* somatic symptom disorders?
   A. conversion disorder
   B. body dysmorphic disorder
   C. illness anxiety disorder
   D. pseudocyesis

4. Which disorder has an equal male-female sex ratio?
   A. illness anxiety disorder
   B. dissociative identity disorder
   C. somatic symptom disorder
   D. dissociative amnesia

5. Nearly constant and distressing pain would most likely occur in_____.
   A. conversion disorder
   B. somatic symptom disorder
   C. illness anxiety disorder
   D. hypochondriasis

6. Which of the following is **not** a conversion symptom?
   A. amnesia
   B. convulsions
   C. paralysis
   D. deafness

7. Somatic symptom disorder can be typed as _____.
   A. symptomatic or asymptomatic
   B. chronic or acute
   C. mild, moderate, severe
   D. care-seeking type, care-avoiding type

8. _____ involves a preoccupation with the fear that one has a serious disease, based on a misinterpretation of body symptoms.
   A. Illness anxiety disorder
   B. Conversion disorder
   C. Pain disorder
   D. Somatic symptom disorder

9. Depersonalization or derealization symptoms have been experienced by what percentage of the U.S. population?
   A. 5
   B. 10
   C. 25
   D. 50

10. People who suffer from conversion disorder also commonly suffer from all **except** which of the following?
    A. depression
    B. anxiety
    C. somatic symptom disorder
    D. alcohol use disorder

11. Dissociative identity disorder may be related to _____.
    A. PTSD
    B. generalized anxiety disorder
    C. body dysmorphic disorder
    D. conversion disorder

12. After seeing his best friend shot and killed, Tom suffered a loss of memory for some but not all events during that particular period of time. This is known as _____.
    A. generalized amnesia
    B. localized amnesia
    C. selective amnesia
    D. declarative amnesia

13. Empirical evidence shows that trauma, in general, _____, which is a major issue in regards to the validity of the concept of repressed memory.
    A. has no effect on memory
    B. contributes to memory loss
    C. impairs memory
    D. enhances memory

14. Which disorder appears to be rarest?
    A. dissociative identity disorder
    B. conversion disorder
    C. somatic symptom disorder
    D. depersonalization/derealization disorder

15. While Jack did not lose contact with reality, he did feel a recurrent feeling of detachment or separation from his body, sort of like watching himself in a movie. This is known as _____.
    A. amnesia
    B. depersonalization
    C. conversion
    D. trance

Additional study resources are available at **www.BVTLab.com**

# CHAPTER OVERVIEW

## CHAPTER OPENER QUESTIONS

Are personality disorders different from other mental disorders?

Can someone have more than one personality disorder? Can the disorders mix together?

Do men and women tend to have different personality disorders?

How do personality disorders begin, and can they be treated effectively?

Were antisocial adults antisocial children?

(Shutterstock)

# Personality Disorders

The mental disorders that have been discussed in earlier chapters describe conditions that seem to intrude on a person's normal functioning. That is, we can talk about them as a change in behavior, which perhaps had an onset triggered by severe stressors or traumas, or which began more gradually and grew worse as a preoccupation with illness or contamination intensified. Sometimes, the clinical symptoms are more evident in particular settings or circumstances, such as high places or social situations.

For some people, their behavior creates problems for themselves or others across many different situations at many different times, because their dysfunctional actions seem to be characteristic of how they move through life. These stable patterns of behaving and of thinking have been fairly consistent throughout their lives, traceable back to adolescence or perhaps childhood. To acquaintances, these consistent tendencies and the problems they cause seem to be "the way a person is" at some fundamental level of personal identity.

> Are personality disorders different from other mental disorders?

The *DSM-III* introduced the notion of separating those disorders that represent changes in a person's functioning from those dysfunctions that have been consistently problematic throughout adult life. Its multiaxial system identified the former as Axis I disorders and the latter as Axis II disorders. The placement of personality disorders on Axis II was a recognition that, in some ways, disturbances of personality are different than other mental disorders. Although Axis I and Axis II distinctions were abandoned in the *DSM-5*, personality disorders continue to present particular challenges for both diagnosis and treatment.

## 8.1 The Concept of Personality

It's important to recognize that **personality** is not a "thing" but rather a way of acting and thinking. As a hypothetical explanatory or descriptive construct within psychology, it has a long and controversial history. Although disputes remain, there is some general consensus among psychologists that individuals tend to develop broadly characteristic ways of viewing and organizing their world, of interacting with others, and of coping with challenges; these approaches to the world tend to become more stable and predictable as people grow from childhood to adolescence to adulthood. This stable and enduring pattern of relating to oneself and to the world has been referred to as the individual's personality.

### 8.1a Assessments of Personality

Psychologists have created several techniques for personality assessment. As described in Chapter 4, projective techniques use vague or unstructured items that are presented to the examinee, who then engages the items to identify a picture, tell a story, complete a drawing or a sentence, or in some other way respond to the stimuli. The assumption of projective testing is that an individual will, often symbolically, project (in the sense of the Freudian defense of projection) important aspects of personality into his or her response.

Trait theorists assume that personality is made of a collection of psychological traits, such as kindness or dependability, which can be identified and measured. In this view, a person may or may not possess the trait of honesty, for example; and that information allows

**Personality**
The stable and enduring pattern of relating to oneself and to the world

**Phrenologists**

Those who attempted to describe personality by feeling the bumps on a person's skull

**Personality inventory**

A self-report questionnaire in which brief responses to a collection of test items are used to assess personal characteristics or behaviors across various personality dimensions

**Factor analysis**

Mathematical technique to analyze a matrix of correlations to reduce dimensions and identify factors that may simplify the relationships

**Neuroticism**

Personality factor associated with the tendency to experience negative emotions

**Extroversion**

Personality factor associated with the tendency to be outgoing or socially gregarious

**Psychoticism**

Personality factor associated with the tendency to show aggressiveness and interpersonal hostility

**Big Five**

Dimensional model of personality that emphasizes the mixture of five main factors: openness to experience, conscientiousness, extroversion, agreeableness, and neuroticism

**Openness to experience**

Personality factor associated with a tendency to show imaginativeness, independence, and preference for variety

(iStock)

some prediction of what that person might do in the future. The **phrenologists** attempted to assess traits by feeling the location of bumps on the skull, which purportedly revealed physical evidence of their presence. Later approaches began measuring traits by a series of questions, and these were combined into large collections called **personality inventories**.

**Factor analysis** developed from mathematical attempts to tease apart the responses given in intelligence testing, and the procedure was soon applied to personality inventories as well. Looking for clusters of inter-correlated items within the tests identifies personality factors. Those clusters are then assumed to reveal information about the underlying foundational tendencies that make up personality. There is no rule about how many factors should be identified; it is mathematically possible to extract several different factor structures from any set of data (Gould, 1981). However, the utility of factor analysis is in the reduction of complexity it may provide. If responses to 100 different questions can be categorized into three or four clusters without too much loss of information, then the procedure may be useful. In other words, the value of identifying personality factors rests in how much variability in test scores each factor "captures" or explains. Over the past 50 years, several factorial models of personality have been proposed, each with support from factor analysis. Eysenck and Eysenck (1969) summarized a three-factor model, arguing that personality consisted of various amounts of **neuroticism** (the tendency to experience negative emotions), **extroversion** (outgoingness and social gregariousness), and **psychoticism** (anger and aggression), and constructed the *Eysenck Personality Inventory* to assess them. Cattell used factor analysis to construct a 16-factor model of personality and devised the *Sixteen Personality Factor Questionnaire* (16-PF) to measure them (Cattell & Stice, 1957). At present, the model endorsed by most psychometricians is a five-factor model, often called the **Big Five**, in which the important components are **openness to experience**, **conscientiousness, extroversion, agreeableness**, and **neuroticism** (McCrae & Costa, 1987). Debate about precisely what those factors measure continues; however, within this perspective, personality consists of the relative degree to which each of these five tendencies is expressed.

Extroversion means outgoingness and social gregariousness.
(iStock)

## 8.1b  Categories or Dimensions

The *DSM-5* is a categorical system of classification. There are 10 primary categories of personality disorders listed, and a person qualifies for a diagnosis depending on how many diagnostic criteria are met according to the judgment of the diagnostician. For example, a history of criminal activity and interpersonal exploitiveness, including at least three of seven criteria involving violations of the rights of others or impulsive and reckless activities, might qualify someone for a diagnosis of antisocial personality disorder within the categorical model. However, the factors presumed to underlie personality are dimensional in structure. That is, people are not either extroverted or introverted but rather can act in either or both ways to various degrees, depending on circumstances. Using a scale of 0 to 10, people might locate themselves along the extroversion-introversion dimension by a score of "2" or "6", for example. Within a dimensional model, certain combinations across the factor dimensions, such as high extroversion and low conscientiousness and agreeableness, would describe antisocial personality.

## 8.1c Classifying Personality Disorders

Distinguishing normal personality from disordered personality may be a complex process. Certainly, the assessment requires accurate information about a person's long-term cognitive and behavioral patterns across many different circumstances and situations. Even if disturbed

Those who are described as introverted tend to prefer solitude or small social groups rather than large social gatherings, and seem more interested in their own thoughts and feelings than the world around them. (Shutterstock)

personalities can be reliably distinguished from the variations of normal ones, the indications of a possible characterological disorder must be separated from distress or impairment that can be explained by a another long-standing condition. Depression, anxiety, or more florid symptoms such as delusional thinking can occur in the context of certain personality disorders, even in the absence of any other diagnosis. Therefore, a clinician must decide if a chronic depressive state is best described by a personality disorder or some other alternative (e.g., dysthymic disorder). The basic criteria for deciding whether a personality disorder exists are described in *DSM-5* General Diagnostic Criteria for a Personality Disorder.

In the *DSM-5*, personality disorders are enduring and inflexible patterns that cause distress either for the person or for other people. They involve disturbances in a combination of areas of global functioning—including mood, cognition, social interactions, and control of impulses—which cannot be better explained by a medical condition, the effects of a

**Conscientiousness**

Personality factor associated with a tendency to be organized, self-disciplined, and responsible

**Agreeableness**

Personality factor associated with a tendency to be caring, helpful, and cooperative

| *DSM-5* | **General Diagnostic Criteria for a Personality Disorder** |
|---|---|

A. An enduring pattern of inner experience and behavior that deviates markedly from the expectations of the individual's culture. This pattern is manifested in two (or more) of the following areas:
1. cognition (i.e., ways of perceiving and interpreting self, other people, and events)
2. affectivity (i.e., the range, intensity, lability, and appropriateness of emotional response)
3. interpersonal functioning
4. impulse control

B. The enduring pattern is inflexible and pervasive across a broad range of personal and social situations.

C. The enduring pattern leads to significant distress or impairment in social, occupational, or other important areas of functioning

D. The pattern is stable and of long duration, and its onset can be traced back at least to adolescence or early adulthood.

E. The enduring pattern is not better accounted for as a manifestation or consequence of another mental disorder.

F. The enduring pattern is not due to the direct physiological effects of a substance (e.g., a drug of abuse, a medication) or to a general medical condition (e.g., head trauma).

Source: Reprinted with permission from the *Diagnostic and Statistical Manual of Mental Disorders,* Fifth Edition, (Copyright 2013). American Psychiatric Association.

substance, or another mental disorder. They are long-standing conditions that can be traced back, if not to childhood patterns, at least to adolescence or early adulthood.

The process of diagnosing personality disorders is made more challenging by certain complications that may not be present in other diagnoses. For example, some personality-disordered individuals are not particularly bothered by their own personality patterns, which likely cause more distress for others. They may not seek, accept, or cooperate with clinical involvement. In other personality disorders, exaggeration of symptoms is among the defining features, obviously contributing to the difficulty of accurate diagnosis.

It is common for people in treatment to have two or more disorders concurrently, and these may interact in complex ways that contribute to the severity of each. In addition, there are significant overlaps among the symptoms of the ten *DSM-5* personality disorders, so that mixed types and/or comorbid personality disorder diagnoses are frequent. In fact, Zimmerman, Rothschild, and Chelminski (2005) used a structured interview for *DSM-IV* personality disorders to assess 859 patients and found that whenever the diagnostic criteria for one personality disorder were met, the majority of patients were diagnosed with more than one.

As might be expected from these issues, reliability problems have plagued the personality disorder classifications. The *DSM-III* reliability field trials found kappa values of 0.56 and 0.65 across the two phases (American Psychological Association, 1980). Even lower values were found in the *ICD-10* field trials more than a decade later when reliability was 0.47 for personality disorders as a group with only 0.12 for histrionic personality disorder and 0.33 for dependent personality disorder (Sartorius, et al., 1993). The *DSM-5* field trials found the reliability for borderline personality disorder to be "questionable" at 0.36, while the even lower 0.31 for obsessive-compulsive personality disorder was based on too few subjects to be considered an accurate estimate (Regier et al., 2013). Such poor levels of diagnostic reliability raise serious questions about the value of these classifications within the *DSM* system, a point to which we shall return later.

> Can someone have more than one personality disorder? Can the disorders mix together?

Another diagnostic consideration involves the increasing tendency to apply these diagnoses to adolescents. Although many psychologists have argued that infant temperaments and early childhood events form the structure of later adult personality, most psychologists assume that the pervasive patterns of thought and behavior that are called personalities develop gradually as individuals mature. Strictly speaking, the *DSM-5* requires onset of most personality disorders by early adulthood, but it does not rule out use of these labels beforehand. In the relatively rare instances in which a child or adolescent under the age of 18 is diagnosed with a personality disorder, the problematic features must have persisted for at least 1 year (American Psychiatric Association, 2013). One examination of the application of personality diagnoses in adolescents, ages 14–18, found an over-diagnosis of antisocial and avoidant personality disorders when the *DSM-IV* criteria were applied to that age group (Western, Shelder, Durrett, Glass, & Martens, 2003).

Personality disorders appear to be very common among the mental health population. Nearly one-third of the patients interviewed by Zimmerman and his colleagues (2005) met the criteria for at least one personality disorder; and when the "Personality Disorder Not Otherwise Specified" category was included, the rate increased to almost half of the group. The incidence in the general population of any personality disorder was recently estimated at just over 9%, based on sub-sample of the National Comorbidity Survey Replication (Lenzenweger, Lane, Loranger, & Kessler, 2007).

Recognizing the overlap of personality disorders around certain symptom typologies, the *DSM-5* loosely organizes the 10 disorders into three clusters. The personality disorders within *Cluster A* (paranoid, schizoid, schizotypal) tend to present symptoms that observers consider odd or eccentric. Those within *Cluster B* (antisocial, borderline, histrionic, narcissistic) are associated with dramatic, emotional, and erratic symptoms. In *Cluster C* disorders (avoidant, dependent, obsessive-compulsive), people present symptoms that generally appear avoidant or fearful. The *DSM-5* cautions that this clustering system, "although useful in some research and educational situations, has serious limitations and has not been consistently validated" (American Psychiatric Association, 2013, p. 646). The terms are used here for simplifying the presentation; but, as we will see, ongoing research continues to recognize those limitations.

## **8.1d**  Treating Personality Disorders

By their chronicity, stability, and involvement in several life areas, personality disorders are difficult to treat. As mentioned above, many people with these disorders resist or refuse treatment or disagree with the need for change; they may enter therapy only because of social or legal coercion (Meyer & Deitsch, 1996). They may also sabotage therapy. Social relationships are usually severely disrupted, and often the characteristics that produce interpersonal difficulties also interfere with the client-therapist connection. Much effort is required to forge a therapeutic relationship, and clinicians are frequently confronted with boundary concerns and transference and counter-transference issues.

> **Do men and women tend to have different personality disorders?**

The complex combinations of overlapping personality disorders and other disorders provide unique treatment challenges. Comorbidity is quite common: up to 50% of patients with either schizotypal personality disorder or borderline personality disorder also meet the criteria for a depressive disorder (Woo-Ming & Siever, 1998). Usually, the presence of a personality disorder is associated with poorer outcome of treatment for the comorbid condition, although this is not invariably true (Crits-Christoph & Barber, 2002; Levenson, Wallace, Fournier, Rucci, & Frank, 2012).

In many cases, treatment is directed at particular deficits or symptoms rather than any underlying condition. Psychological interventions may be long-term and often include either marital or family therapy (Meyer & Deitsch, 1996) to address social dysfunction. Pharmacological interventions for personality disorders may be tailored to specific signs of depression, anxiety, impulsivity, or panic, guided by symptom presentation. Overall, *Cluster A* symptoms appear to be best treated with atypical antipsychotic drugs, whereas SSRIs are most readily prescribed for those in *Clusters B* and *C* (Grossman, 2004). In general, there has been very little controlled research on the relative effectiveness of treatments for personality disorders, with the few exceptions that will be noted below.

Many people with personality disorders resist or refuse treatment or disagree with the need for change; they may enter therapy only because of social or legal coercion. When they do begin regular treatment sessions, personality disorder patients may even sabotage their own therapy. (iStock)

## **8.2**  *Cluster A* Personality Disorders

*Cluster A* personality disorders involve symptoms that are described as odd or eccentric. Normally, these symptoms are not of sufficient intensity to include delusions and hallucinations; however, when individuals are under sufficient stress, brief psychotic states (ranging from minutes to hours) may occur. These disorders invariably involve restriction of social connection with others. Lenzenweger and his colleagues (2007) estimate that 5.7% of the population meets the criteria for at least one of the *Cluster A* diagnoses. An overview of the personality disorders included in *Cluster A* is shown in Table 8-1.

> **How do personality disorders begin, and can they be treated effectively?**

**Table 8-1**   DSM-5 *Cluster A* Personality Disorders

| Disorder | Key Descriptions | Sex Ratio |
|---|---|---|
| Paranoid personality disorder | Pervasive distrust and suspiciousness | More common among males |
| Schizoid personality disorder | Pervasive social detachment, emotional restriction | Slightly more common among females |
| Schizotypal personality disorder | Pervasive social and interpersonal deficits, with cognitive or perceptual distortions and eccentric behavior | Slightly more common among males |

Source: Reprinted with permission from the *Diagnostic and Statistical Manual of Mental Disorders*, Fifth Edition, (Copyright 2013). American Psychiatric Association.

## 8.2a   Paranoid Personality Disorder

People with paranoid personality disorder (see *DSM-5* Diagnostic Criteria for Paranoid Personality Disorder) are distrustful, suspicious, and expect others to take advantage of them in nearly all circumstances. They do not show a sense of humor and rarely relax or let down their guard in social situations. They take offense readily and hold grudges easily for some unintentional slight that they have interpreted as malevolent. Others may describe them as angry, litigious, hostile, stubborn, or sarcastic. These characteristics help to keep them isolated from others, and typically they have few or no close friend or confidants.

Jealousy and envy, together with an excessive view of one's own self-importance, are characteristic. The paranoid pattern of interacting with others may be traceable to childhood but must begin by early adulthood for the diagnosis. During periods of stress, those with paranoid personality disorder sometimes experience brief psychotic episodes. Co-occurring disorders often include major depressive disorder, agoraphobia, obsessive-compulsive disorder, and substance disorders. National surveys have estimated the prevalence of paranoid personality disorder at between 2.3% and 4.4% of the general population. Paranoid personality disorder is more commonly diagnosed among males (American Psychiatric Association, 2013).

| *DSM -5* | Diagnostic Criteria for Paranoid Personality Disorder |
|---|---|

301.0 (F60.0) Paranoid Personality Disorder

A. A pervasive distrust and suspiciousness of others such that their motives are interpreted as malevolent, beginning by early adulthood and present in a variety of contexts, as indicated by four (or more) of the following:

1. Suspects, without sufficient basis, that others are exploiting, harming, or deceiving him or her.
2. Is preoccupied with unjustified doubts about the loyalty or trustworthiness of friends or associates.
3. Is reluctant to confide in others because of unwarranted fear that the information will be used maliciously against him or her.
4. Reads hidden demeaning or threatening meanings into benign remarks or events.
5. Persistently bears grudges, i.e., is unforgiving of insults, injuries, or slights.
6. Perceives attacks on his or her character or reputation that are not apparent to others and is quick to react angrily or to counterattack.
7. Has recurrent suspicions, without justification, regarding fidelity of spouse or sexual partner.

B. Does not occur exclusively during the course of schizophrenia, a bipolar disorder or depressive disorder with psychotic features, or another psychotic disorder and is not attributable to the physiological effects of another medical condition.

**Note:** If criteria are met prior to the onset of schizophrenia, add "premorbid," i.e., "paranoid personality disorder (premorbid)."

Source: Reprinted with permission from the Diagnostic and Statistical Manual of Mental Disorders, Fifth Edition, (Copyright 2013). American Psychiatric Association.

## Causal Factors

There is some evidence that paranoid personality disorder is more likely when a history of either schizophrenia or delusional disorder, persecutory type, exists within the family (American Psychiatric Association, 2013). Psychological mistreatment or trauma in childhood and particular cultural experiences might play a role in its development. However, the causes of paranoid personality disorder remain unknown.

## Treatment of Paranoid Personality Disorder

No controlled studies have been completed on either pharmacological or psychological treatment outcomes for paranoid personality disorder. Cognitive therapy may be of value although the only available data are from case study methods (Crits-Christoph & Barber, 2002). A general approach in psychotherapy requires careful work at relationship building, collaboration in planning the goals of therapy, avoidance of techniques that emphasize vulnerability (such as hypnosis), and gradual challenging and testing of beliefs (Meyer & Deitsch, 1996). Antipsychotic medications may be prescribed to target symptoms of paranoid ideation. However, there are no data concerning the relative effectiveness of such approaches.

# 8.2b Schizoid Personality Disorder

Those diagnosed with schizoid personality disorder (see *DSM-5* Diagnostic Criteria for Schizoid Personality Disorder) show a pervasive detachment from social relationships and a restricted range of emotional expression with others. They may appear cold or aloof and seem to have little interest in relationships with families or friends. In fact, they prefer to be alone and choose activities that will keep them so, including night jobs. Their lack of emotional expression is notable; they react passively to important events around them and are not easily aroused to anger or any emotional display. They are not interested in sexual relationships or experiences; in the rare event that they date or marry, it is because they passively accept the initiation by others.

These people are largely indifferent to the praise or criticism of others—unlike paranoid personality disorder where the response to even slight criticism is overblown. In both types of disorders, social relationships are impaired. People with schizoid personality disorder are loners who seem oblivious to social cues or normal social customs such as greetings.

| *DSM-5* | Diagnostic Criteria for Schizoid Personality Disorder |
|---|---|

301.20 (F60.1) Schizoid Personality Disorder

A. A pervasive pattern of detachment from social relationships and a restricted range of expression of emotions in interpersonal settings, beginning by early adulthood and present in a variety of contexts, as indicated by four (or more) of the following:

1. Neither desires nor enjoys close relationships, including being part of a family.
2. Almost always chooses solitary activities.
3. Has little, if any interest in having sexual experiences with another person.
4. Takes pleasure in few, if any, activities.
5. Lacks close friends or confidants other than first-degree relatives.
6. Appears indifferent to the praise or criticism of others.
7. Shows emotional coldness, detachment, or flattened affectivity.

B. Does not occur exclusively during the course of schizophrenia, a bipolar disorder or depressive disorder with psychotic features, another psychotic disorder, or autism spectrum disorder and is not attributable to the physiological effects of another medical condition.

**Note:** If criteria are met prior to the onset of schizophrenia, add "premorbid," i.e., "schizoid personality disorder (premorbid)."

Source: Reprinted with permission from the *Diagnostic and Statistical Manual of Mental Disorders,* Fifth Edition, (Copyright 2013). American Psychiatric Association.

Prevalence of the disorder is between 3% and 5% of the population, and it is diagnosed slightly more often in males (American Psychiatric Association, 2013).

### Causal Factors

There may be an increased prevalence of schizoid personality disorder in families where schizophrenia or schizotypal personality disorder is present (American Psychiatric Association, 2013). Such overlap may suggest common biological or environmental factors. However, the involvement of those factors in the development of schizoid personality disorder remains unclear.

### Treatment of Schizoid Personality Disorder

It is rare for people with schizoid personality disorder to seek treatment, and few case studies have been reported. No controlled studies have been completed on either pharmacological or psychological treatment outcomes for schizoid personality disorder. Psychological interventions may focus on social skills training and increasing social involvement; however, in most cases, the individual is not interested in increased social connection.

## 8.2c Schizotypal Personality Disorder

Schizotypal personality disorder (see *DSM-5* Diagnostic Criteria for Schizotypal Personality Disorder) involves social deficits and social discomfort, combined with distortions of perception and cognition and eccentric behavior. Those who qualify for the diagnosis find close relationships uncomfortable and usually, like with schizoid personality disorder, do not have close friends or confidants outside of family members. However, they are not cold or aloof but instead feel anxious in social settings because they do not feel like they "fit in." Their thinking and perception would seem unusual to other people. They may believe that they can cause events by thinking about them or have the idea that events in their surroundings have a special meaning for them (**ideas of reference**). In addition, they may dress and speak

**Ideas of reference**

False interpretation of events in terms of special meaning for the self

---

| *DSM-5* | **Diagnostic Criteria for Schizotypal Personality Disorder** |
|---|---|

301.22 (F21) Schizotypal Personality Disorder

A.  A pervasive pattern of social and interpersonal deficits marked by acute discomfort with, and reduced capacity for, close relationships as well as by cognitive or perceptual distortions and eccentricities of behavior, beginning by early adulthood and present in a variety of contexts, as indicated by five (or more) of the following:

1.  Ideas of reference (excluding delusions of reference).
2.  Odd beliefs or magical thinking that influences behavior and is inconsistent with subcultural norms (e.g., superstitiousness, belief in clairvoyance, telepathy, or "sixth sense"; in children or adolescents, bizarre fantasies or preoccupations).
3.  Unusual perceptual experiences, including bodily illusions.
4.  Odd thinking and speech (e.g., vague, circumstantial, metaphorical, overelaborate, or stereotyped).
5.  Suspiciousness or paranoid ideation.
6.  Inappropriate or restricted affect.
7.  Behavior or appearance that is odd, eccentric, or peculiar.
8.  Lack of close friends or confidants other than first-degree relatives.
9.  Excessive social anxiety that does not diminish with familiarity and tends to be associated with paranoid fears rather than negative judgment about self.

B.  Does not occur exclusively during the course of schizophrenia, a bipolar disorder or depressive disorder with psychotic features, another psychotic disorder, or autism spectrum disorder.

**Note:** If criteria are met prior to the onset of schizophrenia, add "premorbid," i.e., "schizotypal personality disorder (premorbid)."

Source: Reprinted with permission from the *Diagnostic and Statistical Manual of Mental Disorders,* Fifth Edition, (Copyright 2013). American Psychiatric Association.

in unusual ways ( for example, clothes that do not fit together or loosely connected speech). Superstitions are common, and the individual may claim clairvoyance or telepathic abilities. None of these unusual beliefs quite reaches delusional proportions, however.

The term "schizotypal" reveals the assumed connection of this personality disorder to schizophrenia and to schizoid personality disorder, as well. Indeed, some have suggested that the *Cluster A* disorders occur within a *schizophrenic spectrum* of related conditions (e.g., (Siever & Davis, 2004). In many ways, the pattern of behavior described here is a "sub-threshold" version of schizophrenia, and similar symptoms were diagnosed in the *DSM-II* as "latent" schizophrenia. It seems surprising, then, that only a small percentage of these people later develop schizophrenia (American Psychiatric Association, 2013). It does frequently co-occur with schizoid personality disorder. The diagnoses share several similar criteria (social deficits, lack of close friends other than family and restricted range of emotions), and these two disorders had the highest comorbidity rate of all personality disorders (37%) in the Zimmerman, et al. (2005) study. There is also a high prevalence of depressive disorder in schizotypal individuals. If there is a gender imbalance, it is in favor of males; and it may affect about 4% of the population (American Psychiatric Association, 2013).

## Causal Factors

Schizotypal personality disorder tends to run in families, especially those in which schizophrenia is present (American Psychological Association, 2000), leading most to conclude that at least a modest genetic vulnerability exists. Siever and Davis (2004) note increased evidence of shared genetic, metabolic, and behavioral abnormalities between these disorders, as well as distinctive developmental paths that may actually result in some protection for those with schizotypal personality disorder from schizophrenia.

## Treatment of Schizotypal Personality Disorder

The commonalities between schizotypal personality disorder and schizophrenia suggest that antipsychotic medications could be useful in treatment. Limited studies have found a modest and generalized response to low-dose antipsychotic medication such as haloperidol in mixed groups of schizotypal and borderline personality disorders; results with antidepressant medications appear less certain (Koenigsberg, Woo-Ming, Siever, & Siever, 2002). There have been no controlled treatment outcome studies of psychotherapies for schizotypal personality disorder.

# 8.3 *Cluster B* Personality Disorders

An overview of the personality disorders listed in *Cluster B* is shown in Table 8-2. These disorders tend to involve symptom presentations that may be dramatic, emotional, or erratic.

*Table 8-2*   **DSM-5 *Cluster B* Personality Disorders**

| Disorder | Key Descriptors | Sex Ratio |
|---|---|---|
| Antisocial personality disorder | Pervasive and reckless disregard of others, violations of rules or laws, impulsiveness, deceitfulness | More common among males |
| Borderline personality disorders | Pervasive instability in relationships, self-image, and feelings | More common among females |
| Histrionic personality disorder | Pervasive, excessive emotionality and attention seeking | Slightly more common among females |
| Narcissistic personality disorder | Pervasive exaggerated sense of self-importance, lack of empathy, and need for admiration | More common among males |

Source: Reprinted with permission from the *Diagnostic and Statistical Manual of Mental Disorders*, Fifth Edition, (Copyright 2013). American Psychiatric Association.

Threats of suicide, frequently of a manipulative nature, or self-mutilating acts are common. A factor-analytic study of the *Cluster B* personality disorders (Fossati, et al., 2007) suggests that the main components of all Cluster B diagnoses include impulsivity, aggressiveness, and novelty-seeking. Among the specific disorders, impulsiveness was more strongly associated with borderline personality disorder, while aggression correlated more strongly with antisocial and narcissistic diagnoses. The National Comorbidity Survey Replication found that *Cluster B* personality disorders, as a group, may affect about 1.5% of the general population (Lenzenweger, Lane, Loranger, & Kessler, 2007) although other estimates, including those given in the *DSM-5*, tend to be much higher.

## 8.3a Antisocial Personality Disorder

Common descriptors of those who display antisocial personality disorder (see *DSM-5* Diagnostic Criteria for Antisocial Personality Disorder) include deceitful, aggressive, manipulative, irresponsible, impulsive, and reckless. These people routinely violate the rights of others and appear to show no empathy, sympathy, or concern for the people around them. At the same time, they can be superficially charming and use this ability to exploit relationships and situations. They have a long history of such activities dating back to age 15 and evidence before that of conduct disorder (which involves patterns of serious rule violations, aggressiveness, deceitfulness, and destructiveness during adolescence). As adults, they commonly engage in acts for which they could be arrested.

Antisocial individuals may use dramatic acts in manipulative ways, such as threatening violence or suicide, in order to exploit others or to achieve some goal. At the same time, they are at higher risk for suicide than the general population (Duberstein & Conwell, 1997). As a rule, those with antisocial personality disorder are irresponsible parents and poor role models, and their offspring are subject to higher risk of mental disorders. Abuse or neglect of children is common. Histories of violence and exploitive sexuality, together with lack of remorse and indifference to the suffering of others, contribute to stormy and assaultive relationships.

Children and young adults that show a pattern of violence toward others, destruction of property or vandalism, theft or bullying, may be at risk for developing antisocial personality disorder. (iStock)

| DSM-5 | Diagnostic Criteria for Antisocial Personality Disorder |
|---|---|

301.7 (F60.2) Antisocial Personality Disorder

A. There is a pervasive pattern of disregard for and violation of the rights of others occurring since age 15 years, as indicated by 3 (or more) of the following:
  1. Failure to conform to social norms with respect to lawful behaviors as indicated by repeatedly performing acts that are grounds for arrest.
  2. Deceitfulness, as indicated by repeated lying, use of aliases, or conning others for personal profit or pleasure.
  3. Impulsivity or failure to plan ahead.
  4. Irritability and aggressiveness, as indicated by repeated physical fights or assaults.
  5. Reckless disregard for the safety of self or others.
  6. Consistent irresponsibility, as indicated by repeated failure to sustain consistent work behavior or honor financial obligations
  7. Lack of remorse, as indicated by being indifferent to or rationalizing having hurt, mistreated, or stolen from another.
B. The individual is at least age 18 years.
C. There is evidence of a conduct disorder with onset before age 15 years.
D. The occurrence of antisocial behavior is not exclusively during the course of schizophrenia or a bipolar disorder.

Source: Reprinted with permission from the *Diagnostic and Statistical Manual of Mental Disorders*, Fifth Edition, (Copyright 2013). American Psychiatric Association.

They are often in trouble with the law or are unemployed and may have spent long periods incarcerated in prisons or being homeless (American Psychiatric Association, 2013). They can also be quite effective at gaming the system: among a group of 115 opioid-dependent patients in clinical methadone maintenance trials, those with antisocial personality disorder were 5 times more likely to be receiving physical disability benefits than were the patients without the disorder (Byrne, Cherniack, & Petry, 2013).

Although it is tempting to equate a repeated pattern of criminal activity with antisocial personality disorder, it is not accurate to say that all career criminals can be so diagnosed. In fact, a sub-clinical label that better applies to many such persons is "adult antisocial behavior," a *DSM-5* listing meant to apply to situations in which the focus of clinical attention is antisocial behavior that is not due to a mental disorder. Distinguishing adult antisocial behavior from antisocial personality disorder requires sufficient information to diagnose a personality disorder, in addition to evidence of a conduct disorder before age 15.

Antisocial personality disorder is estimated to occur in 3% of males and 1% of females in the general population—although females may be under-diagnosed because of male aggression bias in the conduct disorder diagnosis. However, it is much more prevalent (over 70%) in certain settings, such as substance abuse treatment groups among the legally incarcerated (American Psychiatric Association, 2013). The behavior patterns characteristic of antisocial personality disorder have been the focus of, perhaps, more attention from psychologists than other personality disorders, and so a review of that history is worthwhile.

## Background of the Diagnosis

In 1835 Pritchard described a kind of "moral insanity" in which intellect seemed unimpaired but moral principles were "perverted or depraved," the "power of self-government" was lost or diminished, and the person was incapable of "conducting himself with decency and propriety in the business of life." Later writers used the term *constitutional psychopathic inferiority* to refer to this pattern of behavior, strongly implying a biological and possibly hereditary etiology. Until the 1960s, the term *psychopathic personality* (or just **psychopath**) was the most common label. The *DSM* described the pattern as "antisocial personality disorder" in its diagnostic series, although the term *psychopath* is still widely used.

Writers have compiled lists of varying lengths to describe the essential features of the psychopathic or antisocial personality. The following six characteristics represent a synthesis of earlier descriptions by various authors, especially Cleckley (1976), and McCord and McCord (1964).

1.  *Lack of conscience or feelings of remorse*   When most of us have violated some moral standard, especially if we have hurt another person physically or emotionally, we are likely to feel some regret, remorse, or "twinge of conscience." The psychopath does not. One psychopath describes how he murdered three people: "The two little kids started crying, wanting water. I gave them some and she [their mother] drove a while—and I turned around and started shooting in the back seat and then turned back and shot her. She fell over against me and onto the floor" (Symkal & Thorne, 1951, p. 311). After giving the children a drink of water, he shot them and later related the story without compassion or remorse. In psychoanalytic terminology, the psychopath has little or no superego and no guilt feelings about wrongdoing.

2.  *Impulsivity; inability to delay gratification*   Psychopaths tend to act upon the impulse of the moment. They seem unable or unwilling to delay gratification for more long-term rewards. Therefore they are likely to commit impulsive, poorly planned criminal acts, flit from one mate to another (with or without marriage), quit or be fired from job after job because they cannot stand the restrictions or demands of ordinary work, and, in general, lead erratic and unstable lives. When frustrated in seeking immediate gratification, they are likely to respond with aggression or violence against their perceived frustrators.

**BVT** *Lab*

Visit **www.BVTLab.com** to explore the student resources available for this chapter.

**Psychopath**

Antisocial personality, involving characteristics such as lack of empathy or concern for others, frequent rule violations, impulsivity, and superficial charm

3. *Inability to profit from mistakes*   Most people, caught in some criminal or antisocial act and given some appropriate punishment, either develop their criminal expertise so that they are less likely to get caught the next time or give up criminal activities. Not so with psychopaths. Although they may be caught in many crimes and receive varying kinds of punishment, they do not seem to learn from these experiences and frequently repeat the same antisocial behavior in the future.

4. *Lack of emotional ties to other people*   Psychopaths are loners; they seem incapable of binding ties or loyalties to other people. Although they may form fleeting attachments, these lack emotional depth and tenderness—and not uncommonly end abruptly in aggressive explosions. They can behave as callously toward their own wives, children, or parents as toward anyone else. Other people are treated as objects to be manipulated for the psychopaths' own pleasure.

5. *Stimulus seeking*   Most psychopaths become bored quickly with the humdrum of everyday life. They search constantly for new thrills and experiences—daring robberies, impersonations, confidence games, new varieties of drugs, and deviant sexual behavior.

6. *Ability to make a good impression on others*   There is no reason to believe that psychopaths, on the average, are any more or less intelligent than the rest of us. Many of them have learned as part of their manipulative strategies to appear intelligent, likable, charming, and witty. Frequently they talk their way out of tight spots, "con" people into dubious investments, or convince judges, juries, probation officers, or therapists of their good intentions for the future.

Studies at that time suggested that the psychopath's inability to profit from mistakes derived from a lack of anxiety about future punishment and an impaired ability to learn responses motivated by avoidance of pain or other forms of punishment. Punishment is effective in deterring most people from repeating undesired behavior because the person learns to respond with anxiety in anticipation of being caught. In a study by Hare (1965a), the subjects watched consecutive numbers 1 to 12 appear on a display. They were told that each time the number "8" appeared they would receive an electric shock equal in intensity to one earlier determined to be the strongest they could tolerate. Both normals and nonpsychopathic criminals showed anticipatory rises in palmar sweat gland activity (*galvanic skin response*, or GSR), but psychopathic criminals did not.

Given a relative lack of anticipatory anxiety, one would expect psychopaths to learn conditioned electrodermal (GSR) responses less well than nonpsychopaths. This was shown to be the case (Hare, 1965b); GSR responses were conditioned to auditory stimuli, preceded by electric shock as the unconditioned stimulus (see Figure 8-1). Other work similarly showed that psychopaths demonstrate poorer learning in shock avoidance experiments (Lykken, 1957; Schmauk, 1970). A general conclusion might be that psychopaths, defined according to

Ted Bundy, convicted and executed for the serial murders of women, is often cited as an example of antisocial personality. (AP Wide World)

Cleckley's (1976) criteria, show less anxiety than nonpsychopaths in stressful situations, perhaps contributing to psychopaths' willingness to indulge in risky behavior and their difficulty in learning to inhibit antisocial behavior.

Quay (1977) theorized that a primary characteristic of psychopaths that might explain much of their behavior is an inordinate need for increases or changes in stimulation. Others suggested that psychopaths are physiologically under-aroused and thus seek stimulation to bring themselves up to an optimal state of pleasurable arousal. Either of these proposals might explain the deficient anxiety conditioning seen in psychopaths. However, Fowles (1993) has suggested that a deficient behavioral inhibition system together with a normal or overactive behavioral activation

**Figure 8-1**
**Conditioning of the**
**Galvanic Skin Response**
**(GSR) in Psychopathic and**
**Nonpsychopathic Criminals**

Source: Adapted from Hare, 1965b. Copyright
1965 by *The Journal Press* and redrawn with
permission.

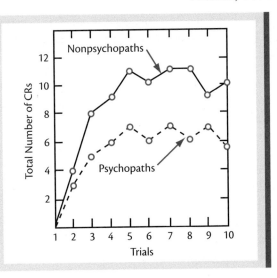

system distinguishes psychopaths. Factor analytic studies remain active as well. Cooke and Michie (2001) suggest the three main factors in psychopathy are Arrogant and Deceitful Interpersonal Style, Deficient Affective Experience, and Impulsive and Irresponsible Behavioral Style.

There are frequent reports of criminals who commit particularly violent or cruel crimes. A commonly cited example of antisocial personality disorder is the intelligent, attractive, and charming Ted Bundy, who was executed in 1989 for serial murders of at least 22 women. Perhaps the most famous and compelling example, however, is that of Charles Manson, who orchestrated bizarre and gruesome murders at several wealthy California households, including the killing of actress Sharon Tate late in her pregnancy. Manson remains incarcerated in a California prison under a life sentence; some information on his early history is provided on the next page.

Charles Mason, convicted of the Tate-LaBianca murders, typifies many features of the antisocial or psychopathic personality.
(AP Wide World)

## Causal Factors

Antisocial personality disorder runs in families and the relatives of females with the condition are at higher risk than are the relatives of antisocial males. Families showing antisocial personality disorder also have higher rates for somatic symptom disorders and substance-related disorders. Both adopted and biological children of parents with antisocial personality disorder show higher risk, indicating both genetic and environmental factors in the cause (American Psychiatric Association, 2013). After reviewing twin and adoption studies, Dahl (1993) concluded that antisocial personality disorder is the only personality disorder to show convincing data for a modest genetic causal influence.

**Were antisocial adults antisocial children?**

Psychoanalytic perspectives have suggested that faulty superego development and the consequent lack of counterbalance for the expression of the id are causal factors in the development of antisocial personality disorder. Environmental influences might include parental abuse, neglect, deficient parenting practices, and inept discipline techniques, all of which can be associated with having antisocial parents. However, the most widely accepted view is probably one of interacting environmental and genetic influences, perhaps similar to those described for aggressive behavior (e.g., Rutter, 1997), within the context of dynamic coercive parent-child interactions and supportive peer-group influences (Granic & Patterson, 2006).

# Case Study 1

**Charles Manson** was born "no name Maddox" on November 12, 1934, in Cincinnati, Ohio, the illegitimate son of a 16-year-old girl named Kathleen Maddox. Relatives said that "Kathleen ran around a lot, drank, and got into trouble." She lived with a succession of men; and William Manson, to whom she was married briefly, provided a last name for young Charles. Kathleen provided little mothering or stability. She would leave the child with obliging neighbors for an hour and then disappear for days or weeks. After a while his grandmother or maternal aunt would pick him up. Most of his early years were spent with one of these two in West Virginia, Kentucky, or Ohio.

In 1939 Kathleen and her brother Luther robbed a service station, knocking out the attendant with coke bottles. They were caught and sentenced to five years in the state penitentiary. While his mother was in prison Charles lived with his aunt, a person who thought all pleasures were sinful but who did give him some love. When his mother was paroled in 1942, she reclaimed him. He was 8 then, and the next several years were spent in a succession of rundown hotel rooms with a variety of newly introduced "uncles."

When Charles Manson was 12, his mother tried to put him in a foster home. None were available, so he was sent to the Gibault School for Boys, a caretaking institution in Indiana. He remained there for 10 months and then ran away and returned to his mother. She did not want him; he ran away again and burglarized a grocery store. Later he broke into several other stores and was finally caught. Placed in the juvenile center in Indianapolis, he escaped the next day. When caught again, the court, erroneously thinking he was Catholic, made arrangements to send him to Father Flanagan's Boys Town.

Four days after his arrival, he and another boy stole a car and drove to the home of the other boy's uncle in Peoria, Illinois. On the way they robbed a grocery store and a gambling casino. Thus Manson committed his first "violent" crime, armed robbery, at the age of 13. The uncle, a criminal in his own right, was glad to see them since they were small enough to slip through skylights. He put them to work immediately—they broke into a grocery store and stole $1,500, for which the uncle permitted them to keep $150. Two weeks later they were caught attempting a similar job. Manson was sent to the Indiana School for Boys at Plainfield.

He stayed there 3 years, running away a total of 18 times. According to his teachers, "He professed no trust in anyone" and "did good work only for those from whom he figured he could obtain something." In early 1951, he and two other 16-year-olds escaped and headed for California, stealing cars for transportation along the way and burglarizing gas stations for needed cash. Near Beaver, Utah, a roadblock set up for a robbery suspect netted them instead. Taking stolen vehicles across a state line is a federal offense, so in March 1951, Manson was sent to the National Training School for Boys in Washington, DC. During Manson's stay there, a psychiatrist wrote "that because of his small stature, illegitimacy, and lack of parental love, he is constantly striving for status with the other boys ... He developed certain facile techniques for dealing with people. These for the most part consist of a good sense of humor, an ability to ingratiate himself ... This could add up to a fairly 'slick' institutionalized youth, but one is left with the feeling that behind all this lies an extremely sensitive boy who has not yet given up in terms of securing some kind of love and affection from the world."

Manson was due for a parole hearing in February 1952; with an offer from his aunt to provide a home and employment for him, the chances looked good. Less than a month before the hearing, however, he took a razor blade and held it against another boy's throat while he sodomized him. As a result, he was transferred to the federal reformatory at Petersburg, Virginia. By August, he had committed eight serious offenses, including three homosexual acts, in his new placement; as a result, he was transferred to an even more secure institution, the Federal Reformatory at Chillicothe, Ohio. There was a marked improvement in his behavior and attitude during the nearly 2 years he spent at Chillicothe, and he raised his educational level from the fourth- to seventh-grade level. In May 1954, he was granted parole.

Manson, however, continued his life of stealing autos, using stolen credit cards, and violating various federal laws such as forging a United States Treasury check and transporting women for the purpose of prostitution across state lines. In July 1961, he found himself back in a federal penitentiary, where he stayed until March 1967.

When released, he was given permission to go to San Francisco—a fateful decision. During this time Manson discovered Haight-Ashbury. Here were young people, naive and eager to believe and to belong. Possibilities were unlimited for any self-styled guru in the making, and Manson quickly sensed that he had stumbled on a unique opportunity. Being an ex-con gave him some automatic status as anti-establishment; and rapping a line of meta-physical jargon that borrowed as much from the drug culture as from Scientology and Buddhism, he had no trouble attracting followers. This combination of familial and historical influences, interacting with the sociological conditions of the drug and counterculture movement of the late 1960s, resulted ultimately in the tragic Tate-LaBianca murders.

## Treatment of Antisocial Personality Disorder

As with other personality disorders, treatment for antisocial personality disorder is difficult; and no treatment evaluations have provided clear evidence of validated approaches. These clients are rarely motivated to attempt real change. Therapists working with them are typically advised to expect resistance and deception, confront deviant behavior, and challenge underlying psychopathic thinking (Meyer & Deitsch, 1996). In controlled settings, such as prisons, some progress is possible with very intensive individual therapies (Salekin, 2002). However, similar approaches are impractical on an outpatient basis, and recidivism rates are high. Targets for treatment often include overt aggression and anger management. Cognitive-behavior therapy appears to be less effective on psychopathic offenders than nonpsychopathic ones (Valliant, Hawkins, & Pottier, 1998). There is a general sense among researchers that treatment is more promising at earlier ages (for adolescent antisocial behavior) than once the pattern becomes more established in adults.

No specific medications are clearly recommended for treatment of antisocial personality disorder. Commonly, drugs are used to target components such as aggressiveness or impulsiveness. A randomized controlled study that included some *Cluster B* patients found the anti-convulsant divalproex, which has also been used for bipolar mania, to be better than placebo in reducing scores on tests measuring aggressiveness and irritability, although those in the drug group discontinued treatment at a higher rate than the placebo group. (Hollander, et al., 2003).

# 8.3b Borderline Personality Disorder

Unstable relationships and emotions characterize borderline personality disorder (see *DSM-5* Diagnostic Criteria for Borderline Personality Disorder). People with this condition can show dramatic shifts in the way they regard others, over brief time periods, from excessive idealization to nearly complete devaluation. They hate being alone and frantically seek to avoid it; they experience chronic feelings of emptiness while their active emotions are very unstable, commonly including anger, guilt, shame, bitterness, and despair. They may frequently shift career plans, life goals, or friends.

Antisocial behavior pattern begins in childhood with apparent lack of remorse or empathy for others, poor behavioral controls—expressions of irritability, impatience, threats, aggression, and inadequate control of anger and temper. (iStock)

Suicidal or self-mutilating acts are common, and at times those with borderline personality disorder may show dissociative symptoms. They may occur as manipulative gestures, designed to prevent abandonment, although they may also reflect genuinely depressed mood. They are at higher risk for completed suicide (Duberstein & Conwell, 1997). Under stress, psychotic-like symptoms may briefly occur. It is estimated that borderline personality disorder affects between 2% and 6% of the general population. About 75% of people diagnosed with this disorder are female (American Psychiatric Association, 2013).

| *DSM-5* | **Diagnostic Criteria for Borderline Personality Disorder** |
| --- | --- |

301.83 (F60.3) Borderline Personality Disorder

A pervasive pattern of instability of interpersonal relationships, self-image, and affects, and marked by impulsivity beginning by early adulthood and present in a variety of contexts, as indicated by five (or more) of the following:

1. Frantic efforts to avoid real or imagined abandonment. (Note: Do not include suicidal or self-mutilating behavior covered in Criterion 5.)
2. A pattern of unstable and intense interpersonal relationships characterized by alternating between extremes of idealization and devaluation.
3. Identity disturbance: Markedly and persistently unstable self-image or sense of self.
4. Impulsivity in at least two areas that are potentially self-damaging (e.g., spending, sex, substance abuse, reckless driving, binge eating). (Note: Do not include suicidal or self-mutilating behavior covered in Criterion 5.)
5. Recurrent suicidal behavior, gestures, or threats, or self-mutilating behavior.
6. Affective instability due to a marked reactivity of mood (e.g., intense episodic dysphoria, irritability, or anxiety usually lasting a few hours and only rarely more than a few days).
7. Chronic feeling of emptiness.
8. Inappropriate, intense anger or difficulty controlling anger (e.g., frequent displays of temper, constant anger, recurrent physical fights).
9. Transient, stress-related paranoid ideation or severe dissociative symptoms.

Source: Reprinted with permission from the *Diagnostic and Statistical Manual of Mental Disorders,* Fifth Edition, (Copyright 2013). American Psychiatric Association.

## Causal Factors

Family members of borderline personality disorder sufferers are 5 times more likely to show the same disorder than the general population. These people are also at increased risk for substance-related disorders, depressive disorders, and antisocial personality disorder (American Psychiatric Association, 2013). Biological factors involved in increased emotional liability (such as increased cholinergic activity) may play a role in symptom presentation (Koenigsberg, Woo-Ming, Siever, & Siever, 2002). Some have proposed that parental neglect or loss during childhood, or a deficient attachment between child and parent, are central to this type of personality development. A model proposing that certain vulnerabilities, such as emotional instability and impulsive tendencies, interact with poor parenting, loss, or trauma to produce borderline personality disorder has been proposed (Paris, 1999). Some studies have described high levels of physical or sexual abuse in childhood among borderline patients (Crits-Christoph & Barber, 2002). However, the cause or causes of borderline personality disorder remain unknown.

## Treatment of Borderline Personality Disorder

Dialectical behavior therapy (DBT)—a complex and eclectic mix of group and individual sessions dealing with interpersonal skills, emotional regulation, problems solving, acceptance, and goal-setting—was effective in reducing some symptoms, compared to standard treatment, for borderline patients who also had drug dependencies (Linehan, et al., 1999). Improvement related to psychodynamic therapy has also been reported in a less controlled outcome study whereas cognitive therapy has been associated with some positive case reports (Crits-Christoph & Barber, 2002). First-line pharmacology for borderline personality disorder involves antidepressants such as the SSRIs and antimanic drugs such as lithium; some studies have reported less solid support for antipsychotic or anti-seizure medications to assist with psychotic symptoms and mood stabilization (Koenigsberg, Woo-Ming, Siever, & Siever, 2002). For example, low doses of the antipsychotic drug clozapine produced improvement in psychotic symptoms, impulsiveness, and depression in a 16-week treatment with a small group of severe borderline personality disorder patients (Bendetti, Sforzini, Columo, Marrei, & Smeraldi, 1998).

# 8.3c Histrionic Personality Disorder

The main features of histrionic personality disorder (*DSM-5* Diagnostic Criteria for Histrionic Personality Disorder) concern excessive emotionality and attention seeking. The rapidly shifting emotions may seem shallow, superficial, and exaggerated to others. Persons showing histrionic personality disorder desire to be the center of attention and act in dramatic ways to bring that about, through both behavioral intensity and physical appearance. They may fish for compliments, act flirtatiously, and pretend that relationships are more intimate than they actually are. Often they assume either a "victim" or a "princess" role in relating to others (American Psychological Association, 2000).

Someone with histrionic personality disorder may assume either a "victim" or a "princess" role in relating to others. (Shutterstock)

People with histrionic personality disorder may be seductive, manipulative, and theatrical in presentation although they are also quite dependent. Manipulative suicidal gestures, often with the goal of attracting attention, are not uncommon. They tend to seek out novelty and excitement, and easily become bored with routine. The general incidence appears to be close to 2% of the population; although the diagnosis is given more often to females, the *DSM-5* notes that the ratio is not significantly different from the proportion of females in treatment, suggesting the diagnostic ratio may be thus slanted in females' favor (American Psychiatric Association, 2013).

## Causal Factors

No information is provided on familial influences for histrionic personality disorder in the *DSM-5*. The condition co-occurs with several other personality disorders, most often narcissistic personality disorder (Zimmerman, Rothschild, & Chelminski, 2005). It is also associated with higher rates of somatic symptom disorder, conversion disorder, and major depressive disorder (American Psychiatric Association, 2013). Various writers have suggested repression or sexual conflicts as underlying causal factors although supporting data are not available.

## Treatment of Histrionic Personality Disorder

No controlled outcome trials have been reported for the treatment of histrionic personality disorder. Attempts at treatment typically target interpersonal relationships, social skills, and

| *DSM-5* | **Diagnostic Criteria for Histrionic Personality Disorder** |
| --- | --- |

301.50 (F60.4) Histrionic Personality Disorder

A pervasive pattern of excessive emotionality and attention seeking, beginning by early adulthood and present in a variety of contexts, as indicated by five (or more) of the following:

1. Is uncomfortable in situations in which he or she is not the center of attention.
2. Interaction with others is often characterized by inappropriate sexually seductive or provocative behavior.
3. Displays rapidly shifting and shallow expression of emotions.
4. Consistently uses physical appearance to draw attention to self.
5. Has a style of speech that is excessively impressionistic and lacking in detail.
6. Shows self-dramatization, theatricality, and exaggerated expression of emotion.
7. Is suggestible (e.g., easily influenced by others or circumstances).
8. Considers relationships to be more intimate than they actually are.

Source: Reprinted with permission from the *Diagnostic and Statistical Manual of Mental Disorders*, Fifth Edition, (Copyright 2013). American Psychiatric Association.

attention seeking. Some believe that hypnosis or placebo treatments that include some level of clinical intensity may be most acceptable to these clients (Meyer & Deitsch, 1996). Apart from scattered case studies, there is very little information about treatment of this group in the literature at present.

# 8.3d Narcissistic Personality Disorder

Those displaying narcissistic personality disorder are self-centered and require the admiration of others. They exaggerate their own self-importance and are preoccupied with fantasies about their own success, brilliance, or beauty. They commonly feel entitled to special treatment; similar to those with antisocial personality disorder, they lack empathy and exploit others for their own purposes. They are described as arrogant, conceited, elitist, and grandiose and can frequently be contemptuous of others (refer to *DSM-5* Diagnostic Criteria for Narcissistic Personality Disorder).

People with narcissistic personality disorder do not care to wait in line or take their turn; they expect special privileges because of their obvious superiority to others. They are condescending and haughty in attitude and behavior. They tend to overstate their accomplishments while underestimating those of others. They may fish for compliments and expect to receive them. Although preoccupied with self-importance, their self-esteem is actually very fragile; criticism may hurt them greatly, leaving them empty and humiliated and primed to counter-attack but also susceptible to depression. To prevent defeat and humiliation, they tend to avoid competitions that they may lose. Narcissistic personality disorder may co-occur with anorexia nervosa and with substance (especially cocaine) use disorders. The diagnosis is more commonly given to males; its prevalence is unclear, with estimates ranging from to as much as 6.2%" (American Psychiatric Association, 2013).

## Causal Factors

The *DSM-5* provides no information about familial influences in narcissistic personality disorder. Psychodynamic theories tend to view it as an outgrowth of the natural ego-centered nature of the child or a defense against feelings of inadequacy; others suggest it may develop from overindulgence by parents. No empirical evidence is available to support either viewpoint.

---

| DSM-5 | Diagnostic Criteria for Narcissistic Personality Disorder |
|---|---|

?01.81 (F60.81) Narcissistic Personality Disorder

...sive pattern of grandiosity (in family and behavior), need for admiration, and lack of ...ty beginning by early adulthood and present in a variety of contexts, as indicated by five (or ...ore) of the following:

1. Has a grandiose sense of self-importance (e.g., exaggerates achievements and talents, expects to be recognized as superior without commensurate achievements).
2. Is preoccupied with fantasies about unlimited success, power, brilliance, beauty, or ideal love.
3. Believes that he or she is "special" and unique and can only be understood by, or associate with, other special or high-status people (or institutions).
4. Requires excessive admiration.
5. Has a sense of entitlement (i.e., unreasonable expectations of especially favorable treatment or automatic compliance with his or her expectations).
6. Is interpersonally exploitive (i.e., takes advantage of others to achieve his or her own ends).
7. Lacks empathy, is unwilling to recognize or identify with the feelings and needs of others.
8. Is often envious of others or believes that others are envious of him or her
9. Shows arrogant, haughty behaviors or attitudes.

Source: Reprinted with permission from the *Diagnostic and Statistical Manual of Mental Disorders*, Fifth Edition, (Copyright 2013). American Psychiatric Association.

*Treatment of Narcissistic Personality Disorder*

There are no established therapies for the treatment of narcissistic personality disorder; indeed, some clinicians consider it even more difficult to engage the narcissistic person in therapy than the antisocial one (Meyer & Deitsch, 1996). Very little information, outside of occasional uncontrolled case studies, exists on psychotherapy or drug therapy with these individuals.

# 8.4 *Cluster C* Personality Disorders

The *Cluster C* personality disorders include those in which symptom presentations tend to be avoidant or fearful. About 6% of the general population displays at least one of the *Cluster C* disorders (Lenzenweger, Lane, Loranger, & Kessler, 2007). An overview of the personality disorders listed in *Cluster C* is shown in Table 8-3.

## 8.4a Avoidant Personality Disorder

Avoidant personality disorder involves social inhibition, hypersensitivity to being evaluated negatively, and feelings of inadequacy (see *DSM-5* Diagnostic Criteria for Avoidant Personality Disorder). These individuals are so preoccupied with, and sensitive to, criticism that they avoid activities where disapproval is possible, including occupational situations and social relationships. They see themselves as inadequate and inferior to others; and they are usually described as shy, lonely, and timid. They resist new relationships or friendships without feeling certain that they will be accepted and liked. Nearly always, they expect others to see their obvious faults, so they resist intimacy and act with restraint, remaining "invisible" in the social background.

Those with avoidant personality disorder take so few risks that they may turn down occupational opportunities or new social relationships because of the possibility of criticism in the future. They may be vigilant in watching for early signs of social disapproval; and their demeanor may evoke a critical reaction from others, which is then seen as confirmation of their self-doubt. Depressive disorders and anxiety disorders, especially social phobia, are often comorbid (American Psychiatric Association, 2013), whereas the most common co-existing personality condition appears to be schizoid personality disorder (Zimmerman, Rothschild, & Chelminski, 2005). No clear gender differences in prevalence are apparent; it appears to affect about 1% of the general population (American Psychiatric Association, 2013).

*Causal Factors*

No information on familial patterns is provided in *DSM-5*, although Dahl (1993) indicates it is more common among close relatives of those with the disorder. The significant overlap of symptoms and high comorbidity between avoidant personality disorder and social phobia may suggest a common biological underpinning (Koenigsberg, Woo-Ming, Siever, & Siever, 2002). Others, however, argue that avoidant personality disorder should be considered within

*Table 8-3*    *DSM-5* **Cluster C Personality Disorders**

| Disorder | Key Descriptions | Sex Ratio |
|---|---|---|
| Avoidant personality disorder | Pervasive social inhibition and feelings of inadequacy | Equal |
| Dependent personality disorder | Pervasive submissive and clinging behavior and fear of separation | More common among females |
| Obsessive-compulsive personality disorder | Pervasive preoccupation with orderliness, details and perfectionism | More common among males |

Source: Reprinted with permission from the *Diagnostic and Statistical Manual of Mental Disorders*, Fifth Edition, (Copyright 2013). American Psychiatric Association.

| DSM-5 | Diagnostic Criteria for Avoidant Personality Disorder |
|---|---|

**301.82 (F60.6) Avoidant Personality Disorder**

A pervasive pattern of social inhibition, feelings of inadequacy, and hypersensitivity to negative evaluations, beginning by early adulthood and present in a variety of contexts, as indicated by four (or more) of the following:

1. Avoids occupational activities that involve significant interpersonal contact, because of fears of criticism, disapproval, or rejection.
2. Is unwilling to get involved with people unless certain of being liked.
3. Shows restraint within intimate relationships because of the fear of being shamed or ridiculed.
4. Is preoccupied with being criticized or rejected in social situations.
5. Is inhibited in new interpersonal situations because of feelings of inadequacy.
6. Views self as socially inept, personally unappealing, or inferior to others.
7. Is unusually reluctant to take personal risks or to engage in any new activities because they may prove embarrassing.

Source: Reprinted with permission from the *Diagnostic and Statistical Manual of Mental Disorders*, Fifth Edition, (Copyright 2013). American Psychiatric Association.

the schizophrenic spectrum (Gooding, Tallent, & Matts, 2007). Possible psychological causes include parental or peer rejection in childhood, although little empirical evidence exists for any specific causal factors.

Avoidant personality disorder involves social inhibition, hypersensitivity to criticism and feelings of inadequacy. These individuals may resist new relationships or friendships when feeling uncertain that they will be accepted or liked. (iStock)

### Treatment of Avoidant Personality Disorder

Pharmacological approaches to treatment of avoidant personality disorder essentially assume that the condition has a common basis with that of social phobia. Case reports suggest certain antidepressant medications (MAO-Is and SSRIs) may be helpful, but controlled studies are needed (Koenigsberg, Woo-Ming, Siever, & Siever, 2002). One randomized controlled trial showed that behavioral treatments that involved graduated exposure and social skills training were more effective than a wait-list control; less rigorous comparative studies and case studies have also supported cognitive therapy and supportive expressive dynamic therapy (Crits-Christoph & Barber, 2002).

## 8.4b  Dependent Personality Disorder

The central characteristic of dependent personality disorder (*DSM-5* Diagnostic Criteria for Dependent Personality Disorder) is an excessive need to be taken care of by others. That persistent need is associated with fears of separation and clinging and submissive behavior designed to evoke care-giving. Individuals with dependent personality disorder are uncomfortable being alone because they fear being unable to care for themselves, so they will urgently seek a replacement relationship if a close relationship ends. Typically, they allow others to make important decisions about most life areas, including employment, use of free time, and choice of friends. They may volunteer to do unpleasant tasks or participate in unwanted activities in hopes of securing the care and support they need. Their pattern of dependency tends to keep them dependent because they do not gain the skills needed for self-support.

People with dependent personality disorder see themselves as inept and totally dependent on the advice and assistance of others. To maintain the dependent bond, they may accept verbal, physical, or sexual abuse. The condition tends to co-occur with borderline personality disorder and with mood and anxiety disorders. It is diagnosed more often among females than males, and its prevalence appears to be less than 1% of the population (American Psychiatric Association, 2013).

| DSM-5 | **Diagnostic Criteria for Dependent Personality Disorder** |

**301.6 (F60.7) Dependent Personality Disorder**

A pervasive and excessive need to be taken care of that leads to submissive and clinging behavior and fears of separation, beginning by early adulthood and present in a variety of contexts, as indicated by five (or more) of the following:

1. Has difficult making everyday decisions without excessive amount of advice and reassurance from others.
2. Needs others to assume responsibility for most major areas of his or her life.
3. Has difficulty expressing disagreement with others because of fear of loss of support or approval. (**Note:** Do not include realistic fears of retribution.)
4. Has difficulty initiating projects or doing things on his or her own (because of a lack of support or approval).
5. Goes to excessive lengths to obtain nurturance and support from others, to the point of volunteering to do things that are unpleasant.
6. Feels uncomfortable or helpless when alone because of exaggerated fears of being unable to care for himself or herself.
7. Urgently seeks another relationship as a source of care and support then a close relationship ends.
8. Is unrealistically preoccupied with fears of being left to take care of himself or herself.

Source: Reprinted with permission from the *Diagnostic and Statistical Manual of Mental Disorders,* Fifth Edition, (Copyright 2013). American Psychiatric Association.

## Causal Factors

The *DSM-5* provides no information about any familial influences in dependent personality disorder. Some have speculated about possible histories of abuse, overprotective parenting, or of delayed "weaning from nurturance" in childhood (Meyer & Deitsch, 1996). However, no empirical evidence appears to support any particular genetic, biological, or psychological causal factors at present.

## Treatment of Dependent Personality Disorder

No evidence is available from controlled reports concerning the relative effectiveness of medication or psychotherapy for dependent personality disorder. Symptomatic treatments for depression or anxiety and directed skills training for assertiveness, independent living, and problem solving may be attempted.

# 8.4c Obsessive-Compulsive Personality Disorder

Obsessive-compulsive personality disorder (*DSM-5* Diagnostic Criteria for Obsessive-Compulsive Personality Disorder) involves a preoccupation with control, orderliness, and perfectionism. People with this condition are over-involved with rules, schedules, and details and are insensitive to the resulting annoyance of others—to the extent that inflexibility of procedure is more important than efficiency. They tend to be stubborn and inflexible about checking details, so that deadlines tend to be missed in spite of excessive devotion to work. The same preoccupation with and dedication to tasks interferes with friendships or leisure activities. Their emphasis is on perfect performance and rigid devotion to principles, and they typically do not trust the abilities of others toward these ends. Consequently, they rarely delegate tasks or collaborate with coworkers.

Unlike obsessive-compulsive disorder (described in Chapter 6), those with obsessive-compulsive personality disorder are not particularly distressed by their condition. In fact, they can appear to be emotionally insensitive and unexpressive. Others may see them as overly conscientious and moralistic. Additionally, those with obsessive-compulsive personality disorder do not display true obsessions or compulsions. According to the *DSM-5*, the condition may be among the most common personality disorders in the general

| **DSM-5** | **Diagnostic Criteria for Obsessive-Compulsive Personality Disorder** |
|---|---|

301.4 (F60.5) Obsessive-Compulsive Personality Disorder

A pervasive pattern of preoccupation with orderliness, perfectionism, and mental and interpersonal control, at the expense of flexibility, openness, and efficiency, beginning by early adulthood and present in a variety of contexts, as indicated by four (or more) of the following:

1. Is preoccupied with details, rules, lists, order, organization, or schedules to the extent that the major point of the activity is lost.
2. Shows perfectionism that interferes with task completion (e.g., is unable to complete a project because his or her own overly strict standards are not met).
3. Is excessively devoted to work and productivity to the exclusion of leisure activities and friendships (not accounted for by obvious economic necessity).
4. Is overly conscientious, scrupulous, and inflexible about matters of morality, ethic, or values (not accounted for by cultural or religious identification).
5. Is unable to discard worn-out or worthless objects even when they have no sentimental values.
6. Is reluctant to delegate tasks or to work with others unless they submit exactly to his or her way of doing things.
7. Adopts a miserly spending style towards both self and others; money is viewed as something to be hoarded for future catastrophes.
8. Shows rigidity and stubbornness.

Source: Reprinted with permission from the *Diagnostic and Statistical Manual of Mental Disorders*, Fifth Edition, (Copyright 2013). American Psychiatric Association.

population, with incidence estimates ranging from 2% to nearly 8%. Its male-to-female ratio is 2:1 (American Psychiatric Association, 2013).

## Causal Factors

No evidence of familial influences is provided in *DSM-5*. People with anxiety disorders may have a higher risk for obsessive-compulsive personality disorder. Many of the features of obsessive-compulsive personality disorder appear to overlap with *Cluster A* rather than *Cluster C* conditions, and there may be an association with eating disorders and depressive disorders (American Psychiatric Association, 2013). Earlier Freudian perspectives invoked fixation at the anal stage of psychosexual development ("anal-retentive" personalities are preoccupied with order and neatness, as compared to "anal-expulsive" personalities that are disorganized and messy), possibly related to over-controlling parents; later perspectives tend to emphasize overuse of defenses. Without empirical data, little is known about these or other possible environmental or familial contributions to this condition.

## Treatment of Obsessive-Compulsive Personality Disorder

There are no controlled outcome studies on either pharmacological or psychological interventions for obsessive-compulsive personality disorder. Therapy may be attempted for relaxation training or to reduce the nearly compulsive preoccupation with detail that is so characteristic of the behavior pattern. Meyer and Deitsch (1996) recommend relaxation, modeling of humor, **bibliotherapy** techniques (use of written materials that may have life significance), and cognitive challenging, although there are no empirical data supporting these interventions for obsessive-compulsive personality disorder.

# 8.5 Other Personality Disorders

## 8.5a Personality Change Due to Another Medical Condition

One new personality disorder classification appears in the *DSM-5*: personality change due to another medical condition. Sometimes, persistent personality changes can be associated

**Bibliotherapy**

The use of selected written materials that may have particular life significance as an adjunct in psychotherapy with chronic medical problems or events such as stroke, head trauma, epilepsy, autoimmune disorders, or other central nervous system dysfunctions. Those afflicted may show emotional instability, aggression, paranoia, apathy, or poor impulse control, among a host of other possible dysfunctions. When these changes can be directly linked to the underlying medical condition, this diagnosis would be appropriate.

## 8.5b   Other Specified Personality Disorder

Quite often, individuals present symptoms that meet the general definition of a personality disorder (see Table 8-1) but do not satisfy the specific criteria for any of the *Cluster A, B, or C* diagnoses. Usually, these appear to be conditions in which the symptoms of different personality disorders are mixed together. In those situations, a diagnosis of "other specified personality disorder" is given. Even when structured clinical interviews are employed in diagnosis, this classification is among the top three personality disorders in terms of prevalence; when interviews are not structured, this is the most common personality disorder diagnosis (Verheul & Widiger, 2004).

## 8.6   Considerations for the Future

The overlap and intermingling of personality disorders with other *DSM* conditions weakens the argument about their independent status, and several writers have called their future status into question. Because categorical diagnoses of many of these disorders involve matching client symptoms to "3 of the following 7" or "5 of the following 9" criteria, there can be a very large range of variability in the expression of any single personality disorder. Thus, two persons with the same diagnosis may behave in different ways (a challenge to convergent validity), while others with different diagnoses may act similarly (a challenge to divergent validity). Factor-analytic studies of the 10 personality disorders did not support their categorical organization in the *DSM-IV* (Sheets & Craighead, 2007), and one evaluation of convergent and divergent validity and correspondence to the Big Five personality factors in the *DSM-IV* classification system indicated that only borderline personality disorder met all criteria for a useful and valid classification that identifies functional impairment (Ryder, Costa, & Bagby, 2007). Others suggested that substantial revisions were needed in paranoid personality disorder because of poor validity (Bernstein & Useda, 2007).

The broad and persistent criticism of the personality disorders led the *DSM-5* task force to consider major changes in their classification. In preparation for *DSM-5*, proposals to rethink the personality disorders by shifting to diagnosis based on five-factor models of personality appeared (Widiger, Costa Jr, & McCrae, 2002). Among the other options mentioned for the *DSM-5* taskforce to consider were whether to abandon the classifications altogether or to redefine personality disorders as either early onset or chronic variants of existing *DSM* conditions (Widiger, 2007). It appeared certain that the *DSM-5* would move toward a more dimensional, and less categorical, model for diagnosis of personality disorders (Regier, Narrow, Kuhl, & Kupfer, 2009); and early drafts of the *DSM-5* proposed sweeping changes including reducing the number of disorders from 10 to 6 and adding a dimensional assessment component based on a five-factor model of personality (curiously, not identical to the well-researched Big Five model). However, the proposed changes were so extensive that many balked at what appeared to be confusing and time-consuming assessments, and in the final draft the sweeping changes were voted down. Consequently, the *DSM-5* retains the *DSM-IV* personality disorder categories with almost no changes, although the alternative personality trait model was placed in Section III for further study. Given the continued dissatisfaction with their current status, the personality disorders will most likely be revamped with the next update of the *DSM* (version 5.1).

# Chapter Review

## TO SUM UP ...

- Personality disorders are enduring and stable styles of thinking, perceiving, and behaving across many settings and situations that are evident at least since early adulthood and that cause distress for the person or for others.

- Personality disorders may affect 9% of the population. Within clinical samples, nearly one-half of persons receiving any *DSM* diagnosis also meet the criteria for some type of personality disorder diagnosis.

- Personality disorder symptoms generally cluster into three groups: those that are odd or eccentric; those that are dramatic, emotional, or erratic; and those that are anxious or fearful.

- Very little is known about the causes of personality disorders, which are presumed to originate in adolescence. Family studies tend to support either weak or only moderate genetic influences.

- There is significant overlap between the different personality disorders and between personality disorders and several other mental disorders. The degree of comorbidity raises questions about the validity of the personality disorder categories. Diagnostic reliability also continues to be a problem for these conditions.

- Mathematical studies of personality assessments tend to support a dimensional model of personality disorders rather than the current categorical model of personality disorders used by *DSM-5*.

- Treatment of personality disorders is difficult. People diagnosed with these conditions often do not seek treatment and may be uncooperative patients. Several psychological and pharmacological interventions have been attempted, but there is only limited evidence of their effectiveness.

## KEY TERMS

Agreeableness   191

Bibliotherapy   210

Big Five   190

Conscientiousness   191

Extroversion   190

Factor analysis   190

Ideas of reference   196

Neuroticism   190

Openness to experience   190

Personality   189

Personality inventories   190

Phrenologists   190

Psychopath   199

Psychoticism   190

# QUESTIONS FOR STUDY

- Discuss how a dimensional method of personality disorder diagnosis might work and whether it would be an improvement over a categorical one.

- Imagine that you are hosting a large party, and you have invited people with each of the personality disorders. Which ones will accept your invitation, and which ones will refuse your invitation, and why?

- Try to describe a person who would meet the diagnostic criteria for two personality disorders simultaneously.

# POP QUIZ

1. Dr. Brown believes that personality is a collection of psychological characteristics, such as kindness or dependability, which can be identified and measured. She would be best described as a _____.
   A. trait theorist
   B. humanist
   C. phrenologist
   D. psychoanalyst

2. The *DSM-5* lists _____ different primary personality disorders.
   A. three
   B. six
   C. ten
   D. twelve

3. _____ personality disorders tend to present symptoms that observers consider odd, or eccentric.
   A. *Cluster D*
   B. *Cluster C*
   C. *Cluster B*
   D. *Cluster A*

4. Personality disorders are difficult to treat because of all of the following reasons **except** their _____.
   A. stability
   B. chronicity
   C. medical basis
   D. involvement in several life areas

5. Which of the following personality disordered individuals would have recurrent suspicions, without justification, regarding the fidelity of a spouse or sexual partner?
   A. obsessive-compulsive personality disorder
   B. histrionic personality disorder
   C. schizoid personality disorder
   D. paranoid personality disorder

6. People with _____ are largely indifferent to criticism.
   A. dependent personality disorder
   B. obsessive-compulsive personality disorder
   C. borderline personality disorder
   D. schizoid personality disorder

7. _____ individuals initially diagnosed with schizotypal personality disorder go on to develop schizophrenia.
   A. Very few
   B. Nearly a third of
   C. Half of
   D. Most

8. The *Cluster B* personality disorders include individuals who may be described as _____.
   A. odd or eccentric
   B. emotional or dramatic
   C. avoidant or fearful
   D. psychotic

9. One characteristic of antisocial personality disorder is _____ as these individuals frequently talk their way out of difficult situations and may "con" others into believing their good intentions for the future.
   A. the inability to profit from mistakes
   B. the need for admiration
   C. impulsivity
   D. the ability to make a good impression on others

10. Of those diagnosed with borderline personality disorder, _____ are female.
    A. 75%
    B. 50%
    C. 25%
    D. 5%

11. Frank believes he is more important than he really is. He has a grandiose sense of self-importance, and is preoccupied with fantasies about his own success and brilliance. Frank would best be described as having _____.
    A. narcissistic personality disorder
    B. histrionic personality disorder
    C. dependent personality disorder
    D. obsessive-compulsive personality disorder

12. In the general population, ___ display at least one of the personality disorders.
    A. 1%
    B. 4%
    C. 6%
    D. 9%

13. The most common personality disorder diagnosis is most likely _____.
    A. paranoid personality disorder
    B. dependent personality disorder
    C. other specified personality disorder
    D. schizoid personality disorder

14. The use of written materials that may have life significance is called
    _____.
    A. bibliotherapy
    B. biotherapy
    C. autobibliotherapy
    D. biblicotherapy

15. Dialectical behavior therapy (DBT) is effective in treating which of the following?
    A. antisocial personality disorder
    B. borderline personality disorder
    C. obsessive-compulsive personality disorder
    D. dependent personality disorder

Additional study resources are available at **www.BVTLab.com**

# CHAPTER OVERVIEW

# CHAPTER OPENER QUESTIONS

What is normal sexual functioning? How can it become impaired?

How common are sexual dysfunctions? How effective is treatment?

What are paraphilics? Are they dangerous?

What is gender dysphoria? Is it different from homosexuality?

Can people change from male to female or from female to male?

(Shuttertock)

# Sexual and Gender Disorders

Scientific study of human sexual behavior is a recent endeavor. However, ideas about connections between sexuality and abnormality are much older and have played a large role in the very development of psychology and psychiatry. Especially among Western Christian cultures, sexual activity was something that authorities, concerned with proper conduct, viewed warily. Many religious leaders advised that if sex was necessary at all, it should occur as rarely as possible and should not be enjoyed because it was a sin of the flesh. Some influential men of science, such as Krafft-Ebing (1840–1902), considered all variations from "normal" sexuality to be diseases. Recall from Chapter 2 that masturbation was considered a cause of insanity by the founder of American psychiatry, Benjamin Rush; and physicians of the eighteenth, nineteenth, and twentieth centuries recommended (sometimes extreme) measures to protect against "self-abuse." By the time of Freud, sexual appetites, fantasies, and conflicts came to be viewed on one hand as central to all human psychological functioning, and on the other hand, the source of most psychological disturbance.

These views began to change with increased scientific interest in sexuality, evident only within the past few generations. Kinsey and his colleagues (1948; 1953) were among the first to collect data on the prevalence of different kinds of sexual behavior such as masturbation, marital and premarital heterosexual intercourse, and homosexuality. Although their surveys were not representative of the general population, their findings clearly indicated that sexual activities were more varied than most Americans at the time believed. As perspectives on sexuality became more open over the past half-century, the *DSM* system adopted broader views of sexual variations and dysfunctions as well. Homosexuality, once considered a mental disorder, was not listed among the *DSM-III* conditions. Sexual variations are no longer considered deviations or disorders *a priori*; instead, they must, in most cases, be recurrent, persistent, and distressing to the individual in order to earn a *DSM* label.

The *DSM-5* divides psychosexual disorders into three general categories: sexual dysfunctions (which are associated with disturbances of the sexual response cycle, or with painful intercourse); paraphilias (which concern intense urges, fantasies, or behaviors involving unusual targets of sexual arousal); and gender dysphoria (in which there is strong and persistent sense of incongruence between one's assigned gender and one's gender identity). The field trial data from *DSM-III* indicated that diagnostic reliability for the psychosexual disorders was good to excellent overall,

Sexual orientation is no longer considered a defining factor in mental disorder. (s_buckley/ Shutterstock.com)

> What is normal sexual functioning? How can it become impaired?

with a range of 0.92 to 0.75 across Phases 1 and 2 (American Psychiatric Association, 1980). However, those estimates actually result from averaging across two very reliable categories and one very unreliable category. The *DSM-5* field trials did not include assessments of any of these disorders. Each will be considered in turn, but first a review of normal sexual functioning is in order.

# 9.1 Human Sexual Functioning

Masters and Johnson (1966), in their pioneering study of human sexuality, greatly increased our knowledge about physiological aspects of sexual functioning. Unlike the researchers before them, Masters and Johnson did not simply interview people about their sexual activities. They instead made direct observations, in a laboratory setting, of over 10,000 episodes of sexual activity involving 312 men and 382 women, ranging in age from early adulthood to age 89 and engaged in either solitary sexual activity or sexual interactions with a partner. They recorded physiological responses such as heart rate and muscle tension and contractions by using special equipment, some of which was placed over the penis or inside the vagina during sexual stimulation. Of course, the people who volunteered for these observations did not comprise a representative sample of the population: they were less sexually inhibited, more sexually experienced, and probably more liberal in their sexual attitudes than most Americans. Still, it is not unreasonable to assume that the behavioral and physiological responses observed are applicable to general human sexual functioning, and this ground-breaking research still forms the foundation of our knowledge of human physiological sexual response.

One of their findings was that the basic sexual response cycle is the same for men and women and consists of four phases. The *excitement phase* begins with whatever is sexually stimulating and arousing for the particular person. Blood rushes into the genitals (**vasocongestion**), causing penile erection in males and vaginal lubrication and clitoral swelling in females. If the stimulation continues, excitement builds quickly to a point called the *plateau phase*, in which the sexual arousal is maintained and intensified. If stimulation is terminated or ceases to be effective at this point, the person will not experience orgasm but will enter a prolonged period of gradually decreasing sexual tensions. The *orgasmic phase*, the shortest period of the cycle, consists of those few seconds when the bodily changes resulting from stimulation reach their maximum intensity. Orgasm involves muscular contractions of the pelvic area. In males, it consists of a stage of *ejaculatory inevitability*, after which the second stage, ejaculation of semen, cannot be controlled. Women do not report a corresponding point of inevitability before their orgasms, which include clusters of contractions that are intense and close together. During the *resolution phase*, sexual tensions decrease as the person returns to the unstimulated state. Women are capable of having another orgasm if effective stimulation is continued. For men, on the other hand, there is a period of time, which varies among individuals, when re-arousal and orgasm are impossible. This period is called the **refractory period**; its duration varies widely, from minutes to hours, influenced by many factors including the male's age and novelty of the sexual practice.

Scientific study of sexual behavior is a recent endeavor. (iStock)

Masters and Johnson's findings also corrected some previously held fallacies about human sexuality, as noted below.

**Vasocongestion**

Increased blood flow to, and swelling of, localized tissues and organs

**Refractory period**

Period following orgasm in males during which further sexual arousal and orgasm are not possible

1. ***Myth #1: Direct stimulation of the clitoris is essential for the attainment of orgasms.*** In the female the clitoris is the organ that is most sensitive to sexual stimulation. It had been widely believed that continuous and direct clitoral stimulation is important for the attainment of orgasms. This is not so, said Masters and Johnson. In fact, during the plateau phase the clitoris retracts and becomes relatively inaccessible to stimulation by either hand or penis. Actually, the clitoris is stimulated during intercourse without any special effort because every thrust exerts pressure indirectly on this organ. Furthermore, many women find direct

stimulation of the head of the clitoris irritating and prefer either stimulation on the side of the clitoral shaft or the general genital area.

2. ***Myth #2: Vaginal orgasms are better than clitoral orgasms.*** Freud proposed that vaginal orgasms represent a more mature level of psychosexual functioning than clitoral orgasms, a viewpoint widely held in psychoanalytic circles. Part of the reasoning was that females who masturbated via clitoral stimulation were using the clitoris as a substitute penis, an expression of penis envy. Although various writers, ( for example, Ellis, 1962) had argued against this idea, it remained for Masters and Johnson to disprove it conclusively. Physiological recording reveals only one kind of female orgasm, and clitoral stimulation plays an important role in it. In fact, the women in their study frequently reported that orgasms resulting from masturbation or manual manipulation by a partner, both of which tend to focus on the clitoris, were more intense than orgasms achieved in intercourse.

3. ***Myth #3: Simultaneous orgasms represent a superior sexual accomplishment.*** The older marriage manuals stated that the couple's achievement of simultaneous orgasms was a mark of superior sexual accomplishment. Masters and Johnson did not find this to be so. In fact, preoccupation with achieving simultaneous orgasms could cause partners to direct their attention to the adequacy of their performance rather than losing themselves in the feelings of lovemaking. Assuming the *spectator role*, as Masters and Johnson call this attitude, can lead to erectile difficulties in men and failure to have orgasm in women.

4. ***Myth #4: Size of penis contributes importantly to female sexual enjoyment.*** In a study of 80 men, Masters and Johnson found remarkably little variation in size of erect penises. Even though there is some small range in size, the authors draw attention to the fact that during entry the vaginal walls expand just enough to accommodate the penis, so that the friction between penis and vagina should not be much affected by penile size.

The observational studies of Masters and Johnson also led to the development of specific therapeutic techniques that continue to be used in sex therapy today. They suggested, for example, that many sexual dysfunctions have their origins in **performance anxiety**. Both men and women can become preoccupied with "producing" or "performing," the man with satisfying the woman, the woman with having an orgasm—the overt expression of which she sees as important in satisfying her male partner as well as herself. Fears of not being able to perform increase the likelihood of failure; and each new failure increases the worries of failing next time, resulting in a vicious circle. The woman, blaming herself to some extent for the man's failure, may become even more concerned that she is not performing adequately. One or both individuals may take on a spectator role, in which they are critically observing their performance rather than unselfconsciously participating in lovemaking. The identification of performance anxiety as etiologically important for sexual dysfunction resulted in the creation of anxiety-reduction approaches to sex therapies that are widely used today. Recent research continues to implicate performance anxiety as central to the development and maintenance of all sexual dysfunctions in both men and women (McCabe, 2005).

The work of Masters and Johnson shed less light on the causes and treatments of the paraphilias or of gender dysphoria. It also may have produced an under-appreciation of the possible biological causes of sexual disorders. There are now many biological factors known to cause or contribute to sexual dysfunction. Any physical disorder that involves the circulatory system, for example, can affect sexual performance. There are a variety of medical conditions, hormonal influences, and medication side effects that can directly produce sexual impairment. Efforts to treat these conditions pharmacologically have increased dramatically in the past two decades, as discussed below. The psychological treatment of sexual problems, however, owes more to the contributions of Masters and Johnson than to any other single source.

**BVT** *Lab*

Flashcards are available for this chapter at **www.BVTLab.com**.

**Performance anxiety**

Fear of not being able to perform sexually, which in turn hinders sexual performance, and may be central to the development of sexual dysfunctions

# 9.2 Sexual Dysfunctions

In the *DSM-5*, a sexual dysfunction is a disturbance in a person's sexual response or experience of sexual pleasure. A broad range of disorders, representing all stages of the sexual response cycle, are included. The diagnosis of sexual dysfunction requires clinical judgment that the impairment is not a normal variation in response, considering the age and experience of the person, the adequacy of the sexual stimulation involved (lack of knowledge about sexual anatomy and sexual techniques can play a role in development of sexual disorders, in some cases), and the level of subjective distress. Inter-rater diagnostic reliability was excellent for the sexual dysfunctions in the *DSM-III* field trials, ranging from 1.0 to 0.86 across the two phases.

> How common are sexual dysfunctions? How effective is treatment?

Each of the dysfunctions can be classified with certain clinical specifiers:

a. Lifelong Type vs. Acquired Type—Some dysfunctions may be life-long, occurring since the age of puberty. Others develop at some point after a period of normal sexual functioning.

b. Generalized Type vs. Situational Type—Generalized sexual dysfunctions occur in many or all types of circumstances, regardless of sexual stimulation, situations, or partners. Situational dysfunctions are limited to particular circumstances or to particular partners.

c. Severity (Mild, Moderate, or Severe)—Ratings of severity are based on the degree to which the symptoms cause distress.

The *DSM-5* reorganized *DSM-IV*'s sexual dysfunctions by making the categories gender-specific when possible and moving away from linking disorders to parts of the sexual response cycle. Emphasis is more strongly placed on the degree of distress caused by the symptoms, and diagnosis requires at least 6 months. The primary categories of sexual dysfunctions (i.e., those that are not induced by the effects of a medication or substance) are summarized in Table 9-1. Isolated or occasional symptoms, such as these, are common in both men and women and do not necessary indicate the presence of a disorder. To meet criteria for one of these conditions, symptoms must cause significant distress for the person; be persistent or recurrent; and not be due to another mental disorder (such as depression), medical disorder (such as a circulatory

### Table 9-1   DSM-5 Sexual Dysfunctions

| Disorder | Key Symptoms | Minimum Duration Required for Diagnosis |
|---|---|---|
| Delayed ejaculation | Marked delay, reduction in, or absence of ejaculation | 6 months |
| Erectile disorder | Marked difficulty attaining or retaining erection during sexual activity | 6 months |
| Female orgasmic disorder | Marked delay, reduction in, or absence of orgasms | 6 months |
| Female sexual interest/ arousal disorder | Absent or reduced sexual interest or sexual arousal | 6 months |
| Genito-pelvic pain/ penetration disorder | Persistent or recurrent vaginal or pelvic pain during sexual activity | 6 months |
| Male hypoactive sexual desire disorder | Persistent or recurrent deficiency in or absence of sexual desire | 6 months |
| Premature ejaculation | Persistent or recurrent pattern of ejaculating before the person wishes during sexual activity | 6 months |

Source: Reprinted with permission from the *Diagnostic and Statistical Manual of Mental Disorders*, Fifth Edition, (Copyright 2013). American Psychiatric Association.

problem), or the effect of a substance or medication. The *DSM-5* also provides a classification for substance/medication induced sexual dysfunction, which will be discussed later.

# 9.2a  Female Sexual Interest/Arousal Disorder

A woman's persistent or recurrent deficiency in the desire for sexual activity, and in normal sexual fantasies or thoughts, that causes significant distress is diagnosed as female sexual interest/arousal disorder. This new category (see *DSM-5* Diagnostic Criteria for Female Sexual Interest/Arousal Disorder) is intended to encompass those women who in the *DSM-IV* would be diagnosed with Hypoactive Sexual Desire Disorder and Female Sexual Arousal Disorder. The low arousal or lack of desire may be generalized to all sexual activities or it may be situational, involving only one partner or a specific activity such as intercourse. Typically the person does not seek or initiate sexual interaction but may participate reluctantly after partner initiation. To make the diagnosis, the clinician must consider gender, age, health, and cultural contexts of the level of desire, as well as the context of the interpersonal relationships that are affected.

Decreased sexual interest is a common issue among women. Representative national samples indicate one-third of U.S. women experience problems with low sexual desire, and 20% of females report arousal problems (American Psychiatric Association, 2000). However, there

Decreased sexual interest is a common issue among women: Representative national samples indicated 20% of United States women experience problems with low sexual desire. (Shutterstock)

| DSM-5 | Diagnostic Criteria for Female Sexual Interest/Arousal Disorder |
|---|---|

302.72 (F52.22) Female Sexual Interest/Arousal Disorder

A.  Lack of, or significantly reduced, sexual interest/arousal, as manifested by at least three of the following:
  1.  Absent/reduced interest in sexual activity.
  2.  Absent/reduced sexual/erotic thoughts or fantasies.
  3.  No/reduced initiation of sexual activity, and typically unreceptive to a partner's attempts to initiate.
  4.  Absent/reduced sexual excitement/pleasure during sexual activity in almost all or all (approximately 75%–100%) sexual encounters (in identified situational contexts or, if generalized, in all contexts).
  5.  Absent/reduced sexual interest/arousal in response to any internal or external sexual/erotic cues (e.g., written, verbal, visual).
  6.  Absent/reduced genital or nongenital sensations during sexual activity in almost all or all (approximately 75%–100%) sexual encounters (in identified situational contexts or, if generalized, in all contexts).

B.  The symptoms in Criterion A have persisted for a minimum duration of approximately 6 months.

C.  The symptoms in Criterion A cause clinically significant distress in the individual.

D.  The sexual dysfunction is not better explained by a nonsexual mental disorder or as a consequence of severe relationship distress (e.g., partner violence) or other significant stressors and is not attributable to the effects of a substance/medication or other medical condition.

Specify whether:
Lifelong: The disturbance has been present since the individual became sexually active.
Acquired: The disturbance began after a period of relatively normal sexual function.
Specify whether:
Generalized: Not limited to certain types of stimulation, situations, or partners.
Situational: Only occurs with certain types of stimulation, situations, or partners.
Specify current severity:
Mild: Evidence of mild distress over the symptoms in Criterion A.
Moderate: Evidence of moderate distress over the symptoms in Criterion A.
Severe: Evidence of severe or extreme distress over the symptoms in Criterion A.

Source: Reprinted with permission from the *Diagnostic and Statistical Manual of Mental Disorders*, Fifth Edition, (Copyright 2013). American Psychiatric Association.

is much variation in female sexual interest across ages and cultures. The incidence of the newly combined *DSM-5* category is unknown. Decreased sexual desire can be associated with other mental disorders, such as depressive disorders, as well as with relationship problems. The diagnosis is not given in the absence of significant distress; a persons who self-identifies as "asexual" would not receive the label (American Psychiatric Association, 2013). Although it can begin at any time after puberty, most frequently deficit sexual desire develops after a period of relatively normal sexual interest, in connection with interpersonal problems and/or stressful events (American Psychiatric Association, 2000).

This condition may involve the recurrent inability to attain an adequate lubrication-swelling response in sexual excitement or inability to maintain the arousal long enough for the completion of sexual activity. Normally, sexual arousal in women involves vasocongestion, producing vaginal lubrication and swelling of the external genitals. To make the diagnosis, the clinician first considers issues such as age and health status and determines that the lack of arousal is not due to inadequate sexual stimulation. Female sexual interest/arousal disorder can be accompanied by orgasm disorders, and it may result in painful intercourse and avoidance of sexual situations. In earlier classifications, the condition was referred to by the pejorative term *frigidity*.

The male equivalents of female sexual interest/arousal disorder consist of two diagnoses, male hypoactive sexual desire disorder and erectile disorder, which will be described next.

# 9.2b Male Hypoactive Sexual Desire Disorder

Male hypoactive sexual desire disorder describes a condition of recurrent deficiency in (or absence of) sexual desire and erotic thoughts or fantasies, persisting at least 6 months and causing significant distress. The individual's age health, and social/cultural context are taken into consideration when giving the diagnosis. Men with this disorder may no longer initiate sexual activity with a partner, or participate only minimally in response to another's initiation. Some sexual activities, including masturbation, may continue in the absence of desire. Like women, men show cross-cultural variations in low sexual desire; and problems with sexual desire may affect a significant proportion of older men, although the persistent lack of desire appears to characterize only a small segment (less than 2%) of males aged 16–44 (American Psychiatric Association, 2013).

# 9.2c Erectile Disorder

The defining symptom of erectile disorder (see *DSM-5* Diagnostic Criteria for Erectile Disorder) is persistent or recurrent difficulty in attaining an adequate erection for sexual activity or in maintaining the erection until the activity is completed. Some men are unable to obtain any erection from the onset of the sexual event, while others may attain an initial erection but lose tumescence before penetration or during thrusting. Erectile problems may be generalized to all sexual situations or may be specific to certain ones ( for example, some may awake with morning erections or maintain erection only during solitary masturbation). Affected men may experience anxiety about sexual performance and fear of failure. Depression and substance disorders may co-occur, each of which has also been associated with erectile difficulties (American Psychiatric Association, 2000). National representative survey data suggest that 10% of males report erectile problems; however, age is a significant factor, with incidence rising from about 5% at age 40 to 15% by age 70 (Segraves & Althof, 2002). In earlier classifications, the condition was referred to by the pejorative term, *impotence*.

## Causal Factors

More research is needed to define the specific causes of deficient sexual desire. A variety of factors are associated with reduced desire, including medical conditions such as arthritis or irritable bowel syndrome, other mental disorders such as depression, and previous history

| DSM-5 | Diagnostic Criteria for Erectile Disorder |

302.72 (F52.21) Erectile Disorder

A. At least one of the three following symptoms must be experienced on almost all or all (approximately 75%–100%) occasions of sexual activity (in identified situational contexts or, if generalized, in all contexts).

   1. Marked difficulty in obtaining an erection during sexual activity.

   2. Marked difficulty in maintaining an erection until the completion of sexual activity.

   3. Marked decrease in erectile rigidity.

B. The symptoms in Criterion A have persisted for a minimum duration of approximately 6 months.

C. The symptoms in Criterion A cause clinically significant distress in the individual.

D. The sexual dysfunction is not better explained by a nonsexual mental disorder or as a consequence of severe relationship distress or other significant stressors and is not attributable to the effects of a substance/medication or other medical condition.

Specify whether:

Lifelong: The disturbance has been present since the individual became sexually active.

Acquired: The disturbance began after a period of relatively normal sexual function.

Specify whether:

Generalized: Not limited to certain types of stimulation, situations, or partners.

Situational: Only occurs with certain types of stimulation, situations, or partners.

Specify current severity:

Mild: Evidence of mild distress over the symptoms in Criterion A.

Moderate: Evidence of moderate distress over the symptoms in Criterion A.

Severe: Evidence of severe or extreme distress over the symptoms in Criterion A.

Source: Reprinted with permission from the *Diagnostic and Statistical Manual of Mental Disorders,* Fifth Edition, (Copyright 2013). American Psychiatric Association.

of sexual or physical abuse (American Psychiatric Association, 2013). Ironically, the most common pharmacological treatments for depression, the SSRIs, may themselves result in decreased desire (Fava & Rankin, 2002). Sexual desire tends to decrease with age for both men and women. The androgen hormone testosterone plays a significant role in male sexual interest, and both androgens and estrogens are involved in female libido. When levels of these hormones drop (during aging, after menopause), sexual desire often declines (LeVay & Valente, 2006). Psychological factors may reduce sexual desire, including relationship difficulties, stress, and negative attitudes about sex.

Sexual arousal problems, on the other hand, have been the source of much attention in the professional literature. According to psychoanalytic theory, men and women show inhibited sexual excitement because unconsciously they perceive sexual activity as dangerous. The physical inhibition of sexual response is, thus, a defense against the threatening impulse. In this view, anxiety over sexual expression stems from the Oedipal conflict, which in men leads to intense castration anxiety. As Fenichel (1945) put it, "In the simplest and most typical cases, impotence is based on persistence of an unconscious sensual attachment to the mother. Superficially no sexual attachment is completely attractive because the partner is never the mother; in a deeper layer, every sexual attachment has to be inhibited because every partner represents the mother" (p. 170).

and Johnson (1970) suggested that in addition to performance anxiety, social learning histories contribute to the dysfunction. In their study and treatment of men with primary impotence, 3 of the 32 subjects reported having had clearly seductive mothers. In each instance the son had slept in the mother's bedroom at least through puberty; and although there had been no actual intercourse, the relationship had involved strong erotic features. The father in these families had been either absent or ineffective. These three cases are consistent with an Oedipal interpretation. Six men came from a background in which there was a strong religious belief that sex was sinful. It is of interest that these men married wives with equally restrictive religious backgrounds, five of whom had vaginismus (involuntary contraction of the pelvic/vaginal muscles making intercourse painful). Another six men had had homosexual attachments as teenagers and still considered themselves basically homosexual in orientation. Three of these homosexually inclined men had had domineering mothers, but the other three reported nothing unusual in the family pattern. Four other impotent men had had humiliating initial sexual experiences with prostitutes. The squalid quarters, repelling physical appearance of the women, and the amusement and derision of the prostitutes had made sexual arousal impossible and destroyed their self-confidence. No two of the remaining 13 men reported similar histories, either in terms of initial sexual trauma or features of family beliefs or interaction. Interviews with sexually dysfunctional women revealed a similar variety of social learning experiences that may have contributed to their difficulty.

Especially for men, arousal problems increase with age. Several biological factors are known to influence sexual arousal, including any condition that affects the circulatory system and many types of medications and drugs. Lower urinary tract symptoms can affect female desire, lubrication, and orgasm (Cohen, Barboglio, & Gousse, 2008). Among males, erectile disorder has been linked to nicotine (smokers have twice the rate of erection problems as nonsmokers), alcohol (at higher doses), obesity, diabetes, spinal cord injury, stress, anxiety, and depression (LeVay & Valente, 2006). Antipsychotic medications are known to produce sexual dysfunction, including erectile problems, as side effects (Baggaley, 2008). Antidepressant medications, especially the SSRIs, produce sexual side effects as well (Rivas-Vazquez, Blais, Rey, & Rivas-Vazques, 2000), including erectile dysfunction, reduced sexual interest, and ejaculatory difficulties.

## Treatments for Deficient Sexual Desire

Intervention is difficult for low or absent sexual desire. No established pharmacological treatments exist. There are no aphrodisiacs or other medications that can create sexual desire in an individual, although there is some evidence that testosterone supplementation may increase sexual desire in men and women who have lower than normal levels (LeVay & Valente, 2006). Others suggest that high doses of androgens may improve low sexual interest in females (Segraves, 2003). Psychotherapy appears to be modestly effective, with between 50% and 70% of patients showing improvement, although only half maintain improvement three years after therapy (Segraves & Althof, 2002). Often, therapy involves marital or relationship counseling.

Couples counseling is moderately effective for both men and women in treating low sexual interest. (iStock)

## Treatments for Deficient Sexual Arousal

Wolpe (1958) was among the first to apply systematic desensitization to sexual dysfunctions. He pointed out that his counter-conditioning approach to sexual inhibitions seemed especially appropriate since anxiety inhibits sexual responding in a direct way. Pre-orgasmic sexual arousal is predominantly parasympathetic in nature, whereas anxiety almost always involves strong sympathetic arousal. Thus anxiety would directly inhibit the parasympathetic activation necessary for effective sexual responding. On the other hand, if the parasympathetic sexual arousal could be made to be stronger than the competing anxiety response, then the former—in time—should replace the latter. Wolpe had individuals conduct their own desensitization *in vivo*, that is, at home with a cooperative partner, usually a spouse. The basic strategy was to have the person determine at what point in the sequence of sexual activity that anxiety began and to go beyond that point only gradually and in small steps, permitting the anxiety associated with each stage to be successfully counter-conditioned. It was important that both partners understood and accepted that no particular level of performance was expected. Over periods of up to 25 sessions, the partners would gradually increase contact and activity while maintaining a relaxed state. On the basis of his clinical records, Wolpe (1973) concluded that 14 of 18 impotent men recovered to the extent of achieving "entirely satisfactory sexual performance." Another three attained a level that was acceptable to their partners.

Obler (1973) reported a controlled study of systematic desensitization in the treatment of sexual dysfunctions. Twenty-two matched individuals with sexual dysfunctions (premature ejaculation and secondary impotence in males and secondary orgasmic dysfunction in females) were assigned to each of three conditions: systematic desensitization plus assertiveness training, psychodynamically oriented group therapy, and a no-treatment control group. The systematic desensitization plus assertiveness training group showed marked improvement over the 15 sessions in terms of the percentage of successful sexual attempts; both the individuals in group therapy and the members of the no-treatment control group showed little or no increase on this measure. The improvements in the behaviorally treated group were maintained at an 18-month follow-up.

Masters and Johnson (1970) similarly sought to reduce anxiety that interferes with arousal through *sensate focus*, which progresses through three phases: pleasuring (in which the couple is instructed to gently touch and caress, but not to have intercourse or orgasm); genital stimulation (involving light genital play but again without any orgasm or intercourse); and nondemand intercourse, increasing gradually from brief penetration to full thrusting. They reported improvement for nearly 75% of males with acquired erectile dysfunction. Other psychotherapy studies have confirmed that significant gains and long-term improvements are realized by up to two-thirds of patients who undergo treatment (Segraves & Althof, 2002).

Biological approaches, however, have received much more attention in recent years. Earlier biological interventions for male erectile disorder included prosthetic devices, such as semi-rigid rods or inflatable tubes, which were surgically implanted to provide erection for intercourse. Vacuum devices, placed over the penis to draw blood into the organ and produce an erection, have been available for years. A tension band placed over the base of the penis kept blood from flowing out. Vasodilating medications such as papaverine, injected directly into the penis, produce erections within 15 minutes, although treatments involving this approach have high dropout rates (Segraves & Althof, 2002).

The biggest advance in biological treatment has been the development of an oral medication, sildenafil, which relaxes a valve in the penis to allow increased blood flow. Pfizer introduced the drug in 1998 as Viagra; unlike papaverine, it produces an erection only if sexual excitement is present (the drug does not produce desire or excitement itself). Several similar drugs are now on the very lucrative market for pharmaceutical treatment of erectile dysfunction. Clinical trials have shown response rates of nearly 70% although there are concerns about its use in those with heart conditions, and controlled studies

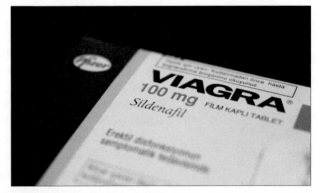

Sales of Viagra® and related products exceed one billion dollars globally. (Shutterstock)

of long-term use are not yet available. Some research suggests that sildenafil plus a time-limited group psychotherapy technique, or psychotherapy alone, produce significantly better results than sildenafil given orally on demand (Melnik & Abdo, 2005). A similar comparison study of sildenafil alone with sildenafil plus cognitive-behavior therapy in combination, involving 53 couples, found those receiving the combined treatments showed better results (Banner & Anderson, 2007). Sildenafil may also be helpful for erectile problems resulting from antidepressant medications, although more data are needed on their interactions (Fava & Rankin, 2002).

To date, results with sildenafil in the treatment of female sexual arousal problems have been less promising. The availability of water-based lubricant jellies and crèmes can significantly relieve friction during intercourse for effective symptomatic relief. Alternative preparations, including herbal extracts, remain largely untested. In one assessment of ginkgo biloba extract for treatment (as a blood-flow enhancer) of female sexual arousal disorder, Meston, Rellini, and Telch (2008) found it was not better than placebo and did not enhance sex therapy, which was effective separately.

## 9.2d Female Orgasmic Disorder

Women with female orgasmic disorder may experience normal sexual desire and excitement phases, but they also experience a recurrent absence or delay of orgasm either in specific

Partners who don't experience normal sexual desire or are frustrated by a recurrent absence or delay of orgasm can easily become discouraged or depressed. This can cause significant distress or interpersonal problems or a sense of distance in the relationship. (iStock)

sexual circumstances (Situational Type), or in all sexual activities (Generalized Type), persisting at least 6 months and causing significant distress. The diagnostic process requires careful consideration of factors such as age, sexual history, and whether the sexual stimulation received is adequate in focus, duration, and intensity for orgasm. The female capacity for orgasm tends to increase with sexual knowledge and experience; once acquired, the ability is rarely lost. Therefore, most cases of female orgasmic disorder may be lifelong rather than acquired (American Psychiatric Association, 2000). In situational cases, females may be able to reach orgasm during solitary masturbation but not with a partner. Inhibited orgasm is a relatively common problem among females; estimates are that from 10% to 41% of women report orgasm difficulty, and about 10% do not have orgasms during their lifetimes (American Psychiatric Association, 2013). However, not all of these women report significant distress; some report satisfaction with their sexual lives even with few or no orgasms.

## 9.2e Delayed Ejaculation

Like its female counterpart, delayed ejaculation involves an inability to reach orgasm or a delay in reaching orgasm that follows a normal phase of sexual excitement. The absence or delay of ejaculation is recurrent and persistent (lasting at least 6 months) and results in marked distress. The orgasmic dysfunction is not due to inadequate sexual stimulation, a medical condition, or the effects of a substance. Age is a diagnostic consideration since as males age they tend to require longer periods of stimulation before reaching orgasm. Most cases appear to be situational, such as orgasm being inhibited during intercourse but occurring in masturbation or oral sex. About 10% of males report occasional problems with inhibited ejaculation (American Psychiatric Association, 2000), but less than 1% report problems persisting more than 6 months, making delayed ejaculation the least common male sexual complaint (American Psychiatric Association, 2013).

## 9.2f Premature (Early) Ejaculation

Males diagnosed with premature ejaculation show almost the opposite symptoms from delayed ejaculation. Instead, orgasm and ejaculation occur with minimal sexual stimulation, within approximately 1 minute of vaginal penetration or before the person wishes it in the case of nonvaginal sexual activities. Ejaculation may occur before penetration is achieved or shortly thereafter. The pattern must be recurrent and persistent, and associated with significant distress. When giving the diagnosis, the clinician must consider factors such as age, length of excitement phase, novelty of the practice or partner, and the frequency of sexual activities. Premature ejaculation is most often seen in young men, and onset tends to date to their earliest attempts at intercourse. Most males with the disorder can inhibit orgasm during masturbation longer than during intercourse. About 27% of males indicated problems with early ejaculation in a representative national sample (American Psychiatric Association, 2000), making it among the most common sexual complaints. However, it is estimated that only 1%–3% of men would meet the duration requirements (ejaculation in less than 1 minute, persistent for at least 6 months) of the *DSM-5* diagnosis (American Psychiatric Association, 2013).

## Causal Factors

Orgasm difficulties can result from medication use, as previously mentioned. In males, prostate inflammation can result in rapid ejaculation (LeVay & Valente, 2006). In many cases of orgasmic dysfunction, there is inadequate knowledge of sexual anatomy, and therefore inadequate experience in providing sexual stimulation sufficient

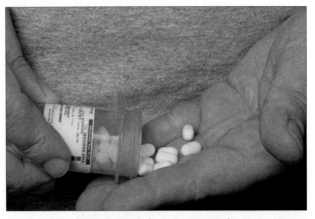

Orgasm difficulties can result from various medications. (Shutterstock)

to produce orgasm. Because of large differences in masturbatory experience, males have greater experience with orgasm at earlier ages. At the same time, the majority of female college students report faking an orgasm (Elliott & Brantley, 1997), which might give false feedback to partners about the ineffectiveness of their sexual techniques, which may further degrade the quality of stimulation. Other possible causal factors include emotional conflicts over sexuality, relationship difficulties, or fear of pregnancy. One perspective of premature ejaculation suggests that young males learn to masturbate to orgasm quickly in order to avoid detection, and this could shape faster ejaculations. No empirical evidence exists in support of any particular causal theory for orgasm disorders. The *DSM-5* suggests a moderate genetic contribution to premature ejaculation, but not for delayed ejaculation or female orgasmic disorder (American Psychiatric Association, 2013).

## Treatment of Orgasmic Disorders

Interventions derived from Masters and Johnson (1970) are widely viewed as effective. For deficient orgasm, sensate focus may be combined with education about sexual anatomy and masturbation training. The assumption is that solitary masturbatory practice, without demand components, could shape orgasm techniques that could then be transferred to activity with a partner. Lobitz and LoPiccolo (1972), for example, incorporated a nine-step masturbation program for women who had never experienced orgasm and reported 100% success in treating 13 women. Several studies have confirmed the effectiveness of masturbatory training for orgasmic disorder (Chambless, et al., 1998; Segraves & Althof, 2002). Sotile and Kilmann (1977) reviewed a large number of studies and concluded that various methods of systematic desensitization are also successful in treating orgasmic dysfunctions.

For men with premature ejaculation, the couple is usually taught the **squeeze technique** whereby the partner stimulates the penis until the man is about to ejaculate and then squeezes on the top and bottom surfaces immediately below the head of the penis. This stops the ejaculatory process, and after a brief pause stimulation can be resumed. In this way the man comes to recognize the impending signs of ejaculation and can learn to increasingly delay the point of inevitability. Masters and Johnson report moderately high success rates, but subsequent evaluations suggest that gains are not maintained well over the long term (Segraves & Althof, 2002).

Pharmacological interventions for premature ejaculation seem to have followed from the recognition that several psychiatric drugs have the unintended side effect of delaying orgasm. A variety of antipsychotic and antidepressant drugs have been used, with double-blind trials showing drugs superior to placebos (Segraves & Althof, 2002). SSRIs appear to

**Squeeze technique**

Method for treating premature ejaculation in which the penis is squeezed below the head just before ejaculation to stop the ejaculatory process

be more effective in delaying ejaculation if taken daily, rather than on-demand, and topical anesthetics may also delay ejaculation (Waldinger, 2007). Pharmaceutical interest and activity is high in this area, raising concern among some researchers (e.g., Rowland & Burek, 2007) that it is distracting from work toward an important biobehavioral understanding of the condition.

## 9.2g  Genito-Pelvic Pain/Penetration Disorder

Genito-pelvic pain/penetration disorder involves pain, or the fearful anticipation of pain, during intercourse or vaginal penetration. The *DSM-5* disorder replaces two sexual pain disorders in the *DSM-IV*, dyspareunia (painful intercourse) and vaginismus. The pain may occur during intercourse or persist afterwards and is not caused by lack of lubrication, a general medical condition, the effects of a substance, or another mental disorder. Involuntary contraction of the perineal muscles surrounding the outer vagina, in response to attempts to penetrate the vagina, is sometimes involved. It may be triggered by actual or anticipated penetration by a penis, finger, speculum, or tampon. In sexual interactions the contracted muscles prevent intercourse and may sometimes prevent normal gynecological examination as well. Normal sexual responses are usually not impaired unless penetration is attempted or anticipated. However, sufferers tend to avoid intimate circumstances and sexual opportunities, often creating difficulties in relationships. The specifiers for this disorder do not include Generalized vs. Situational Type, as it is assumed that the dysfunction occurs in each sexual situation. The course of the disorder is largely unknown, as women may not seek treatment until other problems (e.g., conception issues) occur; however, genito-pelvic pain complaints tend to peak in early adulthood and near menopause (American Psychiatric Association, 2013). Trauma, such as rape or sexual assault, can be causal for sexual pain disorders, although Meyer and Deitsch (1996) consider the primary causes to be painful childbirth, inadequate lubrication, and abrasion by pubic hair.

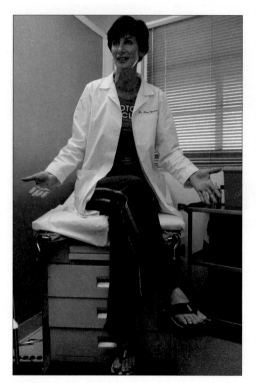

Dr. Sharon Mitchell is a clinical sexologist and director of the Adult Industry Medical Healthcare Foundation in Sherman Oaks, California. Sexologists study, among other things, sexual dysfunctions and disorders, and treat patients. (AP Wide World)

### *Treatment of Sexual Pain Disorders*

Sotile and Kilmann (1977) reviewed the literature and found that systematic desensitization could be used effectively for dyspareunia and vaginismus in women. Relaxation, sensate focus, and general counseling are usually part of psychological approaches to treatment. Vaginismus can be effectively treated by a combination of relaxation training and **Kegel exercises** (which tense and release the vaginal muscles) followed by the self-insertion of a graduated series of dilators into the vagina. Success rates reported for these interventions range from 83% to 100% at 1-year follow-up (Segraves & Althof, 2002).

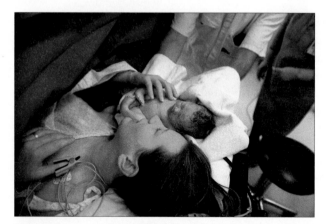

Trauma from a painful childbirth that leads to a sexual pain disorder would be diagnosed as a "sexual dysfunction due to a general medical condition." (Shutterstock)

## 9.2h  Other Sexual Dysfunctions

**Kegel exercises**

Exercises to tense and release vaginal muscles

Substance/medication-induced sexual dysfunction occurs when there is a significant impairment in sexual function that results from intoxication, withdrawal, or exposure to a medication or other substance capable of producing the symptoms. Among the possible substances are alcohol, opioids, sedatives, amphetamine, and cocaine, as well as antidepressants and antipsychotics, which frequently produce sexual side-effects. Some substances may not have their effects on sexual functioning until after a long delay (as in alcohol and nicotine), while others may produce dysfunction quickly (within 8 days of antidepressant use). There is no duration requirement, but the dysfunction must cause distress and not occur exclusively during delirium. The likelihood of the disorder appears to increase with age (American Psychiatric Association, 2013).

*Other specified sexual dysfunction* is available as a category to include dysfunctions that do not meet any other disorder's criteria. An example might include symptoms of sexual aversion disorder, a former *DSM-IV* category that was discontinued due to its rarity. In this condition, individuals not only show a lack of interest in sexual activity but also an active aversion to, and avoidance of, sexual contact with a partner. Sufferers react with disgust, fear, anxiety, and occasionally panic attacks when faced with a sexual situation involving the opportunity for sexual contact; these reactions cause significant distress. Individuals may avoid possible sexual partners or situations by occupying nearly all their time in work, school, or family; or they may travel or attempt to make themselves unappealing through dress or habits. The reactions can be specific to certain aspects of sexual activity or generalized to nearly all sexual stimuli, including kissing (American Psychiatric Association, 2000).

## 9.2i Future Considerations in the Treatment of Sexual Dysfunctions

There are a variety of clearly effective psychotherapies for sexual dysfunctions. The techniques pioneered by Masters and Johnson have proven to be valuable although other therapists have not matched their reported rates of success (see Table 9-2).

Behavioral and cognitive-behavioral approaches to treatment of sexual dysfunctions continue to produce solid outcomes. Sarwer and Durlak (1997) report that "field" behavioral sex therapy produced success rates of 65% in 365 married couples presenting a range of sexual dysfunctions, and outcomes did not vary as a function of diagnosis. More recently, Stravynski and his colleagues (2007) randomly assigned 49 single women with various sexual dysfunctions (most common were orgasm difficulties, arousal difficulties, and low desire) to one of four treatment conditions: (a) behavioral therapy providing social skills training;

*Table 9-2*   Results of Therapy for Sexual Dysfunctions

| Results of Sex Therapy at the Masters & Johnson Institute | | | |
|---|---|---|---|
| | N[a] | Failures | Successes[b] | Success Rates |
| Primary impotence | 65 | 21 | 44 | 67.7% |
| Secondary impotence | 674 | 134 | 540 | 80.1% |
| Premature ejaculation | 543 | 35 | 508 | 93.6% |
| Ejaculation incompetence | 113 | 27 | 86 | 76.1% |
| Male totals | 1395 | 217 | 1178 | 84.4% |
| Anorgasmia | 811 | 207 | 604 | 74.5% |
| Vaginismus | 130 | 2 | 128 | 98.5% |
| Female totals | 941 | 209 | 732 | 77.8% |
| Combined Totals | 2236 | 426 | 1910 | 81.8% |

[a] Cases seen between 1959 and 1985.

[b] A case was categorized as successful only if the change in sexual function was unequivocal and lasting. For all patients seen before 1973, follow-up lasted five years. From 1973, the follow-up period was reduced to two years. If a patient was successful during the two-week sex therapy program but then slipped back into dysfunction, the case was listed as a failure.

Source: Masters, W. H., Johnson, V. E., and Kolodny, R. C., (1992). *Human Sexuality* (4th Edition). New York, NY: Harper Collins Publishers, Inc. Reprinted with permissions.

(b) dysfunction-targeted behavior therapy involving sensory awareness, fear reduction, education, and masturbatory training; (c) a combination of both behavioral treatments; or (d) a waiting list control group. Therapy was provided in small groups over 15 weeks. Compared to the waiting list controls, general improvements in sexual desire, sexual experience, and sexual satisfaction were evident in all treatment groups with no significant difference between treatment methods seen. The authors interpret the findings to indicate that behavior therapy is broadly effective for sexual dysfunctions in single women although the degree of improvement was below that reported for males.

Regardless of the evidence of the effectiveness of psychotherapy, there is a clear and concerning trend toward medicalization of the sexual dysfunctions (Rowland, 2007). The shift from the biopsychosocial perspective toward a medical model of dysfunction, is apparent in the rapid introduction of new drugs for sexual problems, driven by an aggressive pharmaceutical industry. The danger is that the exclusive push to market and prescribe very profitable new medications that provide temporary symptom relief will indirectly hinder the development and use of effective psychotherapies, as well make research into biopsychological foundations of sexual dysfunctions more difficult. An increased reliance on empirical verification of interventions and controlled comparisons between different treatments might be one effective response on the part of sex therapists.

## 9.3 Paraphilic Disorders

The paraphilic disorders are disorders in which the disturbance concerns the focus or target of sexual desire. The diagnostic criteria describe intense and recurrent sexual fantasies, sexual urges, or sexual behaviors involving objects, children, non-consenting persons, or suffering and humiliation. For some people with paraphilias, the fantasies or stimuli may be necessary in order to become sexually aroused; others may engage in them more episodically. Several of the paraphilias, involving children or non-consenting persons, involve criminal offenses in addition to mental disorders. The legal system may be the source of referral of many of these people into treatment. The paraphilic disorders are summarized in Table 9-3.

> **What are paraphilics? Are they dangerous?**

As is apparent in Table 9-3, all of the paraphilic disorders are much more common among men than women. In fact, it is rare for women to receive any of these diagnoses. Paraphilias must be distinguished from non-pathological sexual fantasies and practices, which can show wide variation. In broad terms, these disorders can be clustered as courtship disorders, conditions that involve pain or suffering, and disorders involving unusual preferences in desire. The key factor is that paraphilic disorders involve clinically significant distress or impairment, such as when they are experienced as obligatory for arousal, involve non-consenting victims, create legal difficulties, or interfere with interpersonal relationships. In the *DSM-III* field trials, diagnostic reliability for paraphilias was excellent (1.0) in Phase 1; no figure is available for Phase 2, indicating no other patients were evaluated with these disorders. The prevalence of paraphilias in the population is not well documented, but the substantial pornography market catering to paraphilic imagery suggests that paraphilic disorders may be under-diagnosed. Approximately 50% of those seen clinically are married (American Psychiatric Association, 2000).

## 9.3a Exhibitionistic Disorder

The defining pattern of exhibitionistic disorder is the recurrent fantasy, urge, or behavior of exposing one's genitals to an unsuspecting stranger. These fantasies, urges, or actions are experienced as sexually arousing and persist over a period of at least 6 months. The diagnosis can be made either if the person acted on the urges or if the urges and fantasies

*Table 9-3*   DSM-5 Paraphilic Disorders

| Disorder | Key Symptoms | Minimum Duration Required for Diagnosis | Sex Ratio |
|---|---|---|---|
| Exhibitionistic Disorder | Exposure of genitals to unsuspecting stranger | 6 months | Much more common among males |
| Fetishistic Disorder | Sexual arousal involving nonliving objects | 6 months | Much more common among males |
| Frotteuristic Disorder | Sexual arousal involving touching un-consenting persons | 6 months | Much more common among males |
| Pedophilic Disorder | Sexual arousal involving prepubescent child | 6 months | Much more common among males |
| Sexual Masochism Disorder | Sexual arousal involving self-humiliation or self-suffering | 6 months | Much more common among males |
| Sexual Sadism Disorder | Sexual arousal involving the humiliation or suffering of others | 6 months | Much more common among males |
| Transvestic Disorder | Sexual arousal involving cross-dressing | 6 months | Much more common among males |
| Voyeuristic Disorder | Sexual arousal involving secret observation of others who are naked or sexually engaged | 6 months | Much more common among males |

Source: Reprinted with permission from the *Diagnostic and Statistical Manual of Mental Disorders*, Fifth Edition, (Copyright 2013). American Psychiatric Association.

cause the person significant distress or interpersonal difficulty. Specifiers can be used to indicate whether the target was prepubertal children, physically mature individuals, or both. Additional *DSM-5* specifiers are "in a controlled environment" (where opportunities to expose are limited) and "in full remission" (symptom-free for 5 or more years). Occasionally the exhibitionist masturbates during the act of exposure or while fantasizing about the exposure later. Most typically, no further attempt is made for sexual contact with the unsuspecting victim. Some exhibitionists report that the shock or surprise of the victim is sexually arousing; others fantasize that the victim will become sexually aroused (American Psychiatric Association, 2000).

Exhibitionism frequently takes place in some isolated place such as a park, a darkened movie theater, or a parked car. It is one of the most common sexual offenses reported to the police in the United States. These individuals are frequently introverted and quietly appropriate in ordinary social relationships. Onset is usually before age 18, and it may decrease in incidence as one ages. The incidence in the population is not known, but it is unlikely to be higher than 2%–4% of the male population (American Psychiatric Association, 2013). Exhibitionistic disorder may be associated with significant impairment; in one study of 25 males with the disorder, over 90% had comorbid conditions including depression, substance abuse, and personality disorders; and suicidal ideation was common (Grant, 2005).

## 9.3b  Fetishistic Disorder

In fetishistic disorder, sexual interest becomes focused on non-living objects such as fur, underwear, leather items, high-heeled shoes, or stockings, or on specific non-genital body parts such as feet or toes. The person experiences recurrent, intense, sexually arousing fantasies, urges, or behaviors involving these objects in sexual contexts, usually masturbating while fondling or smelling them, or having the person's partner wear them. The diagnosis requires that these urges, fantasies, or behaviors persist for at least 6 months and are distressing or cause interpersonal problems. The fetish does not include items used in cross-dressing (transvestic disorder) or items specifically designed to provide sexual arousal (e.g., sex toys). Most commonly, the fetish object becomes a required or strongly preferred aspect of sexual functioning; and, in its absence, males may experience erectile difficulties (American Psychiatric Association, 2000). The *DSM-5* diagnosis can be specified by object: body parts, nonliving objects, or other. It is still almost exclusively a male disorder (American Psychiatric Association, 2013).

Fetish interests are increasingly catered to by the pornography industry, in which fetish-related videos may comprise one-fourth of the output of some large companies, and the Internet, which has played a major role in connecting fetishists to each other (LeVay & Valente, 2006). Although the paraphilia is not in itself illegal, occasionally individuals with fetishism come to the attention of legal authorities because large collections of shoes, panties, bras, or other items are discovered in their homes after reports of stolen items from apartments, clotheslines or laundromats.

Typically, the act of frotteurism disorder occurs in a crowded settings such as subways, elevators, sporting events, and busy sidewalks. (Shutterstock)

## 9.3c Frotteuristic Disorder

The essential feature of frotteuristic disorder is intense sexual arousal from touching or rubbing against a non-consenting person, persisting at least 6 months. The diagnosis can be made either if the individual has committed the act or if the urges and fantasies cause distress or impairment. Typically, the touching occurs in crowded settings—such as subways, elevators, sporting events, and busy sidewalks. The individual may rub his or her genitals or hands against the victim's thighs, buttocks, or breasts, and then escape into the crowd without making further contact with the victim. A male frotteurist may wear a protective cover, such as a plastic bag, over his penis at the time of his act to prevent his ejaculate from staining his clothes (LeVay & Valente, 2006). At the time of contact, frotteurists sometimes fantasize about having a close relationship with the victim. Frotteurism usually begins in adolescence and peaks between ages 15–25 before becoming less frequent (American Psychiatric Association, 2000). The disorder can be specified as in a controlled environment or in full remission. Frotteuristic acts such as inappropriate touching occur in almost a third of the male population; the incidence of the disorder is assumed, however, to be much lower than that, perhaps below 10% (American Psychiatric Association, 2013).

Christopher Paul Neil, a Canadian schoolteacher, is escorted by law officers out of a conference. Neil, 32, who has become the world's most wanted suspected pedophile, was arrested in Thailand, where he was hiding with a Thai friend who had arranged his sexual liaisons with young boys. (AP Wide World)

## 9.3d Pedophilic Disorder

Pedophilic disorder involves intense sexual arousal to prepubescent children, persisting at least 6 months. The diagnosis requires that the person has either acted on these urges or is distressed or impaired by the urges or fantasies. To distinguish it from other forms of child sexual contact, in pedophilia the person must be at least age 16 and must be 5 or more years older than the child, who is generally 13 or younger. The disorder can be subtyped as "exclusive" (in which case sexual attraction is limited to children) or "nonexclusive" (in which case sexual attraction has included adults). Girls are the victims of pedophiles more often than boys. Pedophilia can also be specified as "limited to incest" (which generally refers to first-degree relatives) or by victim category ("sexually attracted to males," "sexually attracted to females," "sexually attracted to both"); (American Psychiatric Association, 2013).

Some who act on pedophilic urges limit contact to undressing the child and looking; others fondle the child, or expose themselves and masturbate. Oral-genital contact or penetration can occur, as can intercourse, but these actions are less common (Fagan, Wise, Schmidt, & Berlin, 2002). Pedophiles may rationalize their behavior as being educational or pleasurable for the child or claim they were being provoked. Those with the disorder may take jobs or engage in hobbies or activities that bring them into contact with children, and they may engage in very complex steps to get access and to prepare or "groom" their victims. The course of pedophilia tends to be more chronic, and the relapse rate appears to be higher in those who are attracted to males (American Psychiatric Association, 2000). Its incidence is unlikely to be higher than 3%–5% of the male population, with the female incidence at only a fraction of that (American Psychiatric Association, 2013).

Pope Benedict XVI, left, shown here with Irish Bishop John Magee at the Vatican. Benedict XVI accepted the resignation of Bishop John Magee, a former papal aide who stands accused of endangering children by failing to report suspected pedophile priests to police. (AP Wide World)

Pedophilic disorder may have received more attention than other paraphilias in the research literature. A review of 170 cases revealed that homosexual or bisexual pedophiles tend to be later in birth order than heterosexual pedophiles—in concordance with other birth order research that indicates that homosexuality incidence increases with birth order (Bogaert, Bezeau, Kuban, & Blanchard, 1997). A reanalysis of data involving over 7,000 sexual offenders and over 18,000 comparison participants for whom intelligence test data were available confirms that male sex offenders tend to have lower IQ scores than non-offenders; and among sex offenders, those who sexually abuse children have lower scores than offenders of adult victims (Cantor, Blanchard, Robichaud, & Christensen, 2005). The relation between IQ and offender status is shown in Figure 9-1.

The diagnosis of pedophilic disorder is complicated by the fact that the behavior is criminal; and mandatory reporting laws require, with few exceptions, notification of legal authorities. Within that context, individuals with pedophilia rarely give honest or accurate reports of the extent of their activities and deny, frequently, any involvement whatsoever. The practice of **plethysmographic assessment** (i.e., measuring changes in penile circumference in response to visual and auditory stimuli of a sexual nature) has been used to assist in diagnosis; typically, pedophiles show more arousal to child-related stimuli than adult-related stimuli. Perhaps it is no surprise that those arrested for child pornography offenses show phallometric response patterns similar to pedophiles when presented with slides and audio narratives of nude prepubescent children, suggesting that a legal record of child pornography can serve as a valid indicator of pedophilia (Seto, Cantor, & Blanchard, 2006). Besides lower IQ, pedophilia also appears to be associated with poorer recall memory and lower right-handedness, both brain-related correlates that may or may not have causal status (Cantor, et al., 2004).

**Plethysmographic assessment**

Assessment of sexual arousal by measurement of genital blood flow

The actual incidence of pedophilia in the population is not known. However, for reasons that are not clear, substantiated cases of child sexual abuse appear to have declined by over 50% since 1990 (Finklehor & Jones, 2006). Female pedophilia is rare, which may be why occasional cases receive widespread coverage in the media. It is also possible that the male victims of

Blood flow through the genitals, measured with a vaginal plethysmograph (a) or a penile plethysmograph (b), can provide objective assessment of sexual arousal. (Wikimedia Commons)

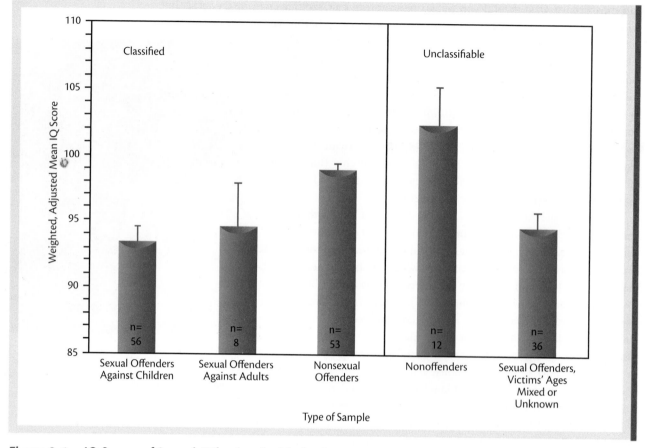

**Figure 9-1**   *IQ Scores of Sexual Offenders by Victims' Age Group*

IQ scores are adjusted for two covariates, the year and the data format of the report providing the data. The numbers appearing at the bottom of each bar represent the number of samples making up each group. The five groups represent 3,187 sexual offenders against children, 302 sexual offenders against adults, 16,222 nonsexual offenders, 432 nonoffenders, and 2,158 sexual offenders with victims' age groups unknown.

Source: Cantor, J. M., Blanchard, R., Robichaud, L. K., and Christensen, B. K. (2005). Quantitative reanalysis of aggregate data on IQ in sexual offenders. *Psychological Bulletin*, 131, 555–568. Reprinted with permission.

female pedophiles are less likely to report the abuse or to view it as damaging. That notion is supported by the controversial meta-analysis of the effects of childhood sexual abuse by Rind, Tromovitch, and Bauserman (1998). They conclude that child sexual abuse is not typically related to serious difficulties later in life for female victims, and the risk of psychological damage is lowest for male victims of female perpetrators. However, physical abuse, whether sexual or nonsexual, and incest are associated with a more damaging outcome.

## 9.3e  Sexual Masochism Disorder

**Masochism**

Preferences for obtaining sexual gratification by experiencing pain inflicted on oneself

**Asphyxiophilia**

Intentional deprivation of oxygen to increase intensity of sexual arousal or orgasm

The person with sexual **masochism** obtains intense sexual arousal through fantasies, urges, or behaviors involving the act of being bound, beaten, humiliated, or otherwise forced to suffer. Masochistic fantasies may involve being whipped, tortured, beaten, raped, pierced, shocked, or subject to other forms of physical or verbal abuse or humiliation; they must have persisted for 6 months and must cause distress or interpersonal problems to qualify for the diagnosis. In some cases, individuals act on these urges or fantasies during solitary sexual behavior, while others seek masochistic acts with partners. The course tends to be chronic, and the activities may remain relatively mild or may increase in intensity and dangerousness. Specifiers include in a controlled environment and in full remission. It can also be specified for one type of masochistic act, **asphyxiophilia**, which involves oxygen depriving activities such as choking, hanging, or suffocating; several accidental deaths occur from these practices each year in the United States (American Psychiatric Association, 2000). Prevalence estimates of about 2% of males and 1% of females have been reported in Australia, but the U.S. incidence of the disorder is unknown (American Psychiatric Association, 2013). It is possible that the interest is masochism and sadism (below) is increasing, as indicated by widely-available sadomasochistic pornography and best-selling novels such as *Fifty Shades of Gray.* Some information exists that masochists are more common among higher socioeconomic levels, and many are highly educated and successful at work (Levitt, Moser, & Jamison, 1994).

## 9.3f Sexual Sadism Disorder

The term **sadism** comes from the name of the Marquis de Sade (1740–1814) who achieved sexual gratification by inflicting pain on his partners. Sexual sadism disorder involves intense sexual arousal and fantasies, persisting for 6 months, about causing physical or psychological suffering to others. To receive the diagnosis, the person either has committed the act on a nonconsenting person or is distressed and impaired by the urges. Sadistic fantasies involve themes of dominance and control over another person and typically include bondage, whipping, spanking, burning, torturing, raping, or otherwise inflicting suffering. The course tends to be chronic, and the activities may remain relatively mild or may increase in intensity and dangerousness; when severe, especially involving those with antisocial personality disorder, victims may be seriously injured or killed (American Psychiatric Association, 2000). The condition can be specified as in a controlled environment or in full remission. The prevalence is unknown, but less than 10% of civilly committed sex offenders carry the diagnosis (American Psychiatric Association, 2013).

Mistress Iridium reaches for a glowing candle preparing to dribble hot wax on their fellow performer Miko at the restaurant La Nouvelle Justine in New York. In addition to the performance, customers can purchase $20 services from the "special fare" menu, such as spanking from a vinyl-clad waiter or waitress. (AP Wide World)

## 9.3g Transvestic Disorder

The essential feature of transvestic disorder is recurrent, intense, sexually arousing fantasies, urges, or behaviors that involve cross-dressing. The pattern must persist for at least 6 months and must be associated with distress or social impairment. The transvestic act may range from occasionally wearing a single object of women's clothing to complete cross-dressing with make-up, female mannerisms, and habits. Most individuals with transvestic disorder experience the sexual arousal by imagining they are females, often visualizing female genitalia. In the *DSM-IV* diagnosis, the disorder, by definition, occurred only in heterosexual males. The *DSM-5* no longer carries that requirement. It is distinguished from the cross-dressing that may be involved in gender dysphoria, which is not done for purposes of sexual arousal. It is a rare disorder in males, and extremely rare in females, but actual incidence is not known. It can be specified with fetishism or with autogynephilia (arousal at thinking of self as a female), and if in a controlled environment or in full remission (American Psychiatric Association, 2013).

Most cases of transvestic disorder involve males who cross-dress as females. (Corbis)

**Sadism**
Preference for obtaining sexual gratification by inflicting pain on one's partner

# 9.3h Voyeuristic Disorder

Individuals with voyeuristic disorder experience intense sexual arousal connected to observing an unsuspecting person who is naked, disrobing, or engaged in sexual activities. The diagnosis requires that the person has either acted on these urges or that the urges cause the person distress or impairment, and signs of voyeurism must persist for 6 months. Typically, the voyeur does not seek sexual contact with the observed person although he may harbor a fantasy of such activity. It is the violation of privacy that seems to be most arousing to the voyeur, who may masturbate during the viewing or at a later time while recalling the event. Voyeurism usually begins by age 15, tends to have a chronic course, and may be the person's exclusive sexual outlet when severe (American Psychiatric Association, 2000). The diagnosis can be specified if in a controlled environment or in full remission. Prevalence could be as high as 12% in males and one-third that for females (American Psychiatric Association, 2013).

# 9.3i Other Specified Paraphilic Disorder

There are many additional forms of paraphilic conditions—all having in common the intense sexual arousal associated with urges, fantasies, and acts involving unusual sources of attraction. If these are recurrent and persist for six months, and cause distress or social problems, they may be coded as *other specified paraphilic disorder*. Some examples that have been reported include zoophilia (animals), necrophilia (corpses), coprophilia (feces), and klismaphilia (enemas).

## *Causal Factors*

The fantasies and behaviors involved in the paraphilias often first appear during childhood and become elaborated in adolescence and adulthood (American Psychiatric Association, 2013). For example, both masochistic and sadistic fantasies are likely to have been present in childhood. Psychoanalytic perspectives suggest that paraphilias result from regression or fixation at earlier stages of psychosexual development: The individual reverts to sexual habits that aroused earlier in life. Other psychoanalysts consider them expressions of hostility to obtain revenge for a childhood in which parents punitively inhibited budding sexuality (Masters, Johnson, & Kolodny, 1992). Biological speculations have included excessive exposure to male hormones, focal brain damage, and chromosomal abnormalities; however, evidence is lacking to support any of these possibilities.

Most of the data on the development of the various paraphilic disorders derive from retrospective reports of the individuals involved. These reports suggest that learned anxiety or inhibition with respect to more conventional heterosexual behavior might be mixed with positive experiences associated with particular pedophilic sexual expression in childhood. In one conditioning model, McGuire and his colleagues (1965) stress the importance of some early experience with the deviant sexual behavior followed by a period of time during which the person masturbates while fantasizing about the deviant object or behavior. The repeated masturbation is thought further to condition sexual arousal to the particular fantasized stimulus. These authors suggest that without the subsequent pairing of masturbation with the fantasized object, the deviant behavior would probably not develop.

McGuire and his associates report several examples where such conditioning could have occurred. Two exhibitionists reported similar experiences in which they had been urinating in a semipublic place when a woman passing by surprised them. They felt no sexual arousal at the time; rather they were embarrassed and left hurriedly. It was only later that the sexual significance of the encounter occurred to them, and each had then masturbated frequently to the memory of the incident. Eventually the thought of self-exposure became so sexually arousing that each had acted upon the idea. In another case, a 17-year-old male had seen, through a window, a girl dressed only in her underwear. He was sexually aroused and later masturbated repeatedly to this memory. In time the memory of the actual girl became vague, but advertisements and shop window displays continually reminded him of underwear; his masturbating fantasies gradually fixated on female underwear. Three years later he had no sexual interest at all in girls but was sexually aroused by female underwear, which he bought or stole.

In accordance with a conditioning model, sexual arousal has been established to formerly neutral stimuli through classical conditioning procedures. Rachman (1966), for example, paired a photographic slide of black boots with a slide of an attractive nude woman. Subjects subsequently showed penile arousal when the pictures of boots were presented alone. Those results were later replicated, but certain methodological problems in these studies prevent clear conclusions. For example, the control procedures were inadequate; specifically, arousal to boots was not assessed before pairing them with the nude picture. More recent controlled research has demonstrated, however, that male sexual arousal can be classically conditioned (Gaither, Rosenkranz, & Plaud, 1998).

Social learning models proposed that lack of parental care, physical punishment, and aggressive behavior within the family increase the chances of pedophilic development. People raised in such homes may demonstrate the low self-esteem, limited capacity for affection and intimacy, and impaired ability to postpone gratification that is reported among sexual offender samples (Maletzky, 2002). In a different take on self-esteem, LaTorre (1980) reported that college students who had been rejected for dates responded more positively to pictures of women's legs and panties, and less positively to pictures of women, than did other men who had not been rejected, suggesting rejection as a factor in fetish development. At this point, conditioning and learning models remain plausible accounts for paraphilia development, but further controlled studies are necessary.

## Treatment of Paraphilic Disorders

People with paraphilias do not often seek treatment unless mandated by legal authorities and may claim that therapy is not needed. Lack of motivation for change represents a serious impediment to therapy; in fact, those in treatment may make deliberate attempts to fool the therapist into believing that the problem has improved when, in fact, it hasn't (Masters, Johnson, & Kolodny, 1992). Published reports on the treatment of most paraphilias are based on case studies, providing little guidance for identifying effective therapies.

Some medication approaches appear to be partly directed by the apparent similarity of the paraphilic behavior to obsessive-compulsive disorder, which may be responsive to SSRIs. As such, antidepressants form one general thrust of pharmacotherapy for paraphilias. Other pharmacological approaches attempt to inhibit sexual arousal by giving estrogen-like or progestin-like hormones to males. These drugs reduce the production and action of androgens; and they have been associated with reduced sexual activity, including masturbation, in small group trials (e.g., (Cooper, Sandhu, Losztyn, & Cernovsky, 1992). The limited data available are perhaps stronger in support of antiandrogens although controlled comparative research is needed (Gijs & Gooren, 1996).

Behavioral treatments for paraphilias tend to include masturbatory retraining or aversion techniques. Masturbatory retraining may involve instructing the person to masturbate while engaged in the paraphilic fantasy and to continue masturbating for a much longer time (e.g., 1–2 hours) than is pleasurable, even after ejaculating. Most males experience continued stimulation, such as this, as very uncomfortable; the goal is to make the paraphilic fantasy aversive. This technique can be combined, at other times, with masturbation to nondeviant stimuli, in which case masturbation stops after ejaculation. There have been positive case reports based on this type of orgasmic reconditioning, which has been termed masturbatory satiation or masturbatory extinction (Gaither, Rosenkranz, & Plaud, 1998). Aversion approaches attempt to reduce sexual arousal to deviant stimuli by pairing them with aversive events such as electric shock or noxious odors. Data appear more convincing for olfactory aversive therapy, which has been found useful in several studies. In one successful treatment example (Earls & Castonguay, 1989), an adolescent pedophile was presented sexual stimuli relating to children and to adults while undergoing plethysmographic assessment. An aversive odor (ammonia) was presented contingent on penile arousal to the child stimuli, but not after arousal to adult stimuli. Post-treatment assessments and follow-up indicated increased arousal to adult images and dramatic decreases in arousal to children.

A different type of aversive therapy involves covert sensitization in which imagery of the paraphilic act is paired with an anxiety-inducing or nausea-inducing verbal description. Typically, the person imagines engaging in the paraphilia and then imagines a very unpleasant outcome. Imagery of appropriate behavior is paired with descriptions of positive outcomes. An early example comes from Hayes, Brownell, and Barlow (1978). The client was an adult male with a history of attempted rape, exhibitionism, and sadistic fantasies. The exhibitionist scenes involved imagery of exposing himself, in which he was identified by his victim and then located by police who arrest him at home in front of his crying wife. The imagined scene was constructed to maximize the aversive consequences he most feared. Similar scenes were prepared for sadistic imagery. The results are shown in Figure 9-2.

### Figure 9-2   *Treatment of Paraphilias with Covert Sensitization*

Obtained in response to exhibitionistic, sadistic, and heterosexual stimuli during baseline, treatment, and follow-up phase. Card sort data are daily averages in the baseline and treatment phases, and weekly averages in the follow-up phase.

Source: Hayes, S. C., Brownell, K. D., and Barlow, D. H. (1978). The use of self-administered covert sensitization in the treatment of exhibitionism and sadism. *Behavior Therapy, 9,* 283–289. Reprinted with permissions.

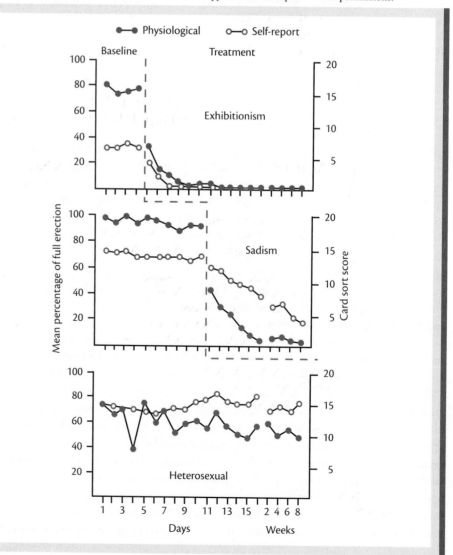

The degree of arousal was assessed in two ways: the physiological assessment of penile erection and the self-report using a card-sort technique with cards that described various sexual situations. The covert sensitization procedure appears effective during therapy and across an eight-week follow-up in reducing arousal to paraphilic stimuli while arousal to normal heterosexual stimuli did not change. A diverse set of cognitive-behavioral procedures—involving cognitive restructuring, relapse prevention, and empathy training (identification with the victim)—have also been employed in individual case studies with some positive results. These approaches may focus on identifying and correcting cognitive distortions, assumptions, and justifications for paraphilic acts. Combining these techniques with behavioral or conditioning approaches can result in better outcomes (Maletzky, 2002).

The promising results from case studies involving either psychotherapy or pharmaceutical treatments have not been supplemented by well-controlled or double-blind trials, and comparison group data are lacking. Recidivism continues to be a serious problem in the treatment of sex offenders, and most interventions are not seen as alternatives to incarceration for those groups. Relapse appears to be high when medications are discontinued, and combination therapies do not allow partition of the effective components. There is obviously a need for more careful research to refine the treatment of paraphilias.

# 9.4 Gender Dysphoria

In gender dysphoria, both (a) strong and persistent cross-gender identification and (b) persistent discomfort with one's assigned sex or with the gender role associated with it occur. As a result, the person experiences clinically significant distress or impairment in functioning. The disorder is diagnosed somewhat differently for children than for adults; the criteria for gender dysphoria in children are shown in *DSM-5* Diagnostic Criteria for Gender Dysphoria in Children. Children with gender dysphoria may express the wish to grow the genitals of the other sex; they prefer

> **What is gender dysphoria? Is it different from homosexuality?**

---

| *DSM-5* | **Diagnostic Criteria for Gender Dysphoria in Children** |
|---|---|

302.6 (F64.2) Gender Dysphoria in Children

A.  A marked incongruence between one's experience/expressed gender and assigned gender, of at least 6 months duration, as manifested by at least 6 of the following (one of which must be Criterion A1):
1.  A strong desire to be of the other gender or an insistence that one is the other gender (or some alternative gender different from one's assigned gender).
2.  In boys (assigned gender), a strong preference for cross-dressing or simulating female attire; or in girls (assigned gender), a strong preference for wearing only typical masculine clothing and a strong resistance to wearing feminine clothing.
3.  A strong preference for cross-gender roles in make-believe play or fantasy play.
4.  A strong preference for the toys, games, or activities stereotypically used or engaged in by the other gender.
5.  A strong preference for playmates of the other gender.
6.  In boys (assigned gender), a strong rejection of typically masculine toys, games, and activities and a strong avoidance of rough-and-tumble play; or in girls (assigned gender), a strong rejection of typically feminine toys, games, and activities.
7.  A strong dislike of one's sexual anatomy.
8.  A strong desire for the primary and secondary sex characteristics that match one's experienced gender.

The condition is associated with clinically significant distress or impairment in social, school, or other important areas of functioning.

Specify if:
With a disorder of sex development (e.g., a congenital adrenogenital disorder such as 255.2 [E25.0] congenital adrenal hyperplasia or 259.50 [E34.50] androgen insensitivity syndrome).
Coding note: code the disorder of sex development as well as gender dysphoria.

Source: Reprinted with permission from the *Diagnostic and Statistical Manual of Mental Disorders,* Fifth Edition, (Copyright 2013). American Psychiatric Association.

the stereotypic play, mannerisms, and attire of the other gender. Boys may enjoy feminine toys and playing house, often role-playing female figures such as mothers or sisters. They prefer girls as playmates to other boys. They may also adopt feminine mannerisms such as sitting down to urinate. Girls may refuse to attend school or social events in which feminine attire is required, may cut their hair short, and may take on a boy's name. They show little interest in dolls or typical girls' toys and prefer boys as playmates, enjoying rough-and-tumble play and contact sports. In adolescents and adults with gender dysphoria, there is frequent expression of the desire to live as or to become the other sex, including interest in sex-change surgery or hormonal treatments. Gender dysphoria in adolescents and adults can be specified if post-transition (that is, living as the other gender and preparing for or having had some medical procedure to alter gender). Often, effective cross-dressing allows some people with this disorder to pass convincingly as a member of the other sex. Gender identity disorder appears to be quite rare, although little data exist; in clinical settings, males with the disorder outnumber females by a factor of least 2 or 3 in the U.S., although in some countries (e.g., Japan and Poland) females with the condition may outnumber males (American Psychiatric Association, 2013).

The diagnosis of gender identity disorder (also called **transsexualism**) in the *DSM-IV* was not given if there was a concurrent intersex condition, although this is no longer the case for gender dysphoria in the *DSM-5*. There are some biological conditions that affect the development of sex characteristics in the fetus; and, as a result, some people may have genitals that appear to have both male and female characteristics. In one of these intersex conditions, **congenital adrenal hyperplasia** (CAH, also termed *adrenogenital syndrome*), a genetic female (XX) fetus is exposed to high levels of androgens during fetal development. This may cause elongation of the clitoris to resemble a penis and fusion of the labia to resemble a scrotal sac; thus, the external genitals appear masculine. In another intersex condition, **androgen insensitivity syndrome**, a genetic male (XY) fetus shows general insensitivity during fetal development to androgens and is born with undeveloped sexual structures that by default resemble the external female genitalia. In cases of these and other pseudohermaphroditic conditions, individuals troubled by persistent cross-gender identity may be diagnosed with gender dysphoria with the specifier "with a disorder of sex development."

Accurate diagnosis of gender dysphoria may be difficult. Reliability data from field trials indicated that the *DSM-III* diagnostic criteria showed very poor reliability (from −0.001 to −0.002 in the two phases). In the *DSM-5*, it must be distinguished from simple nonconformity to stereotypic sex roles, and the cross-gender identification must not be based merely on the cultural advantages of being the other sex. The cross-dressing involved must be distinguished from transvestic disorder (in which case cross-dressing produces sexual arousal), and the conviction of belonging to the other sex cannot be delusional, as may occur in schizophrenia. In addition, sexual attraction to others of the same biological gender, which those experiencing gender dysphoria may consider normal heterosexual attraction for someone who identifies with the other sex, must be distinguished from homosexuality, in which there is not gender discomfort.

The course of gender dysphoria is variable. Two trajectories are highlighted in the *DSM-5*: early onset gender dysphoria starts in childhood, while late-onset dsyphoria begins at or after puberty over time, cross-gender behaviors tend to decline for most children with the disorder, perhaps due to social and parental shaping. It tends to be more persistent in girls. Most boys (two-thirds or more) who do not persist in gender dysphoria identify as gay or homosexual; girls who do not persist in the disorder identify as lesbian at lower rates. Adults may show fluctuating course with late-onset females more likely to engage in transvestic activities for arousal. People with gender dysphoria often feel socially isolated and may experience concurrent anxiety disorders or depression (American Psychiatric Association, 2013).

## Causal Factors

Although chromosomal sex is determined at the time of conception, gender identity develops in early childhood and is usually established by age 3, suggesting that causal factors for

**Transsexualism**

Condition in which sexual identity is contrary to biological gender

**Congenital adrenal hyperplasia**

Condition in which fetal exposure to androgens results in masculinization of the genitals of a genetic female

**Androgen insensitivity syndrome**

Condition in which a genetically male fetus is insensitive to the effects of androgen and develops genitalia resembling a female

gender identity disorder are located in prenatal or early postnatal development. No research has established specific biological factors in the development of gender identity disorder.

However, animal research has demonstrated that masculine behavior can be increased in female animals by providing high levels of male hormones in the prenatal environment, while male animals behave more like females when not given sufficient amounts of male hormones prenatally. Goy (1970), for example, injected pregnant rhesus monkeys with the male hormone testosterone. Masculinized female infants were born with genitals that included both male and female characteristics. When these females grew up, they showed more rough-and-tumble play and were more masculine than normal females in other social behaviors.

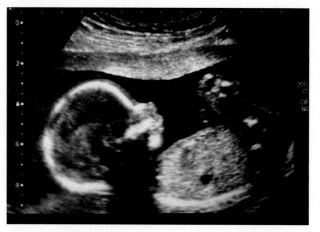

Chromosomal sex is determined at conception and gender identity is usually established by age 3. However, research in animals has established that prenatal exposure to unusual levels of male or female hormones can affect gender development. (iStock)

Similar effects have been noted in human female children. During the 1950s, a number of pregnant women were treated with synthetic progestin (a hormone that prepares the uterus for pregnancy) in order to reduce miscarriages. An unexpected side effect of this drug was that it caused an excess of male hormones and, thereby, affected the development of female fetuses. Compared with matched control girls, these girls had more "masculine" interests, gave higher priority to a career over marriage, were less interested in participating in baby care of a younger sibling or a neighbor's child, and preferred to play with boys' toys such as cars, guns, and trucks rather than dolls (Erhardt, 1973). The prenatal exposure of male fetuses to female hormones (estrogen and progesterone) has also been reported to produce feminization in boys (Yalom, Green, & Fisk, 1973). However, there is no direct evidence that hormonal exposure causes gender identity disorder in humans, and there are no clear hormonal distinctions between those with gender identity disorder and people with normal gender identity.

> **Can people change from male to female or from female to male?**

Coolidge, Thede, and Young (2002) report that analysis of twin research supports a strong heritable component in gender identity disorder. However, Segal (2006) reports non-concordance of female-to-male transsexualism in two pairs of identical twins, suggesting prenatal hormonal influences as possible causal factors. The *DSM-5* describes the evidence of familial transmission as weak, with stronger support for prenatal hormonal influences (American Psychiatric Association, 2013). Psychoanalytic models tend to emphasize issues in parental relationships in which children over-identify with the opposite sex parent. No clear evidence exists to support any particular causal theory.

## Treatment of Gender Dysphoria

Sex reassignment surgery appears to be among the only effective treatments for chronic gender dysphoria in adults. It is recommended that the person preparing for sex reassignment first complete 1 year of life-experience as the other sex and 6 months on continuous hormone treatments in order to be a candidate for surgery. Male-to-female operations typically involve plastic surgery for creating a vagina and labia from penile and scrotal skin and modifying the remnant penis into a sensitive clitoris. The female-to-male operation is less well established, but can involve creating a phallus with skin from the forearm (Sohn & Bosinski, 2007). Sexual sensitivity can be maintained by using the clitoris as a base for the neophallus. Reviews of outcome literature reveal that most transsexuals are satisfied with the outcome of sex reassignment surgery (LeVay & Valente, 2006).

# Chapter Review

## TO SUM UP ...

- The normal sexual response cycle consists of four phases: the excitement phase, the plateau phase, the orgasmic phase, and the resolution phase.

- Masters and Johnson's research helped to dispel previously held fallacies about direct stimulation of the clitoris, clitoral versus vaginal orgasms, simultaneous orgasms, and the relationship between size of the penis and sexual enjoyment.

- Sexual dysfunctions are disorders in which there is a disturbance in the sexual response cycle or pain occurs during sexual activity. Sexual dysfunctions are relatively common among the population.

- Anxiety about sexuality plays an important role in the development of these dysfunctions. Masters and Johnson especially emphasize performance anxiety and a spectator role.

- There are a variety of effective psychotherapies for the sexual dysfunctions. Medications are increasingly used to provide symptom relief as well. Some sex therapists are concerned about the growing medicalization of treatment for sexual dysfunctions.

- Paraphilias are disorders in which the disturbance concerns the focus or target of sexual desire. They are much more common among males than females. Some paraphilic disorders involve activities that are illegal.

- Behavioral approaches to treating paraphilic disorders appear promising, especially those involving covert sensitization and orgasmic reconditioning.

- Gender dysphoria involving persistent cross-gender identification and discomfort with or rejection of one's biological sex is very rare. Unlike sexual dysfunctions and paraphilic disorders, which may display high diagnostic reliability, the gender identity disorders historically show very low diagnostic reliability.

- The causes of and treatments for gender identity disorder remain unclear. Most adults who undergo sex reassignment surgery are satisfied with the outcome.

# KEY TERMS

Androgen insensitivity
    syndrome   240

Asphyxiophilia   234

Congenital adrenal hyperplasia   240

Kegel exercises   228

Masochism   234

Performance anxiety   219

Plethysmographic assessment   233

Refractory period   218

Sadism   235

Squeeze technique   227

Transsexualism   240

Vasocongestion   218

# QUESTIONS FOR STUDY

- Discuss Masters and Johnson's pioneering studies of human sexuality. How was therapy for sexual disorders influenced by their work?

- Suggest a possible explanation for the large gender difference in the diagnosis of paraphilias.

- Describe the differences between transvestic fetishism and transsexualism.

# POP QUIZ

1. The human sexual response cycle was defined by _____.
   A. Benjamin Rush
   B. Alfred Kinsey
   C. Masters and Johnson
   D. Sigmund Freud

2. The proper order of the sexual response cycle consists of which of the following?
   A. plateau phase, orgasmic phase, resolution phase, excitement phase
   B. excitement phase, plateau phase, orgasmic phase, resolution phase
   C. excitement phase, orgasmic phase, plateau phase, resolution phase
   D. plateau phase, orgasmic phase, excitement phase, resolution phase

3. Which phase do men experience, but not women?
   A. plateau phase
   B. orgasmic phase
   C. resolution phase
   D. refractory period

4. Sally has experienced sexual dysfunctions since she was 13 years old. The *DSM-5* specifier choice for Sally's situation is _____.
   A. Early Remission vs. Full Remission
   B. Lifelong Type vs. Acquired Type
   C. Generalized Type vs. Situational Type
   D. Due to Psychological or to Combined Factors

5. To meet criteria for a sexual dysfunction disorder, the minimum duration of dysfunction must be _____.
   A. There is no minimum duration of dysfunction required.
   B. 1 month
   C. 3 months
   D. 6 months

6. The hormone _____ may increase sexual desire in men and women who experience sexual desire disorders.
   A. progesterone
   B. estrogen
   C. adrenaline
   D. testosterone

7. About _____ of American women report some difficulties with low sexual desire.
   A. one-tenth
   B. one-third
   C. one-half
   D. two-thirds

8. According to psychoanalytic theory, men and women with deficient sexual arousal show inhibited sexual excitement because unconsciously they perceive sexual activity as _____.
   A. dangerous
   B. odd
   C. confusing
   D. dirty

9. An effective treatment for deficient arousal in males is _____.
   A. sildenafil
   B. aphrodisiacs
   C. alcohol
   D. ginkgo biloba extract

10. Seth is fascinated by women's shoes and stockings. He has recurrent, intense sexually arousing fantasies, urges, or behaviors that revolve around high heels, panty hose, and patent leather. He has 20 pairs of shoes and has stolen shoes from women's dressing rooms and from female coworkers. He often masturbates from merely smelling them or when a partner wears them. He would be diagnosed with _____.
    A. fetishistic disorder
    B. exhibitionistic disorder
    C. frotteuristic disorder
    D. voyeuristic disorder

11. John has recently incorporated the masochistic act of _____ into his sexual life. This involves oxygen depriving activities such as choking, hanging or suffocating.
    A. areophila
    B. coprophilia
    C. asphyxiophilia
    D. klismaphilia

12. Jane gets sexual gratification by inflicting pain on her partner through whippings and beatings with various hard leather objects, and by inserting blunt objects into various orifices. She would be diagnosed with _____.
    A. transvestic disorder
    B. sexual masochism disorder
    C. frotteuristic disorder
    D. sexual sadism disorder

13. A pharmaceutical treatment for males with paraphilic disorders is to give hormones in an attempt to reduce sexual arousal. These drugs reduce the production and action of _____
    A. oxytocin
    B. progestins
    C. estrogens
    D. androgens

14. When a genetic male fetus is insensitive to the effects of androgen and develops genitalia resembling a female, this is known as _____.
    A. androgen insensitivity syndrome
    B. adrenogenital syndrome
    C. congenital adrenal hyperplasia
    D. Klinefelter's syndrome

15. It is recommended that the person preparing for sex reassignment first complete ____ months of life experience as the other sex and ___ months on continuous hormone treatments in order to be a candidate for surgery.
    A. 3, 6
    B. 6, 6
    C. 12, 6
    D. 12, 9

Additional study resources are available at www.BVTLab.com

# CHAPTER OVERVIEW

# CHAPTER OPENER QUESTIONS

What are the signs of psychosis?

How do various psychotic disorders differ?

Can schizophrenia be reliably diagnosed?

How strong are genetic influences in the development of schizophrenia?

What non-genetic factors seem to contribute to psychosis?

What is the dopamine hypothesis?

Can psychotic disorders be treated?

(Wikimedia Commons)

# chapter

# Schizophrenia and Psychotic Disorders

The disorders considered in this chapter represent severe forms of psychopathology that are usually labeled psychoses. As distinguished from the Freudian, anxiety-driven **neurosis** that can result when id impulses threaten to overwhelm the ego, **psychosis** concerns a more serious pathology that involves a loss of contact with reality. The *DSM-5* category of Schizophrenia Spectrum and Other Psychotic Disorders includes several distinct diagnoses; the most well-known is schizophrenia, which has been the focus of clinical and research attention for well over 100 years. Lay terms for these conditions often include "madness" or "insanity" (the latter actually has a specific legal meaning which will be discussed in a later chapter); they are distinctly different in scope and impairment from the disorders considered thus far. To better understand these psychotic disorders, a general overview of psychotic symptoms follows.

## 10.1  Psychosis

The presence of psychosis is inferred in the same way as all other mental disorders: from what people say during an interview and how they act when observed. Some symptoms—such as delusions, hallucinations, and grossly impaired speech or movement—are considered direct evidence of psychosis, almost as if bizarre attributes have been added to a person's psychological repertoire. Other symptoms provide indirect evidence of psychosis: impairment in self-care, restricted range of emotion, poverty of speech content, inability to initiate goal-directed behavior. In a sense, these indirect symptoms seem as if something has been lost or removed from a person's psychological state. The direct (or positive) symptoms and indirect (or negative)

Disturbances in thinking and language are among the key symptoms of psychosis. (iStock)

symptoms can be described as disturbances of language and thought, disturbances of sensation and perception, disturbances of motor behavior, emotional disturbances, and social withdrawal.

> **What are the signs of psychosis?**

## 10.1a  Disturbances in Language and Thought

### Loosening of Associations

One aspect of psychosis is a tendency toward loose, disjointed expression in speech. Bleuler (1950) referred to this problem as the "derailment of associations" by which he meant that the person becomes distracted by irrelevant associations, cannot suppress them, and as a consequence wanders farther and farther off the subject. Some writers for example, (Meehl, 1962) have used phrases like "cognitive slippage" to describe how the schizophrenic's train of thought seems to slip away from its intended goal. Others refer to these aspects of impaired communication as "tangentiality" because the speaker seems to follow tangents in the original utterance that lead loosely to other semantic pathways.

**Neurosis**

Anxiety-driven condition that results when id impulses threaten to overwhelm the ego

**Psychosis**

Severe psychological disturbance involving personality disorganization and loss of contact with reality

Intruding associations may sometimes be highly personal and result in speech that is egocentric or autistic and, in extreme instances, almost totally unintelligible. The following example, from 65 years ago, remains as illustrative as ever:

*Interviewer*: Why are you in the Hospital?

*Patient*: I'm a cut donator, donated by double sacrifice. I get two days for everyone. That's known as double-sacrifice; in other words, standard cut donator. You know, we considered it. He couldn't have anything for the cut, or for these patients.

*Interviewer*: Well, what do you do here?

*Patient*: I do what is known as the double criminal treatment. Something that he badly wanted, he gets that, and seven days' criminal protection. That's all he gets, and the rest I do for my friend.

*Interviewer*: Who is the other person that gets all this?

*Patient*: That's the way the asylum cut is donated.

*Interviewer*: But who is the other person?

*Patient*: He's a criminal. He gets so much. He gets twenty years criminal treatment, would make forty years; and he gets seven days criminal protection and that makes 14 days. That's all he gets.

*Interviewer*: And what are you?

*Patient*: What is known as cut donator Christ. None of them couldn't be able to have anything; so it has to be true works or prove true to have anything, too. He gets two days; and that twenty years makes forty years… (Cameron, 1947, pp. 466–467)

Note that the patient's sentence structure or syntax is not impaired; there is no evidence of educational or intellectual difficulties that might make communication ineffective. Instead, although the form of language appears normal, the content is unusual; and the meaning seems lost. The parts may be loosely connected. For instance, the "double sacrifice" seems associated with the doubling of 20 years to 40 years and the doubling of 7 days to 14 days. However, in the utterance, the contribution of this connection to the information is obscure. To many clinicians, such impaired communication has been considered evidence of a formal thought disorder.

The *DSM-5* distinguishes between loose associations or derailment, which involve shifts between clauses of topics or referential frames, and incoherence, which concerns shifts within clauses (American Psychiatric Association, 2000). The unusual results of loose language associations have sometimes been described as "word salad"—that is, psychotic speech can almost seem as if a collection of words were thrown together and tossed, like a salad, before presentation. Of course, for the psychotic speaker, words may be associated in ways of which the listener is unaware. One example is called **clanging**, which involves the use of a word not because of its meaning, but because of its sound (such as in rhyming or punning). In other cases, a psychotic speaker employs the use of neologisms, or "new words" that the speaker invents. Consider this letter from Larry P., as written to the author in request for release from the hospital:

"The Physcological Sanity of my mind is conducted with Reason of sanity justice sedetating attempt to cooperated a sanity of justice deal of ordain lane, attempt of shock treatment of tolerating allergic reactions of dust acid attacks.

This is my offering of justice answerable logic which says I'm sanity but I can't conduct, so please excuse this era of joint settlement of joint delusion, I'm still please to hear of this place but I would like some kind of discussion about this reason of jure demand."

**Clanging**

The use of a word
because of its sound,
rather than its meaning

Other characteristics of psychotic language use include **alogia**, or impoverished speech. Replies to questions may be very brief and convey little information; speech may be repetitive, stereotyped, and non-spontaneous. Sometimes, psychotic language appears to be over-generalized and hyper-metaphorical. An interesting observation comes from Luria (1982), who proposes that in response to the question "What is a dog?" those of low intelligence would give a concrete and one-dimensional answer, such as "a dog barks" or "a dog has four legs"; a normal person might give a categorical response, "a dog is a mammal" or "a dog is a pet"; and a schizophrenic person might give an over-generalized response, such as "a dog is mass, attracted by gravity to the earth's core." Hyper-metaphorical speech is a form of overgeneralization: instead of reporting, "My arm fell asleep," a psychotic person might report, "My arm died" (taking the sleep metaphor too far). Conversely, other psychotic speech shows **echolalia**, in which the person repeats whatever someone else says.

Note extensive religious themes in this drawing by a schizophrenic patient. (Courtesy of Dr. Charles Lyons)

## Delusions

By definition, **delusions** are not beliefs shared by other members of a culture or articles of religious faith shared by believers. Instead, they are extreme convictions that are firmly held in spite of what nearly everyone else in the subculture would consider incontrovertible evidence to the contrary. They are distinguished from ideas by their fixedness. For clinical purposes, delusions can be subdivided into several types, which are presented next.

*Bizarre delusions* involve false beliefs that could not possibly be true, given what is known about the world. For example, a woman who insists she is pregnant, in spite of a series of negative tests, may be delusional; but the delusion is not a bizarre one. It is possible that a mistake was made; false negatives are not unknown. However, a man who insisted that he was pregnant is endorsing a belief that could not conceivably be true. Similarly, the delusion of being followed by the CIA is not completely implausible, but a man who believes that his head is switched onto other bodies at night while he sleeps is engaging in a bizarre delusion.

*Delusional jealousy* involves the incorrect conviction that a person's spouse or sexual partner has been or is being unfaithful. Unlike "normal" suspicion about infidelity, delusional jealousy is unreasonably held even in the face of proof or evidence to the contrary.

*Erotomanic delusions* are patently false beliefs that another person, often someone famous or of higher status or authority, is in love with the individual.

*Grandiose delusions* involve grossly inflated self-importance, fame, power, wealth, or knowledge. They may involve special relationships with powerful or holy entities, or identification with a great person from history such as a political, military, or religious leader.

*Mood-congruent delusions* concern content that is entirely consistent with expressed mood. For example, the belief that one is responsible for a deadly tornado, or that one's body is rotting, would be congruent with depressed mood (as would other themes of death, guilt, or failure).

*Mood-incongruent delusions* involve content that is not consistent with the prevailing mood. Beliefs of unlimited wealth and power would be incongruent with depressed mood.

*Delusions of being controlled* involve the belief that some external force or agent is manipulating one's movements, thoughts, speech, or emotions. People may believe that a murderous impulse, a sexual fantasy, or an urge to commit suicide is imposed from the outside. The controlling agents may be gods, demons, parents, political groups, or a vague "they." The mechanism of control is sometimes spelled out—for example, hypnotism, extrasensory perception, or influencing machines such as a television set or an X-ray device.

**Alogia**

Impoverished speech which conveys little information

**Echolalia**

Repetition of words or phrases spoken by another person

**Delusion**

False belief that is firmly held, contrary to the consensus of other people

*Delusions of reference* are false beliefs that events, people, or things in the immediate environment have a special and unique significance for the individual. For example, a person may believe that graffiti refers specifically to the private events of an individual's life, or that a song broadcast on the radio was meant to send a specific message to the person alone.

*Persecutory delusions* concern the theme of being plotted against, attacked, cheated, threatened, or persecuted in some way by other various people or groups, such as neighbors, competitors, bosses, politicians, or the FBI. People holding such beliefs may find confirmation in seeing a group of people laughing among themselves, or in the frown of a passing pedestrian.

People with schizophrenia or other psychotic disorders tend to perceive things differently than others do. (Shutterstock)

*Somatic delusions* are false convictions that concern the body. Examples include the belief that one is changing sexes, is pregnant, or that internal organs are rotting.

*Thought broadcasting delusions* involve the belief that others can hear or receive one's thoughts.

*Thought insertion delusions* concern the belief that some external person or agency is inserting thoughts into one's consciousness. In some cases, the delusion involves receiving special broadcasts through a special receiver planted within the brain.

These categories of delusions are organized conceptually and are not mutually exclusive. Persecutory delusions, for example, could be mood-congruent with depression while also being bizarre.

## 10.1b Disturbances in Sensation and Perception

Psychotic individuals often report perceptual distortions. The world may seem flat, unreal, or remote; objects seem unusually large or small; or time passes with unusual slowness or rapidity. One patient described how other people appeared distorted:

> *" ... people look confusing ... they look almost like they're made up ... like they're real people ... and people I know, but they have masks on or they're disguising themselves. It's like a big play ... "*
>
> (Freedman & Chapman, 1973, p. 52).

Even more dramatic than perceptual distortions are false sensory experiences called **hallucinations**. The person hears voices, sees visions, smells odors, or has sensations of touch for which there are no identifiable external stimuli. Hallucinations must be distinguished from **illusions**, in which an actual sensory stimulus is perceived incorrectly. (In the dark bedroom, clothes hanging in the closest may be misperceived as a lurking killer, but this is not hallucinatory.) They also are distinguished from the strange sensory experiences that are sometimes associated with falling asleep, dreaming, or awakening.

Hallucinations can involve any sensory system:

**Hallucinations**

Sensations or perceptions in the absence of an external source

**Illusions**

The incorrect perceptions of sensory stimuli

- In *auditory hallucinations*, the person hears voices that may condemn, praise, direct, or accuse. They may be identified with a specific agent such as God, the devil, parents, past acquaintances, or unspecified "others." While experiencing a hallucination, the person may or may not realize it is unreal; often it may seem to come from an external source. The individual may listen passively to the voices, act upon their commands, or talk back to them—arguing, pleading, or cursing them.

Interestingly, brain imaging studies have shown that individuals experiencing auditory hallucinations display activation in the expressive rather than receptive language areas of the brain (Cleghorn, et al., 1992); in many ways auditory hallucinations appear to involve faulty interpretation and monitoring of self-talk (Allen, Aleman, & McGuire, 2007).

- *Visual hallucinations* can include lights, moving objects, places, and people. In some cases they may appear as cartoon objects or as unformed images.

- *Gustatory hallucinations* involve the perception of a taste, such as blood. Most often the taste is unpleasant.

- *Olfactory hallucinations* involve odors, usually unpleasant, such as decaying matter, or burning hair or rubber.

- *Somatic hallucinations* concern false sensations experienced as coming from inside the body, such as electricity or pressure.

- *Tactile hallucinations* concern the false feeling of being touched or having something just beneath the skin, such as splinters or crawling insects.

Andrea Yates, convicted in 2002 of murdering her five children, was later found not guilty by reason of insanity. She reportedly suffered from auditory hallucinations. (AP Wide World)

Hallucinations can also be considered as mood-congruent or mood-incongruent. Any type of hallucination can occur in psychotic individuals, but certain types may be more common in some disorders. For example, the hallucinations most commonly reported in schizophrenia are auditory although other types can also occur; drug-induced psychoses can involve strong, visual hallucinations. Tactile hallucinations may be more typical of drug withdrawal. Damage to any sensory areas of the brain could result in hallucinatory responses involving those areas; gustatory and olfactory hallucinations may often be more characteristic of medical conditions or localized brain impairments, such as temporal lobe epilepsy, than of schizophrenia (American Psychiatric Association, 2000).

## 10.1c Disturbances in Motor Behavior

Psychotic persons may engage in strange, stereotyped gestures, postures, or facial grimaces, referred to as **catatonia**. Occasionally they may cease bodily movements altogether in catatonic immobility or become wildly excited, at the other extreme, and move violently or unpredictably in catatonic excitement. Sometimes, a waxy flexibility is present, in which a catatonic person can be molded into a posture that may be rigidly maintained over long periods of time. Other forms of catatonic behavior include apparently motiveless resistance to instructions or attempts to be moved, stupor, refusal to speak (**mutism**), and **echopraxia**, in which a person imitates the movements of others. Some become unable (or unwilling) to dress, undress, feed themselves, or attend to their toileting needs. Ordinary inhibitions may be lost so that they urinate, defecate, or masturbate in public.

Catatonia can occur within several disorders. The *DSM-5* has added it as a specifier, defined by the presence of at least three catatonic symptoms, for other psychotic disorders, other mental disorders, and other medical conditions. For example, catatonia can be a characteristic of schizophrenia or other psychotic disorders, major depressive disorder, or bipolar disorder; it can also occur with head injuries and neurological diseases. In these conditions, the appropriate *DSM-5* diagnosis would be catatonia associated with another mental disorder, catatonic disorder due to another medical condition, or unspecified catatonia (when the underlying condition is unclear).

**Catatonia**

Unusual movement or immobility associated with psychosis

**Mutism**

Refusal to speak

**Echopraxia**

Repetitively imitating the movements of others

## 10.1d Emotional Disturbance

Frequently, the emotional state in psychotic conditions is described as shallow, flattened, or blunted. **Affective flattening** is characterized by a lack of range of emotions. The lack of enjoyment in all aspects of life that often characterizes the schizophrenic person is sometimes referred to as **anhedonia.** In some psychoses, emotions are expressed inappropriately. People may laugh, cry, giggle, or rage with no clear relationship to events in the social environment.

## 10.1e Social Withdrawal

Schizophrenic individuals tend to avoid close interpersonal relationships, spend much of their time alone, and retreat more and more into their own fantasy world. The withdrawal is both physical and psychological. Their unintelligible speech and inappropriate emotional expression can keep them as psychologically distant from others as would miles of physical space. There may be confusion about personal identity, gender, and sense of self that add to disrupted social relationships. In addition, volition (or goal-directed behavior) seems impaired, so that work and self-care responsibilities are not completed, further isolating the individual from others.

## 10.2 Diagnosis of Psychotic Disorders

Although the psychotic disorders are discussed together in the *DSM-5*, there is no assumption that these disorders share a common cause, a common pathway, or even a common fundamental set of symptoms. Psychotic symptoms can appear briefly (transiently) during periods of stress in individuals with many different conditions and do not, in themselves, verify the presence of a psychotic disorder. The symptom patterns and degree of impairment differ within the psychotic disorders as well.

The main psychotic disorders are summarized in Table 10-1. Not listed is schizotypal personality disorder (refer to Chapter 8), which the *DSM-5* considers within the schizophrenia spectrum but also describes among the personality disorders (American Psychiatric Association, 2013). The distinction between schizophrenia, schizophreniform disorder, and brief psychotic disorder is one of duration. The involvement of significant mood components distinguishes schizoaffective disorder. In delusional disorder, the psychotic symptoms are largely limited to delusions; and, in that sense, individuals may show less overall impairment in daily living.

There are also many medical conditions that can produce psychotic symptoms. Neurological conditions (such as epilepsy and multiple sclerosis), endocrine disorders (including hypothyroidism), metabolic conditions, fever, and nearly any other disorder with

**Affective flattening**

Lack of range of emotions

**Anhedonia**

Loss of interest or pleasure in all aspects of life

*Table 10-1*　DSM-5 Psychotic Disorders

| Disorder | Key Symptoms | Minimum Duration Required for Diagnosis | Sex Ratio |
|---|---|---|---|
| Schizophrenia | Delusions, hallucinations, disordered speech and behavior | 6 months | More common among males |
| Schizophreniform Disorder | Same as schizophrenia, but duration less than 6 months | 1 month | Slightly more common among males |
| Schizoaffective Disorder | Mood episode and hallucinations/delusions occurring together | 2 weeks | More common among females |
| Brief Psychotic Disorder | Delusions, hallucinations, disorganized speech but duration less than 1 month | 1 day | More common among females |
| Delusional Disorder | Non-bizarre delusions without other symptoms | 1 month | Equal |

Source: Reprinted with permission from the *Diagnostic and Statistical Manual of Mental Disorders,* Fifth Edition, (Copyright 2013). American Psychiatric Association.

central nervous system involvement could be responsible for psychotic states. In addition, a wide variety of legal and illegal substances can produce hallucinations, delusions, verbal incoherence, and other psychotic behavior as a direct result of use or upon abrupt withdrawal. The appropriate diagnostic categories for these conditions are "psychotic disorder due to another medical condition," and "substance/medication induced psychotic disorder," respectively.

## 10.2a  Schizophrenia

Probably no mental disorder has received as much attention within the professional literature as schizophrenia. The disorder represents a puzzle that has so far defied solution, in spite of the focused effort of medical and psychological science. Much important knowledge has been gained, yet much more information is needed to understand this extreme condition.

A wide variety of legal and illegal substances can produce hallucinations, delusions, and other psychotic behavior as a direct result of use or upon abrupt withdrawal. This must be considered when attempting to diagnose a psychotic disorder. (Wikimedia Commons)

### History of the Diagnosis

As noted in Chapter 2, Kraepelin used the term *dementia praecox* to refer to a syndrome that involved an early, usually gradual, onset and a progressive deterioration of mental functioning. Bleuler (1950) introduced the term *schizophrenia* in 1911, to refer to essentially the same pattern of psychological symptoms. He drew upon the Greek words for "split mind" to refer to a split between thought processes and emotions or to a general disorganization in thought and behavior. This kind of splitting is not the same as that in the dissociation reactions of fugue, amnesia, or multiple personality. In those conditions, the split is between different states of consciousness (or different selves) rather than between thought and emotion. Bleuler did not believe that schizophrenia began in childhood or adolescence, necessarily, or that it necessarily progressed to an irreversible dementia.

> **Can schizophrenia be reliably diagnosed?**

European and American psychiatrists diverged in their diagnostic practices with respect to schizophrenia. The Europeans stayed rather close to Kraepelin's original concept and tended not to give this diagnosis to individuals who abruptly developed acute schizophrenic-like symptoms but recovered from the episode within a few months. European psychiatrists were also more inclined to diagnose patients as manic-depressive (or bipolar) who would have been diagnosed schizophrenic in this country. American psychiatrists, on the other hand, were more influenced by Bleuler and so did not insist on a chronic course of the disorder; further, their approach explicitly stated that the diagnosis of manic-depressive disorder should be made only if the diagnosis of schizophrenia had definitely been ruled out. A demonstration of how the diagnosis of schizophrenia increased from the 1930s to the 1950s in the United States is provided by Kuriansky and his colleagues (1974), who showed that only 28% of the patients at the New York State Psychiatric Institute were diagnosed schizophrenic between 1932 and 1941, compared to an astounding 77% between 1947 and 1956.

After 1980, some of these differences began to disappear. By employing the more precise diagnostic system of *DSM-III*, the number of people with schizophrenia in the U.S. was cut in half: acute schizophrenic-like episodes lasting less than 6 months were classified as schizophreniform disorders, while those with strong mood components were more likely diagnosed with schizoaffective disorder. Those who might have been labeled with "simple schizophrenia" or "latent schizophrenia" in the *DSM-II* were likely, instead, to be called borderline personality disorder and schizotypal personality disorder. The diagnostic reliability improved significantly, to 0.81 in both phases of the *DSM-III* reliability field trials. In the *DSM-5* field trials, the pooled kappa of 0.46 for schizophrenia was considered to indicate "good" reliability (Regier, et al., 2013).

Currently, the diagnosis of schizophrenia (refer to *DSM-5* Diagnostic Criteria for Schizophrenia) requires two psychotic symptoms during a 1-month active phase, one of which must be delusions, hallucinations, or disorganized speech. In earlier versions of the

---

### *DSM-5*  Diagnostic Criteria for Schizophrenia

295.90 (F20.9) Schizophrenia

A. Two (or more) of the following, each present for a significant proportion of time during a 1-month period (or less if successfully treated). At least one of these must be (1), (2), or (3):

1. Delusions.
2. Hallucinations.
3. Disorganized speech (e.g., frequent derailment or incoherence).
4. Grossly disorganized or catatonic behavior.
5. Negative symptoms (i.e., diminished emotional expression or avolition).

B. For a significant portion of the time since the onset of the disturbance, level of functioning in one or more major areas, such as work, interpersonal relations, or self-care, is markedly below the level achieved prior to the onset (or when the onset is in childhood or adolescence, there is failure to achieve expected level of interpersonal, academic, or occupational functioning).

C. Continuous signs of the disturbance persist for at least 6 months. This 6-month period must include at least 1 month of symptoms (or less if successfully treated) that meet Criterion A (i.e., active-phase symptoms) and may include periods of prodromal or residual symptoms. During these prodromal or residual periods, the signs of the disturbance may be manifested only by negative symptoms or by two or more symptoms listed in Criterion A present in an attenuated form (e.g., odd beliefs, unusual perceptual experiences).

D. Schizoaffective disorder and depressive or bipolar disorder with psychotic features have been ruled out because either 1) no major depressive or manic episodes have occurred with the active-phase symptoms, or 2) if mood episodes have occurred during active-phase symptoms, they have been present for a minority of the total duration of the active and residual periods of the illness.

E. The disturbance is not attributable to the physiological effects of a substance (e.g., a drug of abuse, a medication) or another medical condition.

F. If there is a history of autism spectrum disorder or a communication disorder of childhood onset, the additional diagnosis of schizophrenia is made only if prominent delusions or hallucinations, in addition to the other required symptoms of schizophrenia, are also present for at least 1 month (or less if successfully treated).

Specify if:

The following course specifiers are only to be used after a 1-year duration of the disorder and if they are not in contraindication to the diagnostic course criteria.

**First episode, currently in acute episode:** First manifestation of the disorder meeting the diagnostic symptom and time criteria. An *acute episode* is a time period in which the symptom criteria are fulfilled.

**First episode, currently in partial remission:** *Partial remission* is a period of time during which an improvement after a previous episode is maintained and in which the defining criteria of the disorder are only partially fulfilled

**First episode, currently in full remission:** *Full remission* is a period of time after a previous episode during which no disorder-specific symptoms are present.

**Multiple episodes, currently in acute episode:** Multiple episodes may be determined after a minimum of two episodes (i.e., after a first episode, a remission and a minimum of one relapse).

**Multiple episodes, currently in partial remission:**

**Multiple episodes, currently in full remission:**

**Continuous:** Symptoms fulfilling the diagnostic criteria of the disorder are remaining for the majority of the illness course, with subthreshold symptom periods being very brief relative to the overall course.

**Unspecified**

Specify if:

**With catatonia** (refer to the catatonia criteria associated with another medical disorder for definition).

**Coding note:** Use additional code 293.89 (F06.1) catatonia associated with schizophrenia to indicate the presence of the comorbid catatonia.

*Specify* current severity:

Severity is rated by a quantitative assessment of the primary symptoms of psychosis, including delusions, hallucinations, disorganized speech, abnormal psychomotor behavior, and negative symptoms. Each of these symptoms may be rated for its current severity (most severe in the past 7 days) on a 5-point scale ranging from 0 (not present) to 4 (present and severe).

**Note:** Diagnosis of schizophrenia can be made without using the severity specifier.

*DSM*, the diagnosis could be given with only one active psychotic symptom, if a "cardinal" or "indicator" symptom was present. Those special symptoms were either bizarre delusions or auditory hallucinations that have the form of a running commentary or conversation. The *DSM*-5 removed this provision in large part because it was difficult to distinguish bizarre and non-bizarre delusions reliably. In addition to active indicators, negative symptoms are quite frequent and can account for much of the impairment associated with the disorder. Affective flattening is usually present, making the person appear unresponsive. Alogia results in decreased fluency in communication. Often, **avolition** is manifested by sitting for long periods of time with little or no interest in work or social activities. (The negative symptoms of schizophrenia must be distinguished from those that occur with depression or as side effects of medication.) Schizophrenia involves either a decline from a prior level of function or a failure to meet expected levels, and this change is usually apparent to others who know the person. As a condition of the diagnosis, signs of disorder must persist for at least 6 months; however, for much of that time (except for 1 month), the symptoms can be either residual (attenuated symptoms that follow an active phase) or prodromal (symptoms that precede an active phase).

Earlier versions of the *DSM* classified schizophrenia by its subtype: paranoid, disorganized, catatonic, undifferentiated, or residual. This practice was discontinued in the *DSM-5* because the subtypes didn't appear to be stable, reliable, or valid, and added little to treatment—although catatonia is offered as a specifier for the diagnosis. Other specifiers describe the course of schizophrenia as first episode, multiple episodes, or continuous, and whether the condition is in full or partial remission. In place of the subtypes, the *DSM-5* encourages a dimensional rating of severity.

Although most cases have onset between the late teens to mid-30s, schizophrenia can be diagnosed at any age. Men have somewhat earlier age of onset than women, who tend to show better outcome. Men also tend to show more negative symptoms, whereas women are more likely to display paranoid delusions, mood symptoms, and hallucinations. Rates for co-morbid substance-related disorders, especially nicotine dependence, are quite high. Risk of suicide is also elevated; up to 20% make at least one suicide attempt, and about 5%–6% of schizophrenics eventually succeed. Schizophrenia is slightly more common among males as well. Most estimates have put the rate at about 1% of the population, although the *DSM-5* gives somewhat lower estimates of 0.3% to 0.7% (American Psychiatric Association, 2013).

## Earlier Perspectives on Schizophrenic Spectra

"[Madness] rais'd on a sudden from some solemn evident, as from a vehement passion, is much safer than invading by degrees." This observation—that a gradual onset of psychotic behavior was indicative of a more severe and chronic course than that associated with an abrupt onset—was made in 1685 by Willis in *The London Practice of Physick* (Wedner, 1963). Both Bleuler and Kraepelin (in his later writings) were aware that not all patients diagnosed as schizophrenic showed an irreversible course toward total deterioration. Historically there have been two interpretations of this fact: (1) These patients must have been misdiagnosed in the first place since, by definition, schizophrenia is a progressive and incurable disorder; or (2) there are two types of schizophrenia, one type showing the progressive deterioration and the other showing the capacity for recovery.

The latter point of view led to the distinction between process and reactive schizophrenias, the former with a poor prognosis for recovery and the latter with a good prognosis. (See Kantor, Wallner, & Winder, 1953, for an early attempt to make this distinction.) Process schizophrenia is further characterized by an early and gradual onset of symptoms; the person develops little social or intellectual competence and shows, eventually, more and more withdrawal and disorganization. Reactive schizophrenia, on the other hand, is marked by relatively normal social and intellectual development and appears abruptly in the form of an acute reaction, frequently in response to known life stressors. The person with such an acute reaction may be severely disturbed, delusional, confused, and disorganized, but has a

**Avolition**

Inability to initiate and complete goal-directed activities

good chance of recovery. Another alternative sub-classification focuses on the distinction between positive and negative symptoms. In this framework, Type I schizophrenia describes cases of the disorder in which active signs predominate, such as prominent delusions and hallucinations. In Type II schizophrenia, negative symptoms—such as flat affect, avolition, alogia, and social withdrawal—predominate. The overlap with the process-reactive dimension is not complete, but generally Type I would resemble the reactive subgroup and Type II would resemble the process subgroup. Outcome measures are more positive for Type I patients.

Related to these attempts to conceptualize different types of schizophrenia is a long history of research that related premorbid adjustment to outcome in those with the disorder. An individual with low premorbid adjustment usually has not been married, has never worked at one job for 2 years or more, has had no academic or vocational training after high school, did not date steadily as a teenager, and has never been deeply in love and told the person about it. Ratings of the patient's social and heterosexual adjustment prior to hospitalization were found to be highly predictive of recovery from the first hospitalization for schizophrenia (Phillips, 1953; Stephens, O'Connor, & Wiener, 1968). Researchers also found that poor-premorbid patients are more deviant in their language and thought processes and possibly have a stronger genetic disposition to the disorder than do good-premorbid patients (Gottesman & Shields,

This painting reflects the interaction between a hallucinating individual and non-reality. The real shadow of the hallucinating person transforms into the corporal image of the perceived individual. (Corbis)

1972; Maher, McKean, & McLaughlin, 1966).

There is now general recognition that rapid or acute onset of positive and florid symptoms, occurring later in life in someone with good premorbid adjustment, is associated with better prognosis for recovery than a gradual, insidious onset of negative symptoms, beginning earlier in life in someone with poor premorbid adjustment.

# 10.3  Other Psychotic Conditions

There are various other psychotic disorders in the *DSM-5* that can be distinguished from schizophrenia in terms of duration of the disturbance or severity of symptoms.

## 10.3a  Schizophreniform Disorder

Schizophreniform disorder involves symptoms that are identical to those of schizophrenia's Criterion A, including hallucinations, delusions, disorganized speech and behavior, and negative psychotic symptoms. However, the diagnosis of schizophreniform disorder is given only if the duration of symptoms is at least 1 month but less than 6 months. Impaired social or occupational functioning is not required for the diagnosis, but it may occur in people with schizophreniform disorder. Presumably, all schizophrenics move through a period of schizophreniform disorder before their condition has persisted for 6 months. However, the *DSM-IV-TR* suggests the incidence is only one-fifth that of schizophrenia. It also estimates that two-thirds of those with schizophreniform disorder will likely develop either schizophrenia or schizoaffective disorder (American Psychiatric Association, 2013). Specifiers available for the diagnosis are "with good prognostic features" or "without good prognostic features"; the

> **How do various psychotic disorders differ?**

distinction essentially concerns the presence or absence of the factors associated with better outcomes in schizophrenia, as described above.

## 10.3b  Schizoaffective Disorder

Those with schizoaffective disorder show a combination of symptoms of both psychosis and mood disorder. There must be a major depressive episode or a manic episode, concurrent at some point with the symptoms listed in Criterion A of schizophrenia. However, there also must be a period of 2 weeks or more in which the psychotic symptoms are present but the major mood symptoms are absent. Overall, mood symptoms must be present a majority of the time. The disorder is coded, according to its mood symptoms, as either bipolar type or depressive type. Additional specifiers (course, severity) are the same as for schizophrenia. Females are more likely than males to receive the diagnosis of schizoaffective disorder, largely because females tend to show more frequent mood disorder, and the depressive subtype of schizoaffective disorder is most common. The prevalence of schizoaffective disorder is about one-third that of schizophrenia (American Psychiatric Association, 2013).

An obvious difficulty involves reliably distinguishing schizoaffective disorder from schizophrenia (in which there may be mood symptoms) and mood disorder with psychotic features (which may include hallucinations and delusions). The distinctions concern how prominent the relative mood and psychotic indicators are and their duration relative to each other; misdiagnosis has not been uncommon. In fact, according to the *DSM-5*, "there is growing evidence that schizoaffective disorder is not a distinct nosological category" (American Psychiatric Association, 2013, pp. 89–90). Still, diagnostic reliability, at 0.50, was about equal to that for schizophrenia in the *DSM-5* field trials (Regier, et al., 2013). Age of onset is usually young adulthood, and prognosis tends to be better than that for schizophrenia, but worse than that for mood disorders.

## 10.3c  Brief Psychotic Disorder

Brief psychotic disorder involves the sudden onset of psychotic symptoms that last more than 1 day but do not persist more than a month, with eventual return to full functioning. The psychotic indications involve at least one positive symptom (delusions, hallucinations, disorganized speech, or disorganized or catatonic behavior) and are not explained by the effects of drugs, medical conditions, or another mental disorder that can cause transient psychosis. Usually people displaying brief psychotic disorder are experiencing severe stress or turmoil in their lives, and they appear overwhelmed and confused. The disorder can be specified "with marked stressors," "without marked stressors," or "with postpartum onset" (if the condition began within 4 weeks of giving birth). Up to 9% of cases of first-onset psychosis may be accounted for by brief psychotic disorder. It is twice as common among females as males. Prognosis tends to be much better than for other psychotic conditions. However, in their acutely disturbed state, people with this condition may be at much higher risk for suicide (American Psychiatric Association, 2013).

## 10.3d  Delusional Disorder

In comparison with schizophrenia, delusional disorder involves a more limited range of psychotic symptoms. The delusions may be bizarre (this was disallowed for the *DSM-IV* diagnosis) but may not include prominent auditory or visual hallucinations. Although the delusions are persistent (at least 1 month in duration), they are focused on a theme apart from which there may be little impairment in behavior or functioning. In delusional disorder (called "paranoid disorder" in the *DSM-III*), the delusions usually concern being followed, poisoned, deceived, infected, or loved at a distance. The diagnosis is subtyped according to the predominant theme—erotomanic, grandiose, jealous, persecutory, somatic, mixed,

**BVT** *Lab*

Visit **www.BVTLab.com** to explore the student resources available for this chapter.

or unspecified. Other specifiers include "with bizarre content" if the delusions are clearly implausible. Remaining specifiers for course and severity are the same as for schizophrenia.

Some individuals develop delusions of grandeur in which they see themselves endowed with special abilities or as having been called by God to lead mankind to salvation. Others feel they have made some great invention that the world ignores no matter how hard they try to promote it. Commonly, delusions of persecution and grandiosity are present together. It is easy to see how persecutory themes can quickly develop in the context of grandiose beliefs. The establishment rarely welcomes religious messiahs, and inventions that cannot be proved to work likely elicit rebuff.

Delusional persons may respond to these criticisms by constructing more elaborate beliefs about special groups whose whole purpose is to persecute them. Much of the delusional thinking and behavior is logical if one accepts a basic premise—for example, that a certain group is conducting a conspiracy. Attempts to dissuade the delusional person of such false beliefs by logical argument and questioning of the evidence are likely to fail. In fact, the attempt may be seen as part of the conspiracy.

Delusional disorders appear to be uncommon with population incidence as low as 0.2%. Delusional disorder seems to occur at equal rates in males and females, although males may be more likely to show the jealous subtype (American Psychiatric Association, 2013). Diagnoses of delusional disorder are rare, in part, because such individuals do not seek help. In spite of a chronic course, the disorder does not seem to interfere with other aspects of the individual's thinking and behavior; the disorganization in these areas evident in schizophrenia or the extremes of elation and depression seen in the mood disorders are not present. Except for those parts of life related to the delusional beliefs, many affected persons may seem normal. Others, however, may show serious disruption if the delusion intersects important domains of daily occupational and interpersonal life.

The persecutory subtype of delusional disorder may be difficult to differentiate from paranoid personality disorder. Perhaps the most crucial distinguishing feature is that a paranoid personality lacks an enduring, well-formulated delusional belief. It may also be difficult to define the boundaries between delusional disorder, somatic type and either illness anxiety disorder or body dysmorphic disorder, especially if those beliefs are held with delusional intensity (American Psychiatric Association, 2000).

Another variant involves shared delusional disorder, which would be listed in the *DSM-5* under "other specified schizophrenia spectrum and other psychotic disorders." There is little known about shared delusional disorder, which occurs when an individual develops a delusion in the context of a close personal relationship with another person who already has an established delusion. The delusion is similar in content to the already-established delusion held by the other person (sometimes called the "inducer"), who most often is dominant in the relationship. Shared delusional disorder can involve groups of people, such as families, but most often includes only two who share the delusional beliefs. It appears to be rare and may be more common in females although very little information is available. Most cases seem to involve an inducer who is schizophrenic and who shares the delusion with a person of close blood relation or connected by marriage, often in conditions of relative social isolation (American Psychiatric Association, 2000).

## 10.3e Additional Psychotic Disorders

As noted above, psychoses can be caused by medical conditions or use of substances, and these would be labeled "psychotic disorder due to a general medical condition" or "substance/medication-induced psychotic disorder." Obviously, these diagnoses require knowledge of the etiological significance of the medical condition or substance. These disorders may be responsible for many psychotic symptoms. *DSM-IV-TR* notes, "It has been suggested that 9 out of 10 nonauditory hallucinations are the product of a Substance-Induced Psychotic Disorder or a Psychotic Disorder Due to a General Medical Condition" (American Psychiatric

Association, 2000, p. 339). The remnant category, "unspecified schizophrenia spectrum and other psychotic disorder," applies to psychotic presentations that do not meet the criteria for a defined psychotic disorder.

Under Section III in the *DSM-5*, one additional proposed psychotic disorder remains under consideration. Attenuated psychosis syndrome is a proposed label for those individuals who show subthreshold psychotic symptoms, but do not fall into any other category of psychosis. It is thought that they may be at increased risk for transitioning into a psychotic mental disorder in the future. However, Gaudiano and Zimmerman (2013) evaluated 1,257 people seeking out-patient treatment for psychotic symptoms and were unable to clearly identify a single person for whom the diagnosis would apply, calling into question its usefulness.

# 10.4  Causal Factors in Psychotic Disorders

Nearly all research on psychotic disorders has concerned schizophrenia. Over the course of many years, several psychological, biological, and genetic theories have been advanced to explain that disorder. To date, however, the etiology of schizophrenia remains unclear. A very active program of research has generated hypotheses about its genetic, neurochemical, anatomical, environmental, social, and psychological foundations, across many decades. Each of these strands of inquiry will be considered within some historical perspective.

> **How strong are genetic influences in the development of schizophrenia?**

## 10.4a  Biological Factors

### Heredity

Accumulated evidence points strongly to a genetic contribution to schizophrenic disorders. For example, schizophrenia occurs at a significantly higher rate in the close relatives of schizophrenic individuals than in the population at large; first-degree relatives have a risk that is 10 times greater than that of the general population (American Psychiatric Association, 2000). Further, the risk increases as the degree of genetic relatedness to the schizophrenic person increases (Gottesman I. I., 1991): first-degree relatives (parents, siblings, children) show higher risks than second-degree (grandchildren, nephews), who show slightly higher risk than third-degree relatives (first cousins). A genetic vulnerability to schizophrenia has been demonstrated by both twin and adoption studies.

### Twin Studies

Twin studies, dating back nearly a century, have consistently found identical twins to be concordant for (share a diagnosis of) schizophrenia more often than fraternal twins. The concordance estimates, however, have varied widely, partly because of uncertainty about twin zygosity but also because of varying definitions of schizophrenia employed (see Table 10-2). For example, estimates published before 1960 indicated that two-thirds or more of identical, or monozygotic, twins were concordant for schizophrenia; studies after 1960 tend to report lower concordance rates.

More recent estimates using stricter definitions and better methodology tend to estimate concordance at less than half; Gottesman (1991) reported the risks between identical twins as 48%, a figure that continues to be widely cited as the best measure of heritability. However, it has become apparent that the concordance estimates have been consistently overstated. A careful review of the more methodologically sound studies, reported by Torrey and his colleagues (1994), concluded that the best estimate of concordance for identical (MZ) twins is approximately 28% (that is, when one twin is schizophrenic, in 28% of cases the other twin is schizophrenic as well). For fraternal (DZ) twins, the concordance rate is about 6% (see Figure 10-1).

*Table 10-2*   Concordance Rates for Schizophrenia in Early Twin Studies

| | Number of Pairs | | Concordance Percentages | |
|---|---|---|---|---|
| | Identical | Fraternal | Identical | Fraternal |
| ***Early Studies*** | | | | |
| Luxenberger (1928), Germany | 19 | 13 | 58 | 0 |
| Rosanoff et al. (1934), U.S. and Canada | 41 | 53 | 61 | 13 |
| Essen-Möller (1941), Sweden | 11 | 27 | 64 | 15 |
| Kallmann (1953), New York State | 174 | 517 | 69 | 10 |
| Slater (1953), England | 37 | 58 | 65 | 14 |
| ***Recent Studies*** | | | | |
| Inouye (1961), Japan | 55 | 11 | 60 | 18 |
| Kringlen (1967), Norway | 55 | 90 | 25 | 4 |
| Tienari (1971), Finland | 19 | 20 | 16 | 5 |
| Fischer (1973), Denmark | 21 | 41 | 24 | 10 |
| Gottesman & Shields (1972), England | 24 | 33 | 42 | 9 |

These results consistently show a higher MZ concordance than DZ concordance, providing strong evidence for a genetic influence in schizophrenia. Of course, if only genetic features cause schizophrenia, the concordance rate among genetically identical twins would be 100%. These data, therefore, also confirm very substantial non-genetic contributions to the disorder. However, the consistent MZ/DZ differences in these studies are entirely supportive of a genetic liability.

In some twin research, the data are more difficult to interpret. Kläning (1999) reported that DZ twins were statistically much more likely to be admitted for treatment of schizophrenia than MZ twins, based on Danish twin records—a result that seems surprising in the face of such strong evidence of genetic factors. In fact, even the revised concordance estimates may overstate the genetic contribution. Uncertainty about whether the twins are truly identical contributes to overestimation: lower MZ concordance is found in studies that use laboratory measures to confirm zygosity (Walker, Downey, & Caspi, 1991).

*Figure 10-1*   **Pairwise Twin Concordance Rates for Schizophrenia from Methodologically Adequate Studies**

Source: From Torrey, E. F., Bowler, A. E., Taylor, E. H., & Gottesman, I. I., (1994). *Schizophrenia and manic-depressive disorder: The biological roots of mental illness as revealed by the landmark study of identical twins.* New York, NY: Basic Books. Reprinted with permissions.

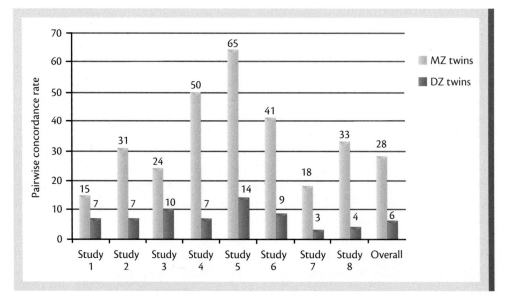

Another important factor in twin concordance concerns the intrauterine environment. In fraternal (DZ) twins, two separate eggs are fertilized; each develops within its own placental sac, surrounded by its own chorionic membrane. Identical twins are produced from a single egg; approximately two-thirds of MZ twin pairs share the same placenta and same blood circulation (Phelps, Davis, & Schartz, 1997), while the other one-third is dichorionic (see Figure 10-2). Davis, Phelps, and Bracha (1995) attempted to retrospectively identify chorionic status of concordant and disconcordant MZ twins and found that twins without evidence of having shared a placenta showed about 10% concordance, while those with evidence of shared placenta showed 60% concordance for schizophrenia. The shared circulatory and placenta features of the womb for monochorionic twins could be responsible for similarities between MZ twins due to shared environment, rather than shared genetics. Thus, the amount of similarity (concordance) ascribed to genetics would be overestimated. Typically, twin studies have not reported on chorionic status.

## Adoption Studies

Evidence from adoption studies also supports a heritable factor in the development of schizophrenia. Heston (1966) found that children born to schizophrenic mothers and placed in foster or adoptive homes within the first 3 days after birth had a significantly higher incidence of schizophrenia as young adults than did a control group of foster or adoptive children whose parents were not schizophrenic. Five of the 47 children whose biological mothers were schizophrenic were diagnosed, without knowledge of the group to which they belonged, as schizophrenic; none of the children in the control group was so diagnosed. Although the absolute number of children who became schizophrenic is small, the chance of all five coming from the experimental group was less than 2.5 times in 100 ($p < 0.025$). Rosenthal and his colleagues (1975) obtained similar results in a study conducted in Denmark, where it was possible through a central psychiatric registry to determine who had been adopted at an early age and who among the biological parents, either father or mother, had been diagnosed as schizophrenic.

In another variation using the same psychiatric register in Denmark, Kety and his colleagues (1976) identified a group of early adoptees that had become schizophrenic. They then tracked as many of the biological parents of the adoptees as possible to see what proportion of them were schizophrenic. The results are summarized in Table 10-3 where it can be seen that the diagnosis of schizophrenia (or the suspicion) was highest, about 14%, in the biological parents of schizophrenic adoptees, than for any other group of parents.

### Figure 10-2 *Chorionic Arrangements in Twins*

Chorionic arrangements in twins: (a) Dichorionic Twins have separate placentas and separate fetal circulation. (b) Monochorionic twins share placenta and circulation.

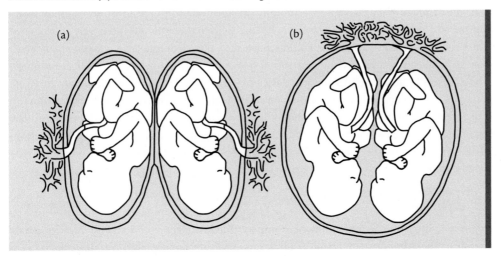

*Table 10-3*    Percentage of Parents Diagnosed as Having Either Definite or
                Uncertain Schizophrenia

| Type of Parent | N | Percentage Schizophrenic |
|---|---|---|
| Biological parents of schizophrenic adoptees | 173 | 13.9 |
| Biological parents of control adoptees | 174 | 3.4 |
| Adoptive parents of schizophrenic adoptees | 74 | 2.7 |
| Adoptive parents of control adoptees | 91 | 5.5 |

Source: Kety, S. S., Rosenthal, D., Wedner, P. H., & Schulsinger, F. (1976).

The results of these adoption studies are difficult to explain by environmental factors since the early removal of the child from the biological family should prevent the psychological transmission of the disorder from the biological parents. It would be necessary to show that the adoptive environments of the experimental children were more pathology-inductive than those of the control children, and there was no reason to suspect that might be the case.

Many adoption and family studies tend to show a greater than expected proportion of biological parents or other relatives of schizophrenic children have schizophrenia spectrum disorders such as schizotypal personality disorder and schizoaffective disorder; the evidence is more limited for schizoid, paranoid, and avoidant personality disorders (American Psychiatric Association, 2000). This suggests the possibility that some aspect of the genetic disposition to schizophrenia may, in weaker form, manifest itself in these diverse disturbances.

In summary, both the twin studies and the adoption studies indicate that genetic factors contribute substantially to the development of schizophrenia, although estimates of the degree of influence have moderated somewhat over the past few decades. Ongoing research is attempting to identify specific chromosomes or genes that could be responsible for increased risk for the disorder.

> **What non-genetic factors seem to contribute to psychosis?**

### Genetic Linkage Studies

Tracing the disorder within a pedigree, or deciphering DNA segments that may affect the production of various neurotransmitters, are among the techniques employed to search for the genes that impact schizophrenia. Many studies have been conducted, and many more are underway, in this endeavor. Researchers looking for marker genes have implicated multiple sites on at least 10 chromosomes; increasingly, the developing view is that the disorder is very complex genetically. In fact, no single gene has been consistently associated with increased risk for schizophrenia in spite of very intensive research (Tandon, Keshaven, & Nasrallah, 2008). According to one estimate, of the 325 possible dopamine-related polymorphisms that are candidates in Caucasian risk, only 19 have been evaluated in methodologically appropriate ways; and satisfactory conclusions about their involvement are still elusive (Talkowski et al., 2007). Genome studies have also revealed small but significant genetic overlap between schizophrenia and other major mental disorders, notably depression, bipolar disorder, autism, and attention-deficit hyperactivity disorder (Smoller, et al., 2013). At present, the most accurate description of research is that the genetic mechanisms producing schizophrenia are unknown but probably involve a broad spectrum of both common and uncommon alleles, each contributing to a small degree (American Psychiatric Association, 2013). For perspective on the difficulty of genetic research into the disorder, Cromwell (1993) noted that 89% of schizophrenics have no known relative with schizophrenia.

### Neurochemistry

One possibility is that genetic influences impact the risk of schizophrenia by modifying bio-chemical processes in the central nervous system, especially those related to neurotransmission (see Figure 10-3). This idea of a biochemical imbalance in psychopathology has an old and honorable tradition that goes back to Grecian theories of "humors" in the blood and more recently to Kraepelin, who believed that dementia praecox was probably caused by toxic substances secreted from the sex glands. The fact that certain chemicals, such as hallucinatory and stimulant drugs, can produce striking changes in mental experiences that resemble the schizophrenic reaction lends credence to the hypothesis that in schizophrenia the body

### Figure 10-3   *Release of Neurotransmitters*

Molecules of chemical neurotransmitters, such as dopamine and norepinephrine, are released at the nerve ending, travel across the synaptic cleft, attach themselves to receptor sites on a succeeding neuron, and thus active an electrical impulse that travels along that neuron. After performing this function, most neurotransmitter molecules, including those of dopamine and norepinephrine, are released and reabsorbed in the original nerve ending.

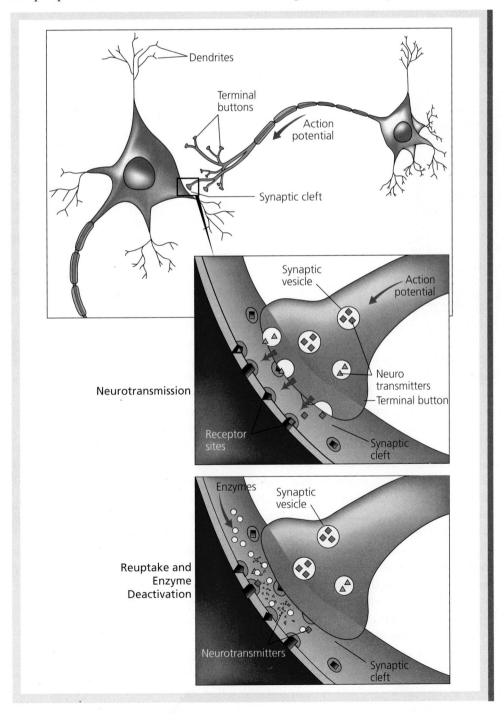

may be producing its own toxic substances. The search for that toxin included the *taraxin hypothesis*, which proposed that copper-proteins in the blood of schizophrenics produced a toxin that interfered with normal brain function. Kidney dialysis was utilized as a treatment for schizophrenia until 1977, under the assumption that the toxin could be removed. Others proposed that a naturally produced psychedelic substance was overabundant in the brain of schizophrenics. After 50 years of work, one of the most consistently supported findings has been evidence implicating the role of excessive activation of neuronal tracts that use the neurotransmitter dopamine. this is not the cause (may play a role)

The **dopamine hypothesis,** which proposed that schizophrenia resulted from a relative excess of dopamine activity in the brain, was an outgrowth of the attempt to explain the action of the antipsychotic medications that began appearing in the 1950s. Although the drugs from the phenothiazine class, with the first product marketed as Thorazine, were originally used for

> What is the dopamine hypothesis?

tranquilizing properties prior to surgery, they were inadvertently determined to reduce several signs of psychosis—including delusions, emotional flattening, catatonia, and to a lesser extent hallucinations. Research into their mechanism of action indicated that they appeared to block dopamine receptor sites on post-synaptic neurons in brain networks now thought to participate in attentional, motivational, and emotional activities. The drugs were assumed to be effective because they counteracted the cause of schizophrenia: too much dopaminergic activity.

Several lines of evidence support the dopamine hypothesis. First, among the frequent side effects of heavy and prolonged use of phenothiazines for schizophrenia are symptoms resembling Parkinson's disease: rhythmic tremors accompanied by difficulty in controlling body movements. The dopamine tract has been shown to degenerate in Parkinson's disease; and the disease can be successfully treated with L-dopa, an amino acid that replenishes the available supply of dopamine. Thus, the phenothiazines, in all likelihood, are in some way reducing activity in dopamine neurons and mimicking, in part, the symptoms of Parkinson's disease.

The dopamine hypothesis also receives support from research with amphetamine drugs. These stimulant drugs produce two effects related to schizophrenia: (1) In large and continuing doses amphetamines elicit a psychosis that can be indistinguishable from acute paranoid schizophrenia. (2) In very small doses they exacerbate certain symptoms of schizophrenic patients. Finally, the phenothiazines have a calming effect on amphetamine psychosis (Snyder, 1974).

The 2001 film *A Beautiful Mind* is loosely based in the life of John Forbes Nash, Jr., a genius mathematician. The film shows how Nash develops paranoid schizophrenia as a young man and endures the loss and burden his condition brings to his wife and friends. (Corbis)

This evidence provides a strong, though indirect, indication that some kind of overactivation of dopaminergic neurons is associated with schizophrenia. At first, it was assumed that the disorder involved excessive production of dopamine. Research, however, cast doubt on this possibility. Post and his colleagues (1975), for example, found no difference in levels of homovanillic acid (one of the substances resulting when dopamine is metabolized) in the cerebrospinal fluid of acute schizophrenics and various comparison groups. Findings of this kind led investigators (Bacopoulos, Spokes, Bird, & Roth, 1979; Post, Fink, Carpenter, & Goodwin, 1975) to suspect that oversensitivity in the dopamine receptors, rather than excessive amount, may account for the inferred unusual degree of activation in the dopaminergic neurons. More recent work suggests that an excess of particular types of dopamine receptors, called D2 receptors, are present in the brains of schizophrenics (Abi-Dargham, 2004).

**Dopamine hypothesis of schizophrenia**

Proposed that the disorder was caused by excessive dopamine activity in the brain (Hence, DA-blocking drugs like Thorazine were useful)

As promising as the dopamine hypothesis is in explaining schizophrenia, there are data that do not appear to support it. For one-third of schizophrenics, dopamine-blocking drugs are unhelpful. For those who do respond, it may take weeks to show improvement, even though the receptors are blocked almost immediately. Other neurotransmitters have been implicated, including glutamate (which may alter dopamine transmission), serotonin, and the inhibitory transmitter GABA (Goff & Coyle, 2001). Newer antipsychotic drugs may only weakly block dopamine and have most of their effects on these other neurotransmitters, yet they seem to be about equally effective as the original phenthiazines. The dopamine hypothesis is now considered a part of the neurochemical description of schizophrenia, but not the entire story.

## Neuroanatomy

The brains of schizophrenic patients reveal no specific anatomical deviations or lesions that consistently distinguish them from the brains of normals. However, evidence collected over the past 50 years does suggest some possible impairment in brain functioning in schizophrenia. Ricks and Nameche (1966), for example, found evidence for "soft signs" of neurological impairment (abnormal speech, abnormal gait, poor coordination, impaired attention span, and hyperactivity) when they examined guidance clinic records of adolescents who were subsequently hospitalized for schizophrenia. Subsequently, EEG studies (e.g., Itil, 1977) suggested higher incidence of abnormal brain wave patterns among schizophrenics, along with evidence that points to dysfunction in the left hemisphere of the brain in samples of schizophrenic patients (Buchsbaum, 1977). None of these findings, in small groups of subjects, was consistent enough to be useful in diagnosis.

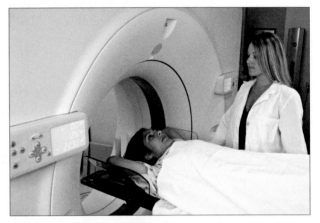

With improvement in brain imaging, research turned to CAT, PET, MRI, and fMRI scanning to identify differences between schizophrenic and normal brains. Some schizophrenics show evidence of enlarged brain ventricles. (iStock)

With improvement in brain imaging, research turned to CAT, PET, MRI, and fMRI scanning to identify differences between schizophrenic and normal brains, with mixed results. Some proportion of schizophrenics, variously estimated at between 25% and 60%, show evidence of enlarged brain ventricles. Unfortunately, brain ventricle enlargement is not unique to schizophrenia; it occurs in several other conditions, including chronic alcoholism, Huntington's disease, and Alzheimer's disease. Enlargement may also not correlate well with psychotic symptoms, sometimes appearing in the well twin or the healthy siblings of schizophrenics (Staal, et al., 2001).

Other neurological reports suggest that some schizophrenics show cerebral atrophy (Keller, et al., 2003), decrease in the size of the thalamus (Staal et al., 2001), and reduction in size of the hippocampus (Velakoulis, et al., 2006). Special caution is needed in interpreting the results because brain changes are known to result from prolonged use of neuroleptic medications, such as the phenothiazines, which might be confused for separate evidence of the disorder. Torrey (2002) concludes that evidence for brain abnormalities is strong and not related to medication use. However, no anatomical marker specific to schizophrenia, or necessary for its occurrence, is known.

## 10.4b  The Search for Neurobehavioral Markers

Since the 1930s, researchers have employed the techniques of experimental psychology to ascertain differences between schizophrenic and normal subjects on common cognitive tasks such as memory, reaction time, and attention. Over the years, a vast literature has accumulated. Numerous neurobehavioral deficits have been identified in schizophrenic samples, but their severity has varied widely. It was hoped that these deficits might serve as markers for the disorder (**endophenotypes**), valuable as risk indicators either in predicting onset or prognosis of the disorder, or in identifying neurological facets that may identify genetic foundations of schizophrenic functioning.

**Endophenotypes**

Observable traits that can serve as biomarkers for a disorder

Shakow (1961) was among the first to report large differences in a simple reaction time experiment. Reaction time was measured when a subject was asked to lift a finger from a telegraph key as soon as a light came on. Schizophrenics were markedly slower on this task than normals, with process schizophrenics showing greater impairment than reactive or paranoid schizophrenics. Numerous subsequent studies found similar results. Asarnow and his colleagues (1977) reported foster children whose biological mothers were schizophrenic showed greater deficits in paying attention than various comparison groups. Attentional dysfunction can also be observed in schizophrenics whether they are on medication or off medication (Finkelstein, Cannon, Gur, Gur, & Moberg, 1997). These results suggest that attention deficit might be a useful marker for schizophrenia. A common interpretation of these findings is that schizophrenics become distracted by irrelevant stimuli, either from the external environment or from their own thought processes. An unusual susceptibility to distraction by irrelevant stimuli might be a basic feature in the schizophrenia-prone individual, present before the full-blown disorder develops and after recovery from an acute phase of the disorder. However, in spite of consistent evidence of attention problems, the nature of the deficit is still not well understood (Gold & Thaker, 2002).

There are other possible neuropsychological markers for schizophrenia as well. Working memory deficits may be a useful indicator (Barch, 2005), perhaps related to the attention deficit. Errors in smooth pursuit eye movements have been noted for some time (e.g., Holzman & Levy, 1977); schizophrenics tend to track a moving target with frequent interruptions and numerous rapid movements. There also appears to be an association between impaired eye-tracking and schizotypal features in community samples, suggesting the measure could be valuable as an endophenotype for liability to schizophrenia (Lenzenweger & O'Driscoll, 2006). Some evidence suggests that the impairment is evident in family members. However, Boudet and his colleagues (2005) found eye-tracking impairment in schizophrenics but not in their first-degree relatives, thus calling its usefulness as a marker into question.

Finally, it is important to note that some schizophrenic patients show no obvious evidence of these or other endophenotypes. Palmer and his colleagues (1997) found that almost 30% of schizophrenics given a comprehensive neuropsychological evaluation produced normal profiles that could not be distinguished from a control group by experienced neuropsychologists. The measures employed included verbal and cognitive ability, attention, memory, sensory function, and motor skills. Research continues to be brisk in this area, but to date the marker candidates are not useful for diagnosis or identification of at-risk individuals.

Since genetic makeup is precisely the same in discordant monozygotic twins, different environmental influences must account for the development of schizophrenia in one twin and not another. (Shutterstock)

## 10.4c Environmental Factors

The strongest evidence for an environmental influence in the etiology of schizophrenia is the fact that concordance rates for identical twins are much less than 100%. Since genetic makeup is precisely the same in discordant monozygotic twins, different environmental influences must account for the difference. It does not necessarily follow, however, that the environmental influences are psychological or social in nature. The biological context—such as different intrauterine environments, birth complications, or subsequent diseases—might contribute to the development of schizophrenia in one twin and not the other.

One research strategy that seems promising is the study of identical twins that are discordant for schizophrenia. Environmental factors should be highlighted in this situation where one identical twin becomes schizophrenic and the other does not since the two individuals begin life with exactly the same genetic dispositions. Some early studies found evidence suggestive of the possibility that the twin who became schizophrenic had experienced more central nervous system illnesses, suffered from more complications or asphyxias at birth, or had a lighter birth weight (Pollin & Stabenau, 1968).

Those observations have been expanded in subsequent years, consistently implicating the prenatal and perinatal period as important. Schizophrenia appears to be more common in those whose mothers had viral infections during the second trimester of pregnancy (Brown, et al., 2000); and perhaps relatedly, more schizophrenics are born during the winter and spring months (Davies, Wellham, Chant, Torrey, & McGrath, 2003), after the peak of seasonal virus such as cold and influenza. In addition, Buka and his colleagues (2008) report that offspring of mothers who were infected with herpes simplex virus at the end of pregnancy were at increased risk for later development of schizophrenia. Certainly, the findings of higher concordance rates in monochorionic than dichorionic MZ twins by Davis et al. (1995) are also consistent with a **viral risk hypothesis**. These observations point to the importance of early developmental factors in the complex etiological picture of the disorder.

More generally, a variety of birth factors associate with schizophrenia. McNeil, Cantor-Graae, and Ismail (2000) note that obstetric complications, reduced head circumference, and minor physical abnormalities of the head and limbs are all significantly associated with offspring who later became schizophrenic. These findings are supported by a meta-analysis of population-based studies by Cannon, Jones, and Murray (2002), confirming that complications during pregnancy, complications during delivery, and abnormal fetal growth and development were risk factors associated with schizophrenia. There is also newer evidence from a population-based study in Denmark that viral or bacterial infection during childhood, serious enough to warrant hospitalization, is associated with a 50% increase in the likelihood of developing schizophrenia (Lowry, 2013).

Outside of early childhood, increasing attention is being given to adolescent development. Poor academic achievement and social adjustment in the adolescent years precede onset of schizophrenia. Some data implicate cannabis use as a risk factor for schizophrenia. Use in adolescence is associated with some increase in incidence, but the cause and effect relationship is unclear at this point (e.g., Tandon, Keshaven, & Nasrallah, 2008).

## 10.4d Psychosocial Factors

Because schizophrenia was known early in the history of psychology, much attention was historically afforded to finding possible psychological causes of the condition, especially in the mother-child or family relationship.

Psychoanalytic theory long held that schizophrenia reflects a weak ego that can no longer contain the expression of ordinarily unconscious id impulses. The combination of weak ego and fixations at the oral stage leads to a regression to this early level of development. Schizophrenic persons were also said to have withdrawn their libidinal attachments from other people and turned this energy inward on themselves. Thus, they become detached from other people and autistically preoccupied with their own inner world. However, these views stimulated little research, and schizophrenics were rarely targets for psychoanalysis.

### Family Influences

**Schizophrenogenic Mothers**  Neo-Freudian writers on schizophrenia, less tied to the concepts of orthodox psychoanalytic theory, stressed the importance of the early relationship with the mother (for example, Sullivan, 1953). In fact, certain mothers thought to have special "talent" for producing schizophrenic offspring were called *schizophrenogenic*. The central feature of the schizophrenogenic mother is extreme overprotectiveness and intrusiveness. This "engulfing" mother infantilizes the child, tells the child what to think or feel, and in general prevents the child from growing up as a separate person with a sense of personal identity and autonomy. The lack of separation between the mother and child is

**Viral risk hypothesis**
Theory that schizophrenia may be caused *in utero* by viral infection of the mother

thought to reflect the mother's perception of the child as an extension of herself. The child cannot escape this relationship and contributes, in a way, to its continuation.

The lack of separation between the mother and child is thought to reflect the mother's perception of the child as an extension of herself. Some early theories suggested that extreme overprotectiveness and intrusiveness may contribute to the development of schizophrenia. (iStock)

Several early studies found that, relative to mothers of normal offspring, mothers of schizophrenics answered questionnaire items about child-rearing attitudes in a direction more consistent with overcontrolling, intrusive behavior (e.g., Mark, 1953). Further, studies that measured children's perceptions of maternal behavior seemed to show consistently that mothers of schizophrenics are perceived by their schizophrenic children as being intrusively overcontrolling (e.g., Heilbrun, 1960; McKinley, 1963). Of course, having a seriously disturbed child may elicit more overprotective responses from a mother, confounding the direction of causality.

Murray Bowen, in the early 1950s, was one of the first persons to conduct systematic clinical studies in which he and his staff directly observed the interaction of families that included a schizophrenic son or daughter. Beginning at the Menningers' Clinic and continuing later at the National Institute of Mental Health in Bethesda, Maryland, he brought the mothers and families of schizophrenic young adults to live on the grounds in cottages or in special apartments on the hospital wards. On the basis of his observations Bowen (1978) described a phenomenon that he called the *transfer of anxiety*. The mother, for example, would become anxious and then focus her thinking on the sickness of her child, repeatedly verbalizing how disturbed the child was. Soon the mother's anxiety would be less and the patient's psychotic symptoms would be worse. In other less common instances, the son or daughter would make positive steps toward recovery and the mother would show increasing signs of anxiety, perhaps taking to her bed with some kind of physical illness. More generally Bowen proposed that when one member in an overly attached relationship functioned at a level less than the person's capacity, the other individual functioned in an over-adequate fashion. As with anxiety, occasionally the roles of under-adequate and over-adequate would be exchanged. Overt schizophrenic symptoms might then be one manifestation of under-adequate functioning.

## Family Dynamics

The phenomenon of the transfer of anxiety was just one aspect of the kind of family relationships that existed in enmeshed families (that were too closely knit in an emotional sense). Theodore

The phenomenon of the transfer of anxiety was just one aspect of the kind of family relationships that existed in enmeshed families (that were too closely knit in an emotional sense). (iStock)

Lidz and his colleagues (1965) conducted intensive studies of the families of 17 schizophrenic patients and found "whole family" psychopathology in all of them. The mothers were seen as unstable, strange persons who had difficulties setting boundaries between themselves and the disturbed child. The fathers tended to be either aggressive and paranoid, or passive and ineffectual. Although none of the parents had been hospitalized, in 60% of the families at least one parent was considered to be virtually psychotic or paranoid; and in the remaining families, one or both parents maintained a precarious adjustment involving considerable distortion of reality. Generational boundaries were always breached, either because one parent acted like a rival sibling or because a parent used a child as an emotional replacement for a spouse. Marital problems were present in most families; and the remaining families showed a pattern called marital skew, in which the serious psychopathology of the dominant parent was passively accepted by the other. Lidz especially emphasized the transmission of irrationality that occurred in such a family, in which members deny and distort the obvious interpretations of experiences; act as though certain disturbing situations did not exist; talk to each other in vague, amorphous, or fragmented ways; and are impervious to the child's own feelings and desires. The effects of these family patterns on the child were thought to include the production of schizophrenic symptoms.

**The Double Bind**    Bateson and his colleagues (1956) proposed that one kind of parent-child interaction is especially important in the development of schizophrenia, the double bind. The double bind arises when (1) the child is emotionally dependent upon the parent, and it is therefore extremely important for him or her to understand communications accurately and respond appropriately; and (2) the parent expresses two contradictory messages. The content of what the parent says may be the opposite of the message contained in tone of voice or facial expression, or the content itself may simply consist of two incompatible messages. The child cannot comment on the incongruous messages, withdraw from the situation, or ignore the messages. Caught in a bind from which there is no escape, the child uses "crazy" thinking and actions to cope with this intolerable situation.

The double bind. (iStock)

The double bind notion thus proposed that psychotic symptoms were a form of adaptation to an impossible situation. Working from a similar perspective, Laing and Esterson (1971) studied the families of 11 schizophrenic women. In each case they felt there was strong evidence that family environment could account for the patient's schizophrenic behavior. Their basic thesis is that the behavior and thought processes of people diagnosed as schizophrenic, indeed, seem crazy outside of the family context, but seen from the family perspective are not crazy or irrational at all. In fact, such behavior is just how a person might rationally react to such an environment.

The reports of Bateson and his colleagues (1956), Bowen (1978), Laing and Esterson (1971), and a number of other authors seemed to make a plausible case for family determinants of schizophrenia. These hypothesized family influences could be conceptualized within the framework of social learning theory. Parents might model and perhaps reinforce disturbed communication and peculiar ideas; then punish attempts at interpersonal intimacy, "straight" communication, and developing a distinct identity, ultimately forcing the child to withdraw in order to escape this aversive experience.

**Controlled Research on Family Correlates**    Although these sorts of theories (the double bind, the schizophrenogenic mother, the transmission of irrationality) and other family-oriented views of the origins of schizophrenia initially seemed useful, controlled research provided only partial support for these views. Some researchers sought clues in information about family characteristics obtained before the child was diagnosed as schizophrenic. McCord and his colleagues (1962) made use of an extensive body of information that had been gathered on a large sample of boys as part of a delinquency prevention study. Later 12 of these boys became psychotic, and their family backgrounds were compared with a group closely matched on such variables as socioeconomic class and ethnic background of parents, presence of psychoses or neuroses in parents, neurological signs and glandular imbalances, and race. The comparison showed that a higher percentage of mothers of the psychotic sons were rated as overcontrolling (67%) than were mothers of the control group (8%). Although based on a small sample, the results appeared consistent with the "schizophrenogenic" mother hypothesis.

In a similar study, Waring and Ricks (1965) compared records of 50 children who had been treated at the Judge Baker Guidance Center in Boston and who later became schizophrenic as adults with records of a control group of children who were also treated at the center but who did not become schizophrenic. The two groups were matched on age, sex, IQ, presenting symptoms, socioeconomic class, and ethnic background. Like others, Waring and Ricks found a higher proportion of psychotic parents in the schizophrenic group than in the control group. Absence of disturbed family environment was characteristic of 48% of the nonschizophrenic control families, but all of the families of schizophrenics were identified as disturbed. A related finding was that there were no healthy marriages in the schizophrenic groups compared with 15% healthy marriages in the control group.

These data provided support to the idea that future schizophrenics grow up in severely disturbed family environments, but other researchers reached different conclusions. For example, Jacob (1975), surveyed the research based on direct observation of family interaction and found no consistent evidence that families of schizophrenics were different from normal control families in the amount of conflict, expression of positive or negative emotion, or in relative dominance of father and mother. Even in supportive studies, no one pattern of family interaction related to the subsequent development of schizophrenia.

The reports of communication disturbance in the families of schizophrenics are, of course, consistent with the psychological transmission of this disturbance. However, these results are equally consistent with genetic transmission. Parents who are not overtly schizophrenic themselves but carry a genetic disposition to schizophrenia may manifest their "schizotypal" tendency in the form of somewhat impaired communication skills. The basic disposition to become schizophrenic, however, may be transmitted through the genes rather than through mystifying communication. Assessing communication deviance in the adoptive parents of children who become schizophrenic is one test of these two alternative theories. If psychological transmission is important, then these adoptive parents should show more disturbances in communication than adoptive parents of children who do not become schizophrenic. In two studies designed to test this hypothesis, one (Wynne, Singer, & Toohey, 1976) supported it and the other (Wender et al., 1977) did not. Since that time, the overall adoption research seems to provide more evidence for genetic transmission than for the influence of pathological families.

### Recent Research on Family Influences

At the same time, more recent research has provided strong data that family interactions contribute to the reappearance of symptoms following improvement, if not to their initial onset. Brown (1959) had noted that after discharge from treatment, schizophrenics who had only limited subsequent contact with relatives did better than those who spent more time with their families. Over the next twenty years, he refined his explanation for this difference in outcome by proposing that *expressed emotion* (EE) in the family home was the important factor. Expressed emotion consists of criticism, hostility, and emotional over-involvement (intrusiveness). When EE levels in the family were high, patients were more prone to relapse. Many studies have subsequently confirmed that high EE situations do lead to reappearance or worsening of psychotic symptoms. Levels of EE can also be used to predict relapse (Butzlaff & Hooley, 1998). In addition, the effect of close family contact on a schizophrenic person interacts with the emotional climate of the family: patients who have more than 35 contact hours per week with the family have the highest risk of relapse in high EE families, but have the lowest relapse risk in low EE families (Beggington & Kuipers, 1994).

The effect of EE on relapse might explain certain cultural differences in outcome in schizophrenia. As a general rule, those individuals with schizophrenia in the developing world tend to have a more acute course, and a better outcome, than schizophrenics in the industrialized world such as the United States (American Psychiatric Association, 2000). Jenkins and Karno (1992) noted that higher levels of family EE are present among British and Anglo-American cultures, with lower EE levels in Mexican and Indian cultures. Family levels of EE might explain some of the differences in relapse across various cultures.

## Cultural Influences

Schizophrenia apparently exists in all cultures, from the most "primitive" to the most "advanced." Global incidence appears to be up to 0.7% of the population (American Psychiatric Association, 2013). However, the incidence rates and character of the symptoms do vary widely from culture to culture. Murphy (1968), for example, reported unusually high incidence rates of schizophrenia in several subcultures. Tamil Indians living in Singapore showed a higher rate than their Chinese and Malay counterparts; Irish Catholics in southern Ireland had higher rates than those in England. Differences of this kind could conceivably reflect differences in genetic makeup of the populations, although that seemed unlikely with large populations that have not been isolated.

Murphy then compared rates of schizophrenia in three "traditional" French Canadian communities with rates in other French Canadian communities where traditions were changing and had less hold. The prevalence of schizophrenia in women was found to be extremely high in the traditional communities and was especially apparent in two subgroups of women: married women over age 35 and young unmarried women. Schizophrenia was almost nonexistent among younger married women in traditional settings.

Murphy (1968) suggested that the unusual prevalence of schizophrenia among the young single and older married women might be explained by cultural factors. The traditional communities considered the ideal woman as one who gets married early, has many children, is hardworking, patient, and submissive to her husband. The idea of an independent career for women, outside of religious orders, was only just beginning to be accepted as a possibility. For some women, according to Murphy, the conflict between satisfying the expectation of the community and pursuing interests of their own became sufficiently acute to precipitate the schizophrenic reactions—reactions that tended to occur either at the time they were entering the marriageable age period or later as their children were growing up and the satisfactions derived from the family were diminishing.

It is also known that there are differences in the onset, symptom presentation, and the course of schizophrenia across different cultures (American Psychiatric Association, 2013). In an early examination of the differences, Murphy and his colleagues (1963) surveyed psychiatrists in 27 countries representing the major regions of the world, collecting information about schizophrenic patients they had seen, including ethnic and religious background and the frequency of various symptoms. Social and emotional withdrawal, auditory hallucinations, delusions, and flatness of affect were broadly seen among patients. Other features, however, varied markedly in the different cultures. For example, two kinds of delusions showed an especially strong relationship to the world's religions—delusions with religious content and delusions of destruction. The highest percentage of religious delusions was found for Roman Catholics, the lowest for Judaism and Buddhism.

Murphy and his colleagues (1963) proposed that religious delusions and delusions of destruction were positively correlated with the extent to which religions induce a sense of guilt. Also, they suggested that Eastern religions such as the Hindu, Buddhist, and Shinto types promote a more passive acceptance of fate and an emotional detachment from

Eastern religions such as the Hindu, Buddhist, and Shinto types promote a more passive acceptance of fate and an emotional detachment from life. (iStock)

life. Consistent with the latter point was the finding that social and emotional withdrawal occurred most frequently as a symptom among the Japanese and Okinawans. The authors note that the low frequencies of religious delusions and delusions of destruction among the Jewish schizophrenics were inconsistent with his general interpretation, but they were unable to offer any alternative explanation.

## Socioeconomic Influences

It has long been known that rates of schizophrenia are highest in the lowest socioeconomic social classes. It is also well established that risk of schizophrenia is higher for those raised in urban environments (Pederson & Mortensen, 2001). Two fundamentally different hypotheses have been proposed for such social influences: (1) The stresses associated with the extremes of social disorganization, poverty, and harshness found in the lowest socioeconomic level (and urban slums) are a cause or partial cause of schizophrenia. (2) Schizophrenic or schizophrenia-prone individuals tend to drift into these slum areas because they are unable to function effectively in the rest of society.

Rates of schizophrenia are higher among those in lower socioeconomic classes and urban areas. (iStock)

Studies dating back several decades have supported both positions. In support of the "drift" hypothesis, Gerard and Houston (1953) found that the excess of schizophrenics from slum areas resulted almost entirely from young schizophrenics who had left home and rented rooms in rundown sections of town. Goldberg and Morrison (1963) obtained information on the occupations of the fathers of male schizophrenics in England and Wales. They found that although the occupations of schizophrenic sons were concentrated in the lowest social class, the occupations of the fathers were not, implying a downward drift on the part of the sons. Turner and Wagonfeld (1967) reported similar results.

However, Brenner (1973) presented data showing a strong relationship between times of economic hardship and first-admission rates to mental hospitals (including schizophrenia) in New York State, with evidence extending to 1841. Furthermore, in the 1841–1915 data the relationship was much higher for farmers, laborers, and salesmen than for individuals in more economically secure professions, such as lawyers and doctors. The stress of an economic downturn should fall most heavily on the former groups.

Correlational findings, of course, are subject to many interpretations. One possibility is that during times of relative prosperity, individuals who are already schizophrenic are supported and cared for by relatives. In hard times, however, the relatives find they can no longer provide for such persons and commit them to a mental hospital, thus increasing the first-admission rates. Brenner, however, offers several bits of evidence against such an interpretation. First, admissions of patients who are totally dependent on others were not more affected by economic changes than were admissions of individuals who had some savings and at least marginal capacity for earning a living. Second, admissions to private hospitals showed a similar relationship to economic cycles. The cost of private hospitalization is considerably higher than the cost of keeping the patient at home. Third, hospitalization rates for the criminally insane showed the same relationship. In these cases, the commission of a crime triggered hospitalization, not the need of a family to economize. The analysis of over a century of data by Brenner supported a stress interpretation and suggested that economic conditions can make a difference as to whether certain people become schizophrenic or not.

Mintz and Schwartz (1971) offered an alternative interpretation of the relationship between social class and schizophrenia. These authors pointed out that the most impoverished areas of large cities are likely to include a mixture of people with different ethnic backgrounds. When people live in an area in which their own ethnic group is few in number, they may be especially subject to conflicting cultural traditions and expectations. Mintz and Schwartz found a significant negative correlation between the incidence of schizophrenia in people of Italian descent and the number of other people of Italian descent who lived in the community: the fewer the number of other Italians, the higher the rate of schizophrenia. The ethnic makeup was more important than the affluence of the neighborhood, which proved, in fact, to have no relationship to the incidence of schizophrenia within these particular groupings of Italian-Americans.

These findings suggest that separation from a cohesive and supportive culture may be a more important correlate of schizophrenia than poverty itself. They also appear to be partially confirmed by recent findings of Cantor-Graae and Selten (2005) that first- and second-generation immigrants have much higher rates of schizophrenia than the general population. If these immigrants would also be more likely to live in urban areas and be of lower socioeconomic class, it would be additional support for socio-cultural factors such as stress or adversity influencing schizophrenia.

## Trauma and Abuse

Read and his colleagues (2005) reviewed the professional literature between 1872 and 2004 that involved child physical abuse or child sexual abuse, and either schizophrenia or psychosis. They report a large and significant relationship exists between abuse in childhood and later development of schizophrenia or psychosis. In studies that included those terms, more than half of psychotic men and women had a history of physical or sexual abuse in childhood. Further, most psychiatric patients had suffered serious physical assaults as adults; approximately one-third of female patients had been raped. As stronger evidence about the causal role of abuse, the authors identify a "dose effect"—more severe abuse is associated with a larger number and greater severity of psychotic symptoms, including hallucinations and delusions. In fact, the content of hallucinations was so strongly linked to the severity of abuse that Read et al. propose that hallucinations are essentially dissociative memories of traumatic abuse, experienced as decontextualized "flashbacks." Delusions, then, might be explanations imposed by the psychotic person to account for the decontextualized trauma memories.

Some researchers (e.g., Read et al., 2005) have reported that a large and significant relationship exists between physical or sexual abuse in childhood and later development of schizophrenia or psychosis. (iStock)

Read and his colleagues interpret the evidence as supporting a causal role for childhood trauma in the development of schizophrenia, even in the absence of any genetic predisposition. The authors note that trauma produces activation of the HPA axis and that prolonged or severe stress also elevates dopamine levels in the brain, which have been implicated in schizophrenia. According to their argument, childhood trauma could thus produce long-term dysregulation of the dopaminergic system, leading directly to psychosis.

In arguing that schizophrenia, like PTSD, may be a product of the long-term effects of severe trauma, Read et al. make a strong case that psychological factors do play a role in the development of psychosis. A limitation of their analysis is that very few of the studies reviewed were well controlled. However, most of the recent studies with better methodology have also supported the association between physical or sexual abuse and psychosis. Whitfield and his colleagues (2005) reviewed over 17,000 subjects in California and found that adverse childhood events were associated with hallucinations in a dose-response relationship (Whitfield et al., 2005). A recent study of over 6,400 children in England (Schreier, et al., 2009) reported an increased risk of psychotic symptoms in those children who were victims of peer bullying, further extending the range of traumatic triggers of psychotic disorders.

A recent study of over 6,400 children in England reported an increased risk of psychotic symptoms in those children who were victims of peer bullying. (iStock)

# 10.4e  Causal Factors in Psychosis: A Summary

The emerging picture from decades of research into the causes of schizophrenia is complex and puzzling, allowing for some range in etiological opinion. On one end, a strong medical-model perspective considers schizophrenia to be a biological disease of the brain, unrelated to psychological influences, in which a genetic predisposition is triggered by a biological event such as a viral infection either *in utero* or in infancy (Torrey, Bowler, Taylor, & Gottesman, 1994). On another end, some schizophrenia cases are considered to be the direct result of childhood trauma and abuse, even in the absence of genetic susceptibility (Read, Van Os, Morrison, & Ross, 2005). A more centrist position is represented by those who believe that a simple neurodevelopmental model cannot explain many factors about onset and severity and look, instead, to a dopamine dysfunction that can have multiple causes—including genetic, environmental, social, and psychological ones (Broome, et al., 2005).

The current state of affairs is one of a wealth of data, but a poverty of conclusions. Thousands of research studies have been published in the past 20 years, examining the multitude of genetic, neurochemical, neuroanatomical, and developmental facets of the disorder. Still, the important answers elude us. As Tandon and his colleagues (2008) summarize the situation:

> *Although it appears that our understanding of the causation of schizophrenia has substantially increased over the past two decades, what we can confidently assert is essentially the same—both genetic and environmental factors are important, but exactly which specific exposures and exactly how they cause schizophrenia is still unknown.*
>
> (p. 12).

It appears at this point that more certain pronouncements and convictions are premature. Even after 30 years of intensive work, the most practical view of schizophrenia etiology remains the diathesis-stress model (Zubin & Spring, 1977), which proposed that the disorder is triggered by stressful events in someone with a diathesis (that is, a predisposition or a vulnerability) to the disorder. Vulnerability within the diathesis-stress model could be traced to genetic, biological, or psychological history.

## One Disorder

One source of difficulty in explaining schizophrenia is that people vary greatly in their psychotic presentations—one schizophrenic may appear very different from others. There are many deficits and abnormalities that describe some subsets of patients, but no finding seems central to all. To put it another way, much has been learned about contributory causes, but no necessary conditions for schizophrenia have emerged. Instead, the evidence gives the impression that there are many paths to the disorder. Is it possible that there are several different conditions, with different etiologies, that the *DSM-5* includes among the schizophrenia spectrum? Various writers have suggested that the negative (or "deficit") form of schizophrenia may represent a fundamentally different disorder from the positive type, based on differences in symptom presentation, neurological signs, and medication response (Kirkpatrick, Bunchana, Ross, & Carpenter, 2001). In fact, season of birth also appears to differ for deficit compared to non-deficit cases (Messias, et al., 2004), supporting the idea that they may be distinct conditions. If, under the same umbrella, many different disorders have been collected, then the task of finding a universal cause may be an impossible one, and a radical rethinking of the issue is in order.

# 10.5  Treatment of Psychotic Disorders

*CBT helps immensly long term.*

## 10.5a  Biological Therapy

Efforts in the first half of the twentieth century to treat schizophrenia or other psychoses generally involved the somatic therapies (coma therapy, psychosurgery, or electroconvulsive therapy) or the use of strong opiates and sedative drugs for calmative purposes. As noted earlier, a treatment breakthrough occurred with the widespread use of the phenothiazine drugs, beginning with the commonly used variety chlorpromazine, sometimes called by its trade name, Thorazine.

> **Can psychotic disorders be treated?**

Several well controlled, double blind studies supported the effectiveness of this drug to reduce schizophrenic symptoms. In one study involving 692 schizophrenic patients from 37 different Veterans Administration hospitals, Casey et al. (1960) found chlorpromazine to be much more effective than phenobarbital (a sedative) or a placebo over a 12-week course of treatment. Other phenothiazines and similar compounds were quickly introduced (see Chapter 3). These dopamine-blocking drugs reduced the severity of the most disabling active symptoms and allowed many seriously psychotic people to leave the institutions that had housed them in their more confused states (see Figure 10-4).

Hogarty and Ulrich (1977) provide evidence on the relapse rate for schizophrenic patients maintained on either chlorpromazine or placebo after discharge from a hospital. At the end of 2.5 years post-discharge, 86% of placebo-treated patients had relapsed, compared with 55% of the chlorpromazine group (see Figure 10-5). Although chlorpromazine was more effective than a placebo, the greater than 50% relapse rate for the former casts some doubt on the ability of the phenothiazine drugs to prevent relapse in many patients.

More than 100 studies have shown that the "typical" antipsychotic drugs (as chlorpromazine and other drugs with similar pharmacological activity are called) are more effective than placebos and a number of other drugs, with about 60% of treated subjects showing

---

**Figure 10-4**  *Inpatient Population of Mental Hospitals*

Inpatient population of state and county mental hospitals rose steadily from the turn of the century until 1955, after which it has decreased sharply.

Source: Bassuk & Gerson (1978). Copyright ©1978 by *Scientific American*. Used with permissions

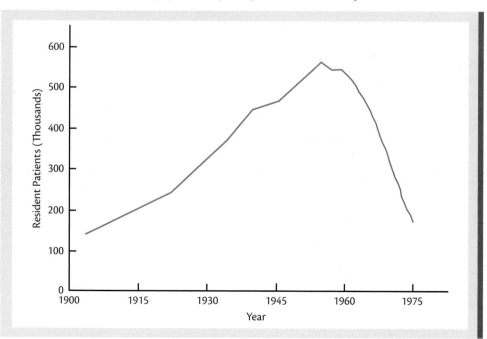

*Figure 10-5* **Effectiveness of Chlorpromazine**

Percentage of patients not relapsing on a 30-month post-discharge period who continued to receive either chlorpromazine (a phenothiazine) or placebo

Source: Hogarty & Ulrich (1977) Copyright ©1977 American Medical Association. Used with permissions

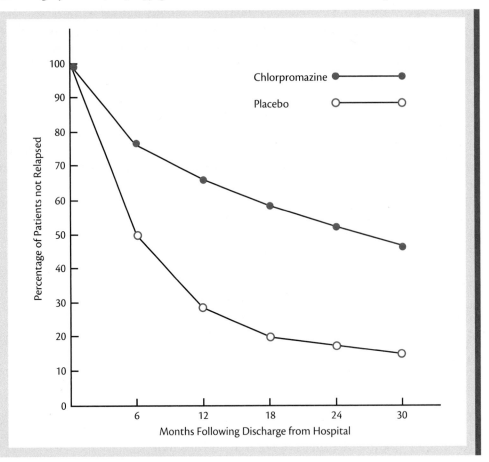

improvement in positive symptoms within 6 weeks (Sheitman, Kinon, Ridgway, & Lieberman, 1998). However, phenothiazines are not universally successful in reducing schizophrenic symptomatology. Some patients show only limited improvement, and a substantial number require continued hospitalization. Relapse also continues to be a significant issue.

A major problem contributing to this high relapse rate is patient discontinuation of medications. Many patients do not like taking these drugs since there are many troublesome side effects of phenothiazines. Drowsiness, constipation, fine motion tremor, nausea, dizziness, jaundice, and weight gain are among the more common ones. A serious and irreversible side effect that has been found to develop in some patients given long-term phenothiazine treatment is **tardive dyskinesia**, an untreatable symptom pattern consisting of involuntary slow, rhythmical, stereotyped movements of the legs, arms, or trunk, as well as oral movements such as lip smacking. In addition to these troubling side effects, antipsychotic medications produce sexual dysfunctions in between 30% and 80% of patients (Baggaley, 2008).

A new generation of antipsychotic medication was introduced in the 1980s. These drugs (which include clozapine, rispiradone, and olanzapine, sold as Clozaril, Resperdal, and Zyprexa, respectively) block a broader range of receptors than the first generation drugs, and have less serious side effects. Originally targeted for treatment-resistant patients, these have become first-line medications for schizophrenia. They appear to be as effective as the typical anti-psychotics (both classes are more effective on positive rather than negative symptoms) but perhaps are more easily tolerated because of milder side effects. However, weight gain and sexual dysfunctions remain common; and although the atypical anti-psychotics do not produce tardive dyskinesia, they can result in a potentially fatal blood disease called

**Tardive dyskinesia**

Occasional long-term side effect of phenothiazine treatment of schizophrenia and involves rhythmical, stereotyped movements and lip smacking

agranulocytosis in a small percentage of patients. Drug discontinuation remains a major problem in treatment; one recent investigation found that schizophrenics take medication for only an average of 6 months in any single year, and this "light use" was related to higher risk of hospitalization and longer hospital stays (DosReis, et al., 2008).

*these drugs dont cure, help manage.*

A meta-analysis of the treatment literature published from 1895 through 1991 was conducted by Hegarty and his colleagues (1994). Their database included 320 studies involving almost 52,000 subjects, in which outcome data were reported for at least 1 year. The mean proportion of patients showing improvement at follow-up was 40.2%. (If broad diagnostic criteria were used, favorable outcome was closer to 47%.) Although favorable outcome percentages increased from the 1920s to the 1970s, they declined thereafter; after 1986, mean favorable outcome was similar to that found in the first half of the twentieth century (36.4%). The atypical anti-psychotics may improve on that outcome, largely because their side effect profiles lead to less discontinuation; but without question, pharmacological treatment for schizophrenia involves temporary management of symptoms, at best.

## 10.5b  Psychosocial Therapy

### Psychoanalytic Therapy *not very helpful*

Freud and many of his psychoanalytic colleagues were skeptical of the value of psychoanalysis for schizophrenic patients. The extreme psychological withdrawal seemed to be an effective barrier against the intimate interpersonal interchanges and transference reactions considered so essential for psychoanalytic treatment. However, some therapists, notably Harry Stack Sullivan and Frieda Fromm-Reichmann, felt that with several major modifications psychoanalytic therapy *could* be used successfully with schizophrenic patients.

Studies with adequate controls have not shown insight-oriented psychotherapy to be particularly effective with schizophrenic patients. For example, May and his colleagues (1967) found the phenothiazine drugs alone were just as effective as phenothiazine drugs plus psychotherapy, and both of these treatments were more effective than psychotherapy alone. Grinspoon and his colleagues (1968) used experienced psychoanalytic therapists and also found that psychotherapy added little if anything to phenothiazine treatment. Later evaluations were less than supportive: Mueser and Berenbaum (1990) suggested that some groups of patients get worse under psychodynamic therapy.

### Family Therapy *helpful (sometimes)*

Because expressed emotion (EE) is a factor in predicting relapse, family intervention approaches have been developed to enhance communication and interaction between members. Components typically include education about schizophrenia, assistance in utilizing community supports, decreasing emotional over-involvement, and stress-management. A key feature in effectiveness appears to be duration: at least 9 months of family sessions are needed for improved outcomes to develop (Kopelowicz, Liberman, & Zarate, 2002). These family approaches have produced positive impacts on rehospitalization and relapse, but not on other measures (Bustillo, Lauriello, Horan, & Keith, 2001).

Because expressed emotion is a factor in predicting relapse, family intervention approaches have been developed to enhance communication and interaction between members. (Shutterstock)

### Behavioral Therapy

Paul and Lentz (1977) pioneered social learning approaches for changing behavior within groups of schizophrenic patients. They employed a structured token economy as an incentive system and focused interventions on social skills, self-care, and participation in activities in inpatient settings, with positive results. Subsequent interventions targeted behavioral deficits, conversational skills, medication management, disruptive activities, and most symptoms associated with schizophrenia; hundreds of studies have supported the value of such interventions as a component of treatment programs (Kopelowicz, Liberman, & Zarate, 2002).

An interesting application of acceptance and commitment therapy (ACT) for use in treating psychotic patients comes from Bach and Hayes (2002). Patients were randomly assigned to either treatment as usual or four brief sessions of ACT therapy, in which patients were taught to accept the occurrence of troubling but unavoidable private events (such as hallucinations and delusions), "just noticing" them without taking them to be literally true, while also working toward valued goals. The patients who received ACT reported being less troubled by psychotic symptoms and were rehospitalized at less than half the rate of those receiving treatment as usual (which commonly encourages patients to actively suppress the symptoms).

## Cognitive Therapy

Hogarty and his colleagues (2004), in a randomized study, compared cognitive enhancement therapy for schizophrenia to enriched supportive therapy. The cognitive enhancement technique employed computer-assisted training in cognitive tasks such as attention, memory, and problem solving, and cognitive small group training in social skills and problem solving. Both groups showed significant long-term improvement in symptom and cognitive measures, although cognitive enhancement therapy also resulted in improvements in a processing speed measure. Other reviews (Bustillo, Lauriello, Horan, & Keith, 2001) suggest that cognitive-behavioral techniques may enhance standard social skills training for schizophrenics. It may also be possible to use cognitive behavioral therapy (CBT) to help prevent the development of schizophrenia in high-risk individuals. Of 201 patients classified as high-risk for psychosis based on family history, the presence of subclinical symptoms, or having experienced a brief (less than 1 week) psychotic episode, those who received CBT targeting cognitive biases as an adjunct to treatment were 50% less likely to progress to psychosis compared to those who received treatment as usual (van der Gaag, et al., 2012).

# Chapter Review

## TO SUM UP ...

- The psychotic disorders are severe disturbances involving loss of contact with reality.

- "Positive" symptoms of schizophrenia include hallucinations, delusions, disorganized speech, and disorganized behavior. The "negative" symptoms include social withdrawal, lack of self-care, emotional blunting, poverty of speech, and lack of interest in goal-directed activities.

- Schizophrenia differs from schizophreniform disorder and brief psychotic disorder largely on the basis of duration.

- Delusional disorder involves fixed non-bizarre delusions, without significant impairment in other areas of life.

- Schizophrenia affects less than 1% of the population, and it is somewhat more common in males.

- Twin and adoption studies indicate a significant genetic risk factor for schizophrenia. However, the substantial non-concordance in MZ twins indicates significant non-genetic causal factors as well.

- Many consider schizophrenia to be a biological brain disease, but there are no laboratory tests or medical examinations that can verify the diagnosis. Some, but not all, schizophrenics show neurological abnormalities or brain structural changes.

- Environmental risk factors for schizophrenia include maternal viral infections during pregnancy and complications of pregnancy or delivery.

- Psychosocial risk factors for schizophrenia include poverty, immigration, and childhood abuse.

- Prognosis in schizophrenia is better when presentations involve acute or rapid onset, positive symptoms, and later age of onset. Prognosis is poor when the presentation involves early onset, gradual worsening, and the preponderance of negative symptoms.

- Drug therapies have been shown effective in reducing the symptoms of schizophrenia in many patients. However, some patients show only limited improvement and still cannot get along outside the hospital. Relapse rate is high, and the medications may produce troublesome side effects.

- Psychosocial interventions involving family communication, social skills training, and various cognitive-behavioral procedures targeting symptom severity have been shown to be useful in the overall treatment of people with schizophrenia.

- Although intensive research on schizophrenia has produced thousands of studies over many decades, the cause or causes of schizophrenia remain unclear. Any underlying genetic, biological, neurochemical, developmental, or psychosocial factors necessary for the disorder are unknown at this time.

## KEY TERMS

Affective flattening   252

Alogia   249

Anhedonia   252

Avolition   255

Catatonia   251

Clanging   248

Delusion   249

Dopamine hypothesis of
    schizophrenia   264

Echolalia   249

Echopraxia   251

Endophenotypes   265

Hallucinations   250

Illusions   250

Mutism   251

Neurosis   247

Psychosis   247

Tardive dyskinesia   276

Viral risk hypothesis   267

## QUESTIONS FOR STUDY

- John has been diagnosed with schizophrenia. Are there any physical or psychological tests that can support the diagnosis? Are there any physical or psychological tests that can confirm or refute the diagnosis?

- Suggest three reasons why twin studies have varied so much in their reports of twin concordance for schizophrenia.

- Describe the dopamine hypothesis of schizophrenia, and discuss evidence for and against this hypothesis.

- If the Rosenhan study involving pseudopatients (Chapter 4) were repeated today, would the fakers be more easily detected? Why or why not?

## POP QUIZ

1. Symptoms such as delusions, hallucinations, and grossly impaired speech or movements are considered _____ evidence of psychosis.
   A. direct or positive
   B. inadequate
   C. indirect or negative
   D. latent

2. A psychotic speaker may employ _____, which involves the use of a word not because of its meaning but because of its sound.
   A. derailment
   B. clanging
   C. alogia
   D. word salad

3. Dr. Napen had a difficult time interviewing the patient who kept repeating everything that Dr. Napen asked. The patient was presenting with

   _____.
   A. neologism
   B. echolalia
   C. word salad
   D. alogia

4. Robert believed that Britney Spears was in love with him, even though she has never met him. Robert's delusions are best described as _____.
   A. bizzare
   B. somatic
   C. erotomanic
   D. grandiose

5. Which is *not* an example of catatonia?
   A. grimacing
   B. waxy flexibility
   C. unpredictable movements
   D. laughing

6. Who introduced the term schizophrenia in 1911 to refer to a split between thought processes and emotions or to a general disorganization in thought and behavior?
   A. Bleuler
   B. Kraepelin
   C. Blauler
   D. Kroplin

7. Many people with schizophrenia have difficulty showing an interest in work or in completing goal-directed activities. This is known as _____.
   A. alogia
   B. avolition
   C. atonia
   D. affective flattening

8. Brief psychotic disorder involves the sudden onset of at least one positive psychotic symptom that lasts more than _____ but does not persist more than

   _____.
   A. 1 day, 1 week
   B. 1 day, 1 month
   C. 1 week, 1 month
   D. 1 week, 6 months

9.  The best estimate of the concordance rate for schizophrenia between monozygotic twins is _____.
    A. 10%
    B. 28%
    C. 48%
    D. 75%

10. Among the frequent side effects of heavy and prolonged use of _____ for schizophrenia are symptoms which resemble Parkinson's Disease.
    A. SSRIs
    B. MAO-inhibitors
    C. benzodiazepines
    D. phenothiazines

11. Which groups in the U.S. show higher rates of schizophrenia than the general population?
    A. rural residents
    B. first- and second-generation immigrants
    C. upper-middle class
    D. all of the above

12. Schizophrenia, like _____, may be a product of the long-term effects of severe trauma.
    A. OCD
    B. depression
    C. GAD
    D. PTSD

13. The first medication used widely to treat schizophrenia was _____.
    A. mellaril
    B. risperidone
    C. thioridazine
    D. chlorpromazine

14. In delusional disorder, which of the following occurs?
    A. The person behaves relatively normally.
    B. Delusions and hallucinations predominate.
    C. Delusions usually include sensory misperceptions.
    D. Disorganized speech is often the only obvious symptom.

15. Expressed emotion in families is thought to influence which of the following?
    A. development of schizophrenia
    B. content of delusions shown by schizophrenic patients
    C. display of positive or negative symptoms by schizophrenic patients
    D. probability of relapse by schizophrenic patients

# CHAPTER OVERVIEW

# CHAPTER OPENER QUESTIONS

What are mood episodes, and how are they used in diagnosis?

What are the causes of the depressive and bipolar disorders?

How are mood disorders different from normal variations in mood? How common are mood disorders?

Do mood disorders improve without treatment?

Does medication work better than psychotherapy for depression?

Is mania treated differently than depression?

How common is suicide? Who is at greatest risk?

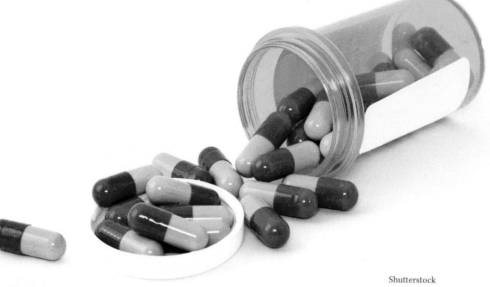

Shutterstock

# 11

# Mood Disorders and Suicide

Our life experiences typically involve subjective feelings and emotions that serve, in part, to provide us with feedback about the outcomes of our efforts. Success, progress, frustration, and failure usually are accompanied by different emotions, ranging from joy and euphoria, to a sense of satisfaction and well-being, to irritability, anger, sadness, or despair. Emotions are clearly adaptive for all species that display them (Darwin, 1872). However high levels of emotionality in humans can become maladaptive, causing major problems in social, occupational, and interpersonal functioning, and significantly increasing the risk of attempted or completed suicide. The mood disorders describe conditions in which the intensity of emotion and affect create significant problems for individuals and the people around them.

Disturbances in mood have been long recognized as disabling. For example, **melancholia** (a particularly deep depression) formed one of the four humors of early Greek medicine (Chapter 2). Mood disorders (also sometimes called affective disorders) are among the most common diagnoses in the *DSM-5*, where they are broadly classed as Depressive Disorders, and as Bipolar and Related Disorders. They include the widest range of affect, from those who find nothing whatsoever pleasurable in life to those who seek as much immediate gratification as possible.

## 11.1 Diagnosis of Mood Disorders

### 11.1a Mood Episodes

In the *DSM-5*, the mood disorders are largely defined by various combinations of mood episodes

**What are mood episodes, and how are they used in diagnosis?**

that function somewhat like diagnostic building blocks. These components include the major depressive episode, the manic episode, and the hypomanic episode. They do not constitute diagnoses in themselves, but their presence or absence is essential in most mood disorder diagnoses.

In a major depressive episode, sleep is usually disturbed either through insomnia or by waking early and being unable to return to sleep.
(Shutterstock)

### Major Depressive Episode

The criteria for a major depressive episode are shown below in the *DSM-5* Criteria for a Major Depressive Episode. The episode involves a 2-week period of nearly constant depressive symptomatology: sadness, loss of interest or pleasure, changes in weight, changes in sleep, loss of energy, agitated or slow movement, difficulty concentrating, guilt, and/or thoughts of death. Obviously, many people experience occasional depressed mood, including some of these symptoms. A major depressive episode is distinguished by its duration (nearly

**Melancholia**

Particularly deep level of depression characterized by absence of interest or pleasure in all things, changes in sleep, changes in weight, and/ or excessive guilt

constant for 2 weeks), the degree of disturbance (at least five of the symptoms are present), and the impairment that it causes in life. To be considered as part of a major depressive episode, the symptoms must represent a change from previous functioning (American Psychiatric Association, 2013).

| *DSM-5* | **Criteria for a Major Depressive Episode** |
| --- | --- |

**Major Depressive Episode**

A. Five (or more) of the following symptoms have been present during the same 2-week period and represent a change from previous functioning; at least one of the symptoms is either (1) depressed mood or (2) loss of interest or pleasure.

**Note:** Do not include symptoms that are clearly attributable to another medical condition.

1. Depressed mood most of the day, nearly every day, as indicated by either subjective report (e.g., feels sad or empty) or observations made by others (e.g., appears tearful). (**Note:** In children and adolescents, can be irritable mood.)
2. Markedly diminished interest or pleasure in all, or almost all, activities most of the day, nearly every day (as indicated by either subjective account or observation).
3. Significant weight loss when not dieting or weight gain (e.g., a change of more than 5% of body weight in a month), or decrease or increase in appetite nearly every day. (**Note:** In children, consider failure to make expected weight gain.)
4. Insomnia or hypersomnia nearly every day.
5. Psychomotor agitation or retardation nearly every day (observable by others; not merely subjective feelings of restlessness or being slowed down).
6. Fatigue or loss of energy nearly every day.
7. Feelings of worthlessness or excessive or inappropriate guilt (which may be delusional) nearly every day (not merely self-reproach or guilt about being sick).
8. Diminished ability to think or concentrate, or indecisiveness, nearly every day (either by subjective account or as observed by others).
9. Recurrent thoughts of death (not just fear of dying), recurrent suicidal ideation without specific plan, or a suicide attempt or a specific plan for committing suicide.

B. The symptoms cause clinically significant distress or impairment in social, occupational, or other important areas of functioning.

C. The episode is not attributable to the direct physiological effect of a substance or another medical condition.

Source: Reprinted with permission from the *Diagnostic and Statistical Manual of Mental Disorders*, Fifth Edition, (Copyright 2013). American Psychiatric Association.

Most commonly, the depressive episode involves loss of interest or pleasure in activities that used to be enjoyable. Appetite is nearly always affected; most often it is reduced, but some people increase their food intake. Weight may change in accordance with the alteration in eating patterns. Similarly, sleep is usually disturbed, either in terms of insomnia or by wakening early and being unable to return to sleep. Others, however, increase their sleep duration. People feel fatigued, tired, and find common tasks exhausting. Concentration is difficult, and thinking may seem to be slowed; tasks that are intellectually demanding are not completed or attempted. Sufferers may be preoccupied with personal failure and blame themselves for any non-positive event they encounter; the sense of guilt and worthlessness can combine with feelings of hopelessness and helplessness and extend to thoughts of suicide and death.

At times during a major depressive episode, some people may experience psychotic symptoms. Guilt may be of delusional proportions, such as feeling responsible for global problems or natural disasters. When psychotic features are present, the additional symptoms they produce are not included in the identification of the episode. For example, an individual may hold the delusion that falling asleep will cause other people to die; any resulting loss of sleep would not be counted as evidence of meeting the diagnostic criterion of insomnia because the sleep disturbance is caused by the delusion itself. The presence of psychotic symptoms in a major depressive episode requires differentiation from schizoaffective disorder, in which psychotic symptoms are also present in the absence of the mood episode.

A distinction must be made between a major depressive episode and the normal depressive symptoms associated with bereavement. As discussed in Chapter 5, the normal grief reaction following death of a loved one generally does not include a strong sense of worthlessness, suicidal ideation, psychosis, or extreme impairment, as is shown in major depressive episodes. As such, in the *DSM-IV* a major depressive episode was not diagnosed if the depressive symptoms could be better accounted for by bereavement. The *DSM-5* discontinued this practice of "bereavement exclusion," because bereavement often extends for over a year and can itself serve as a trigger for a major depressive episode. The issue for the clinician would be to distinguish normal grief from a grief-related depression. The *DSM-5* notes, for instance, that depression usually involves a loss of interest in almost all things, while those in grief may still experience positive emotions, such as fond memories (American Psychiatric Association, 2013).

## Manic Episode

The key feature of a manic episode is a distinct period (at least 1 week in duration, unless the person has already required hospitalization) of expansive, elevated, or irritable mood. In many ways, the manic episode (*DSM-5* Diagnostic Criteria for a Manic Episode) is nearly the opposite of a major depressive episode. The elevated mood is usually experienced as enjoyable or euphoric; to observers who know the person, it seems excessively so. When mood is expansive, the individual may seem overly enthusiastic and intrusive in social interactions. Irritability is also common, perhaps related to a blocking of the person's wishes, and frequently there are mood swings between irritability and euphoria (American Psychiatric Association, 2013).

During the manic episode, people evidence grandiose or inflated self-esteem, little need for sleep, pressured speech, flight of ideas, and distractibility. They multi-task several activities at once and seek out pleasurable activities that provide immediate gratification, without regard for consequences. They are usually very sociable and, frequently, sexually indiscriminate. However, the excessive social involvement typically becomes demanding and

---

| **DSM-5** | **Diagnostic Criteria for a Manic Episode** |
| --- | --- |

Manic Episode

A. A distinct period of abnormally and persistently elevated, expansive, or irritable mood and abnormally and persistently increased goal-directed activity or energy, lasting at least 1 week and present most of the day, nearly every day (or any duration if hospitalization is necessary).

B. During the period of mood disturbance and increased energy or activity, three (or more) of the following symptoms have persisted ( four if the mood is only irritable) are present to a significant degree and represent a noticeable change from usual behavior:
   1. Inflated self-esteem or grandiosity.
   2. Decreased need for sleep (e.g., feels rested after only 3 hours of sleep).
   3. More talkative than usual or pressure to keep talking.
   4. Flight of ideas or subjective experience that thoughts are racing.
   5. Distractibility (i.e., attention too easily drawn to unimportant or irrelevant external stimuli), as reported or observed.
   6. Increase in goal-directed activity (either socially, at work or school, or sexually) or psychomotor agitation (i.e., purposeless non-goal-directed activity).
   7. Excessive involvement in activities that have a high potential for painful consequences (e.g., engaging in unrestrained buying sprees, sexual indiscretions, or foolish business investments).

C. The mood disturbance is sufficiently severe to cause marked impairment in social or occupational functioning or to necessitate hospitalization to prevent harm to self or others, or there are psychotic features.

D. The episode is not attributable to the physiological effect of a substance (e.g., a drug of abuse, a medication, other treatment) or another medical condition.

domineering. Angry outbursts and hostility may be part of the nearly constant flow of verbal output, some of which is so tangential as to be incoherent. Consider the letter below written after a patient in a manic state was involuntarily hospitalized.

The manic person's demeanor is typically flamboyant or dramatic, and judgment is poor; illegal activities and arrest are not uncommon. Shopping sprees may occur, in which an individual may squander life savings or purchase large quantities of unneeded items without the ability to pay. Sometimes, manic individuals become aggressive and assaultive and increase their use of alcohol or drugs.

Manic episodes typically begin rapidly and may follow exposure to stressors. The symptoms build quickly and usually escalate over several days. They tend to be briefer than major depressive episodes, but can last several weeks.

### Hypomanic Episode

The remaining mood episode in the *DSM-5* concerns symptoms that are similar to, but less severe than, a manic episode. The criteria identifying a hypomanic episode are displayed in *DSM-5* Diagnostic Criteria for a Hypomanic Episode. At least three symptoms of elevated, expansive, or irritable mood are required, lasting at least 4 days; no psychotic symptoms are allowed by the diagnostic criteria. A variety of manic-like activities may occur, but they are less bizarre and more organized than those within a manic episode. In addition, impairment resulting from the episode is minimal, and hospitalization is not required. Nonetheless, the episode represents a change in functioning that is observable by other people. Hypomanic episodes tend to begin abruptly and may last from weeks to months; frequently a major depressive episode either precedes or follows the experience. Up to 15% of sufferers eventually develop a manic episode as well (American Psychiatric Association, 2013).

The *DSM-IV* included a mixed episode involving alternation between a major depressive episode and a manic episode, nearly every day, during a 1-week period. This was removed in the *DSM-5* and replaced with a specifier, "with mixed features," that can be added to manic or hypomanic episodes to indicate that depressive features are also present, or to depressive episodes to indicate manic or hypomanic features are involved.

These three mood episodes are combined in various ways to describe the *DSM-5* mood disorders, summarized in Table 11-1. As can be seen, the presence of any manic episode results in the diagnosis of bipolar I disorder. A major depressive episode can occur in major depressive disorder or in bipolar I or II disorder. Dysthymic disorder and cyclothymic disorder involve less severe depressive states; a hypomanic episode characterizes bipolar II disorder and, to a lesser extent, cyclothymic disorder.

These conditions occur at relatively high rates in the population. Kessler, Berglund, and their colleagues (2005) indicated that lifetime prevalence for any mood disorder is 20.8%. Sex ratios for the unipolar (depressed) conditions are decidedly in female favor, by a factor of 2 or 3 times the rates for males. Sex ratios are approximately equal for bipolar I disorder and cyclothymic disorder. However, it is expected that more boys than girls will receive the

Letter sent by a patient in a manic episode (Courtesy of Dr. Charles Lyons)

| *DSM-5* | **Diagnostic Criteria for a Hypomanic Episode** |
|---------|--------------------------------------------------|

Hypomanic Episode

A. A distinct period of abnormally and persistently elevated, expansive, or irritable mood and abnormally and persistently increased activity or energy, lasting at least 4 consecutive days and present most of the day, nearly every day.

B. During the period of mood disturbance and increased energy and activity, three (or more) of the following symptoms (four if the mood is only irritable) have persisted, represent a noticeable change from usual behavior, and have been present to a significant degree:

  1. Inflated self-esteem or grandiosity.
  2. Decreased need for sleep (e.g., feels rested after only 3 hours of sleep).
  3. More talkative than usual or pressure to keep talking.
  4. Flight of ideas or subjective experience that thoughts are racing.
  5. Distractibility (i.e., attention too easily drawn to unimportant or irrelevant external stimuli), as reported or observed.
  6. Increase in goal-directed activity (either socially, at work or school, or sexually) or psychomotor agitation.
  7. Excessive involvement in activities that have a high potential for painful consequences (e.g., engaging in unrestrained buying sprees, sexual indiscretions, or foolish business investments).

C. The episode is associated with an unequivocal change in functioning that is uncharacteristic of the individual when not symptomatic.

D. The disturbance in mood and the change in functioning are observable by others.

E. The episode is not severe enough to cause marked impairment in social or occupational functioning, or to necessitate hospitalization. If there are psychotic features, the episode is, by definition, manic.

F. The episode is not attributable to the physiological effects of a substance (e.g., a drug of abuse, a medication, other treatment).

Source: Reprinted with permission from the *Diagnostic and Statistical Manual of Mental Disorders,* Fifth Edition, (Copyright 2013). American Psychiatric Association.

diagnosis of disruptive mood dysregulation disorder (American Psychiatric Association, 2013). Of course, premenstrual dysphoric disorder is only diagnosed in females.

Diagnostic reliability varies among the mood disorders. Brown and his colleagues (2001) reported good to excellent reliability when a general mood disorder was the principal *DSM-IV* diagnosis (up to 0.72) and good reliability for the specific diagnosis of major depressive disorder. The reliability for dysthymic disorder (0.22) was poor, however. In the

## *Table 11-1*    DSM-5 Depressive and Bipolar Disorders

| Disorder | Key Symptoms | Minimum Duration Required for Diagnosis | Sex Ratio |
|----------|-------------|------------------------------------------|-----------|
| Major depressive disorder | Presence of major depressive episode | 2 weeks | More common among females |
| Persistent depressive disorder (dysthymia) | Persistent depressed mood, usually including major depressive episode | 2 years | More common among females |
| Premenstrual dysphoric disorder | Mood lability and irritability during most menses | 1 year | None |
| Disruptive mood dysregulation disorder | Before age 10, recurrent severe temper outbursts | 3 or more times per week, for 12 months | More common among males |
| Bipolar I disorder | Presence of manic episode | 1 week | Equal |
| Bipolar II disorder | Major depressive episode plus hypomanic episode | 2 weeks | More common among females |
| Cyclothymic disorder | Recurrent depression and hypomania, without major depressive or manic episodes | 2 years | Slightly more common in females |

Source: Reprinted with permission from the *Diagnostic and Statistical Manual of Mental Disorders,* Fifth Edition, (Copyright 2013). American Psychiatric Association.

*DSM-5* field trials, a kappa reliability of only 0.25 was found for major depressive disorder, earning a "questionable" rating, while bipolar I disorder produced a "good" kappa of 0.56 (Regier, et al., 2013).

The mood disorders include a variety of qualifiers that further describe their onset, pattern, or severity, in addition to the "with mixed features" specifier described above. With the exception of the less extreme disorders (e.g., dysthymic and cyclothymic disorders), the qualifiers can include a rating of severity (mild, moderate, or severe); if the severity is high, an indication is included as to whether psychotic symptoms are present or not. If echolalia, **echopraxia**, or disturbances in motor activity are dominant among the symptoms of bipolar I disorder or major depressive disorder, the qualification "with catatonic features" can be added. The "melancholic features" qualifier describes particularly deep depression, which tends to be worse in the morning and is characterized by loss of pleasure in nearly all things, significant anorexia or weight loss, psychomotor changes, and early morning wakening. (In practice, the melancholic qualifier may be seen as an indication of need for more active intervention, including electroconvulsive therapy.) If the mood disorder has onset within 4 weeks of childbirth, the qualifier "with postpartum onset" is added. In some recurrent mood conditions, symptoms appear to cycle with the time of year; these can be indicated by a "seasonal pattern" qualifier. Most often, the seasonal forms of mood disorders are more severe in the winter months, corresponding to a shorter period of daylight. The *DSM-5* added an "anxious distress" specifier for mood conditions with anxiety symptoms.

## 11.2 Depressive Disorders

### 11.2a Major Depressive Disorder

Major depressive disorder is the most commonly diagnosed disorder among adults (Craighead, Hart, Craighead, & Ilardi, 2002). As many as 1 in 4 females experience major depressive disorder at some point in their lives; the risk for males is about half of that. The average age of onset is in the mid-20s, but the condition can appear at any point in life. Generally, younger people tend to have higher overall rates of depression than those in later life. The diagnosis requires the presence of a major depressive episode, which itself has a 2-week duration requirement, without any history of either manic or hypomanic episodes. The condition may consist of a single depressive episode, which remits and never recurs. More commonly (in some 60% of cases), a second episode occurs although the episodes may be separated by several years. Depression becomes more likely to recur with each additional episode that an individual suffers. Of those having a second episode, 70% have a third; of those having three episodes, 90% have a fourth (American Psychiatric Association, 2000).

Major depressive disorder can be associated with general medical conditions and health status; up to a fourth of those with diabetes, cancer, or heart conditions develop depression during the course of their medical problems. It may be preceded, or followed, by dysthymic disorder, and almost 10% of those having a single episode of major depressive disorder eventually develop a manic episode (and bipolar I disorder). Depression commonly co-occurs with certain anxiety disorders (e.g., panic disorder), substance use disorders, eating disorders, and some personality disorders. Homosexual males and females report a much higher rate of major depression than do heterosexuals (Cochran, Sullivan, & Mays, 2003). A significant risk of mortality exists: up to 15% of those with major depressive

Homosexual males and females report a much higher rate of major depression than do heterosexuals. (Shutterstock)

**Echopraxia**

Repetitively imitating the movements of others

disorder die by suicide (American Psychiatric Association, 2000). Major depressive disorder has a 12-month prevalence of about 7% in the United States; it is 3 times more prevalent in young adults than in the elderly (American Psychiatric Association, 2013).

## 11.2b Persistent Depressive Disorder (Dysthymia)

The symptoms of persistent depressive disorder can be as severe as, and longer in duration than, major depressive disorder. The condition, new to the *DSM-5*, essentially combines major depressive disorder with the more persistent but milder *DSM-IV* diagnosis of dysthymic disorder. It involves a nearly continuous state of depressed mood that has lasted for 2 years without much respite. As mentioned above, dysthymic disorder appeared less reliable than other mood disorders. The *DSM-5* task force concluded that there was little to support the separation of the two disorders. As now conceptualized, persistent depressive disorder requires fewer of the symptoms than are required for a major depressive episode (that is, a major depressive episode is not a requirement for the diagnosis), but does not limit the number of symptoms experienced; thus, most will probably experience major depressive episodes during the 2-year course, and in fact, may continuously meet the full criteria for that period (i.e., chronic major depressive disorder). *DSM-5* estimates 12-month prevalence to be 0.5% for persistent depressive disorder and 1.5% for chronic major depressive disorder (American Psychiatric Association, 2013).

*wears you out. Always gloomy. Not as severe as major.*

## 11.2c Disruptive Mood Dysregulation Disorder

Another new diagnosis in the *DSM-5* is disruptive mood dysregulation disorder (see *DSM-5* Diagnostic Criteria for Disruptive Mood Dysregulation Disorder). The condition involves chronic, severe irritability, manifested by temper outbursts beginning before 10 years of age and extending to age 18. Temper may be expressed verbally or physically, involving aggression against people or physical objects. Outbursts must be persistent (three times per week or more), and cross-situational (in at least two settings). In large part, the condition was introduced to stem the increasing diagnosis of bipolar I disorder in children, by offering a category that covered non-episodic irritability. Although the criteria give an age window of 6 to 18, it is not recommended for children under age 7. Age of onset must be by 10 years of age. The prevalence is estimated at 2%–5%. Children with disruptive mood dysregulation disorder often show the symptoms of attention-deficit/hyperactivity disorder as well, and are at risk for depressive and anxiety disorders as adults (American Psychiatric Association, 2013).

## 11.2d Premenstrual Dysphoric Disorder

Premenstrual dysphoric disorder graduated from a proposed diagnosis in the *DSM-IV* to a depressive disorder in *DSM-5*. It concerns mood lability, irritability, and depressive symptoms during most menstrual periods during the preceding year. The symptoms, which can include anger, anxiety, tension, and at least one physical sign of depression, must be present before menses, improve after menses onset, and become minimal by a week after menses. According to the *DSM-5*, this is not a culture-bound condition and occurs around the globe, although culture may influence the expression of symptoms. Its incidence may be as high as 5.8% of menstruating women (American Psychiatric Association, 2013). Some research has indicated that women with the condition have lower pain thresholds

Premenstrual dysphoric disorder (commonly known as premenstrual syndrome or PMS) is a new depressive diagnosis in the *DSM-5*. (Shutterstock)

| DSM-5 | Diagnostic Criteria for Disruptive Mood Dysregulation Disorder |

296.99 (F34.8) Disruptive Mood Dysregulation Disorder

A. Severe recurrent temper outbursts manifested verbally (e.g., verbal rages) and/or behaviorally (e.g., physical aggression toward people or property) that are grossly out of proportion in intensity or duration to the situation or provocation.

B. The temper outbursts are inconsistent with developmental level.

C. The temper outbursts occur, on average, three or more times per week.

D. The mood between temper outbursts is persistently irritable or angry most of the day, nearly every day, and is observable by others (e.g., parents, teachers, peers).

E. Criteria A–D have been present for 12 or more months. Throughout that time, the individual has not had a period lasting 3 or more consecutive months without all of the symptoms in Criteria A–D.

F. Criteria A and D are present in at least two or three settings (i.e., at home, at school, with peers) and are severe in at least one of these.

G. The diagnosis should not be made for the first time before age 6 years or after age 18 years.

H. By history or observation, the age of onset of criteria A–E is before 10 years.

I. There has never been a distinct period lasting more than 1 day during which the full symptom criteria, except duration, for a manic or hypomanic episode have been met.
Note: Developmentally appropriate mood elevation, such as occurs in the context of a highly positive event or its anticipation, should not be considered as a symptom of mania or hypomania.

J. The behaviors do not occur exclusively during an episode of major depressive disorder and are not better explained by another mental disorder (e.g., autism spectrum disorder, posttraumatic stress disorder, separation anxiety disorder, persistent depressive disorder [dysthymia]).
Note: This diagnosis cannot coexist with oppositional defiant disorder, intermittent explosive disorder, or bipolar disorder, though it can coexist with others, including major depressive disorder, attention-deficit/hyperactivity disorder, conduct disorder, and substance use disorders. Individuals whose symptoms meet the criteria for both disruptive mood dysregulation disorder and oppositional defiant disorder should only be given the diagnosis of disruptive mood dysregulation disorder. If an individual has ever experienced a manic or hypomanic episode, the diagnosis of disruptive mood dysregulation disorder should not be assigned.

K. The symptoms are not attributable to the physiological effects of a substance or to another medical or neurological condition.

Source: Reprinted with permission from the *Diagnostic and Statistical Manual of Mental Disorders,* Fifth Edition, (Copyright 2013). American Psychiatric Association.

and experience pain more intensely; this is associated with lower beta-endorphin levels in the blood (Straneva, et al., 2007). A survey of 3,965 women in the U.S. indicated that women with premenstrual dysphoric disorder were more likely to experience suicidal ideation and more likely to make suicide attempts than those without the disturbance (Pilver, Libby, & Hoff, 2013).

# 11.2e Other Depressive Disorders

Many different medications and drugs, and medical conditions such as hypothyroidism, can also produce severe depressive episodes. If the mood disturbance can be traced to substance intoxication, substance withdrawal, or exposure to a medication (e.g., alcohol, hallucinogen, opioid, L-dopa) the appropriate diagnosis would be substance/medication-induced depressive disorder. If it can be directly linked to a medical condition such as Huntington's disease, stroke, or brain injury, the diagnosis would be depressive disorder due to another medical condition.

| **DSM-5** | **Diagnostic Criteria for Premenstrual Dysphoric Disorder** |
| --- | --- |

625.4 (N94.3) Premenstrual Dysphoric Disorder

A. In the majority of menstrual cycles, at least five symptoms must be present in the final week before the onset of menses, start to improve within a few days after the onset of menses, and become minimal or absent in the week post menses.

B. One (or more) of the following symptoms must be present:
   1. Marked affective lability (e.g., mood swings, feeling suddenly sad or tearful, or increased sensitivity to rejection).
   2. Marked irritability or anger or increased interpersonal conflicts.
   3. Marked depressed mood, feelings of hopelessness, or self-depreciating thoughts.
   4. Marked anxiety, tension, and/or feelings of being keyed up or on edge.

C. One (or more) of the following symptoms must additionally be present, to reach a total of five symptoms when combined with symptoms of Criterion B above.
   1. Decreased interest in usual activities (e.g., work, school, friends, hobbies).
   2. Subjective difficulty in concentration.
   3. Lethargy, easy fatigability, or marked lack of energy.
   4. Marked change in appetite, overeating, or specific food cravings.
   5. Hypersomnia or insomnia.
   6. A sense of being overwhelmed or out of control.
   7. Physical symptoms such as breast tenderness or swelling, joint or muscle pain, a sensation of "bloating," or weight gain.
   **Note:** The symptoms in Criteria A–C must have been met for most menstrual cycles that occurred in the preceding year.

D. The symptoms are associated with clinically significant distress or interference with work, school, usual social activities, or relations with others (e.g., avoidance of social activities; decreased productivity and efficiency at work, school, or home).

E. The disturbance is not merely the exacerbation of the symptoms of another disorder, such as a major depressive disorder, panic disorder, persistent depressive disorder (dysthymia), or a personality disorder (although it may co-occur with any of these disorders).

F. Criterion A should be confirmed by prospective daily ratings during at least two symptomatic cycles. (**Note:** The diagnosis may be made provisionally prior to this confirmation.)

G. The symptoms are not attributable to the physiological effects of a substance (e.g., a drug of abuse, a medication, other treatment) or another medical condition (e.g., hyperthyroidism).

Source: Reprinted with permission from the *Diagnostic and Statistical Manual of Mental Disorders,* Fifth Edition, (Copyright 2013). American Psychiatric Association.

# 11.3 Causal Factors in Depressive Disorders

The causes of major depressive disorder (which has received much more attention) and persistent depressive disorder have been the targets of much research over the past century. There is strong evidence for biological and psychological involvement in the development of depression,

> **What are the causes of depressive and bipolar disorders?**

although (like schizophrenia) no necessary or sufficient causal influences have been identified. Nonetheless, several contributory causal conditions have been identified.

## 11.3a Biological Components

*Genetic Factors*

Major depressive disorder occurs more commonly within families, and its prevalence may be 3 times higher among first-degree relatives of people with the condition. Twin and family studies show a moderate degree of genetic influence, with heritability estimates of about 42% for females and about 29% for males, based on Swedish twin studies (Kendler, Gatz, Gardner, & Pederson, 2006). There have been many genetic investigations into depression, but no specific genetic basis for depression has been reliably supported. A recent example involves the 5-HTT serotonin-transporter gene on chromosome 17, which was apparently associated (in its short homozygote form) with increased risk of depression following stressful life events (Caspi, et al., 2003). The usefulness of this genotype in predicting depression after stress was partially confirmed by other studies as well (Goldberg D., 2006). However, a newer meta-analysis of published data involving the 5-HTT gene and depression found no evidence that the genotype was associated with depression in men or women or that the genotype improved the prediction of depression over that of stressful life events alone (Risch, et al., 2009).

Major depressive disorder occurs more commonly within families, and its prevalence may be 3 times higher among first-degree relatives of people with the condition. (Shutterstock)

## Biochemical Factors

The biochemical basis of depression has been intensively studied since the development of the early antidepressant medications. Like the dopamine hypothesis in schizophrenia, the **monoamine hypothesis** of depression developed out of attempts to understand how antidepressant medications worked in the brain. In the early 1950s, a chemical called iproniazid was synthesized for the treatment of tuberculosis. Physicians noticed that this drug seemed to make some patients mildly euphoric. When iproniazid was given to depressed patients, it was, indeed, found to be moderately successful in relieving their symptoms.

Animal research indicated that iproniazid increased the concentration of the neurotransmitters norepinephrine (NE) and serotonin (5-HTT) in the brain. These neurotransmitters are members of the catecholamine and indolamine classes of the biogenic amines. (Dopamine, the neurotransmitter implicated in schizophrenia, is a catecholamine neurotransmitter as well.) These bioamines are synthesized from amino acid precursor substances (see Figure 11-1). Although the activity of the biogenic amines cannot be directly measured in real time in a living person, their metabolites (MHPG, HVA, and 5-HIAA) can be measured in spinal fluid, blood, and urine.

**Monoamine hypothesis**

Hypothesis that depression is caused by a deficiency of certain monoamine neurotransmitters in the brain

It was subsequently discovered that iproniazid had its effect on monoamine levels by inhibiting an enzyme, monoamine oxidase, that breaks down NE and 5-HT in the synapse as part of the neurotransmitter metabolism and re-uptake cycle. By preventing the breakdown of these amines, iproniazid effectively increased their concentration in the synapse. Other drugs that inhibited monoamine oxidase were also found to be useful in reducing depression in some patients. At about the same time, it was noticed that a new drug being used to treat high blood pressure, reserpine, occasionally induced depressive reactions. Animal studies showed reserpine depleted norepinephrine and serotonin in the brain. The finding that drugs that increase monoamines alleviate depression, while drugs that deplete monoamines induce depression, produced the monoamine hypothesis, which proposes that depression is caused by a relative depletion of monoamines in the brain.

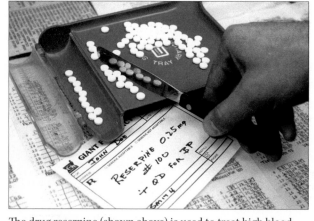

The drug reserpine (shown above) is used to treat high blood pressure, but can occasionally induce depressive reactions. Animal studies showed that reserpine depleted norepinephrine and serotonin in the brain which led to a depressed mood. (Wikimedia Commons)

Other antidepressant drugs, the tricyclics, were later developed and were found to increase the available amounts of NE. Unlike the monoamine oxidase inhibitor

*Figure 11-1*  **Precursors and Metabolic Products of Two Groups of Biogenic Amines**

Source: Adapted from Akiskal, H. S., & McKinney, W. T. (1975). Overview of recent research on depression. *Archives of General Psychiatry, 32,* 285–304.

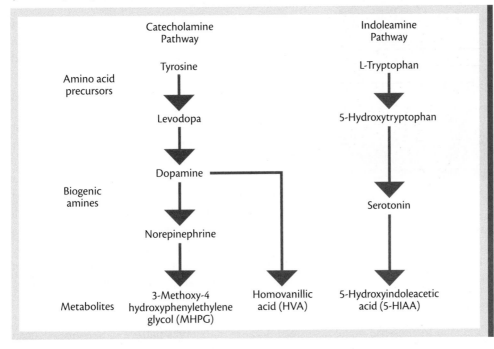

(MAO-I) drugs, the tricyclic drugs block the reuptake process and, thereby, also increase the synaptic levels of norepinephrine. More recent medications, the selective serotonin reuptake inhibitors (SSRIs), have less effect on NE and more on 5-HT re-uptake.

It is easy to imagine how the depletion of a neurotransmitter could produce symptoms of depression. If the number of neurons being activated is greatly reduced, one might expect to see the cognitive and behavioral slowing, the reduction in energy, and the unresponsiveness observed in depression. Conversely, if the number of neurons being activated is greatly increased, the overactivity associated with mania might be expected. Evidence in support of the monoamine hypothesis has been inconsistent, however. There is little indication that depression can be directly linked to levels of monoamines; in fact, studies often find normal levels of NE and 5-HT in depressed groups, and serotonin depletion manipulations do not reliably produce depression (France, Lysaker, & Robinson, 2007). Further, there is no logical requirement that the effect of a medication reveals the underlying cause of a disorder; aspirin relieves headaches, but headaches are not, therefore, caused by a lack of aspirin. Reviewing the monoamine hypothesis and other chemical imbalance theories of depression, Valenstein (1998) concludes that while many in the pharmaceutical industry confidently assert that neurochemical imbalances cause depression, the evidence is often directly contradictory to that claim.

## Hormonal Dysregulation

The relationship between depression and stressful events indicates that the hypothalamic-pituitary-adrenal (HPA) axis (see Chapter 5) plays an important role in mood disorders. Conditions such as Cushing's syndrome and hypothyroidism, which affect the endocrine system and the adrenal cortex, are associated with increased risk for depression. The stress hormone cortisol is elevated in the blood of a sizable proportion of depressed patients; about half with major depressive disorder show abnormalities in the HPA system (Peterson & Benca, 2006).

Those observations led to searches to find a biological test for depression that could serve as a marker to distinguish those who became depressed after stressful life events ("reactive" or "exogenous" depressions) from those who became depressed due to internal biological dysfunctions ("endogenous" depressions). The *dexamethasone suppression test* (DST) was one such attempt. Dexamethasone is a synthetic hormone that normally suppresses the secretion of cortisol and reduces HPA activity. In some depressed people, however, dexamethasone fails to have this effect. Those nonresponders were presumed by DST proponents to be endogenously depressed (and, therefore, in need of medication rather than psychotherapy). Subsequent work, however, failed to support the DST as a specific marker for depression; instead, nonsuppression occurs in many other conditions including panic disorder (as well as in 10% of normals) and appears to be a general index of level of distress. As a result, the DST is no longer considered a useful marker (Valenstein, 1998). The reactive-endogenous distinction has also been largely abandoned because life events were found to be involved in the onset of most depressions first considered to be "endogenous." At this point, it appears likely that chronic stress can produce long-term HPA dysregulation in many people with major depressive disorder.

It is possible that hormonal factors underlie the gender differences in the incidence of depressive mood disorders. Because of its cyclic pattern in females, estrogen level has been implicated in risk for depression. (Shutterstock)

It is possible that hormonal factors underlie the gender differences in the incidence of unipolar (depressive) mood disorders. Because of its cyclic pattern in females, estrogen level has been implicated in risk for depression (Goldberg D., 2006). This hormone impacts neurotransmitter function, and fluctuating levels may confer susceptibility for mood changes. Mood disorders become more common in females after menarche and occur in the context of hormone-related changes such as in premenstrual dysphoric disorder, post-partum onset depression, and menopause (Steiner, Dunn, & Born, 2003). However, because hormonal levels fluctuate in all women, the unique nature of their involvement in the subset of women who become depressed remains uncertain.

> How are mood disorders different from normal variations in mood? How common are mood disorders?

## Sleep Dysregulation

The insomnia or hypersomnia characteristic of a major depressive episode suggest that sleep disturbances may play a role in depressive onset. There is evidence that the sleep cycle is disturbed in specific ways among depressed patients, and these disturbances may be seen even during periods of remission (Peterson & Benca, 2006). Normal sleep cycles progress through four stages of increasingly low-frequency brain waves (as seen on an electroencephalograph, or EEG), followed by a period of rapid eye movement (REM), all within a 90-minute cycle that repeats through the night. Among depressed people, the latency to REM onset is shortened (that is, REM begins more quickly after falling asleep), and REM sleep periods tend to last longer. Decreased time to REM onset is one of the most reliable sleep disturbances associated with depression. However, the significance of the sleep pattern differences in depression is not clear, and sleep dysregulation does not appear to distinguish unipolar from bipolar mood disorders.

## Neuroanatomy

Because it is known that some types of brain damage are associated with increased depressive symptomatology, efforts to identify abnormalities in the brains of depressed persons are continuing. Findings of reduced activity in the prefrontal cortex are consistent with other studies suggesting reduced volume of that area among depressed patients (Davidson, Pizzagalli, Nitschke, & Putnam, 2002). Evidence of various other differences in activity in the hippocampus, the amygdala, and the anterior cingulate cortex indicate that the brain is working differently in depressed people compared to normal people. EEG differences in activity between the brain hemispheres have also been found in some, but not all, studies with lowered left hemisphere activity more characteristic of depression. In general, depression appears to be associated with increased activity in the limbic system, perhaps together with decreased activity in areas that regulate limbic activity (Gotlib & Hamilton, 2008). However, none of these differences appear to be necessary for the disorder, and it remains unclear whether these neuroanatomical indicators precede depression onset, co-occur with the disorder, or result from expression of the disorder (Davidson, Pizzagalli, Nitschke, & Putnam, 2002).

## 11.3b Psychosocial Components

### The Psychoanalytic View

The psychoanalytic view stresses the significance of intrapsychic processes that originate early in life in the development of depression. Events that happen in the oral stage of psychosexual development are considered important in creating a susceptibility to later depressive reactions. According to this perspective, young infants' early interactions with their mothers inevitably involve both satisfactions and frustrations. Although mothers feed and hold infants, providing warmth, stimulation, and relief from painful stimuli, they cannot always provide satisfaction immediately or with total success. Infants, then, begin to perceive mothers as both good and bad. In this early stage of development, infants do not make a clear distinction between the external world (mother, in this case) and their own selves. One way the infants learn to deal with the world is by taking it inside; the process is called **introjection** or the early beginnings of identification. Thus they introject the image of the good-bad mother into their own self-image.

Decreased time to REM onset is one of the most reliable sleep disturbances associated with depression. (Shutterstock)

Introjection need not lead to serious psychological problems later unless the infant has experienced an unusually intense love for the "good" mother and hate for the "bad" mother. Psychoanalytic theory states, however, that when such an intensely ambivalent image of the good-bad mother has been introjected, then later in life when the child or adult experiences a loss, this intense love-hate conflict from early infancy is reactivated. The anger and hatred become directed inward against that part of the individual that is the introjected bad mother. This inward turning of aggression, then, presumably explains the depressed person's self-derogatory attitude that finds its ultimate expression in suicidal impulses. Some combination of the mother's actual behavior (severe deprivation, perhaps, or overindulgence mixed with occasional frustrations) and the infant's fantasies would determine whether such a depression-producing introjection occurs.

No empirical evidence is available to support or refute the psychodynamic perspective of depression as aggression-turned-inward. It is difficult, of course, to test a theory that rests on the mental imagery of infants.

### Infant-Mother Attachment

Others consider the child-mother relationship important in the development of mood disorders independent of the psychoanalytic perspective. Spitz (1946) observed infants of unwed mothers in an institutional nursery. Although the mothers were encouraged to spend considerable time with their babies, some had to be away from their infants for long

**Introjection**

In psychoanalytic theory, part of the process of identification, whereby a person incorporates or internalizes the characteristics of others

periods. From a sample of 123 infants observed during the first year of life, 19 were reported to have developed an obvious syndrome of depression. Sad facial expression, weeping, lack of responsiveness to environmental events, slowness of movement, loss of muscle tone, refusal to eat, insomnia, withdrawal, and apathy were evident. When their mothers came back, the children eventually returned to normalcy. This reaction occurred only in some infants whose mothers had to be away from them for about 3 months when the infants were between 6 and 10 months of age, but not in all such infants.

The quality of mother-infant attachment may be a contributing factor for depression. (Shutterstock)

In a later experimental study, Kaufman and Rosenblum (1967) separated four infant monkeys from their mothers but kept them with the father and another adult female. During separation, which lasted for 4 weeks, the infants displayed loud screams, agitated pacing and searching, and distress calls. These behaviors lasted for 24 to 36 hours, during which time the infants did not sleep. Afterward, three monkeys became inactive, stopped responding to or making social gestures, and ceased play behavior. They frequently sat hunched over, almost in a ball, with their heads between their legs. Their facial muscles sagged, and they presented the classical facial configuration of human dejection. They occasionally emitted a plaintive cooing sound. The monkeys gradually began to recover, and by the end of the month of separation the infants had almost returned to normal.

These early studies supported the view that the quality of the maternal relationship influenced risk for depression. Besides mother-infant separation early in life, the quality of infant-child attachment continues to be seen as a contributing factor for depression. Disruptions in attachment—including emotional detachment, maternal abuse, or maternal depression—serve to increase risk for depression (Goldberg D., 2006). However, there is much variability between individuals in the strength of these associations (Willerman & Cohen, 1990).

## Reduction of Positive Reinforcement

Since Skinner (1953), the behavioral perspective has assumed that depression is related to a relative loss of positive reinforcement and pleasure. Ferster (1973) and Lewinsohn (1974) suggested that the apathy and lack of responsiveness associated with depression result from a lack of contingent positive reinforcement for nondepressed behavior. In some ways, then, depression is similar to being in a state of extinction. This situation could come about in several ways:

(a) Few events may be reinforcing. Some depressed persons may simply experience attention or social responsiveness as less reinforcing than do other people. As a result, the motivation to act is not present.

(b) Fewer reinforcing events are available. Depressed persons may have fewer friends and others to whom they can turn for reinforcing interaction. The death of a loved one or the breakup of a relationship, for example, might be especially devastating to a person who has few alternative sources for interpersonal satisfactions.

(c) Social reinforcements may be available and, in fact, reinforcing, but the depressed person may lack the social skills necessary to obtain these reinforcements.

(d) Persons may not only lack skill in initiating and maintaining enjoyable social interaction, they may also have developed response styles that are aversive to others and that actually drive people away. This effect was shown in an experiment conducted by Coyne (1976). Female college students were asked to talk for 20 minutes on the telephone to a depressed female outpatient, a non-depressed female outpatient, or a normal control female. Afterward, subjects who had talked to the depressed patients reported themselves to be significantly more depressed, anxious, and hostile than subjects who had talked to either of the other two types. They also were more rejecting of the depressed patients, expressing less willingness to interact with them in the future. If depressed persons manage to make talking to them an aversive experience, it would not be surprising if people began to avoid them, reducing even further their sources of social reinforcement.

(e) A final circumstance associated with low rates of positive social reinforcement is one in which an unusually high proportion of a person's behavior is controlled by negative reinforcement that is aimed at avoiding aversive consequences. A student, for example, spends long hours studying because she is afraid of the disapproval and criticism that accompany low grades or not completing college or not getting into graduate school. As another example, Forrest and Hokanson (1975) suggest that depressed individuals may have learned to make self-punitive responses in order to avoid aggressive responses from others. A life that is dominated by aversive control and has relatively little positive reinforcement might, in time, lead to depression.

## Cognitive Processes

Cognitive theorists, however, argue that it is the other way around: Persons feel depressed because they engage in depressed ways of thinking. Beck (1976) emphasized the role of cognitions in producing and maintaining depression. According to Beck these inner statements take three forms: (1) The person may *exaggerate the magnitude of obstacles*, responding to any minor frustration with thoughts such as "I might as well give up." (2) The person may *interpret relatively trivial events as important losses*. A wealthy businesswoman regards herself as poor whenever she hears of someone making more money than she does; a man who has to wait thirty seconds for an elevator thinks, "I'm losing valuable time." (3) The person may be continually *self-disparaging, magnifying criticisms and insults*. An outstanding student thinks whenever a teacher calls on another student, "She doesn't really think I'm smart or she would have called on me." A student who has difficulty getting a date on a single occasion thinks, "I must be repulsive to girls." Beck believes that persistent thoughts of this kind cause the person to feel and act in a depressed manner.

These inner statements, or **automatic thoughts**, tend to be pessimistic and negative. Rather than considering positive interpretations for events, the depressed person selectively accepts the most negative interpretation available and assumes that things will only get worse in the future. So, for Beck, a depressive cognitive triad characterizes depressive thinking: negative thoughts about the self, negative thoughts about the present, and negative thoughts about the future.

## Learned Helplessness

Seligman (1975) proposed a cognitive-behavioral theory of depression that centers on the person's belief that he or she has little control over the important events in his or her life. Seligman used the term **learned helplessness** to refer to this learned belief or expectation that there is nothing one can do to improve a bad situation. The idea of learned helplessness originated in animal experiments in which Seligman and his colleagues were studying the relationship of fear conditioning to instrumental learning. They found that dogs that received inescapable painful electric shocks (while restrained in a harness) were impaired in learning a future task in which they could avoid shock by jumping

**Automatic thoughts**

Covert self-statements, often pessimistic and negative, that occur readily and may contribute to depression

**Learned helplessness**

The theory that depression is caused by a lack of connection between responses and their outcomes (i.e., a lack of control over events)

Generally, animals with learned helplessness training show several symptoms similar to human depression, including loss of appetite, loss of sleep, passivity, and weight loss. (iStock)

over a barrier from one side of the box to another at a given signal. Similar impairment did not occur in naïve dogs, or in animals that had received prior escape training.

Subsequent work by Seligman and others, using variations of the triadic design methodology described in Chapter 5, explored the helplessness effect in different types of situations with different species. Generally, animals with learned helplessness training show several symptoms similar to human depression, including loss of appetite, loss of sleep, passivity, and loss of weight. Seligman (1975) concluded that depression was caused not by lack of reinforcement but by learning that responses have no connection with outcomes—the result of which is helplessness in future situations.

There is considerable animal research showing that the unavoidable stress that produces learned helplessness also produces lowered levels of brain norepinephrine. Although different investigators disagree as to whether the helplessness is first learned and then produces the lowered levels of NE, or the lowered levels of NE come first and cause the observed helplessness (Seligman M. P., 1975; Weiss, Kruger, Danielson, & Elman, 1974), there is agreement that uncontrollable and/or unpredictable environmental stresses cause NE depletion, providing a good model of how psychological events can impact brain chemistry.

Learned helplessness as an explanation of human depression, however, received considerable criticism (e.g., Wortman & Dintzer, 1978). It was reformulated as an **attribution model of depression** by Abrahamson, Seligman, and Teasdale (1997). They proposed that attributions about the causes of events are made across three dimensions: internal-external, stable-unstable, and global-specific. If an attempt to do something ends in failure, people can attribute the failure to internal factors ("I'm stupid") or to external factors ("the task was impossible"); to stable conditions ("it's the way I am") or to unstable conditions ("I did not sleep well"); and to global ("I'm not capable") or to specific ("I had the wrong tools") factors. In this cognitive form of the model, depression is caused by a pessimistic attribution style that employs internal, stable, and global accounts of personal problems.

Students gather in Holden Hall during the massacre at Virginia Tech on April 16, 2007. More attention is being paid to such incidents usually regarding the perpetrator's mental health. (Wikimedia Commons)

enviroment plays a role.
malibu vs.
chicago.

**Attribution model of depression**

View that depression is caused by a pessimistic attribution style that emphasizes internal, stable, and global factors to explain personal problems

### Other Psychosocial Factors

There appear to be many other life events that can contribute to risk for unipolar mood disorders. Stressful life events are strongly related to onset of depression, especially when they are experienced as uncontrollable or unpredictable. For example, sexual or physical abuse in childhood is clearly related to later depressive conditions (Goldberg D., 2006). Further, the number of stressful life events is directly associated with the incidence of depression (Risch, et al., 2009). The intensity of stressors required to trigger depression appears to be less for each successive recurrence of the depressive episode, and recurrent depression is related to a reduction in volume of the hippocampus, presumably as the result of toxic stress hormones (Monroe & Harkness, 2005). Much attention has turned to the serious impacts of bullying, following highly publicized school shootings across the United States. Interestingly, in a Danish sample of 2,348 boys, those who frequently bullied others at age 8 were more likely to show depression and suicidal activity by age 18; however, the victims of bullying were not themselves at increased risk (Klomek, et al., 2008).

## 11.4 Treatment of Depressive Disorders

There is a strong tendency toward "spontaneous" recovery and recurrence in the mood disorders. Morrison, Winokur, Crowe, and Clancy (1973) reported follow-up ratings on 87 patients with bipolar disorders, 202 with unipolar depression, and 183 poor-premorbid schizophrenics. The results are striking. After 5 years, approximately 80% of the patients with mood disorders had recovered, compared to less than a third of those with poor-premorbid or process schizophrenia (see Figure 11-2). These patients were hospitalized before either electroconvulsive treatment or antidepressive drugs were used at their hospital; thus these data tend to show the "natural" or untreated course of the disorders.

Recent work employing more precise diagnostic criteria finds similar remission rates for major depressive disorder (between 70% and 75% for both genders over a 2-year period), although remission is slowed when a personality disorder is also present (Grilo, et al., 2005). Bipolar remission rates are lower, however, with about half of the patients showing sustained remission or improvement over a 10-year period (Goldberg & Harrow, 2004). It should be remembered that for the majority of sufferers, mood disorders are recurrent, dramatically increasing their impact on public health. Still, in the context of such levels of "spontaneous" improvement, it might be expected that treatment effects could be overestimated. In fact, the placebo response is quite high in outcome studies of depression, making the identification of effective treatments more difficult. However, a variety of biological and psychological interventions have been shown to be effective in treating the unipolar depressions.

> **Do mood disorders improve without treatment?**

## 11.4a  Biological Treatments

### Medication

Antidepressant medications are demonstrably effective in many randomized, placebo-controlled studies although no particular antidepressant has been consistently shown to be more effective than others (Nemeroff & Schatzberg, 2002). Typically, medication is effective for 50%–70% of outpatients in alleviating depression (Thase & Kupfer, 1996). All of these medications work to increase the levels of neurotransmitters (especially NE and

*Figure 11-2*
**Percentage of Recovery in Patients Over Time**

Follow-up information was obtained at different times for different groups of patients, so each point on the curves represents a different group of patients.

Source: Adapted from Morrison, J., Winokur, G., Crowe, R., & Clancy, J. (1973). The Iowa 500: The first follow-up. *Archives of General Psychiatry, 29,* 678–682.

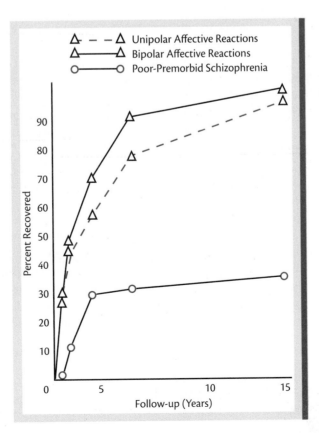

5-HT) within the synaptic cleft. The primary differences between the different classes of antidepressants concern side effects and safety. Tricyclics and MAO-Is are less well tolerated by patients because of a variety of unpleasant side effects, including dry mouth, blurred vision, constipation, and weight gain. They are also less effective for depression with psychotic features. MAO-Is have the disadvantage of requiring multiple doses per day. Further, to prevent possibly serious hypertensive crises, patients on these drugs must avoid certain foods that contain the amino acid tyramine, including chocolate, cheese, and some meats and wines. With these side effects and restrictions, the tricyclics and MAO-Is are associated with poorer patient compliance in treatment. In addition, the antidepressive effects of medication are typically not seen for several weeks. Because depressed patients are at increased risk of suicide, overdose is an important consideration with these classes of antidepressants since a fatal overdose may require less than a 2-week supply of pills.

For those reasons, SSRIs are generally the first-line medical treatments for depression at present, and they are among the most widely prescribed of all drugs. Studies comparing the effectiveness of SSRIs and tricylics generally indicate similar rates of improvement, with SSRIs showing lower discontinuation rates due to intolerance. They also present a much lower risk of overdose and produce milder side effects (which can include nervousness, insomnia, nausea, and sexual dysfunction). Either alone or in combination with other antidepressants, these therapies have received research support in the treatment of major depressive disorder and dysthymic disorder. However, relapse remains a significant problem—especially when medication is discontinued; the risk can be reduced, but not eliminated, by continuation of pharmacotherapy (Thase & Kupfer, 1996).

Unfortunately, in such a lucrative pharmaceutical market, there have been some troubling revelations about outcome research on antidepressant medications. A study by Turner and his colleagues (2008) reviewed the data on outcome trials involving 12,564 patients, submitted by pharmaceutical companies to the Food and Drug Administration (FDA) between 1987 and 2004 as part of the drug approval process. The data contained outcome results for 12 different medications, including widely prescribed drugs marketed as Zoloft, Prozac, and Effexor by major drug companies (Eli Lilly, Pfizer, and Wyeth, respectively). Some of these trials submitted to the FDA reported positive outcomes while others did not. Turner and his colleagues (2008), however, found a strong publication bias in the professional literature: 37 of 38 trials reporting positive results for antidepressants were subsequently published in psychiatric journals; yet of the 36 studies that reported negative or questionable outcomes, only 14 made it into print, and those that did were worded to convey the impression of positive outcomes. Put another way, 48 of 51 published studies (94%) reported positive outcomes, while the FDA database registered only 38 of 74 studies (51%) as reporting positive results. According to the authors, the effect of such selective publication is to over-inflate each drug's reported superiority to placebo in the literature.

High rates of placebo response in studies of antidepressant medication were already a concern, although the placebo condition is not the same as no-treatment, since patients receive much contact and attention from staff, which may alone have therapeutic benefit (Nemeroff & Schatzberg, 2002). Kirsch and his colleagues (2002) reviewed data submitted to the FDA for the top six antidepressant medications between 1987 and 1999, and concluded that only 18% of the response to medication was the result of the pharmacological components; the remaining effect was duplicated in placebo groups. They concluded that the clinical significance of the slight superiority of drugs over placebo was questionable. These issues notwithstanding, the SSRIs remain among the most widely prescribed of all medications and are routinely given to depressed patients as the first (and often only) treatment intervention.

## Electroconvulsive Therapy

Two Italian psychiatrists, Cerletti and Bini, first introduced **electroconvulsive therapy (ECT)** in 1933. In the original treatment, two electrodes were placed on either side of the head at the temples, and a voltage of about 100 volts AC was applied briefly ( from 0.1 to 0.5 of a second).

**Electroconvulsive therapy (ECT)**

Therapeutic induction of convulsive seizures by applying electrical current to the head; found to have some effectiveness with severe depressions

*Non-drug treatments are healthier and more effective in the long run.*

The electric current produced a convulsive seizure (similar to *grand mal epilepsy*) that lasted for 40 to 60 seconds. Patients lost consciousness immediately and did not regain it for several minutes. They were likely to be somewhat confused and dazed for an hour or so afterward.

The procedure has been refined so that it is no longer as unpleasant or as likely to cause physical injury to the patient. ECT is now typically applied unilaterally rather than bilaterally, most often over the non-dominant hemisphere of the brain. A short-acting sedative drug and a muscle relaxant are frequently administered intravenously before treatment, putting the person to sleep so that the strong muscle contractions will not fracture any bones. Ordinarily treatments are given two to five times a week for a total of 2 to ten treatments, depending on how quickly improvement occurs.

Although ECT has many critics, it seems to work more quickly and possibly with a higher percentage of patients than do the antidepressant drugs (Avery & Winokur, 1977). At one time, in the 1940s and 1950s, ECT enjoyed widespread use with almost all forms of psychotic disorders, including schizophrenia. Research, however, consistently showed that its effectiveness is limited to severe depressive and obsessive-compulsive symptoms. Memory loss as a side effect has long been a significant problem for some patients. Ernest Hemingway received two series of electroconvulsive treatments and complained bitterly to his friend and biographer, A. E. Hotchner (1966), about how his memory was wrecked and how he was ruined as a writer. "What is the sense of ruining my head and erasing my memory, which is my capital, and putting me out of business?"

Still, ECT works quickly for depression, and ECT response rates for those who do not respond to medication range from 50%–60% (Thase & Kupfer, 1996). ECT has been shown to be superior to antidepressant medications or placebos in controlled randomized trials, and remains important in the treatment of severe and resistant forms of depression (Pagnin, de Queiroz, Pini, & Cassano, 2004). It remains an effective intervention, although the mechanisms of its action are unclear and the relapse rate after treatment is high. In recent years it has been used much less commonly and after other interventions have been unsuccessful.

### Transcranial Magnetic Stimulation

As noted in Chapter 3, there are a variety of new brain stimulation techniques, including vagus nerve stimulation and **transcranial magnetic stimulation (TMS)**, which seek the effectiveness of ECT without producing seizures. Repetitive transcranial magnetic stimulation (rTMS) uses several short pulses of magnetic stimulation, at sub-seizure thresholds, to stimulate areas of the cortex. Several demonstrations of effective use of rTMS are available in the literature, and some reviewers conclude the approach is promising in depression treatment (e.g., Marangell, Martinez, Jurdi, & Zboyan, 2007). Other reviews, however, have concluded that it is no more effective than sham therapy (Couturier, 2005). In a recent randomized controlled trial, rTMS was much less effective in producing short-term relief than ECT (Knapp, et al., 2008). Neither approach produced long-term improvements. However, newer data have been reported that indicate daily TMS for 4 to 6 weeks was effective in treatment-resistant patients with unipolar, nonpsychotic depression, and improvements were maintained at a 1-year follow-up (Cassels, 2013).

## 11.4b Psychological Treatments

A variety of psychotherapies have been demonstrated effective in the treatment of unipolar depression. Chambless and his colleagues (1998) include interpersonal therapy, behavioral therapy and cognitive therapy among the well-established psychological interventions for depression, and brief dynamic therapy, self-control therapy, and social problem-solving therapy as probably efficacious treatments. Several reviews have concluded that certain psychotherapies are equally effective as medication and have lower risk of relapse in the treatment of unipolar depression.

**BVT** *Lab*

Visit **www.BVTLab.com** to explore the student resources available for this chapter.

**Transcranial magnetic stimulation (TMS)**

Pulsed magnetic stimulation of the brain, as a treatment for severe depression

## Cognitive Therapy

Beck's cognitive-behavior therapy has been the most extensively evaluated treatment, and several controlled trials support its effectiveness as at least equivalent to standard antidepressant medications (Craighead, Hart, Craighead, & Ilardi, 2002). It appears to have a protective effect against relapse, with 1-year relapse rates of approximately 25%, compared to 50% for antidepressant medication (Gloaguen, Cottraux, Cucherat, & Blackburn, 1998). The therapy typically involves identifying and challenging dysfunctional belief patterns (or schemas) about the self and the world, which are characteristic of depressive thinking. Through a process of testing the validity of these depressive cognitions and engaging in more objective evaluation of events, depressive thinking can be modified. It is often combined with behavioral "homework" to increase activity levels, practice newly acquired personal skills, and counteract the prevailing perspective of self-failure. The evidence supporting cognitive therapy for depression has made it the "gold standard" against which other psychotherapies have been compared.

Cognitive therapy typically involves identifying and challenging dysfunctional belief patterns (or schemas) about the self and the world, which are characteristics of depressive thinking.
(Shutterstock)

## Behavioral Therapy

Consistent findings also support behavioral therapy as effective for depression (Craighead, Hart, Craighead, & Ilardi, 2002). Several positive reviews have recently appeared comparing behavioral approaches with other psychotherapies. A literature review of randomized trials by Ekers, Richards, and Gilbody (2007), for example, concluded that behavioral therapy was superior to brief psychotherapy and supportive therapy, yet equivalent to cognitive therapy, leading the authors to question whether adding cognitive components to a simpler behavioral intervention would be useful in treatment of most patients.

A variety of techniques are used within behavioral therapy approaches to treating depression, including self-reinforcement and social skills training. In an early illustration, Fuchs and Rehm (1977) devised a training procedure to increase self-reward and decrease self-punishment among depressed subjects. First, they taught their depressed women to attend more to positive or successful events, to set realistic, step-by-step goals for behavioral change, and to provide themselves with generous, self-administered rewards contingent on successfully completing each small step toward their goals. This 6-week program resulted in significant decreases in both self-report and behavioral measures of depression.

Behavioral activation seeks to institute behavior change by increasing activity levels and by encouraging approach, rather than avoidance, of difficult situations (Dimidjian, Martell, Addis, & Herman-Dunn, 2008). It teaches coping skills with the goal of increasing behavior in contexts where reinforcing results are likely. Techniques include self-monitoring, scheduling of goal-directed activities, and addressing specific behavioral deficits. In a recent controlled study involving 241 subjects with major depressive disorder, behavioral activation was equivalent to antidepressant medication and superior to cognitive therapy in acute intervention for more severely depressed persons (Dimidjian, et al., 2006). A subsequent randomized trial comparing cognitive therapy, antidepressant medication, and behavioral activation by Dobson and his colleagues (2008) found both cognitive therapy and behavioral activation at least as effective as continued medication at a 1-year follow-up, as well as a 2-year follow-up, after medication was discontinued. Cognitive therapy and behavioral activation also showed lower risk of relapse compared to medication. Behavioral activation appeared more effective than cognitive therapy with the more severely depressed patients, but it did not differ significantly from cognitive therapy in other outcome measures. Dobson and his colleagues (2008) conclude that behavioral activation is a relatively simple, cost-effective and enduring intervention. Other meta-analyses of treatment literature (Cuijpers, Van Straten, & Warmerdam, 2005) also support the effectiveness of behavioral activation as an uncomplicated and efficient treatment for depression that produces enduring improvement.

## Other Psychotherapies

Interpersonal therapy focuses on identification and improvement of a person's difficulties in interpersonal functioning (including grief, isolation, disputes, and role transitions), especially with family members. It has been demonstrated in randomized controlled trials to be effective in major depressive disorder (Craighead, Hart, Craighead, & Ilardi, 2002). Other newer psychotherapies are demonstrating effectiveness as well. Acceptance and commitment therapy was equivalent to cognitive therapy for depression in a recent randomized controlled trial (Forman, Herbert, Moitra, Yeomas, & Geller, 2007). Seligman, Rashid, and Parks (2006) outline an approach to treating depression that does not focus on depressive cognitions but rather on positive thinking about events. "Positive psychotherapy" seeks to increase engagement and positive emotions through practice. Specific exercises are designed to encourage the depressed person to identify personal strengths, focus on and savor good things in life, and to cultivate positive attitudes such as optimism, forgiveness, attachment, and gratitude. Initial reports by the authors suggest significant improvement in depression measures for those completing the course of treatment.

## Other Treatments for Depression

Sleep deprivation is one of the most rapid, but least commonly used, interventions to treat depression. Preventing REM sleep can produce a 50% decrease in symptom severity within a few hours for between 30% and 60% of patients although the improvement is short-lived; relapse occurs after even a brief nap. Relatedly, most antidepressant medications are REM sleep suppressors (Peterson & Benca, 2006). **Phototherapy** with bright, broad-spectrum lighting has been effective in treating seasonal recurrent depression, although in a recent comparison study CBT produced fewer relapses and lower symptom severity than light therapy, both after treatment and at 1-year follow-up (Rohan, Roecklein, Lacy, & Vacek, 2009). Evidence is inconsistent for light therapy alone in the treatment of non-seasonal depression, with about half of recent studies finding evidence of effectiveness and half finding no support (Even, Schroder, Friedman, & Rouillon, 2008).

Phototherapy with bright, broad-spectrum lighting has been effective in treating seasonal recurrent depression.
(Wikimedia Commons)

## 11.4c Summary of Treatment for Unipolar Depression

A large number of controlled studies have demonstrated that there are several effective interventions for the treatment of unipolar depression. Medication is the most common intervention, and effective antidepressants have been developed that have milder side-effect profiles than earlier-generation drugs. These medications also reduce the risk of relapse as long as they continue to be administered. However, medication discontinuation is associated with significant recurrence of depression. ECT is an effective and rapid intervention for severe depression, but it is associated with memory loss and high rates of relapse. Several psychotherapies appear to be as effective for depression

**Does medication work better than psychotherapy for depression?**

**Phototherapy**

Use of board-spectrum light to treat seasonal depression

as medication, including cognitive therapy, behavioral therapy, and interpersonal therapy. In general, psychotherapy is associated with lower risk of relapse when compared to antidepressant medication. The existence of a significant placebo response, and a high rate of natural remission, may influence reported rates of effectiveness, as may selective publication of research presenting the positive, but not negative, outcomes in medication trials.

# 11.5 Bipolar Mood Disorders

## 11.5a Bipolar I Disorder

Bipolar I disorder is distinguished from the other mood disorders by the occurrence of manic episode at some point in the condition. As noted earlier in *DSM-5* Diagnostic Criteria for a Manic Episode, the manic episode is characterized by excessive elation, irritability, talkativeness, flight of ideas, and accelerated speech and motor behavior. In some cases of bipolar I disorder, a single manic episode is experienced without any recurrence; however, this is a relatively rare situation: more than 9 of 10 have a second episode. Most (60%–70%) of these individuals will also experience a major depressive episode, thus the term **bipolar** referring to the two

**Is mania treated differently than depression?**

poles of mania and depression. On average, people with bipolar I disorder experience about four recurrences in 10 years. If there are cycles of both manic and major depressive episodes (a condition formerly termed *manic-depressive*), the condition is described by its most recent expressed episode (hypomanic, manic, or depressed). When the "with rapid cycling" specifier applies, at least four mood episodes have been experienced within the past year. Additional moods may be experienced concurrently with a manic episode as well, and their presence determines whether the bipolar I disorder is specified with mixed features. In these cases, mood shifts may be rapid between the manic and depressed states with each sometimes lasting only a few hours (American Psychiatric Association, 2013).

Bipolar I disorder occurs in approximately 0.6% of the population, an incidence similar to that of schizophrenia. The incidence appears to be about equal in males and females. It can develop at any age, but the average age of onset is 18. Typically there is disruption in several interpersonal and occupational areas of functioning; work difficulties and divorce are common. Substance use disorders often co-occur with the disorder, and the conditions may exacerbate each other. As many as 15% of people with bipolar I disorder successfully commit suicide, and the condition may be responsible for 25% of all completed suicides (American Psychiatric Association, 2013). However, a long-term mortality study found that suicides were more common in patients with unipolar depression than in those with either bipolar I or bipolar II disorder (Angst, Stassen, Clayton, & Angst, 2002). The reliability estimate for bipolar I disorder in the *DSM-5* field trials, pooled from two sites, is 0.56, rated as "good" (Regier, et al., 2013).

## 11.5b Bipolar II Disorder

In contrast, bipolar II disorder does not involve a manic episode. Instead, bipolar II individuals experience the less severe hypomanic episode, interspersed with major depressive episodes. In other words, the mood swings are less extreme on the high (manic) end of the mood spectrum. In addition, a major depressive episode is necessary for the diagnosis of bipolar II, unlike bipolar I. Bipolar II disorder tends to involve a greater number of mood episodes than bipolar I disorder, although bipolar I may actually include more hypomanic episodes. It usually begins with a depressive episode, and as a result the diagnosis may be missed until a hypomanic episode occurs. Perhaps related to the major depressive component, bipolar II disorder is more common among females than males, and its incidence is about half that of bipolar I disorder (American Psychiatric Association, 2013).

**Bipolar**

Referring to the two extreme poles of mood: mania and depression

A recent comparison of natural outcomes of bipolar I and bipolar II disorders (Mantere, et al., 2008) found that bipolar II patients may actually be more impaired, spending about 40% more time in depressive states than bipolar I patients because of a higher number of depressive phases over an 18-month period. The diagnostic reliability of bipolar II disorder is not well established (Simpson, et al., 2002). Several efforts to improve diagnostic reliability have included the use of structured and semi-structured interviews although in one recent study these two instruments agreed only in 51% of cases (Benazzi, 2003). One possible reason for reliability problems concerns the heterogeneity of symptom presentation possible in the bipolar disorders. According to Lieberman, Peele, and Razavi (2008), there are mathematically as many as 163 symptom combinations that could qualify as a manic episode and more than 37,000 for a *DSM-IV* mixed episode, before specifiers are applied; total possible combinations for all of the bipolar conditions exceeds five billion.

## 11.5c Cyclothymic Disorder

The remaining bipolar spectrum disorder, cyclothymic disorder, does not involve manic, hypomanic, or major depressive episodes (see *DSM-5* Diagnostic Criteria for Cyclothymic Disorder). Instead, hypomanic symptoms (that never meet the full criteria for a hypomanic episode) alternate with depressive symptoms that do not meet the full criteria for a major depressive episode. The mood swings are, therefore, less intense than the other bipolar conditions. In cyclothymic disorder, these mood swings last at least 2 years and cause significant distress or dysfunction for the individual. The condition tends to begin in adolescence and follows a persistent course.

Cyclothymia appears to be relatively rare in the general population, but prevalence figures vary. Estimates from a representative sample of over 9,000 people in the United States estimated lifetime prevalence of 1% for bipolar I disorder, 1.1% for bipolar II disorder, and 2.4% for subthreshold bipolar spectrum disorders (Merikangas, et al., 2007). The *DSM-5* places the prevalence of cyclothymic disorder occurring at about the same rate as bipolar I disorder, although it is found more commonly (up to 5%) among those in treatment for mood disorders. It is diagnosed more commonly in females, perhaps because they are more likely to present for treatment. Between 15% and 50% of those with cyclothymic disorder subsequently develop either bipolar I or bipolar II disorder, both of which share family linkage with the condition (American Psychiatric Association, 2013).

| *DSM-5* | **Diagnostic Criteria for Cyclothymic Disorder** |
| --- | --- |

301.13 (F34.0) Cyclothymic Disorder

A. For at least 2 years (at least 1 year in children and adolescents) there have been numerous periods of hypomanic symptoms that do not meet the criteria for a hypomanic episode and numerous depressive symptoms that do not meet the criteria for a major depressive episode.

B. During the above 2-year period (1 year in children and adolescents), the hypomanic and depressive periods have been present for at least half of the time and the individual has not been without the symptoms for more than 2 months at a time.

C. Criteria for a major depressive, manic, or hypomanic episode have never been met.

D. The symptoms in Criterion A are not better explained by schizoaffective disorder, schizophrenia, schizophreniform disorder, delusional disorder, or other specified or unspecified schizophrenia spectrum and other psychotic disorder.

E. The symptoms are not attributable to the physiological effects of a substance (e.g., a drug of abuse, a medication) or another medical condition (e.g., hyperthyroidism).

F. The symptoms cause clinically significant distress or impairment in social, occupational, or other important areas of functioning.

Specify if:

**With anxious distress**

## 11.5d Other Bipolar Disorders

As in the case of other *DSM-5* categories, bipolar disturbances can result from substances or other medical conditions. These can be diagnosed, accordingly, as substance/medication-induced bipolar and related disorder and bipolar and related disorder due to another medical condition. The remaining bipolar disorders that cannot otherwise be classified may include conditions in which hypomanic episodes are of brief duration or do not occur with depressive episodes, or cyclothymia that does not persist for a full 2 years. These would be listed as other specified bipolar and related disorder.

# 11.6 Causal Factors in Bipolar Disorders

The evidence for genetic etiology is stronger for bipolar I disorder than for other mood disorders. Many studies have indicated that the disorder runs in families, with relatives of bipolar I individuals having as much as 10 times the risk for also showing a bipolar condition as the general population (American Psychiatric Association, 2013). A large Danish twin study indicated 62% concordance in MZ twins versus 8% concordance in DZ twins. The risk for bipolar II disorder is increased in the relatives of those with bipolar I disorder, as well (Potash & DePaulo, 2000). The search for contributing genes has been very active, although several candidate sites identified (and enthusiastically introduced) over the past 30 years have not received subsequent support. Current attention is directed at possible sites implicated on chromosomes 4, 12, 18, and 21, as well as the X chromosome, and for genes related to the serotonergic and dopaminergic systems (Potash & DePaulo, 2000). However, despite very intensive effort, at this point no gene has consistently been implicated as causal for bipolar I or bipolar II disorder; and the current picture suggests multiple genes interacting with each other and with the environment in complex and unknown ways (Payne, Potash, & DePaulo, 2005).

Like unipolar depression, bipolar I disorder is characterized by abnormalities in HPA activity, and increased cortisol levels may precede manic episodes (Daban, Vieta, Mackin, & Young, 2005). Stressful life events accordingly tend to correspond with the onset of mania in people with bipolar I disorder. Interestingly, bipolar I disorder is twice as common in high-income countries as low-income countries (American Psychiatric Association, 2013). There is evidence for the role of brain norepinephrine in the onset of bipolar cycles. Bunney and his colleagues (1972) carefully followed the transition from depression to mania, and from mania to depression, for 10 patients. Urinary levels of various neurotransmitters were measured on a daily basis. Only NE showed a clear and significant increase on the day before the behavioral symptoms of mania appeared. The level of NE remained high during the manic phase and returned somewhat more gradually to its previous low level when mania switched to depression. Each of nine patients for whom this measure was obtained showed an increase in NE levels on the day preceding the onset of mania. Since NE levels and HPA activity are responsive to psychological events, it is possible that various environmental triggers could precipitate mania recurrence. Sleep loss is also a trigger for manic episodes in these patients (Peterson & Benca, 2006).

## 11.6a Treatment of Bipolar Disorders

### *Medication*

Lithium (a light metal) may have been naturally present in certain Roman spas known for their calming properties; it was in use for the treatment of mania in Europe by the early 1950s. Its introduction in the U.S. was resisted for two decades because it had previously been dispensed as a salt substitute (lithium chloride) for those seeking to reduce sodium intake. Several cases of lithium toxicity resulted, effectively closing the door for American use until the 1970s.

Lithium carbonate has long been shown to be more effective than placebo in treating the manic phase of bipolar I disorder (Goodwin & Athanasios, 1979; Keck & McElroy, 2002).

**BVT** *Lab*

Improve your test scores. Practice quizzes are available at **www.BVTLab.com**.

Besides reducing the acute symptoms of bipolar affective disorders, maintenance doses of lithium can reduce or prevent recurrences (Prien, 1979) and are strongly associated with a reduced risk of suicide (Fountoulakis, Grunze, Panagoitidis, & Kaprinis, 2008). Unfortunately, a significant percentage of patients do not respond well to maintenance therapy (Keck & McElroy, 2002). Toxicity can still be a problem, so blood levels of lithium are typically monitored to maintain concentration within a therapeutic window. Side effects can be troubling; and at the same time, many bipolar patients find the manic state to be enjoyable. Because there are no effective long-acting versions of the drug available (as there are for several antipsychotic medications), treatment compliance is a constant issue. Furthermore, Lithium response rates currently are 40%–50%, compared to earlier expectations of 80%–90%; the change in response may be due to factors such as earlier onset, increased comorbid drug use, and shorter hospital stays (Thase & Kupfer, 1996). Recurrence of mania during prophylactic medication ranges from 40%–60%, most often related to drug noncompliance. As a result, the anticonvulsant medications such as carbamazepine and valproate are increasingly used in maintenance therapy, often in combination with lithium.

Lithium, valproate, and carbamazepine—the three mood-stabilizing agents—are not particularly effective against the depressed state in bipolar disorders. For these symptoms, antidepressant medication is usually added (Keck & McElroy, 2002). However, the value of antidepressants in bipolar depression is controversial because of possible drug interactions and concerns that manic states may be re-triggered (Fountoulakis, Grunze, Panagoitidis, & Kaprinis, 2008), and they should be used with caution.

After 50 years of research, lithium's mode of action is still not completely understood. Animal experiments show that the drug decreases levels of brain norepinephrine—findings that support an association between high levels of NE and manic behavior. As previously mentioned, urinary levels of NE have also been found to increase as individual patients change from depressed to manic states. One theory, supported by indirect evidence, is that lithium carbonate reduces abnormally high levels of intraneuronal sodium, which has been preventing the reuptake of NE and thus causing excessive amounts of this neurotransmitter to accumulate (Goodwin & Athanasios, 1979). Current reviews suggest a more complex effect of lithium on several neurotransmitter-signaling networks (Lenox & Hahn, 2000).

## Psychosocial Treatments

Generally, there are no psychotherapies that are effective alone in the treatment of bipolar mania or psychotic depression, and withholding somatic treatments may be considered malpractice among physicians (Thase & Kupfer, 1996). There is evidence that psychoeducation improves medication compliance. Cognitive-behavioral therapy addressing problem solving, stress management, communication skills, and relapse prevention may be helpful in overall treatment adherence (Craighead, Miklwitz, Fank, & Vajk, 2002). Cognitive therapy may also be beneficial component of treatment. Over a 30-month period of treatment and follow-up, a cognitive therapy plus medication group had lower risk of relapse than a medication-only group (Lam, Hayward, Watkins, Wright, & Sham, 2005). Additional studies have supported adjunctive interpersonal therapy for stabilizing daily routine and improving depressive phases, and marital/family therapy for reducing relapse and improving communication (Craighead, Miklwitz, Fank, & Vajk, 2002).

# 11.7 Suicide

Suicide is by no means always associated with severe depression, but it is clear that a much higher proportion of individuals with diagnosed depressions commit suicide than in the population at large. As core symptoms for the mood disorders—or in association with substance use disorders, eating disorders, psychoses, anxiety, or personality disorders—emotions such as hopelessness and despair are often present in a suicidal crisis. In the United

States, suicide ranks among the top 10 leading causes of death. It has become a serious problem for the military, which had more suicides than combat deaths in Afghanistan during 2012 (CBS News, 2013). A recent study found that bipolar disorder was associated with the highest risk of suicide among male veterans, while among female veterans the highest risk was among those with substance use disorders (Ilgen, et al., 2010).

> How common is suicide? Who is at greater risk?

Not everyone is at equal risk for suicide, however; there are strong gender and ethnic associations with completed suicide. A gender distinction is evident at all ages and across all groups, based on the CDC statistics for suicides in 2005 in the United States (see Figure 11-3). Males succeed at suicide at nearly 4 times the rate of females and represent almost 80% of suicide deaths.

Although males complete suicide more often, females make nearly 3 times as many suicide attempts. The different mortality rates are partly due to method: most males used firearms, while the most common female attempts involved poisoning. In the state of Oregon between 2003 and 2010, for example, 62% of male suicides (compared to 31% of female suicides) involved guns; the leading suicide method for females was poisoning (41% of deaths, compared to 13% of male suicides). An equal percentage of both male and female suicides (18%) involved hanging or suffocation (Shen & Millet, 2012). Suicide rates are also much higher among White and Native American/Native Alaskan males than other groups.

Age is a more significant factor in the likelihood of male suicide than female suicide (Figure 11-4). For White males, the risk of suicide increases throughout life, reaching its highest levels after age 65. In stark contrast, suicide risk in American Indians/Alaska Natives is highest before age 25 and declines thereafter. Female rates show a decline after age 65. The *DSM-5* notes that the likelihood of suicide attempts drops as people move beyond middle age, but the risk of completed suicide does not (American Psychiatric Association, 2013).

Suicide rates are much higher among White and Native American/Native Alaskan males than other groups. Age is a significant factor regarding suicide rates, and the risk in American Indians/Alaska Natives is highest before age 25. (iStock)

## 11.7a  Psychological Correlates

Many investigators have tried to determine the type of personality traits or life experiences that are associated with individuals who attempt suicide. For example, Paykel and his colleagues (1975) compared reports of stressful life events during the 6-month period preceding a suicide attempt for 53 individuals who attempted suicide with 53 depressive control patients who had not attempted suicide, matched individually for age, sex, marital status, and race. Data were also obtained on a matched sample from the general population. Those who had attempted

*Figure 11-3*
***Age-Adjusted Rates of Completed Suicide in 2005 by Gender and Ethnic Groups***

Source: Centers for Disease Control

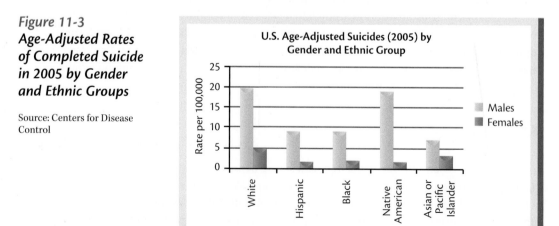

*Table 11-2*    Frequency of Stressful Events Preceding Suicide Attempts

| Event | Suicide Attempts (N = 53) | Depressives (N = 53) | General Population (N = 53) |
|---|---|---|---|
| Serious argument with spouse | 19 | 8 | 0 |
| New person in home | 11 | 4 | 0 |
| Engagement | 7 | 0 | 4 |
| Serious illness of close family member | 17 | 7 | 4 |
| Serious personal physical illness | 15 | 5 | 1 |

Source: Adapted from Paykel, E. S., Prusoff, B. A., & Myers, J. K. (1975). Suicide attempts and recent life events. *Archives of General Psychiatry*, 32, 327–331.

suicide reported 4 times as many stressful life events as did individuals in the general population sample and 1.5 times as many as in the depressed sample. Some of the specific life events that were significantly different in frequency are shown in Table 11-2. These results suggest that two general types of events were present more often in the lives of the suicide attempters: interpersonal conflicts (as suggested by "arguments with spouse" and "new person in the home") and serious illness in a close family member or themselves.

Baechler (1979) studied 127 cases of suicide and proposed that suicidal acts could be grouped into four categories according to their meaning to the person: (1) For many, perhaps most, suicide represents an escape from an intolerable situation. The person may be experiencing intense shame, guilt, fear, or physical pain and sees suicide as the only way out. (2) For some individuals the main motive for suicide is aggression—to seek vengeance on others, to make them feel remorse. (3) Yet others commit suicide as an act of sacrifice or in relation to some higher values. The immolations of Buddhist monks, or devout suicide bombers, would be examples. (4) Finally, there are suicides performed in the context of games or undergoing an ordeal in order to prove oneself. Russian roulette is an example of the former. These categories may not capture all the variations in suicidal motivation, but they do serve to remind us that people commit suicide for a variety of reasons.

## 11.7b  Risk Factors for Suicide

A variety of risk factors for suicide have been identified. The most widely supported indicators for inpatients are similar to those for general public, including:

    a.    Previous suicide attempt—This is the strongest single predictor of suicidal activity.

    b.    Contemplated method at hand—Those who have planned the method of suicide, and have the means or materials needed to carry it out, are at highest risk.

*Figure 11-4*
***Rates of Completed U.S. Suicide in 2005 by Age, Gender, and Ethnic Group***

Data for Native Alaskan/Indian males aged 65+ were not available

Source: Centers for Disease Control

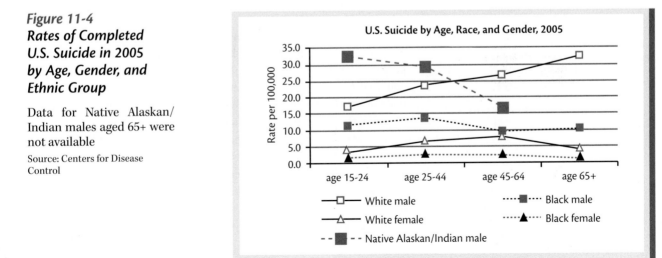

c. Male gender—Males are much more likely to succeed at suicide, compared to females.

d. Hopelessness—A hopeless attitude is related to lifetime risk of suicide.

e. Diagnosis of mood disorder or schizophrenia—Along with anorexia nervosa, epilepsy, personality disorder, and obsessive-compulsive disorder, these conditions are associated with increased risk of successful suicide.

f. Previous psychiatric admissions—especially if multiple admissions (Cassells, Paterson, Dowding, & Morrison, 2005).

Other conditions increasing the risk for suicide include the presence of alcohol or drugs because substances can reduce ability to inhibit self-damaging impulses. Functional physical and psychological limitations, resulting from chronic health problems, are also significantly associated with increased risk (Kaplan, McFarland, Huguet, & Newsom, 2007). Data from the National Comorbidity Study, taken from a representative sample of nearly 8,100 respondents, indicated that the people most likely to attempt suicide were males with fewer years of education, living in the Western or Southwestern U.S., and without active religious affiliation (Nock & Kessler, 2006). Other predictors included psychiatric disorders, substance abuse or dependence, mania (which increased risk ninefold), and a history of multiple (but not single episode) rapes or sexual molestations. Interestingly, the risk for suicide is higher among female physicians than among females in the general population, based on a study of doctors in England and Wales (Hawton, Clements, Sakarovitch, Simkin, & Deeks, 2001). The risk is also increased for mothers who were infected with *Toxoplasma gondii*, a parasite common in cats, near the time of giving birth (Pedersen, Mortensen, Norgaard-Pedersen, & Postolache, 2012). Among adolescents, Goldstein, Bridge, and Brent (2008) found that those who completed suicide were more likely to have displayed a sleep disturbance (including insomnia) within 1 week of the suicide than control subjects, suggesting that sleep problems may serve as an effective warning sign.

A sign advising of the phone number for a suicide-prevention hotline is shown on the Aurora Bridge in Seattle. The signs, along with telephone call boxes, were put up as efforts to reduce the number of people who jump to their deaths from the bridge. Eight people committed suicide here in 2006. (AP Wide World)

## 11.7c  Suicide Prevention

In assessing suicide potential, protective factors are considered as well. Family support, employment, significant relationships (including marriage), having future plans, and being in treatment—all serve to reduce the risk of completed suicide (Sánchez, 2001). A person is usually intensely suicidal for only a short period of time; if that time can be gapped by the support of others and by resorting to remaining strengths, the suicidal crisis can pass.

Suicide prevention is one important goal of crisis intervention in community mental health services. The aim is to help a person contemplating suicide to consider other alternatives and to direct the person to resources for psychotherapeutic or other forms of help. A common model of crisis intervention (e.g., Slaikeu, 1990) involves first making psychological contact with the person, actively listening and exploring the dimensions of the problem, and helping with solutions to immediate issues covering the next 12 hours or so. At times of imminent danger, actions might be necessary without the person's consent (such as protective custody). If the person can be supported and assisted through the brief period in which risk of suicide is highest, then additional resources can come into play to work on the longer-term issues, such as relationships, unemployment, and health problems.

Many suicides cannot be prevented. However, the availability of rapid-response crisis intervention services saves many lives each year.

# Chapter Review

## TO SUM UP ...

- Mood episodes include the major depressive episode, the manic episode, and the hypomanic episode. Mood disorders are diagnosed, in large part, by the presence or absence of these components.

- The depressive disorders include major depressive disorder, persistent depressive disorder, disruptive mood dysregulation disorder, and premenstrual dysphoric disorder. They are characterized, in general, by depressive or irritable mood and loss of pleasure in activities.

- The bipolar disorders include bipolar I disorder, bipolar II disorder, and cyclothymic disorder. They are characterized by increased activity and talkativeness, inflated self-esteem, decreased need for sleep, and elated or expansive mood sometimes alternating with depression.

- Episodic mood disorders are characterized by a tendency toward spontaneous recovery and recurrences.

- There is evidence of genetic involvement in the development of mood disorders. The genetic factor appears to have a much greater influence in the bipolar conditions than in the unipolar conditions.

- Effective antidepressant and antimanic medications began to appear in the 1950s. Newer medications may not be more effective, but they do have milder side effects.

- Explanations for the mode of action of antidepressant medications led to the hypothesis that depression is caused by a relative depletion of neurotransmitters such as NE and 5-HT. The evidence for this theory is inconsistent.

- A variety of theories exist concerning the psychological causes of depression, including intrapsychic aggression turned inward, disrupted maternal-child relationship, reduced rate of reinforcement, effect of uncontrollable stressors, and depressive attributional cognitive style. Effective psychotherapies have developed that include behavioral therapy, cognitive therapy, and interpersonal therapy.

- In treatment of unipolar depression, medications and psychotherapies can produce approximately equal results. Risk of relapse appears to be less for psychotherapy than for pharmacotherapy.

- ECT is effective for short-term relief of serious depression. It may also produce some memory loss, and relapse rate is high.

- Lithium is effective in treating bipolar affective disorders. It reduces active manic symptoms and decreases risk of suicide. However, treatment compliance is a problem.

- Psychotherapy may be useful as an adjunct to mood stabilizing medication in bipolar I disorder.

- People with mood disorders, as well as other mental disorders, are at increased risk for suicide.

- Males are much more likely to commit suicide than females although females make more attempts. The highest risk groups for suicide in the U.S. are older white males and younger Native American-Native Alaskan males.

## KEY TERMS

Attribution model of depression   300

Automatic thoughts   299

Bipolar   306

Echopraxia   290

Electroconvulsive therapy (ECT)   302

Introjection   297

Learned helplessness   299

Melancholia   285

Monoamine hypothesis   294

Phototherapy   305

Transcranial magnetic stimulation (TMS)   303

## QUESTIONS FOR STUDY

- Compare unipolar and bipolar mood disorders in terms of their incidence, gender ratio, genetic loading, and effective treatment.

- Give examples of the internal, global, and stable attributions that characterize depressive thinking.

- You are interviewing a patient who has attempted suicide. Describe three factors that might lead you to worry about increased risk of completing suicide, and three factors that might lead you to conclude that risk is lower for completed suicide.

## POP QUIZ

1.  The depressive episode includes all of the following **except** _____.
    A.  distractibility
    B.  sleep disturbance
    C.  fatigue
    D.  indecisiveness

2. The key feature of a manic episode is a distinct period (at least _____ ) of expansive, elevated, or irritable mood.
   A. 1 week
   B. 2 weeks
   C. 4 days
   D. 5 days

3. The hypomanic episode **cannot** include which symptom?
   A. inflated self-esteem
   B. distractibility
   C. decreased need for sleep
   D. delusional grandiosity

4. The presence of a manic episode results in the *DSM-5* diagnosis of _____.
   A. bipolar I disorder
   B. bipolar II disorder
   C. major depressive disorder
   D. cyclothymic disorder

5. If echolalia, echopraxia, or disturbances in motor activity are dominant among the depressive symptoms, which specifier applies?
   A. "with melancholic features "
   B. "with catatonic features"
   C. "with postpartum onset"
   D. "with a seasonal pattern"

6. Temper outbursts in disruptive mood dysregulation disorder must persist for

   _____ .
   A. 1 month
   B. 6 months
   C. 1 year
   D. 2 years

7. The prevalence of premenstrual dysphoric disorder is close to ____ % of women.
   A. 1
   B. 6
   C. 10
   D. 20

8. Learned helplessness is the theory that depression is caused by a lack of connection between responses and their outcome, which was proposed by

   _____ .
   A. Seligman
   B. Beck
   C. Freud
   D. Skinner

9. Lithium is recommended for which disorder?
   A. bipolar I disorder
   B. bipolar II disorder
   C. cyclothymic disorder
   D. major depressive disorder

10. Which class of antidepressants shows lower discontinuation rates due to intolerance and is generally the first-line medical treatment for depression?
    A. tricyclics
    B. TPAs
    C. MAO-Is
    D. SSRIs

11. Which of these disorders is most common?
    A. bipolar I disorder
    B. bipolar II disorder
    C. cyclothymic disorder
    D. major depressive disorder

12. Which disorder shows an equal sex ratio?
    A. major depressive disorder
    B. disruptive mood dysregulation disorder
    C. bipolar I disorder
    D. bipolar II disorder

13. One of the most reliable sleep disturbances associated with depression is _____.
    A. shorter latency to REM
    B. longer latency to REM
    C. early evening awakening
    D. late evening awakening

14. The attributional style of depressed individuals is characterized by a tendency to make _____ attributions for negative events.
    A. internal, stable, specific
    B. external, unstable, global
    C. internal, unstable, specific
    D. internal, stable, global

15. Among adolescents, those who completed suicide were more likely to have displayed a/an _____ within 1 week of the suicide, suggesting that it may serve as an effective warning sign.
    A. eating disturbance
    B. motor disturbance
    C. sleep disturbance
    D. visual disturbance

# CHAPTER OVERVIEW

# CHAPTER OPENER QUESTIONS

How do substance use and substance-induced disorders differ?

How common are substance-related disorders?

What is the difference between dependence and abuse?

Is one born an addict? What is withdrawal? What is tolerance?

What causal factors influence the development of substance dependence?

What disorders are triggered by chronic drug use?

Which treatments are effective for substance use disorders?

(iStock)

# Substance-Related and Addictive Disorders

# chapter 12

A Guatemalan Indian, when asked why he drank so much of the local beverage (aguardiente) replied: "A man must sometimes take a rest from his memory." The need to forget our cares seems to be universal; in almost all cultures throughout recorded history, one way of achieving this has been by using substances that have **psychoactive** properties—that can modify mood, perception, or brain function.

The Greek historian Herodotus writes of the Scythians reaching certain pleasurable states by casting hemp seeds over open fires and inhaling the vapors. The Aztecs described, in great detail, their ritual drugs: teonanacatl (psilocybin), peyotl (peyote), ololiuqui (morning glory seeds), piecetl, and toloatzin. In many South American countries, away from the cities, individuals prepare a potent hallucinogenic drink from the plant *Banisteriopsis caapi*, which they call ayahuasca or caapi. Inhabitants of the South Pacific Islands use a drug called kava; people in the East Indian archipelago ingest nutmeg; people of the West Indies use cohoba snuff; both the Siberians and the Norsemen swallowed small amounts of the potentially deadly *Amanita muscaria* or fly agaric mushroom, which reportedly passes through the kidneys unchanged so that one could drink one's own urine (or a friend's) and regain the effect. Finally, fruits or vegetables fermented into some variant of alcohol are probably among the earliest known intoxicants.

The drug that has been used most effectively as an **analgesic** (pain reducer) throughout the centuries is opium. Both the Egyptians and the Persians used it medicinally, and the Greek physician Theophrastus mentions its effectiveness as a sleep inducer and pain reliever. In addition, opium became the standard therapeutic agent for cough and hysteria. Despite its wide medicinal use, its potential for producing psychological and physiological dependency was unnoticed by the medical profession. In fact, addiction to opium did not become widespread until the British East India Company imported the drug on a large scale into Europe during the nineteenth century (Maurer & Vogel, 1954).

> **Psychoactive**
> Altering mood, perception, or brain function
>
> **Analgesic**
> A drug that reduces pain
>
> **Addiction**
> Chronic pattern of habitual maladaptive behavior, often experienced as compulsive and uncontrollable, that tends to provide immediate gratification

There are, then, an impressive number of substances that have been used by human beings to alter thinking, mood, and perception. Some of these have been used in religion or medical treatment, and others, with less official sanction, in an attempt to attain a degree of euphoria. Almost every society appears to allow, if not directly employ, one or more mind-altering substances for certain segments of the population. In American culture today, use of legal and illegal substances is a leading social and health problem—implicated in a large proportion of crime, occupational and interpersonal dysfunction, disease, disability, and death each year. Yet nearly all of these impacts might be preventable—if we can understand how substance use begins, how it is maintained, and how it can be treated.

Substance involvement ranges from occasional intake to a complete dependency on and compulsive use of drugs that literally destroy the person's life. Although the term **addiction** is widely used to describe particularly chronic patterns of substance use, the *DSM-5* does not include the word in its diagnostic terminology "because of its uncertain definition and its potentially negative connotation" (American Psychiatric Association, 2013, p. 485). Curiously, it nonetheless names the general category of these conditions "Substance-related and Addictive Disorders."

In the nomenclature of the *DSM-5*, substance-related disorders are divided into substance use disorders (which describe the pathological pattern of behaviors related to the use of a substance) and substance-induced disorders (which include the results of substance use: intoxication, withdrawal, and induced mental disorders). In revising these classifications, the *DSM-5* abandoned the distinction, fundamental in *DSM-IV*, between substance *dependence* and substance *abuse*. Instead, the behaviors to which these terms referred are incorporated into the criteria for substance use disorders.

> **How do substance use and substance-induced disorders differ?**

# 12.1 Substance Use Disorders

The general criteria used for diagnosing substance use disorders are summarized in General Diagnostic Criteria for *DSM-5* Substance Use Disorders. *DSM-5* considers symptoms loosely organized into four general clusters: impaired control over use of the substance; social impairments that result from use; risky use of the substance; and pharmacological criteria, namely tolerance and withdrawal. **Tolerance** is a need for increasing amounts of a substance in order to have the desired effect, or the diminishing effects produced by the same amount of the drug. **Withdrawal** is a specific psychological and physiological reaction to discontinuation of a substance which taking the substance can relieve. Neither tolerance nor withdrawal is required for the diagnosis of a substance use disorder; indeed, not all substances are associated with withdrawal (e.g., phencyclidine and other hallucinogens, or inhalants). Importantly, tolerance and withdrawal symptoms that occur during "appropriate medical treatment with prescribed medications ... are specifically not counted when diagnosing a substance use disorder" (American Psychiatric Association, 2013, p. 484).

> **How common are substance-related disorders?**

Generally, at least two of the criteria in *DSM-5* General Diagnostic Criteria for Substance Use Disorders within a 12-month period are needed to meet the criteria for a diagnosis. Severity of the disorder is specified in terms of how many symptoms are present: "Mild" severity is indicated by two to three symptoms, "Moderate" by four to five symptoms, and "Severe" by six or more symptoms. Other course specifiers allow one to distinguish whether the disorder is in early or sustained remission, in a controlled environment (where the substance is unavailable), or on maintenance therapy, meaning symptoms are controlled by an agonist drug (a chemical that acts on the same receptors and, in effect, substitutes for the drug, as methadone does for heroin).

The diagnostic criteria of alcohol use disorder are shown in *DSM-5* Diagnostic Criteria for Alcohol Use Disorder. In form and content, these criteria are almost identical to those for any other substance, with a few minor substance-specific alterations. Typically the person continues to use the substance even while knowing that a persistent physical or

**Tolerance**

Need for increasing amounts of a substance to have the desired effect

**Withdrawal**

A specific psychological and physiological reaction to discontinuation of a substance

| *DSM-5* | **General Diagnostic Criteria for Substance Use Disorders** |
|---|---|

General Diagnostic Criteria for *DSM-5* Substance Use Disorders

*Symptoms of impaired control*

Use of substance in larger amounts or over longer period than intended

Persistent desire or attempts to cut down or regulate use, often unsuccessfully

Much time spent acquiring and using the substance, or recovering from its effects

Craving for the drug

*Symptoms of social impairment*

Failure to fulfill major obligations due to substance use

Continued use despite resultant social or interpersonal problems

Relinquishing important activities because of substance use

*Risky use of the substance*

Recurrent use in situations where it is physically dangerous

Continued use in spite of physical or psychological problems caused or worsened by the substance

*Pharmacological criteria*

Tolerance (diminished substance effect from the same dosage)

Withdrawal (syndrome of substance-specific symptoms that develop upon cessation of use)

Source: Reprinted with permission from the *Diagnostic and Statistical Manual of Mental Disorders*, Fifth Edition, (Copyright 2013). American Psychiatric Association.

psychological problem is being caused or made worse. The pattern of use produces significant social or occupational problems, or interferes with fulfilling major role obligations in life. For example, a person may repeatedly be too intoxicated to provide adequate parental care or to operate machinery at work. Legal problems are often involved because of criminal activity, such as driving under the influence of intoxicants or the possession or distribution of illegal drugs. It is this continued use of the substance despite significant distress or impairment it causes that is central to the diagnosis (American Psychiatric Association, 2013).

**What is the difference between dependence and abuse?**

---

**DSM-5** | **Diagnostic Criteria for Alcohol Use Disorder**

Alcohol Use Disorder

A. A problematic pattern of alcohol use leading to clinically significant impairment or distress, as manifested by at least two of the following, occurring within a 12-month period:

1. Alcohol is often taken in larger amounts or over a longer period than was intended.
2. There is a persistent desire or unsuccessful efforts to cut down or control alcohol use.
3. A great deal of time is spent in activities necessary to obtain alcohol, use alcohol, or recover from its effects.
4. Craving, or a strong desire or urge to use alcohol.
5. Recurrent alcohol use resulting in a failure to fulfill major role obligations at work, school, or home.
6. Continued alcohol use despite having persistent or recurrent social or interpersonal problems caused or exacerbated by the effects of alcohol.
7. Important social, occupational, or recreational activities are given up or reduced because of alcohol use.
8. Recurrent alcohol use in situations in which it is physically hazardous.
9. Alcohol use is continued despite knowledge of having a persistent or recurrent physical or psychological problem that is likely to have been caused or exacerbated by alcohol.
10. Tolerance, as defined by either of the following:
    a. A need for markedly increased amounts of alcohol to achieve intoxication or desired effect.
    b. A markedly diminished effect with continued use of the same amount of alcohol.
11. Withdrawal, as manifested by either of the following:
    a. The characteristic withdrawal syndrome for alcohol (refer to Criteria A and B for the criteria set for alcohol withdrawal).
    b. Alcohol (or a closely-related substance, such as a benzodiazepine) is taken to relieve or avoid withdrawal symptoms.

*Specify* if:

**In early remission:** After full criteria for alcohol use disorder were previously met, none of the criteria for alcohol use disorder have been met for at least 3 months but for less than 12 months (with the exception that Criterion A4, "Craving, or a strong desire or urge to use alcohol," may be met).

**In sustained remission:** After full criteria for alcohol use disorder were previously met, none of the criteria for alcohol use disorder have been met at any time during a period of 12 months or longer (with the exception that Criterion A4, "Craving, or a strong desire or urge to use alcohol," may be met).

*Specify* if:

**In a controlled environment:** This additional specifier is used if an individual is in an environment where access to alcohol is restricted.

**Code based on current severity: Note** for ICD-10-CM codes: If an alcohol intoxication, alcohol withdrawal, or another alcohol-induced mental disorder is also present, do not use the codes below for alcohol use disorder. Instead, the comorbid alcohol use disorder is indicated in the 4th character of the alcohol-induced disorder code (see the coding note for alcohol intoxication, alcohol withdrawal, or a specific alcohol-induced mental disorder). For example, if there is comorbid alcohol intoxication and alcohol use disorder, only the alcohol intoxication code is given, with the 4th character indicating whether the comorbid alcohol use disorder is mild, moderate, or severe: **F10.129** for mild alcohol use disorder with alcohol intoxication or **F10.229** for a moderate or severe alcohol use disorder with alcohol intoxication.

*Specify* current severity:

**305.00 (F10.10) Mild:** Presence of 2–3 symptoms.

**303.90 (F10.20) Moderate:** Presence of 4–5 symptoms.

**303.90 (F10.20) Severe:** Presence of 6 or more symptoms.

Source: Reprinted with permission from the *Diagnostic and Statistical Manual of Mental Disorders*, Fifth Edition, (Copyright 2013). American Psychiatric Association.

The substance use disorder category has been a reliable one, with the *DSM-III* field trials showing diagnostic reliability of 0.80 or above on both phases. The *DSM-5* field trials found a kappa of 0.40 for alcohol use disorder, which was considered "good" reliability (Regier, et al., 2013). Although the ratio varies by substance, males are more likely to receive substance-related diagnoses than females (American Psychiatric Association, 2013). Substance use disorders are common; estimates of their lifetime incidence rates in recent nationally representative surveys range from 13.2%–17.8% for alcohol abuse and 5.4%–12.5% for alcohol dependence (Hasin, Stinson, Ogburn, & Grant, 2007; Kessler, et al., 2005). The *DSM-5* indicates the 12-month prevalence rate for alcohol use disorder is in adults is 8.5% (American Psychiatric Association, 2013). Alcohol use disorders were the most common mental health problems among college students, with a combined incidence of just over 20%—significantly higher than that of their non-college-attending peers (Blanco, et al., 2008). People ages 18–24 have high prevalence rates of nearly all substance use disorders, relative to other ages, although rates vary widely across different substances (American Psychiatric Association, 2013).

## 12.2 Substance-Induced Disorders

The other class of substance-related disorders involves not the maladaptive pattern of substance use itself but rather the syndromes and consequences produced as a result of recurrent ingestion. These are the substance-induced disorders that consist of intoxication, withdrawal, and a series of substance-induced mental disturbances: delirium, dementia, psychotic disorders, mood disorders, anxiety disorders, sexual dysfunctions, and sleep disorders. They can arise, in various combinations, as a consequence of repeated exposure to several different substances and toxins.

> Is one born an addict? What is withdrawal? What is tolerance?

### 12.2a Substance Intoxication

Substance **intoxication** is a reversible change in behavior and cognition that occurs within a short time after ingestion of a substance and is a result of the substance's physiological effect on the central nervous system. Its onset typically occurs within minutes of use and resolves as the body metabolizes the substance. To continue with the example of alcohol, the diagnostic criteria of alcohol intoxication are shown in *DSM-5* Diagnostic Criteria for Alcohol Intoxication.

Not all substances that lead to dependence cause intoxication. For example, no such syndrome is identified for tobacco. The manifestations of intoxication can vary widely between individuals taking the same substance, affected by factors such as dosage, tolerance to the substance, and the person's expectation of the substance's effect. Intoxication symptoms can also vary widely across substances (e.g., alcohol intoxication can include *nystagmus*, involuntary movements of the eyes, while cocaine intoxication is associated with pupillary dilation), although different classes of substances can produce similar symptoms of intoxication as well (e.g., alcohol and sedatives).

### 12.2b Substance Withdrawal

Substance withdrawal is a substance-specific syndrome—involving behavioral, psychological, and cognitive changes—that occurs after the cessation or reduction of substance use, following a period of prolonged use (see *DSM-5* Diagnostic Criteria for Alcohol Withdrawal for the example of alcohol withdrawal). The symptoms of withdrawal are usually the opposite of the symptoms of intoxication. It is nearly always accompanied by craving for the substance, the administration of which reverses the withdrawal syndrome.

Withdrawal syndromes occur with many, but not all, substances of abuse; in the case of caffeine, a withdrawal syndrome is identified but no caffeine use disorder yet exists (it is under

**Intoxication**

A reversible problematic change in behavior and cognition following ingestion of a substance

| *DSM-5* | **Diagnostic Criteria for Alcohol Intoxication** |
| --- | --- |

Alcohol Intoxication

A. Recent ingestion of alcohol.

B. Clinically significant problematic behavioral or psychological changes (e.g., inappropriate sexual or aggressive behavior, mood lability, impaired judgment) that developed during, or shortly after, alcohol ingestion.

C. One (or more) of the following signs or symptoms developing during, or shortly after, alcohol use:
   1. Slurred speech
   2. Incoordination
   3. Unsteady gait
   4. Nystagmus
   5. Impairment in attention or memory
   6. Stupor or coma

D. The signs or symptoms are not attributable to another medical condition and are not better explained by another mental disorder, including intoxication with another substance.

   **Coding note:** The ICD-9-CM code is **303.00**. The ICD-10-CM code depends on whether there is a comorbid alcohol use disorder. If a mild alcohol use disorder is comorbid, the ICD-10-CM code is **F10.129**, and if a moderate or severe alcohol use disorder is comorbid, the ICD-10-CM code is **F10.229**. If there is no comorbid alcohol use disorder, then the ICS-10-CM code is **F10.929**.

Source: Reprinted with permission from the *Diagnostic and Statistical Manual of Mental Disorders,* Fifth Edition, (Copyright 2013). American Psychiatric Association.

| *DSM-5* | **Diagnostic Criteria for Alcohol Withdrawal** |
| --- | --- |

Alcohol Withdrawal

A. Cessation of (or reduction in) alcohol use that has been heavy and prolonged.

B. Two (or more) of the following, developing within several hours to a few days after the cessation of (or reduction in) alcohol use described in Criterion A:
   1. Autonomic hyperactivity (e.g., sweating or pulse rate greater than 100 bpm)
   2. Increased hand tremor
   3. Insomnia
   4. Nausea or vomiting
   5. Transient visual, tactile, or auditory hallucinations or illusions
   6. Psychomotor agitation
   7. Anxiety
   8. Generalized tonic-clonic seizures

C. The signs or symptoms in Criterion B cause clinically significant distress and impairment in social, occupational, or other important areas of functioning.

D. The signs or symptoms are not attributable to another medical condition and are not better explained by another mental disorder, including intoxication or withdrawal from another substance.

*Specify* if:

   **With perceptual disturbances:** This specifier applies in the rare instance when hallucinations (usually visual or tactile) occur with intact reality testing, or auditory, visual, or tactile illusions occur in the absence of a delirium.

   **Coding note:** The ICD-9-CM code is **291.81**. The ICD-10-CM code for alcohol withdrawal without perceptual disturbances is **F10.239**, and the ICD-10-CM code for alcohol withdrawal with perceptual disturbances is **F10.232**. Note that the ICD-10-CM code indicates the comorbid presence of a moderate or severe alcohol use disorder, reflecting the fact that alcohol withdrawal can only occur in the presence of a moderate or severe alcohol use disorder. It is not permissible to code mild alcohol use disorder with alcohol withdrawal.

Source: Reprinted with permission from the *Diagnostic and Statistical Manual of Mental Disorders,* Fifth Edition, (Copyright 2013). American Psychiatric Association.

consideration in *DSM-5*'s Section III). The *DSM-5* does not identify a substance withdrawal classification for either hallucinogens or inhalants (including solvents). Withdrawal symptoms can be severe and may be associated with perceptual disturbances and seizures (as can occur in alcohol withdrawal). In many cases, however, withdrawal symptoms are mild or minimal, involving restlessness and perhaps insomnia. The most intense withdrawal symptoms generally subside within a few days after appearing although subtler symptoms can persist for weeks (American Psychiatric Association, 2000). Withdrawal syndromes are described in the *DSM-5* for alcohol, caffeine, cannabis, tobacco, stimulants, opioids, and sedatives, hypnotics, or anxiolytics (antianxiety drugs).

The substance-related disorders can involve a wide variety of legal and illegal drugs and toxins. Some commonly abused drugs and their characteristics are included in Table 12-1.

In addition to intoxication and withdrawal, the substance-induced disorders includes conditions in which other mental disorders, such as depression and anxiety, are induced by substances, as has been noted in prior chapters. In general, the more sedating drugs tend to induce depressive disorders, while the more stimulating drugs tend to induce psychotic disorders; both can produce sleep and sexual dysfunctions (American Psychiatric Association, 2013).

## 12.3   Development of Substance-Use Disorders

Some substances are associated with greater risk of dependence and abuse than others. Generally, faster-acting substances present more of a risk of dependence than slower-acting ones, and methods of administration that deliver the psychoactive components of the drug to the brain more quickly are associated with higher degrees of dependence. Figure 12-1 illustrates the substances that are considered by addiction workers as the easiest upon which to become dependent and the most difficult from which to abstain or discontinue, once dependence is established.

Nicotine, a legal and widely available substance, tops the list of most dependence-producing substances. Nicotine is also noteworthy in the devastation it produces, even though its psychotropic properties may seem mild compared to other substances. According to the Centers for Disease Control and Prevention, tobacco use (the main source of nicotine) accounts for 442,000 deaths annually (CDC, 2011). To put that number into perspective, nicotine dependence is connected to nearly 1 in 5 of all deaths in the country, making it the leading preventable cause of death. In contrast, alcohol consumption directly caused 85,000 deaths, or 3.5% of the total (Mokdad, Marks, Stroup, & Gerberding, 2004). Tobacco kills more Americans than human immunodeficiency virus (HIV), illegal drug use, alcohol use, motor vehicle injuries, suicides, and murders—*combined*—each year.

## 12.3a   Causal Factors for Substance Dependence

Although it is now generally understood that biological and psychological factors interact in the development of substance dependence, a continuing controversy has involved the extent to which a "disease" conceptualization is accurate in explaining the disorder. Early versions of a disease model of addiction appeared in the United States shortly after the Civil War, when morphine use became associated with widespread addiction, known as "the soldier's disease" (Kleber, 1990). It was generally viewed as "evidence of a character weakness, not of criminality" and evoked "pity rather than contempt," at least toward former soldiers and rural white women suffering from opiate-medicine addiction (Kleber, 1990, p. 58). However, as drug abuse became more widely associated in later decades with the use of cocaine by Southern Blacks and the smoking of opium by Chinese immigrants, stronger and more negative views developed, leading to legislation outlawing drug and alcohol use.

> **What causal factors influence the development of substance dependence?**

*Table 12-1*    Drugs with Abuse Potential and Their Characteristics

| Official Name of Drug or Chemical | Method of Taking | Medical Use | Withdrawal | Usual Short-Term Effects | Possible Long-Term Effects |
|---|---|---|---|---|---|
| *Alcohol* <br> Whiskey, gin, beer, wine | Swallowing liquid | Rare; sometimes used as a sedative (for tension). | Yes | Depression of central nervous system. Relaxation (sedation). Drowsiness. Impairment in judgment, reaction time, coordination, and emotional control. Frequent aggressive behavior and driving accidents. | Irreversible damage to the brain, and liver. Severe withdrawal, dementia; amnestic, psychotic, mood, anxiety, and sleep disorders; sexual dysfunctions. |
| *Sedatives* <br> Barbiturates, Nembutal, Seconal, Phenobarbital, Doriden, Chloral hydrate, Meprobamate, Miltown, Equinil, Valium, Librium, Quaalude (Sopors) | Swallowing pills or capsules | Treatments of insomnia and tension. Induction of anesthesia. | Yes | Depression of central nervous system. Sleep, relaxation (sedation), or drowsiness. Sometimes euphoria. Impaired judgment, reaction time, coordination, and emotional control. Relief of anxiety tension. Muscle relaxation. | Irritability, weight loss. Severe withdrawal, dementia; amnestic, psychotic, mood, anxiety, and sleep disorders; sexual dysfunctions. |
| *Stimulants* <br> Caffeine <br> Coffee, tea, Coca-Cola No-Doz | Swallowing Liquid | Mild stimulant; treatment of some forms of coma. | Yes | Stimulation of central nervous system. Increased alertness. Reduced fatigue. | Anxiety and sleep disorders. |
| *Nicotine* <br> Cigarettes, cigars | Smoking (inhalation) | None | Yes | Stimulation of central nervous system. Relaxation or distraction due to the process of smoking. | Cancer, cardiovascular disease, lung disease. Smoker's cough. Sexual dysfunctions. |
| *Amphetamines* <br> Benzedrine <br> Dexedrine <br> Methamphetamine | Swallowing pills or capsules, snorting, smoking, or injecting in veins. | Treatment of obesity, narcolepsy, fatigue, attention deficit | Yes | Stimulation of central nervous system. Increased alertness, reduction of fatigue, loss of appetite, insomnia. Often euphoria. | Irritability, weight loss. Psychotic, mood, anxiety, and sleep disorders; sexual dysfunctions. |
| *Cocaine* | Snorting or injecting in veins. | Anesthesia of eye and throat | Yes | Stimulation of central nervous system. Increased alertness, reduction of fatigue, loss of appetite, euphoria. | Respiratory problems, weight loss, cardiovascular problems. Psychotic, mood, anxiety, and sleep disorders; sexual dysfunctions. |
| *Cannabis sativa* <br> *(marijuana)* | Smoking (inhalation) or swallowing | Potential for appetite enhancement, glaucoma, some neuro-degenerative conditions, may relieve side effects of chemotherapy | Yes | Relaxation, euphoria, increased appetite. Some alteration of time perception, impaired judgment, lethargy. | Chronic cough, lung diseases. Psychotic and anxiety disorders. |
| *Opiates (narcotics, analgesics)* <br> Opium, Heroin, Methadone, Morphine, Oxycodone Codeine, Percodan, Dermerol | Swallowing pill or capsule, smoking, injecting in muscle or vein. | Treatment of severe pain, diarrhea, and cough. | Yes | Depression of central nervous system. Sedation, euphoria, relief of pain. Impaired intellectual functioning and coordination. | Constipation, loss of appetite, weight loss, temporary impotency and sterility. Psychotic, mood, and sleep disorders; sexual dysfunctions. |
| *Hallucinogens* <br> LSD, Psilocybin, Mescaline, STP, MDA | Swallowing liquid, capsules, or pill (or sugar cube), or chewing plant | Experimental study of mind and brain function | No | Production of visual imagery, increased sensory awareness. Anxiety, nausea, impaired coordination. | Psychotic, mood, and anxiety disorders; flashbacks. |
| *Miscellaneous* <br> Volatile solvents (glue, gasoline, nutmeg) | Variable; usually inhalation (sniffing or "huffing") | None | No | Euphoria. Can produce delirium and delusional reaction. | Sometimes serious damage to liver and kidneys. Reports of brain damage. Dementia. Psychotic, mood, and anxiety disorders. |
| *Phencyclidin (PCP)* <br> Keptamine | Swallowing, snorting, smoking | None | No | Euphoria. Can produce delirium and delusional reaction. | High blood pressure, seizures, respiratory problems. Psychotic, mood, and anxiety disorders. |

**Figure 12-1**

**Substances to Which It Is Easiest to Form an Addiction and to Which It Is Most Difficult to Quit**

The substances that are most easy to get "hooked" on, and the most difficult to quit, according to a 0–100 scale ranked by experts in substance dependence

Source: Adapted from Hastings, J. (1990, November/December). Easy to get hooked on, hard to get off. *Health*, p. 37.

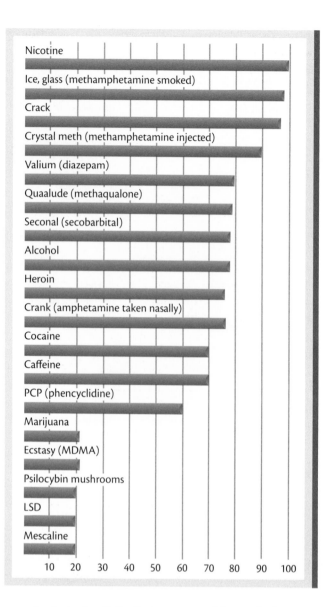

Addiction to drugs came to represent criminal activity that was caused by weak character and a lack of moral fiber.

This "moral failure" model was contrasted with a physical disease model proposing that alcoholism (or alcohol dependence) was internal to the individual due to underlying and presumably genetically transmitted predisposing factors. Jellenek (1960) described alcoholism as a progressive, degenerative disease that passes through four stages: the *pre-alcoholic*, in which social drinking becomes more frequent and tolerance increases; the *prodromal*, characterized by gulping of drinks, preoccupation with alcohol and occasional black-outs; the *crucial*, in which binging and loss of control occurs and the individual is unable to stop drinking until intoxicated; and finally the *chronic*, when the person is openly intoxicated in most settings and lives only to drink.

The disease conception is well conveyed by Mann (1968) in the following:

> *"Alcoholism is a disease which manifests itself chiefly by the uncontrollable drinking of the victim, who is known as an alcoholic. It is a progressive disease, which, if left untreated, grows more virulent year by year, driving its victims further and further from the normal world and deeper and deeper into an abyss which has only two outlets: insanity or death."*

(p. 3)

A congenital biological disposition to be an alcoholic is clearly stated, as follows, by Kessel (1962):

> **❝** *Since some people apparently blessed with everything that should save them from alcoholism … take to drink uncontrollably, whereas others much less well endowed by fate can drink without crossing the fatal frontier, a certain conclusion is inevitable: One does not become an alcoholic. One is born an alcoholic.* **❞**
>
> (p. 128)

In the disease view, alcoholics are unable to control their drinking due to the influence of powerful internal physiological forces. Although the diagnosis could be given only on the basis of behavioral criteria, once diagnosed the drinker became separated from the behavior: Compulsive drinking was a sign of alcoholism, but non-drinking was not a sign of its absence. There was no cure; those who remained abstinent from alcohol, even for decades, were still in recovery. For the past half-century, the disease model of addiction has often been portrayed as the only alternative to the moral failure model (Lyons, 2006).

Gradually, the role of environmental context and learning history in the development of substance use problems began to be appreciated. Central to most concepts of addiction are the inability to stop the addictive behavior and the high rate of recidivism or relapse that follows attempts to quit. Similarities in relapse rate curves across different addictive substances have been noted for decades (see Figure 12-2), implying that common mechanisms of addiction could be identified.

The U.S. Surgeon General's report on smoking, in 1979, saw these (and other) similarities as etiologically significant. It termed smoking "the prototypic substance dependence" (U.S. Department of Health, Education, and Welfare, 1979), suggesting that as we learn about one addiction, we learn about others as well. In 1988, the Surgeon General's report went further, concluding the following:

1. The pharmacological and behavioral processes that determine tobacco addiction are similar to those that determine addiction to drugs such as heroin and cocaine.

2. Environmental factors, including drug-associated stimuli and social pressure, are important influences on initiation, patterns of use, quitting, and relapse to use of opioids, alcohol, nicotine, and other addicting drugs (U.S. Department of Health and Human Services, 1988).

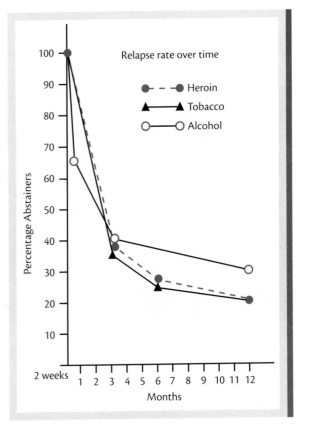

### Figure 12-2    *Relapse Rates*

Relapse rates are similar for persons dependent on alcohol, tobacco, or heroin.

Source: Adapted from Hunt, W. L., Barnett, W., & Branch, L. G. (1971). Relapse rates in addiction programs. *Journal of Clinical Psychology*, 27, 455–465.

With increased attention to the environmental contributions to substance disorders and better understanding of genetics, the disease concept of addiction is gradually being modified into a more interactive perspective. Although the saying "No one chooses addiction" is still commonly used to promote the disease notion, the behavioral dynamics of choice are actually very informative to the analysis of how addiction develops and how it is treated (Heyman, 2009). The complex interplay of short- and long-term behavioral consequences, biological systems, and environmental context is now the target of significant psychological research. It is interesting how different from the views of Mann and Kessel (quoted above) is the more recent appraisal by Moore (2001) in his review of the nature-nurture issue:

> *"Drug abuse must reflect both biological and psychological factors that together have produced a brain that craves certain drugs. After all, experience with drugs always precedes addiction to drugs, and an addiction certainly influences subsequent experiences. Ultimately, there is little reason to think that drug abuse is any more of a genetically produced "disease" than is fast skiing; in both cases, a brain forged by gene-environment interactions motivates its body to seek out particular kinds of stimulation."*

(p. 224; italics in original)

## 12.3b Biological Components

Much of the research on genetic and biological foundations of substance abuse and dependence has concerned alcohol; findings involving that substance are consequently given greater space here. Nonetheless, it is assumed that although substance-specific factors are important, there are also many cross-substance similarities, as noted in the Surgeon General's report.

Much of the research on genetic and biological foundations of substance abuse and dependence has been concerned with alcohol. (iStock)

### Genetics

Because psychoactive substances have their effects at the synapses of the brain, genetic factors influence the response to drugs and contribute to variations in substance involvement between people. There is little doubt that alcohol dependence tends to run in families. Winokur and his colleagues (1970) found that about 40% of 259 hospitalized alcoholics had a parent, usually the father, who was an alcoholic. Adoption studies have more clearly suggested a role for heredity. Goodwin and his colleagues (1973) found that sons of alcoholics placed in foster homes early in life were nearly 4 times more likely to develop alcoholism than were adoptees without known alcoholism in their biological parents. The adoptive parents of the two groups (all living in Denmark) did not differ in socioeconomic backgrounds, rates of alcoholism, or other psychological disorders. Goodwin and his colleagues (1977) in a similar adoption study found inconclusive results for a genetic factor in the daughters of alcoholics, however.

Twin studies support a modest genetic effect. A comparison of 3,516 male twins revealed a concordance rate of 58% MZ twins compared to 50% DZ twins for either alcohol abuse or alcohol dependence. Analysis suggested 48%–58% of the variability in the disorder could be accounted for by genetic factors, with the remainder ascribed to non-shared environment (Prescott & Kendler, 1999). Hughes (1986) has suggested a similar heritability estimate for smoking. However, a meta-analysis by Walters (2002) of 50 studies found a more modest heritability estimate of 30%–38% for alcohol misuse. A stronger genetic influence for males than for females was also reported.

The apparently stronger heritability of alcohol dependence in males may partly explain the sex ratio in the diagnosis. These findings correspond to general differences between genders in the rate of substance consumption. Globally, a greater proportion of abstainers from alcohol are females than are males (World Health Organization, 2004); there is no country in which males abstained at an appreciably higher rate than females. Males also metabolize alcohol in the liver more rapidly than females, on average; a similar amount of alcohol will have a greater effect in females, even after controlling for differences in body weight.

Several candidate genes that may confer susceptibility to dependence on various substances have been proposed, but there is no general consensus on the genetic foundation of dependence or abuse. Some studies have reported that certain genes related to dopamine synthesis and expression, such as the DRD2 receptor gene, are associated with increased risk of alcohol dependence. A recent follow-up of 838 persons involved in a longitudinal study of problem behavior, however, found no evidence of DRD2 linkage with alcohol abuse or dependence (Haberstick, et al., 2007).

Any genetic influence may be specific for particular substances. There is some evidence that the children of alcohol-dependent parents are at higher risk for alcohol dependence but not dependence on other substances (American Psychiatric Association, 2000). It is also possible that some of the familial clustering of substance dependence may be due to its linkage with other disorders (e.g., antisocial personality disorder) that themselves predispose people to substance abuse and dependence.

### Neurological Factors

Generally, all psychoactive drugs affect brain function and appear to have their effects mediated by the mesocorticolimbic dopamine pathway (sometimes called the "pleasure pathway") that is activated by pleasurable or reinforcing events. According to current biological models of addiction, repeated exposure to a biological agent (a drug) affects the brain over time, producing adaptations in individual neurons, which in turn alter the functioning of the neural circuits in which those neurons operate (Nestler & Aghajanian, 1997).

> **What disorders are triggered by chronic drug use?**

Chronic drug use produces long-lasting, physical modifications in this pathway; thus, use that was once "voluntary" becomes compulsive. The brain responds to the artificially higher levels of neurotransmitters produced by the drug by downregulating that neurotransmitter's "natural" activity. This can lead, eventually, to tolerance, withdrawal, and craving—the components of substance dependence.

## 12.3c  Psychosocial Components

### Cultural Factors

There are wide variations between racial and ethnic groups in terms of the amounts of substances consumed. In the case of alcohol, for example, annual consumption per person ranges from nearly zero in several countries (e.g., Kuwait, Somalia, Bangladesh, Saudi Arabia) to the equivalent of almost 19.5 liters of pure alcohol per capita in Uganda. In the United States, per capita annual consumption is 8.51 liters of pure alcohol equivalent; the consumption rate in Ireland (14.45) is more than 7 times the rate of consumption in Ecuador (1.99), according to data collected by the World Health Organization (2004).

Similarly, tobacco consumption varies widely between different racial and cultural groups (Substance Abuse and Mental Health Sevices Administration, 2006). Within the U.S., American Indians or Alaskan Natives have the highest rate of smoking and Asians have the lowest rates; within the Asian culture, those of Korean background smoke at more than 3 times the rate of those of Chinese background.

Some cultural differences may be tied to biological and genetic factors, as well. One speculation has been that some individuals are protected from alcoholism because they inherit a tendency to respond to even small amounts of alcohol with very unpleasant reactions, which would tend to inhibit extensive drinking or perhaps any drinking at all. Research has shown that about three-fourths of Asian people respond to alcohol in this negative fashion—a fact that may account for the low rate of alcoholism among Asians (Wolff, 1972). It now appears that 50% of Japanese, Chinese, and Korean people have a deficiency in an enzyme (aldehyde dehydrogenase) that assists in the breakdown of alcohol during early metabolism. As a result, they tend to experience unpleasant palpitations and flushing of the face when consuming alcohol, and these reactions serve as a natural unpleasant consequence that deters drinking. Asian groups have a lower risk for alcohol use disorder (American Psychiatric Association, 2013).

It is also apparent that different social and religious customs and practices encourage or discourage involvement with particular substances. In the U.S., for example, Mormon culture discourages the non-medical use of all substances, including caffeine, alcohol, and tobacco; other religious groups are less restrictive, and even employ certain substances in religious rituals.

## Drugs as Reinforcers

By virtue of their physiological properties on the reward pathways in the brain, many drugs are powerful, unconditioned reinforcers. As such, their effects reward the use of the substances and the environmental stimuli associated with drugs take on value—as discriminative stimuli setting the occasion for use, as conditioned stimuli eliciting craving, and as conditioned reinforcers maintaining the chain of behaviors leading to drug ingestion.

Research with animals demonstrates conditioning as an important influence in drug-related behavior. Davis and Smith (1979) showed that a stimulus paired with a drug (either morphine or amphetamine) could be used as a conditioned reinforcer to maintain operant responding, and its reinforcing strength was directly related to the dose with which it was paired. Stimuli paired with a drug can also be used to alleviate narcotic withdrawal in rats (Lal, Miksic, Drawbaugh, Numan, & Smith, 1976), and conditioned stimuli associated with various drugs can acquire the ability to increase dopamine metabolism (Perez-Cruet, 1976).

An example of the reinforcing value of a drug comes from a study with monkeys in which lever pressing provided an intravenous dose of nicotine on a fixed-interval schedule of reinforcement (Goldberg, Spealman, & Goldberg, 1981). The value of nicotine in maintaining the responding is evident in Figure 12-3. Mecamylamine is a chemical that blocks nicotine receptor sites in the brain, and it can be seen here to reduce the reinforcing value of nicotine. A brief visual stimulus paired with nicotine became a conditioned reinforcer; when it was omitted, responding declined even though nicotine was still delivered. Nicotine also functions as a reinforcer in humans (Hughes, Pickens, Spring, & Keenan, 1985; Harvey, et al., 2004). For a person who smokes one pack of cigarettes per day, assuming that each cigarette yields 10 puffs or nicotine "shots," smoking is an activity that is emitted and reinforced 73,000 times per year. Few other activities are so consistently and powerfully strengthened across a wide variety of settings (Lyons, 1991).

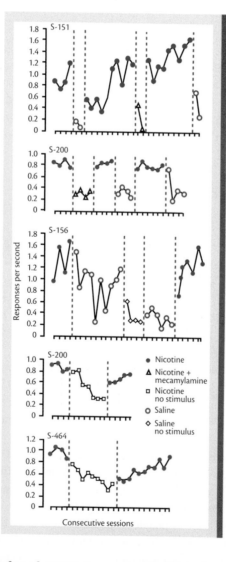

**Figure 12-3**
**Nicotine Reinforces Lever Pressing in Monkeys**

Effects of substituting saline for nicotine injections (open circles), treatment with mecamylamine before the session (open triangles), or omitting the brief stimulus during the FI fixed-interval reinforcement schedule (open squares) on responding under the second-order schedule of intravenous nicotine injection for individual monkeys.

Source: Adapted from Goldberg, S. R., Spealman, R. D., & Goldberg, D. M. (1981) Persistent behavior at high rates maintained by intravenous self-administration of nicotine. *Science, 214,* 573–575.

## Conditioning Factors

Conditioning influences extend to fundamental properties of substance dependence such as tolerance and withdrawal. Siegal, Hinson, Krank, and McCully (1982) demonstrated the conditioning of opiate tolerance in rats. Noting that some overdose fatalities involved experienced drug users who died after a dose that had not previously been lethal, the authors proposed that drug overdose might often be a failure of tolerance. Pavlovian conditioning principles suggested that environmental cues present during drug administration (conditioned stimuli) are paired with the onset of drug effect (the unconditioned stimulus) and, subsequently, elicit the anticipatory physiological responses that the body uses to counteract the drug. These compensatory physiological responses are evident as drug tolerance. According to this conditioning analysis, drug tolerance is a response that becomes conditioned to the stable environmental stimuli that have reliably accompanied recurrent drug use in the past. If so, tolerance would be modulated by drug cues, and overdose might be more likely when drugs are taken under novel conditions.

Rats were injected with heroin in a gradually increasing series of 15 dosages, given every other day. One group (N = 37) received the doses in their normal colony room while another group (N = 42) received the drug during a two-hour stay in a different, novel room filled with white noise. Then, each group received a final dose, larger than they had previously received, in one of the 2 environmental settings. A third group of control animals (N = 28) also received this large dosage although they had not previously been exposed to heroin.

The results are summarized in Table 12-2. The large injection of heroin was fatal to nearly all (96.4%) of control animals, which had established no tolerance for the drug. Among the experimental groups, the mortality rate was lower because prior drug exposure had produced tolerance, but mortality was twice as high when animals received the large dose in a different environmental setting than the one in which the drug was previously experienced. Siegal et al. concluded that tolerance had been conditioned to the environmental cues that predicted the drug and that in the absence of these cues (in the different setting or DT group) tolerance was reduced, resulting in higher mortality.

Siegal (1999) expanded these and other experimental observations into a more comprehensive Pavlovian analysis of tolerance, craving, and withdrawal. The cues that predict the onset of drug effect—including the environmental setting, the procedures of administration, and the interoceptive stimuli accompanying the entry of the drug into the body and the onset of its effects—all serve as conditioned stimuli that elicit anticipatory homeostatic responses as the body prepares to compensate for the drug. These compensatory responses are, generally, the opposite of the unconditioned response caused by the drug itself and produce tolerance to the drug effect. However, if the drug does not follow the predictive stimuli, the compensatory responses are experienced as craving and withdrawal symptoms. The analysis also explains the observation that tolerance and withdrawal are less pronounced in individuals who receive a drug passively, compared to those who self-administer the drug. This is because the act of self-administration involves additional internal or interoceptive cues predicting the drug, which combine with the external cues of the situation. As a result, tolerance is stronger, and withdrawal symptoms are more evident, in self-administering

*Table 12-2*   Rat Mortality After Large Dose of Heroin

Rat mortality after large dose of heroin, given either in the same setting (ST) or different setting (DT) as previous injections.

| Group | Mortality |
|---|---|
| ST | 32.4% |
| DT | 64.3% |
| Control | 96.4% |

Source: Adapted from Siegel, S., Hinson, R. E., Krank, M. D., & McCully, J. (1982). Heroin "over-dose" death: Contribution of drug-associated environmental cues. *Science, 216,* 436–437.

subjects. Once such conditioning is in place, re-exposure to drug-related cues, even after a long period of abstinence, can produce craving for the drug, withdrawal symptoms, and relapse to drug use.

## Expectancy

Substance use and preference are affected by beliefs and expectancies held by an individual. For example, evidence shows that it is alcoholics' beliefs about whether they are drinking alcohol that are more highly associated with desire for additional drinks than whether, in fact, they are drinking alcohol. Marlatt and his colleges (1973) used a taste preference task and found that whether alcoholics were given an initial drink of actual alcohol or plain tonic did not affect their subsequent drinking (suggesting that exposure to alcohol itself did not cause loss of control). However, alcoholics who were told that they were receiving alcohol drank more than those who were told they were not receiving alcohol, whether or not alcohol was actually included in the drink.

Instructions can also alter the value of nicotine as a reinforcer. Hughes and his colleagues (1985) showed that nicotine-dependent subjects preferred to chew a nicotine gum to a placebo gum. However, the preference could be reversed if subjects were given false descriptions of the placebo gum as being a new nicotine gum with fewer side effects.

## Social Influences

Characteristics of the immediate social community have a powerful influence on the initiation and maintenance of drug behavior. Potential drug abusers are likely to be strongly affected by the availability of certain drugs and the modeling and social reinforcement by peers for drug usage. Several longitudinal studies have shown that variables such as perceived drug use in the peer group and perceived peer tolerance for drug use predict future drug use in adolescents before they have begun using drugs (Kandel, Kessler, & Margulies, 1978).

The effect of drug availability, setting, and peer group behavior is powerfully shown in a study that compared American soldiers in Vietnam with a matched control group (Robins, *The interaction of setting a predisposition in explaining novel behavior: Drug initiations before, in, and after Vietnam,* 1978). The initiation of narcotic drug use ( for example, heroin) increased dramatically during the soldiers' stay in Vietnam and returned to a level somewhat lower than their pre-Vietnam level after they were discharged. The control group showed no comparable change (see Figure 12-4).

Robins, Helzer, and Davis (1975) also found that relapse rates among these Vietnam veterans differed greatly, depending on the environment in which drug use was acquired. Among those veterans who initiated narcotic use in Vietnam less than 10% resumed use within 6 months of release from treatment in federal hospitals, while 70% of persons who acquired addiction to the same drugs in the U.S. relapsed after treatment. In other words, relapse was much more likely if patients were discharged into the same environment in which the addiction was established.

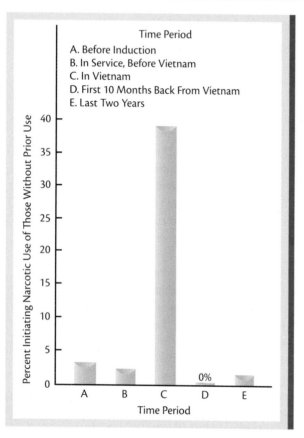

**Figure 12-4   *Vietnam Veterans and Narcotic Use***

Percentage of veterans initiating narcotic use (usually heroin) during five time periods before, during, and after tours in Vietnam. The percentages are based on the number of veterans without prior narcotic use who initiated use in that time period. The number of veterans without prior use would, of course, decrease across the different time periods.

Source: Adapted from Robins, L. N. (1978). *The interaction of setting and predisposition in explaining novel behavior, in, and after Vietnam.* Washington, DC: Hemisphere.

Modeling effects have long been recognized as important in substance abuse. Smart and Fejer (1972) found a positive relationship between the parents' use of tranquilizing drugs, alcohol, and tobacco (as reported by the students) and the students' use of drugs of all kinds. Peers also strongly influence substance use. As peer group deviancy increases, adolescent alcohol and drug use increases; as parental monitoring and support increases, alcohol and drug use decreases (Barnes, Hoffman, Welte, Farrell, & Dintcheff, 2006). These observations imply that improvement of parenting skills may be an important component in prevention and treatment.

## 12.3d  Summary

Evidence appears to support substantial contributions from both genetics and environment to the development of substance use disorders. Biological susceptibility to the unconditioned effects of drugs can be influenced by a history of drug experiences to produce alterations in the brain's response to a substance. The reinforcing value of drugs strengthens and maintains drug use. As use continues, tolerance, withdrawal, and craving can be produced as anticipatory responses of the brain as it attempts to compensate for the onset of drug effects. These brain responses can be elicited by stimuli that have accompanied and predicted drug onset in the past, such that tolerance can be associated with the settings of drug use, and withdrawal, craving, and relapse can be triggered when drug cues are not followed by the drug. The development of these bio-behavioral patterns is a function, in part, of genetic history, cultural influence, environmental setting, drug availability and experience, and the degree of parental and peer-group support.

# 12.4  Development of Substance-Induced Disorders

As previously discussed, both substance intoxication and substance withdrawal are reversible, substance-specific syndromes related to recent ingestion of a substance or to cessation of the substance after a prolonged period of heavy use. The other substance-induced disorders may develop more gradually, but specific drugs or toxins are etiologically important in their initiation, maintenance, or worsening. There is great variation among substances in the disorders they induce. Again, however, much research to date has involved the persisting effect of alcohol.

The substance-induced disorders concern substance-specific intoxication and withdrawal; substance-induced mental disorders—such as psychotic, mood, anxiety, sleep, or sexual dysfunctions; and substance-induced neurocognitive disorders, such as delirium or major neurocognitive disorder. The particular set of disorders will be discussed by substance.

## 12.4a  Alcohol-Induced Disorders

Alcohol use is associated with some of the most severe and long-lasting substance-induced disorders. Alcohol intoxication is probably the most well-known effect of consumption; the impairment it produces is a major contributor to death or injury in automobile accidents, violence, and suicide. Alcohol appears to be involved in up to 55% of fatal automobile accidents and more than one-half of all murders (American Psychiatric Association, 2000). Sometimes, intoxication is associated with amnesia for events that occurred during the intoxicated state. Level of impairment is related to blood

Alcohol intoxication is a major contributor to death or injury in automobile accidents, violence, and suicide. (iStock)

alcohol concentration—which, in turn, is determined by the amount of alcohol consumed, the rate of consumption, body weight, gender, and food intake, among other factors. Most states define legal intoxication as a blood alcohol concentration of 0.08 g/100mL, a level that can be reached at the rate of two or three standard "drinks" (a **standard drink** is the equivalent of 12 oz. of beer, 4 oz. of table wine, or 1.5 oz. of 80-proof liquor) within 1 hour for most average-sized men and women. Blood alcohol concentrations in excess of 0.30 to 0.40 g/100mL can cause respiratory failure and death in non-tolerant individuals (see Figure 12-5).

The *DSM-5* provides the specifier "alcohol intoxication delirium" within the neurocognitive disorders for delirium (Chapter 15) to describe conditions in which consumption of alcohol results in symptoms in excess of normal intoxication, serious enough to warrant clinical attention. "Alcohol withdrawal delirium" involves similar symptoms of delirium that have onset during withdrawal from alcohol. Both disorders may involve perceptual disturbances with auditory, tactile, or visual hallucinations. Alcohol withdrawal delirium with perceptual disturbances (*delirium tremens*, or "DTs") occurs in less than 10% of strongly dependent individuals during withdrawal when the alcohol level in the blood drops suddenly (American Psychiatric Association, 2013). Initially the person is restless, cannot sleep, and is made nervous by slight noises. Left untreated, a psychological disturbance of psychotic proportions may develop, in which the person becomes disoriented in place and time, has visual hallucinations (frequently of fast-moving animals such as rats, cockroaches, snakes, or spiders that seem to swarm over the wall, bed, or the person's body), develops

**Standard drink**

Standard ethanol content, or the amount of alcohol in 12 oz. of beer, 4 oz. of wine, or 1.5 oz. of liquor

*Figure 12-5*    ***Correlation of Automobile Accidents and Blood Alcohol Level***

Relative probability that a driver causes and is involved in a crash as a function of blood alcohol level. For example, a risk of 5 means that a driver has a 5 times greater risk of causing a crash than a driver whose blood alcohol level is less than 0.03%.

Source: Aarens, M., Cameron, T., Roizen, J., Roizen, R., Schneberk, D., & Wingard, D.

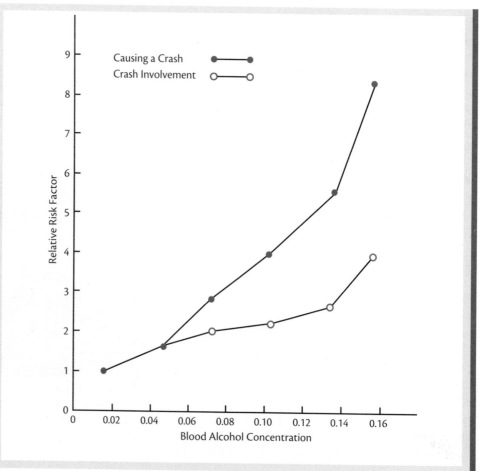

gross tremors of the arms and legs, sweats profusely, and has a fast but weak heartbeat. The person may react with terror to the hallucinated animals, hiding under the bedcovers or desperately fighting them off. The acute phase of the DTs, which usually lasts from 3 to 6 days, is likely related to a serious medical problem such as liver failure or hypoglycemia. In the past, approximately 10% of individuals with this disorder died as a result of convulsions, heart failure, and other complications. Recent drugs, however, have reduced the death rate.

Continued use of alcohol in large quantities has a variety of physical consequences on major organ systems in the body, the least serious of which is the chronic irritation of the stomach lining, resulting in indigestion or ulceration. Extensive use also results in the accumulation of fat in the liver, reducing its functioning and eventuating, if continued, in a marked impairment of this organ called hepatic **cirrhosis**.

Imaging procedures have shown that cerebral atrophy is associated with extensive and chronic alcoholic abuse (Fox, Ramsey, Huckman, & Proske, 1976). In some cases this cerebral atrophy can be reversed, as indicated by brain X-rays taken before and after periods of 1 to 4 months of abstinence (Carlen, Wortzman, Holgate, Wilkinson, & Rankin, 1978). The reversible atrophy occurred only in individuals who showed improvement in psychological functioning during the abstinent period. The authors speculate that many brain neurons had been only partially damaged and that new dendrites had "sprouted" on the still viable axons.

Figure 12-6 shows, in this comparison, reduced brain volume and size, and cortical atrophy in the image of an alcoholic subject. Brain effects such as these can underlie several different substance-induced disorders. Alcohol-induced persistent major neurocognitive disorder (also known as Korsakoff's syndrome), first described by the Russian psychiatrist Korsakoff in 1887, afflicts about 1% of chronic alcoholics. It involves a defect in remembering recent events. The person, however, fills in the gaps in memory with imaginary happenings, a process usually referred to as **confabulation**. These patients are also likely to show polyneuritis, the inflammation of a large number of peripheral nerves. Korsakoff's syndrome is thought to result from a deficiency of vitamin B (thiamine) associated with the alcoholic's poor dietary habits over a long period of time. Massive doses of thiamine may help to prevent or treat the amnestic condition although, once established, impairment can be quite severe and persist indefinitely.

A variety of other debilitating and potentially lethal consequences can also follow chronic and extensive alcohol use, including damage to the cardiovascular system and the development of a life-style that renders the chronic abuser vulnerable to a variety of serious diseases. How much these effects are due to the direct pharmacologic effect of alcohol and how much to the life-style that accompanies chronic and protracted use is not always clear. It has been shown that alcohol has a direct effect upon cells taken from rat embryos, retarding both their growth and rate of differentiation (Brown, Goulding, & Fabro, 1979). Women who drink during pregnancy are more likely to have babies with physical and behavioral deviations, including mental retardation and neurodevelopmental disorders. **Fetal alcohol syndrome** (FAS)—a constellation of fetal abnormalities, impairments in growth, and central

**Cirrhosis**

Degenerative chronic disease in which liver cells are replaced by scar tissue

**Confabulation**

Filling gaps in memory with imaginary recollection

**Fetal alcohol syndrome**

Constellation of fetal abnormalities resulting from maternal alcohol use during pregnancy

*Figure 12-6*
**Comparison of MRI Images of Two Females, One Alcoholic and One Normal Control**

Source: Images Courtesy of National Institute on Alcohol Abuse and Alcoholism.

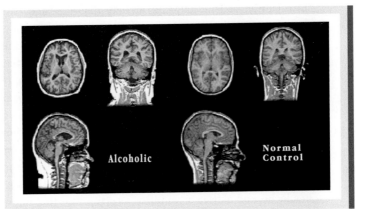

nervous system problems caused by alcohol exposure *in utero*—is now recognized as the leading preventable cause of birth defects (Wedding, et al., 2007).

# 12.4b Stimulant-Induced Disorders

First synthesized in the 1920s, the amphetamines initially found their way into approved medical use as the active ingredients in nasal decongestant inhalers. Soon they were recognized as potent central nervous system **stimulants**. They produce increased alertness, wakefulness, euphoria, and an increased ability to concentrate. Amphetamines were used widely by truck drivers attempting to make up time on long hauls, students cramming for examinations, and executives facing a strenuous week. They also served to inhibit appetite and were frequently prescribed for that reason as components of weight-loss programs or to treat depression. They retain valid medical uses for certain conditions such as narcolepsy and attention deficit/hyperactivity disorder. However, they are widely abused; and especially when they are smoked or injected, they are associated with violent and aggressive behavior.

The *DSM-5* identifies stimulant intoxication and stimulant intoxication delirium, stimulant withdrawal, and stimulant-induced psychotic, mood, anxiety, or sleep disorders, as well as stimulant-induced sexual dysfunction, as induced disorders associated with this substance. During intoxication, individuals may experience euphoria, hypervigilance, anger, anxiety, rapid heartbeat, chills, nausea or confusion. Perceptual distortions, including hallucinations, can occur, and judgment is impaired.

Most complications reported in regard to stimulant abuse result from chronic consumption. When dosage is kept within the medically therapeutic range (5–15 mg), tolerance to the drugs develops slowly. However, progressive increments in dose levels accelerate the development of tolerance to amounts hundreds of times greater than the therapeutic dose, often without apparent serious physiological effects (Carey & Mandel, 1968). An unusual feature of amphetamine tolerance is that the cardiovascular system becomes tolerant to large doses rather rapidly, so that heartbeat and blood pressure may not be significantly increased in chronic abusers. However, amphetamines, and especially methamphetamine, can cause long-term injury to the brain, including persistent abnormal brain chemistry and psychotic conditions that persist for months or years (Ernst, Chang, Leonido-Yee, & Speck, 2000).

During intense amphetamine intoxication, auditory and tactile hallucinations and paranoia can occur, as can extreme anger and threats. The psychotic state may be nearly indistinguishable from paranoid schizophrenia, except that the reaction disappears some 3 to 6 days after discontinuation of the drug. During amphetamine withdrawal, symptoms can resemble a major depressive episode (American Psychiatric Association, 2013).

# 12.4c Caffeine-Induced Disorders

Caffeine is associated with four substance-induced disorders in the *DSM-5*: caffeine intoxication, caffeine-induced anxiety disorder, and caffeine-induced anxiety and sleep disorders. The drug is widely consumed cross-culturally, with more than 80% of adults using caffeine during the past year. Intake is increasing as high-caffeine products are marketed, especially in younger people. Caffeine intoxication may impact 7% of the population. Intoxication tends to involve nervousness, restlessness, diuresis, excitement, and—occasionally—mild sensory disturbances. At normal levels of intake, no medical difficulties are consistently associated with caffeine use. Heavy use may exacerbate anxiety or gastrointestinal problems or produce cardiac arrhythmia; very large doses can provoke seizures or respiratory failure. Use of oral contraceptives increases the risk of intoxication, as they tend to decrease the elimination of caffeine (American Psychiatric Association, 2013).

Caffeine withdrawal disorder lists marked fatigue and drowsiness, depressed mood, headache, and nausea or vomiting as symptoms that follow the abrupt cessation of caffeine

**Stimulants**

Drugs that stimulate the CNS and produce wakefulness, alertness, and ability to concentrate

after prolonged daily use. As always, the diagnosis would require that the symptoms cause significant distress or impairment in social, occupational, or interpersonal functioning. Symptoms usually peak within 1 to 2 days of abstinence (American Psychiatric Association, 2013). As noted earlier, a proposed category of caffeine use disorder is placed in Section III of the *DSM-5* for further study. As currently organized, it would involve having three of nine symptoms common to the substance use disorders within a 12-month period.

## 12.4d  Cannabis-Induced Disorders

Cannabis intoxication, cannabis intoxication delirium, cannabis-induced psychotic disorder, cannabis-induced anxiety disorder, and cannabis induced sleep disorders, as well as cannabis withdrawal—all are included in the *DSM-5*. Cannabis (most often in the form of marijuana that is smoked or eaten) is the most widely used illicit drug in the United States. Nearly one-third of Americans have ingested a cannabinoid at some point. A 1992 U.S. survey indicated that lifetime prevalence of cannabis use disorders was nearly 5% (American Psychiatric Association, 2000); a representative sample of Australians found that about 2.2% of the adult population met criteria for a cannabis use disorder (Teesson, Lynskey, Manor, & Baillie, 2002). Reliable data on the extent of impairment produced by cannabis use are difficult to collect: Individuals with cannabis use disorders appear to be less likely to seek treatment than those with other substance use disorders. However, the rate of cannabis use disorders is increasing (American Psychiatric Association, 2013).

Cannabis is the most widely used illicit drug in the United States. (iStock)

Cannabis intoxication occurs within minutes of smoking, or within a few hours of oral ingestion, and typically includes euphoria, altered time judgment, anxiety, and increased heart rate. At higher doses, perceptual disturbances including hallucinations may occur, as well as paranoid ideation and experiences of depersonalization. Among regular users, nearly one-third report mild depression, anxiety, or irritability (American Psychiatric Association, 2000). There has been increasing interest in the connection between cannabis use in adolescents and subsequent development of schizophrenia, although it is not clear if the association is a causal one (Tandon, Keshaven, & Nasrallah, 2008). A large prospective study in New Zealand found that heavy cannabis use in adolescence was associated with a drop in IQ scores (as much as 8 points) at age 38, emphasizing the potential neurotoxic risk of cannabis to the developing brain (Meier, et al., 2012).

## 12.4e  Cocaine-Induced Disorders

Cocaine comes from the coca plant in South America and was first isolated in 1865. It became widely used as a mild stimulant and anesthetic in the United States (and an early stimulating ingredient of Coca-Cola). Cocaine is associated with several substance-induced disorders—including cocaine intoxication and intoxication delirium, cocaine withdrawal, and cocaine-induced psychotic, bipolar, depressive, anxiety, and sleep disorders, and cocaine-induced sexual dysfunctions. It produces strong euphoric effects, and dependence can develop rapidly; because it has a short half-life, there is frequent re-dosing. Cocaine is usually snorted or injected. In an easily vaporized form called "crack," it has an extremely rapid onset and a very high level of associated dependence.

The diagnostic criteria for cocaine intoxication are identical to those for the amphetamines. Stimulant effects are most commonly seen. Dramatic behavioral changes can take place; and psychotic symptoms, including hallucinations and delusions, can occur.

Sudden death from cardiac or respiratory arrest or stroke has been reported in otherwise healthy people using cocaine. Withdrawal develops within hours of cessation of heavy use and can include intense dysphoria and suicidal behavior (American Psychiatric Association, 2013). Those with cocaine-induced psychotic disorder may appear similar to those with paranoid schizophrenia. Depressive mood is common among cocaine-dependent individuals. Other induced symptoms resemble panic disorder or generalized anxiety disorder.

## 12.4f Hallucinogen-Induced Disorders

The **hallucinogens** comprise a class of drugs that produce marked changes in mood and sensory perception. They include a wide variety of substances with very different chemical and pharmacologic properties and form a class only because of the general similarity of their effects. These drugs range from the naturally occurring variants such as peyote, psilocybin, and amanita muscaria to laboratory synthesized substances such as lysergic acid diethylamide (LSD), mescaline, and the "letter" or "alphabet" drugs such as STP, MDMA ("Ecstasy"), and PCP. Up to 10% of the population has experienced a hallucinogen, but lifetime prevalence of hallucinogen abuse or dependence appears to be less than 1% (American Psychiatric Association, 2000).

LSD, first synthesized by Hoffman, a Swiss chemist, was introduced into this country in the early 1950s. It was initially used in research because it was thought to produce a model of the schizophrenic reaction. Subsequently, researchers have concluded that the LSD experience is quite different from schizophrenia. For a time, LSD was used as an adjunct in the treatment of neuroses, psychoses, and alcoholism; but later it was determined to be unhelpful.

The most striking effects of the drugs are sensory and perceptual. Perceptions seem intensified, objects become sharper and brighter, and details not ordinarily noticed become clear. Hallucinations and illusions are central to the intoxication. Physical symptoms such as pupil dilation, rapid heartbeat, sweating, and tremors typically occur. There may be evidence of tolerance with repeated use, but the hallucinogens do not appear to produce a significant withdrawal syndrome.

Phencyclidine (PCP) is a hallucinogen originally developed as an anesthetic that shortly became a drug of abuse. It and related substances, such as ketamine, can be swallowed, smoked, or injected. Phencyclidine intoxication generally involves agitation, belligerence, impaired judgment, and assaultiveness, combined with physical disturbances (numbness, rapid heartbeat, muscle rigidity, seizures, and involuntary movements of the eyes). Slurred speech, slowed reaction time, and disorganized thinking are also present. At higher doses, psychotic symptoms, including hallucinations, occur. Phencyclidine-induced intoxication delirium, psychotic disorder, mood disorder, and anxiety disorder have been described. Rates of dependence are not clear, but about 2.5% of the population report use on at least one occasion (American Psychiatric Association, 2013).

The induced disorders associated with these substances include intoxication, hallucinogen persisting perception disorder (**flashbacks**), and hallucinogen-induced psychotic, mood, or anxiety disorders. Hallucinogen persisting perception disorder involves the re-experiencing of some of the symptoms of intoxication, in the absence of recent ingestion, in episodes that can last several months. It may occur in just over 4% of hallucinogen users (American Psychiatric Association, 2013).

## 12.4g Inhalant-Induced Disorders

Inhalant use typically involves toxins or solvents such as paint thinner, gasoline, glue, or paint, or other volatile compounds containing toluene, benzene, acetone, and other substances. Typically the substances are concentrated on a rag or in a paper bag and inhaled. Intoxication is rapid and can involve euphoria, perceptual disturbances, dizziness, impaired judgment, slurred speech, and stupor. Besides inhalant intoxication, the *DSM-5* recognizes

**Hallucinogens**

Drugs that produce marked changes in perception

**Flashbacks**

Re-experiencing some of the symptoms of intoxication in the absence of recent ingestion

inhalant intoxication delirium, inhalant-induced persisting dementia, and inhalant-induced psychotic, mood, and anxiety disorders.

The inhaled toxic substances can cause permanent damage to various organ systems, leading to kidney or liver failure. Neurological deficits are common in chronic users, contributing to a persisting dementia, and sudden death can occur from heart or respiratory failure. About 10% of 13-year-old children have used inhalants at least once, but only about 0.4% of teenagers develop inhalant-related disorders (American Psychiatric Association, 2013).

Apart from intoxication, inhalant-induced conditions include psychotic, depressive, anxiety, and neurocognitive disorders. However, inhalant withdrawal has not been identified.

## 12.4h  Tobacco-Induced Disorders

As discussed previously, nicotine dependence is the single greatest cause of preventable death in the nation. Up to 43% of the adult population have used cigarettes, and up to half of daily smokers may have tobacco use disorder (American Psychiatric Association, 2013); those figures would make it the most common form of substance dependence. Nicotine is a stimulant drug that has also been used in the past as an insecticide. Although it affects mood via several different neurotransmitters, it also increases dopamine levels in the reward pathways of the brain; and, as such, it is a powerful unconditioned reinforcer. The most serious health-related effects are due not to nicotine per se but the use of tobacco as a vehicle for its delivery.

The only substance-induced disorders associated with nicotine are tobacco withdrawal and tobacco-induced sleep disorder. Usually, withdrawal involves irritability, depressed mood, restlessness, difficulty concentrating, insomnia, and/or increased appetite. Craving for tobacco is nearly always reported. Symptoms may begin within hours of cessation of smoking and last for several days. The large majority of smokers (80%) have attempted to quit, and 60% of those relapse within a week while only about 5% remain abstinent—but because of their repeated attempts, about half of tobacco users eventually abstain (American Psychiatric Association, 2013).

## 12.4i  Opioid-Induced Disorders

Opiates—or **narcotics**, to use the common term—are **depressants** that have their major effect on the central nervous system and respiration. They are most commonly used as analgesics, or painkillers, although they are also frequently prescribed for use in cough suppressants and for diarrhea. For centuries the most frequently used medications throughout the civilized world contained high concentrations of opium. Morphine, a more potent alkaloid form of opium, was isolated in Germany in 1804. This compound, like heroin almost a century later, was originally hailed as a cure for the opium habit since

The drug that has been used most effectively as an analgesic (pain reducer) throughout the centuries is opium. (iStock)

morphine could be substituted for opium without any signs of withdrawal. Interestingly, it was long felt by physicians that the administration of morphine hypodermically was a means of avoiding addiction. Today, prescription opioids (synthetic opium) such as oxycodone are responsible for more overdose deaths than any other substance, twice as many as cocaine and heroin combined (Okie, 2010).

Opioid-induced disorders include opioid intoxication, opioid withdrawal, opioid intoxication delirium, and opioid-induced psychotic, and mood, sexual, and sleep disorders. During intoxication, the pupils become constricted, and drowsiness, slurred speech, and impairment of memory or attention occur. With chronic use the individual becomes constipated; depression and insomnia are frequently present. Sexual and reproductive

**Narcotics**

Opiate drugs that produce stupor and pain relief

**Depressants**

Drugs that depress the CNS and produce drowsiness, and sedation

dysfunctions are common; in women, menstruation becomes irregular or ceases, and men experience frequent erectile dysfunction. In effect, many of the bodily functions are slowed down.

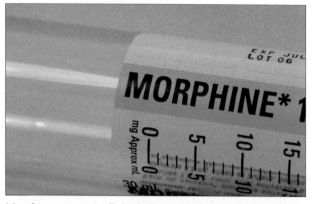

Morphine was originally hailed as a cure for the opium habit.
(iStock)

Initially, individuals tend to experience increasing euphoria as they increase the dose and the frequency of administration. Most chronic users report that after a period of use they cease even attempting to obtain the high and use the drug just to "feel right" or avoid withdrawal symptoms. Withdrawal involves anxiety, restlessness, craving, and increased sensitivity to pain. Dysphoria, nausea, muscle aches, diarrhea, fever, and insomnia are present in some combination. Acute withdrawal subsides within a week. Opioid use disorder occurs at a prevalence of less than 1% of the population, with lower rates among African Americans and higher rates for Native Americans. More males than females use opiates; the male-to-female ratio for heroin use is 3:1 (American Psychiatric Association, 2013).

## 12.4j   Sedative, Hypnotic or Anxiolytic-Induced Disorders

Sedative or tranquilizing drugs have been widely prescribed for relief of anxiety and insomnia. These substances include barbiturates, benzodiazepines, and hypnotic compounds that produce sleep or have anti-anxiety effects. The drugs are very widely used, with about 15% of adult Americans ingesting them within the past year (American Psychiatric Association, 2000). Unlike with the other substances considered, women may have a higher incidence of substance use disorder in this class than men. The incidence of sedative, hypnotic, or anxiolytic use disorder appears to be lower than 0.5% (American Psychiatric Association, 2013).

The sedative, hypnotic, or anxiolytic-induced disorders are intoxication, intoxication delirium, withdrawal, withdrawal delirium, persisting dementia, persisting amnestic disorder, and induced psychotic, mood, anxiety, sexual, and sleep disorders. Intoxication involves clouding of consciousness, impairment in memory or attention, disequilibrium, poor judgment, slurred speech, and stupor. The symptom presentation resembles several aspects of alcohol intoxication.

In chronic users, severe depression and suicidal behavior can occur. The combination of these substances with other drugs, especially alcohol, dramatically increases risk of death. Abrupt withdrawal of barbiturates from a heavily dependent individual produces a withdrawal syndrome that is severe and potentially lethal. Close medical observation is required to slowly decrease in the amount of barbiturates administered daily. In intoxication delirium, auditory, tactile, and visual hallucinations may occur.

## 12.5   Treatment of Substance-Related Disorders

Many different therapeutic approaches have been applied to substance abuse and substance dependence. Treatment can be particularly difficult, in part because of the relapsing nature of the disorders and because many individuals are not motivated to change, in fact continuing to deny that a serious problem exists. Often, events such as health crises, arrests, or major disruptive events precipitate the entry into treatment. Treatment of some substance dependencies

**Which treatments are effective for substance use disorders?**

may require detoxification periods in which medical personnel closely monitor gradual withdrawal. For alcohol-related treatment, however, there appears to be little difference in outcome of inpatient versus outpatient treatment settings (Finney & Moos, 2002). In nearly all programs, treatment compliance is a problem, and dropout rates from therapy are high. Nonetheless, a variety of demonstrably effective interventions are available.

# 12.5a Biological Treatments

## Agonist and Antagonist Therapies

As mentioned earlier, **agonists** are chemicals that can substitute for other drugs by having similar effects on receptor sites. Methadone, a synthetic narcotic related to heroin, has been used with some success in the treatment of heroin dependency. Methadone is an opiate agonist that does not produce the same euphoric reaction as heroin but does provide analgesic and sedative effects, and it reduces the craving for heroin. When methadone treatment is combined with vocational and personal counseling, it is relatively effective. It has enabled many former heroin addicts to become productive and responsible members of their communities. There is also evidence that urban crime rates have decreased in areas where methadone has been used (Dupont & Katon, 1971). Methadone maintenance treatment has been shown to reduce heroin use and criminal behavior among addicts waiting for admission into more comprehensive treatment programs (Schwartz, Jaffe, Highfield, Callaman, & O'Grady, 2007). However, methadone itself produces strong dependence. In essence, dependency on one drug, methadone, is substituted for dependency on another, heroin.

Other opiate agonists, including buphrenorphine, have come into use recently and have been tested in controlled clinical trials. Buphrenorphine is a partial opiate **antagonist**, meaning it also blocks receptor sites that opiates activate and, as a result, may make relapse less likely by reducing the effects of opiates when it is present. Both methadone and buphrenorphine have shown documented effectiveness in treating opiate dependence, especially when combined with therapy (Herveck, Hser, & Teruyan, 2008).

Other antagonist drugs have targeted different substances. Naltrexone is an opiate receptor-site blocker that may also reduce alcohol use among opioid addicts and has been established as an effective treatment in alcohol dependence (O'Brien & McKay, 2002). However, compliance issues moderate its usefulness (Modesto-Lowe & Van Kirk, 2002). Efforts continue to find substances that can remove craving and decrease relapse by blocking the pharmacological effect of drugs of abuse. An apparent GABA agonist, acamprosate, has been associated with positive outcomes and appears promising in the treatment of alcohol dependence.

A common approach for tobacco use disorder is to provide supplemental nicotine in forms other than tobacco to control craving, while smoking cessation programs move the smoker toward abstinence; then, nicotine is tapered off gradually by reducing supplemental doses. Most often, nicotine is supplied either in chewing gum form or as a skin patch. Earlier studies found both techniques effective in assisting with initial smoking cessation (O'Brien & McKay, 2002), although a newer, prospective study that followed nearly 800 people over several years found no difference in relapse rates between those who used nicotine replacement therapy (NRT) and those who did not. In fact, relapse was higher among those who had used NRT for any length of time without professional counseling (Alpert, Connolly, & Biene, 2013).

## Aversion Therapies

The drug Antabuse (disulfiram) has also been used to control alcohol use disorder. The presence of this drug in the bloodstream produces extremely unpleasant effects (such as nausea and cold sweats) when alcohol is consumed. The person, therefore, tends to remain abstinent in order to avoid the discomfort that drinking would produce. The problem with Antabuse is that the person must be motivated to take the drug every 2 to 3 days. When compliance can be assured (such as in a comprehensive program involving compliance checking), disulfiram has demonstrated its effectiveness in reducing drinking (Herveck, Hser, & Teruyan, 2008).

**Agonist**

Chemical that can substitute for another substance at receptor sites

**Antagonist**

Chemical that blocks receptor sites for another substance

However, the drug is associated with some negative side effects, and it does not appear to be equally effective with all users. Further, its value in restricting alcohol use is present only as long as the drug is taken; relapse is likely when the drug is withdrawn unless other therapeutic efforts can prevent it.

# 12.5b Psychological Treatments

Several attempts have been made recently to identify empirically supported psychotherapies for the treatment of substance abuse and dependence. It is becoming clear that some interventions seem to be more effective than others although methodological problems prevent indisputable conclusions. The more common therapies with some empirical support involve skills training, peer support, and therapy that addresses not only substance use but also coping skills in the context of daily life.

## Alcoholics Anonymous

In the early 1930s, Bill W. overcame his alcoholism through a basic spiritual change. He immediately sought out his friend Dr. Bob and was able, also, to help him achieve recovery. Both began to help other alcoholics, partly as a self-help program to keep themselves from relapsing; and in 1935 they formed Alcoholics Anonymous (AA). Since then AA has grown to over 10,000 groups located around the world with more than a million members.

The AA approach may be likened to a combination of religious belief and group therapy. Several tenets are fundamental to AA: Persons must admit that they are powerless over alcohol, must turn the direction of their lives over to God as they understand Him, must recognize that they can never drink again, must concern themselves with going for one day at a time without alcohol rather than with the long-term problem of alcoholism, and must seek to help other alcoholics. At weekly meetings, which have an inspirational quality, close bonds are developed among members; testimonials and confessions are made. When members feel on the verge of succumbing to the temptation to drink, they learn to contact another member for emotional support. Helping other members in this way probably bolsters their own "will power." In general, AA not only attempts to stop members from drinking but also, and perhaps most importantly, provides social relationships and responsibilities to replace the frustrations and emptiness that usually have come to characterize the alcoholic's life. Put somewhat differently, AA provides other responses that can be substituted for drinking.

The AA model has been extended to many other types of substance dependence and impulse control problems, including Narcotics Anonymous, Gamblers Anonymous, Overeaters Anonymous, and Sexaholics Anonymous. All share a common commitment to peer support and a 12-step approach, but they also encourage individuals to admit their powerlessness in self-control. Some people have objected to this approach while others may not share the spiritual or religious components of the program.

For those who may object to the disease perspective of AA or its reliance on religious intervention for sobriety, B. F. Skinner (1987) offered a reworded 12 steps that do not require a person to give up responsibility to a higher authority and, in fact, keeps the responsibility for sobriety on the drinker. His alternative steps are compared to the original in Table 12-3.

Research on the effectiveness of AA is mixed, in large part because the organization is loosely based in community chapters and collects no scientific data. However, two multi-site assessments have suggested that AA's effectiveness is about equal to cognitive-behavioral interventions (Finney & Moos, 2002). A meta-analysis of 361 controlled studies evaluating the effectiveness of treatment for alcohol use disorders did not list AA among the more effective treatments, largely because of an absence of studies comparing it to no-treatment or other treatments as controls. However, AA is readily available throughout the country at no cost and may be the most widely consumed intervention for alcohol problems.

*Table 12-3*    The 12 Steps of Alcoholics Anonymous and Skinner's Alternative 12 Steps

| The Twelve Steps | The Alternative 12 Steps |
|---|---|
| 1. We admitted we were powerless over alcohol ... that our lives had become unmanageable. | 1. We accept the fact that all our efforts to stop drinking have failed. |
| 2. Came to believe that a Power greater than ourselves could restore us to sanity. | 2. We believe that we must turn elsewhere for help. |
| 3. Made a decision to turn our will and our lives over to the care of God as we *understood* Him | 3. We turn to our fellow men and women, particularly those who have struggled with the same problem. |
| 4. Made a searching and fearless moral inventory of ourselves | 4. We have made a list of the situations in which we are more likely to drink. |
| 5. Admitted to God, to ourselves, and to another human being the exact nature of our wrongs. | 5. We ask our friends to help us avoid these situations. |
| 6. Were entirely ready to have God remove all these defects of character. | 6. We are ready to accept the help they give us. |
| 7. Humbly asked Him to remove our shortcomings. | 7. We earnestly hope that they will help. |
| 8. Made a list of all persons we had harmed, and became willing to make amends to them all. | 8. We have made a list of the persons we have harmed and to whom we hope to make amends. |
| 9. Made direct amends to such people wherever possible, except when to do so we injure them or others. | 9. We shall do all we can to make amends, in any way that will not cause further harm. |
| 10. Continued to take personal inventory and when we were wrong promptly admitted it. | 10. We will continue to make such lists and revise them as needed. |
| 11. Sought through prayer and meditation to improve our conscious contact with God as we understood Him, praying only for knowledge of His will for us and the power to carry that out. | 11. We appreciate what our friends have done and are doing to help us. |
| 12. Having had a spiritual awakening as the result of these steps, we tried to carry this message to alcoholics and to practice these principles in all our affairs. | 12. We, in turn, are ready to help others who may come to us in the same way. |

Source: Skinner, B. F., (1987). A humanist alternative to A.A.'s Twelve Steps: A human centered approach to conquering alcoholism. *The Humanist*, July/August 1987, 47, 5.

## Motivational Interviewing

A brief and uncomplicated intervention for substance use disorders is motivational interviewing (Miller & Rollnick, 1991). In this approach, the therapist is empathetic but seeks to divert the client from apathy about the situation. The goal is that the client comes to be the one to suggest change, without pressure or coercion. The therapist presents information that may highlight discrepancy of symptoms and likely outcomes of continued use, but he/she offers no diagnostic labels and presents no arguments about the need for change. Motivational interviewing, as a very brief intervention, has been found to be effective in promoting behavior change when compared against alternative therapies or no treatment (Miller & Wilbourne, 2002). In one example, a two-session component of motivational interviewing, combined with advice on cognitive-behavioral techniques to reduce cannabis use, was as effective as 12 sessions of cognitive-behavioral relapse prevention group training in reducing use and symptoms of dependence in cannabis users (Stephens, Roffman, & Curtin, 2000). Both treatment groups improved compared to wait-list controls.

## Contingency Management

Several behavioral interventions attempt to modify the pattern of substance use by employing reinforcement contingencies that provide external incentives for improvement. With motivated clients, simple forms of contingency management have proven quite effective in modifying substance intake. Foxx and Rubinoff (Foxx & Rubinoff, 1979) used small monetary rewards in a changing-criterion design to gradually decrease caffeine intake for three dependent females. The results for one subject are shown in Figure 12-7. Subjects deposited

*Figure 12-7    Daily Caffeine Intake*

Subject's daily caffeine intake (mg) during baseline, treatment, and follow-up. The criterion level for each treatment phase was 102 mg of caffeine less than the previous treatment phase.

Source: Adapted from Foxx, R. M., & Rubinoff, A. (1979). Behavioral treatment of caffeinism: Reducing excessive coffee drinking. *Journal of Applied Behavior Analysis, 12*, 335–344.

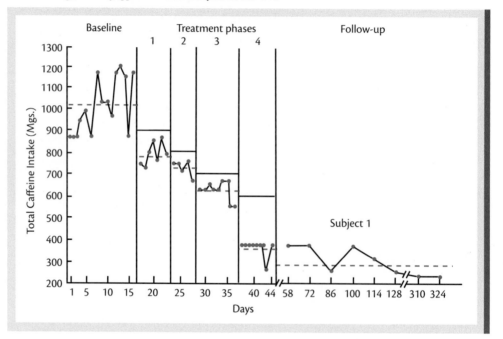

a small amount of money at the end of baseline and then received portions of the deposit back for each phase in which they did not exceed criterion. A bonus payment was available for consecutive phases in which criterion was not exceeded. All three subjects reduced intake dramatically and maintained lower levels during extended follow-up.

Could the same improvements be shaped in those with alcohol dependency? That was the goal of efforts to produce controlled social drinking. The social drinking intervention includes education about alcohol effects, self-monitoring of consumption, self-control techniques to slow and pace alcohol intake, and blood alcohol concentration discrimination training. Sobell and Sobell (1973) reported evidence suggesting that some alcoholics can become controlled drinkers. In their study, alcoholics who indicated a desire to become controlled drinkers and who had available significant outside social support to help maintain controlled drinking were candidates for the controlled drinking condition. The other alcoholics were assigned to a non-drinking condition. Individuals considered appropriate for controlled drinking training were then randomly assigned to either the controlled drinking condition or to the usual hospital treatment, which consisted of a combination of AA vocational training, medication, and group therapy—all of which emphasized abstinence. During the 6-month period at the end of a 2-year follow-up, individuals in the controlled drinking group had been functioning well (either abstinent or drinking moderately) on 87% of the days compared with 44% of the days for the control group. These results clearly implied that some alcoholics could learn to drink in moderation. Vogler, Weissbach, and Compton (1977) also were successful in training younger alcoholics to become controlled drinkers.

Others, especially those within the disease-model tradition who argued that abstinence was the only legitimate goal for addiction treatment, challenged these results. The controversy, which has involved fraud charges against the Sobells at one point but later exoneration, continues to this day. However, follow-up of the original sample and subsequent research by others support the position that some people with moderate alcohol problems can learn to control drinking at social levels (Sobell & Sobell, 1995).

**BVT** *Lab*

Improve your test scores. Practice quizzes are available at www.BVTLab.com.

## Relapse Prevention

Marlatt and his colleagues examined circumstances under which alcoholics relapsed after treatment. Most commonly they had taken their first drink in one of three situations: interpersonal conflicts in which they had had to cope with frustration and anger; negative emotional states such as anxiety, depression, loneliness, and boredom; or social pressures by friends or others to have a drink. These and related observations began to reveal the interacting factors—individual, environmental, and physiological—that contribute to relapse and that suggest pathways for its prevention.

The relapse prevention approach begins by acknowledging that relapse is a very likely outcome during attempts to remain abstinent. Rather than giving up and concluding that treatment has failed (the "**abstinence violation effect**," which can actually encourage resumption of substance abuse), those in relapse prevention training come to view relapse as a "slip" or "bump in the road" that does not necessarily predict program failure. Individuals learn about recognizing and coping with relapse triggers, including emotional states, high risk situations, and "apparently irrelevant decisions" (such as taking a walk that happens to lead past a bar) that set up a relapse. Further, they practice abstinence skills in relapse-prone situations (because success in those situations makes one more likely to remain abstinent in the future, compared to success only in "easy" circumstances). Relapse prevention is now widely included as a component of nearly all substance abuse treatment. Its techniques have also been used in bipolar I disorder patients, as a means to prevent or lessen manic episodes.

## Competing Reinforcement

Several very promising results have been reported for techniques that approach substance disorders in terms of competing motivations. The use of a drug is immediately reinforced by the drug's effect, but there are negative consequences associated with drug use as well. Conversely, there are consequences of remaining abstinent and of engaging in alternative activities. If the overall motivation for not using drugs exceeded the overall motivation for using, people might end their drug dependency, or at least alter usage. The community reinforcement model (Azrin, 1976) uses social, familial, vocational, and recreational reinforcers to motivate clients to reduce alcohol consumption. Techniques include problem solving, living skills, assertiveness training, goal setting, anti-abuse compliance, job skills experiences, and alternative reinforcing activities. In several reviews and replications, it has been found to be effective (Finney & Moos, 2002; Miller & Wilbourne, 2002), even among homeless alcohol-dependent persons (Smith, Meyers, & Delaney, 1998).

Using a community reinforcement approach, Higgins and his colleagues (1993) provided behavioral treatment that included "incentive vouchers" contingent on cocaine-free urine samples, which were collected unpredictably three times per week. The first clean urine sample earned the equivalent of $2.50, with higher monetary values for each consecutive clean sample, as well as a bonus each time three consecutive clean samples were collected. Subjects could accumulate nearly $1,000, in voucher value if they remained continuously abstinent during the 12-week treatment period. After week 12, each clean urine sample earned a state lottery ticket. Comparison subjects received standard drug abuse counseling treatment, which provided supportive therapy and counseled that drug abuse was a treatable but incurable disease. These comparison subjects received $5.00 for each urine sample regardless of outcome. The results (see Figure 12-8) showed that those in the behavioral treatment group achieved significantly higher rates of abstinence and maintained abstinence longer throughout the 24-week treatment period.

Budney, Moore, Rocha, and Higgins (2006) used a similar abstinence voucher reinforcement method to treat cannabis dependence. Voucher incentives were as effective as cognitive-behavior therapy during treatment, but the combination of the two approaches enhanced success at abstinence during follow-up. Other voucher programs are being tested on nicotine dependence as well.

**Abstinence violation effect**

The tendency of an abstainer to conclude that relapse indicates the failure of treatment

*Figure 12-8*   *Competing Reinforcement Treatment for Cocaine*

Abstinence from cocaine among cocaine-dependent outpatients given behavioral treatment (incentive vouchers for clean urine) or standard drug abuse counseling

Source: Adapted from Higgins, S. T., Budney, A. J., Bickel, W. K., Hughes, J. R., Foerg, F., & Badger, G. (1993) Achieving cocaine abstinence with a behavioral approach. *Journal of American Journal of Psychiatry, 150,* 736–769.

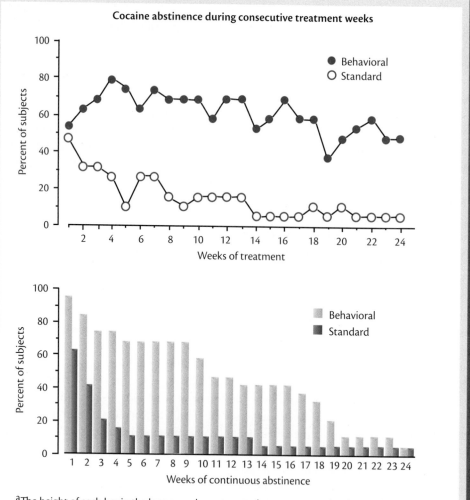

[a]The height of each bar in the lower graph represents the percentage of patients who achieved a duration of abstinence greater than or equal to the number of weeks indicated.

## Cognitive-Behavioral Therapy

Multi-component cognitive-behavior therapy involves the combination of skills training, stress management, identification of high-risk situations, relapse prevention, and cognitive restructuring. This approach has been well established for smoking cessation and appears helpful for cocaine dependence as well (Chambless, et al., 1998). When combined with community reinforcement and behavioral marital therapy, its use appears very promising in treatment of alcohol dependence (Finney & Moos, 2002).

A novel study by Clifasefi, Bernstein, Mantonakis, and Loftus (2013) attempted to modify drinking preference by implanting false taste aversion memories. Participants who received the suggestion that they had become sick after drinking rum or vodka before age 16 became more confident that the suggestion was true and subsequently reported reduced preference for that particular beverage. Possibly, the induction of false memories could be a useful adjunct in therapy for substance use disorders.

# 12.6 Gambling Disorder

Unlike the conditions we have considered thus far in the chapter, gambling disorder resembles an addiction without a substance. During the development of the *DSM-5*, proposals were made to include a category of "behavioral addictions" to include uncontrolled internet use, compulsive pornography use, shopping addiction, and possibly several other non-substance related disorders. Eventually, these plans were shelved until further research could accumulate about the addictive nature of people's involvement with these pleasurable activities. Gambling disorder remains the only "addictive" behavior to earn inclusion into the *DSM-5*.

In gambling disorder (see *DSM-5* Diagnostic Criteria for Gambling Disorder), individuals repeatedly engage in gambling that is persistent and maladaptive, as evidenced by preoccupation with gambling, unsuccessful attempts to either stop or control gambling, and interpersonal, occupational, and social disruption resulting from the activity. The individual frequently "chases" losses over the long term and may commit crimes or lie to family members to get money as the financial situation worsens. Many individuals seek excitement though gambling, and larger bets may be needed to achieve the same level of excitement over time. Others, however, gamble to escape problems or to relieve unpleasant moods (such as guilt or depression).

The prevalence of gambling disorder (called pathological gambling in the *DSM-IV*) may be increasing as more opportunities for legal gambling become available. It may affect as many as 7% of the population within certain areas such as Australia (American Psychiatric Association, 2000); a commonly accepted figure for the general U.S. population is about 3%, although *DSM-5* reduces the estimate for gambling disorder to no more than 1% lifetime

---

**DSM-5** | **Diagnostic Criteria for Gambling Disorder**

312.31 (F63.0) Gambling Disorder

A. Persistent and recurrent problematic gambling behavior leading to clinically significant impairment or distress, as indicated by the individual exhibiting four (or more) of the following in a 12-month period:
  1. Needs to gamble with increasing amounts of money in order to achieve the desired excitement. tolerance
  2. Is restless or irritable when attempting to cut down or stop gambling. withdrawl
  3. Has made repeated unsuccessful efforts to control, cut back, or stop gambling.
  4. Is often preoccupied with gambling (e.g., having persistent thoughts of reliving past gambling experiences, handicapping or planning the next venture, thinking of ways to get money with which to gamble).
  5. Often gambles when feeling distressed (e.g., helpless, guilty, anxious, depressed).
  6. After losing money gambling, often returns another day to get even ("chasing one's losses").
  7. Lies to conceal the extent of involvement with gambling.
  8. Has jeopardized or lost a significant relationship, job, or educational or career opportunity because of gambling.
  9. Relies on others to provide money to relieve desperate financial situations caused by gambling.

B. The gambling behavior is not better explained by a manic episode.

C. *Specify* if:
  **Episodic:** Meeting diagnostic criteria at more than one point, with symptoms subsiding between periods of gambling disorder for at least several months.
  **Persistent:** Experiencing continuous symptoms, to meet diagnostic criteria for multiple years.

*Specify* if:
  **In early remission:** After full criteria for gambling disorder were previously met, none of the criteria for gambling disorder have been met for at least 3 months but for less than 12 months
  **In sustained remission:** After full criteria for gambling disorder were previously met, none of the criteria for gambling disorder have been met at any time during a period of 12 months or longer.

*Specify* current severity:
  **Mild:** 4–5 criteria met
  **Moderate:** 6–7 criteria met
  **Severe:** 8–9 criteria met

Source: Reprinted with permission from the *Diagnostic and Statistical Manual of Mental Disorders*, Fifth Edition, (Copyright 2013). American Psychiatric Association.

risk in the general population. The condition appears to be 3 times more common among males, who tend to have adolescent onset and gamble for excitement; females have later onset and tend to gamble for escape. Pathological gamblers are often highly competitive and easily bored, and involvement tends to increase under times of stress or depression for most problem gamblers (American Psychiatric Association, 2013). Those with pathological gambling often report increased rates of other mental disorders as well. When Lyons (2002) asked psychologists about comorbid conditions for their clients who carried a primary *DSM-IV* diagnosis of pathological gambling, major depressive disorder and substance use disorders were listed as the most common co-occurring diagnoses (see Figure 12-9).

Pathological gambling was first included as a mental disorder in the *DSM-III* and defined largely in terms of the disruption and damage that the activity can cause to personal, occupational, and social functioning. The diagnostic criteria were revised in the *DSM-III-R* and intentionally patterned after those for substance dependence, introducing aspects suggesting both tolerance and withdrawal (Rosenthal, 1992). The *DSM-IV* diagnosis, requiring 5 of 10 criteria, was modified in the *DSM-5* to require four criteria within a 12-month period. Because only four of nine possible indications of maladaptive play are required, there are a great number of different combinations of criteria that could result in the diagnosis. Not all of the criteria appear to be equally predictive of problems, however. Of those gamblers who meet at least one of the criteria, "chasing losses" is most commonly reported; however, this characteristic does not distinguish social players from pathological ones. The indicator most predictive of serious difficulties was criminal behavior (such as theft) driven by gambling losses; together with loss of control and damage to relationships, these three criteria form the characteristics of the most serious problem gamblers (Toce-Gerstein, Gerstein, & Volberg, 2003).

## Causal Factors

The cause of pathological gambling remains unclear although speculation has followed paradigmatic lines for many years. As in the case of substance use disorders, moral weakness was widely accepted as the critical variable distinguishing compulsive gamblers from social players before the "enlightened" view of the Freudians, who by the middle of the twentieth century spoke of "neurotically sick" gamblers driven by unconscious impulse toward ruin. According to Bergler (1957):

### Figure 12-9    Co-occurring Disorders Among Pathological Gamblers

Co-occurring disorders present among pathological gamblers, as reported by their psychologists.
Source: Lyons, 2002

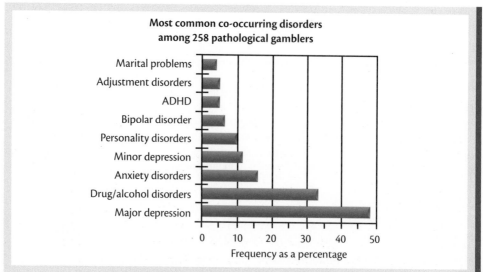

I submit that the gambler is not simply a rational though "weak" individual who is willing to run the risk of failure and moral censure in order to get money the easy way, but a neurotic with an unconscious wish to lose ... The act of gambling in itself is a denial of the 'reality principle.' In this act of denial, the gambler is expressing his neurotic aggression against those who have taught him the 'reality principle,'—in most cases his parents ... For him, losing is essential to his psychic equilibrium. (p. vii, 19, italics in original)

Bergler's psychodynamic assessment of pathological gambling was widely cited and was influential in psychiatry's conception of compulsive gambling as a symptom of an underlying disease, as well as the development of Gambler's Anonymous, which is based on the 12-step AA model (Porter & Ghezzi, 2006). About the same time, however, a very different perspective on pathological gambling had appeared, from Skinner (1953):

Slot machines, roulette wheels, dice cages, horse races, and so on pay off on a schedule of variable-ratio reinforcement. Each device has its own auxiliary reinforcements, but the schedule is the important characteristic ... The ratio is varied by one of several "random" systems. The pathological gambler exemplifies the result. Like the pigeon with its five responses per second for many hours, he is the victim of an unpredictable contingency of reinforcement. The long-term net gain or loss is almost irrelevant in accounting for the effectiveness of this schedule. (p. 104)

Obviously, these etiological perspectives show some fundamental differences. Bergler's concept led to the biomedical view that compulsive gambling is an addictive disease within the person, while Skinner's notion led to behavioral perspectives that consider problem gambling to be the result of experiences with unpredictable payoffs. These opposing views are still evident within the scientific literature.

Among possible biological contributions, there is some evidence that gambling problems run in families and cluster with alcohol use disorders (American Psychiatric Association, 2013). Twin studies suggest both environmental and genetic contributions, but quantification is hampered by concerns that pathological gambling may include several subtypes with possibly differing etiologies (Pallanti, Rossi, & Hollander, 2006). Further clarification within the diagnosis may help to untangle various causal contributions.

Weatherly and Dixon (2007) have proposed an integrated behavioral model of problem gambling that emphasizes the interaction of contingencies of monetary reinforcement, verbal **rule-governed behavior** (including inaccurate cognitions about probability), a tendency to steeply discount delayed rewards (so that smaller amounts of money today are valued more highly than larger amounts of money tomorrow), and the non-monetary rewarding consequences if gambling (such as excitement or escape). When these influences intersect with known risk factors for compulsive gambling (e.g., SES, gender, ethnic membership, and age), gambling problems may be a likely outcome, according to this model.

## Treatments for Gambling Disorder

There are no adequate controlled medication studies involving gambling disorder. Antidepressant medications, particularly SSRIs, as well as mood stabilizers (such as lithium and valproate), have produced some positive results; the opiate antagonist naltrexone also appears useful in some patients. However, outcomes have been inconsistent, placebo response has been high, and treatment compliance has been problematic. Other promising results have been reported using cognitive-behavioral interventions that involve reinforcement for alternative activities, identification of triggers leading to gambling, stress management, and addressing cognitive distortions (such as the **gambler's fallacy** that past losses change the likelihood of a future win) although these data are also preliminary (Petry & Roll, 2006). The disorder is attracting increased attention from researchers and clinicians, which should help refine and improve interventions and identify the most effective therapies.

**Rule-governed behavior**

Behavior that is controlled by the verbal description of a contingency rather than the contingency itself

**Gambler's fallacy**

The inaccurate belief that past losses alter the future likelihood of a win

# Chapter Review
## TO SUM UP ...

- Psychoactive drugs have been used throughout recorded history as an escape or relief from the strains and frustrations of life.

- Substance use disorders involve pathological patterns of substance use that cause impairment in important areas of functioning.

- Substance-induced disorders are conditions that are brought on by recurrent substance use. They include substance intoxication, substance withdrawal, and a variety of cognitive disturbances and disorders including psychotic, mood, anxiety, and sleep disorders, and sexual dysfunctions.

- Tolerance is said to occur when a larger dose of a drug is required to produce the same effect. Withdrawal is a syndrome with effects opposite those of intoxication. Both can occur in response to recurrent drug use and, subsequently, become conditioned to drug cues, which are stimuli that precede and predict drug onset.

- Many different substances are associated with problematic use. Nicotine appears to be particularly dependence-producing, and tobacco use is the largest preventable cause of death in the U.S.

- Both genetics and environmental factors make substantial contributions to the development and maintenance of substance-related disorders.

- Some substances produce widespread neurological damage and are associated with several serious substance-induced disorders, including persisting neurocognitive syndromes. Other substances induce fewer or less severe conditions. Alcohol use can produce a variety of severe conditions, and drinking during pregnancy is the largest preventable cause of birth defects in the U.S.

- The empirically validated treatments for substance disorders include both biological and psychosocial interventions. These may be used in combination and, most often, include a relapse-prevention component.

- Among the biological approaches, methadone and buphrenorphine for opiate dependence, naltrexone for opiate or alcohol dependence, and disulfiram for alcohol dependence have been shown effective in controlled trials.

- Among the psychotherapies, motivational interviewing, contingency management, community reinforcement, social skills interventions, and cognitive-behavioral therapies have demonstrated effectiveness in clinical trials.

- There is no clear indication that inpatient treatment is more effective than outpatient treatment. Alcoholics Anonymous may be effective, but controlled trials are needed to test the approach.

## KEY TERMS

## QUESTIONS FOR STUDY

- Defend, and criticize, the disease model of addiction, citing evidence where possible.

- Explain how tolerance and withdrawal can both be conceptualized as compensatory conditioned responses.

- Describe several of the newer biological and psychosocial treatments for substance-related disorders.

- Investment in the stock market is in some ways like gambling. Discuss what might be involved in a gambling disorder in which the game was market investment.

## POP QUIZ

1. _____ is a need for increasing amounts of a substance in order to have the desired effect.
   A. Addiction
   B. Withdrawal
   C. Tolerance
   D. Psychological need

2. A(n) _____ drug is a chemical that acts on the same receptors and, in effect, substitutes for the drug.
   A. agonist
   B. antagonist
   C. preagonist
   D. protagonist

3. Which of the following occur in confabulation?
   A. Gaps in memory are filled with imaginary happenings.
   B. Gross tremors of the arms and legs develop.
   C. Auditory and tactile hallucinations and paranoia can occur.
   D. The person becomes disoriented in place and time.

4. The "pleasure pathway" is another name for the _____ pathway.
   A. mesocorticolimbic serotonin
   B. mesocorticolimbic norepinephrine
   C. mesocorticolimbic GABA
   D. mesocorticolimbic dopamine

5. Which is linked to the highest number of deaths?
   A. nicotine
   B. alcohol
   C. suicide
   D. methamphetamine

6. Tolerance is stronger, and withdrawal symptoms are more evident, in which of the following people?
   A. those who receive the drug at random intervals
   B. those who passively receive the drug
   C. those who self-administer the drug
   D. those who receive the drug in novel settings

7. Jerry failed his breathalyzer test as his blood alcohol concentration level was over the legal intoxication level of _____.
   A. 0.80g/100mL
   B. 0.10g/100mL
   C. 0.01g/100mL
   D. 0.08g/100mL

8. Which of the following is true when relapse rate curves are compared?
   A. Smokers relapse at a higher rate than all others.
   B. Alcoholics relapse at a higher rate than all others.
   C. Opioid users relapse at a higher rate than all others.
   D. Relapse rates are quite similar across addictions.

9. _____ initially found their way into approved medical use as the active ingredients in nasal decongestant inhalers.
   A. Hallucinogens
   B. Inhalants
   C. Amphetamines
   D. Opioids

10. Nearly _____ of Americans have ingested a cannabinoid at some point.
    A. one-fourth
    B. one-third
    C. one-half
    D. two-thirds

11. Which of the following involves the re-experiencing of some of the symptoms of hallucinogen intoxication, in the absence of recent ingestion, in episodes that can last several months?
    A. Hallucinogen-induced psychotic disorder
    B. Hallucinogen withdrawal
    C. Hallucinogen persisting perception disorder
    D. Hallucinogen intoxication delirium

12. Opiates produce stupor and pain relief and depress the _____ nervous system.
    A. peripheral
    B. central
    C. somatic
    D. parasympathetic

13. Alcoholics Anonymous was formed by two men looking to overcome their alcoholism in _____.
    A. 1911
    B. 1935
    C. 1955
    D. 1975

14. A recent behavioral intervention for cocaine abusers has shown promising results using which technique?
    A. "vouchers" for consecutive clean urine samples
    B. nausea-producing drugs paired with cocaine
    C. motivational interviewing to encourage controlled use
    D. covert sensitization

15. The _____ effect is the tendency of an abstainer to relapse completely after a minor transgression.
    A. abstinence promotion
    B. abstinence violation
    C. resilience violation
    D. compliance violation

Additional study resources are available at **www.BVTLab.com**

# CHAPTER OPENER QUESTIONS

How is intellectual disability diagnosed?

What causes Down syndrome?

Do we know what causes stuttering? Can we help the stutterer to speak in a normal way?

Can autism be treated?

Which childhood disorders are the most common?

(Shutterstock)

# Neurodevelopmental and Disruptive Disorders

# chapter 13

As children and adolescents mature into adults, their rates of development vary. We can define developmental milestones for abilities—such as academic skills, language, motor development, and social development—based on how the majority of children of different ages acquire them; and those milestones can help identify those who need additional attention and assistance. The disorders described in this chapter include dysfunctions that first appear during childhood, reflecting issues of both physical and psychological maturation. For some of them, the disturbance is considered to be one of the developmental process; for others, the problems involve deficient self-control of emotions and behavior.

In the *DSM-IV*, these conditions were considered within a larger category "Disorders of infancy, childhood, or adolescence." The *DSM-5* revision moved several of those disorders to other areas—for example, separation anxiety disorder and selective mutism were relocated to the anxiety disorders, pica and rumination disorder were moved to the feeding and eating disorders, and reactive attachment disorder was placed among the trauma- and stressor-related disorders. Two new classifications were organized: one describes neurodevelopmental disorders, spanning childhood and adolescence; the other describes disruptive, impulse-control, and conduct disorders, a category created by merging the impulse control dysfunctions with the disruptive conditions of childhood.

## 13.1 Neurodevelopmental Disorders

The neurodevelopmental disorders all have their onset during the period of biological development before the brain and nervous system are complete; yet they are quite varied in their symptoms, etiologies, and treatments. The various disorders covered in this category are listed in Table 13-1. We have much more information on etiology and treatment for some of these conditions than others, as reflected in the coverage to follow. We do know, however, that boys are much more at risk than girls in several categories

One severe developmental disorder from the *DSM-IV*, Rett's disorder, was removed from the list of mental disorders. At first in Rett's disorder, there is a normal period of growth and development, with normal sensorimotor development and head growth through the first 5 months of life. Then, between 5 and 48 months of age, head growth decelerates, and previously acquired language, social, and psychomotor abilities are lost. It is a rare condition and occurs almost exclusively among females. A mutation in a dominant X-linked allele appears to be involved in about 90% of Rett's cases (Armstrong, 2005). Presumably, this is now viewed as a condition that can cause mental disorders, rather than as a mental disorder in itself. Rett's disorder can be indicated within specifiers for some of the neurodevelopmental disorders in the *DSM-5*.

*Table 13-1*  DSM-5 Neurodevelopmental Disorders

| Disorder | Key Symptoms | Age or Duration Requirement | Sex Ratio |
|---|---|---|---|
| Intellectual disability (intellectual developmental disorder) | Deficits in intellectual and adaptive functioning | Onset during the developmental period | More common among males |
| Language disorder | Difficulties in language use and acquisition | Onset in early developmental period | Unclear |
| Speech sound disorder | Difficulties in speech sound production | Onset in early developmental period | Unclear |
| Childhood-onset fluency disorder (stuttering) | Disturbance in fluency and time patterning of speech | Onset in early developmental period | Unclear |
| Social (pragmatic) communication disorder | Deficits in social communication | Onset in early developmental period | Unclear |
| Autism spectrum disorder | Deficits in social communication and interaction, restricted activities | Onset in early developmental period | More common among males |
| Attention-deficit hyperactivity disorder (ADHD) | Multiple symptoms of inattention or hyperactivity | Several symptoms prior to age 12 | More common among males |
| Specific learning disorder | Difficulties learning and using academic skills | 6 months | More common among males |
| Developmental coordination disorder | Deficit in motor skills development, clumsiness | Onset in early developmental period | More common among males |
| Stereotypic movement disorder | Repetitive purposeless behavior | Onset in early developmental period | Unclear |
| Tic disorders | Rapid, recurrent motor movements or vocalizations | 1 year; onset before age 18 | More common among males |

Source: Reprinted with permission from the *Diagnostic and Statistical Manual of Mental Disorders,* Fifth Edition, (Copyright 2013). American Psychiatric Association.

# 13.1a  Intellectual Disability (Intellectual Developmental Disorder)

Intellectual disability is diagnosed when there is evidence that intellectual abilities are significantly below average, and important adaptive skills are also impaired. Intellectual functioning is assessed, in part, by an individually administered standardized test of intelligence; and the resulting score must be among the lowest 2.5% of the population. Level of adaptive functioning can

**How is intellectual disability diagnosed?**

also be assessed by standardized measures or clinical examination across three domains: conceptual (academic), social, and practical. For the diagnosis to be given, there must also be adaptive dysfunction in at least one of these domains that results in failure to acquire normal milestones in personal independence and social responsibility, including language and communication, academic abilities, independent care skills, money management, and social judgment. The deficit in adaptive function must be evident in multiple environments and require ongoing support by others. Deficits that require ongoing support must also be present in at least one area of adaptive daily functioning, across multiple environments. Intellectual disability can be specified as mild, moderate, severe, or profound, defined in terms of the degree of adaptive impairment. The incidence may be 1% of the population, with males diagnosed more often than females (American Psychiatric Association, 2013).

Intelligence is formally measured by intelligence tests (which were described in Chapter 4). The tests assess a variety of abilities including vocabulary, comprehension, general information, short-term memory, and analytic skills; and the resulting scores are compared with those of same-age peers. The **IQ**, or intelligence quotient, is a standard score calibrated

**IQ**

Intelligence quotient, a standard score indicating intellectual functioning as compared to others in the population with a mean (or average) of 100 and a standard deviation of 15 (see Figure 13-1). In a normally distributed distribution such as IQ, 95% of scores fall within two standard deviations of the mean, or between 70 and 130. Individuals who score between about 85 and 70 may meet the definition of borderline intellectual functioning; it is not a disorder, but it may be a focus of clinical attention. Those with IQs less than 65–75 (two standard deviations below the mean, with a 5-point error range), who also show significant impairment in adaptive functioning, meet the criteria for intellectual disability.

# 13.1b  Mild Intellectual Disability

Mildly disabled individuals make up the vast majority (perhaps 85%) of those with this condition. During the preschool years, these individuals develop social and communication skills and show little or no impairment in motor activities. They are often not distinguished from normal children until a later age. Their subnormal intelligence becomes apparent during the school years, and they tend to fall behind their age group. With persistence they can learn academic skills roughly comparable to a sixth-grade level by their late teens. Problem solving tends to involve concrete approaches. Socially these individuals may form friends easily, but social interactions may be immature; they may also misperceive social cues. With extended education and assistance, independence in several areas can be achieved; however, on-going support is needed. As adults they can usually acquire vocational skills necessary for economic independence.

American actor Tom Hanks played the lead character in the film *Forrest Gump*. The character is written to be well below average intelligence statistically, and yet proves himself to possess great integrity and love for the people he encounters despite his handicap. (Getty Image)

# 13.1c  Moderate Intellectual Disability

These individuals with moderate intellectual disability represent about 10% of the people with intellectual disability. They usually learn to talk during the preschool years, but at a later time and more slowly than normal children. In addition, their academic abilities are markedly below peers. They are likely to show impairments in sensorimotor development, such as poor coordination; and their social skills are likely to be limited. They gain little at all from the usual academic instruction at school but can, in special classes, profit from training in social and occupational skills. Social judgment is also limited, and behavioral problems can create social difficulties. They can care for personal needs, such as hygiene and dressing, with extended training and frequent reminders. As adults they are unlikely to achieve complete independence but can contribute to their own support in the protective environment of sheltered work conditions.

*Figure 13-1*
***Distribution of IQ Scores in the General Population***

The normal bell-shaped distribution of 10 scores in the general population. An IQ of 65–75 arbitrarily divides the range of intellectual disability.

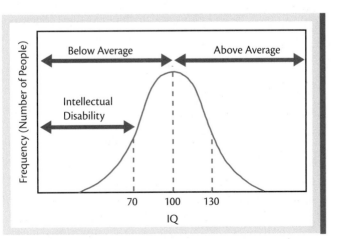

## 13.1d  Severe Intellectual Disability

Those with intellectual disability require assistance in areas of independent functioning. (AP Wide World)

People with severe intellectual disability make up about 3.5% of those with intellectual development disorder. Impaired development is apparent in infancy or early childhood in the form of poor motor development, minimal speech, and fairly often the presence of physical deformities. They do not profit as much from training as the moderately retarded, although as they get older many can learn to talk in simple words and phrases and learn elementary health and grooming habits. They remain dependent on others in problem solving and personal hygiene areas, requiring support and assistance at all times. As adults they may learn to perform certain routine tasks and develop recreational interests, but generally require complete supervision and economic support. Maladaptive behavior becomes increasingly problematic.

## 13.1e  Profound Intellectual Disability

The smallest group with intellectual disability (about 1.5% of the total) is profoundly disabled. Extreme deficits in both intellectual and sensorimotor functions are apparent early in life. Conceptual abilities are limited largely to the physical world. Some limited goals of habit training may be achieved in the older child, but usually these people will require total care for the rest of their lives. Many have physical or sensory dysfunctions that further restrict their capacity to walk or otherwise cope with environmental demands.

Before the *DSM-II*, particularly pejorative terms were used for subtypes of intellectual disability. Those currently labeled as having a mild disability were termed "morons" or "feeble-minded," those with moderate disability were termed "imbeciles," and those with what is now severe or profound intellectual disability were called "idiots." Those conditions were subsequently renamed mild, moderate, severe, and profound mental retardation, which in the *DSM-IV* were determined by IQ level. As described above, the distinctions in severity of intellectual disability are no longer based on IQ score, but rather on level of adaptive functioning.

## 13.1f  Causal Factors in Intellectual Disability

A variety of factors are linked to intellectual disability, including heredity, problems in embryonic development, environmental influences, other mental disorders, pregnancy or perinatal problems, and acquired medical conditions. No specific causal factors are identified in 30%–40% of the cases (American Psychiatric Association, 2000). Generally, specific organic factors are more likely to be associated with profound and severe levels of disability. Zigler (1967) suggested that if the distribution of IQ scores was plotted from a sample of the total population, including those in institutions for the mentally retarded, it would form the usual bell-shaped normal curve except at the very low end, where there tends to be a bump (see Figure 13-2).

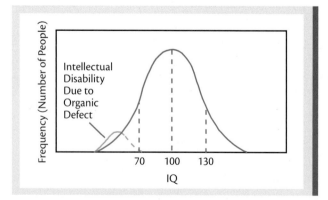

*Figure 13-2*  ***Distribution of IQ Scores***

The distribution of IQ scores, showing the sub-distribution thought to reflect individuals whose intellectual disability results from specific organic defect.

### Heredity

At the gene level there are numerous recessive inherited conditions associated with intellectual disability. One of the best known of the recessive syndromes is **phenylketonuria** (**PKU**), an inherited error in protein metabolism. The genetic site associated with PKU is located on chromosome 12. In PKU, the individual lacks liver enzymes necessary to convert the amino acid phenylalanine, which is found in many foods, into another amino acid, tyronine. As a result, phenylalanine accumulates and is converted into phenylpyruvic acid and other abnormal metabolites that cause brain damage, hyperactivity, and seizures. Newborns are routinely screened for PKU by blood tests. If an infant is homozygous for PKU, following a special low-phenylalanine diet that restricts or eliminates fish, chicken, dairy products, and other high-phenylalanine foods can prevent retardation. This dietary adjustment, which must be maintained throughout life, prevents the buildup of phenylalanine in the brain.

The most common heritable condition associated with intellectual disability is **fragile X syndrome**, involving a nearly separated segment of the long arm of the X chromosome (see Figure 13-3). The disorder, due to a mutation on the FMR-1 gene site, produces retardation and subtle physical characteristics such as an elongated face and large ears. It is also associated with hyperactivity, self-injurious behaviors, and emotional difficulties (Schwarte, 2008). Fragile X can be detected through blood tests or prenatally though **amniocentesis** or chorionic villus sampling, which collects fetal cells. Males are disproportionately affected by this condition because they carry only one X chromosome while females carry two, giving greater variability in the disorder's expression. For example, Mazzocco, Freund, Baumgardner, Forman, and Reiss (1995) describe monozygotic 16-year-old female twins who were concordant for fragile X but disconcordant for mental retardation: one sister's IQ was measured at 47, while the unaffected sister scored 105. The retardation associated with fragile X is often less apparent in younger children, although there are delays in developmental milestones such as sitting up and talking. However, IQ tends to decline as fragile X individuals age, not because of loss of abilities, but rather due to suboptimal growth (Schwarte, 2008).

Other recessive conditions associated with retardation are *galactosemia* and *Tay-Sach's* disease (also identifiable prenatally through amniocentesis). Among the dominantly inherited forms, *tuberous sclerosis* (epiloia) is probably the most widely known. This condition, caused by tuberous calcifications in the brain, produces intellectual disability and epilepsy. More recently, the cumulative impact of multiple genes has received increasing attention. Two general polygenetic effects appear to be related to intellectual disability. In one, sets of genes that are responsible for brain development produce structural

Kenneth Allen (left) and his brother Hunter both suffer from phenylketonuria (PKU), a genetic disorder that prevents them from digesting an essential amino acid. (AP Wide World)

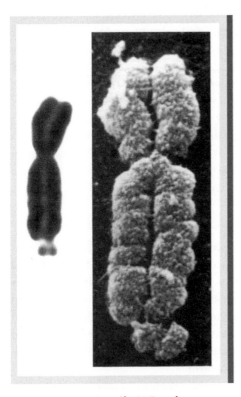

***Figure 13-3    Fragile X Syndrome***

In fragile X syndrome, material on the long area of the X chromosome is nearly or completely detached.

Source: Images courtesy of the Fragile X Foundation

**Phenylketonuria (PKU)**

Rare single-gene recessive metabolic disorder that results in intellectual disability

**Fragile X syndrome**

Condition in which the tip of the X chromosome is at risk of separation

**Amniocentesis**

Taking a sample of amniotic fluid to conduct genetic tests on a fetus

abnormalities in the brain; in the other, genetic variations decrease the normal neural and synaptic plasticity that characterizes learning (Valliant, Hawkins, & Pottier, 1998).

**What causes Down syndrome?**

## Alterations of Embryological Development

The best-known chromosomal abnormality is **Down syndrome**, a common disability caused by the presence of an extra chromosome. In most cases, the extra chromosome results from the failure of the twenty-first pair of the mother's chromosomes to separate during meiosis (cell division). These two chromosomes then join with the single twenty-first chromosome of the father to give three number 21 chromosomes, sometimes referred to as *trisomy 21* (see Figure 13-4). The trisomy can be detected prenatally through fetal screening procedures such as amniocentesis. Down syndrome is associated with intellectual impairment as well as a wide variety of physical anomalies: a large fissured tongue that tends to protrude from the mouth, almond shaped eyes, flat nasal bridge, a short crooked fifth finger, and broad hands with a crease running across the palm. Down syndrome occurs once in about 700 births, but the risk is strongly linked to maternal age. The incidence increases from 1 in 2,000 births for 20-year-old mothers to 1 in 25 for mothers older than 45 years of age.

The condition was given the name *mongolism* or *mongoloid idiocy* more than a century ago because of the superficial facial resemblance of affected persons to Asians of Mongolian origin, together with the prevailing racist attitudes about presumed inherent mental inferiority of non-Caucasians (Gould, 1981). In fact, the condition is easily recognizable in Asian children as well. IQs of these individuals tend to range from the 30s to the 70s. They are at increased risk for several medical conditions, including ear infections and hearing loss, mitral valve prolapse, sleep apnea, and obesity (Davis, 2008).

The leading cause of preventable intellectual disability is the effect of maternal alcohol consumption on the developing embryo. As discussed in Chapter 12, fetal alcohol syndrome produces characteristic biological and psychological impairments, including mild to moderate intellectual disability. In the *DSM-5*, the behavioral ramifications of fetal alcohol syndrome would be diagnosed as "neurodevelopmental disorder associated with prenatal alcohol exposure". Although the risk of fetal alcohol syndrome appears greatest with significant alcohol consumption during the first trimester, no "safe" level of maternal drinking has been identified.

**Down syndrome**

A condition associated with mental retardation caused by trisomy of chromosome 21

### Pregnancy or Perinatal Problems

During pregnancy the embryo and fetus may be exposed to a variety of harmful biological influences. Those that have been either directly or indirectly associated with intellectual dysfunction are poor maternal health—including acute and chronic maternal infections, maternal-fetal blood incompatibility, anoxia, radiation, drugs, and premature birth.

The most common prenatal infections associated with intellectual disability are rubella, toxoplasmosis, syphilis, and cytomegalovirus. Rubella produces dysfunction by infection of the fetus through the mother during the first 3 months of pregnancy. Immunization is available against

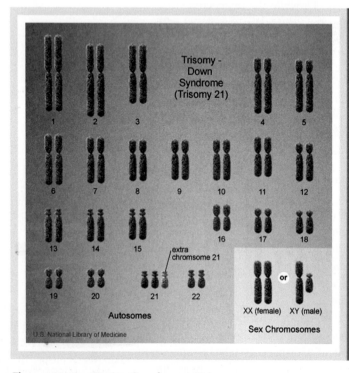

*Figure 13-4*   **Down Syndrome Trisomy**

Source: U.S. National Library of Medicine

this dreadful disease. Rh disease, the best known of the blood incompatibilities, occurs only when the mother's blood lacks a certain chemical factor that is in the fetus's blood: the mother is Rh negative and the fetus is Rh positive. Typically in later-born pregnancies, the mother's body mobilizes against the Rh factor, causing destruction of red blood cells, lack of oxygen, and a toxic state that can result in both mental and motor handicap. Rh disease has been treated by blood transfusions at birth and during the pregnancy itself, as well as by medications.

**Prematurity** refers to preterm delivery and low birth weight. Premature infants have greater health risks in many areas and are at increased risk for intellectual disability and other developmental disorders. Prematurity is related to a pregnant woman's general state of health, particularly her diet and smoking. Medical interventions have significantly improved the survival ability of premature infants; but they remain at higher risk of cognitive impairment, sensory impairment, and various conditions of the central nervous system (Allen, 2008).

*Cretinism* is stunted physical and mental development caused by impaired functioning of the thyroid gland, one cause of which is an iodine-deficient diet. Certain characteristic physical features—including stunted growth, dry skin, coarse hair, and a large head—usually accompany severe intellectual disability. Preventive efforts, such as the wide availability of iodized salt, have led to the virtual elimination of this kind of disability in the Western world. Even when cretinism occurs, most of the impairment can be avoided if a thyroid supplement is added to the infant's diet early enough.

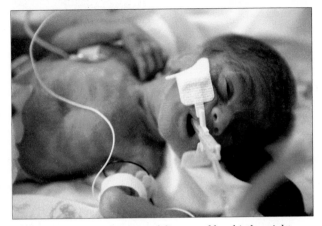

Prematurity refers to preterm delivery and low birth weight. Premature infants have greater health risks in many areas and are at increased risk for mental retardation and other development disorders. (iStock)

## Acquired Medical Conditions

Adverse biological events occur postnatally as well as during pregnancy and at birth. Infectious diseases that involve the brain, such as **encephalitis** and **meningitis**, are probably the most important retardation-producing conditions; other postnatal causes are head trauma, lead poisoning, brain tumors, and epilepsy. There is also the very important question of whether infant diets deficient in protein may impair mental development, if not actually cause intellectual disability. Injuries from "shaken baby syndrome" can include brain damage and cognitive impairment.

Much public attention has recently been focused on lead encephalitis, a complication of lead poisoning. This is a brain condition that can result from prolonged contact with or ingestion of lead-based materials. In the United States, a continuing federal effort has reduced or eliminated lead from paint, gasoline, children's toys, and other sources to reduce lead exposure. About 6% of children treated for lead poisoning are found to have severe intellectual disability.

Cranial abnormalities, often of unknown origin, can also cause cognitive limitations. Both *macrocephaly* (large-headedness) and *microcephaly* (small-headedness) are associated with brain changes that involve intellectual impairment. In addition, increased accumulation of cerebrospinal fluid in the ventricles of the brain produces *hydrocephaly* and damages brain tissue.

## Environmental Influences

Psychological and social factors can produce deficits in intelligence as well. Rare cases of deprivation and abuse have been discovered, in which environmental improvement resulted in increases in IQ. Koluchova (1976) reported one such case involving 7-year-old identical twin boys who were rescued from severely abusive conditions that involved extreme deprivation, isolation and beatings. At first, they could barely walk and had very limited speech. When

**Prematurity**

Preterm delivery and low birth weight, may be associated with multiple impairments in behavioral, cognitive, sensory, and CNS functioning

**Encephalitis**

Inflammation of the brain

**Meningitis**

Inflammation of the meninges, the protective covering of the brain and spinal cord

tested at age 8, they scored in the moderately retarded range. After 7 years of environmental enrichment and therapy, the IQ rose to the normal range (see Figure 13-5).

Kokuvi, a 17-year-old student at the Volta School for the Mentally Challenged who has microcephaly. (Wikimedia Commons)

Environmental influences interact with genetic influences to produce both normal and abnormal levels of intelligence. In extreme circumstances such as these, the impact of deprivation appears obvious; however, prevailing conditions that involve persisting limited cognitive stimulation can produce broadly lower levels of intelligence as well. Inadequate intellectual stimulation may stem from limited opportunity, lack of exposure, or lack of support for academic training and achievement. In addition, impoverished environments are associated with increased exposure to crime, drug abuse, teenage pregnancy, and inadequate school funding. Perhaps not surprisingly, intelligence test scores are generally found to be correlated with social class, and individuals at the lowest socioeconomic levels tend to perform most poorly.

The quality of parental influence and stimulation within the home are also factors that shape intellectual development of the child. Polansky and his colleagues (1972) studied impoverished families in rural Appalachia and identified a particular constellation of maternal characteristics (lack of motivation to acquire competence, apathy, feelings of futility, absence of meaningful personal relationships) that seemed to be especially related to developmental difficulties in the children. Within the sample of 65 mother-child pairs studied (all living at or below the poverty level), they found that the more common these characteristics, the lower the child's IQ. In addition, maternal apathy-futility was correlated positively with lethargic, withdrawn, dependent, and clinging children.

# 13.2 Treatment for Intellectual Disability

## 13.2a Prevention

Obviously, it is important to act to control as many of the conditions that cause intellectual dysfunction as possible. Family planning should include consideration of maternal age; and during pregnancy the fetus must be properly nourished while exposure to alcohol or other toxins is eliminated. Maternal health should be monitored and infections avoided. After birth, an enriched and stimulating environment is important, both in schools and at home.

*Figure 13-5*
**IQ Changes in Twin Boys Rescued at Age 7 from Abuse**

Source: Koluchova, J. (1976). A report on the further development of twins after severe and prolonged deprivation. In A. M. Clarke & D. B. Clarke (Eds.), *Early experience: Myth and evidence* (pg. 55–66). New York, NY: The Free Press.

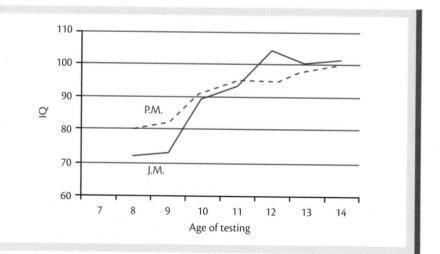

## Early Intervention Programs

Treatment for intellectually disabled children involves providing the kind of early childhood environments that will help them develop cognitive resources more fully and to emulate desirable peer and adult models. This goal is most likely to be achieved through special home intervention programs and participation in preschool day nurseries (child development centers). Heber and his associates (Garber & Herber, 1978; Heber & Garber, 1980) assessed an intensive early intervention program among at-risk families in an impoverished area of Milwaukee, Wisconsin. Children of low-IQ mothers (mothers had IQ of 75 or less) were randomly assigned to an experimental or control condition (20 in each group). At 3 months of age, children in the experimental group began attending a special enrichment program at a nearby school facility, which targeted perceptual-motor, cognitive-language, and social-emotional development. The program continued all day, 5 days a week, and 12 months a year until the children entered school at age 6. In addition, mothers were given some remedial academic training, together with instruction in parenting skills, homemaking and vocational training. Various measures of intelligence were obtained at 6-month intervals for both groups. Experimental children averaged over 20 IQ points higher between 2 and 10 years of age. At age 6 the average IQ for the experimental children was 121 and for the control children was 87, over 30 points difference. At age 10, 4 years after all intervention had stopped, the average IQs were 105 and 85, respectively—still a large and significant difference between the groups.

Other early intervention programs have demonstrated their effectiveness in reducing the risk of cultural-familial retardation. The federal Head Start program, for example, has been successful in improving school readiness and decreasing problem behaviors for at-risk children (e.g. Abbot-Shim, Lambert, & McCarty, 2003). In schools, special education opportunities are available for children with intellectual disability. Mainstreaming, an effort to keep the disabled child with normal peers as much as possible, is a common approach to foster both social and academic improvement.

## Other Treatments and Facilities

In more serious cases of intellectual disability, treatment occurs within residential living facilities, in treatment facilities, or institutions that support persons with severe disabilities. Structured behavior modification is very useful in training important skills such as self-care, language, and daily living abilities. One serious problem associated with severe intellectual disability is self-injurious behavior. A comprehensive review of behavioral interventions for self-injury, involving mostly persons with severe or profound intellectual disability, found both reinforcement- and punishment-based techniques effective (Kahng, Iwata, & Lewin, 2002).

## Pharmacological Treatments

There are no medications that treat intellectual disability although there are a variety of antipsychotic, sedative, and tranquilizing drugs that can be used to control behavioral problems. These medications are widely employed to control aggressive and challenging behaviors in retarded individuals although no clear empirical support exists for their use. Data on the effectiveness of various drug therapies offer only weak support at best (Petty & Oliver, 2005). A recent comparison study tested a first generation antipsychotic, haloperidol, against a newer antipsychotic medication, respiradone, and placebo in 86 retarded men with aggressive problem behavior. Aggression decreased substantially in all groups, but placebo was linked to a somewhat greater improvement and fewer treatment problems than either medication (Tyrer, et al., 2008). Nonetheless, use of these and similar medications to control challenging behavior in those with intellectual disability remains common.

BVT Lab

Flashcards are available for this chapter at www.BVTLab.com.

# 13.3 Specific Learning Disorders

*Specific learning disorders* combine the *DSM-IV* diagnoses of *reading disorder, mathematics disorder, disorder of written expression, and learning disorder not otherwise specified.* The diagnosis requires difficulties in learning and academic skills involving reading, spelling, writing, or mathematics, in which measured abilities are below what would be expected by the student's chronological age. The difficulties are not due to intellectual disability, and they must have persisted for 6 months or more, in spite of attempts to remediate them. The diagnosis includes specifiers for areas of impairment (with impairment in reading, with impairment in written expression, with impairment in mathematics) and severity (mild, moderate, or severe).

Reading difficulties may involve errors in comprehension, slow reading, and oral substitutions, distortions or omissions. This condition has also been called "dyslexia." As many as 80% of persons with these learning disorders are males, although there may be reason to believe that bias in diagnosis is partly responsible: boys are more likely to show disruptive behavior along with the reading dysfunction, thereby attracting diagnostic attention (American Psychiatric Association, 2000). Mathematical difficulties can include the linguistic, perceptual, attentional, and computational skills involved in mathematic achievement. Disorder of written expression is characterized by deficient writing skills, often including combinations of poor handwriting, poor grammar and punctuation, common spelling errors, and poor organization of paragraphs or sentences. It can be associated with perceptual-motor or language deficits. Less is known about disorder of written expression than the other learning disorders, in part because standardized testing of reading and math skills is easier than for writing abilities. Together, specific learning disorders may affect 5% to 15% of the population (American Psychiatric Association, 2013).

## 13.3a Causal Factors for Learning Disorders

The *DSM-5* defines specific learning disorder as having a biological origin causing a dysfunction in the brain, without being more specific. Prematurity, low birth weight, and prenatal exposure to nicotine are listed as risk factors, however. Specific learning disorders involving reading and math especially tend to run in families (American Psychiatric Association, 2013). Genetic factors doubtlessly influence learning abilities, perhaps in a general rather than ability-specific way. Plomin and Kovas (2005) conclude that the genes affecting one learning disorder affect others as well, resulting in substantial overlap and generalist gene effect. When learning disorders are co-morbid with attention-deficit/hyperactivity disorder (ADHD), outcomes tend to be poorer (American Psychiatric Association, 2013). There are also significant correlations between the specific learning disorders that may suggest they interrelate at a more basic level. Wolf and Bowers (1999), for example, propose that phonological deficits that impede word recognition and deficits in rapid recognition and naming of stimuli are both core deficits in reading disorder.

Specialized remedial programs have produced significant gains in severely delayed reading and math abilities using behavioral, fluency-based individualized instruction (e.g., Johnson & Layng, 1992). However, learning disorder symptoms may persist into adulthood for up to 4% of the population (American Psychiatric Association, 2013).

# 13.4 Motor Disorders

The neurodevelopmental disorders also include a set of motor disorders, conditions in which a deficit in motor coordination or delay in meeting motor development milestones interferes with academic or daily life. These include developmental coordination disorder, stereotypic movement disorder, and the tic disorders.

# 13.4a  Developmental Coordination Disorder

Poor motor coordination may be indicated by clumsiness, dropping things, below average sports skills, or poor handwriting; delays may occur in walking, sitting, or crawling. The clumsiness of developmental coordination disorder is not due to a physical disability such as cerebral palsy or muscular dystrophy, nor is it characteristic of the motor difficulties associated with intellectual disability. Instead, the ability to execute coordinated motor skills is below that expected by the person's age. For the diagnosis to qualify, the motor deficiencies must be severe enough to interfere with the normal activities of daily living. The *DSM-5* reports the prevalence at between 5% and 6% of children ages 5–11 (American Psychiatric Association, 2013). Little information is available on causal factors or treatments for those with developmental coordination disorder, and in some cases it persists into adulthood.

# 13.4b  Stereotypic Movement Disorder

Motor behavior that is nonfunctional and repetitive is the key feature of stereotypic movement disorder. Movements often consist of body rocking, hand waving, or shaking; however, all types of movements may be involved. Some repetitive activities are also physically damaging: eye-poking, head-banging, face-slapping, and self-biting can cause serious injury and may persist for years. Risk factors may include social isolation or environmental stress. Some neurogenetic conditions such as Rett's syndrome also contribute to stereotypic movement disorder (American Psychiatric Association, 2013).

Prevalence may be between 10%–15% of those with intellectual disability who are living in residential facilities. While there may be gender differences in the expression of particular symptoms (e.g., self-biting may be more common among females than males with the disorder) the overall gender ratio appears to be equal (American Psychiatric Association, 2000).

Treatment information is limited for non-tic movement disorders, although there is substantial literature supporting behavioral methods that provide aversive consequences contingent on self-injurious acts while simultaneously shaping competing responses (Matson & LoVullo, 2008). Antipsychotic medication has not been particularly effective apart from tranquilization. However, small case reports have indicated that the opiate receptor site blocker naltrexone has been useful for some individuals with self-injurious behavior (Symons, et al., 2001).

# 13.4c  Tic Disorders

The *DSM-5* motor disorders category includes four disorders involving verbal tics, motor tics, or a combination of the two. **Tics** are sudden, stereotyped motor movements or vocalizations that are rapid, recurrent, non-rhythmic, and experienced as irresistible. Simple motor tics include eye blinking, facial grimacing, and neck jerking; they may last less than a second. Complex motor tics, which tend to last at least several seconds, can include hand gestures, squatting, twirling, retracing one's steps, smelling objects, jumping, or making obscene gestures. Simple vocal tics may involve clearing the throat, grunting, or snorting. Complex vocal tics include words; phrases; changes in the volume, emphasis, or pitch of language; or **coprolalia**, verbal obscenities or socially unacceptable verbalizations.

Tics often occur in bouts, separated by minutes or hours, which may vary in intensity and frequency across different contexts and settings. They can be temporarily suppressed with varying success in certain circumstances, such as at school or when a person is engaged in directed activity; and they usually cease during sleep.

## *Tourette's Disorder*

In Tourette's disorder, both multiple motor and vocal tics have persisted for at least a year. Symptoms must have begun before the age of 18; and the tics, which typically happen many

**Tics**
Involuntary muscular twitching, usually in the facial muscles

**Coprolalia**
Verbal obscenities or socially unacceptable verbalizations, often emitted as vocal tics

times each day, cannot be attributable to a general medical condition or a substance. Tics usually begin by age 6, and can wax and wane in a course that tends to diminish in severity as the person ages into adulthood (American Psychiatric Association, 2013). In less than 10% of persons, coprolalia occurs; but more often vocal tics consist of coughing, barking, or grunting. About half of the cases begin with a simple motor tic such as blinking (American Psychiatric Association, 2000).

Persons with Tourette's disorder often feel discomfort, shame, or social embarrassment over their condition, especially if they are older; impairment in functioning is not among the diagnostic criteria for this condition. Obsessions or compulsions may be present. About one-half of people with Tourette's disorder also have ADHD, and the stimulants used to treat ADHD have been associated in some studies with increased tic incidence and severity (Pidsosny & Virani, 2006). Tourette's disorder also may co-occur with obsessive-compulsive disorder. The diagnosis is given to men between 2 and 5 times more often than women. It is a rare condition with an upper prevalence estimate of about 8 school-aged children per 1,000 (American Psychiatric Association, 2013). There appears to be a substantial genetic component to the disorder, although the mechanism is unknown; and some individuals with Tourette's disorder show no evidence of familial pattern. Medications including older and newer antipsychotic drugs (e.g. haloperidol and respiradone) are useful in treatment but have significant side effects, including weight gain (Swain, Scahill, Lombroso, King, & Leckman, 2007). Recently, behavioral techniques including habit reversal therapy (involving awareness training and competing response training) and exposure and response prevention have been proposed for inclusion among the well-established psychotherapies (Cook & Blacher, 2007). A recent randomized controlled trial found behavior therapy as effective as antipsychotic medications for treating Tourette's disorder in children (Piacentini, et al., 2010).

### Persistent (Chronic) Motor or Vocal Tic Disorder and Provisional Tic Disorder

Persistent chronic motor or vocal tic disorder involves either vocal tics or motor tics, but not both. It differs in this way from Tourette's disorder, which requires the presence of each at some point. Like Tourette's disorder, symptoms must persist for a year, and have onset before age 18. In provisional tic disorder, single or multiple vocal or motor tics occur but have persisted less than 12 months.

## 13.5 Communication Disorders

Four specific disorders of expressive or receptive language are classified by the *DSM-5*. While the *DSM-IV* noted that these disorders were more common among males, the *DSM-5* now indicates that sex ratios are unclear. All of these disorders also appear to aggregate within families although specific genetic, neurological, or environmental causes are unknown.

## 13.5a Language Disorder

Language disorder involves language use and acquisition that is substantially below that expected from an individual's chronological age. The language impairments are not due to intellectual disability, or to auditory or visual impairment or a motor dysfunction. Expressively, this is shown by limited vocabulary, word recall difficulty, shortened or overly simplistic sentences, errors in verb tense, or in a deficiency of understandable discourse. Receptive communication may also be affected, involving difficulties understanding words or sentences, or particular types of word phrases (such as "if-then" statements). As a result of this comprehension deficit, it may appear as if the person has not heard, or attended to, a comment or question; he or she may seem shy or confused, or give inappropriate or tangential responses to questions. All language modalities may be involved: expression of written language, spoken language, and sign language can be impaired. The course is variable, although some difficulties tend to persist into adulthood; those with receptive language deficits appear to have a poorer prognosis (American Psychiatric Association, 2013).

## 13.5b Speech Sound Disorder

Speech sound disorder is an articulation disorder in which persons fail to use the speech sounds that are normal for their developmental level. Difficulties may occur in knowledge of the correct phonological sounds or in the motor coordination required for speaking (which involves movements of the jaw, mouth, lips, and tongue, as well as controlled airflow). For example, sounds may be difficult to produce (*th*, *ch*), substituted for one another (*t* for *k*) or omitted. Lisping is also common. Speech therapy is helpful; and articulation tends to improve over time—although if language disorder is also present, the prognosis is less optimistic (American Psychiatric Association, 2013).

## 13.5c Childhood-Onset Fluency Disorder (Stuttering)

Childhood-onset fluency disorder (stuttering) is a disturbance in speech fluency typically characterized by speech blocks, repetitions of words or syllables, and prolongations of speech sounds. Approximately 1% of all children are persistent stutterers; and another 4%–5% show transitory stuttering when young, but outgrow it in time (American Psychiatric Association, 2000). Children with the condition often find the dysfunction embarrassing; and they may avoid speaking opportunities or limit speech to short, simple utterances. The difficulties increase under conditions of stress or anxiety. Stuttering almost always starts before the age 7, but it can be coded for adult onset; usually, the onset is gradual (American Psychiatric Association, 2013). In families in which the father has a history of stuttering, 10% of daughters and 20% of sons also stutter (American Psychiatric Association, 2000).

> Do we know what causes stuttering? Can we help the stutterer to speak in a normal way?

Stuttering has received perhaps more historical attention from psychologists than the other communication disorders. Psychodynamic theorists emphasized the symbolic meaning of stuttering: one psychoanalytic scholar, Fenichel (1945), suggested that stuttering stems from conflict around the expression of anal-sadistic impulses. Speaking became associated with the utterance of obscene, especially anal, words and the expression of verbal aggression.

> The same motives which in childhood were directed against pleasurable playing with feces make their appearance again in the form of inhibitions or prohibitions of the pleasure of playing with words. The expulsion and retention of feces, and actually the retention of words, just as previously the retention of feces, may either be the reassurance against possible loss or a pleasurable auto-erotic activity. One may speak in stuttering, of a displacement upwards of the functions of the anal sphincters. (pp. 311–312)

Other less complex psychological theories tended to emphasize factors that create anxiety or concern about speaking properly (Bloodstein, 1975; Johnson W. , 1959; Sheehan, 1975). Consistent with an anxiety or tension theory, Lanyon (1978) suggested that the stuttering act is preceded and accompanied by a physical struggle to speak. It can involve excessive muscle tension, especially in speech-related areas, along with breathing irregularities and a variety of extraneous body movements. According to Lanyon, the stuttered word appears to be the end point of a chain of events, of which the initial event appears to be the perception that a disruption in fluency is about to occur. This perception has become conditioned to elicit the physical struggle that eventuates in the stuttered response.

## *Treatment for Stuttering*

Half or more of the individuals who begin to stutter will recover with little or no professional help, and this is especially true for the younger child (Wingate, 1976). According to the *DSM-5*, 65%–85% of stutterers recover from the dysfluency (American Psychiatric Association, 2013). Stutterers themselves are usually aware of circumstances in which their dysfluency disappears or is greatly diminished. Bloodstein (1949) found that at least 90% of the stutterers sampled reported substantial reduction in stuttering when reading in chorus, speaking to an animal or to an infant, singing, swearing, speaking to a rhythmic swing of the arm or foot tapping, or imitating a regional or foreign dialect.

A number of techniques, some similar to those reported above by stutterers, have been shown to reduce stuttering although generalization to more normal ways of speaking outside of the clinic can be a problem. One technique that has been found consistently to produce an immediate reduction in stuttering is delayed auditory feedback. When non-stutterers talk while hearing their own speech played back through earphones with about a 1/10 second delay, they tend to show marked disruptions in speech similar to stuttering. Paradoxically, when a stutterer's speech is delayed in this fashion, the stuttering is almost completely suppressed. Another example is rhythmic cuing, in which the person is asked to speak in a rhythmical, singsong fashion, usually with the aid of a metronome. Wingate (1976) has suggested that the important common factor in these and other procedures found to reduce stuttering is a slowing down of speech that permits a deliberate substitution of a nonstuttered utterance.

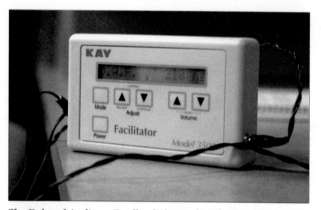

The Delayed Auditory Feedback device (DAF) allows the speaker to hear his or her own voice with a time delay, which helps stutterers to speak more clearly. (AP Wide World)

More recently, Wagaman, Miltenberger, and Arndorfer (1993) trained eight children to detect any instance of stuttering, to regulate breathing from the diaphragm, and to exhale slightly before beginning to speak. Subjects practiced speaking during natural exhalation, beginning with short conversational phrases. If a stutter occurred, subjects stopped speaking immediately and reinstated the breathing technique. Parents assisted in practice, kept records of progress, and offered social praise. Improvement was significant and sustained for all children outside of the treatment setting. Both parents and speech pathologists reported that the children's speech was unimpaired and natural after treatment (see Figure 13-6).

## 13.5d Social (Pragmatic) Communication Disorder

New to the *DSM-5* is social (pragmatic) communication disorder, a condition in which basic practical social communication skills—such as greetings, taking turns in conversation, asking for clarifications, or matching speech styles to the context of the listener (for example, playground vs. classroom)—are impaired. Children with this condition have difficulty telling stories, making inferences, distinguishing humor, and understanding common metaphors, resulting in social and academic difficulties. Social (pragmatic) communication disorder is not due to intellectual deficiency, autism spectrum disorder, or other mental disorders; however, it does occur more commonly in families that have histories of autism, communication disorders, or learning disorders (American Psychiatric Association, 2013).

## 13.6 Autism Spectrum Disorder

One particularly controversial change made during the development of the *DSM-5* involves the decision to combine four of *DSM-IV*'s pervasive developmental disorders into a single

*Figure 13-6    Behavioral Treatment for Stuttering*

Percentage of stuttered words in four subjects. The arrows represent treatment sessions. The squares are generalization probes.

Source: Adapted from Wagaman, J. R., & Arndorfer, R. E. (1993). Analysis of a simplified treatment for stuttering children. *Journal of Applied Behavior Analysis, 36,* 53–61.

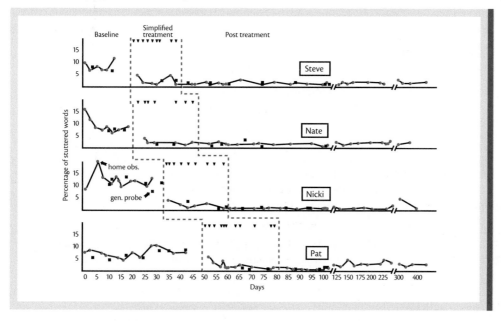

spectrum diagnosis. These conditions included autistic disorder, Asperger's disorder (in which language was not delayed), childhood disintegrative disorder (in which individuals show normal development for the first 2 years of life, then lose previously acquired abilities), and pervasive developmental disorder not otherwise specified. Research had not consistently supported a clear separation between the conditions. For example, Miller and Ozonoff (2000) reported that those with Asperger's disorder have a higher IQ than autistics; once IQ is controlled, however, comparisons on visual-perceptual skills show no clear differences between children with the two conditions. Consequently, the authors saw little evidence that Asperger's disorder was a separate condition from high-IQ autism requiring a separate diagnosis. The distinctions between the former pervasive developmental disorders are now considered to be differences in severity of the same core symptoms: deficits in social communication and interactions, and restrictive, repetitive behaviors.

Autism spectrum disorder (see *DSM-5* Diagnostic Criteria for Autism Spectrum Disorder) involves problems in social interactions, communication, or play. Socially, there is little reciprocal interaction: younger autistic individuals have few or no friendships, rarely engage in communicative eye contact, and generally seem unaware of others. Older children with autistic disorder may be interested in friendships, but lack the social understanding involved in establishing them. Language is usually delayed or absent; when it is present, it often seems abnormal in pitch, tone, or rhythm. Range of interests and activities is narrow, and often the individual repetitively engages in structured routines such as arranging toys in very specific ways. These routines tend to be inflexible, and changes can produce great distress. Stereotypic movements, such as flapping of hands or rocking, are often present. The person may be preoccupied with inanimate objects or parts of objects, or with very narrow interests such as dates or phone numbers. The severity of autism spectrum disorder is specified by the degree of deficits shown, indicated by "requiring support" (e.g., difficulty initiating social interactions), "requiring substantial support" (e.g., marked deficits even with supports in place, frequent and obvious repetitive behaviors) or "requiring very substantial support" (e.g., minimal response to social overtures, repetitive behaviors markedly interfere with functioning).

In infancy, the autistic child may show an indifference or aversion to physical contact such as cuddling and a failure to respond to the voices and social invitations of parents, leading many parents to initially be concerned that the child is deaf. Self-injurious behavior may occur, ranging from mild to severe forms of head banging or self-biting. Most autistic individuals also have some degree of intellectual disability, but the level of cognitive skills is uneven across abilities. About one-fourth of people with fragile X meet the diagnostic criteria for autism spectrum disorder, and its presence is associated with lower development and generally poorer outcome (Schwarte, 2008).

| *DSM-5* | **Diagnostic Criteria for Autism Spectrum Disorder** |
|---|---|

299.00 (F84.0) Autism Spectrum Disorder

A. Persistent deficits in social communication and social interaction across multiple contexts, as manifested by the following, currently or by history (examples are illustrative, not exhaustive; see text):

1. Deficits in social-emotional reciprocity, ranging, for example, from abnormal social approach and failure of normal back-and-forth conversation; to reduced sharing of interests, emotions, or affect; to failure to initiate or respond to social interactions.

2. Deficits in nonverbal communicative behaviors used for social interaction, ranging, for example, from poorly integrated verbal and nonverbal communication, to abnormalities in eye contact and body language or deficits in understanding and use of gestures; to a total lack of facial expressions and nonverbal communication.

3. Deficits in developing, maintaining, and understanding relationships, ranging, for example, from difficulties adjusting behavior to suit various social contexts; to difficulties in sharing imaginative play or in making friends; to absence of interest in peers.

*Specify* current severity:

**Severity is based on social communication impairments and restrictive, repetitive patterns of behavior.**

B. Restricted, repetitive patterns of behavior, interests, or activities, as manifested by at least two of the following, currently or by history (examples are illustrative, not exhaustive; see text):

1. Stereotyped or repetitive motor movements, use of objects, or speech (e.g., simple motor stereotypies, lining up toys or flipping objects, echolalia, idiosyncratic phrases).

2. Insistence on sameness, inflexible adherence to rules, or ritualized patterns of verbal or nonverbal behavior (e.g., extreme distress at small changes, difficulties with transitions, rigid thinking patterns, greeting rituals, need to take same route or eat same food every day).

3. Highly restricted, fixated interests that are abnormal in intensity or focus (e.g., strong attachment to or preoccupation with unusual objects, excessively circumscribed or perseverative interests).

4. Hyper- or hyporeactivity to sensory input or unusual interest in sensory aspects of the environment (e.g., apparent indifference to pain/temperature, adverse response to specific sounds or textures, excessive smelling or touching of objects, visual fascination with lights or movement).

*Specify* current severity:

**Severity is based on social communication impairments and restrictive, repetitive patterns of behavior.**

C. Symptoms must be present in the early developmental period (but may not become fully manifest until social demands exceed limited capacities, or may be masked by learned strategies in later life).

D. Symptoms cause clinically significant impairment in social, occupational, or other areas of current functioning.

E. These disturbances are not better explained by intellectual disability (intellectual developmental disorder) or global developmental delay. Intellectual disability and autism spectrum disorder frequently co-occur; to make comorbid diagnoses of autism spectrum disorder and intellectual disability, social communication should be below that expected for general developmental level.

Note: Individuals with a well-established *DSM-IV* diagnosis of autistic disorder, Asperger's disorder, or pervasive developmental disorder not otherwise specified should be given the diagnosis of autism spectrum disorder. Individuals who have marked deficits in social communication, but whose symptoms do not otherwise meet criteria for autism spectrum disorder, should be evaluated for social (pragmatic) communication disorder.

*Specify* if:

**With or without accompanying intellectual impairment**

**With or without accompanying language impairment**

**Associated with a known medical or genetic condition or environmental factor**

**Associated with another neurodevelopmental, mental, or behavioral disorder**

**With catatonia**

Source: Reprinted with permission from the *Diagnostic and Statistical Manual of Mental Disorders,* Fifth Edition, (Copyright 2013). American Psychiatric Association.

The reliability of the diagnosis of autistic disorder was assessed in *DSM-IV* field trials as good to excellent, with kappa values generally in the 0.70–0.80 range (Klin, Lang, Cicchetti, & Volkmar, 2000). In the *DSM-5* field trials, pooled reliability for autism spectrum disorder was very good at 0.69 (Regier, et al., 2013). Autism spectrum disorder is at least 4 times more common in males, although females with the condition are more likely to show intellectual disability (American Psychiatric Association, 2013). Prevalence rates of autistic disorder increased from 1 in 2,500 to 1 in 500 in the past 20 years (Kabot, Masi, & Segal, 2003), and the *DSM-5* estimates the autism spectrum disorder frequency at nearly 1% of the population (American Psychiatric Association, 2013). It is not clear whether this reflects a true increase in the occurrence of the disorder, an improvement in methods of detection and diagnosis, or an increased recognition of autism spectrum conditions (Volker & Lopata, 2008).

Some people with autism spectrum disorder may have particularly strong abilities in very narrow areas. Perhaps 10% of autistic individuals show **savant syndrome**, or evidence of exceptional skills in mathematics, music, drawing, calculation of dates, mechanical aptitude, or memory (Miller, L. K., 1999). One clear example is Nadia (see Figure 13-7), an autistic female with exceptional drawing ability (Selfe, 1977). However, the great majority of autistic individuals do not show savant syndrome.

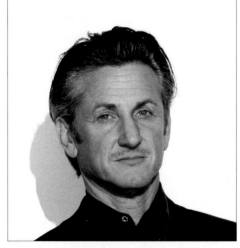

In the 2001 film *I am Sam,* actor Sean Penn portrays an autistic adult. The academy award nominated film shows what severe emotional hardship a developmental disability can cause for those suffering from the condition and for their loved ones. (AP Wide World)

## 13.6a  Causal Factors

### Heredity

Autism spectrum disorder tends to run in families, with about 5% of siblings of autistic persons also showing the condition (American Psychiatric Association, 2000). Twin studies

**Savant syndrome**

Exceptional ability in a narrow area

## Figure 13-7   *Extraordinary Drawing Ability in an Autistic Child*

Drawings that Nadia made at age 3-1/2 (right) and age 5-1/2 (left)

Source: Selfe, L. (1977). *Nadia: A case of extraordinary drawing ability in an autistic child.* New York, NY: Academic Press. Reprinted with permission.

support a substantial genetic contribution, and there have been positive linkage reports for every chromosome; at least 188 candidate sites are being investigated although none have been confirmed (Volker & Lopata, 2008). *DSM-5* reports that about 15% of cases are known to be associated with specific genetic mutations, with the remaining risk polygenetic and diffuse (American Psychiatric Association, 2013).

## Neurological Factors

Autism spectrum disorder has been associated with some abnormalities of brain function or structure. It has been observed that those with the condition have higher serotonin levels than unaffected persons. It has also been reported that brain growth for autistic infants is accelerated in the first 2 years, followed by a slower-than-normal growth period, so that brain size is in the normal range by early adolescence. Abnormalities of the cerebellum and amygdala have also been reported (Kabot, Masi, & Segal, 2003; Volker & Lopata, 2008). However, no consistent and unique abnormality is present, and it is not possible to diagnose autism spectrum disorder by means of any anatomical or biochemical marker.

## Psychosocial Factors

Leo Kanner (1943), a child psychiatrist, first formulated the concept of early infantile autism on the basis of a careful study of 11 children, all of whom showed a strange indifference to people. Kanner noted that the parents of the children in his original sample appeared to be rather cool and distant in their interpersonal relationships. Other writers, for example J. L. Despert (1951), developed psychological theories of autism in which the parents' aloofness was thought to produce the lack of responsivity in the child. Subsequent research did not support the notion of lack of warmth in parents of autistic children (Cantwell, Baker, & Rutter, 1978; DeMeyer, et al., 1972). Psychodynamic clinicians speculated that the autistic child's self-destructive behavior reflects underlying feelings of worthlessness and self-hate (Bettelheim, 1967), although no empirical evidence exists for that explanation.

An autistic child learns to communicate using visual symbols.
(iStock)

Some investigators have suggested that other deficits, probably associated with biological abnormalities, are fundamental to autistic disorder. Lovaas, Koegel, and Schreibman (1979) proposed that many of the autistic child's difficulties result from "**stimulus over-selectivity**," or a tendency to selectively respond to only part of the relevant cues in the environment. In some instances, the autistic child responds selectively to minor or even irrelevant aspects of the stimulus situation. Lovaas and his associates report a number of studies demonstrating the autistic child's difficulty in responding to multiple cues. For example, autistic and normal children were reinforced for responding to a complex stimulus that included a visual, auditory, and tactile component, each presented simultaneously. Later, when these components were presented separately, the autistic children tended to respond to only one component and ignore the other two. The normal children responded to each component equally. Lovaas et al. suggest that an extreme tendency to ignore many aspects of relevant environmental information could result in many of the symptoms seen in autism and in the difficulty in teaching such children the use of language and other skills.

Other researchers suggest that the central deficit in autism is a "**theory of mind**," or the ability to attribute mental states to the self or others. A meta-analysis of the literature indicated that individuals with autistic disorder performed less well than persons with intellectual disability or normal individuals in tasks such as understanding false belief, taking the perspective of others, or understanding picture stories in which mental state is a

**Stimulus over-selectivity**

Selectively responding to specific, often minor aspects of the stimulus situation

**Theory of mind**

Ability to recognize or attribute mental states in others

central component (Yirmiya, Erel, Shaked, & Solomonica-Levi, 1998). The assumption is that deficiencies in the skills subsumed under "theory of mind" produce impairments in social interactions, communication, and play such as that seen in autism spectrum disorder.

Based on the success of applied behavior analysis in treating autism, Bijou and Ghezzi (1999) introduced a model, the "behavior interference theory," that describes how a sequence of interconnected biobehavioral developments might produce autism onset. According to the theory, there is first a tendency to escape or avoid tactile or auditory stimuli, which the child finds unpleasant. This tendency interferes with the development of important social discriminative and reinforcing stimulus functions that ordinarily originate within the interactions between the mother and her baby. This in turn leads to abnormal development of social-emotional and communicative behavior, which then gives rise to stereotypic behavior as compensation for the lack of social-emotional and communicative behavior.

## Vaccines

Several studies have examined the possibility that the increase in autism spectrum disorder over the past 25 years could be due to the increased use of medical vaccinations, such as the measles, mumps, and rubella (MMR) vaccine. Some proponents of the argument point to the fact that a mercury substance has been used in the vaccine's production and that mercury is a toxin, which could impact the central nervous system. There have been several large-scale evaluations of that possibility. To date, none have found any evidence that vaccinations or mercury exposure is associated with autism. In fact, Honda, Shimizu, and Rutter (2005) found that terminating a large-scale MMR vaccination program had no impact, more than a decade later, on the increasing autism rates in Japan.

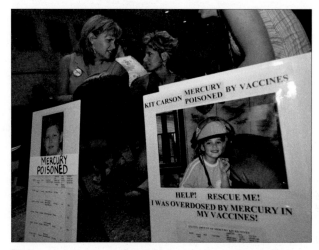

"Moms against mercury" activists at a news conference on vaccines and child health. Several studies have examined the possibility that the increase in autism over the past 25 years could be due to the increased use of medical vaccinations. To date, none have found any evidence that vaccinations or mercury exposure is associated with autism. (AP Wide World)

# 13.6b  Treatment of Autistic Disorder

## Pharmacological Approaches

Stimulant medications and newer antipsychotic drugs such as respiradone have been used in treating autism spectrum clients, especially those with hyperactive symptoms, self-injury, and aggression. Additionally, SSRIs have been prescribed to reduce repetitive or compulsive-like behaviors. However, there is no consensus on the relative effectiveness and safety of these approaches. Several studies have reported methylphenidate, the stimulant most often prescribed for ADHD, reduced symptoms of hyperactivity among autistic subjects. However, this population may also be more susceptible to troubling side effects of the medication (e.g., Handen, Johnson, & Lubetsky, 2004).

## Behavioral Approaches

Significant developments have occurred in the behavioral treatment of autism over the past three decades. Lovaas (1987) demonstrated the effectiveness of an intensive 40 hour per week behavior modification program that targeted language and social skills on a 1:1 basis. Parents received training in the program and assumed therapist duties in the home, following initial treatment in the clinic and at school. After treatment, 47% of the experimental group of children attained normal social and academic functioning and were indistinguishable from peers; their gains were maintained at multi-year follow-ups. Since that time, intensive behavioral interventions for autism have been refined and replicated. A review by Howard,

Former Miami Dophins star and autism activist Dan Marino speaks before Florida Governor Charles Crist on May 20, 2008. (AP Wide World)

Sparkman, Cohen, Green, and Stanislaw (2005) found this type of intervention more effective, both after treatment and at follow-up, than eclectic mixed therapies or public special education classes. Several other investigators have confirmed the value of this approach (sometimes called simply *applied behavior analysis* or ABA treatment), especially when interventions begin at very early ages and parents are involved as therapists, making more naturalistic training settings possible. Comprehensive evaluations have subsequently concluded that both structured and naturalistic behavioral approaches were effective in increasing communication, peer interactions, and social interactions, and reducing problem behaviors (Dawson, et al., 2010; Volker & Lopata, 2008).

## Other Treatments

A variety of other treatments have been promoted, including vitamins and minerals, special sugar-free or gluten-free diets, chelation therapy (to remove heavy metals from the body), auditory integration therapy, craniosacral manipulation, secretin, sensory integration, facilitated communication, and holding therapy. There is a paucity of research, and no substantial empirical support, for any of these interventions (Kabot, Masi, & Segal, 2003).

**Can autism be treated?**

# 13.7  Attention-Deficit/Hyperactivity Disorder

Attention-deficit/hyperactivity disorder (see *DSM-5* Diagnostic Criteria for Attention-Deficit/Hyperactivity Disorder) is the leading source of referrals for youth to mental health care. The condition has been identified for many years. Early in the twentieth century, the terms "minimal brain damage" and "minimal brain dysfunction" were employed to describe a hyperactive condition presumably caused by damage to the developing brain, especially

---

| *DSM-5* | **Diagnostic Criteria for Attention-Deficit/Hyperactivity Disorder** |
| --- | --- |

Attention-Deficit/Hyperactivity Disorder

A.  A persistent pattern of inattention and/or hyperactivity-impulsivity that interferes with functioning or development, as characterized by (1) and/or (2):

1.  **Inattention**: Six (or more) of the following symptoms have persisted for at least 6 months to a degree that is inconsistent with developmental level and that negatively impacts directly on social and academic/occupational activities:

**Note**: the symptoms are not solely a manifestation of oppositional behavior, defiance, hostility, or failure to understand tasks or instructions. For older adolescents and adults (age 17 and older), at least five symptoms are required.

    a.  Often fails to give close attention to details or makes careless mistakes in schoolwork, at work, or during other activities (e.g., overlooks or misses details, work is inaccurate).

    b.  Often has difficulty sustaining attention in tasks or play activities (e.g., has difficulty remaining focused during lectures, conversations, or lengthy reading).

    c.  Often does not seem to listen when spoken to directly (e.g., mind seems elsewhere, even in the absence of any obvious distraction).

    d.  Often does not follow through on instructions and fails to finish schoolwork, chores, or duties in the workplace (e.g., starts tasks but quickly loses focus and is easily sidetracked).

    e.  Often has difficulty organizing tasks and activities (e.g., difficulty managing sequential tasks; difficulty keeping materials and belongings in order; messy, disorganized work; has poor time management; fails to meet deadlines).

    f.  Often avoids, dislikes, or is reluctant to engage in tasks that require sustained mental effort (e.g., schoolwork or homework; for older adolescents and adults, preparing reports, completing forms, reviewing lengthy papers).

g. Often loses things necessary for tasks or activities (e.g., school materials, pencils, books, tools, wallets, keys, paperwork, eyeglasses, mobile telephones).

h. Is often easily distracted by extraneous stimuli ( for older adolescents and adults, may include unrelated thoughts).

i. Is often forgetful in daily activities (e.g., doing chores, running errands; for older adolescents and adults, returning calls, paying bills, keeping appointments).

2. **Hyperactivity and impulsivity:** Six (or more) of the following symptoms have persisted for at least 6 months to as degree that is inconsistent with developmental level and that negatively impacts directly on social and academic/occupational activities:

**Note:** The symptoms are not merely a manifestation of oppositional behavior, defiance, hostility, or failure to understand tasks or instructions. For older adolescents and adults (age 17 and older), at least five symptoms are required.

a. Often fidgets with or taps hands or feet or squirms in seat.

b. Often leaves seat in situations when remaining in seat is expected (e.g., leaves his or her place in the classroom, in the office or other workplace, or in other situations that require remaining in place).

c. Often runs about or climbs in situations where it is inappropriate. (**Note:** In adolescents or adults, may be limited to feeling restless).

d. Often unable to play or engage in leisure activities quietly.

e. Is often "on the go," acting as if "driven by a motor" (e.g., is unable to be or uncomfortable being still for an extended time, as in restaurants, meetings; may be experienced by others as being restless or difficult to keep up with).

f. Often talks excessively.

g. Often blurts out an answer before the question has been completed (e.g., completes people's sentences, cannot wait for turn in conversation).

h. Often has difficulty waiting his or her turn (e.g., while waiting in line).

i. Often interrupts or intrudes on others (e.g., butts into conversations, games, or activities; may start using other people's things without asking or receiving permission; for adolescents and adults, may intrude into and take over what others are doing).

B. Several inattentive or hyperactive-impulsive symptoms were present prior to the age of 12 years.

C. Several inattentive or hyperactive-impulsive symptoms are present in two or more settings (e.g., at home, school, or work; with friends or relatives; in other activities).

D. There is clear evidence that the symptoms interfere with, or reduce the quality of, social, academic, or occupational functioning.

E. The symptoms do not occur exclusively during the course of schizophrenia or another psychotic disorder and are not better explained by another mental disorder (e.g., mood disorder, anxiety disorder, dissociative disorder, personality disorder, substance intoxication or withdrawal).

F. *Specify* whether:

**314.01 (F90.2) Combined presentation:** If both Criterion A1 (inattention) and Criterion A2 (hyperactivity-impulsivity) are met for the past 6 months.

**314.00 (F90.0) Predominantly inattentive presentation:** If both Criterion A1 (inattention) is met but Criterion A2 (hyperactivity-impulsivity) is not met for the past 6 months.

**314.01 (F90.1) Predominantly hyperactive/impulsive presentation:** If Criterion A2 (hyperactivity-impulsivity) is met and Criterion A1 (inattention) is not met for the past 6 months.

*Specify* if:

**In partial remission:** When full criteria were previously met, fewer than the full criteria have been met for the past 6 months, and the symptoms still result in impairment in social, academic, or occupational functioning.

*Specify* current severity:

**Mild:** Few, if any, symptoms in excess to those required to make the diagnosis are present, and symptoms result in no more than minor impairments in social or occupational functioning.

**Moderate:** Symptoms or functional impairment between "mild" and "severe" are present.

**Severe:** Many symptoms in excess of those required to make the diagnosis, or several symptoms that are particularly severe, are present, or the symptoms result in marked impairment in social or occupational functioning.

Source: Reprinted with permission from the *Diagnostic and Statistical Manual of Mental Disorders,* Fifth Edition, (Copyright 2013). American Psychiatric Association.

from encephalitis or injuries associated with birth. Brain damage could not be substantiated, however; the term "minimal cerebral dysfunction" was later used, followed by "hyperactive child syndrome." By the time of *DSM-II*, it was called

**Which childhood disorders are the most common?**

"hyperkinetic reaction." The *DSM-III* recognized two forms, attention deficit disorder and attention deficit disorder with hyperactivity. The *DSM-IV* diagnosis, attention-deficit/hyperactivity disorder, allowed for prominent symptoms of inattention, hyperactivity-impulsivity, or a combination of the two. That practice was continued in the *DSM-5*. At least some symptoms must have caused impairment before age 12, compared to age 7 in the *DSM-IV*; they must be present in at least two different settings; and they must interfere with academic, occupational, or social functioning.

Inattention may be obvious in several situations. Academic work tends to be messy or careless, reflecting disorganization and a lack of attention to detail; and school grades are usually poor. Affected individuals may appear easily distracted or forgetful. They avoid tasks requiring sustained mental effort. Hyperactivity appears as a high level of bodily activity—the person cannot sit still, fidgets, wriggles, and is constantly on the move from one place of interest to another. Young children may climb on furniture and appear constantly driven; older adolescents feel restless and have a difficult time remaining in quiet activities. Impulsivity may appear as impatience and intrusiveness. ADHD individuals tend to interrupt others, make comments out of turn, and act before considering immediate consequences.

The disorder is much more commonly diagnosed in males than females, at approximately a 2:1 ratio (American Psychiatric Association, 2013) although estimates given in the *DSM-IV* were as high as 9:1 (American Psychiatric Association, 2000). Most often, the condition becomes apparent when a child enters school and is required to remain seated for long periods of time. Prevalence is estimated at about 5% of school-aged children (American Psychiatric Association, 2013). Usually, as children mature, the condition becomes less obvious and often attenuates significantly by late adolescence. However, some individuals continue to show signs of ADHD into adulthood. ADHD is highly co-morbid with other conditions including learning disorders, oppositional defiant disorder, and conduct disorder (Kessler, Chiu, Demler, Merikangas, & Walters, 2005). It occurs more often in families where mood disorders, anxiety disorders, substance use disorders, and antisocial personality disorder are present (American Psychiatric Association, 2000).

## 13.7a Causal Factors

Family and twin studies indicate a strong genetic component to ADHD, although strong family, school, and peer influences are also important in its occurrence. Neurological studies have suggested that reduced levels of activity in particular areas of the brain, including the frontal lobe, basal ganglia, and the cerebellum, occur with ADHD (Barkley, et al., 2002). Possibly, underactivity in certain brain areas produces deficiencies in attention and in the ability to inhibit certain activities, resulting in hyperactivity and impulsivity. There have been frequent suggestions of relationship between ADHD and diet (including sugar and food dyes), but these have not been accompanied by any controlled supporting data. A recent review of health and nutrition data from a nationally representative sample of the U.S. found that both maternal smoking during pregnancy and increased lead concentration in the blood were both associated with ADHD (Froehlich, et al., 2009). The *DSM-5* reports that low birth weight may be associated with a threefold increase in risk (American Psychiatric Association, 2013). However, the specific cause or causes of ADHD remain unidentified.

## 13.7b Treatment for ADHD

Stimulant medications such as methylphenidate (marketed as Ritalin) have been shown to reduce the symptoms of ADHD in the short term; and they are effective for about 70% of children, compared to about 10% for placebo (Greenhill & Ford, 2002). Nearly all ADHD children in the U.S. are prescribed medication as the first-line treatment for the condition. Some slower-release medications and non-stimulant alternatives have also been introduced, but no differences in effectiveness among these drugs are apparent (Furman, 2008). Behavior therapy and contingency management programs have empirical support for treating ADHD. Although short-term effect sizes reported in controlled studies appear to favor medication for reducing symptoms (Hinshaw, Klein, & Abikoff, 2002), they favor behavior therapy for treatment of impairments and associated difficulties. While useful in the short term, the medications do not appear to have long-term effectiveness, and they may stunt growth. A 3-year follow-up of the Multimodal Treatment Study of Children with ADHD found that although medication produced greater improvements than behavior therapy at the conclusion of treatment, there were no group differences between medication, behavior therapy, or a combination of those on any measure 2 years later (Jensen, et al., 2007). However, there was a significant stimulant-related decrease in growth rates, including both height and weight, among medicated children across the 3-year period (Swanson, et al., 2007). Contrary to frequent assertions in the pharmacological and professional literature, there is no evidence that treatment with stimulant medication is associated with a reduction in later risk for substance abuse (Humphreys, Eng, & Lee, 2013). The American Psychological Association's task force on pharmacological, psychosocial, and combined interventions for childhood disorders, after weighing the risks and benefits of effective treatments, recommended that children should first receive a trial of psychosocial intervention for ADHD before medication is initiated (American Psychological Association, 2006).

## 13.7c  ADHD Controversies

The reliability and validity of the ADHD diagnosis continues to be a source of controversy. The incidence of ADHD has increased dramatically over the past three decades. The increase may stem in part from practices intended to improve diagnostic reliability through the use of standardized rating scales. Healey, Miller, Castelli, Marks, and Halperin (2008) note that ADHD rating scales, which focus only on symptom presence, result in many false positives. However, the diagnosis did well in the *DSM-5* field trials, with a pooled reliability of 0.61 (Regier, et al., 2013).

Although it is observed in other countries, American children are more likely than others to receive the diagnosis, and 80%–90% of global methylphenidate is prescribed for American children (Stolzer, 2007). Roughly 1 in 25 U.S. children receive stimulant medication for ADHD; and medication expenditures were $2.3 billion in 2003 (Furman, 2008), in spite of the lack of evidence of long-term effectiveness. Because of these facts, some researchers are concerned that the disorder is being over-diagnosed and over-medicated, in part because of the significant financial benefits involved for pharmaceutical companies who both produce the medications and promote a disease-model view of the condition. One problem is that the medications are not specific for ADHD. Normal men and boys respond similarly to stimulant drugs as ADHD boys, showing decreases of activity and greater attention to tasks (Rapoport, Buchsbaum, & Weingartner, 1980). Drug response, therefore, cannot be validation of the diagnosis.

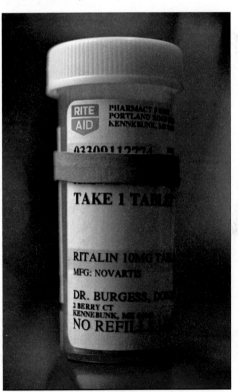

Nearly all ADHD children in the U.S. are prescribed medication as the first-line treatment for the condition. (Wikimedia Commons)

A more contentious issue involves the validity of the diagnosis itself. Although ADHD is presented as a neurological disease, there are no laboratory tests, neurological assessments, physical features, or attentional assessments that are diagnostic for the disorder (American Psychiatric Association, 2013). Concerned about what they consider inaccurate portrayals of the disorder, Barkley and several dozen authorities as co-signers (Barkley, et al., 2002) issued an "international consensus statement" reaffirming their conviction that ADHD is a genuine neurological disease of the brain, with strong genetic influence, that produces serious impairment and is effectively treated by medication. Others have remained unconvinced, however. Timimi and a few dozen cosigners (Timimi & co-signers, 2004) issued a "critique" of the consensus statement, disputing each of the main points. Ongoing disagreement continues to suggest that any "consensus" remains elusive. Coghill (2005) strongly favors the position that ADHD is a valid neuropsychiatric disorder, highly heritable and largely unrelated to parenting. Bailly (2005) notes that there are many non-ADHD causes for hyperactive behavior in children, including sleep disturbances, side effects of asthma medication, hearing impairment, child abuse, inadequate parenting, and onset of other conditions or difficulties. More recently, Furman (2008) reviews the literature and finds the evidence unconvincing, concluding, "It is critical for unbiased clinicians to consider the possibility that ADHD is not a neurobehavioral disease but rather a constellation of symptoms that require attention (no pun intended)" (p. 780).

# 13.8 Disruptive, Impulse-Control, and Conduct Disorders

Other conditions that commonly have childhood or adolescent onset are the disruptive, impulse-control, and conduct disorders. They are not seen as developmental disorders, however. These conditions involve behavior that tends to bring the person into conflict with authority, often shown as impulsive or poorly controlled violations of social rules. Like the neurodevelopmental disorders, they are all more common in males than females. Included in this section (and double-listed in the *DSM-5*) is antisocial personality disorder, which was described with the other personality disorders in Chapter 8. These disorders are summarized in Table 13-2.

## 13.8a Oppositional Defiant Disorder

The distinguishing features of oppositional defiant disorder are recurrent defiance and hostility—including arguing, being spiteful, refusing to comply with requests, and intentionally annoying others—toward authority figures. These individuals are unwilling to compromise and are stubborn, resistant, and defiant—most often with adults or peers that they know well. Diagnostic criteria also include losing one's temper, often blaming others for one's mistakes, and being easily annoyed. Of course, one must distinguish the disorder from similar behavior that may be normal for a particular developmental level. The diagnosis requires the weekly presence of four such symptoms for a period of at least 6 months, involving anyone other than a sibling; if the person is under 5 years in age, then symptoms are required nearly every day to qualify for the diagnosis. The severity of oppositional defiant disorder can be specified with the descriptors "mild" (symptoms in only one setting), "moderate" (symptoms in two settings), and "severe" symptoms in three or more settings (American Psychiatric Association, 2013).

*Table 13-2*   DSM-5 Disruptive, Impulse-Control, and Conduct Disorders

| Disorder | Key Symptoms | Age or Duration Requirement | Sex Ratio |
|---|---|---|---|
| Oppositional defiant disorder | Angry defiant behavior | 6 months | More common among males |
| Conduct disorder | Persistent violations of social norms or rules | 12 months | More common among males |
| Intermittent explosive disorder | Recurrent impulsive aggressive outbursts | 12 months, onset after age 5 | More common among males |
| Antisocial personality disorder | Pervasive violation of the rights of others | Onset by age 15, current age at least 18 | More common among males |
| Pyromania | Recurrent fire-setting | None | More common among males |
| Kleptomania | Recurrent impulsive theft | None | More common among females |

Some samples have reported incidence as high as 11%, but the average is about 3.3%. Before puberty, the disorder is more common in males; however, males and females show about equal rates after puberty. Usually, onset is before age 8, and it commonly precedes the development of conduct disorder. It is strongly co-morbid with both ADHD and conduct disorder (American Psychiatric Association, 2013). Diagnostic reliability, assessed in the *DSM-5* field trials, was "good" at 0.40 (Regier, et al., 2013). Effective treatments for oppositional defiant disorder are similar to those for conduct disorder (below), usually involving parent and child training and family interventions (American Psychological Association, 2006; Webster-Stratton & Hammond, 1997). Training programs for parents of children with oppositional defiant disorder are listed among the well-established, empirically validated treatments by Chambless and his colleagues (1998).

The distinguishing features of oppositional defiant disorder are recurrent disobedience and hostility towards authority figures. (Shutterstock)

## 13.8b  Conduct Disorder

Another common disruptive pattern of behavior is conduct disorder (see *DSM-5* Diagnostic Criteria for Conduct Disorder). It involves repetitive and persistent violations of rules, socially appropriate norms, and the rights of others, often taking the form of aggression, damage to property, deceitfulness and theft, and serious rule violations. The pattern is usually evident in a variety of settings over a 12-month period; and it must cause serious impairment in academic, occupational, or social functioning. In many ways, conduct disorder is a childhood version of antisocial personality disorder—and, in fact, evidence of conduct disorder before age 15 is a requirement for the antisocial personality disorder diagnosis. Conduct disorder may be diagnosed in adults, but only in the absence of adult antisocial personality disorder.

Individuals with conduct disorder are often bullies, and they have little empathy or concern for the feelings of others. Feelings of guilt are rarely associated with the acts committed. The *DSM-5* added a new specifier to conduct disorder, "with limited prosocial emotion," to designate those cases in which persons show little or no evidence of guilt, empathy, or concern for the feelings, wishes, and well-being of others. Frequently, those with conduct disorder are also reckless and irritable. Smoking, early sexual activity, and use of illegal substances are common. The prognosis appears poorer in childhood-onset type and in relation to the "with limited prosocial emotions" specifier. The condition commonly co-occurs with ADHD and is also associated with mood disorders, anxiety disorders, learning disorders, and substance use disorders. Incidence appears to have increased in the past few decades and may be as high as 10% in the general population, although median estimates are closer to 4% (American Psychiatric Association, 2013).

### Causal Factors

Conduct disorder tends to run in families and is more likely when parents or siblings have antisocial personality disorder or conduct disorder, substance use disorder, mood disorders, or ADHD. Other predisposing factors include parental rejection or neglect, use of harsh discipline, physical or sexual abuse, lack of supervision, peer rejection, below-normal IQ, and early institutional living. Both genetic and environmental factors are thought to be involved in its development (American Psychiatric Association, 2013).

Certain behaviors consistent with conduct disorder are serious rule violations, social deviancy, and aggression. Smoking, sexual activity, and use of illegal substances are common and begin at a young age. (iStock)

| *DSM-5* | **Diagnostic Criteria for Conduct Disorder** |

Conduct Disorder

A. A repetitive and persistent pattern of behavior in which the basic rights of others or major age-appropriate societal norms or rules are violated, as manifested by the presence of at least three of the following 15 criteria in the last 12 months from any categories below, with at least one criterion present in the past 6 months:

**Aggression to People and Animals**

1. Often bullies, threatens, or intimidates others.
2. Often initiates physical fights.
3. Has used a weapon that can cause serious physical harm to others (e.g., a bat, brick, broken bottle, knife, gun).
4. Has been physically cruel to people.
5. Has been physically cruel to animals.
6. Has stolen while confronting a victim (e.g., mugging, purse snatching, extortion, armed robbery).
7. Has forced someone into sexual activity.

**Destruction of Property**

8. Has deliberately engaged in fire-setting with the intention of causing serious damage.
9. Has deliberately destroyed others' property (other than by fire setting).

**Deceitfulness or Theft**

10. Has broken into someone else's house, building, or car.
11. Often lies to obtain goods or favor or to avoid obligations (i.e., "cons" others).

**Serious Violations of Rules**

13. Often stays out at night despite parental prohibitions, beginning before age 13 years.
14. Has run away from home overnight at least twice while living in the parental or parental surrogate home, or once without returning for a lengthy period.
15. Is often truant from school, beginning before age 13 years.

B. The disturbance in behavior causes clinically significant impairment in social, academic, or occupational functioning.

C. If the individual is age 18 years or older, criteria are not met for antisocial personality disorder.

*Specify* whether:

**312.81 (F91.1) Childhood-onset type:** Individuals show at least one symptom characteristic of conduct disorder prior to age 10 years.

**312.82 (F91.2) Adolescent-onset type:** Individuals show no symptom characteristic of conduct disorder prior to age 10 years.

**312.89 (F91.9) Unspecified onset:** Criteria for a diagnosis of conduct disorder are met, but there is not enough information available to determine whether the onset of the first symptom was before or after age 10 years.

*Specify* if:

**With limited prosocial emotions:** To qualify for this specifier, an individual must have displayed at least two of the following characteristics persistently over at least 12 months and in multiple relationships and settings. These characteristics reflect the individual's typical pattern of interpersonal and emotional functioning over this period and not just occasional occurrences in some situations. Thus, to assess the criteria for the specifier, multiple information sources are necessary. In addition to the individual's self-report, it is necessary to consider reports by others who have known the individual for extended periods of time (e.g., parents, teachers, co-workers, extended family members, peers).

**Lack of remorse or guilt:** Does not feel bad or guilty when he or she does something wrong (exclude remorse when expressed only when caught and/or facing punishment). The individual shows a general lack of concern about the negative consequences of his or her actions. For example, the individual is not remorseful after hurting someone else or does not care about the consequences of breaking rules.

**Callous lack of empathy:** Disregards and is unconcerned about the feelings of others. The individual is described as cold and uncaring. The person appears more concerned about the effects of his or her actions on himself or herself, rather than their effects on others, even when they result in substantial harm to others.

**Unconcerned about performance:** Does not show concern about poor/problematic performance at school, at work, or in other important activities. The individual does not put forth the effort necessary to perform well, even when expectations are clear, and typically blames other for his or her poor performance.

**Shallow or deficient affect:** Does not express feelings or show emotions to others, except in ways that seem shallow, insincere, or superficial (e.g., actions contradict the emotion displayed, can turn emotions "on" or "off" quickly) or when emotional expressions are used for gain (e.g., emotions displayed to manipulate or intimidate others).

*Specify* current severity:

**Mild:** Few if any conduct problems in excess of those required to make the diagnosis are present, and conduct problems cause relatively minor harm to others (e.g., lying, truancy, staying out after dark without permission, other rule breaking).

**Moderate:** The number of conduct problems and the effect on others are intermediate between those specified in "mild" and those in "severe" (e.g., stealing without confronting a victim, vandalism).

**Severe:** Many conduct problems in excess of those required to make the diagnosis are present, and conduct problems cause considerable harm to others (e.g., forced sex, physical cruelty, use of a weapon, stealing while confronting a victim, breaking and entering).

Granic and Patterson (2006) described a behavioral model of antisocial behavior, emphasizing the dynamic interplay between parents and the child. Based on coercion theory, the model proposes that parents and children train each other, through ongoing dynamic responding, in ways that increase aggressive and oppositional behavior by the adolescent. In one example interaction, a parent may request compliance from an adolescent engaged in an inappropriate activity. The adolescent then responds coercively, escalating the problem behavior to the point that the parent, frustrated, withdraws. The child senses the parent's acquiescence and reduces the problem activity. The child's escalation of misbehavior is reinforced by the withdrawal of parental demands for compliance, while the parental withdrawal is thus reinforced by the temporary improvement in behavior. The cumulative effect of many such exchanges over many situations is to produce more coercive behavior on the part of the adolescent, and less monitoring and discipline on the part of the parents. Inept discipline and monitoring from parents, together with rejection by normal peers and increasing adolescent commitment to deviant peer groups, further contribute to the development of antisocial behavior and delinquency.

## Treatment for Conduct Disorder

Behavioral techniques have been effectively employed for the treatment of antisocial and oppositional conduct in children and adolescents. One key part of the interventions is training of parents in behavior management skills, along with training both parents and children in problem solving approaches. Especially when instituted in families early after the onset of conduct disorder in young children, child training (e.g., modeling problem solving, social skills, and coping with stressful situations) and parent training (e.g., modeling of parenting skills and solutions for interpersonal problems) are effective in significantly reducing problem behaviors. Improvements have been maintained at 1-year follow-up (Kazdin, 1998; Webster-Stratton & Hammond, 1997).

Both parent training and community-based prevention programs have been shown to be effective (American Psychological Association, 2006; Farmer, Compton, Burns, & Robertson, 2002), but there are concerns that group-based treatments can have iatrogenic effects. That is, group treatments may result in increased rather than decreased problem behavior by inadvertently reinforcing deviant values, increasing contact with peers who model inappropriate behaviors, and normalizing skewed perceptions about the prevalence of delinquent activities. Several reports of increased deviancy in delinquent or at-risk youth undergoing peer-group treatment formats in community or school setting are available, including some evidence of increased likelihood of substance use following participation in Drug Abuse Resistance Education (DARE) programs (Rhule, 2005). It is important to be aware of these possibilities, in order to modify programs and delivery methods that present such risks.

# 13.8c Intermittent Explosive Disorder

Intermittent explosive disorder describes recurrent outbursts of verbal or physical aggressiveness involving failure to resist aggressive impulses. The aggression may include destruction of property, physical attacks that injure others, or verbal threats of assault. Outbursts are not pre-planned and are not attempts to achieve any clear objective such as intimidation. They are sometimes accompanied by strong emotions such as rage, grossly out of proportion to any provocation or precipitating stress. These episodes are often very distressing to the individual; and their consequences can involve loss of employment, interpersonal difficulties, divorce, legal problems, or serious injuries. The diagnosis cannot be given before age 6. Onset of the condition is usually in late childhood (American Psychiatric Association, 2013).

Because aggressive acts may occur in many mental disorders, careful diagnosis is required to rule out alternative conditions that can account for the behavior, such as antisocial or other personality disorders, conduct disorder, ADHD, or manic episodes. Most people with intermittent explosive disorder also have other disorders (Coccar & Danehy,

2006), complicating the diagnostic process. Similarly, the diagnosis requires that the aggression not be explainable by the effects of a substance or a general medical condition (such as head trauma).

Those with intermittent explosive disorder may have childhood histories of tantrums and sometimes also experience mood, anxiety, or substance use disorders, or other impulse control conditions. Data from a representative sample of over 9,000 adults found lifetime prevalence rates of 7.3% of the population, with average onset at age 14, and (for those affected) a lifetime average of 43 attacks (Kessler, et al., 2006). There is limited information on the etiology or treatment of intermittent explosive disorder although some evidence exists supporting the effectiveness of relaxation training, cognitive-behavioral therapy, and SSRI antidepressants in reducing aggressive behavior and improving affect (Coccar & Danehy, 2006).

Some authorities complained that the diagnostic reliability and validity of the intermittent explosive disorder diagnosis was poor because many impulsively aggressive persons would not be captured within the *DSM-IV* criteria for the disorder, which required a sense of increasing tension, relieved by the outburst. Coccaro, Kavoussi, Berman, and Lish (2006) proposed a set of revised diagnostic criteria that include rate (twice per week) and duration (1 month) criteria, together with removing the rule-out regarding other conditions (like antisocial personality disorder) that might better explain the aggression. These new criteria were tested on a group of 188 personality-disordered individuals and were found to have good inter-rater reliability and construct validity, and they were subsequently incorporated into the *DSM-5*.

## 13.8d Kleptomania

Kleptomania involves an impulsive urge to steal items that are not needed either for personal use or for their value. The theft is not driven by anger or a sense of vengeance, nor is it in response to delusions or hallucinations. In kleptomania, the person experiences a growing sense of tension before stealing, which is replaced by pleasure and relief after the theft occurs. Items are stolen impulsively with little preplanning and hold little value to the individual, who subsequently may discard them or give them away to others. People with this disorder know that the theft is wrong, and they may fear being caught and arrested; they often feel guilty afterward. However, stealing may be chronic and continue for years, despite a series of arrests and convictions. Kleptomania may occur in a significant minority of shoplifters, but its prevalence in the general population is less than 1%. Three-fourths of those with kleptomania are female (American Psychiatric Association, 2013).

As with intermittent explosive disorder, kleptomania must be distinguished from stealing that can occur in the context of conduct disorder, antisocial personality disorder, or a manic episode. Comorbid conditions most often include major depressive disorder, anxiety and eating disorders, and other impulse control disorders. Compulsive buying may be present as well (American Psychiatric Association, 2013). There is a high rate of hoarding of items by those with kleptomania, but often individuals report amnesia for the theft event (Grant, 2006). The condition usually begins by adolescence.

Little is known about etiology or effective therapy. Most individuals report shoplifting for 10 or more years before entering treatment. Some positive reports involving naltrexone (an opiate receptor blocker) for reducing urges to steal have been reported, but overall data are mixed; no pharmacological treatment is supported by controlled studies. Similarly, there are case reports suggesting covert sensitization and exposure and response prevention have been effective behavioral interventions, but no well-controlled studies have been published (Grant, 2006).

## 13.8e Pyromania

Pyromania involves multiple episodes of intentional fire setting. The urge to start a fire is accompanied by increasing tension or arousal, and pleasure or relief accompanies the fire and its aftermath. Individuals with pyromania do not set fires for monetary gain, to conceal a crime, as expressions of anger or vengeance, or for social or political reasons. Fire setting is also not a result of impaired judgment such as that associated with intoxication, limited intellectual functioning, or dementia. Instead, individuals with pyromania are fascinated by fire and are attracted to and curious about all aspects of fire, including fire-fighting paraphernalia, fire alarms, and fire-fighting. Some people with the disorder affiliate themselves with local fire departments and may actually become firefighters in order to be close to their source of fascination.

Although pyromania is an impulse control disorder, fires are not often set on impulse but rather after advance preparation that may be considerable. However, the person is frequently indifferent to the possible loss of life or destruction of property that may result. The condition is more common among males with poor social skills or learning difficulties, and in juveniles it is associated with conduct disorder and ADHD (American Psychiatric Association, 2000). It is also common for fire-setters to have a history of alcohol use disorder. Its prevalence is unknown in the population, but 3.3% of fire-setters in the criminal justice system may qualify for the diagnosis (American Psychiatric Association, 2013).

Individuals with pyromania are fascinated by, attracted to, and curious about all aspects of fire. Pyromania involves multiple episodes of intentional fire setting. (Shutterstock)

Classic psychoanalytic theory considered pyromania to be a symbolic sexual act; Freud considered it the equivalent of masturbation. Occasional case studies have reported sexual arousal in both male and female arsonists, suggesting that pyromania sometimes occurs in the context of fetishism (e.g., Balachandra & Swaminath, 2002). Others have proposed that it is a form of communication, aggression, or self-destructiveness by juveniles with limited social skills; suicidal thoughts or acts are very common among arsonists (Lejoyeux, McLoughlin, & Ades, 206). A few case studies have reported positive outcomes with behavioral interventions such as aversion therapy. However, very little systematic work is available on the etiology or treatment of pyromania.

# Chapter Review

## TO SUM UP ...

- The neurodevelopmental disorders involve dysfunctions relating to the developmental process. The disruptive, impulse-control, and conduct disorders involve deficient self-control of emotions and behavior.

- Intellectual disability is significantly below average intellectual functioning, combined with impairment in adaptive skills. Its causes include genetics, embryological errors, prenatal or postnatal conditions or injuries, environmental restrictions, or any conditions that prevent normal brain development.

- Although medications are commonly used in treating symptoms related to intellectual disability and autism spectrum disorder, there is little evidence for their effectiveness. Intensive behavioral intervention is helpful in treating many children with autistic disorder, especially if intervention begins at very young ages and includes parents as therapists.

- Several communication disorders may have onset during childhood or adolescence, and impair academic and social functioning. These conditions tend to improve as individuals get older.

- Tic disorders involve sudden, rapid motor movements or vocalizations that are experienced as irresistible.

- The most common childhood disorders involve disruptive behavior such as that seen in ADHD, conduct disorder, and oppositional defiant disorder. Although both genetic and environmental factors are involved in the development of these disorders, their specific causes are unknown.

- ADHD is controlled by stimulant medication and behavioral therapy during the short-term. However, there is no evidence that medications have long-term value for ADHD, and stimulants appear to inhibit physical growth. Behavior therapy and family therapy have been demonstrated as effective in treating conduct disorder and oppositional defiant disorder.

- Conduct disorder is a disruptive condition that involves violations of rules and the rights of others. It is a prerequisite for later development of antisocial personality disorder.

- There is much overlap and comorbidity between ADHD, oppositional defiant disorder, and conduct disorder.

- Both kleptomania and pyromania are impulse control disorders in which rising tension is relieved by the impulsive act.

# KEY TERMS

| | |
|---|---|
| Amniocentesis   359 | Phenylketonuria (PKU)   359 |
| Coprolalia   365 | Prematurity   361 |
| Down syndrome   360 | Savant syndrome   371 |
| Encephalitis   361 | Stimulus over-selectivity   372 |
| Fragile X syndrome   359 | Theory of mind   372 |
| IQ   356 | Tics   365 |
| Meningitis   361 | |

# QUESTIONS FOR STUDY

- Identify three preventable causes of intellectual disability.

- Discuss controversies involved in the diagnosis and treatment of ADHD.

- Distinguish the symptoms of two common disorders from two uncommon or rare disorders described in the chapter.

- Describe the disorders in which criminal behavior may be present.

# POP QUIZ

1. The specifiers for intellectual disability (mild, moderate, severe, profound) are based on which of the following?
   A. IQ scores
   B. degree of impairment in adaptive functioning
   C. the number of symptoms that occur
   D. the number of settings in which the disability is apparent

2. A standard score on intelligence test has a mean of _____ and a standard deviation of _____.
   A. 100; 15
   B. 100; 50
   C. 50; 15
   D. 50; 5

3. Among children, the most frequent psychological referral to mental health facilities occurs for which disorder?
   A. ADHD
   B. oppositional defiant disorder
   C. conduct disorder
   D. stuttering

4. How do psychostimulant drugs affect normal children?
   A. They induce a period of depression.
   B. They increase energy but decrease alertness.
   C. They improve attention and decrease motor activity.
   D. They have no observable effects on normal children.

5. _____, associated with intellectual disability, is also called trisomy 21.
   A. Fragile X syndrome
   B. PKU
   C. Rett's disorder
   D. Down syndrome

6. The wide availability of _____ has led to the virtual elimination of cretinism in the Western world.
   A. lithium
   B. iodized salt
   C. MMR vaccine
   D. folic acid

7. Harry is given a series of tests. His reading and writing results are significantly below those predicted by his intelligence and education. He would most likely be diagnosed as having _____.
   A. intellectual disability
   B. ADHD
   C. language disorder
   D. specific learning disorder

8. In families in which the father has a history of stuttering, _____% of daughters and _____% of sons also stutter.
   A. 20, 40
   B. 20, 30
   C. 10, 30
   D. 10, 20

9. What is savant performance?
   A. extreme sociability
   B. an exceptional skill in a specific area
   C. self-injurious behavior
   D. very high IQ

10. Which of the following disorders is more likely to involve coprolalia?
    A. language disorder
    B. conduct disorder
    C. Tourette's disorder
    D. Rett's disorder

11. Brain growth may be unusually rapid for the first 2-3 years in children with _____.
    A. autism spectrum disorder
    B. fragile X syndrome
    C. stereotypic movement disorder
    D. ADHD

12. Delayed auditory feedback helps to reduce _____.
    A. language disorder
    B. childhood-onset fluency disorder
    C. social (pragmatic) communication disorder
    D. speech sound disorder

13. Tim has been diagnosed as having oppositional defiant disorder; Vince has been diagnosed as having conduct disorder. What is the major difference between these two boys?
    A. Tim is older than Vince.
    B. Compared to Tim, Vince has a much better prognosis.
    C. Vince has engaged in more serious forms of rule violations than has Tim.
    D. They demonstrate the same symptoms, but Tim is more likely to be intellectually disabled.

14. Which of the following disorders is more common among females?
    A. conduct disorder
    B. pyromania
    C. autism spectrum disorder
    D. kleptomania

15. Although considered an impulse-control disorder, _____ actually includes planning and preparation for the act.
    A. kleptomania
    B. pyromania
    C. intermittent explosive disorder
    D. none of the above

# CHAPTER OVERVIEW

## CHAPTER OPENER QUESTIONS

What is the relationship between eating disorders, culture, and gender?

How are anorexia nervosa and bulimia nervosa different? Which is easier to treat?

What are parasomnias and dyssomnias?

What are the most common sleep disorders?

Can someone fall asleep in the middle of a conversation?

Do people sleepwalk because they are dreaming?

Do some people act out their dreams?

What treatments are effective for elimination disorders?

(Shutterstock)

# Eating, Sleep, and Elimination Disorders

# chapter 14

The dysfunctions we examine in this chapter involve basic biological processes necessary for human life: eating, sleeping, and eliminating waste. Many of the conditions involve the patterning of the activity, although symptoms of excess and deficiency are diagnostic. The largest category, the sleep-wake disorders, concerns dissatisfaction with the quality, timing, or amount of sleep. The smallest classification, the elimination disorders, consists only of two conditions involving inappropriate toileting. We begin here with the feeding and eating disorders.

## 14.1 Feeding and Eating Disorders

Among the feeding and eating disorders are conditions that can seriously impair physical and psychological health. They involve patterns of altered consumption, some of which affect

> **What is the relationship between eating disorders, culture, and gender?**

the absorption of nutrients. Pica and rumination disorder were moved from "Conditions first diagnosed in infancy, childhood, or adolescence" in the *DSM-IV* to join anorexia nervosa and bulimia nervosa, as well as binge-eating disorder (a formerly provisional diagnosis) and a new condition, avoidant/restrictive food intake disorder, in defining this category. The various feeding and eating disorders are displayed in Table 14-1.

The feeding and eating disorders do not include obesity, currently not listed as a mental disorder. According to the *DSM-5*, "Obesity (excess body fat) results from the long-term excess of energy intake relative to energy expenditure. A range of genetic, physiological, behavioral, and environmental factors that vary across individuals contributes to the development of obesity; thus, obesity is not considered a mental disorder" (American Psychiatric Association, 2013, p. 329). However, since all of the conditions we have been considering develop from a range of genetic, physiological, behavioral, and environmental factors, the distinction is less than clear. Presumably, the more pertinent issue would be that obesity is defined not in terms of the behavior that produces it, but rather in terms of its product, excess body fat—rather analogous to the relationship between smoking (the behavior) and lung cancer (its product).

Diagnostic reliability in the *DSM-III* field trials for eating disorders (at that time, only anorexia nervosa and bulimia nervosa were defined) was 0.59 for adults, but stronger reliability was recorded for children and adolescents. The reliability appears to have improved under the *DSM-IV*. Especially when structured interviews are used, the overall reliability for eating disorder diagnoses is high (Kutlesic, Williamson, Gleaves, Barbin, & Murphy-Eberenz, 1998). Brody, Walsh, and Devlin (1994) assessed binge eating disorder criteria at 0.70, indicating good reliability for this provisional diagnosis. The *DSM-5* field trials found "good" reliability for both binge eating disorder (0.56) and avoidant/restrictive food intake disorder (0.48), but other feeding and eating disorders were not assessed (Regier, et al., 2013).

## 14.1a Anorexia Nervosa

The condition now diagnosed as anorexia nervosa is one that has been recognized for well over 100 years. It appears to have been exceedingly rare until the mid-twentieth century

*Table 14-1* DSM-5 Feeding and Eating Disorders

| Disorder | Key Symptoms | Minimum Duration Required for Diagnosis | Sex Ratio |
|---|---|---|---|
| Anorexia nervosa | Restriction of energy intake, plus intense fear of gaining weight | None | More common among females |
| Bulimia nervosa | Recurrent binges and compensatory behaviors | 3 months | More common in females |
| Binge-eating disorder | Recurrent binges without compensatory behaviors | 3 months | More common in females |
| Avoidant/restrictive food intake disorder | Persistent failure to meet nutritional needs | None | Equal |
| Pica | Eating nonfood substances | 1 month | Unclear |
| Rumination disorder | Repeated regurgitation of food | 1 month | Unclear |

Source: Reprinted with permission from the *Diagnostic and Statistical Manual of Mental Disorders,* Fifth Edition, (Copyright 2013). American Psychiatric Association.

when its incidence increased, particularly among young females in Western industrialized countries. Self-starvation had been known for many years in early religious literature, but the clinical syndrome was first described and named by doctors in Paris and London in the nineteenth century. William Gull (1888) reported a case of a teenage girl who had nearly starved herself to death "without apparent cause"; she was treated effectively by light feeding every few hours (see Figure 14-1).

> How are anorexia nervosa and bulimia nervosa different? Which is easier to treat?

Anorexia nervosa, as currently defined, (see *DSM-5* Diagnostic Criteria for Anorexia Nervosa) involves three main features: restricted calorie intake insufficient to maintain normal body weight, intense fear of gaining weight, and a disturbance in the perception of body size. The fear of weight gain and the inaccurate perception that one's body is too

*Figure 14-1* **Before and After Anorexia Treatment**

Anorexic teenager before treatment (left) and after recovery (right) (W. Gull, 1888).
Source: Images courtesy U.S. National Library of Medicine

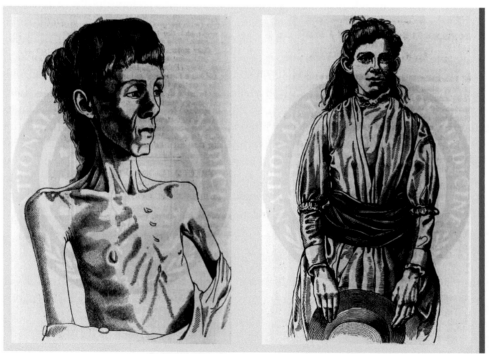

| DSM-5 | Diagnostic Criteria for Anorexia Nervosa |

Anorexia Nervosa

A. Restriction of energy intake relative to requirements, leading to a significantly low body weight in the context of age, sex, developmental trajectory, and physical health. Significantly low weight is defined as a weight less than minimally normal or, for children and adolescents, less than that minimally expected.

B. Intense fear of gaining weight or of becoming fat, or persistent behavior that interferes with weight gain, even though at a significantly low weight.

C. Disturbance in the way in which one's body weight or shape is experienced, undue influence of body weight or shape on self-evaluation, or persistent lack of recognition of the seriousness of the current low body weight.

**Coding note:** The ICD-9-CM code for anorexia nervosa is **307.1**, which is assigned regardless of subtype. The ICD-10-CM code depends on the subtype (see below).

*Specify* whether:

**(F50.01) Restricting type:** During the last 3 months, the individual has not engaged in recurrent episodes of binge eating or purging behavior (i.e., self-induced vomiting or the misuse of laxatives, diuretics, or enemas). This subtype describes presentations in which weight loss is accomplished primarily through dieting, fasting, and/or excessive exercise.

**(F50.02) Binge-eating/purging type:** During the last 3 months, the individual has engaged in recurrent episodes of binge eating or purging behavior (i.e., self-induced vomiting or the misuse of laxatives, diuretics, or enemas).

*Specify* if:

**In partial remission:** After full criteria for anorexia nervosa were previously met, Criterion A (low body weight) has not been met for a sustained period, but either Criterion B (intense fear of gaining weight or of becoming fat or behavior that interferes with weight gain) or Criterion C (disturbances in self-perception of weight and shape) is still met.

**In full remission:** After full criteria for anorexia nervosa were previously met, none of the criteria have been met for a sustained period of time.

*Specify* current severity:

The minimum level of severity is based, for adults, on current body mass index (BMI; see below) or, for children and adolescents, on BMI percentile. The ranges below are derived from World Health Organization categories for thinness in adults; for children and adolescents, corresponding BMI percentiles should be used. The level of severity may be increased to reflect clinical symptoms, the degree of functional disability, and the need for supervision.

**Mild:** BMI ≥ 17 kg/m$^2$

**Moderate:** BMI 16–16.99 kg/m$^2$

**Severe:** BMI 15–15.99 kg/m$^2$

**Extreme:** BMI < 15 kg/m$^2$

Source: Reprinted with permission from the *Diagnostic and Statistical Manual of Mental Disorders*, Fifth Edition, (Copyright 2013). American Psychiatric Association.

fat result in behaviors to prevent weight gain, even though the individual may already be emaciated. Two eating patterns are characteristic of those with anorexia nervosa. In one, the "restricting type," the individual diets, fasts, or exercises excessively, so that intake of food is inadequate to maintain current weight. In the less common "binge-eating/purging type," the individual regularly consumes food, often in large quantities, but then compensates by inducing vomiting or by misusing laxatives, enemas, or diuretics to produce weight loss.

Most often, weight loss is achieved by severe restriction in diet. As certain food items are restricted in the person's diet, the range of acceptable foods can become very narrow: sometimes, only a few leaves of lettuce comprise the daily menu. Typically, food becomes a pre-occupation for those with anorexia nervosa, often with obsessive-compulsive intensity. The person thinks of food most of the time and may hoard food items or even collect food recipes (American Psychiatric Association, 2013). However, the strict control of eating and the achievement of continued weight loss are considered to be personal accomplishments and a source of pride for the anorexic individual.

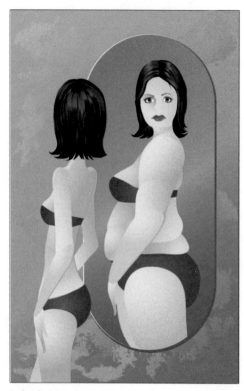

In both anorexia nervosa and bulimia nervosa, self-evaluation is unduly influenced by body weight or shape. (iStock)

Concern about weight, body shape, and especially fear of gaining weight are central features of anorexia nervosa. Body size and shape are very important to the self-image of those with the disorder, and perceptions of body image are distorted such that individuals feel fat even when weight is significantly below normal. They tend to view themselves in mirrors frequently, scanning for parts of their bodies that they feel are too heavy or fat in appearance.

Onset of the disorder usually occurs in adolescence; in no case was onset age later than the mid-20s in the National Comorbidity Study, a nationally representative survey (Hudson, Hiripi, Pope, & Kessler, 2007). The course is highly variable, and many who begin with the restricting type of the disorder shift to binge eating/purging type. A variety of physical disruptions consequent on starvation are evident in those with anorexia nervosa. Menstruation often ceases (or is delayed in prepubertal females); the *DSM-IV* diagnosis required cessation of menstruation for at least three consecutive menstrual cycles. **Amenorrhea** is no longer listed among the diagnostic criteria for the disorder, however. There may be intolerance to cold, loss of strength, abdominal pain, constipation, and heart irregularities. **Purging** behaviors may cause loss of tooth enamel and other dental problems, as well as osteoporosis, anemia, electrolyte imbalances, and dehydration. Hospitalization may become necessary, and mortality may be up to 5% per decade (American Psychiatric Association, 2013). Fortunately, average lifetime duration of anorexia appears to be much shorter than for the other eating disorders, averaging only 1.7 years (Hudson, Hiripi, Pope, & Kessler, 2007).

The incidence of anorexia nervosa is much higher among young females in Western industrialized nations where food is plentiful. It appears to be linked to cultural views about beauty and thinness, and driven by widespread media representations of increasingly thin models as images of perfection in fashion. The influence of culture can be seen in the fact that immigrants' risk for the disorder increases as they become more enmeshed in American life (American Psychiatric Association, 2013). Lucas, Beard, O'Fallon, and Kurland (1991) reported that the prevalence of anorexia nervosa over a 50-year period in Minnesota, from 1935 to 1984, rose linearly among females ages 15 to 24, with incidence increasing 36% every 5 years during that period. In the same period, incidence of the disorder did not change for males or older females. Overall, female rates were nearly 12 times higher than male rates of anorexia nervosa during 1980–1984. Since that time, the rate of increase has slowed.

Lifetime prevalence rates now appear to be about 0.9% for women and 0.3% for men (Hudson, Hiripi, Pope, & Kessler, 2007). Male cases tend to be associated with homosexuality (Russell & Keel, 2002). Those at highest risk are white females ages 15–24; in contrast, anorexia nervosa appears to be extremely rare among Black American females (Hoek, 2006). One possible explanation for such racial disparity is that risk for the disorder is greater among those of higher socioeconomic status (Striegel-Moore & Bulik, 2007).

Anorexia nervosa commonly occurs in conjunction with other mental disorders. In a sample of 101 adolescent females in treatment for anorexia nervosa, over 73% were diagnosed with at least one other disorder, most often mood or anxiety disorders. The binge eating/ purging type is associated with significantly greater risk of substance use disorders than the restricting type (Salbach-Andre, et al., 2008). The binge eating/purging type is also linked to significantly greater likelihood of suicide attempts (Bulik, et al., 2008).

## Causal Factors

The etiology of anorexia nervosa remains unknown. Psychoanalytic writers proposed that anorexic individuals, when faced with the anxiety-arousing prospect of genital sexuality

**Amenorrhea**

Absence of menstruation in a woman of reproductive age

**Purging**

A compensatory activity intended to reverse the effects of eating, usually involving self-induced vomiting or use of laxatives

at adolescence, regress to already existing oral fixations. Denial of eating is thought to reflect denial of sexuality or, even more specifically in some cases, guilt over the unconscious wish to be impregnated through the mouth. Family systems therapists have emphasized conflicts around issues of independence and changing from childhood to adult ways. Anorexic children are likely to appear in families that are excessively enmeshed—emotionally speaking—have overprotective parents, and lack effective ways of directly resolving conflicts. Thus the anorexic girl may be seen as asserting her independence in the only way she can, by refusing to eat.

Biological and cultural influences interact in the development of the disorder. Anorexia nervosa runs in families, and concordance rates are higher in MZ than DZ twins (American Psychiatric Association, 2013). Concordance has been reported as high as 55% for MZ twins, versus 5% for DZ twins (Fairburn & Harrison, 2003), suggesting substantial genetic contribution to risk for the disorder. Offspring of mothers with anorexia

Anorexia appears to be linked to cultural views about beauty and thinness, and driven by widespread media representations of increasingly thin models as images of perfection in fashion. (Shutterstock)

nervosa are at high risk for the disorder as well (Striegel-Moore & Bulik, 2007). However, its strong association with cultural portrayals of beauty in terms of thinness also indicates very important contributions from environmental factors. This may explain the significant variations in prevalence among different ages, ethnic groups, and sexual orientations. As noted above, homosexual orientation is a significant risk factor for eating disorders in males. Greater emphasis on physical attractiveness among gay men places them, like heterosexual women, at higher risk for attitudes and behaviors related to eating disorders (Siever, 1994). Among heterosexual adolescent males, the factors increasing the risk of eating disorders similarly involve low self-esteem and peer pressure to lose weight, although body image issues tend to involve male pursuit not of thinness but of muscularity (Ricciardelli & McCabe, 2004). Certain athletes, especially those involved in aesthetic performance (such as figure skating or gymnastics) or those emphasizing a specific weight (such as judo or wrestling) are at higher risk for eating disorders (Sundgot-Borgen, 1994).

## Treatment for Anorexia Nervosa

Outcome of treatment for anorexia nervosa did not improve much throughout the twentieth century: Steinhausen (2002) reports that even after 1950, mortality remained significantly high (ranging up to 22% in some studies), and less than one-half of patients fully recovered. More recently, some promising results have been reported for a particular form of conjoint family therapy for adolescents, in which parents are coached in how to assume control over the anorexic child's eating and weight. External controls are then gradually reduced as the child complies with parental authority so that increasing autonomy is linked with improved eating patterns (Wilson, Grilo, & Vitousek, 2007). However, this approach is less beneficial with older persons or if the disorder has persisted beyond a few years.

Medications are rarely used as the sole therapeutic approach and there is no clear evidence that antidepressants, which are widely prescribed for the condition, have any value over placebo (Wilson, Grilo, & Vitousek, 2007). No drug has been found to promote weight gain for these patients (Fairburn & Harrison, 2003). Inpatient treatment, which allows for close monitoring, nutritional counseling, and specific behavioral contingencies, can be effective in restoring body weight. However, the addition of medication does not add to outcome, and "at present, there is no specific role for pharmacology in the treatment of anorexia nervosa" (Wilson, Grilo, & Vitousek, 2007, p. 577).

**BVT** *Lab*

Flashcards are available for this chapter at www.BVTLab.com.

*more common than Anorexia.*

## 14.1b Bulimia Nervosa

Certain athletes, especially those involved in aesthetic performance (such as figure skating or gymnastics) or those emphasizing a specific weight (such as judo or wrestling) are at higher risk for eating disorders. (Shutterstock)

The condition known as bulimia nervosa (see *DSM-5* Diagnostic Criteria for Bulimia Nervosa) differs substantially from anorexia nervosa. Instead of weight loss and strict control of eating associated with a sense of achievement, bulimia nervosa involves a sense of lack of control related to recurrent episodes of eating large quantities of food. The binge episode is then followed by some attempt to compensate, such as purging, fasting, or excessive exercise. Like anorexia nervosa, those with bulimia nervosa fear gaining weight, are dissatisfied with their bodies, and base their self-evaluation on weight and body shape.

**Binge eating** involves amounts of food larger than others would normally eat in a given time. It usually includes high-calorie foods such as cookies, cakes, and ice cream; Fairburn and Harrison (2003) estimate that between 1,000 and 2,000 food calories are typically consumed during the binge event. Binge eating usually takes place rapidly, in secret, and continues until the individual becomes uncomfortably full. The person often reports feeling out of control during a binge event although he or she is able to stop the act if suddenly interrupted by others. Once the binge eating concludes, the person may employ several techniques to compensate for the binge in order to avoid weight gain. Most commonly vomiting is self-induced, often by

**Binge eating**

Eating much larger amounts of food than normal within a given time

---

| *DSM-5* | **Diagnostic Criteria for Bulimia Nervosa** |
| --- | --- |

307.51 (F50.2) Bulimia Nervosa

A. Recurrent episodes of binge eating. An episode of binge eating is characterized by both of the following:
   1. Eating, in a discrete period of time (e.g., within any 2-hour period), an amount of food that is definitely larger than what most individuals would eat in a similar period of time under similar circumstances.
   2. A sense of lack of control over eating during the episode (e.g., a feeling that one cannot stop eating or control what or how much one is eating).
B. Recurrent inappropriate compensatory behaviors in order to prevent weight gain, such as self-induced vomiting, misuse of laxatives, diuretics, or other medications; fasting; or excessive exercise.
C. The binge eating and inappropriate compensatory behaviors both occur, on average, at least once a week for 3 months.
D. Self-evaluation is unduly influenced by body shape and weight.
E. The disturbance does not occur exclusively during episodes of anorexia nervosa.

*Specify* if:

   **In partial remission:** After full criteria for bulimia nervosa were previously met, some, but not all, of the criteria have been met for a sustained period of time.

   **In full remission:** After full criteria for bulimia nervosa were previously met, none of the criteria have been met for a sustained period of time.

*Specify* current severity:

   The minimum level of severity is based on the frequency of inappropriate compensatory behaviors (see below). The level of severity may be increased to reflect other symptoms and the degree of functional disability.

**Mild:** An average of 1–3 episodes of inappropriate compensatory behaviors per week.

**Moderate:** An average of 4–7 episodes of inappropriate compensatory behaviors per week.

**Severe:** An average of 8-13 episodes of inappropriate compensatory behaviors per week.

**Extreme:** An average of 14 or more episodes of inappropriate compensatory behaviors per week.

Source: Reprinted with permission from the *Diagnostic and Statistical Manual of Mental Disorders*, Fifth Edition, (Copyright 2013). American Psychiatric Association.

*both binging and purging.*

use of fingers or instruments to trigger a gag reflex; one-third of those with bulimia nervosa also use laxatives to compensate for binge eating (American Psychiatric Association, 2013). Non-purging methods employ fasting for a day or more, or excessive exercise.

Bulimia nervosa is more common than anorexia nervosa, affecting up to 1.5% of females; the female-to-male ratio is 10:1 (American Psychiatric Association, 2013). Most receiving the diagnosis are white. Onset is usually 5 years later than that for anorexia nervosa, and average duration of the disorder is much longer, about 8.3 years (Hudson, Hiripi, Pope, & Kessler, 2007). Although bulimia may persist for several years, over the longer term symptoms tend to diminish (American Psychiatric Association, 2013). Unlike anorexia nervosa, which tends to occur among individuals of higher socioeconomic status, bulimia nervosa is not related to SES (Striegel-Moore & Bulik, 2007).

The purging behavior is associated with several negative physical consequences—including disturbed electrolyte balance, extensive dental erosion, stomach problems, and diarrhea. Dependence on laxatives for bowel movements may develop in those who use that technique for purging. Bulimia nervosa is often associated with mood disorders, and up to one-third of sufferers also have substance use disorders, usually involving alcohol or stimulants (American Psychiatric Association, 2013).

## Causal Factors

Risk for bulimia nervosa is elevated among victims of childhood physical or sexual abuse (American Psychiatric Association, 2013). There are data suggesting familial aggregation in bulimia nervosa, and some studies have suggested heritability estimates between 50% and 83% (Striegel-Moore & Bulik, 2007). However, clinical studies showing 35% concordance in MZ twins versus 30% concordance in DZ twins seem to indicate a weaker genetic link than for anorexia nervosa (Fairburn & Harrison, 2003).

The cultural factors affecting one's tendency to relate body image to self-esteem in bulimia nervosa are assumed to be similar to those for anorexia nervosa. At least among college students, exposure to mass media (especially magazines) that promote thin-beauty ideals is associated with increased likelihood of disordered eating (Harrison & Cantor, 1997). Stice (2001) outlined one pathway by which this may occur in vulnerable individuals: Exposure to thinness-promoting media, particularly in young people who value appearance highly, leads to acceptance (internalization) of these ideals of beauty. Together with a social pressure to be thin, these internalized ideals of beauty lead to dissatisfaction with one's appearance. Because these ideals are unattainable for nearly everyone, negative self-affect develops, leading to dieting and restriction, and thereby increasing the chance that binging will occur in response to severe hunger.

Bulimia nervosa, more common than anorexia nervosa, affects about 1.5% of females. (iStock)

## Treatments for Bulimia Nervosa

A greater number of controlled interventions have been conducted with bulimia nervosa than with anorexia nervosa, and the outcome data are more promising, with evidence supporting the use of both medications and psychotherapy. Antidepressant medications produce greater improvements in both binge-eating and purging than placebos (Wilson & Fairburn, 2002). They also improve mood and tend to work rapidly. However, medications are not associated with sustained improvement or with effect sizes equal to those of cognitive-behavioral therapies (Fairburn & Harrison, 2003).

Among psychotherapies, interpersonal therapy focuses on how the person's relationships with other people contribute to the eating disorder. It has shown some evidence of effectiveness but requires further evaluation (2007). The identified treatment of choice for bulimia nervosa is cognitive-behavioral therapy, under which about half of patients cease binge eating and purging, and many report improvement in depressive symptoms and self-esteem (Wilson & Fairburn, 2002; Wilson, Grilo, & Vitousek, 2007).

One example of a comprehensive CBT intervention for bulimia nervosa comes from Spangler (1999). The 20-week program begins by establishing a regular eating pattern. First, a detailed food record is kept in which the person records each instance of food consumption, including what and how much is eaten, time of day, and context. Foods and situations that the client reports as "low risk" and "high risk" for binge eating are identified. Then, the client begins a defined schedule of normal eating, involving three meals and two snacks per day, so that the person is eating something every 3 to 4 hours. Many bulimics fear that eating on a regular basis will result in weight gain. However, their practice of restriction actually leads to increased hunger, setting the stage for binge eating. Regular eating patterns reduce binge events.

A list of pleasant activities (bathing, phone conversations, gardening) is compiled with the instruction that the client must engage in one immediately after finishing a normal meal to reduce the opportunity and the temptation to engage in compensatory acts. The person is instructed to eat at specified times, whether hungry or not, followed immediately by a pleasant activity (rather than remaining in the kitchen area). As a normal pattern of eating is resumed, the client experiences less hunger and therefore fewer urges to binge and less temptation to purge after normal portions. Weekly weighing reveals that resumption of a regular eating schedule produces little if any weight gain, removing a source of anxiety about normal eating patterns. An educational component adds information about nutrition and contradicts commonly held false beliefs about vomiting (which does not expel the majority of calories consumed) and laxative use (which expels even fewer calories).

Next, Spangler (1999) begins a process to counter the cognitive components of bulimia nervosa by attempting to modify the client's beliefs about body shape and weight, body dissatisfaction, and binging. Through example-giving and standard cognitive disputation, the importance of physical appearance to self-esteem and self-worth is challenged. Food tolerance is increased with the gradual addition of some "high-risk" foods to the daily diet. This shows the client that normal portions of forbidden foods can be consumed without a binge ensuing. Homework assignments might include activities to reveal the body, such as swimming, as a way to reduce the importance of concerns about appearance as well as to promote normal exercise. Stress-reduction and problem-solving skills are also taught as alternatives to binge eating during times of stress. Finally, a relapse prevention component is added. The client lists a set of clues or markers, such as changes in eating pattern or the presence of certain moods, which might increase the chance of relapse. Then a plan is drawn up for the client to follow if the clues or markers appear, including activities in which to engage or family or friends to contact. Spangler (1999) reports improvement that persists during long-term follow-up for clients using interventions of this type.

## 14.1c Binge-Eating Disorder

The diagnostic criteria for binge-eating disorder include recurrent episodes of binge eating associated with both a sense of lack of control and rapid consumption. Other symptoms are eating until uncomfortably full, eating large amounts when not hungry, eating alone because of embarrassment about eating patterns, and guilt after overeating. Binge-eating disorder requires that binges average at least once a week for a 3-month period, and they must be associated with marked distress. Binges are not accompanied by compensatory behaviors (as in bulimia nervosa) and, as such, the condition is frequently associated with varying degrees of obesity (American Psychiatric Association, 2013).

Most people showing this condition have long histories of unsuccessful dieting. The eating pattern tends to be chronic and is often associated with depression, anxiety, and negative self-image. Unlike anorexia nervosa and bulimia nervosa, which tend to have onset during adolescence, binge-eating disorder may not appear until well into adulthood. Although some earlier studies suggested that binge-eating disorder is more common among whites than other ethnic groups (Brody, Walsh, & Devlin, 1994), later studies report that the condition is not linked to racial/ethnic status (Striegel-Moore & Bulik, 2007). Nationally representative data show higher lifetime incidence among women (3.5%) than men (2%), a significant but less extreme gender difference than those of other eating disorders (Hudson, Hiripi, Pope, & Kessler, 2007). The *DSM-5* provides 12-month prevalence rates at 1.6% for adult females and 0.8% for adult males (American Psychiatric Association, 2013). In a sample of persons with eating disorders, binge-eating disorder was twice as common as bulimia nervosa (Kutlesic, Williamson, Gleaves, Barbin, & Murphy-Eberenz, 1998).

Some evidence suggests that, like those with other eating disorders, persons with binge-eating disorder may harbor dysfunctional attitudes about body shape and size that excessively influence self-evaluation (Hrabosky, Masheb, White, & Grilo, 2009). Although not all binge eaters engage in such overvaluation, those who do show higher levels of disordered eating and depression (Grilo, et al., 2008). Binge-eating disorder appears to be different from a related pattern of disordered eating, **night eating syndrome**, in which individuals consume more than half of their daily calories in late-night binges. Subjects with either condition show greater depressive symptomatology than a comparison group, but those with binge-eating disorder engage in more binging episodes and feel less control over eating (Allison, Grilo, Masheb, & Stunkard, 2005). In *DSM-5*, night eating syndrome would be diagnosed as in the category "other specified feeding or eating disorder."

Treatments for binge-eating disorder include antidepressant medications and psychotherapy. Cognitive-behavior therapy is generally associated with high treatment completion rates, remission of binge eating in over half of subjects, and improvement in accompanying depression. Antidepressant medications are superior to placebo in reducing binging and in weight loss; however relapse rates are high, and discontinuation of treatment remains problematic (Wilson, Grilo, & Vitousek, 2007). Those who respond rapidly to either type of treatment (that is, show a two-thirds reduction in binge eating within 4 weeks) are more likely to show remission of the disorder and greater weight loss (Grilo, Masheb, & Wilson, 2006).

*[handwritten margin note: therapies help. meds associated w/ high relapse rates.]*

## 14.2  Avoidant/Restrictive Food Intake Disorder

Those with avoidant/restrictive food intake disorder do not eat enough food to meet their energy or nutritional needs. A significant weight loss, nutritional deficiency, dependence on supplemental feeding, or marked interference in normal functioning is needed for the diagnosis. Like anorexia nervosa, this disorder is associated with malnutrition that can be life threatening. Unlike anorexia, the lack of appetite or avoidance of food does not involve body shape or image. The condition cannot be associated with lack of available food, gastrointestinal disorders, or a general medical condition, or occur exclusively during anorexia or bulimia. The new *DSM-5* diagnosis replaced the *DSM-IV* condition "feeding disorder of infancy or early childhood," which required childhood onset. Infant feeding disorder may account for half of hospital admissions for failure to thrive, which itself may have community incidence of 3% and appears to be equally prevalent in males and females (American Psychiatric Association, 2000). The avoidance or restriction of food might be attributable to Pavlovian conditioning, in the sense that an aversive experience (such as vomiting or choking) may be paired with particular food-related stimuli. Then, the avoidance of food may emerge as an anticipatory conditioned response, sometimes termed *functional dysphagia* (American Psychiatric Association, 2013).

## 14.2a  Pica

Pica essentially involves the persistent (at least 1 month) eating of non-nutritive, nonfood substances such as soil, paint, cloth, string, chalk, and pebbles. The substances eaten

**Night eating syndrome**

Eating pattern in which individuals consume more than half of their daily calories in late-night binges

tend to vary with age—with younger children more likely to eat paint or plaster, hair, and cloth, whereas older children are more likely to consume pebbles, animal droppings, sand, and leaves. The eating of these substances must be inappropriate to developmental level (very young children normally put almost anything into their mouths); and it must not be a culturally sanctioned practice. A variety of physical and medical complications can develop among individuals with pica. Some materials eaten may be toxic or may cause gastrointestinal problems—including infections, perforations, and blockages. Typically the condition remits after several months or a few years. Pica is more commonly found in association with intellectual disability, where its incidence can be as high as 15% (American Psychiatric Association, 2000). It is also sometimes seen in females during pregnancy (American Psychiatric Association, 2013).

Ferreri, Tamm, and Wier (2006) describe an intervention for pica involving a 4-year-old autistic boy who had engaged in toy pica for the previous year. The boy would place various plastic toys into his mouth, sucking on and chewing the edges until pieces could be bitten off and swallowed. He became aggressive when attempts were made to remove the toys. The treatment program involved dipping the toys into tapioca pudding, which the boy disliked, before they were made available to him. Pica ceased almost immediately and did not recur after the tapioca dipping was discontinued. The boy continued to use the toys during normal play, however.

## 14.2b Rumination Disorder

In rumination disorder, individuals repeatedly regurgitate their food. There is no nausea associated with the process. The material is then either discarded or, more commonly, re-chewed or re-swallowed. The condition must persist for a month and not be associated with a general medical condition or neurodevelopmental disorder, or occur as part of anorexic or bulimic patterns. Rumination disorder usually occurs in infants, with onset before 1 year of age. Some older individuals, especially those with intellectual disability, may also show the condition. Malnutrition and weight loss are associated difficulties; it can be fatal in infants if untreated. Rumination disorder appears to be rare (American Psychiatric Association, 2013).

## 14.3 Sleep-Wake Disorders

**Polysomnography**

Using a polygraph to make a continuous record during sleep of multiple physiological variables (such as breathing, heart rate, EEG, and muscle contractions)

**Dyssomnias**

Sleep disorders that are concerned with abnormal sleep amount, quality, or timing

**Parasomnias**

Sleep disorders that are concerned with abnormal events or behaviors involving the sleep cycle or sleep-wake transitions

Humans spend about one-third of their lives in sleep. However, the *DSM* system did not identify a separate classification of sleep disorders until the *DSM-IV*, and these mental disorders remained less familiar to many clinicians than other diagnoses. The category was reworked in the *DSM-5* as the sleep-wake disorders, with the intention of making the classifications useful both to mental health professional and to general medical practitioners. Consequently, the conditions include a wider range of supporting biological validators than are found elsewhere in the manual. In some instances, formal sleep studies (**polysomnography**) are required for diagnostic determination.

Optimal sleep is considered to be restful and refreshing under most circumstances with good sleep continuity (few periods spent in wakefulness), efficiency (most relative time in bed spent asleep), and short latency (the number of minutes required to fall asleep). Disturbances of sleep in the *DSM-IV* were described in broad terms as the **dyssomnias** (conditions involving abnormal sleep amount, quality, or timing) and the **parasomnias** (concerned with abnormal events or behaviors involving the sleep cycle or sleep-wake transitions). Although that distinction is no longer central to the *DSM-5* organization, the terms retain their descriptive value in discussing the sleep/wake disorders (see Table 14-2).

What are parasomnias and dyssomnias?

People with sleep-wake disorders can have significant life impairment, similar in degree to chronic health conditions like diabetes, heart disease or arthritis (Sateia & Nowell, 2004).

*Table 14-2*    DSM-5 Sleep-Wake Disorders

| Disorder | Key Symptoms | Minimum Duration Required for Diagnosis | Sex Ratio |
|---|---|---|---|
| Insomnia disorder | Dissatisfaction with sleep amount or quality | 3 months | More common among females |
| Hypersomnolence disorder | Excessive sleepiness despite getting at least 7 hours sleep | 3 months | Equal |
| Narcolepsy | Recurrent irrepressible need to sleep | 3 months | Slightly more common among males |
| Obstructive sleep apnea hypopnea | Nocturnal breathing pauses due to obstruction | None | More common among males |
| Central sleep apnea | Nocturnal breathing pauses not due to obstruction | None | More common in males |
| Sleep-related hypoventilation | Decreased respiration with elevated $CO_2$ levels | None | Unclear |
| Circadian rhythm sleep-wake disorders | Persistent sleep disruption due to misalignment of circadian rhythm and sleep-wake schedule | None | Unclear |
| Non-rapid eye movement sleep arousal disorders | Repeated partial wakening with sleepwalking or night terrors | None | Unclear |
| Nightmare disorder | Repeated distressing nightmares | None | More common among females |
| Rapid eye movement sleep behavior disorder | Repeated arousal with complex activity during REM sleep | None | More common among males |
| Restless legs syndrome | Frequent urges to move legs, especially at night | 3 months | More common among females |

Source: Adapted from the *Diagnostic and Statistical Manual of Mental Disorders,* Fifth Edition, (Copyright 2013), American Psychiatric Association.

Often, the symptoms presented by people with sleep disorders resemble those of other mental disorders—such as panic, anxiety, and depression—and may be misidentified as a result. Correct diagnosis may be difficult, requiring extensive information about history and evaluation in a sleep laboratory. Nonetheless, structured interviews using *DSM-III-R* criteria produced good to excellent inter-observer agreement across different disorders, with highest agreement on insomnia and hypersomnia; the only category with poor reliability was circadian rhythm sleep disorder (Schramm, et al., 1993). Sleep-wake disorders were not assessed in the *DSM-5* field trials.

Many people experience periodic sleep disruption or unusual sleep experiences but rarely seek treatment for the condition. Because sleep patterns are so variable and symptoms are so common, the prevalence of most sleep disorders is uncertain. Diagnoses of these conditions should be restricted to those individuals for whom the sleep disturbances produce significant distress or impairment in important areas of functioning. Still, sleep problems are notable among the elderly with almost 50% complaining about chronic sleep difficulties (Cooke & Ancoli-Isreal, 2006). It is likely that these conditions are under-diagnosed among the general population.

# 14.4 Dyssomnias

## 14.4a Insomnia Disorder

In insomnia disorder, individuals have difficulty falling asleep or remaining asleep, or they are unable to get back to sleep after early-morning wakening. They commonly complain that the sleep they achieve is *nonrestorative*—that is, restless and of poor quality. Daytime fatigue is often problematic as a result. To qualify for diagnosis, the sleep disturbance cannot be due to a general medical condition, the effects of a substance, or another mental disorder. Insomnia disorder must persist for at least 3 months, occur 3 nights per week, and cause significant distress or impairment in functioning. It can be specified as being comorbid with non-sleep mental disorders, other medical disorders, or other sleep disorders. Specifiers are also provided to indicate if the condition is episodic (1–3 months of symptoms), persistent (more than 3 months of symptoms), or recurrent (two or more episodes within 1 year). It is the most prevalent sleep disorder: a third of adults complain about insomnia, and perhaps 10% of the population would meet the diagnostic criteria for insomnia disorder (American Psychiatric Association, 2013).

**What are the most common sleep disorders?**

People with insomnia often find themselves trapped in a vicious cycle, in which distress at not being able to sleep increases their level of arousal, which in turn makes sleeping less probable. Often, they acquire maladaptive sleep habits, such as napping during the day, that add further to the disturbance. In their attempt to bring on sleep, they may use medications or alcohol to induce drowsiness, followed later by stimulant drugs to combat fatigue the next morning. As a result, substance dependence may develop. Other conditions associated with primary insomnia include mood and anxiety disorders (American Psychiatric Association, 2000).

Nearly 1 in 5 people who consult a physician indicate that insomnia is problematic (Vgontz & Kales, 1999). Onset is rare in childhood or adolescence. Insomnia increases with age, affecting 25% of the elderly population. Generally, younger people report problems falling asleep whereas older people experience more difficulty remaining asleep. The disorder occurs more often in women; for them, first onset is often reported following the birth of a child, or menopause. The course is variable, but over half of people with chronic complaints of insomnia continue to experience symptoms for more than 1 year (American Psychiatric Association, 2013).

Sleep restriction can cause a variety of neurobehavioral symptoms, including memory impairment, depressed mood, and lapses of concentration. These effects accumulate across several days of sleep restriction until they equal the approximate deficits associated with 3 days of total sleep deprivation (Banks & Dinges, 2007). Insomnia disorder may also be related to a range of serious medical conditions, including hypertension, heart disease, and conditions involving muscular or skeletal pain.

### Causal Factors

Problems with disrupted sleep run in families, but the genetic contributions to insomnia disorder are unclear (American Psychiatric Association, 2013). Many physical and medical conditions can precipitate the condition; "primary" insomnia (not related to other conditions or causes) makes up only about 15% of chronic insomnia cases (Sateia & Nowell, 2004).

Psychological distress is the most common cause of primary insomnia (Vgontz & Kales, 1999). Development may begin with any specific event or stressor that disrupts sleep. If the disruption continues, the person becomes frustrated, anxious, and concerned about his or her inability to sleep, increasing the emotional arousal and further interfering with sleep. Individuals often attempt to force sleep by remaining in bed longer, but that serves to associate the bed with arousal and wakefulness. The resulting conditioning of arousal is evident, as people may sleep better when not trying to sleep (for example, when watching TV), or when they are in different sleep environments (such as a hotel).

### Treatments for Insomnia Disorder

Benzodiazepines are widely used to promote sleep, but they are not recommended for long-term use. Antidepressants may also be helpful. However, pharmacotherapy for insomnia degrades over time (Vgontz & Kales, 1999). The naturally occurring hormone melatonin has been shown in randomized, controlled trials to improve sleep in chronic insomniacs, with few side effects and no withdrawal symptoms after discontinuation (Lemoine, Nir, Laudon, & Zisapel, 2007). Non-pharmacological interventions include stimulus control (restricting use of bedroom to sleep-related activities only); sleep restriction via a regular sleep-wake schedule without napping; relaxation training; and control of stimulants such as caffeine. Regular exercise, not close to bedtime, is also helpful. Cognitive-behavioral treatment including several of these components can be robust, effective, and durable (Sateia & Nowell, 2004).

## 14.4b Hypersomnolence Disorder

Hypersomnolence disorder consists of excessive sleepiness despite receiving at least 7 hours of sleep during the main sleep period. Those with the condition may sleep for more than 9 hours without finding sleep refreshing and then have difficulty awakening. Daytime naps are not experienced as restorative or refreshing. Unintentional sleep may occur, especially when the person is in low-stimulation or inactive situations. Individuals struggle to remain alert, but efficiency, concentration, and memory are typically impaired, as are social and occupational functions. Specifiers for the condition include comorbidity with another mental disorder, medical condition, or sleep disorder; duration specifiers for acute (less than 1 month), subacute (1–3 months) and persistent (more than 3 months); and severity indicators for mild (alertness difficulties 1–2 days/week), moderate (alertness difficulties 3–4 days/week) and severe (alertness difficulties 5–7 days/week) (American Psychiatric Association, 2013). During one type of recurrent hypersomnolence disorder (called Kline-Levin syndrome), individuals may spend as much as 20 hours per day in bed (American Psychiatric Association, 2000).

For some people experiencing recurrent hypersomnolence, the sleepiness is associated with disinhibition of sexuality, compulsive overeating, or impulsive behavior. Mood disorders and substance dependence (related to stimulant use) may be more common among those with hypersomnolence disorder, but much is unknown about comorbidity with other disorders. The prevalence for males and females is approximately equal. Hypersomnolence runs in families, but its causes are not clear. Onset is usually between ages 15 and 30, and the course tends to be chronic and stable, sometimes for decades. Its incidence is about 1% in the population, but as many as 10% of individuals presenting at sleep clinics complain of hypersomnolence (American Psychiatric Association, 2013). Treatment usually includes stimulant drugs.

## 14.4c Narcolepsy

People with narcolepsy experience repeated, irrepressible sleep or the need for sleep, occurring at least three times per week for at least 3 months. The sleep is unintended and may occur in inappropriate situations, such as when driving a car, attending a meeting, or engaging in a conversation. In addition to sleep attacks, the diagnosis of narcolepsy requires either **cataplexy** (sudden loss of muscle control without loss of consciousness; in children, grimaces or jaw opening with tongue thrusting, symptoms that have been called "cataplectic faces"), a deficiency of hypocretin (a hypothalamic neurotransmitter associated with arousal) measured in the cerebrospinal fluid, or short latency (15 minutes or less) to rapid eye movement, or **REM, sleep**. Between 20% and 60% experience **sleep paralysis** (being awake, but unable to move or speak). A significant proportion of sufferers also experience REM intrusions, which produce vivid dreamlike imagery just as one is falling asleep (*hypnagogic hallucinations*) or just after awakening (*hypnopompic hallucinations*). The condition is quite rare (0.04% of the population or less) and may be slightly more common among males (American Psychiatric Association, 2013).

Cataplexy is often precipitated by strong emotions such as anger, laughter, or surprise. Cataplexy occurs outside of sleep attacks, and can range from subtle signs that may not be obvious to others (such as drooping eyelids or a sagging jaw) to dropping items and falling to the ground. Full consciousness is maintained during the episode, which typically lasts only a few seconds or minutes. REM sleep intrusion is associated with intense dreamlike

**Can someone fall asleep in the middle of a conversation?**

**Cataplexy**
Sudden loss of muscle control without loss of consciousness

**REM sleep**
Sleep phase that involves rapid eye movements, often associated with vivid dreaming

**Sleep paralysis**
Being awake but unable to move, just at the junction of sleep and wakefulness

imagery that may be visual, auditory, or kinetic, often incorporating components from the surrounding environment ( for example, movement within a picture hanging on the wall). REM intrusion also results in sleep paralysis in nearly half of those with narcolepsy. Sometimes these combine into frightening experiences of being unable to move while unusual events are unfolding. However, hypnagogic and hypnopompic hallucinations occur in about 15% of the general population; and up to 50% have experienced sleep paralysis, so these REM-related symptoms are not unique to the disorder (American Psychiatric Association, 2000).

Those with narcolepsy typically experience sleepiness daily, and some may take voluntary naps in attempt to manage sleepiness. However, involuntary episodes can present serious risk of harm to self or others: two-thirds of those with narcolepsy have fallen asleep while driving (Aldrich, 1992). Social activities may be curtailed out of fear of sleep attacks or of emotional arousal that may precipitate an episode of cataplexy (in fact, joking and laughing are the most typical triggers for cataplexy). Affected individuals may also have a history of mood or anxiety disorders, as well as obesity (American Psychiatric Association, 2013).

### Causal Factors

Narcolepsy is a serious problem that persists throughout life. People with narcolepsy are often overweight or obese and have elevated risk for type II diabetes, but their eating patterns are not abnormal when compared to controls (Dahmen, Becht, Engel, Thommes, & Tonn, 2008). Up to one-half of first-degree relatives of those with narcolepsy also show symptoms of sleepiness and up to 15% have the disorder, suggesting a strong genetic contribution (American Psychiatric Association, 2000). Recently, the risk of narcolepsy among first-degree relatives of those with the disorder was calculated to be 75 times higher than the risk in the general population (Ohayon & Okun, 2006). However, MZ twins have high non-concordance rates (Vgontz & Kales, 1999), indicating unknown environmental contributions to the disorder as well. Because of an association with a specific pattern of human leukocyte antigen (HLA) response, some have proposed that narcolepsy may arise as part of an autoimmune condition (Erman, 2006), although many in the population share similar HLA patterns without narcolepsy. Manipulation of genes controlling production of hypocretin can produce narcoleptic states in dogs and mice, and there is a deficiency of hypocretin in the spinal fluid of some narcoleptics (Nishino, Ripley, Overeem, Lammers, & Mignot, 2000). Increasingly, it appears that narcolepsy may be due to an autoimmune-related loss of neurons in the hypothalamus that produce hypocretin (Dauvilliers, Arnulf, & Mignot, 2007). As noted above, a hypocretin deficiency now satisfies one of the criteria for narcolepsy in the *DSM-5*.

### Treatment of Narcolepsy

Therapeutic naps for 10–60 minutes daily may be of benefit in management of the condition. Stimulant drugs are typically used to stave off sleep attacks; methylphenidate is the preferred drug for preventing sleep onset (Vgontz & Kales, 1999). Antidepressant medications may help reduce cataplexy in patients with narcolepsy.

## 14.4d  Breathing-Related Sleep Disorders

The central feature of a breathing-related sleep disorder is sleep disruption (leading to excessive sleepiness or insomnia) caused by a breathing difficulty. Most often, the breathing difficulty is **sleep apnea**, in which breathing ceases during sleep. Essentially, the sleeping individual stops breathing, begins to suffocate, and then rouses from sleep briefly to gasp for breath. In addition to apnea, *hypopnea* (a reduction in airflow, related to unusually slow or shallow breathing) and *hypoventilation* (abnormal blood levels of oxygen and carbon dioxide) also constitute the respiratory events that may disturb sleep in these conditions. These ventilation cycles may occur more than 15 times per hour, so that the individual partially awakens from sleep hundreds of times throughout the night. As a result, sleep is not

**Sleep apnea**

Frequent cessation of breathing during sleep

experienced as restful or restorative, and symptoms similar to those of insomnia are evident (poor concentration, irritability, mood disturbances, and memory disturbances).

The most common form of breathing-related sleep disorder is obstructive sleep apnea hypopnea, involving repeated obstructions of the upper airway, accompanied by loud snoring. The *DSM-5* diagnosis requires at least five apneas or hypopneas per hour of sleep, verified by polysomnography, that result in nocturnal breathing disturbance or daytime fatigue, or evidence of 15 or more apneas or hypopneas per hour of sleep regardless of resulting symptoms. It can be specified according to severity, based on the degree of reduced blood oxygen saturation. Obstructive sleep apnea is more common in overweight individuals, for whom soft tissues in the neck can block the airway; those with large necks over 16–17 inches are at greater risk. In less obese persons, obstructions can be related to tonsil size, abnormal growths, or nasal airway obstruction.

People with breathing-related sleep disorders (as well as those with hypersomnolence disorder) often experience a dull headache on awakening, sometimes accompanied by **sleep drunkenness** (difficulty wakening, confusion, and inappropriate behavior, also called *sleep inertia*). They often are excessively sleepy during the day and may involuntarily fall asleep at inappropriate times, in extreme cases, similar to those with narcolepsy. Naps are usually not refreshing. Mood and anxiety disorders are often associated with breathing-related sleep disorders.

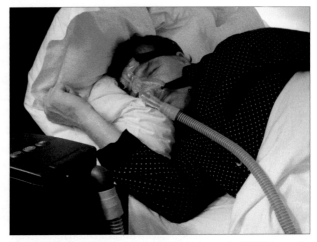

The nasal continuous positive airway pressure (nCPAP) is used to treat severe sleep apnea by delivering a continuous flow of air to the nostrils through a nose mask. (iStock)

Obstructive sleep apnea hypopnea is more common among middle-aged, overweight males and in children with enlarged tonsils (who, unlike adults, may not snore). It occurs in up to 15% of the adult population, with higher rates (more than 20%) among the elderly (American Psychiatric Association, 2013). Interestingly, sleep-disordered breathing is significantly less common in children who were breastfed for at least two months (Montgomery-Downs, Crabtree, Capdevila, & Gozal, 2007). Obstructive sleep apnea hypopnea tends to have a gradual onset and a chronic course, and it can contribute to premature death by heart arrhythmia or cardiovascular disease. Weight loss and continuous positive airway pressure or other techniques to keep the airway open are the most effective treatments (Vgontz & Kales, 1999).

A much more rare breathing-related sleep disorder is central sleep apnea, in which there are five or more apneas per hour of sleep, not related to obstruction. Snoring is much less common in this condition. The periodic breathing pattern that occurs in central sleep apnea can be subtyped as idiopathic, comorbid with opioid use (which impacts respiratory rhythm), or related to Cheyne-Stokes breathing, an increasing/decreasing air intake pattern that is tied to the development of heart failure. It appears most often in users of long-acting opioids, such as methadone, and in association with renal failure or stroke (American Psychiatric Association, 2013).

Sleep-related hypoventilation need not involve apneas but rather shallow or decreased breathing that leads to elevated levels of carbon dioxide ($CO_2$) levels in the blood. Sufferers complain of frequent wakening, sleepiness, insomnia, and headaches. The condition is thought to be uncommon, but may be increasing related to rising obesity and chronic obstructive pulmonary disease (COPD) rates (American Psychiatric Association, 2013).

## 14.4e Circadian Rhythm Sleep-Wake Disorders

Circadian rhythm sleep-wake disorders involve a persistent sleep disturbance due to a mismatch between the person's internal 24-hour sleep-wake cycle (the circadian sleep-wake pattern) and the schedule required by the person's environment. As a result of the mismatch

**Sleep drunkenness**
Difficulty awakening from sleep, often including confusion and inappropriate behavior

in cycles, affected people usually experience insomnia at some times of the day and sleepiness at other times, with significant distress or impairment of functioning evident (for example, falling asleep at inappropriate times). In some types of Circadian rhythm sleep-wake disorders, an individual may feel "locked in" to a cycle of unusually late sleep and awakening, unable to adjust the cycle to an earlier one such as that required for a job (delayed sleep phase type). In other cases, people may experience earlier sleep onset and awakening, with the inability to adjust to the conventional later sleep/wake times (advanced sleep phase type). The condition may be generated by certain work schedules, especially night shifts (shift work type), or appear as a lack of discernible sleep-wake rhythm, with sleep fragmented into at least three different periods during the day (irregular sleep-wake type). In another pattern (non-24-hour sleep-wake type), the sleep phase gradually increases and drifts out of 24-hour alignment, so that sleep time moves into daytime hours. This subtype is particularly common in blind or visually handicapped persons, for whom the incidence approaches 50% (American Psychiatric Association, 2013).

Persons diagnosed with the delayed sleep phase type of the disorder typically have great difficulty shifting the sleep-wake cycle forward; but once sleep is initiated, it is normal. They feel continually sleep-deprived due to the need to maintain social or occupational obligations, except on weekends or during vacations, when they tend to shift back to a later cycle. Shift work type may be most common among those on nightshift or rotating-shift schedules; shorter sleep duration and more frequent awakenings are often accompanied by difficulties pertaining to family demands and environmental disturbances during sleep times (such as traffic noises and telephones). In addition to sleep disruption, other symptoms associated with circadian rhythm sleep disorders include headache, fatigue, impaired coordination, decreased appetite, and indigestion. All forms of the disorder produce difficulties in concentration and memory, attention, and performance; and depressive symptoms are not uncommon.

The severity of the sleep disruption appears to increase with age. Some forms (e.g., shift work type) show reversal of symptoms with schedule changes, while the delayed sleep phase type may last for decades. The prevalence of circadian rhythm sleep-wake disorders is unknown. More than 7% of adolescents may experience delayed sleep phase type, and more than 10% of night shift workers may experience shift work type. Some types appear to aggregate within families (American Psychiatric Association, 2013). Melatonin, secreted by the pineal gland, helps to regulate sleep-wake cycle rhythm; it appears to be beneficial in the treatment of circadian rhythm sleep-wake disorders (Pandi-Perumal, Srinivasan, Spence, & Cardinali, 2007).

# 14.5  Parasomnias

## 14.5a  Non-Rapid Eye Movement Sleep Arousal Disorders

The non-rapid eye movement sleep arousal disorders involve incomplete awakening from sleep, accompanied by sleepwalking or sleep terrors (see *DSM-5* Diagnostic Criteria for Non-Rapid Eye Movement Sleep Arousal Disorders). The *DSM-5* diagnostic category is a combination of two separate *DSM-IV* disorders, sleepwalking disorder and sleep terror disorder. Usually, the incomplete awakening occurs in the first third of the sleep episode and tends to be brief (less than 10 minutes), although longer (up to 1 hour) events may occur. Typically, in the sleepwalking type, the eyes are open; the event may begin simply and become progressively more complex, including getting out of bed and leaving the room. Sleep terrors involve a strong sense of dread and a compulsion to escape, but the person usually does not wake completely and returns to sleep. In both types of episodes, persons do not remember the event the next morning.

**Do people sleepwalk because they are dreaming?**

Sleepwalking involves repeated episodes of complex motor activities which begin during slow wave non-REM sleep. Depending on the severity, the motor activities can range from sitting up in bed to carrying on conversations, eating food, leaving a building, or even operating machinery. Episodes usually terminate with return to full sleep (sometimes in new or unfamiliar locations). If awakened (which is difficult), the sleepwalker is typically confused for several minutes and does not report dreaming or awareness of the event. During a sleepwalking episode, the individual commonly has a blank face and is relatively unresponsive to attempts to communicate or be awakened by others. The person may talk or even answer questions, but a genuine dialogue is usually not established. Although their eyes are typically open, sleepwalkers may be clumsy (Plante & Winkelman, 2006). Some injure themselves by walking into walls or falling through windows. Occasionally, sleepwalkers may strike out at others, particularly if sleep terrors are also present.

People with sleep terror disorder do not recall dreaming, apart from fragment images and a sense of terror. (iStock)

There have been reports of complex sexual or violent behaviors, including homicide and rape, occurring during episodes of sleepwalking (Cartwright, 2004; Rosenfeld & Elhajjar, 1998). Actually, a full range of directed sexual activities with self or partners (**sexomnia**) has been reported in sleeping individuals—including masturbation, fondling, sexual verbalizations, and intercourse—with complete amnesia for the episodes reported after awakening the next morning. These types of complex acts are not limited to sleepwalking disorder; they have also occurred within other parasomnias such as REM sleep behavior disorder (below) and confused arousals associated with sleep apnea as well (Schenck, Amulf, & Mahowald, 2007). Although traditionally considered extremely rare, sleep-related violence may be greatly under-reported, with as much as 2% of the population enacting some form of violence during sleep (Lettieri & Williams, 2011). However, the majority of such cases occur in young to middle-aged men with a history of sleepwalking (Plante & Winkelman, 2006). Sleep-related eating may also occur during sleepwalking episodes, especially among females, with varying degrees of amnesia. Inappropriate foods may be consumed at these times as well (American Psychiatric Association, 2013).

**Sexomnia**

Sexual activities during sleep, without conscious awareness

---

| **DSM-5** | **Diagnostic Criteria for Non-Rapid Eye Movement Sleep Arousal Disorders** |
|---|---|

Non-Rapid Eye Movement Sleep Arousal Disorders

A. Recurrent episodes of incomplete awakening during sleep, usually occurring during the first third of the major sleep episode, accompanied by either one of the following:
   1. **Sleepwalking**: Repeated episodes of rising from bed during sleep and walking about. While sleepwalking, the individual has a blank, staring face; is relatively unresponsive to the efforts of others to communicate with him or her; and can be awakened only with great difficulty.
   2. **Sleep terrors**: Recurrent episodes of abrupt terror arousals from sleep, usually beginning with a panicky scream. There is intense fear and signs of autonomic arousal, such as mydriasis, tachycardia, rapid breathing, and sweating, during each episode. There is relative unresponsiveness to efforts of others to comfort the individual during the episodes.
B. No or little (e.g., only a single visual scene) dream imagery is recalled.
C. Amnesia for the episodes is present.
D. The episodes cause clinically significant distress or impairment in social, occupational, or other important areas of functioning.
E. The disturbance is not attributable to the physiological effects of a substance (e.g., a drug of abuse, a medication).
F. Coexisting mental and medical disorders do not explain the episodes of sleepwalking or sleep terrors.

**Coding note:** For ICD-9-CM, code 407.46 for all subtypes. For ICD-10-CM, code is based on subtype

*Specify* whether:

   **307.46 (F51.3) Sleepwalking type**

   *Specify* if

      **With sleep-related eating**

      **With sleep-related sexual behavior (sexomnia)**

   **307.46 (F51.4) Sleep terror type**

Source: Reprinted with permission from the *Diagnostic and Statistical Manual of Mental Disorders*, Fifth Edition, (Copyright 2013). American Psychiatric Association.

In sleep terrors, individuals awake from sleep abruptly, usually with a cry or panicky scream. They show intense fear and autonomic arousal—such as rapid heartbeat, rapid breathing, pupil dilation (mydriasis), and sweating—and are generally unresponsive to efforts by others to awaken them. They may actively resist attempts to comfort or hold them by swinging, punching, or rising from the bed and fleeing; these acts can result in physical injury to self or others. In most episodes, individuals do not fully awaken and return to sleep. However, if they fully waken, they do not recall dreaming, apart from fragmented images and a sense of terror. The next morning there is amnesia for the episode, which usually does not occur more than once in a night. Episodes recur after several days or weeks and are made more likely by fatigue, stress, and alcohol or sedative use.

Usually, non-rapid eye movement sleep arousal disorders begin before age 12 and resolve during adolescence and thereafter, declining from an incidence of perhaps 5% among children to less than 1% in adults (American Psychiatric Association, 2013). Much is unknown about the causes or treatments for the condition. In one study involving three boys with histories of recurrent sleep terrors, scheduled awakenings 30 minutes before expected occurrence of sleep terrors were effective in reducing their frequency (Durand & Mindell, 1999). Especially in adults, sleep terror is related to higher incidence general psychopathology, including PTSD, mood and anxiety disorders, and some personality disorders. A family history of sleepwalking or sleep terror is present in up to 80% of cases (American Psychiatric Association, 2013).

## 14.5b  Nightmare Disorder

Those with nightmare disorder repeatedly experience frightening dreams that result in awakening. Individuals rapidly become alert and oriented after waking and can recall the nightmares in detail. Most often, the nightmares involve threats to the person's safety, security, or self-esteem; and these intense dreams (or the sleep disruption they produce) cause significant distress or impairment for the individual.

The dreams in nightmare disorder usually last longer than 10 minutes and happen during REM sleep, which increases in the second half of the night. The nightmares often are lengthy, elaborate, and terrifying, and may recur several times in a night. Themes about attack, injury, pursuit, and personal failure or embarrassment are typical. Upon awakening, the person may be anxious and fearful, and can recall the sequence and imagery of the dream in detail. The most common impact of recurrent nightmares is subjective distress; some individuals may avoid sleeping, and daytime functioning may then be impaired as a result of sleepiness.

Nightmare disorder most often occurs in children who have been exposed to severe psychosocial stressors. The dreams usually begin between 3–6 years of age and increase in prevalence and severity into early adulthood. Females experience nightmare disorder up to 2 times more often than males (American Psychiatric Association, 2013). Depression, substance use disorders, and personality disorders may be associated with the condition; but PTSD is accompanied by nightmares nearly 5 times more often than any other disorder, and some consider PTSD a predisposing factor for nightmare disorder (Plante & Winkelman, 2006). The incidence of nightmare disorder is unknown although 50% of adults experience occasional nightmares, and up to half of children ages 3–5 experience nightmares severe enough to disturb parents (American Psychiatric Association, 2000).

## 14.5c  Rapid Eye Movement Sleep Behavior Disorder

A provisional condition in the *DSM-IV*, rapid eye movement sleep behavior disorder, was elevated to a parasomnia in the *DSM-5*. It consists of complex motor activity or vocalizations that occur during REM sleep and are associated with vivid dreaming. Normally, skeletal muscles are paralyzed during REM sleep; in those with rapid eye movement sleep behavior disorder, that paralysis is absent, allowing people to essentially act out their dreams. Violent activities such as punching and kicking sometimes occur during episodes; emotion-laden, loud shouting may be present during the episode. The condition may precede or accompany the development of some neurodegenerative conditions, including Parkinson's disease, and it may be more likely in children with autism. Its prevalence about 0.5% of the population (American Psychiatric Association, 2013), but it is more common in the elderly, especially men (Cooke & Ancoli-Isreal, 2006). The disorder appears to have good inter-rater reliability (about 0.65), when assessed among patients with Parkinson's disease (Scaglione, et al., 2004). It can also be induced by a variety of medications, including antidepressants. However, its causes remain uncertain. It is most commonly treated with benzodiazepine medications (Thomas, Bonanni, & Onofrj, 2007)

> Do some people act out their dreams?

## 14.5d Restless Legs Syndrome

Restless legs syndrome was also elevated to a parasomnia from provisional status in the *DSM-IV*. It involves frequent urges to move the legs, especially when resting, in order to relieve unpleasant sensations such as itching, burning, or tingling. The urges are worse in the evening or night and are partly or totally relieved by movement. The urges may interfere with sleep onset or sleep continuity, producing daytime fatigue or sleepiness. Symptoms must occur three times per week for 3 months to qualify for the diagnosis. Between 2% and 7.2% of the population may be affected (American Psychiatric Association, 2013). Other limb movement conditions may occur rhythmically during non-REM sleep, inducing brief arousals that degrade the quality of sleep. Sleep-related limb movement disorders, including restless legs syndrome, increase with age (Cooke & Ancoli-Isreal, 2006). The incidence increases up to about age 60, with the disorder more prevalent in females, especially during pregnancy (American Psychiatric Association, 2013).

Finally, the *DSM* provides the category "substance/medication-induced sleep disorder" to describe the many sleep dysfunctions that can be cause by substance use, intoxication, or withdrawal. A large array of substances, including caffeine, alcohol, tobacco, sedatives, and opioids are associated with sleep dysfunctions; and those with parasomnias and older individuals who take multiple medications may be at greater risk. Women seem more susceptible to substance/medication-induced sleep problems than men, given the same amount and duration of consumption (American Psychiatric Association, 2013).

## 14.6 Elimination Disorders

Only two elimination disorders are listed within *DSM-5*. Both must be distinguished from developmentally appropriate deficiencies in toileting abilities in the youngest children. Thus, these are not diagnosed until after the normal period for attaining continence.

## 14.6a Encopresis

Encopresis involves repeated passage of feces by a person over the age of 4 years into inappropriate places, such as into clothing or onto the floor. Events—which are usually but not always involuntary—must occur at least once a month for at least 3 months and are not due to general medical conditions (other than constipation and its mechanisms) or to use of laxatives. Usually the pattern in encopresis consists of constipation (which can develop in response to anxiety or other psychological states), followed by impaction, further retention, and overflow incontinence. The condition is often associated with embarrassment, social ostracism, and avoidance of social situations. Encopresis may affect 1% of 5-year-olds, and it is more common among males. If events are voluntary or intentional, the disorder may be associated with conduct disorder or oppositional defiant disorder (American Psychiatric

*these are not done as an act of defiance.*

Association, 2000). There are no known pharmacological interventions for encopresis at present (American Psychological Association, 2006). Treatment may involve high-fiber diets, use of laxatives, relaxation training, and behavioral interventions that shape and support regular patterns of toileting. Combinations of behavior techniques with diet and education appear to be helpful (Mikkelsen, 2001).

## 14.6b  Enuresis

Enuresis is repeated voiding of urine into bed or clothes, during day or night, in children age 5 years or older (by which age bladder control would ordinarily have been acquired). The condition is not due to a general medical condition and must occur at least twice a week for 3 months. The diagnosis can be subtyped as nocturnal, diurnal, or both.

Although few consider enuresis in itself to represent a serious disorder, for the young child it can be a source of intense psychological discomfort resulting from the jeers and taunts of unsympathetic peers and the obvious irritation of parents and others who have to cope with frequent changes of bedding. Children may avoid certain activities, such as sleeping at a friend's house, because of the potential embarrassment.

### Causal Factors

Most children with enuresis become continent by adolescence. The prevalence of the disorder may be 10% among 5-year-olds, but falls to half of that by age 10; about 1% of cases continue into adulthood. The condition has strong familial patterns: offspring of an enuretic parent have 5 to 7 times the risk of the general population for developing enuresis, and 75% of children with the disorder have a first-degree relative who was affected (American Psychiatric Association, 2000). Several contributing factors have been proposed for enuresis, including bladder dysfunction, insufficient bladder capacities, disturbance of biological rhythms, poor toilet training, and psychological stress. Psychodynamic theorists considered the meaning of the symptom in terms of intrapsychic conflicts that have their origins in disturbed family relationships. Wetting the bed may be seen, for example, as an unconscious expression of hostility toward a parent, a stubborn refusal to accommodate the parent's demand for more age-appropriate behavior, or a wish to remain infantile.

### Treatment of Enuresis

Oral medications such as antidepressants and desmopressin (a synthetic urine suppressor) are more effective than placebo in reducing enuresis, but relapse is likely when medication is discontinued (Mikkelsen, 2001). Behavioral approaches have involved attempts to condition children to respond to the sensation of a full bladder, and their effectiveness is well validated (Chambless, et al., 1998). The bell and pad method, the best known technique, was developed more than 75 years ago, based on a Pavlovian conditioning model. Urination is an automatic reflex response to a distended bladder. As they grow older, most children learn to inhibit this reflexive response, even while sleeping, and learn to make the response at the right time and place. For the child with nocturnal enuresis, this control is established by conditioning the response of awakening to the stimulus of a full bladder. The procedure itself is quite simple. The child sleeps on a pad that, when moistened by urine, completes an electric circuit, causing a bell to sound, awakening the child. After a few such pairings, the conditioned response (waking up) is triggered by stimuli that predict the bell—that is, by bladder distension. According to Mikkelsen (2001), the bell and pad device is the only treatment that is associated with generalized improvement after the treatment is withdrawn; and although it is the most cost-effective intervention, it remains underused. It is effective in 75% of cases; and compared to medication, it has low risk and high benefit (American Psychological Association, 2006).

**What treatments are effective for elimination disorders?**

# Chapter Review
## TO SUM UP ...

- Anorexia nervosa is a form of self-starvation related to strict control of eating, fear of gaining weight, and disturbed body image. It is associated with below normal body weight and serious physical and medical effects, including death.

- Bulimia nervosa is a loss of control over food intake that occurs in binges. The person either purges the food or engages in excessive exercise or fasting to compensate for binge eating.

- Both anorexia nervosa and bulimia nervosa involve self-evaluation that is too strongly connected to body shape and weight. They are much more common among young white females; and when they occur among males, the eating disorders are likely to be associated with homosexuality or with sports that emphasize aesthetic performance or weight limits.

- Binge-eating disorder involves repeated food binges without compensatory activities. It is much more common than the other eating disorders and may affect males and females equally.

- Effective treatments for eating disorders include cognitive-behavioral interventions and (to a lesser extent) antidepressant medications.

- There are two general classes of sleep-wake disorders: dyssomnias (with abnormalities in amount, quality, or timing of sleep) and parasomnias (with abnormal behavioral or physiological events occurring during sleep or in the transition between sleep and wakefulness).

- Insomnia disorder is the most common dyssomnia, indicated by difficulty falling asleep or staying asleep. Its likelihood increases with age. Other dyssomnias include conditions of excessive or unexpected sleep, breathing-related sleep disorders, and circadian rhythm sleep disorder.

- Effective treatments include cognitive-behavioral therapies and melatonin for insomnia, stimulant drugs for hypersomnolence disorder and narcolepsy, and positive airway pressure for breathing-related sleep-wake disorder.

- Among the parasomnias, nightmare disorder and REM sleep behavior disorder occur during REM sleep, whereas sleep terrors and sleepwalking occur during non-REM sleep.

- Enuresis and encopresis are disorders involving inappropriate elimination. Enuresis is often effectively treated with the bell and pad method.

## KEY TERMS

Amenorrhea    392

Binge eating    394

Cataplexy    401

Dyssomnias    398

Night eating syndrome    397

Parasomnias    398

Polysomnography    398

Purging    392

REM sleep    401

Sexomnia    405

Sleep apnea    402

Sleep drunkenness    403

Sleep paralysis    401

## QUESTIONS FOR STUDY

- Speculate on reasons why anorexia nervosa has a much shorter average duration than other eating disorders.

- Describe binge eating, and describe the disorders in which it occurs.

- Discuss the role of REM sleep in various parasomnias.

- Distinguish nightmares from sleep terrors.

- Describe how the bell and pad method works.

## POP QUIZ

1.  Which of the following does pica involve?
    A.  regurgitating and re-chewing food.
    B.  eating of non-nutritive substances.
    C.  eating unusually large amounts of food
    D.  purging

2.  Lifetime prevalence rates of anorexia nervosa currently are about _____ of females.
    A.  15%
    B.  10%
    C.  5%
    D.  1%

3. Which of the following are at highest risk for anorexia nervosa?
   A. Caucasian women aged 15–24
   B. African American women aged 13–18
   C. Hispanic women aged 17–24
   D. Caucasian women aged 11–16

4. Which of the following statements is true about eating disorders?
   A. Bulimics maintain below-average body weight.
   B. Anorexics do not engage in binging/purging eating patterns.
   C. Bulimia nervosa is not related to SES.
   D. Mortality rates are similar for bulimia and anorexia.

5. _____are sleep disorders concerned with abnormal sleep amount, quality, or timing whereas _____ are sleep disorders that are concerned with abnormal events or behaviors involving the sleep cycle or sleep-wake transitions.
   A. Hyposomnias; parasomnias
   B. Endosomnias; dyssomnias
   C. Dyssomnias; parasomnias
   D. Parasomnias; dyssomnias

6. Which could not happen during cataplexy?
   A. sleepwalking
   B. falling
   C. being aware of surroundings
   D. feeling emotional distress

7. Nightmare disorder generally has a(n) _____ onset.
   A. childhood
   B. adolescent
   C. young adulthood
   D. mid-life

8. Jack's repeated, irresistible attacks of unintended sleep started to affect his work and family life. Jack went to his doctor, who ordered a sleep study that diagnosed Jack with _____.
   A. central sleep apnea
   B. narcolepsy
   C. hypersomnolence disorder
   D. circadian rhythm sleep-wake disorder

9. Many people experience the sensation of falling out of bed or falling down the stairs as they are starting to fall asleep. This is known as _____.
   A. hypnapompic hallucinations
   B. cateplexy
   C. sleep drunkenness
   D. hypnagogic hallucinations

10. _____ is unusually slow or shallow breathing and may disturb sleep in breathing-related sleep disorder.
    A. Sleep drunkenness
    B. Dyssomnia
    C. Sleep apnea
    D. Hypopnea

11. Melatonin, secreted by the pineal gland, helps to regulate the sleep-wake cycle and appears beneficial in the treatment of _____.
    A. hypersomnolence disorder
    B. central sleep apnea
    C. nightmare disorder
    D. circadian rhythm sleep-wake disorder

12. Sleepwalking involves repeated episodes of complex motor activities which begin during _____.
    A. the first stages of sleep
    B. the later stages of sleep
    C. slow wave REM sleep
    D. slow wave non-REM sleep

13. Which of the following normally occurs during REM sleep?
    A. Skeletal muscles are paralyzed.
    B. Cataplexy occurs.
    C. The eyes are nearly motionless.
    D. Sleep apnea occurs.

14. Enuresis cannot be diagnosed until age _____.
    A. 1
    B. 3
    C. 5
    D. 7

15. The bell and pad device is used to treat _____.
    A. pica
    B. enuresis
    C. rumination disorder
    D. encopresis

Additional study resources are available at **www.BVTLab.com**

# CHAPTER OVERVIEW

# CHAPTER OPENER QUESTIONS

What is delirium?

Can younger people show these symptoms?

What causes neurocognitive disorders?

Is dementia permanent? Can it be prevented?

What treatments are effective for the neurocognitive disorders?

How are the memory impairments of dementia and amnesia different?

take my medication after lunch

I have 4 children

take dog out at 7 am 12 noon and at 3 pm

keys are hanging up by front door

(Shutterstock)

# Neurocognitive Disorders

# chapter 15

The physiological basis of many of the disorders discussed to this point remains unclear and sometimes controversial. As we have seen, the sleep-wake disorders generally include within their definition specific measurements from sleep studies or biochemical assessments; yet for most other *DSM* conditions, the underlying physiological causes have not been unequivocally identified. For the mental disorders considered here, the situation is decidedly different. Delirium, dementia, and the amnestic disorders were categorized as "organic mental disorders" in the *DSM-III*, reflecting their evident connection to brain pathology. That nomenclature was eliminated in the *DSM-IV* due to the growing recognition that all mental disorders have organic or physiological components. The disorders included under the *DSM-5* classification—neurocognitive disorders—are unique in the extent to which their biological etiology can be demonstrated.

Neurocognitive disorders are conditions in which impairment was not present during the developmental period, and so they represent declines in cognitive abilities. In the *DSM-IV*, it was important to distinguish these conditions—all of which involve some degree of memory dysfunction—from the effects of normal aging. As people become older, cognitive abilities such as memory and complex problem solving generally become less efficient. Some people can become easily confused, lost, or forget about where important items are kept. The *DSM-IV* provided a non-disorder listing, "age related cognitive decline," to describe the occasional need for clinical attention by people whose difficulties were within normal limits for persons of similar years. The *DSM-5,* instead, includes these symptoms under the new diagnosis of mild neurocognitive disorder—a decision that has raised some concern about over diagnosis. However, as we will see, the dysfunctions considered here are quite common among the aging population.

## 15.1 Compromised Brain Function

Many pathological conditions of the brain are more common in older persons. The prevalence of dementia, for example, is highest in those over age 85 (American Psychiatric Association, 2000). However, compromise of brain function (and the psychological effects it entails) can occur at any age, resulting from factors such as disease, injury, tumor, inflammation of the brain (**encephalitis**), or a drug or toxin. Some of these conditions are progressive, with continuing decline in cognitive function for the remainder of life. Others are transient and may resolve rapidly and completely. If the underlying organic cause is resolved, the cognitive decline may cease or reverse its course.

As an illustration of the range of the psychological consequences of brain infection, consider the example of the syndrome known as *general paresis*. As noted in Chapter 2, the discovery that general paresis is caused by a syphilitic infection was a landmark in the development of the organic view of psychopathology. Only a small proportion of individuals (less than 5%) who contract syphilis and fail to get treatment ultimately develop the symptoms of general paresis. Once the initial physical signs of infection (chancre, skin rash) subside, a lengthy latency period sets in, during which the infecting spirochetes may invade the heart, spinal cord, brain, or other organs. After this latency period, which can last 10–30 years, overt symptoms of neurosyphilis may begin to appear: failure of the pupil of the eye to contract to light, failure of other reflexes such as the knee jerk reflex, slurred speech, and shaky handwriting. Behavioral changes also occur, often quite slowly. Individuals are likely to become more irritable and have periods

**Encephalitis**

Inflammation of the brain

### Figure 15-1 *Cortical Areas of the Brain*

Cortical areas of the left hemisphere of the brain with shaded areas showing more specialized sections: Broca's area and Wernicke's area are involved in the production and understanding of language; the angular gyrus mediates between visual and auditory information.

Source: Adapted from Geschwind, N. (1979). Specializations of the human brain. *Scientific American, 241,* 180–199.

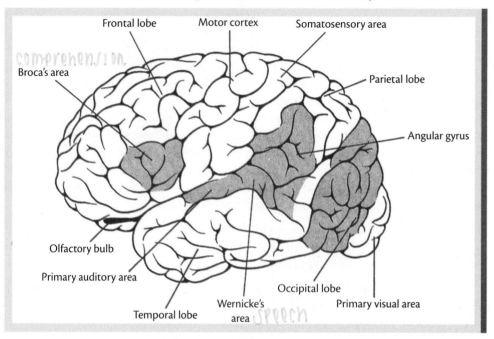

of depression or confusion. As the disease progresses, they may become neglectful of dress, forgetful of social amenities, and lose ordinary inhibitions in the expression of aggressive or sexual impulses. In some cases, grandiose delusions of great power or wealth develop; in other cases, there is simply a progressive dementia or paralysis. Eventually, widespread brain destruction occurs, accompanied by progressive dementia and paralysis.

The nature of the psychological impairment produced by brain dysfunction is related to the area of the brain that is affected. Although the degree of localization of particular cognitive and emotional activities has often been overstated (Kagan, 2007), some broad psychological functions are integrated in specific parts of the brain. General auditory, visual, and spatial orientation is greatly impacted by damage to particular areas of the cortex, for example, see Figure 15-1. Sensorimotor integration related to the sense of touch is richly innervated along the somatosensory cortex; sensation and motor control for different areas of the body and head are mapped onto confined cortical regions. Specific language difficulties can be produced by damage to Broca's area (*Broca's aphasia* involves effortful, slow articulation with little information included) or Wernicke's area (*Wernicke's aphasia* involves fluent speech that conveys little meaning, as well as a profound deficit in speech comprehension). A type of spatial dysfunction is caused by damage to the right parietal lobe of the brain, which controls the left visual field because the optic nerves cross over. The impairment, called **neglect syndrome**, is one in which the left visual field seems to be ignored (see Figure 15-2).

An interesting distinction is apparent between those who experience neglect syndrome (also called *hemineglect* or *unilateral inattention*) because of damage to the left hemisphere as opposed to the right hemisphere. Damage to the right parietal lobe, producing the spatial neglect illustrated in the figure, is frequently accompanied by relative unconcern on the part of the patient, who may consider the condition amusing and seem unaware of its seriousness. Patients with left-hemisphere damage, in contrast, tend to show strong depressive reactions to their conditions (Ogden, 2005).

The different psychological impairments produced by brain damage can be assessed and quantified through various neuropsychological test batteries and mental status

**Neglect syndrome**

A spatial disorder involving inattention to the left visual field due to damage to the right parietal lobe of the brain

examinations. These assessments may involve tasks of verbal or visual memory and can include visual reproduction of standardized complex figures or free-hand drawings, like the clock and flower in Figure 15-2. The accuracy and organization of these reproductions can provide important information about the affected brain areas. Other assessments aim to measure executive control (counting to 10, reciting the alphabet, naming as many animals as possible in 1 minute), short-term memory (recalling a list of digits or pictures following a short delay), visual and auditory recognition (identifying a target stimulus in a list), and the ability to acquire new information (such as learning pairs of words, with one word then serving as a prompt to recall the other). The results from these types of assessments aid in differential diagnosis of the cognitive disorders.

The reliability of organic mental disorders in the *DSM-III* field trials was good with overall kappa values showing highest consistency for the diagnosis of dementia. More recent reviews (Wolfs, Dirksen, Severens, & Verhey, 2006) also indicate good agreement on the dementia category, but not on various dementia subtypes with different etiologies. For example, the *DSM-IV* criteria showed better reliability and validity for dementia of the Alzheimer's type than for vascular dementia (Hogervorst, Bandelow, Combrinck, Irani, & Smith, 2003). The *DSM-5* field trials found test-retest reliability to be "good" (pooled kappa of 0.46) for mild neurocognitive disorder and "very good" for major neurocognitive disorder (pooled kappa of 0.78), but reliability was "questionable" (kappa = 0.36) for mild traumatic brain injury (Regier, et al., 2013). Reliability estimates are harder to find for delirium and amnestic disorders. One reason may be that amnesia can occur in the absence of any biological evidence, as in dissociative amnesia and other dissociative disorders; the issue is further complicated by the high base rate of malingering of amnesia after mild head injury (Larrabee, 2004). Dementia also is more chronic and global in its impact and more consistently observable, in that sense, lending itself to agreement in diagnosis.

In the multiaxial structure of the *DSM-IV*, the mental disorder (e.g., dementia, delirium, or amnestic disorder) was listed on Axis I based on diagnostic criteria that identify its psychological and behavioral characteristics, such as memory or language disturbance. The physical disturbance (e.g., Alzheimer's disease) that causes the mental disorder was separately coded on Axis III as the associated medical condition. The *DSM-5* no longer makes such distinctions: the physical disease is coded along with the mental disorder.

*Figure 15-2* **Neglect Syndrome Due to Damage of the Right Parietal Lobe**

Examples of neglect on drawing test.

Source: Adapted from Strub, R. L., & Black, F. W. (1977). *The mental status examination in neurology.* Philadelphia, PA: F. A. Davis Company.

## 15.2 Delirium

The condition now known as delirium has been recognized for thousands of years. Hippocrates wrote in 500 BC of *phrenitis* (one of several more or less equivalent terms), describing a mental disorder that resulted from poisoning, head injury, or fever. Historically, delirium was associated with incurable madness, poor prognosis, and death. By the nineteenth century, it was understood to have several causes, including alcohol, and was seen as a serious but often transient condition from which full recovery could occur

What is delirium?

*mild: still functioning*
*major: require full*
*time care.*

(Adamis, Treloar, Martin, & MacDonald, 2007). It was known as "acute brain syndrome" in *DSM-I* and has also been called "acute confusional state," "toxic psychosis," and "metabolic encephalopathy" (American Psychological Association, 1980).

As currently defined (see *DSM-5* Diagnostic Criteria for Delirium), **delirium** is a change in consciousness that can involve disorientation, impairment of memory (usually recent), illusions or hallucinations, and reduced attention to the surrounding world. It develops rapidly and can fluctuate in severity at periods throughout the day. By definition, there must be evidence that the disturbance is related to a specific physiological cause, such as a medical condition, a medication, or a substance.

Delirium involves a relatively brief, but global, cognitive impairment of attention and awareness. Delirious individuals often are not oriented to place or time, believing themselves to be at home rather than in the hospital, or confusing day and night. They are easily distracted, and their rapidly shifting attention may make conversation difficult or impossible. There is frequently disruption of the sleep-wake cycle, ranging from hypersomnia to insomnia; sometimes a reduced wakefulness or "clouded consciousness" dominates. Motor activity can vacillate, shifting between hyperactivity and lethargy (American Psychiatric Association, 2000). The course fluctuates during the day, typically becoming worse at night as external stimuli that can provide orienting information become less available (American Psychiatric Association, 2013).

**Delirium**

Rapidly developing change in consciousness and reduced attention

## DSM-5 | Diagnostic Criteria for Delirium

Delirium

A. A disturbance in attention (i.e., reduced ability to direct, focus, sustain, and shift attention) and awareness (reduced orientation to the environment).

B. The disturbance develops over a short period of time (usually hours to a few days, represents a change from baseline attention and awareness, and tends to fluctuate in severity during the course of a day.

C. An additional disturbance in cognition (e.g., memory deficit, disorientation, language, visuospatial ability, or perception).

D. The disturbances in Criteria A and C are not better explained by another preexisting, established, or evolving neurocognitive disorder and do not occur in the context of a severely reduced level of arousal, such as coma.

E. There is evidence from the history, physical examination, or laboratory findings that the disturbance is a direct physiological consequence of another medical condition, substance intoxication or withdrawal (i.e., due to a drug of abuse or to a medication), or exposure to a toxin, or is due to multiple etiologies.

*Specify* whether:

**Substance intoxication delirium:** This diagnosis should be made instead of substance intoxication when the symptoms in Criteria A and C predominate in the clinical picture and when they are sufficiently severe to warrant clinical attention.

**Substance withdrawal delirium:** This diagnosis should be made instead of substance withdrawal when the symptoms in Criteria A and C predominate in the clinical picture and when they are sufficiently severe to warrant clinical attention.

**Medication-induced delirium:** This diagnosis applies when the symptoms in Criteria A and C arise as side effects of a medication taken as prescribed.

**Delirium due to another medical condition:** There is evidence from the history, physical examination, or laboratory findings that the disturbance is attributable to the physiological consequences of another medical condition.

**Delirium due to multiple etiologies:** There is evidence from the history, physical examination, or laboratory findings that the disturbance has more than one etiology (e.g., more than one etiological medical condition, another medical condition plus substance intoxication or medication side effects).

*Specify* if:

**Acute:** Lasting a few hours or days.

**Persistent:** Lasting weeks or months.

*Specify* if:

**Hyperactive:** The individual has a hyperactive level of psychomotor activity that may be accompanied by mood lability, agitation, and/or refusal to cooperate with medical care.

**Hypoactive:** The individual has a hypoactive level of psychomotor activity that may be accompanied by sluggishness and lethargy that approaches stupor.

**Mixed level of activity:** The individual has a normal level of psychomotor activity even though attention and awareness are disturbed. Also includes individuals whose activity level rapidly fluctuates.

Source: Reprinted with permission from the *Diagnostic and Statistical Manual of Mental Disorders*, Fifth Edition, (Copyright 2013). American Psychiatric Association.

Shifting emotional disturbances are typical, including extremes such as euphoria, anger, and depression. Fear is commonly present and sometimes leads to attempts to flee or to attack others perceived to be threatening. People who have experienced states of delirium later report that they felt confused, anxious, and afraid. Visual hallucinations, especially of animals or people, are common and together with delusions are the most significant sources of fear and anxiety (O'Malley, Leonard, Meagher, & O'Keeffe, 2008). Speech disruptions in delirium can include articulation difficulties, inability to name objects, rambling and incoherent verbalizations, repetition, or difficulty understanding words. Writing ability may be impaired as well. These emotional, perceptual, and speech disturbances can resemble other psychotic conditions, except for their fragmented and fluctuating presentation.

Delirium usually follows an **acute** course, developing within hours or days and most often resolving within weeks or, more rarely, months. It can, nonetheless, become chronic if superimposed onto a pre-existing major neurocognitive disorder (see below); and it can progress to stupor, coma, and death for those whose underlying cause remains unrecognized or untreated. Its presence is associated with increased risk of mortality: nearly 40% die within a year of diagnosis. At any one time, delirium may affect between 1% and 2% of the general population; its incidence increases with age, such that nearly one-seventh of those over age 85 are affected. Over half of hospitalized patients display delirium, and 83% of people develop the condition at the end of life (American Psychiatric Association, 2013).

Delirium can occur in all ages, and children (perhaps due to their developing physiology) are at increased risk, especially during illnesses involving fever. The cognitive signs of the disorder may be difficult to identify in children, and their behavior may be misinterpreted as uncooperativeness (American Psychiatric Association, 2000). The elderly are particularly susceptible to multiple influences that can combine to produce the condition. In frail geriatric groups, at least 250 different contributing factors to delirium have been identified, the most common of which are infections, adverse metabolic events, and adverse medication effects (Laurila, Laakkonen, Laurila, Timo, & Reijo, 2008). In addition to advancing age, other risk factors include male gender, alcohol abuse, dementia, and sensory impairment (Bourne, Tahir, Borthwich, & Sampson, 2008).

> **Can younger people show these symptoms?**

Delirium can be caused by exposure to toxins—including fuel, solvents, insecticides, and carbon monoxide—and by medications, drugs or drug abuse, physical damage to the brain, and a host of other events. The *DSM-5* organizes delirium diagnoses according to etiology: substance intoxication delirium, substance withdrawal delirium, medication-induced delirium, delirium due to another medical condition, or delirium due to multiple etiologies. The diagnosis can be specified as acute (lasting a few hours or days) or persistent (lasting weeks or months), and based on the level of psychomotor activity involved (hyperactive, hypoactive, or mixed). The hyperactive subtype appears more commonly when delirium is associated with medication side effects and drug withdrawal (American Psychiatric Association, 2013).

## 15.2a  Substance Intoxication Delirium

Each intoxicating substance produces a characteristic pattern of behavioral disturbances, according to the drug's pharmacology. If the reaction following drug ingestion is significantly different from "normal" intoxication, resulting in cognitive impairment that is excessive and serious enough to warrant clinical attention, then a substance-induced delirium (e.g., alcohol intoxication delirium) may be diagnosed. Besides alcohol, intoxication delirium is associated with amphetamines, cannabis, cocaine, hallucinogens, opioids, PCP, sedatives, anxiolytics, or combinations of drugs and substances. In most conditions, the delirium resolves within a few hours or days as the intoxication dissipates (American Psychiatric Association, 2000).

**Acute**

Type of condition that begins or progresses rapidly, and that tends to end quickly

## 15.2b Substance Withdrawal Delirium

Some substances capable of causing withdrawal can produce substance withdrawal delirium, involving cognitive disturbances in excess of those normally accompanying withdrawal and serious enough to warrant clinical attention. Substance withdrawal delirium develops as tissue concentration of a drug changes following cessation or sharp reduction in use. A well-known example, described in Chapter 12, is alcohol withdrawal delirium (formerly called *delirium tremens*) which can include agitated behavior and vivid visual, tactile, and auditory hallucinations, beginning 2 or 3 days after reduction or cessation of drinking. Alcohol withdrawal delirium occurs in less than 5% of those hospitalized for alcohol dependence and usually runs its course in 2 or 3 days (American Psychiatric Association, 2000). Substance withdrawal delirium has also been identified for the sedative, hypnotic, or anxiolytic drugs. In some longer-acting substances, withdrawal delirium can persist for weeks before resolving.

## 15.2c Medication-Induced Delirium

Many medications—including anesthetics, analgesics, antihistamines, muscle relaxants, heart medications, and some psychotropic medications such as lithium—or their side effects can also cause delirium. Medication-induced delirium usually develops in close accordance to the rate of distribution of the drug in the bloodstream, often within minutes for rapid-acting substances or over longer courses (hours) for drugs that have longer half-lives. Its duration can be affected by rate of both drug absorption and metabolism, as well as by drug interactions (American Psychiatric Association, 2000). Especially among the elderly, polypharmacy is a major risk factor for substance-induced delirium: almost 44% of frail geriatric patients in a recent investigation of delirium prevalence were receiving more than eight regular medications daily (Laurila, Laakkonen, Laurila, Timo, & Reijo, 2008).

## 15.2d Delirium Due to Another Medical Condition

Delirium can develop in the context of a wide range of medical conditions. Specific lesions or tumors of the brain, especially in the parietal or occipital lobe, can produce delirium and so can many disturbances of the central nervous system, metabolic disorders, heart conditions, or systemic illnesses. Delirium may occur in connection with high fevers, encephalitis, fluid imbalances, dehydration, and certain severe vitamin or mineral deficiencies. It may develop post-operatively or in association with hypoxia, shock, or head injury. The specific medical condition (such as an infection of the brain, a stroke, low blood sugar, or a tumor) is noted in the diagnosis (e.g., delirium due to head trauma). Because many of the medical conditions that cause delirium can be treated, delirium due to a general medical condition is frequently resolved rather quickly by interventions for the underlying medical issue.

## 15.2e Delirium Due to Multiple Etiologies

If more than one specific physical factor is known to be involved in the cause of the delirium, delirium due to multiple etiologies can be diagnosed. For example, delirium might result from the combined effects of a liver disease and substance withdrawal. Frequently in the elderly population, medication side effects interact with physical disorders, both of which contribute to delirium. However, the multitude of potential triggers of delirium can also produce a variety of different presentations. "Other specified delirium" describes those cases of delirium not fitting into the above categories, such as delirium that is produced by sensory deprivation or those that do not meet full diagnostic criteria for the condition.

*Treatment for Delirium*

Most people recover fully from delirium whether they receive treatment or not, but intervention shortens the course of disturbance (American Psychiatric Association, 2013). Treatment of the florid and often psychotic symptoms of the disturbance frequently involves sedation, usually via low-dose antipsychotic medication. Some attempts have been made to prevent the development of delirium in high-risk cases through the prophylactic use of antipsychotics or benzodiazepines (Bourne, Tahir, Borthwick, & Sampson, 2008). Of course, careful review of causal factors is important prior to preventative attempts because the medications may themselves contribute to the development of delirium.

# 15.3 Major and Mild Neurocognitive Disorders

The cognitive disturbance associated with neurocognitive disorders involves cognitive decline in one or more cognitive domains. In contrast to delirium, mild and major neurocognitive disorders may have a gradual, slow onset, and more frequently have a **chronic** course.

> **What causes neurocognitive disorders?**

In the *DSM-IV*, major neurocognitive disorder was known as **dementia.** It always involves a memory deficit, most apparent in recent memory and the retention of new learning. For example, a person may lose recently handled items, forget activities that are in progress, or be unable to recall a list of words given moments before. The demented person may become easily lost when walking in unfamiliar settings. When dementia is advanced, memory impairment extends beyond recent events; and people may forget important personal information (such as occupation or even name). Although dementia remains a useful term, the *DSM-5* diagnosis was broadened to include the memory impairments known as amnestic disorders as well.

Neurocognitive disorders are diagnosed on the basis of a decline in functioning in at least one of six cognitive domains:

> **Is dementia permanent? Can it be prevented?**

a. *Complex attention* is the ability to attend to sustained, or multiple, or selective, aspects of an activity. It is demonstrated when a person can remain on task, ignore distractions, and divide attention between two or more things.

b. *Executive function* is the ability to plan tasks, make decisions, manipulate information, solve problems based on feedback, apply complex and effortful solutions, and shift between concepts.

c. *Learning and memory* involve several memory abilities such as short-term recall, delayed recall, cued recall, and recognition, as well as the ability to learn new things.

d. *Language* involves expressive abilities such as naming, word finding, grammar, and syntax, and receptive understanding.

e. *Perceptual-motor abilities* include the ability to navigate, to use tools or devices, and to imitate, draw, or copy.

f. *Social cognition* includes abilities to detect and recognize emotion in others, or to understand another person's point of view.

There are a variety of neuropsychological tests, such as the Halstead-Reitan Neurological Battery, that include specific tasks to measure relative functioning in these areas. Together with intelligence tests and memory instruments, like the Wechsler Memory Scale, they provide a rather thorough indicator of cognitive decline and provide the type of documentation required within the diagnosis.

**Chronic**
Type of condition that begins slowly or gradually, with long duration and/or frequent recurrence

**Dementia**
Global development of multiple cognitive deficits in memory, speech, and executive functioning

The extent of the decline determines whether the neurocognitive disorder is major or mild. In the case of major neurocognitive disorder (see *DSM-5* Diagnostic Criteria for Major Neurocognitive Disorder), the cognitive decline is significant; and the impairments in these areas interfere with independent functioning. In the case of mild neurocognitive disorder, cognitive decline is modest; independent functioning remains adequate. Each disorder can be specified in terms of the causal condition, as well as whether a behavioral disturbance (such as agitation or psychotic symptoms) is also present.

Major neurocognitive disorder includes all of the symptoms of dementia. Some clusters of symptoms that are most frequently seen among the demented include aphasia, apraxia, agnosia, and disturbances in executive function.

**Aphasia** is a language disturbance that involves impairment in understanding or expressing ideas through language. Sentences may appear to be devoid of meaning or empty, and they may be long and disconnected. People may be unable to label common items in the room. References are often vague or indefinite; in severe cases, individuals can become echolalic or mute. Understanding of spoken words is also affected, and individuals may have trouble following instructions or comprehending normal conversation. Both spoken and written language may be impaired in aphasia.

**Apraxia** is manifested by impaired ability to execute motor activities although motor function is intact. For example, individuals may not be able to demonstrate how to comb their hair or brush their teeth, or how to wave good-bye, although they are physically capable

**Aphasia**

A language disturbance involving impairment in understanding or expressing language

**Apraxia**

Impaired ability to execute motor activities although motor functions are intact

---

| *DSM-5* | **Diagnostic Criteria for Major Neurocognitive Disorder** |
|---|---|

Major Neurocognitive Disorder

A. Evidence of significant cognitive decline from a previous level of performance in one or more cognitive domains (complex attention, executive function, learning and memory, language, perceptual-motor, or social cognition) based on:
   1. Concern of the individual, a knowledgeable informant, or the clinician that there has been a significant decline in cognitive function and
   2. A substantial impairment in cognitive performance, preferably documented by standardized neuropsychological testing or, in its absence, another qualified clinical assessment.
B. The cognitive deficits interfere with independence in everyday activities (i.e., at a minimum, requiring assistance with complex instrumental activities of daily living such as paying bills or managing medications).
C. The cognitive deficits do not occur exclusively in the context of a delirium.
D. The cognitive deficits are not better explained by another mental disorder (e.g., major depressive disorder, schizophrenia).

*Specify* whether due to:

| | |
|---|---|
| Alzheimer's disease | Frontotemporal lobar degeneration |
| Lewy body disease | Vascular disease |
| Traumatic brain injury | Substance/medication use |
| HIV infection | Prion disease |
| Parkinson's disease | Huntington's disease |
| Another medical condition | Multiple etiologies |
| Unspecified | |

*Specify*

**Without behavioral disturbance:** If the cognitive disturbance is not accompanied by any significant behavioral disturbance

**With behavioral disturbance:** (specify disturbance): If the cognitive disturbance is accompanied by a clinically significant behavioral disturbance (e.g., psychotic symptoms, mood disturbance, agitation, apathy, or other behavioral symptoms.

*Specify* current severity:

**Mild:** Difficulties with instrumental activities of daily living (e.g., housework, managing money).

**Moderate:** Difficulties with basic activities of daily living (e.g., feeding, dressing).

**Severe:** Fully dependent.

Source: Reprinted with permission from the *Diagnostic and Statistical Manual of Mental Disorders*, Fifth Edition, (Copyright 2013). American Psychiatric Association.

to making those movements. As a result, normal self-care abilities such as dressing and grooming are often disrupted.

**Agnosia** is failure to recognize objects or people that were formerly familiar to the person. Common items such as car keys or pencils might not be identified or labeled verbally. In severe cases of dementia, individuals may not recognize close friends, family members, or even themselves in a mirror.

**Disturbances in executive function** involve impairments in the ability to plan and execute actions. Abstract thinking is deficient, and serial tasks are impaired, such as counting or reciting familiar sequences (e.g., the alphabet). Individuals with disturbed executive function might not recognize error or resist a temptation; they have difficulty with sequences of actions that have not been well practiced.

As the condition progresses, these impairments become more obvious. Individuals may show early symptoms of difficulty with financial issues or with shopping, progressing to problems in daily activities such as dressing, bathing, and eating. They may also lose the ability to use common tools such as telephones. They almost always have impaired judgment and poor insight and may underestimate the dangers of certain activities, such as driving. Delusions (often persecutory) and hallucinations (often visual) can occur; and depending on the causal factor, additional delirium may also be present. In fact, it can be quite difficult to distinguish dementia and delirium in the elderly; the two disorders co-occur in the large majority of hospitalized older patients (Blazer & van Nieuwenhuizen, 2012). However, the dementia must be separable from the effects of any pre-existing delirium before the diagnosis can be applied.

The prevalence of dementia increases rapidly with age, such that 30% of people 85 years of age and older are affected (American Psychiatric Association, 2013). There are many physical conditions known to cause dementia; any condition that is associated with physical damage or deterioration of the brain can be involved. The *DSM-5* diagnosis lists several of the most typical associated conditions within the diagnostic criteria, but their list is not exhaustive. Recently, the link between midlife obesity and later dementia has also become apparent (Loef & Walach, 2013). Some of the conditions are described in more detail below.

A male Alzheimer's patient rests on his bed. Due to his loss of short-term memory, he relies on Post-it® reminders on his dresser drawers to remind him how his clothes are organized. (Getty Image)

# 15.3a Major or Mild Neurocognitive Disorder Due to Alzheimer's Disease

Neurocognitive disorder due to Alzheimer's disease, also called dementia of the Alzheimer's type (DAT), is the most common form of dementia (see *DSM-5* Diagnostic Criteria for Major or Mild Neurocognitive Disorder Due to Alzheimer's Disease); its prevalence is increasing as the population ages, and its numbers are expected to triple by 2050 (Caselli, Beach, Yaari, & Reiman, 2006). Alzheimer's disease accounts for up to 60% of all cases of dementia (Blennow, de Leon, & Zetterberg, 2006). It rarely develops before age 50, but then increases dramatically with age, such that 10% of those in their seventh decade and more than one-fourth in later decades show the disorder. Alzheimer's disease causes a progressive and irreversible dementia that gradually worsens as brain deterioration proceeds, with death occurring on average 10 years after diagnosis (American Psychiatric Association, 2013).

The diagnosis of dementia of the Alzheimer's type is made partly by exclusion—that is, by ruling out other possible causes of dementia such as a stroke or brain tumor, Parkinson's or Huntington's disease, or other conditions that are known to cause dementia. In most cases, there are

*not curable or reversible – can slow it down.*

**What treatments are effective for the neurocognitive disorders?**

**Agnosia**

Failure to recognize familiar objects or people

**Disturbances in executive function**

Involve impairments in the ability to plan and execute actions

| DSM-5 | Diagnostic Criteria for Major or Mild Neurocognitive Disorder Due to Alzheimer's Disease |
|---|---|

Major or Mild Neurocognitive Disorder Due to Alzheimer's Disease

A. The criteria are met for major or mild neurocognitive disorder.

B. There is insidious onset and gradual progression of impairment in one or more cognitive domains (for major neurocognitive disorder, at least two domains must be impaired).

C. Criteria are met for either probable or possible Alzheimer's disease as follows:

*For major neurocognitive disorder:*

**Probable Alzheimer's disease** is diagnosed if either of the following is present; otherwise, **possible Alzheimer's disease** should be diagnosed.

1. Evidence of a causative Alzheimer's disease genetic mutation from family history or genetic testing.

2. All three of the following are present:

a. Clear evidence of decline in memory and learning and at least one other cognitive domain (based on detailed history or serial neuropsychological testing).

b. Steadily progressive, gradual decline in cognition, without extended plateaus.

c. No evidence of mixed etiology (i.e., absence of other neurodegenerative or cerebrovascular disease, or another neurological, mental, or systemic disease or condition likely contributing to the cognitive decline).

*For mild neurocognitive disorder:*

**Probable Alzheimer's disease** is diagnosed if there is evidence of a causative Alzheimer's disease genetic mutation from either genetic testing or family history.

**Possible Alzheimer's disease** is diagnosed if there is no evidence of a causative Alzheimer's disease genetic mutation from either genetic testing or family history, and all three of the following are present:

1. Clear evidence of decline in memory and learning.

2. Steadily progressive, gradual decline in cognition, without extended plateaus.

3. No evidence of mixed etiology (i.e., absence of other neurodegenerative or cerebrovascular disease, or another neurological or systemic disease or condition likely contributing to the cognitive decline).

D. The disturbance is not better explained by cerebrovascular disease, another neurodegenerative disease, the effects of a substance, or another mental, neurological, or systemic disorder.

Source: Reprinted with permission from the *Diagnostic and Statistical Manual of Mental Disorders,* Fifth Edition, (Copyright 2013). American Psychiatric Association.

no "telltale" signs from physical examination (Caselli, Beach, Yaari, & Reiman, 2006). However, the insidious onset and slow progression of DAT may distinguish it from other dementias (such as vascular dementia). The steadily-worsening condition eventually results in extreme cognitive impairment. As the brain disintegration proceeds, memory loss is usually apparent among the earliest symptoms, with increasing degrees of confusion and personality change developing as more of the brain is involved. Patients undergoing personality changes often initially become distrustful and suspicious, but later may be openly belligerent and delusional (Caselli, Beach, Yaari, & Reiman, 2006). In later stages, patients become totally dependent; they often show gait disturbance, become incontinent, and are eventually bedbound and mute (American Psychiatric Association, 2013).

The underlying causal condition, Alzheimer's disease, is a gradual and chronic deterioration of cholinergic neurons (those neurons that use acetylcholine, or ACh, as their neurotransmitter) that innervate the forebrain. As can be seen in Figure 15-3, the microtubules within the axons of these neurons begin disintegrating, and *tau* proteins (which normally stabilize the structure of the neuron) form remnant clumps of material called *neurofibrillary tangles.* In addition, a sticky plaque, consisting of beta amyloid protein fragments and degenerated axon terminals, accumulates in deposits called *senile plaques,* which also damage neurons (see Figure 15-4). There is some evidence that the accumulation of the senile plaques is important in the etiology of DAT, but the plaques do not correlate

*Figure 15-3*

Deterioration of microtubules in the axon, and development of neurofibrillary tangles characteristic of Alzheimer's disease.

Source: National Institute on Aging

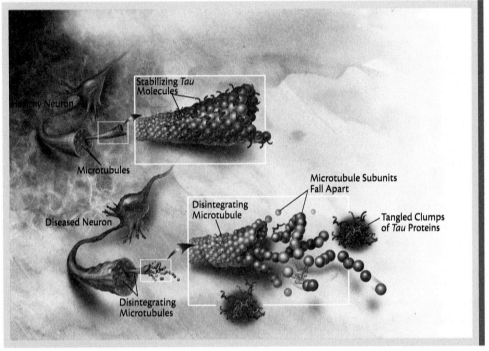

well with the severity of the dementia, while the neurofibrillary tangles do correlate with degree of memory loss (Caselli, Beach, Yaari, & Reiman, 2006). Clearly, both represent major indicators of serious brain pathology.

Early in the course of the disorder, persons are usually able to at least partially compensate (with some effort) for the dysfunctions that involve difficulties in at least two areas, including memory, executive functioning, perceptual motor skills, or language. As Alzheimer's disease progresses, more and more brain areas are impacted; the brain ventricles become enlarged, and the cortex shows clear signs of atrophy. Figure 15-5 shows the appearance of brain slides at different degrees of disease severity. At present, these changes (and the presence of senile plaques and neurofibrillary tangles diagnostic of Alzheimer's disease) can only be verified during autopsy.

As the disorder progresses, reduction in brain activity resulting from neuronal disintegration spreads from the hippocampal and basal forebrain areas to increasingly larger areas of the brain (see Figure 15-6). Recent advances in brain imaging and cerebrospinal fluid analyses (for early indications of beta amyloid deposition) give hope that valid diagnostic markers among living persons may soon be identified (American Psychiatric Association, 2013). To see if biomarkers could predict which of those with milder symptoms progress on to Alzheimer's disease, Prestia and her colleagues (2013) assessed 73 patients with mild cognitive impairment for hippocampal atrophy, amyloid and *tau* protein levels in the cerebrospinal fluid, and decreased brain glucose metabolism. They found that when one

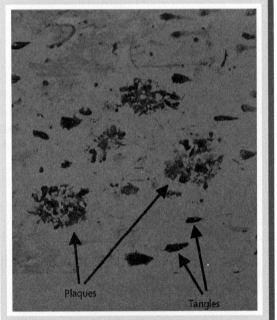

*Figure 15-4*

Plaques and neurofibrillary tangles in the brain of a patient with Alzheimer's disease

Source: Adapted from Blennow, K., de Leon, M. J., & Zetterberg, H. (2006) Alzheimer's Disease. *Lancet, 368,* 387–403.

*Figure 15-5* **Brain Slides Showing the Progression of Alzheimer's Disease**

Progression of Alzheimer's disease as seen in the brain slides showing increased cortical atrophy, enlarged ventricles, and hippocampal shrinkage: (a) shows the brain of patient with pre-clinical Alzheimer's disease; (b) shows the brain affected by mild to moderate Alzheimer's disease, and (c) shows a severely affected brain.

Source: Illustrations from the National Institute on Aging

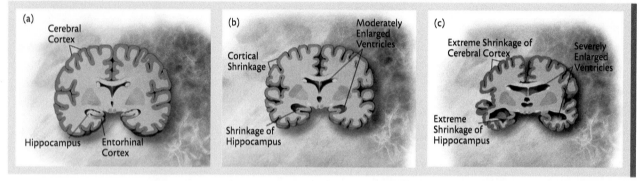

biomarker was present, 4% of patients progressed to Alzheimer's disease; however, when all three markers were positive, 100% subsequently did so.

## Causal Factors

Alzheimer's disease occurs in both familial and sporadic forms. The familial form is rare, with prevalence below 1% (Blennow, de Leon, & Zetterberg, 2006). This form has onset before age 65 and is most closely associated with presenilin1 and presenilin2 genes (see Figure 15-7). There are several known genetic mechanisms that contribute to the sporadic form of Alzheimer's disease, but most cases seem to be associated with the apolipoprotein E (APOE) site on Chromosome 19 (Blennow, de Leon, & Zetterberg, 2006; Caselli, Beach, Yaari, & Reiman, 2006). It is not known specifically how mutations at this site increase risk for DAT, but forms of this gene may be associated with enhanced beta amyloid deposition (Caselli, Beach, Yaari, & Reiman, 2006). However, the association of APOE with DAT is not exclusive, and APOE genetic testing is not yet useful in confirming risk for developing the condition. In the case of the sporadic form of Alzheimer's disease, it appears likely that APOE and several other genes may be involved, each of which confers some risk in complex interaction with environmental factors (Blennow, de Leon, & Zetterberg, 2006).

Several mutations of a beta-amyloid precursor gene, APP, on chromosome 21, have also been linked to Alzheimer's disease (Lendon, Ashall, & Goate, 1997). This may explain the relationship between Alzheimer's disease and Down syndrome, caused by trisomy of

*Figure 15-6* **Progressive Reduction in Brain Activity in Alzheimer's Disease**

(a) shows localized reduction in pre-clinical Alzheimer's disease; (b) illustrates spreading inactivation in mild to moderate Alzheimer's disease; (c) shows widespread metabolic reduction in severe Alzheimer's disease.

Source: Illustrations from the National Institute of Aging

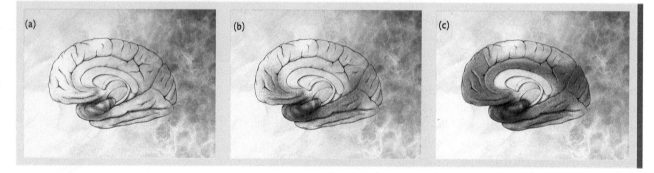

chromosome 21: Alzheimer's disease is almost invariably present in people with Down syndrome after age 45 (Willerman & Cohen, 1990).

## Treatment for Dementia of the Alzheimer's Type

It is not yet possible to stop or reverse the course of Alzheimer's disease or its accompanying dementia. At present, treatment for DAT is focused on techniques to slow the advancement of the deterioration and to improve the quality of life of patients. It is known that destruction of cholinergic neurons in the basal forebrain reduces levels of acetylcholine in the brain and interferes with the functioning of the hippocampus and other areas important to memory. The ACh depletion might be addressed by use of cholinesterase inhibitors, which slow the breakdown of ACh in the synapse, causing levels of the neurotransmitter to decline less steeply. Three cholinesterase inhibitors are currently available: donepezil (sold as Aricept), rivastigmine (Exelon), and galantamine (Reminyl). These drugs can produce modest but measurable effects on cognition, translating into a delayed worsening or temporary slight improvements, in some cases (Caselli, Beach, Yaari, & Reiman, 2006; Evans, Wilock, & Birks, 2004). Some studies, however, have suggested that benefits may be noticeable for as long as a few years (Blennow, de Leon, & Zetterberg, 2006). A fourth medication, memantine, is not a cholinesterase inhibitor but instead blocks a specific glutamate receptor known as NDMA, based on some evidence that glutamate enhancement may play a role in the development of Alzheimer's disease. However, glutamate is the main excitatory neurotransmitter in the central nervous system, and its activity is required for normal brain function; thus memantine is only a partial blocker. It, too, appears to produce small benefits but is significantly superior to placebo (Evans, Wilock, & Birks, 2004).

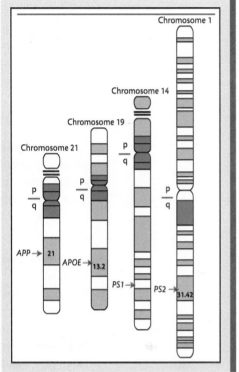

**Figure 15-7    *Genes Associated with Alzheimer's Disease***

Source: Adapted from Lendon, C. L., Ashall, F., and Goate, A. M. (1997). Exploring the etiology of Alzheimer's disease using molecular genetics. *Journal of the American Medical Association, 277,* 825–831.

Standard antipsychotic medications can help with behavioral symptoms but may also contribute to further complications, as well as mortality; their use must be cautious and temporary. A comparison of four atypical antipsychotics (aripiprazole, olanzapine, quetiapine, and respiradone) found a lack of effectiveness and high incidence of adverse side effects in 332 older patients with dementia, psychosis, or PTSD (Jin, et al., 2013). Nonetheless, antipsychotics are widely used to treat dementia in the elderly population. Government investigators reported in 2011 that 83% of Medicare claims for antipsychotic medications were for patients with dementia and that 14% of all nursing home residents were prescribed antipsychotic drugs (Perrone, 2011). SSRIs can reduce depression and anxiety but may cause or worsen sleep disturbances. Other pharmacological interventions may be helpful for physical symptoms, including incontinence and insomnia. An important component of treatment is to take steps that increase the safety of persons with DAT. Automobile driving and gun ownership are both issues, for example, that must be considered for reasons of safety to themselves and others.

Among psychological interventions, therapies that are based on a model of progressively lowered stress thresholds, or that utilize behavioral problem solving techniques, appear to be helpful in managing the disruptive behavior that accompanies dementia (Logsdon, McCurry, & Teri, 2007). These interventions typically involve training of staff or caregivers to observe behavior and identify problem situations and triggers for behavioral disturbances and then to use environmental or scheduling modifications and activity programming to reduce them. Increased behavioral activation, through exercise or scheduling of pleasant events, is also a component in these approaches. These structured efforts have been effective in reducing behavioral disturbances in randomized, controlled clinical trials and are most useful in reducing anxiety and depression among demented patients.

Prevention is also a topic receiving increased attention. Although evidence is preliminary, there may be benefits to nutritional, cognitive, and behavioral strategies to reduce risk of DAT. Aerobic exercise, mental exercise (such as puzzle-solving), vitamin and nutritional supplements, lowering of cholesterol, and regular but moderate ethanol from wine have all been reported as potentially preventative (Caselli, Beach, Yaari, & Reiman, 2006). However, none of these strategies have yet accumulated enough supporting evidence to be recommended as effective.

## 15.3b Other Neurocognitive Disorders

The clinical presentation of dementia is similar across its many various forms, with the possibility of exception of course. As noted above, DAT may be distinguished by slow and gradual onset and progressive decline. Other dementias may show sudden onset or non-progressive course.

### Major or Mild Vascular Neurocognitive Disorder

The symptoms of dementia in vascular neurocognitive disorder and in DAT are essentially identical, except that the onset of the cognitive deficit is usually more abrupt in the former. Vascular dementia is caused by brain damage that results from cardiovascular disease. Essentially, the damage is produced by events in which an interruption of blood supply to the brain (i.e., a **stroke**) leads to an area of dead tissue (an *infarct*). Initial symptoms are likely to include headache, faintness, confusion, memory lapses, aphasia, and—in many cases—temporary paralysis in various body parts. Frequently the person makes a rather good physical and psychological recovery from the first event, but succeeding small strokes can produce accumulating damage that results in dementia, often accompanied by weakness in a limb, difficulties with gait, and problems in motor movement and coordination, or paralysis. The rate of cognitive decline can be highly variable, sometimes evident in a stepwise deterioration in function as each subsequent stroke adds to the overall damage, followed by a plateau in functioning. Late-onset depression and psychomotor slowing, along with personality changes, are common. A single stroke is generally sufficient to produce mild vascular neurocognitive disorder, while two or three are often necessary before major vascular neurocognitive disorder results—depending, of course, on the severity and location of the events. Vascular dementia tends to occur more commonly in males than females (American Psychiatric Association, 2013).

### Major or Mild Frontotemporal Neurocognitive Disorder

Frontotemporal neurocognitive disorder includes either a behavioral variant (shown by three symptoms such as apathy, disinhibition, and compulsive behavior) or a language variant (with obvious decline in language ability or social cognition). Both variants are linked to distinct atrophy in the frontal and temporal lobes of the brain. In large part, however, perceptual motor function is only slightly affected, as is learning and memory. The onset is gradual and insidious. Apathy may show as a lack of interest in socializing with others or in self-care activities. Disinhibition may include changes in habits and social style, including political and religious beliefs. Aphasia is commonly observed. Eating habits may change, and sometimes repetitive or stereotypic behavior appears. There is some indication that males are more likely to display the behavioral variant, and women more likely to show the language variant. Major frontotemporal neurocognitive disorder is associated with faster decline and shorter survival, compared to neurocognitive disorder caused by Alzheimer's disease; however, the differentiation of the conditions can be difficult (American Psychiatric Association, 2013). A variety of degenerative processes may be involved in frontotemporal neurocognitive disorder, including Pick's disease, a progressive neural degeneration (with *tau* protein deposits) typically producing dementia in people in their 50s and 60s. A familial

**Stroke**
Disturbance of blood flow to the brain, resulting in loss of function in the affected brain areas

form of the disorder has been identified, which appears to be linked to genes on chromosome 17 (Greicius, Geschwind, & Miller, 2002). There is increasing recognition that this type of frontal/temporal dementia is more common than once thought, accounting perhaps for 1 in 8 cases of dementia (Ikeda, Ishikawa, & Tanabe, 2004).

## Major or Mild Neurocognitive Disorder Due to HIV Infection

Acquired immune deficiency disease (AIDS) attacks the immune system, and also produces severe neurological damage. Infection with the human immunodeficiency virus (HIV) produces progressive damages to the central nervous system as the body and brain become

increasingly vulnerable to serious infections or tumors resulting from impaired immune function. HIV may also impact brain neurology more directly, causing diffuse cortical and subcortical degeneration (Sadek, et al., 2004). Overall, only a small percentage of those infected with HIV go on to develop dementia. The introduction of newer antiretroviral therapies has reduced the incidence of dementia due to HIV disease by up to 50% and slowed its progress in countries where these drugs are available (McArthur, 2004). Unlike dementias linked to Alzheimer's disease or frontotemporal atrophy, neurocognitive disorder due to HIV infection can have a fluctuating course, and even improve. One-third to one-half of HIV-infected individuals have at least mild cognitive impairment, but fewer than 5% would meet the criteria for major neurocognitive disorder (American Psychiatric Association, 2013).

Closed-head injuries, such as concussions, occur more often in males than females, probably due to different risk-taking. (SwissMacky/Shutterstock.com)

## Major or Mild Neurocognitive Disorder Due to Traumatic Brain Injury

Head injuries can produce brain damage and the associated dementia or amnesia. The severity of neurocognitive disorder resulting from head trauma depends on the location and degree of the injury. Besides memory impairment, head traumas can produce behavioral changes such as aggressiveness or apathy, mood changes—such as depression or affective lability—and personality changes. Usually, dementia caused by head trauma is not progressive (in contrast to dementias related to diseases or repeated strokes), but repeated head injuries, such as those experienced by boxers and football players, may produce some progressive forms. Head trauma also appears to lower the threshold for other dementias, such as DAT, in susceptible persons (Starkstein & Jorge, 2005). Unfortunately, as noted earlier, the diagnostic reliability for the mild form was questionable in the *DSM-5* field trials (Regier, et al., 2013).

Dementia associated with traumatic brain injury was provisionally termed post-concussional disorder in *DSM-IV.* It describes a cognitive impairment that results from a closed-head injury severe enough to cause a cerebral **concussion**, in which the brain is subject to mechanical forces such as rotation, acceleration, or deceleration that do not produce structural damage, but do cause functional impairments. Concussions frequently cause loss of consciousness; upon awakening, the person usually cannot remember the events immediately preceding the injury. Occasionally, seizures can develop as well. Difficulties with attention or memory, headache, sleep disturbance, dizziness, fatigue, unprovoked aggression, affective lability or anxiety, personality changes, or lack of spontaneity are all commonly reported; and effects of a series of minor concussions appear to be cumulative, with increasing serious impairments. Closed-head injuries, such as concussions, occur more often in males than females, probably due to differential risk-taking, and can also be associated with impairments in vision, hearing, olfaction, and loss of interest in food. Over 1.5 million traumatic brain injuries occur annually in the U.S., and about 2% of the population lives with TBI-associated disability (American Psychiatric Association, 2013).

**Concussion**

Closed-head injury in which the brain is subjected to mechanical forces sufficient to cause confusion, temporary incapacity, or temporary loss of consciousness

## *Substance/Medication-Induced Major or Mild Neurocognitive Disorder*

If substance-induced cognitive impairments persist after the usual duration of intoxication or withdrawal, substance/medication-induced neurocognitive disorder may be diagnosed. The specific types of symptoms depend on the type of substance that is involved. Typically, the symptoms are preceded by a long history of drug or medication use; the resulting impairment can show gradual improvement over months, although in some cases symptoms persist even after an extended period of abstinence. Several classes of substances can induce neurocognitive disorders, including alcohol, sedatives and anxiolytics, anticonvulsants, and toxins (including lead, mercury, carbon monoxide, and solvents). Alcohol may be the most common causative substance (American Psychiatric Association, 2013).

> How are the memory impairments of dementia and amnesia different?

Both dementias and **amnestic disorders**, which involve memory impairments that affect the ability to learn and recall new information (i.e., **anterograde amnesia**), can be substance-induced. The ability to recall previously learned material (**retrograde amnesia**) may or may not be affected, depending on severity. Unlike delirium, the memory impairment in amnestic disorders is not associated with impaired consciousness or deficiency in attention; unlike dementia, amnestic disorders are usually not accompanied by cognitive deficits such as aphasia or disturbed executive functioning.

Those with substance-induced amnestic disorders often perseverate (that is, they repeat actions or words). As discussed in Chapter 12, a particularly characteristic symptom is **confabulation**, in which the amnestic person attempts to fill in gaps of memory by inventing stories or explanations which can seem confused, unplanned, often inconsistent, and sometimes exotic. Rather than a conscious attempt to deceive, confabulation appears instead to be a way to avoid uncomfortable uncertainty. The person shows no recognition that the stories may seem outlandish, are incorrect, or may be judged to be falsehoods by the listener.

Confabulation can occur in other memory disturbances, as well, but is most commonly seen as a component of alcohol-induced amnestic confabulatory neurocognitive disorder. Individuals with an alcohol-induced amnestic disorder are able to remember new information for only a short period of time; for example, they can repeat back digits correctly within a few seconds, but are unable to remember anything that happened more than 25 minutes ago. The most well-known example may be alcohol-induced persisting amnestic disorder, which usually occurs in those over age 40 who have histories of heavy alcohol use spanning several years. Often labeled Korsakoff's syndrome, it may be produced by a nutritional deficiency of thiamine (vitamin B-1), as a result of acquiring most daily calories from alcohol rather than necessary foods. The onset may be abrupt, associated with confusion, ataxia, eye-movement difficulties, and other neurological problems. If treated early with large doses of thiamine, the amnestic disturbance can sometimes be prevented. Once established, however, alcohol-induced persisting amnestic disorder continues indefinitely, with some persons showing slight improvement and others exhibiting chronic impairment requiring custodial care. In the case of other substance-induced amnestic conditions (such as those resulting from prolonged heavy use of hypnotics or sedatives), the prognosis may be better: the persisting dementia may improve, and full recovery is often possible (American Psychiatric Association, 2013).

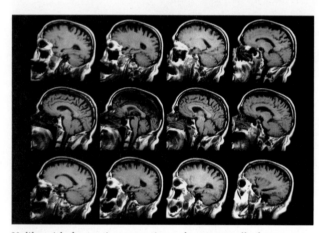

Unlike with dementia, amnestic syndromes usually do not produce specific brain abnormalities evident on CT or MRI scans. (iStock)

**Amnestic disorders**

Disorders in which the ability to learn and recall new information is impaired, without impaired consciousness or cognitive deficits

**Anterograde amnesia**

Loss of ability to form new memories

**Retrograde amnesia**

Inability to recall events that occurred before the onset of the amnesia

**Confabulation**

Filling gaps in memory with imaginary recollection

## 15.3c Other Causal Diseases for Neurocognitive Disorder

### Huntington's Disease *behavioral changes first.*

Huntington's disease is inherited through a single dominant gene on the short arm of chromosome 4; and it causes a progressive degenerative condition affecting cognition, emotion, and movement. The motor dysfunction, which includes involuntary, spasmodic jerking of the limbs, led to the name Huntington's chorea for the condition ("chorea" meaning "dance" in Greek); it is produced by irreversible damage to the brain in the basal ganglia. The children of a parent with this disorder have a 50% chance of being afflicted. However, the symptoms do not ordinarily appear until people are in their thirties or early forties, so many of those affected do not know whether they have the condition until after reaching their reproductive years and perhaps transmitting the gene to their own children. (There are now genetic tests that can confirm whether or not a person carries the genes.) First symptoms appear as slow and insidious changes in mood and behavior but progress to include apraxia, apathy, involuntary tremors in the arms or legs, difficulty in maintaining balance while walking, smacking of the lips and tongue, and disorganized speech and psychotic features. Motor dysfunction eventually makes speech unintelligible, and patients eventually become nonambulatory (American Psychiatric Association, 2013). Postmortem analyses typically show circumscribed cerebral atrophy, especially in the temporal and parietal lobes (Garrett, et al., 1998).

### Parkinson's Disease *body changes first.*

Parkinson's disease is a slowly progressive neurological degeneration that produces major neurocognitive disorder in up to 75% of affected individuals (American Psychiatric Association, 2013). It may be the second most common progressive dementia, after DAT (Greicius, Geschwind, & Miller, 2002). Physical signs include resting motor tremor, rigidity, slow movement, and postural instability. These symptoms are related to destruction of dopamine-producing neurons in the basal ganglia; the resulting decreased dopamine activity can be partially counteracted by administration of the dopamine precursor L-dopa. Cognitive slowing, memory impairment, and disturbance of executive function often associated with depression are also among the psychological symptoms. A minority of Parkinson's disease patients go on to develop dementia, as the degenerative process results in a reduction in volume and atrophy in the amygdala and hippocampus (Bouchard, et al., 2008). Besides loss of dopaminergic neurons, other observable brain changes

Actor Michael J. Fox, who suffers from Parkinson's disease, speaks to the media during a press conference on stem cell research at the United States Capitol in 2005. (AP Wide World)

include deterioration of serotonin neurons (Azmitia & Nixon, 2008) and widespread Lewy body pathology (abnormal accumulations of proteins) in the hippocampus, correlating with cognitive decline (Farlow & Cummings, 2008).

*Lewy Bodies: unhealthy proteins accumulate in the brain. Fast acceleration. symptoms like Alzheimers & Parkinsons.*

### Creutzfeldt-Jakob Disease *type of prion disease.*

Creutzfeldt-Jakob disease is a type of *spongiform encephalopathy* (that is, tiny holes form in the cortex, giving it the appearance of a sponge), caused either by slow viruses or by *prions*, which are abnormal, misshapen proteins. The disease can, therefore, be transmitted to other people; and the responsible agents are resistant to many normal techniques of infection control, including boiling, alcohol, and ultraviolet radiation. (Bleach is effective for decontamination, however). Creutzfeldt-Jakob disease has been transmitted during corneal transplants, neurosurgery

*prion disease: proteins fold over on themselves and then begin to clump in brain. Transmissible. They multiply. Fast acting. No cure.*

*Kuru: eating human brain. type of prion disease.*

and brain biopsy, by human growth factor injection, and (in the case of bovine spongiform encephalopathy) from cattle to humans in food as "mad cow disease." Early signs may be neurocognitive disorder due to prior disease and include fatigue, appetite, sleep problems, or anxiety, followed later by gait and motor difficulties, vision problems, and a rapidly progressing dementia. The rare disorder affects men and women equally; death occurs within 12 months for 90% of affected patients (Greicius, Geschwind, & Miller, 2002). In the *DSM-5*, the diagnosis connected to Creutzfeldt-Jakob disease is neurocognitive disorder due to prion disease.

## 15.3d Major or Mild Neurocognitive Disorder Due to Another Medical Condition

A variety of other medical conditions, including vitamin deficiency, hypoxia, and encephalitis, can produce the dementias and amnestic conditions that comprise neurocognitive disorders. Unlike dementia, there are usually no specific brain abnormalities evident on CT or MRI scans that can be identified as etiologically important in amnesia; instead, careful physical assessment and evidence of a temporal relationship between memory impairment and the medical disorder is important in diagnosing the condition. In some types of general medical conditions (such as hypoxia), the impairments may be broadly generalized. A specific form of transient memory disturbance, termed "transient global amnesia," describes impaired ability to learn new information with variable impairment in recalling events just before or during a stroke. Other types of transient amnesia may be traced to seizures or reversible metabolic conditions (American Psychiatric Association, 2000).

# Chapter Review

## TO SUM UP ...

- The causative events for neurocognitive disorders are identifiable general medical conditions, substances, or medications that affect brain functioning.

- Delirium is a rapidly developing disturbance of consciousness that can result from high fever, metallic poisoning, drugs, and certain kinds of brain injuries. In this condition the person is confused, disoriented, and often incoherent.

- Delirium is a relatively brief disturbance. If the underlying physical problem is resolved, the person usually recovers completely. It is most likely to occur in either children or elderly persons.

- Dementia is a chronic condition involving deterioration from one's previous level of cognitive functioning, memory, abstract thinking, and judgment. This syndrome can result from degenerative processes, infectious diseases, tumors, strokes, and brain injuries. The risk for dementia increases with age.

- Dementia does not involve a disturbance of consciousness, but does involve language and cognitive impairments. Disturbances in the expression or comprehension of language (aphasia), in the ability to execute motor functions (apraxia), in the ability to recognize common objects or familiar people (agnosia), or in the ability to plan and execute complex activities (i.e., executive functioning) are present.

- Alzheimer's disease is a progressive deterioration of the brain that is among the most common causes of dementia. Other causes of progressive dementias include Huntington's disease, Pick's disease, and Creutzfeldt-Jakob disease. Treatment for these conditions attempts to slow the progression of brain damage and to improve the person's life, but the dementia is irreversible.

- Non-progressive dementias include those caused by single strokes or head injuries, or those induced by drugs, medication, or toxins. The extent of dementia is associated with the degree of brain damage; however, the damage does not progress, and the dementia may stabilize or improve.

- Amnestic disorders involve impairments of memory and the ability to learn new information. The amnestic disorders are not associated with the global impairment in cognitive functioning that describes the dementias or with the disturbance of consciousness that defines delirium.

- Amnestic disorders caused by general medical conditions may be transient with later recovery of memory function. Those induced by the persisting effects of alcohol tend to be permanent.

## KEY TERMS

## QUESTIONS FOR STUDY

- Contrast the types of memory impairments associated with delirium, dementia, and amnestic disorders.

- How can dissociative amnesia, amnestic disorder, and malingering be distinguished?

- Describe how a diagnosis of DAT could be confirmed.

- Discuss how dementia differs from amnestic syndrome.

## POP QUIZ

1. The discovery that general paresis is caused by _____ was a landmark in the development of the organic view of psychopathology.
   A. head injury
   B. syphilis
   C. acetylcholine deficiency
   D. lead poisoning

2. Walter is suffering from a spatial disorder in which he is unable to draw anything on his left visual field. He is not able to draw a complete clock, nor is he able to shave his whole face. He is unaware of his deficits and suffers from _____.
   A. neglect syndrome
   B. apraxia
   C. Broca's aphasia
   D. agnosia

3.  A stroke occurs when _____.
    A.  the heart stops beating
    B.  blood flow to the brain is interrupted
    C.  a seizure disrupts neuronal transmissions
    D.  head injury causes damage to the frontal lobe

4.  The emotional, perceptual, and speech disturbances of delirium can resemble other psychotic conditions, except for their _____.
    A.  fragmented and fluctuating presentation
    B.  slow and gradual onset
    C.  psychological stressor origination
    D.  more rational content

5.  Dementia has a(n) _____ course, whereas delirium has a(n) _____ onset.
    A.  chronic, acute
    B.  acute, chronic
    C.  organic, toxic
    D.  chronic, toxic

6.  Larry is unable to recite the alphabet, count backwards from 100, or address an envelope. Larry's impairments would best be described as _____.
    A.  confabulations
    B.  aphasia
    C.  apraxia
    D.  disturbances in executive function

7.  What is the most obvious problem during the beginning stages of dementia?
    A.  inability to recognize faces
    B.  inability to recall distant events
    C.  inability to recall recent events
    D.  inability to care for self

8.  In Alzheimer's disease, beta amyloid protein fragments and degenerated axon terminals accumulate in deposits called _____.
    A.  spongiforms
    B.  prions
    C.  infarcts
    D.  senile plaques

9.  Focal (localized) brain damage is more likely a consequence of _____.
    A.  stroke
    B.  oxygen deprivation
    C.  poison ingestion
    D.  malnutrition

10. The introduction of newer antiretroviral therapies has reduced the incidence of neurocognitive disease due to _____.
    A.  HIV infection
    B.  Huntington's disease
    C.  Parkinson's disease
    D.  Alzheimer's disease

11. Parkinson's disease symptoms are related to destruction of _____ neurons in the basal ganglia.
    A. GABA-producing
    B. dopamine-producing
    C. serotonin-producing
    D. acetylcholine-producing

12. The children of persons who have Huntington's disease have a _____ chance of being afflicted with the disease themselves.
    A. 10%
    B. 25%
    C. 50%
    D. 75%

13. Unlike _____, the memory impairment in amnestic disorders is not associated with impaired consciousness or deficiency in attention.
    A. Pick's disease
    B. delirium
    C. Huntington's disease
    D. dementia

14. When does an individual demonstrate confabulation?
    A. When the individual has impairments in the ability to plan and complete actions.
    B. When the individual repeats actions or words.
    C. When the individual fails to recognize familiar objects or people.
    D. When the individual invents stories and explanations to fill in gaps of memory.

15. Korsakoff syndrome is a disorder usually associated with _____.
    A. stroke
    B. Alzheimer's disease
    C. Lewy bodies
    D. chronic alcoholism

Additional study resources are available at **www.BVTLab.com**

# CHAPTER OVERVIEW

# CHAPTER OPENER QUESTIONS

Who treats mental disorders?

What makes a person incompetent to stand trial?

What is insanity?

Can a person be insane but competent? Incompetent but sane?

How easy is it to escape punishment for a crime by pleading insanity?

How dangerous are ex-mental patients?

How long does involuntary commitment last?

Can people with mental disorders be given treatment against their will?

Should psychologists prescribe medication?

(Shutterstock)

# Legal, Ethical, and Professional Issues in Abnormal Psychology

To this point, we have reviewed the historical development and current status of abnormal psychology, including the nature of mental disorders, their classification, their causes, and their treatments. In Chapter 16 we consider some of the professional issues that come into play in the provision of psychological and psychiatric services to people dealing with these conditions. A variety of legal, ethical, and professional guidelines direct the way recipients are assessed and treated, in both civil and criminal situations. Thus, in this chapter, we also present how these guidelines can impact providers, recipients, and the relationships between them.

## 16.1 Who Treats Mental Disorders?

There are a variety of professionals who have been trained in the assessment and treatment of psychological difficulties. Training beyond a 4-year college degree is necessary in order to

> **Who treats mental disorders?**

be able to work independently as a mental health professional, but there are circumstances in which people with a bachelor's degree can participate in the treatment process. Each state has its own policies that describe the scope of practice of professions like psychology and psychiatry. These general descriptions will illustrate the differences between some of the more common treatment disciplines.

*Psychiatrists* are medical doctors who have completed a specialization in psychiatry, after earning the MD degree (generally, 4 to 6 years of schooling beyond the bachelor's degree). After the appropriate psychiatric rotation and training, and subsequent board certification, they are qualified to independently diagnose and treat mental disorders. Psychiatric treatment typically involves the use of prescription medication although sometimes psychiatrists employ somatic treatments such as ECT and also may provide various types of psychotherapies.

*Clinical Psychologists* have completed doctoral training leading to either the PhD (Doctor of Philosophy) or Psy.D. (Doctor of Psychology) degree, generally 4 to 6 years of schooling beyond the bachelor's degree. Clinical psychologists have also completed a supervised internship; and after earning board certification or licensure to practice, they are qualified to independently diagnose and treat mental disorders. Although they do not currently prescribe medications, a movement in that direction is underway, which would require additional training (this is discussed later in the chapter). Some psychologists hold a Master's Degree (generally, 2 to 3 years of schooling beyond the Bachelor's Degree) and may become licensed as Psychological Associates who can treat mental disorders but may be required to work under the supervision of a PhD or Psy.D.

*Counseling Psychologists* typically hold either doctoral or masters degrees in psychology and may have acquired the credential of Licensed Professional Counselor or Marriage and Family Therapist. They frequently provide assessment and counseling services to those with less severe disturbances such as marital problems and life or career difficulties.

***Psychiatric Nurse Practitioners*** have completed training leading to the MSN (Master of Science in Nursing) degree (generally, 2 to 3 years of training beyond the bachelor's degree). After completing clinical rotation and passing their nursing boards, they are qualified to diagnose and treat mental disorders and may prescribe medication under the periodic supervision of an MD.

***Clinical Social Workers*** have completed training leading to the MSW (Master of Social Work) degree, usually 1 to 2 years of schooling beyond the bachelor's degree. Once they complete the requirements of supervised practice leading to the LCSW (Licensed Clinical Social Worker) credential, they are qualified to provide therapy to those with mental disorders or less severe disturbances.

## 16.2 The Interface of Mental Disorders and the Law

The diagnosis and treatment of mental disorders usually takes place within the general confines of the health industry. The vast majority of individuals with psychological problems can receive assistance from professional clinicians at local community mental health centers or clinics, or in the offices of private practitioners. Distress can be relieved; and functioning can improve through the effective use of therapy, medication, education, and preventative practices.

Sometimes, however, those with mental disorders find themselves involved in the legal system. Perhaps they have acted in ways that led others to doubt their ability to make their own decisions in life, or perhaps their disturbed behavior put others in danger or threatened their own safety. In these situations, laws concerning civil commitment and involuntary hospitalization may be invoked to provide treatment—even if the individual opposes it. Alternatively, a person with a mental disorder may have engaged in actions that violated criminal law. Competency and sanity rulings may then be applied as courts determine whether that person should be held legally responsible for actions that may have occurred as a result of a psychotic misperception of reality or, indeed, whether he or she is even capable of participating in the legal process.

Psychological and psychiatric evaluations are essential for providing critical information needed to render a judgment on commitment, competency, or insanity. Mental health professionals recognize, however, that the people they evaluate can be members of a fragile, distressed population whose legal rights and protections could easily be violated in the context of mandated treatment or involuntary hospitalization. Privacy issues are important in all health matters, but the social stigma associated with mental disorders makes it particularly important that the professionals collecting intimate psychological information follow strict ethical and legal guidelines about how those data are kept secure.

These issues illustrate the interesting and developing area of mental health law and forensic psychology. The rules that govern the process of commitment and the determination of legal responsibility have evolved over the years, and they vary from state to state and between countries. There is much debate about when, or if, a person is not responsible for his or her actions, extending to the very foundation of the notion of "free will," as well as fundamental questions about the extent of the state's responsibility to protect its citizens from themselves. The process of legal determination is also less precise than that of clinical diagnosis, frequently requiring predictions of what might happen or estimates of the probability of dangerous behavior in future situations—issues on which experts in psychology and psychiatry will often disagree.

**Competency**

The mental ability to handle one's own legal affairs, and to understand and assist in legal proceedings

## 16.2a Competency to Stand Trial

**Competency** concerns an individual's mental ability to handle his or her own legal affairs. In the American legal system, a person facing criminal charges has the right to a legal defense during court proceedings before a verdict is rendered. When defendants are mentally disturbed, however, their ability to legally defend themselves may be uncertain, requiring a determination of competence.

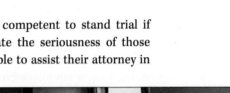

What makes a person incompetent to stand trial?

In most jurisdictions, people charged with a crime are competent to stand trial if they (a) understand the nature of the charges, (b) appreciate the seriousness of those charges and the possible results of a conviction, and (c) are able to assist their attorney in their own defense. Typically, defendants are assumed to be competent, barring arguments and evidence to the contrary. If the issue of trial competency is raised, the court usually orders a psychological evaluation to screen for the presence of a mental disorder and ascertain an individual's level of functioning and understanding of the legal situation. The evaluation may include psychological testing, interviews, observations, and careful consideration of diagnosis in order to reach an opinion about whether or not the individual is too disturbed to participate in legal proceedings. Additional evaluations may be arranged by either the prosecution or the defense. The determination of competency is made by the judge, after receiving the opinions of the evaluators who have examined the person.

Defendants are typically assumed to be competent to stand trial, barring arguments and evidence to the contrary. (iStock)

If the person is ruled to be incompetent to stand trial, the legal proceedings may be put on hold while he or she receives treatment to restore competency. The hope is that after a period of confinement and treatment for their mental disorder, such persons will regain their mental capacities enough to participate in their defense against the charges. Not infrequently, this may take weeks or months, during which time the legal "clock" is stopped, pending a final determination. The issue of guilt or innocence does not arise at this stage of the legal proceeding, only the ability of a person to move through the court process.

This legal procedure has, at times, led to long-term confinement without the safeguards of a trial, as the example of Louis Perroni demonstrates. Perroni operated a filling station in Syracuse, New York. During a 1955 confrontation with developers seeking to build a shopping center on the site where his station was operating, Perroni had fired a warning shot into the air with a rifle. Shortly thereafter he was arrested by police. At the request of the district attorney, the Onondaga County Court judge ordered him to undergo a pretrial psychiatric examination to determine his fitness to stand trial. He was seen by two court-appointed psychiatrists, found incapable of standing trial, and committed to the Matteawan State Hospital. He continually requested to go forward with the legal proceedings, but it was 7 years before he was allowed another hearing on his competency. Despite the fact that for the first time a psychiatrist (Thomas Szasz) retained by the defense testified that Perroni was competent to stand trial, the judge again found him incompetent; and he was sent back to Matteawan State Hospital. Louis Perroni was finally released from Matteawan State Hospital in 1968. He returned to Onondaga County for trial on the original charges, at which time the charges were dismissed. He had been incarcerated for 13 years.

Fortunately, the rights of individuals to be protected from unreasonable detentions based on incompetency to stand trial have been bolstered since the time of Perroni's difficulties. The U.S. Supreme Court (*Jackson v. Indiana*, 1972) considered a case in which an intellectually-deficient defendant, who was both deaf and mute and unable to read or write, was ruled incompetent and held for over 3.5 years on a "treat until competent" order. Had he been found competent and convicted of robbery (the crime with which he was originally charged), he would have instead received a sentence of 60 days. The Court ruled that the length of pretrial confinement should be limited; after some reasonable period of time, if it

BVT *Lab*

Flashcards are available for this chapter at www.BVTLab.com.

appears that the individual is not likely ever to become competent, then either the usual civil commitment procedures for involuntary hospitalization should be initiated, or the person should be released.

Assessing competency is often not an easy task. By virtue of the legal context, some clients are motivated to exaggerate symptoms or malinger, perhaps in the mistaken belief that a ruling of incompetency will make it easy to "beat" the charges. In one review of 105 criminal defendants referred for neuropsychological evaluation, the rate of probable and definite malingered neurocognitive dysfunction was over 50% (Ardolf, Denney, & Houston, 2007). Even when malingering is not involved, competency may be a fluctuating state for some defendants (e.g., those with recurrent episodes of psychosis), itself affected by the stresses of incarceration and the legal process. Not uncommonly, the expert opinions of prosecution evaluators are very different than the expert opinions of defense evaluators.

David Berkowitz, self-styled "Son of Sam," is a good example of the difficulty involved in determining competency to stand trial. Charged with killing six persons and wounding seven others, Berkowitz said that demons, speaking with the voices of barking dogs, had ordered him out on his late-night hunts for victims. Two court-appointed psychiatrists concluded that although he was aware of the murder charges, understood that they were criminal acts, and had the intellectual capacity to understand the legal process, a paranoid psychosis left Berkowitz so "emotionally dead" that he was neither capable of nor interested in assisting in his own defense. Therefore, in their opinion, Berkowitz was incompetent to stand trial. A third psychiatrist, however, maintained that Berkowitz made up the story about the demons and that he was competent to stand trial. The Court agreed with the third psychiatrist, Abrahamsen, and Berkowitz was tried and found guilty. Abrahamsen (1979) based his conclusion on a number of things: the general impression of mental coherence that Berkowitz made on fellow employees, his capacity for careful planning and eventually eluding the police for a long period of time, indications that Berkowitz could decide whether or not to obey the demons, and the report of one attempted murder that happened a year before Berkowitz said that the demons began to talk to him. Abrahamsen was apparently correct in his conclusion: Berkowitz himself, after his conviction, wrote a letter to Abrahamsen in which he said, "Yes, it was all a hoax, a silly hoax, well planned and thought out."

David Berkowitz claimed that demons speaking with the voices of barking dogs had ordered him to kill six persons. The court decided that he was competent to stand trial. (AP Wide World)

Besides criminal charges, there are other situations in which legal competency is an issue for those with mental disorders. A disturbed individual may be incompetent to make treatment choices or to conduct daily affairs (including financial and legal decisions). In these cases, the court may appoint another person (such as a relative, supportive friend, attorney, or clergyman) to be involved in such matters and to make decisions on the person's behalf. A treatment guardian, for example, is often appointed when a person with a mental disorder is too disturbed to make informed decisions about accepting or rejecting proposed treatment plans. Normally, treatment guardians serve until the person can resume personal authority over his or her own affairs.

**Sanity**

The mental ability to distinguish right from wrong, and to form the intent to commit an act such as a crime

## 16.2b  Not Guilty by Reason of Insanity

The matter of **sanity** is a different legal issue from that of competency. Sanity has to do with the person's mental state at the time of the crime, not the trial. Accordingly, the concept is connected to the notion of responsibility over one's actions

**What is insanity?**

and therefore, over guilt or innocence. Again, careful psychological evaluation is necessary to reach an opinion about the defendant's mental state at the time a crime was committed, and the results of these assessments (from experts on both sides of the case) are presented in court. Often, experts disagree on their opinions, and judges and juries must make the final determination of whether or not the person is legally responsible for the crime. It is important to note that a person must first be competent to enter legal proceedings before he or she can be judged not guilty by reason of insanity. It is also apparent that someone could be sane at the time of the offense, but incompetent to stand trial once the proceedings begin. The two issues, therefore, involve independent judgments of mental status at different points in time.

At the very core of the rule of law is the assumption that individuals bear responsibility for their actions; otherwise, the punishments of law would have no value in the deterrence of crime. Still, there is a long tradition in English law that if persons are so mentally deranged that they have no comprehension of the meaning of their criminal acts, then they are not legally responsible for those acts. Like all legal concepts, the notion of insanity has been shaped from a series of case rulings.

One famous case that affected the interpretation of the insanity plea was that of Daniel McNaughton, a Scotsman, who in 1843 was tried for the murder of a man whom he had believed to be the home secretary of the British government. In fact, McNaughton had mistakenly killed the wrong man, a government clerk. He explained his action by saying that he had been "instructed by the voice of God." His clearly deranged behavior was evident to the court, and the verdict was not guilty on the ground of insanity. Queen Victoria, who had herself been the target of at least three previous assassination attempts, was shocked by the finding and asked that it be reviewed. Subsequently, a committee of judges described the criteria that should be applied to such cases in the future: in order for a defendant to be ruled innocent by reason of insanity, it must be shown that "the accused was laboring under such defect of reason from disease of the mind, as not to know the nature and quality of the act he was doing, or as not to know that what he was doing was wrong." The **McNaughton rule**, as it came to be known, with its emphasis on knowing right from wrong, dominated the legal interpretation of mental disorders until recent times and remains an aspect of current insanity law.

Queen Victoria's comment on the attempted assassination of Sir Robert Peel on January 20, 1843, reflected the attitude of many Englishmen. When Daniel McNaughton shot Peel's secretary in the mistaken belief that he had killed the Prime Minister and was absolved of the crime on the ground of insanity, the public was outraged. The controversy continues as to whether a person should or should not be held responsible for a crime because of a mental disorder. (AP Wide World)

The Alabama Supreme Court, in *Parsons vs. State* (1887), expanded the conditions under which the insanity defense might be acceptable. It ruled that even if a person committing a criminal act could tell right from wrong, that person might be not guilty by reason of insanity if a pathological drive or impulse that the individual could not control had compelled the crime. In this **irresistible impulse rule**, the criminal act could be seen as the product of the mental disorder, rather than the person who could not resist acting. The irresistible impulse rule is sometimes referred to as the "policeman over the shoulder" rule, suggesting that a truly unpreventable act would have been committed even if a policeman were looking over the defendant's shoulder at the time. The effect of this, and similar rulings, was to provide a defense for "crimes of passion" or "temporary insanity"—if the irresistible impulse was a momentary one. Of course, a major problem with this standard is the difficulty in distinguishing impulses that a person cannot control from impulses that a person simply does not control.

By the mid-twentieth century, the psychiatric profession had become more and more critical of these approaches. The McNaughton rule, they believed, was based on a conception of people as rational beings who made free choices informed by conscious considerations. Modern psychiatry, influenced by Freud and other adherents of the psychodynamic movement, however, preferred a model that included irrational and unconscious, as well as

**McNaughton rule**

Legal guideline that insanity concerns an individual's inability to distinguish right from wrong in committing the crime

**Irresistible impulse rule**

Legal guideline that insanity concerns a person's inability to resist committing the crime

*insanity defense normally longer sentences.*

conscious, determinants of behavior. The psychiatrists argued that it was difficult for them to testify as to whether a defendant knew right from wrong but that they could bring their expertise to bear on whether the accused was suffering from a mental disturbance. In 1959 Judge Bazelon of the United States Court of Appeals, acknowledging these points, wrote an opinion in the Durham case that formulated a third test of criminal responsibility. The **Durham rule** held that an accused person is not criminally responsible if it is shown that the unlawful act was the product of a mental disease or defect.

In Judge Bazelon's view, however, the Durham rule never accomplished its intended goal; and 18 years later, in 1972, he favored its abandonment (Bazelon, 1974). The basic problem, according to Bazelon, is that when psychiatrists testify, they limit themselves to conclusions (for example, that the defendant is "mentally ill") without providing the jury with understandable evidence to support their conclusion or, for that matter, illuminating what the term "mentally ill" means in a given case. Psychiatric testimony, according to Bazelon, should be submitted to the same scrutiny and examination as any other kind of opinion presented in court. It is not clear what a "product of a mental disorder" is, whereas it is clear that expert psychiatric witnesses disagree about their opinions in such cases.

Further, the Durham rule did not address the issues of "right from wrong" or of irresistible impulse, allowing defendants to claim that simply carrying the diagnosis of any disorder recognized by mental health professionals could be the "cause" of any criminal action they committed.

> Can a person be insane but competent? Incompetent but sane?

In light of the persisting criticism and dissatisfaction with definitions of insanity to that point, the American Law Institute (American Law Institute, 1962) issued a more comprehensive standard in 1962 in its Model Penal Code. The ALI standard stated that:

1. A person is not responsible for criminal conduct if at the time of such conduct, as a result of mental disease or defect, he lacks the substantial capacity either to appreciate the criminality (wrongfulness) of his conduct or to conform his conduct to the requirements of the law.

2. As used in this Article, the terms 'mental disease or defect' do not include an abnormality manifested only by repeated criminal or otherwise antisocial conduct.

**Durham rule**

Legal guideline that insanity concerns the extent to which the criminal act was a product of mental disorder

It is apparent that this standard incorporates components of each of the earlier rulings but also appears to exclude sociopathic behavior, conduct disorder, and antisocial personality disorder from the conditions that qualify for the insanity defense. Later rulings determined that voluntary use of drugs or alcohol could not serve to create a "temporary insanity" defense for a crime under the ALI standard as well. Some legal experts (e.g., Winick, 1995) have suggested that there are also good reasons to exclude personality disorders, impulse control disorders, and most psychosexual paraphilias from meeting the legal requirements of "mental disease," either for the insanity defense or for civil commitment, because their physical status as "illnesses" is questionable. (That legal argument perhaps incorrectly presumes that the "illness" status of other *DSM-IV* conditions has been physically established.)

Most states adopted the ALI standard as a framework for insanity cases. If the capacity to intend to commit a crime (i.e., criminal intent) is diminished by a mental disorder, a defendant could be found not guilty of the crime. However, diminished capacity arguments have continued to be controversial. When John Hinckley Jr. wounded President Ronald Reagan in an assassination attempt in 1981, he had carried a diagnosis of schizophrenia for several years and

John Hinckley Jr., who shot President Reagan in 1981, was found by a jury to be not guilty by reason of insanity. (AP Wide World)

had been obsessed with the actress Jodi Foster, to whom he had been mailing love letters. He explained shooting the President as an attempt to impress Foster so that she would then return his love. A jury found Hinckley not guilty by reason of insanity, accepting the argument that schizophrenia had diminished his capacity to understand the wrongfulness of the act or to conform to the law.

Public criticism of the Hinckley ruling, together with growing dissatisfaction with other verdicts, eventually led to the Federal Insanity Defense Reform Act, passed by the U.S. Congress in 1984, describing the insanity standard for all federal courts to apply. Largely on the recommendation of the American Psychiatric Association (1983, December), the act limited the volitional component of conforming conduct to the law and partially returned to the McNaughton standard:

> *"A person charged with a criminal offense should be found not guilty by reason of insanity if it is shown that, as a result of mental disease or mental retardation, he was unable to appreciate the wrongfulness of his conduct at the time of his offense."*

The insanity defense frequently evokes skeptical reactions in people who wonder if it is not a strategy that clever lawyers use to get guilty clients acquitted. This skepticism is not helped much by the fact that one psychiatric "expert" may testify that a defendant was insane at the time of a crime and another psychiatric expert may testify that the defendant was sane. As one psychiatrist, experienced in legal testimony, put it, "... attorneys for the prosecution and defense will consult privately with as many potential psychiatric witnesses as necessary (when they can afford it) until they find one or two whose opinion they deem useful to their side" (Lunde, 1975).

Actually, the insanity defense is rarely used in the United States and is even more rarely successful; most such defendants are found sane by juries. Generally, only a small percentage of those raising the insanity defense, often less than 12%, are judged by forensic psychologists as meeting the requirements for insanity, although there is much variability between evaluators (Murrie & Wilson, 2005). Some high-profile cases involving successful and unsuccessful use of the insanity defense are shown in Table 16-1.

*Table 16-1*     **Some Famous Cases Involving the Defense of "Not Guilty by Reason of Insanity"**

| Case | Outcome |
| --- | --- |
| *1977*: Francine Hughes poured gasoline over her husband, while he was drunk and asleep, and set him on fire. She claimed she was not responsible due to years of beatings and threats. | Not guilty by reason of insanity |
| *1979*: Kenneth Bianchi claimed he had multiple personality disorder and, therefore, was not responsible for a series of murders and rapes in the Hillside Strangler case. | Guilty |
| *1981*: John Hinckley Jr. attempted to assassinate President Reagan in order to impress actress Jodi Foster. | Not guilty by reason of insanity |
| *1992*: Jeffrey Dahmer tortured, raped, killed, mutilated, and partially ate 15 young men. At trial, he initially entered a plea of not guilty by reason of insanity due to a severe paraphilia and then changed his plea to guilty but insane. | Guilty and sane |
| *1993*: Lorena Bobbitt cut off her husband's penis with a knife while he slept, after he came home drunk and raped her. She claimed depression and PTSD from years of abuse. | Not guilty by reason of insanity |
| *2000*: Michael McDermott gunned down seven co-workers and then claimed that Michael the Archangel had sent him to stop the Holocaust, and to earn a soul, by killing. | Guilty |
| *2001*: Andrea Yates drowned her five children in a bathtub to save them from damnation due to the sinful life she was leading. She had been diagnosed with postpartum psychosis. | Guilty; sentenced to life term in 2002; new trial granted, found not guilty by reason of insanity in 2006 |
| *2002*: Lee Boyd Malvo participated in the Beltway sniper shootings of 12 people in VA and MA. He pled not guilty by reason of insanity because his will was under the complete control of co-shooter John Allen Muhammad. | Guilty |

As is the case in evaluations of competency, sanity examinations must deal with the issues of correct diagnosis and of accurately distinguishing actual from feigned symptoms. When the defendant purportedly suffers from intellectual disability, that determination can be difficult. Of course, someone with significant intellectual deficits could not "fake good" on an intelligence test—yet someone with average or above intelligence could attempt to "fake bad." This becomes important in the light of a U.S. Supreme Court ruling (*Atkins v. Virginia*, 2002) prohibiting the execution of mentally retarded (i.e., intellectually disabled) defendants. The ruling is interesting because it specifies the presence of a condition, rather than a diminished capacity, in assessing legal responsibility (Bonnie, 2004). Unfortunately, standardized intelligence tests are not very sensitive to malingering; and although neuropsychological assessments may be better in that regard, they are not specific to intellectual disability (Graue, et al., 2007). Shandera and her colleagues (2010) administered the Wechsler Adult Intelligence Scale, as well as a series of 10 common neurological screening devices, to 24 adults with intellectual disability and 35 matched community volunteers, 10 of whom answered items honestly while the other 25 were instructed to feign intellectual disability. Of the 11 indicators commonly used to detect neurological or intellectual feigning, only one (the Test of Memory Malingering) showed adequate specificity detecting feigned intellectual disability. Generally, the newer neurological screens were ineffective in distinguishing those with actual intellectual disability and those pretending to have intellectual disability. The authors concluded that there is a need for a new approach for detecting intentional falsification of intellectual disability.

In the past, the end result has been little different for defendants whether they were found sane or insane. In the former case, they spent many years in prison; in the latter case they spent, on the average, about the same number of years confined to a mental hospital (Lunde, 1975). Daniel McNaughton, though found "not guilty," spent the last 22 years of his life in an institution for the criminally insane, where he received essentially no treatment. John Hinckley Jr. remains under the supervision of St. Elizabeth's Hospital, more than 30 years after his attack on Reagan, although he has been allowed furloughs and home visits with his parents since 1999. In fact, there is no legal connection between the hypothetical criminal sentence for an offense and the length of time of commitment. The U.S. Supreme Court ruled that those acquitted by reason of insanity could be held under indefinite commitment until they proved themselves no longer dangerous, even if this is longer than the sentence that conviction would have carried (*Jones v. United States*, 1983).

However, some judicial rulings have made it more difficult to keep individuals involuntarily confined in mental hospitals. For example, in 1974, 200 criminally insane persons were released from Michigan state hospitals because the Michigan Supreme Court ruled that individuals could not be confined if they were not currently mentally disordered (Herbert, 1993). In response to the public outcry that followed, the Michigan legislature changed the law so that a person can be found "guilty but mentally ill." If so convicted, treatment for the mental disorder is provided; when treatment is completed, the person is returned to prison to serve out the remainder of the sentence. Release becomes a decision for the justice system, not the mental health system. Several states now have versions of this approach, which implies responsibility for criminal behavior but attempts, at the same time, to treat whatever mental disorder may be related to the criminal behavior.

> How easy is it to escape punishment for a crime by pleading insane?

Notions of insanity may be quite different in other national jurisdictions. On July 22, 2011, Anders Behring Breivik set off a fertilizer-based car bomb near government buildings in Oslo, Norway, killing 8 and injuring 209. Then, dressed in a police uniform and armed with a rifle and pistol, he boarded a ferry to the island of Utoeya. Nearly 600 young people were staying on the island at a government-sponsored political youth camp. Breivik began shooting at random, killing 69 and wounding more than 33 while he repeated shouted, "You are going to die today, Marxists!" He called Norway's emergency number at least twice during the spree to surrender, hanging up both times, and continued the killing between the phone calls. After more than an hour, he was finally arrested by Norwegian police. Once captured, Breivik admitted his guilt and justified his actions as necessary ones, to prevent the "Islamisation" of Norway. In fact, he had published online a 1,500 page white supremacist, anti-Muslim, anti-feminist manifesto entitled "2083: A European Declaration of Independence" in which he described his preparations and training in the lead-up to the attacks (BBC News, 2011). Under Norwegian law, the McNaughton standard is not recognized; a diagnosis of active psychosis is sufficient for an insanity ruling, without regard for such additional issues as motivation or understanding right from wrong. Two court-appointed psychiatrists evaluated Breivik and found him to be delusional, and diagnosed him with paranoid schizophrenia. At trial, the prosecution asked the court to find Breivik insane. However, a public uproar over the finding erupted, and the court ordered another evaluation. The second team of psychiatrists reported that he was psychologically troubled, but not psychotic. The court ruled that although he showed narcissistic personality features, he was nonetheless sane; and he was imprisoned for a maximum of 21 years.

No doubt, the legal perspective of insanity and criminal responsibility will continue to evolve, through many cases yet to be decided. The *DSM-5* makes this statement in regard to the forensic use of the diagnostic manual:

> **"***In most situations, the clinical diagnosis of a DSM-5 mental disorder such as intellectual disability (intellectual developmental disorder), schizophrenia, major neurocognitive disorder, gambling disorder, or pedophilic disorder does not imply that an individual with such a condition meets legal criteria for the presence of a mental disorder or a specified legal standard (e.g., for competence, criminal responsibility, or disability) … Even when diminished control over one's behavior is a feature of the disorder, having the diagnosis in itself does not demonstrate that a particular individual is (or was) unable to control his or her behavior at a particular time.***"*
>
> (American Psychiatric Association, 2013, p. 25)

## 16.2c Civil Commitment

A much larger group of mentally disturbed individuals (who are accused of no crime) are faced with a different legal procedure, involuntary commitment to treatment facilities. Although many people with mental disorders seek treatment to relieve their distress, some do not. Civil commitment under a state's mental health code allows the state, under certain circumstances, to provide protection and treatment to unwilling persons. In most states, the legal grounds for civil commitment concern the degree to which the disordered person is dangerous to self or others by reason of a mental disorder.

> **How dangerous are ex-mental patients?**

Dangerousness, in this sense, is not limited to actively attempting to hurt other people (assaultiveness, for example) or actively endangering one's own life (i.e., suicidal intention). Self-negligence, lack of shelter, failing to adequately care for personal hygiene, failure to eat, or engaging in harmful activities (walking in traffic, or sleeping on railroad tracks) could also constitute grounds for civil commitment—if the danger to the person is clear and if it is the result of a mental disorder. In these instances, a judge may order that the person is admitted to a treatment facility for various lengths of time in order to receive appropriate evaluation and assistance.

Commitment proceedings vary from state to state. Most states have laws that include provisions for brief, emergency commitments (usually for a few days or up to a week) that are used when immediate action is needed, and a longer period of commitment, if more extended intervention is needed. Typically, one or more persons must file an affidavit containing evidence that the subject suffers from a mental disorder and represents a danger to self or others. A court order is then issued requiring the person named to enter a hospital or other facility for observation and a psychiatric examination; this usually takes approximately 72 hours, but in some cases may take considerably longer. A hearing is then conducted at which testimony is taken from interested parties and from one or more mental health examiners (often psychologists or psychiatrists). The judge makes one of several decisions: (1) to dismiss the person, (2) to hold the person for further observation until the next hearing, or (3) to commit the person for treatment, often for periods of time ranging from 1 month to 6 months.

Of course, the decision to lock an unwilling person into a treatment facility is not taken lightly, and courts require strong grounds for doing so. Because of a history of past abuses and the determined work of such groups as the American Civil Liberties Union, many states have shifted the balance considerably toward the rights of the individual, making involuntary commitments

> **How long does involuntary commitment last?**

more difficult to obtain and making it easier for the patient to get out of the hospital after commitment. This tendency has been reinforced by a decision of the U.S. Supreme Court, which ruled unanimously that people may not be civilly committed to mental institutions unless the state has presented "clear and convincing" evidence that they require involuntary hospitalization (*Addington v. Texas*, 1979). In some cases, the dangerousness to self or others is so immediate and apparent that it is clear that acting swiftly to protect society or the individual is necessary. At other times, however, the degree of dangerousness is inferred, or predicted, based on the current psychological state and previous actions of the person.

Like a meteorologist predicting the weather, the psychologist assessing the likelihood of future violence may issue incorrect forecasts. Meteorology uses very advanced technology and global information capacities to issue forecasts that can be surprisingly accurate; if the chance of rain over the next 24 hours is 70%, rain is measured about 70% of the time—accuracy that may be much better than the prediction of violence by a psychologist or psychiatrist. Yet even in the arguably simpler situation of a nonbiological system like meteorology, the accuracy of weather forecasting falls off sharply a day or so in advance; and predictions more than 6 days in advance are not much better than chance. Psychologists often have much less technical information available to them but are usually asked by courts to predict violence over much longer periods (Monahan & Steadman, 1996).

The prediction of future dangerousness is, therefore, a very inexact science fraught with difficulties, and the results of mistakes can be serious. Concluding that a person is dangerous, when in fact he or she is not, often amounts to violating that person's constitutional rights by forced incarceration in the absence of criminal conviction. On the other hand, concluding that a person is not dangerous, when in fact he or she is, can lead to severe injuries and loss of life, possibly involving many victims. The basic conflict associated with involuntary commitment is thus between the civil liberties of the individual, on the one hand, and concerns of the larger society, protecting itself from dangerous people and providing sustenance and help for those too mentally incapacitated to understand their own plight.

One factor influencing the prediction of violence is the base rate at which it occurs within the population. Although social advocates have long argued that the rate of violence among people with mental disorders was essentially no different than that of the general population, in fact the prevalence of violence among those with a mental disorder is 5 times higher than among those without a mental disorder. Violence is elevated in those diagnosed with schizophrenia, major depression, bipolar disorder, and especially alcohol and drug abuse and dependence. As a result, these disorders are, also, disproportionately represented among the prison and jail populations. Still, more than 90% of those with mental disorders are not violent (Monahan, 1992).

Given the limits of predicting the future, experts testifying about the likelihood of aggression or violence face a very difficult task. Most often, cues such as previous history of aggression, substance abuse, psychotic components such as delusions and hallucinations, level of medication compliance, and conflict within the family are utilized in the predictions, although tests of these predictions indicate they are not significantly related to actual violence (Odeh, Zeiss, & Huss, 2006). Some progress has been made in the use of empirical predictors (Elbogen, 2002), but the current state of the science leaves much to be desired.

## 16.2d The Right to Treatment

Patients who are involuntarily committed are in a special circumstance: their liberty has been denied, but they have not been convicted of a crime and their legal rights remain intact. Court cases over the years have defined those rights to include the right to treatment, the right to receive that treatment in the least restrictive environment that is appropriate, and the right to refuse certain forms of treatment. As in other examples of mental health law, the recognition of these rights grew out of previous rulings involving their abuse.

In 1962 Charles Rouse, age 17, was walking after dark in Washington, D.C. Stopped by a policeman, he was found to be carrying a loaded pistol and some ammunition. Rouse, who already had a modest juvenile arrest record, was acquitted by reason of insanity, declared a "sociopath," and given an indeterminate commitment to St. Elizabeth's Hospital, the capital's main facility for the mentally disturbed. He remained there for 4.5 years before an appeal

reached, by luck, the court of Judge Bazelon. Bazelon sent the case back to the lower court with the injunction that it look into the question of whether Rouse had not, in fact, been deprived of his "right to treatment." The issue was taken up in the lower court although Rouse was freed on other grounds before this particular issue was resolved (Goodman, 1974).

The stage was set, however, for the question of "right to treatment" to be pursued. In 1970 just such a case developed in Alabama. A class action suit (*Wyatt v. Stickney*, 1971) was brought against the state of Alabama for not providing either mental patients or institutionalized mentally retarded individuals with a minimum degree of treatment. Treatment was extremely limited at both kinds of institutions; patients received primarily custodial care and were lucky if they were not abused by the hospital staff. District Judge Frank M. Johnson ruled in the class

St. Elizabeth's Hospital in Washington, DC, a facility for the mentally disturbed. (Wikimedia Commons)

action suit: "To deprive any citizen of his or her liberty upon the altruistic theory that the confinement is for humane therapeutic reasons and then fail to provide adequate treatment violates the very fundamentals of due process" (Goodman, 1974, p. 22).

The landmark *Wyatt* ruling went further, defining minimal physical standards that the institution must meet—including the numbers of showers and toilets, minimum patient-staff ratios, and patient rights concerning access to physical activity, fresh air, and compensation for work performed. It also expanded on the right of patients to receive treatment in the least restrictive conditions necessary for habilitation, and ordered the institutions to attempt to move patients toward less structured living and integration into the community.

George Wallace, then governor of Alabama, appealed the decision, arguing that no federal court has the power to tell a state how to allocate its resources. The Fifth Circuit Court of Appeals, however, supported the original ruling, reaffirming the concept of right to treatment as a matter of constitutional law. (Even before the

**Can people with mental disorders be given treatment against their will?**

appeal decision was reached, Alabama had reduced by 50% the number of patients in mental hospitals and had doubled the state's mental health budget.)

In 1975, the Supreme Court ruled unanimously in the case of Kenneth Donaldson (*O'Connor v. Donaldson*, 1975) that persons who are labeled mentally ill could not be confined against their will without treatment if they are not dangerous to themselves or others and are capable of surviving on the outside. Donaldson was confined involuntarily in a Florida mental hospital for nearly 15 years, during which time he maintained that he received no treatment while the hospital had repeatedly refused his petitions for release. The Court dismissed as "unpersuasive" the hospital superintendent's contention that the courts have no authority to pass on the adequacy of treatment, ruling that this was not the special province of the mental health professional.

The right to treatment and the right to the least restrictive environment have been reaffirmed in other court rulings, and today are well-established along with other protective provisions in the Protection and Advocacy for Mentally ill Individuals Act, passed by Congress in 1986. The act established a protection and advocacy system to safeguard the rights of those with serious mental disorders and to investigate allegations of abuse.

## 16.2e The Right to Refuse Treatment

Most states accept the right of a competent patient to refuse medical treatment. This typically extends, as well, to psychiatric or psychological patients who are voluntarily hospitalized. However, involuntary commitment mandates the state to provide treatment to an unwilling person, making the issue of refusal of treatment for mental disorders a challenging legal question. No clear and general guidelines cover the broad range of situations, except that courts have broadly supported *emergency* treatment, including medication, of violent or dangerous patients without their consent. The right of competent, involuntarily hospitalized patients in non-emergency situations to refuse treatment continues to be the source of some debate.

There have been some state rulings that patients can refuse certain interventions, such as electroconvulsive therapy and psychosurgery. The U.S. Supreme Court ruled (*Washington v. Harper*, 1990) that an incarcerated inmate could be given psychotropic medication against his will because he was dangerous and the pharmacological treatment was in his best interests. It is not clear to what extent the ruling applies in the case of involuntary civil commitment. For example, in a later ruling (*Riggins v. Nevada*, 1992), the Court ruled that a person could not be forced, while he was on trial, to take antipsychotic medication because of the potential for serious side effects such as tardive dyskinesia.

At present, there is no single right to refuse treatment under all situations but rather enormous variations among jurisdictions in many contexts, leaving the general issue of the right to refuse non-emergency treatment by the involuntarily committed unresolved. However, one is led to wonder why a state would involuntarily commit a patient it did not intend to treat; as some point out, nonconsensual treatment is, after all, what involuntary commitment is all about (Applebaum, 1988).

## 16.2f Deinstitutionalization

In practice, the growth of the mental institution as both an asylum for housing the mentally disturbed and a sanctuary for protection of the patient (and of society) was unfortunately accompanied by both neglect and abuse. Inpatient populations increased, conditions were substandard, and limited therapeutic options were available. In fact, many people became less able to function outside of the facilities the longer they were housed there—a process called **institutionalization**.

With the widespread availability of psychotropic medications in the 1950s, it became possible to control some of the florid symptoms of psychosis without confinement. By the 1970s, legal standards concerning the right to treatment in the least restrictive setting were in place as well, and state mental hospitals began to undergo profound change.

**Institutionalization**

The tendency for residents of an institution to become less able to function in the outside world the longer they remain within the institution

Many institutions were closed with the intent of transferring patients into less restrictive community settings. The population of patients housed inside of state hospitals decreased dramatically; by 1992, the number had been reduced by 77%, when compared to the number in 1970 (Witkin, Atay, & Manderscheid, 1996).

By most measures, the deinstitutionalization movement was successful in reintegrating those with mental disorders into supportive community programs where they could receive training in the skills needed for daily living and where outpatient medication management could take place. However, some authorities have questioned whether deinstitutionalization actually put former patients and society at greater risk. Frequently, services for former mental patients are fragmented, and many find themselves homeless without recourse to the asylum. Too often, these people become enmeshed in legal or social conflict and are housed within prisons and jails, choking the penal system (Rollin, 2000). There is also concern that inadequate supervision inhibits the ability to recognize signs of decompensation and suicidal behavior that would have been detected within an inpatient setting (Goldney, 2003).

The data on the potentially damaging effects of decentralizing and downsizing the mental health system have been inconsistent. Although many are concerned about increased risk of violent behavior, victimization, and suicide among former patients, others report more positive outcomes. A recent study in Finland, for example, found a decrease in patient suicides after release from hospitalization (Pirkola, Sohlman, Helia, & Wahlbeck, 2007), compared to rates before deinstitutionalization. Nonetheless, although there are many excellent aftercare programs with dedicated mental health professionals providing compassionate care, few would dispute the inadequacies of outpatient mental health treatment in the United States and elsewhere, or that homelessness and inappropriate legal incarceration have become major problems. With the disappearance of the mental institutions, finding available beds for psychiatric emergencies is now a chronic problem for every community. It is possible that the most compassionate compromise would involve a limited return of the asylum, as a sanctuary for those in critical need (Goldney, 2003).

# 16.3 Ethical Issues for Psychologists

Those who provide mental health treatment are governed by both the legal scope of practice defined for their professions (such as psychology) and by the ethical principles to which the professional group adheres. Psychologists follow the ethical principles adopted by the American Psychological Association (American Psychological Association, 2002), which specify standards involving the practice of psychology.

## 16.3a Confidentiality and Privilege

One of the most important ethical obligations of psychologists is to maintain the privacy of the person seeking treatment. It is unethical to reveal the private communications that take place within therapy or diagnosis to persons outside of the treatment situation. Obviously, it is very important that the person seeking assistance can feel secure in the notion that intimate details about mental or physical health are kept in confidence. **Confidentiality** is thus an ethical obligation on the part of the therapist not to reveal sensitive information to others.

At the same time, the patient holds the privilege to control the release of private information, so that no records are available to others without his or her expressed, written consent. The privilege is the legal authority to release, or to prevent release, of private information. In most cases, the privilege is held by the patient unless the person is a minor, in which case the privilege is held by the parents or legal guardians, or a treatment guardian acting on the patient's behalf. Usually, when a patient discloses information to a therapist for the purposes of assessment or treatment of a mental disorder, that information is a **privileged communication** which legally and ethically should not be revealed.

**Confidentiality**

An ethical obligation on the part of the therapist not to reveal sensitive information to others

**Privileged communication**

Information disclosed to a therapist that cannot be legally revealed without the written consent of the patient

There are important limitations to confidentiality and privilege, however. In some circumstances, such as to protect the client from serious harm, there may be ethical and legal requirements for disclosure to take place. These limitations have gradually been defined by legal cases in which the safety of the client or someone else may be at stake if information is not released. The rules limiting confidentiality and privilege vary from state to state, but there is some general agreement that limits do exist and that therapists are obligated to make their clients aware of these limits.

### Duty to Warn

An illustration of the impact of legal judgments on confidentiality comes from *Tarasoff v. Regents of the University of California* (1976). A graduate student at the University of California at Berkeley, Prosenjit Poddar, had become romantically obsessed with another student, Tatiana Tarasoff (who repeatedly rejected his overtures). On the advice of a friend, who noticed his depression, Poddar sought treatment at the university student health facility. He was seen by both a psychologist and a psychiatrist and was placed on medication with a diagnosis of paranoid schizophrenia. During the course of therapy, Poddar told the psychologist that he intended to kill an unnamed girl (readily identifiable as Tarasoff) after she returned from summer vacation. Concerned about the possibility of violence, the psychologist contacted campus security, informed them that Poddar was dangerous, and recommended that he be detained for civil commitment. The campus police did detain Poddar but released him because he appeared rational and promised to stay away from Tarasoff. Poddar stopped attending therapy sessions. Two months later, after her return to campus, Tarasoff was stabbed to death by Poddar.

At trial, Poddar was found guilty, not of murder, but of manslaughter (the charge was reduced because of a diminished capacity defense). He was jailed, but the conviction was overturned on appeal; Poddar was allowed to return to his native country of India. Tarasoff's parents filed suit for negligence against the university, the psychologist, the psychiatrist, and the campus police.

The California Supreme Court decided the case in 1974, ruling that neither the campus police nor the university was responsible for failing to hospitalize Poddar. However, the psychotherapists were held responsible for failing to warn Tarasoff that her life was in danger. The Tarasoff decision thus established, at least in the state of California, a duty to protect persons who have been specifically threatened, even if the information came out of a confidential therapy session. Many other states have regulations that obligate therapists to act to protect, or to warn, persons against whom specific and credible threats have been made during therapy. Still, there is much uncertainty about the limits of those regulations. For example, it is not yet clear whether a psychologist is obligated to break confidentiality to warn sexual partners of an HIV-infected client (Chenneville, 2000).

### Other Limits on Confidentiality

In general, confidentiality is limited by the obligation of psychologists to protect their clients or others from harm. A psychologist may break confidence to prevent an imminent suicide, for example. Psychologists have a legal obligation to report child abuse or elder abuse as well. If an evaluation is ordered by the court, or if a client raises his or her mental condition as a component of a legal defense, there is no privilege to the communication. In nearly all other therapy situations, the obligation to maintain confidentiality applies.

# 16.4 Should Psychologists Prescribe Medications?

The rapid expansion of psychopharmacology in recent decades has led to a new era in the treatment of mental disorders. It has also vastly increased the consumption of prescription

> **Should psychologists prescribe medication?**

medication. More than 1 in 8 Americans used an antidepressant medication in the last 10 years, and over 3.5 billion doses are consumed annually in the United States; nearly half of those taking antidepressants have been on them for over a year (Antonuccio, Danton, & McClanahan, 2003). Clearly, the pharmaceutical industry has become a major player in the mental health marketplace.

The ability to prescribe psychotropic medications was historically centered on medical doctors with a specialty in psychiatry that were able to use their mental health expertise to assess and treat those with serious disorders. Rather quickly, prescription practices spread to include non-psychiatric physicians, including family therapy doctors (who prescribed antidepressant and antianxiety medications as a component of standard family practice) and to pediatricians (who provided stimulant medications for attention-deficit or hyperactive children). Currently, non-psychiatric physicians prescribe most psychotropic medications (Heiby, DeLeon, & Anderson, 2004).

By the 1980s, non-physicians were gaining limited prescriptive authority. Nurses holding the MSN degree with special training in pharmacology were allowed to prescribe medications as psychiatric nurse practitioners under a doctor's supervision, as were physician assistants. Pharmacists had prescriptive authority in most states as well. The broadening of prescription privileges to some masters-level professionals stimulated psychologists to propose that they, too, could effectively prescribe certain medications, given appropriate pre- and post-doctoral training. Their quest for prescription privileges, opposed by psychiatry, gained momentum in the 1980s and 1990s under a Department of Defense demonstration program that trained 10 psychologists to prescribe psychotropic medications, under the review and supervision of psychiatrists, to patients at military facilities. That program was successful and was extended for several additional years, marking the first professional foray by psychologists into the prescription field.

The American Psychological Association subsequently adopted a policy favoring prescriptive authority in 1996, and proposed training and legislative goals to promote it. Those supporting this position believe it will promote comprehensive, quality care for their clients by allowing psychologists, as trained behavioral scientists, to be active participants in all aspects of treatment. A significant proportion of psychologists opposed the decision, however. Some objected that the proposed training was inadequate (Heiby, DeLeon, & Anderson, 2004), but others objected on the ground that such a path would weaken the integrity of psychological science. Hayes and Heiby (1996) claim that the decision to pursue privileges by doctoral-

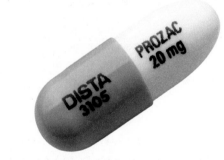

Although psychotropic medications historically were prescribed by medical doctors with a specialty in psychiatry, most are now prescribed by non-psychiatric physicians.

level psychologists is rooted in market issues such as increasing competition from other psychotherapists, the drive of managed-care health providers to lower costs, the dominance of the medical model, and the self-interest of the pharmaceutical industry in expanding the use of medication. The dangers, they suggest, include an undermining of psychological-level analysis, an increased risk of overmedication and medication interactions for clients, and a shift in training emphasis away from science in favor of practice. Nonetheless, psychologist organizations in several states have introduced legislation to allow prescription privileges for psychologists who have specified training, and medical psychologists in Louisiana and New Mexico can now hold limited prescriptive authority. The movement continues to grow, and many feel that it is only a matter of time before clinical psychologists prescribe medication as well as conduct psychotherapy. In 2011, the American Psychological Association, anticipating increased involvement in mediation management by its membership, issued guidelines for prescriptive practices by psychologists (American Psychological Association, 2011).

The pharmaceutical business earns over $400 billion per year globally; and given its rates of return, it may be the most successful industry in the world (Antonuccio, Danton, & McChlanahan, 2003). Not surprisingly, it wields considerable influence in medical practice and research. The ties between psychiatry and the pharmaceutical industry are extensive; quite frequently, researchers reporting the results of drug trials in the psychiatric literature have financial or other relationships with the company that manufactures the drugs being tested. This may have led to publication bias favoring positive results and downplaying negative results, as in the Turner, and his colleagues, (2008) report on FDA antidepressant medication trials discussed in Chapter 11. In fact, a recent publication reporting on the effectiveness of the drug nefazadone was authored by 12 researchers, 11 of whom had financial ties to the manufacturer of the drug. After this and other similar cases, the *New England Journal of Medicine* was forced to relax its own policies against conflicts of interest in order to find enough experts to author studies or write editorials (Antonuccio, Danton, & McChlanahan, 2003).

If prescriptive authority is gained by psychologists, the pharmaceutical industry will gain influence in psychology as well. Antonuccio and his colleagues (2003) propose establishing a "firewall" between psychological science and the pharmaceutical industry as a means to limit that influence. They recommend that drug advertisements not be accepted into scientific journals, that authors declare all conflicts of interest, that drug companies are not allowed to sponsor continuing education credits, that gifts be restricted, and that industry funding not be accepted for training programs. Further, they reiterate that research assessing treatment outcomes should regularly include both placebo and double-blind controls.

Although the outcome of psychology's quest for prescriptive authority is not yet clear, the recommendations of Antonuccio and his colleagues (2003) seem eminently reasonable. Careful, independent research and the empirical validation of psychological interventions should remain the goal of psychological science whether medications form a portion of the practicing psychologist's arsenal or not. There are many important reasons to maintain and expand psychological science and research into non-pharmacological treatments for mental disorders, even if the financial incentives currently lie elsewhere. It remains to be seen how adequate the industry-promoted medical model of psychopathology will prove to be; however, that judgment should be made by the scientific community, rather than by the marketplace.

# Chapter Review
## TO SUM UP ...

- The legal concept of competency to stand trial concerns a person's mental state at the time of legal proceedings. Normally, a competent defendant understands the charges and their seriousness and can assist an attorney in a legal defense.

- The legal concept of insanity concerns a person's mental state at the time of the offense. Although the legal criteria for insanity are still not clearly defined, there is general agreement that insanity involves an inability to distinguish right from wrong and an inability to form specific criminal intent, due to a serious mental disorder.

- Some states have included verdicts such as "guilty but mentally ill" in which the person must serve out a sentence while receiving whatever treatment seems appropriate.

- The process of involuntary commitment involves a conflict between two social concerns: the right of society to protect itself from dangerous persons (and the desire to provide treatment for those who lack sufficient understanding to take care of themselves) versus the civil liberties of the individual.

- Although the vast majority of those with mental disorders are not dangerous to others, the presence of any disorder is associated with a significant increase in the likelihood of violence. The link is strongest for those with substance use disorders.

- The U.S. Supreme Court has ruled that persons who are labeled mentally ill cannot be confined against their will without treatment if they are not dangerous to themselves or others and are capable of surviving on the outside.

- Courts have established a right to treatment for those hospitalized with mental disorders. Courts have also established a right to receive treatment in the least restrictive setting that is appropriate.

- Voluntary, competent patients can refuse treatment for a mental disorder. It is not clear whether involuntarily committed patients can refuse treatment. Courts have supported emergency treatment of involuntary patients who are dangerous, without their consent.

- Psychologists are seeking legislation that would allow them to prescribe psychotropic medications after they receive the necessary training. Limited numbers of psychologists have gained prescriptive authority within a Department of Defense pilot program and in the states of Louisiana and New Mexico. Psychiatry opposes this extension of prescription privileges, as do some psychologists who are concerned about the integrity of psychological science under the influence of the pharmaceutical industry.

## KEY TERMS

Competency   440

Confidentiality   451

Durham rule   444

Institutionalization   450

Irresistible impulse rule   443

McNaughton rule   443

Privileged communication   451

Sanity   442

## QUESTIONS FOR STUDY

- Describe the type of information that a court might need in order to decide on the issue of insanity.

- A psychologist is obligated to protect patient confidentiality except under certain circumstances. Describe several of these limits to confidentiality.

- Discuss how a patient has both a right to treatment, and a right to refuse treatment.

## POP QUIZ

1.  To which of the following does competency refer?
    A. one's ability to succeed at a task
    B. one's current mental state
    C. one's legal responsibility for criminal acts
    D. one's ability to understand legal charges and assist in own defense

2.  Sanity refers to which of the following?
    A. one's ability to succeed at a task
    B. one's current mental state
    C. one's legal responsibility for criminal acts
    D. one's ability to understand legal charges and assist in own defense

3.  In legal terms, "competency" is to "sanity" as _____.
    A. "trial" is to "crime"
    B. "crime" is to "trial"
    C. "private" is to "public"
    D. "public" is to "private"

4. The _____ is a legal guideline that describes insanity in terms of an individual's inability to distinguish right from wrong.
   A. irresistible impulse rule
   B. Durham rule
   C. "policeman over the shoulder" rule
   D. McNaughton rule

5. Who makes the determination of whether a defendant is competent to stand trial?
   A. the judge
   B. the qualified mental examiner
   C. the plaintiff's lawyer
   D. the defendant's lawyer

6. According to the Model Penal Code, which diagnosis would probably be disqualified for a "not guilty by reason of insanity" plea?
   A. antisocial personality disorder
   B. major depressive disorder
   C. sexual sadism disorder
   D. major neurocognitive disorder

7. A person with a mental disorder could be civilly committed if he or she were
   _____.
   A. refusing medication
   B. dangerous to self or others
   C. delusional
   D. abusing drugs

8. A main issue in *Wyatt v. Stickney* (1971) concerned the right to _____.
   A. refuse treatment
   B. be free of mental disorder
   C. receive treatment
   D. trial by jury

9. Overall, the prevalence of violence among those with mental disorders is
   _____ those without a mental disorder.
   A. lower as
   B. equal to
   C. 2 times as high as
   D. 5 times as high as

10. A U.S. Supreme Court ruling (*Atkins v. Virginia*, 2002) prohibits execution of those who are_____.
    A. intellectually disabled
    B. personality disordered
    C. psychotic
    D. severely depressed

11. Which defendant was found not guilty by reason of insanity?
    A. John Hinckley, Jr.
    B. David Berkowitz ("Son of Sam")
    C. Lee Boyd Malvo
    D. Anders Behring Breivik

12. Which of the following is one outcome of the deinstitutionalization movement?
    A. More patients are able to receive treatment.
    B. Fewer patients are treated with medications.
    C. More patients are involved with the penal system.
    D. Fewer patients show signs of serious mental disorders.

13. All of the following are limitations on confidentiality **except** _____.
    A. child abuse
    B. imminent danger to self or others
    C. abuse of the elderly
    D. criminal activity

14. A clear implication of the Tarasoff decision is that the therapist should do which of the following?
    A. inform the police when a client has admitted child abuse
    B. warn the authorities when a client threatens suicide
    C. begin commitment proceedings if a client appears dangerous
    D. warn a person whom the client has specifically threatened to harm

15. Currently, most psychotropic medications are prescribed by _____.
    A. psychiatrists
    B. non-psychiatric physicians
    C. clinical psychologists
    D. psychiatric nurse practitioners

Additional study resources are available at **www.BVTLab.com**

# *DSM-5* Classification

## Neurodevelopmental Disorders

### Intellectual Disabilities
319    (__.__)    Intellectual Disability
315.8    (F88)    Global Developmental Delay
319    (F79)    Unspecified Intellectual Disability

### Communication Disorders
315.39    (F80.9)    Language Disorder
315.39    (F80.0)    Speech Sound Disorder
315.35    (F80.81)    Childhood-Onset Fluency Disorder
315.39    (F80.89)    Social (Pragmatic) Communication Disorder
307.9    (F80.9)    Unspecified Communication Disorder

### Autism Spectrum Disorder
299.00    (F84.0)    Autism Spectrum Disorder

### Attention-Deficit/ Hyperactive Disorder
__.__    (__.__)    Attention-Deficit/ Hyperactive Disorder
*Specify* whether:
314.01    (F90.2)    Combined presentation
314.00    (F90.0)    Predominantly inattentive presentation
314.01    (F90.1)    Predominantly hyperactive/impulsive presentation
314.01    (F90.2)    Other specified Attention-Deficit/ Hyperactivity Disorder
314.01    (F90.9)    Unspecified Attention-Deficit/Hyperactivity Disorder

### Specific Learning Disorder
__.__    (__.__)    Specific Learning Disorder
*Specify* if:
315.00    (F81.0)    With impairment in reading
315.2    (F81.81)    With impairment in written expression
315.1    (F81.2)    With impairment in mathematics

### Motor Disorders
315.4    (F82)    Developmental Coordination Disorder

307.3    (F98.4)    Stereotypical Movement Disorder

### Tic Disorders
307.23    (F95.2)    Tourette's Disorder
307.22    (F95.1)    Persistent (Chronic) Motor or Vocal Tic Disorder
*Specify* if: With motor tics only, With vocal tics only
307.21    (F95.0)    Provisional Tic Disorder
307.20    (F95.8)    Other Specified Tic Disorder
307.20    (F95.9)    Unspecified Tic Disorder

### Other Neurodevelopmental Disorders
315.8    (F88)    Other Specified Neurodevelopmental Disorder
315.9    (F89)    Unspecified Neurodevelopmental Disorder

## Schizophrenia Spectrum and Other Psychotic Disorders
301.22    (F21)    Schizotypal (Personality) Disorder
297.1    (F22)    Delusional Disorder
298.8    (F23)    Brief Psychotic Disorder
295.40    (F20.81)    Schizophreniform Disorder
295.90    (F20.9)    Schizophrenia
__.__    (__.__)    Schizoaffective Disorder
*Specify* if: With bizarre content
295.70    (F25.0)    Bipolar type
295.70    (F25.1)    Depressive type
__.__    (__.__)    Substance/Medication-Induced Psychotic Disorsorder
__.__    (__.__)    Psychotic Disorder Due to Another Medical Condition
*Specify* whether:
293.81    (F06.2)    With delusions
293.82    (F06.2)    With hallucinations
293.89    (F06.1)    Catatonia Associated with Another Mental Disorder (Catatonic Specifier)

293.89    (F06.1)    Catatonic Disorder Due to Another Medical Condition
293.89    (F06.1)    Unspecified Catatonia
298.8    (F28)    Other Specified Schizophrenia Spectrum and Other Psychotic Disorder
298.9    (F29)    Unspecified Schizophrenia Spectrum and Other Psychotic Disorder

## Bipolar and Related Disorders
__.__    (__.__)    Bipolar I Disorder
__.__    (__.__)    Current or most recent episode manic
296.41    (F31.11)    Mild
296.42    (F31.12)    Moderate
296.43    (F31.13)    Severe
296.44    (F31.2)    With psychotic features
296.45    (F31.73)    In partial remission
296.46    (F31.74)    In full remission
296.40    (F31.9)    Unspecified
296.40    (F31.0)    Current or most recent episode hypomanic
296.45    (F31.73)    In partial remission
296.46    (F31.74)    In full remission
296.40    (F31.9)    Unspecified
__.__    (__.__)    Current or most recent episode depressed
269.51    (F31.31)    Mild
296.52    (F31.32)    Moderate
296.53    (F31.4)    Severe
296.54    (F31.5)    With psychotic features
296.55    (F31.75)    In partial remission
296.56    (F31.76)    In full remission
296.50    (F31.9)    Unspecified
296.7    (F31.9)    Current or most recent episode unspecified
296.89    (F31.81)    Bipolar II Disorder
301.13    (F34.0)    Cyclothymic Disorder
__.__    (__.__)    Substance/Medication-Induced Bipolar and Related Disorder
293.83    (__.__)    Bipolar and Related Disorders Due to Another Medical Condition
*Specify* if:
   (F06.33)    With manic features
   (F06.33)    With manic- or hypomanic-like episode
   (F06.34)    With mixed features

296.89 (F31.89) Other Specified Bipolar and Related Disorder

296.80 (F31.9) Unspecified Bipolar and Related Disorder

## Depressive Disorders

296.99 (F34.8) Disruptive Mood Dysregulation Disorder

__.__ (__.__) Major Depressive Disorder

__.__ (__.__) Single episode

296.21 (F32.0) Mild

296.22 (F32.1) Moderate

296.23 (F32.2) Severe

296.24 (F32.3) With psychotic features

296.25 (F32.4) In partial remission

296.26 (F32.5) In full remission

296.20 (F32.9) Unspecified

__.__ (__.__) Recurrent episode

296.31 (F33.0) Mild

296.32 (F33.1) Moderate

296.33 (F33.2) Severe

296.34 (F33.3) With psychotic features

296.35 (F33.41) In partial remission

296.36 (F33.42) In full remission

296.30 (F33.9) Unspecified

300.4 (F34.1) Persistent Depressive Disorder (Dysthymia)

625.4 (N94.3) Premenstrual Dysphoric Disorder

__.__ (__.__) Substance/Medication-Induced Depressive Disorder

293.83 (__.__) Depressive Disorder Due to Another Medical Condition

*Specify* if:

(F06.31) With depressive features

(F06.32) With major depressive-like episode

(F06.34) With mixed features

311 (F32.8) Other Specified Depressive Disorder

311 (F32.9) Unspecified Depressive Disorder

## Anxiety Disorders

309.21 (F93.0) Separation Anxiety Disorder

312.23 (F94.0) Selective Mutism

300.29 (__.__) Specific Phobia

*Specify* if:

(F40.218) Animal

(F40.228) Natural environment

(__.__) Blood-injection-injury

(F40.230) Fear of blood

(F40.232) Fear of injections and transfusions

(F40.233) Fear of injury

(F40.248) Situational

(F40.298) Other

300.23 (F40.10) Social Anxiety Disorder (Social Phobia)

300.01 (F41.0) Panic Disorder

__.__ (__.__) Panic Attack Specifier

300.22 (F40.00) Agoraphobia

300.02 (F41.1) Generalized Anxiety Disorder

__.__ (__.__) Substance/Medication-Induced Anxiety Disorder

293.84 (F06.4) Anxiety Disorder Due to Another Medical Condition

300.09 (F41.8) Other Specified Anxiety Disorder

300.00 (F41.9) Unspecified Anxiety Disorder

## Obsessive-Compulsive and Related Disorders

300.3 (F42) Obsessive-Compulsive Disorder

300.7 (F45.22) Body Dysmorphic Disorder

300.3 (F42) Hoarding Disorder

312.39 (F63.2) Trichotillomania (Hair-Pulling) Disorder

698.4 (L98.1) Excoriation (Skin-Picking) Disorder

__.__ (__.__) Substance/Medication-Induced Obsessive-Compulsive and Related Disorder

294.8 (F06.8) Obsessive-Compulsive and Related Disorder Due to Another Medical Condition

300.3 (F42) Other Specified Obsessive-Compulsive and Related Disorder

300.3 (F42) Unspecified Obsessive-Compulsive and Related Disorders

## Trauma- and Stressor-Related Disorders

313.89 (F94.1) Reactive Attachment Disorder

313.89 (F94.2) Disinhibited Social Engagement Disorder

309.81 (F43.10) Posttraumatic Stress Disorder (includes Posttraumatic Stress Disorder for Children 6 Years and Younger)

308.3 (F43.0) Acute Stress Disorder

__.__ (__.__) Adjustment Disorders

*Specify* whether:

309.0 (F43.21) With Depressed Mood

309.24 (F43.22) With anxiety

309.28 (F43.23) With mixed anxiety and depressed mood

309.3 (F43.24) With disturbance of conduct

309.4 (F43.25) With mixed disturbance of emotions and conduct

309.9 (F43.20) Unspecified

309.89 (F43.8) Other Specified Trauma- and Stressor-Related Disorder

309.9 (F43.9) Unspecified Trauma- and Stressor-Related Disorder

## Dissociative Disorders

300.14 (F44.81) Dissociative Identity Disorder

300.12 (F44.0) Dissociative Amnesia

*Specify* if:

300.13 (F44.1) With dissociative fugue

300.6 (F48.1) Depersonalization/Derealization Disorder

300.15 (F44.89) Other Specified Dissociative Disorder

300.15 (F44.9) Unspecified Dissociative Disorder

## Somatic Symptom and Related Disorders

300.82 (F45.1) Somatic Symptom Disorder

300.7 (F45.21) Illness Anxiety Disorder

300.11 (__.__) Conversion Disorder (Functional Neurological Symptom Disorder)

*Specify* symptom type:

(F44.4) With weakness or paralysis

(F44.4) With abnormal movement

(F44.4) With swallowing symptoms

(F44.4) With speech symptom

(F44.5) With attacks or seizures

(F44.6) With anesthesia or sensory loss

(F44.6) With special sensory symptoms

(F44.7) With mixed symptoms

316 (F54) Psychological Factors Affecting Other Medical Conditions

300.19 (F68.10) Factitious Disorder (includes Factitious Disorder Imposed on Self, Factitious Disorder Imposed on Another)

300.89 (F45.8) Other Specified Somatic Symptom and Related Disorder

300.82 (F45.9) Unspecified Somatic Symptom and Related Disorder

## Feeding and Eating Disorders

307.52 (\_\_.\_\_) Pica
    (F98.3) In children
    (F50.8) In adults

307.53 (F98.21) Rumination Disorder

307.59 (F50.8) Avoidant/Restrictive Food Intake Disorder

307.1 (\_\_.\_\_) Anorexia Nervosa
    *Specify* whether:
    (F50.01) Restricting type
    (F50.02) Binge-eating/purging type

307.51 (F50.2) Bulimia Nervosa

307.51 (F50.8) Binge-Eating Disorder

307.59 (F50.8) Other Specified Feeding or Eating Disorder

307.50 (F50.9) Unspecified Feeding or Eating Disorder

## Elimination Disorders

307.6 (F98.0) Enuresis

307.7 (F98.1) Encopresis

\_\_.\_\_ (\_\_.\_\_) Other Specified Elimination Disorder

788.39 (N39.498) With urinary symptoms

787.60 (R15.9) With fecal symptoms

\_\_.\_\_ (\_\_.\_\_) Unspecified Elimination Disorder

788.30 (R32) With urinary symptoms

787.60 (R15.9) With fecal symptoms

## Sleep-Wake Disorders

780.52 (G47.00) Insomnia Disorder

780.54 (G47.10) Hypersomnolence Disorder

\_\_.\_\_ (\_\_.\_\_) Narcolepsy
    *Specify* whether:

347.00 (G47.419) Narcolepsy without cataplexy but with hypocretin deficiency

347.01 (G47.411) Narcolepsy with cataplexy but without hypocretin deficiency

347.00 (G47.419) Autosomal dominant cerebellar ataxia, deafness, and narcolepsy

347.00 (G47.419) Autosomal dominant narcolepsy, obesity, and type 2 diabetes

347.10 (G47.429) Narcolepsy secondary to another medical condition

## Breathing-Related Sleep Disorders

327.23 (G47.33) Obstructive Sleep Apnea Hypopnea

\_\_.\_\_ (\_\_.\_\_) Central Sleep Apnea
    *Specify* whether:

327.21 (G47.31) Idiopathic central sleep apnea

786.04 (R06.3) Cheyne-Stokes breathing

780.57 (G47.37) Central sleep apnea comorbid with opioid use

\_\_.\_\_ (\_\_.\_\_) Sleep-Related Hypoventilation
    *Specify* whether:

327.24 (G47.34) Idiopathic hypoventilation

327.25 (G47.35) Congenital central alveolar hypoventilation

327.26 (G47.36) Comorbid sleep-related hypoventilation

\_\_.\_\_ (\_\_.\_\_) Circadian Rhythm Sleep-Wake Disorders
    *Specify* whether:

307.45 (G47.21) Delayed sleep phase type

307.45 (G47.22) Advanced sleep phase type

307.45 (G47.23) Irregular sleep-wake type

307.45 (G47.24) Non-24-hour-sleep-wake type

307.45 (G47.26) Shift work type

307.45 (G47.20) Unspecified type

## Parasomnias

\_\_.\_\_ (\_\_.\_\_) Non-Rapid Eye Movement Sleep Arousal Disorder
    *Specify* whether:

307.46 (F51.3) Sleepwalking type

307.46 (F51.4) Sleep terror type

307.47 (F51.5) Nightmare Disorder

327.42 (G47.52) Rapid Eye Movement Sleep Behavior Disorder

333.94 (G25.81) Restless Legs Syndrome

\_\_.\_\_ (\_\_.\_\_) Substance/Medication-Induced Sleep Disorder

780.52 (G47.09) Other Specified Insomnia Disorder

780.52 (G47.00) Unspecified Insomnia Disorder

780.54 (G47.19) Other Specified Hypersomnolence Disorder

780.54 (G47.10) Unspecified Hypersomnolence Disorder

780.59 (G47.8) Other Specified Sleep-Wake Disorder

780.59 (G47.9) Unspecified Sleep-Wake Disorder

## Sexual Dysfunctions

302.74 (F52.32) Delayed Ejaculation

302.72 (F52.21) Erectile Disorder

302.73 (F52.31) Female Orgasmic Disorder

302.72 (F52.22) Female Sexual Interest/Arousal Disorder

302.76 (F52.6) Genito-Pelvic Pain/Penetration Disorder

302.71 (F52.0) Male Hypoactive Sexual Desire Disorder

302.75 (F52.4) Premature (Early) Ejaculation

\_\_.\_\_ (\_\_.\_\_) Substance/Medication-Induced Sexual Dysfunctions

302.79 (F52.8) Other Specified Sexual Dysfunction

302.70 (F52.9) Unspecified Sexual Dysfunction

## Gender Dysphoria

\_\_.\_\_ (\_\_.\_\_) Gender Dysphoria

302.6 (F64.2) Gender Dysphoria in Children

302.85 (F64.1) Gender Dysphoria in Adolescents and Adults

302.6 (F64.8) Other Specified Gender Dysphoria

302.6 (F64.9) Unspecified Gender Dysphoria

## Disruptive, Impulse-Control, and Conduct Disorders

313.81 (F91.3) Oppositional Defiant Disorder

312.34 (F63.81) Intermittent Explosive Disorder

\_\_.\_\_ (\_\_.\_\_) Conduct Disorder
    *Specify* whether:

312.81 (F91.1) Childhood-onset type

312.82 (F91.2) Adolescent-onset type

312.89 (F91.9) Unspecified onset

301.7 (F60.2) Antisocial Personality Disorder

312.33 (F63.1) Pyromania
312.32 (F63.3) Kleptomania
312.89 (F91.8) Other Specified Disruptive, Impulse-Control, and Conduct Disorder
312.9 (F91.9) Unspecified Disruptive, Impulse-Control, and Conduct Disorder

## Substance-Related and Addictive Disorders

### Substance-Related Disorders

#### Alcohol-Related Disorders
__.__ (__.__) Alcohol Use Disorder
*Specify* current severity:
305.00 (F10.10) Mild
303.90 (F10.20) Moderate
303.90 (F10.20) Severe
303.00 (__.__) Alcohol Intoxication
(F10.129) With use disorder, mild
(F10.229) With use disorder, moderate or severe
(F10.929) Without use disorder
291.81 (__.__) Alcohol Withdrawal
(F10.239) Without perceptual disturbances
(F10.232) With perceptual disturbances
__.__ (__.__) Other Alcohol-Induced Disorders
291.9 (F10.99) Unspecified Alcohol-Related Disorder

#### Caffeine-Related Disorders
305.90 (F15.929) Caffeine Intoxication
292.0 (F15.93) Caffeine Withdrawal
__.__ (__.__) Other Caffeine-Induced Disorders
292.9 (F15.99) Unspecified Caffeine-Related Disorders

#### Cannabis-Related Disorders
__.__ (__.__) Cannabis Use Disorder
*Specify* current severity:
305.20 (F12.10) Mild
304.30 (F12.20) Moderate
304.30 (F12.20) Severe
292.89 (__.__) Cannabis Intoxication Without perceptual disturbances
(F12.129) With use disorder, mild
(F12.229) With use disorder, moderate or severe
(F12.929) Without use disorder With perceptual disturbances
(F12.122) With use disorder, mild

(F12.222) With use disorder, moderate or severe
(F12.922) Without use disorder
292.0 (F12.288) Cannabis Withdrawal
__.__ (__.__) Other Cannabis-Induced Disorders
292.9 (F12.99) Unspecified Cannabis-Related Disorder

#### Hallucinogen-Related Disorders
__.__ (__.__) Phencyclidine Use Disorder
*Specify* current severity:
305.90 (F16.10) Mild
304.60 (F16.20) Moderate
304.60 (F16.20) Severe
__.__ (__.__) Other Hallucinogen Use Disorder
*Specify* current severity:
305.30 (F16.10) Mild
304.50 (F16.20) Moderate
304.50 (F16.20) Severe
292.89 (__.__) Phencyclidine Intoxication
(F16.129) With use disorder, mild
(F16.229) With use disorder, moderate or severe
(F16.929) Without use disorder
292.89 (__.__) Other Hallucinogen Intoxication
(F16.129) With use disorder, mild
(F16.229) With use disorder, moderate or severe
(F16.929) Without use disorder
292.89 (F16.983) Hallucinogen Persisting Perception Disorder
__.__ (__.__) Other Phencyclidine-Increased Disorders
__.__ (__.__) Other Hallucinogen-Induced Disorders
292.9 (F16.99) Unspecified Phencyclidine-Related Disorder
292.9 (F16.99) Unspecified Hallucinogen-Related Disorder

#### Inhalant-Related Disorders
__.__ (__.__) Inhalant Use Disorder
*Specify* current severity:
305.90 (F18.10) Mild
304.60 (F18.20) Moderate
304.60 (F18.20) Severe
292-89 (__.__) Inhalant Intoxication
(F18.129) With use disorder, mild
(F18.229) With use disorder, moderate or severe
(F18.929) Without use disorder
__.__ (__.__) Other Inhalant-Induced Disorders

292.9 (F18.99) Unspecified Inhalant-Related Disorder

#### Opioid Related Disorders
__.__ (__.__) Opioid Use Disorder
*Specify* current severity:
305.50 (F11.10) Mild
304.0 (F11.20) Moderate
304.00 (F11.20) Severe
292.89 (__.__) Opioid Intoxication Without perceptual disturbances
(F11.129) With use disorder, mild
(F11.229) With use disorder, moderate or severe
(F11.929) Without use disorder With perceptual disturbances
(F11.122) With use disorder, mild
(F11.222) With use disorder, moderate or severe
(F11.922) Without use disorder
292.0 (F11.23) Opioid Withdrawal
__.__ (__.__) Other Opioid-Induced Disorders
292.9 (F11.99) Unspecified Opioid-Related Disorder

#### Sedative-, Hypnotic-, or Anxiolytic-Related Disorders
__.__ (__.__) Sedative, Hypnotic, or Anxiolytic Use Disorder
*Specify* current severity:
305.40 (F13.10) Mild
304.10 (F13.20) Moderate
304.10 (F13.20) Severe
292.89 (__.__) Sedative, Hypnotic, or Anxiolytic Intoxication
(F13.129) With use disorder, mild
(F13.229) With use disorder, moderate or severe
(F13.929) Without use disorder
292.0 (__.__) Sedative, Hypnotic, or Anxiolytic Withdrawal
(F13.239) Without perceptual disturbances
(F13.232) With perceptual disturbances
__.__ (__.__) Other Sedative-, Hypnotic-, or Anxiolytic-Induced Disorders
292.9 (F13.99) Unspecified Sedative-, Hypnotic-, or Anxiolytic-Related Disorder

#### Stimulant-Related Disorders
__.__ (__.__) Stimulant Use Disorder
*Specify* current severity:
__.__ (__.__) Mild

305.70  (F15.10)  Amphetamine-type
                  substance
305.60  (F14.10   Cocaine
305.70  (F15.10)  Other or unspecified
                  stimulant
__.__   (__.__)   Moderate
304.40  (F15.20)  Amphetamine-type
                  substance
304.20  (F14.20)  Cocaine
304.40  (F15.20)  Other or unspecified
                  stimulant
__.__   (__.__)   Severe
304.40  (F15.20)  Amphetamine-type
                  substance
304.20  (F14.20)  Cocaine
304.40  (F15.20)  Other or unspecified
                  stimulant
292.89  (__.__)   Stimulant Intoxication
                  *Specify* the specific
                  intoxication
292.89  (__.__)   Amphetamine or
                  other stimulant,
                  Without perceptual
                  disturbances
        (F15.129) With use disorder, mild
        (F15.229) With use disorder,
                  moderate or sever
        (F15.929) Without use disorder
292.89  (__.__)   Cocaine, Without
                  perceptual
                  disturbances
        (F14.129) With use disorder, mild
        (F14.229) With use disorder,
                  moderate or severe
        (F14.929) Without use disorder
292.89  (__.__)   Amphetamine or
                  other stimulant,
                  With perceptual
                  disturbances
        (F15.122) With use disorder, mild
        (F15.222) With use disorder,
                  moderate or severe
        (F15.922) Without use disorder
292.89  (__.__)   Cocaine, With
                  perceptual disturbances
        (F14.122) With use disorder, mild
        (F14.222) With use disorder,
                  moderate or severe
        (F14.922) Without use disorder
292.0   (__.__)   Stimulant Withdrawal
        (F15.99)  Amphetamine or other
                  stimulant
        (F14.23)  Cocaine
__.__   (__.__)   Other Stimulate-
                  Induced Disorders
292.9   (__.__)   Unspecified Stimulant-
                  Related Disorders
        (F15.99)  Amphetamine or other
                  stimulant
        (F14.99)  Cocaine

## Tobacco-Related Disorders

__.__   (__.__)   Tobacco Use Disorder
                  *Specify* current severity:
305.1   (Z72.0)   Mild
305.1   (F17.200) Moderate
305.1   (F17.200) Severe
292.0   (F17.203) Tobacco Withdrawal
__.__   (__.__)   Other Tobacco-
                  Induced Disorders
292.9   (F17.209) Unspecified Tobacco-
                  Related Disorders

## Other (or Unknown) Substance-Related Disorders

__.__   (__.__)   Other (or Unknown)
                  Substance Use Disorder
                  *Specify* current severity:
305.90  (F19.10)  Mild
304.90  (F19.20)  Moderate
304.90  (F19.20)  Severe
292.89  (__.__)   Other (or Unknown)
                  Substance Withdrawal
__.__   (__.__)   Other (or Unknown)
                  Substance-Induced
                  Disorders
292.9   (F19.99)  Unspecified Other (or
                  Unknown) Substance-
                  Related Disorders

## Non-Substance-Related Disorders

312.31  (F63.0)   Gambling Disorder

# Neurocognitive Disorders

__.__   (__.__)   Delirium
                  *Specify* whether:
__.__   (__.__)   Substance intoxication
                  delirium
__.__   (__.__)   Substance withdrawal
                  delirium
292.81  (__.__)   Medication-induced
                  delirium
293.0   (F05)     Delirium due to
                  another medical
                  condition
293.0   (F05)     Delirium due to
                  multiple etiologies
780.09  (R41.0)   Other Specified
                  Delirium
780.09  (R41.0)   Unspecified Delirium

## Major and Mild Neurocognitive Disorders

### Major or Mild Neurocognitive Disorder Due to Alzheimer's Disease

__.__   (__.__)   Probable Major
                  Neurocognitive
                  Disorder Due to
                  Alzheimer's Disease
294.11  (F02.81)  With behavioral
                  disturbance

294.10  (F02.80)  Without behavioral
                  disturbance
331.9   (G31.9)   Possible Major
                  Neurocognitive
                  Disorder Due to
                  Alzheimer's Disease
331.83  (G31.84)  Mild Neurocognitive
                  Disorder Due to
                  Alzheimer's Disease

### Major or Mild Fronotemporal Neurocognitive Disorder

__.__   (__.__)   Probable Major
                  Neurocognitive
                  Disorder Due to
                  Frontotemporal Lobar
                  Degeneration
294.11  (F02.81)  With behavioral
                  disturbance
294.10  (F02.80)  Without behavioral
                  disturbance
331.9   (G31.9)   Possible Major
                  Neurocognitive
                  Disorder Due to
                  Frontotemporal Lobar
                  Degeneration
331.83  (G31.84)  Mild Neurocognitive
                  Disorder Due to
                  Frontotemporal Lobar
                  Degeneration

### Major or Mild Neurocognitive Disorder With Lewy Bodies

__.__   (__.__)   Probable Major
                  Neurocognitive
                  Disorder With Lewy
                  Bodies
294.11  (F02.81)  With behavioral
                  disturbance
294.10  (F02.80)  Without behavioral
                  disturbance
331.9   (G31.9)   Possible Major
                  Neurocognitive
                  Disorder With Lewy
                  Bodies
331.83  (G31.84)  Mild Neurocognitive
                  Disorder With Lewy
                  Bodies

### Major or Mild Neurocognitive Disorder Due to Traumatic Brain Injury

__.__   (__.__)   Major Neurocognitive
                  Disorder Due to
                  Traumatic Brain Injury
294.11  (F02.81)  With behavioral
                  disturbance
294.10  (F02.80)  Without behavioral
                  disturbance
331.83  (G31.84)  Mild Neurocognitive
                  Disorder Due to
                  Traumatic Brain Injury

## Substance/Medication-Induced Major or Mild Neurocognitive Disorder

### Major or Mild Neurocognitive Disorder Due to HIV Infection

__.__ (__.__) Major or Mild Neurocognitive Disorder Due to HIV Infection

294.11 (F02.81) With behavioral disturbance

294.10 (F02.80) Without behavioral disturbance

331-83 (G31.84) Mild Neurocognitive Disorder Due to HIV Infection

### Major or Mild Neurocognitive Disorder Due to Prion Disease

__.__ (__.__) Major Neurocognitive Disorder Due to Prion Disease

294.11 (F02.81) With behavioral disturbance

294.10 (F02.80) Without behavioral disturbance

331.83 (G31.84) Mild Neurocognitive Disorder Due to Prion Disease

### Major or Mild Neurocognitive Disease Due to Parkinson's Disease

__.__ (__.__) Major Neurocognitive Disorder Probably Due to Parkinson's Disease

294.11 (F02.81) With behavioral disturbance

294.10 (F02.80) Without behavioral disturbance

331.9 (G31.9) Major Neurocognitive Disorder Possibly Due to Parkinson's Disease

331.83 (G31.84) Mild Neurocognitive Disorder Possibly Due to Parkinson's Disease

### Major or Mild Neurocognitive Disorder Due to Huntington's Disease

__.__ (__.__) Major Neurocognitive Disorder Due to Huntington's Disease

294.11 (F02.81) With behavioral disturbance

294.10 (F02.80) Without behavioral disturbance

331.83 (G31.84) Mild Neurocognitive Disorder Due to Huntington's Disease

### Major or Mild Neurocognitive Disorder Due to Another Medical Condition

__.__ (__.__) Major Neurocognitive Disorder Due to Another Medical Condition

294.11 (F02.81) With behavioral disturbance

294.10 (F02.80) Without behavioral disturbance

331.83 (G31.84) Mild Neurocognitive Disorder Due to Another Medical Condition

### Major or Mild Neurocognitive Disorder Due to Multiple Etiologies

__.__ (__.__) Major Neurocognitive Disorder Due to Multiple Etiologies

294.11 (F02.81) With behavioral disturbance

294.10 (F02.80) Without behavioral disturbance

331.83 (G31.84) Mild Neurocognitive Disorder Due to Multiple Etiologies

### Unspecified Neurocognitive Disorder

799.59 (R41.9) Unspecified Neurocognitive Disorder

## Personality Disorders

### Cluster A Personality Disorders

301.0 (F60.0) Paranoid Personality Disorder

301.20 (F60.1) Schizoid Personality Disorder

301.22 (F21) Schizotypal Personality Disorder

### Cluster B Personality Disorders

301.7 (F60.2) Antisocial Personality Disorder

301.83 (F60.3) Borderline Personality Disorder

301.50 (F60.4) Histrionic Personality Disorder

301.81 (F60.81) Narcissistic Personality Disorder

### Cluster C Personality Disorders

301.82 (F60.6) Avoidant Personality Disorder

301.6 (F60.7) Dependent Personality Disorder

301.4 (F60.5) Obsessive-Compulsive Personality Disorder

### Other Personality Disorders

310.1 (F07.0) Personality Change Due to Another Medial Condition

301.89 (F60.89) Other Specified Personality Disorder

301.9 (F60.9) Unspecified Personality Disorder

## Paraphilic Disorders

302.82 (F65.3) Voyeuristic Disorder

302.4 (F65.2) Exhibitionistic Disorder

302.89 (F65.81) Frotteuristic Disorder

302.83 (F65.51) Sexual Masochism Disorder

302.84 (F65.52) Sexual Sadism Disorder

302.2 (F65.4) Pedophilic Disorder

302.81 (F65.0) Fetishistic Disorder

302.3 (F65.1) Transvestic Disorder

302.89 (F65.89) Other Specified Paraphilic Disorder

302.9 (F65.9) Unspecified Paraphilic Disorder

## Other Mental Disorders

294.8 (F06.8) Other Specified Mental Disorder Due to Another Medical Condition

294.9 (F09) Unspecified Mental Disorder Due to Another Medical Condition

300.9 (F99) Other Specified Mental Disorder

300.9 (F99) Unspecified Mental Disorder

## Medication-Induced Movement Disorders and Other Adverse Effects of Medication

332.1 (G21.11) Neuroleptic-Induced Parkinsonism

332.1 (G21.19) Other Medication-Induced Parkinsonism

333.92 (G21.0) Neuroleptic Malignant Syndrome

333.72 (G24.02) Medication-Induced Acute Dystonia

333.99 (G25.71) Medication-Induced Acute Akathisia

333.85 (G24.01) Tardive Dyskinesia

333.72 (G24.09) Tardive Dystonia

333.99 (G25.71) Tardive Akathisia

333.1 (G25.1) Medication-Induced Postural Tremor

333.99 (G25.79) Other Medication-Induced Movement Disorder

__.__ (__.__) Antidepressant Discontinuation Syndrome

995.29 (T43.205A) Initial encounter

995.29 (T43.205D) Subsequent encounter

995.29 (T43.205S) Sequelae

# Other Conditions That May Be A Focus of Clinical Attention

## Relational Problems

### Problems Related To Family Upbringing

V61.20 (Z62.820) Parent-Child Relational Problems

V61.8 (Z62.891) Sibling Relational Problem

V61.8 (Z62.29) Upbringing Away From Parents

V61.29 (Z62.898) Child Affected by Parental Relationship Distress

### Other Problems Related to Primary Support Groups

V61.03 (Z63.0) Relationship Distress With Spouse or Intimate Partner

V61.03 (Z63.5) Disruption of Family by Separation or Divorce

V61.8 (Z63.8) High Expressed Emotion Level Within Family

V62.82 (Z63.4) Uncomplicated Bereavement

## Abuse and Neglect

### Child Maltreatment and Neglect Problems

#### Child Physical Abuse

*Child Physical Abuse, Confirmed*

995.54 (T74.12XA) Initial encounter

995.54 (T74.12XD) Subsequent encounter

*Child Physical Abuse, Suspected*

995.54 (T76.12XA) Initial encounter

995.54 (T76.12XD) Subsequent encounter

*Other Circumstances Related to Child Physical Abuse*

V61.21 (Z69.010) Encounter for mental health services for victim of child abuse by parent

V61.21 (Z69.020) Encounter for mental health services for victim of nonparental child abuse

V15.41 (Z62.810) Personal history (past history) of physical abuse in childhood

V61.22 (Z69.011) Encounter for mental health services for perpetrator of parental child abuse

V62.83 (Z69.021) Encounter for mental health services for perpetrator of nonparental child abuse

#### Child Sexual Abuse

*Child Sexual Abuse, Confirmed*

995.53 (T74.22XA) Initial encounter

995.53 (T72.22XD) Subsequent encounter

*Child Sexual Abuse, Suspected*

995.53 (T76.22XA) Initial encounter

995.53 (T72.22XD) Subsequent encounter

*Other Circumstances Related to Child Sexual Abuse*

V61.21 (Z69.010) Encounter for mental health services for victim of child sexual abuse by parent

V61.21 (Z69.020) Encounter for mental health services for victim of nonparental child sexual abuse

V15.41 (Z62.810) Personal history (past history) of sexual abuse in childhood

V61.22 (Z69.011) Encounter for mental health services for perpetrator of parental child sexual abuse

V62.83 (Z69.021) Encounter for mental health services for perpetrator of nonparental child sexual abuse

#### Child Neglect

*Child Neglect, Confirmed*

995.52 (T74.02XA) Initial encounter

995.52 (T74.02XD) Subsequent encounter

*Child Neglect, Suspected*

995.52 (T76.02XA) Initial encounter

995.52 (T76.02XD) Subsequent encounter

*Other Circumstances Related to Child Neglect*

V61.21 (Z69.010) Encounter for mental health services for victim of child neglect by parent

V61.21 (Z69.020) Encounter for mental health services for victim of nonparental child neglect

V15.42 (Z62.812) Personal history (past history) of neglect in childhood

V61.22 (Z69.011) Encounter for mental health services for perpetrator of parental child neglect

V62.83 (Z69.021) Encounter for mental health services for perpetrator of nonparental child neglect

#### Child Psychological Abuse

*Child Psychological Abuse, Confirmed*

995.51 (T74.32XA) Initial encounter

995.51 (T74.32XD) Subsequent encounter

*Child Psychological Abuse, Suspected*

995.51 (T76.32XA) Initial encounter

995.51 (T76.32XD) Subsequent encounter

*Other Circumstances Related to Child Psychological Abuse*

V61.21 (Z69.010) Encounter for mental health services for victim of child psychological abuse by parent

V61.21 (Z69.020) Encounter for mental health services for victim of nonparental child psychological abuse

V15.42 (Z62.811) Personal history (past history) of psychological abuse in childhood

V61.22 (Z69.011) Encounter for mental health services for perpetrator of parental child psychological abuse

V62.83 (Z69.021) Encounter for mental health services for perpetrator of nonparental child psychological abuse

## Adult Maltreatment and Neglect Problems

### Spouse or Partner Violence, Physical

*Spouse or Partner Violence, Physical, Confirmed*
995.81  (T74.11XA) Initial encounter
995.81  (T74.11XD) Subsequent encounter

*Spouse or Partner Violence, Physical, Suspected*
995.81  (T76.11XA) Initial encounter
995.81  (T76.11XD) Subsequent encounter

*Other Circumstances Related to Spouse or Partner Violence, Physical*
V61.11  (Z69.11)  Encounter for mental health services for victim of spouse or partner violence, physical
V15.41  (Z91.410) Personal history (past history) of spouse or partner violence, physical
V61.12  (Z69.12)  Encounter for mental health services for perpetrator of spouse or partner violence, physical

### Spouse or Partner Violence, Sexual

*Spouse or Partner Violence, Sexual, Confirmed*
995.83  (T74.21XA) Initial encounter
995.83  (T74.21XD) Subsequent encounter

*Spouse or Partner Violence, Sexual, Suspected*
995.83  (T76.21XA) Initial encounter
995.83  (T76.21XD) Subsequent encounter

*Other Circumstances Related to Spouse or Partner Violence, Sexual*
V61.11  (Z69.81)  Encounter for mental health services for victim of spouse or partner violence, sexual
V15.41  (Z91.410) Personal history (past history) of spouse or partner violence, sexual
V61.12  (Z69.12)  Encounter for mental health services for perpetrator of spouse or partner violence, sexual

### Spouse or Partner Neglect

*Spouse or Partner Neglect, Confirmed*
995.85  (T74.01XA) Initial encounter
995.85  (T74.01XD) Subsequent encounter

*Spouse or Partner Neglect, Suspected*
995.85  (T76.01XA) Initial encounter
995.85  (T76.01XD) Subsequent encounter

*Other Circumstances Related to Spouse or Partner Neglect*
V61.11  (Z69.11)  Encounter for mental health services for victim of spouse or partner neglect
V15.42  (Z96.412) Personal history (past history) of spouse or partner neglect
V61.12  (Z69.12)  Encounter for mental health services for perpetrator of spouse or partner neglect

### Spouse or Partner Abuse, Psychological

*Spouse or Partner Abuse, Psychological, Confirmed*
995.82  (T74.31XA) Initial encounter
995.82  (T74.31XD) Subsequent encounter

*Spouse or Partner Abuse, Psychological, Suspected*
995.82  (T76.31XA) Initial encounter
995.82  (T76.31XD) Subsequent encounter

*Other Circumstances Related to Spouse or Partner Abuse, Psychological*
V61.11  (Z69.11)  Encounter for mental health services for victim of spouse or partner psychological abuse
V15.42  (Z96.411) Personal history (past history) of spouse or partner psychological abuse
V61.12  (Z69.12)  Encounter for mental health services for perpetrator of spouse or partner psychological abuse

### Adult Abuse by Nonspouse or Nonpartner

*Adult Physical Abuse by Nonspouse or Nonpartner, Confirmed*
995.81  (T74.11XA) Initial encounter
995.81  (T74.11XD) Subsequent encounter

*Adult Physical Abuse by Nonspouse or Nonpartner, Suspected*
995.81  (T76.11XA) Initial encounter
995.81  (T76.11XD) Subsequent encounter

*Adult Sexual Abuse by Nonspouse or Nonpartner, Confirmed*
995.83  (T74.21XA) Initial encounter
995.83  (T74.21XD) Subsequent encounter

*Adult Sexual Abuse by Nonspouse or Nonpartner, Suspected*
995.83  (T76.21XA) Initial encounter
995.83  (T76.21XD) Subsequent encounter

*Adult Psychological Abuse by Nonspouse or Nonpartner, Confirmed*
995.82  (T74.31XA) Initial encounter
995.82  (T74.31XD) Subsequent encounter

*Adult Psychological Abuse by Nonspouse or Nonpartner, Suspected*
995.82  (T76.31XA) Initial encounter
995.82  (T76.31XD) Subsequent encounter

*Other Circumstances Related to Adult Abuse by Nonspouse or Nonpartner*
V65.49  (Z69.81)  Encounter for mental health services for victim of nonspousal adult abuse
V62.83  (Z69.82)  Encounter for mental health services for perpetrator of nonspousal adult abuse

## Educational and Occupational Problems

### Educational Problems
V62.3  (Z55.9)  Academic or Educational Problems

### Occupational Problems
V62.21 (Z56.82) Problem Related to Current Military Deployment Status
V62.29 (Z56.9)  Other Problem Related to Employment

### Housing and Economic Problems

#### Housing Problems
V60.0  (Z59.0)  Homelessness
V60.1  (Z59.1)  Inadequate Housing
V60.89 (Z59.2)  Discord With Neighbor, Lodger, or Landlord
V60.6  (Z59.3)  Problem Related to Living in a Residential Institution

Economic Problems

| | | |
|---|---|---|
| V60.2 | (Z59.4) | Lack of Adequate Food or Safe Drinking Water |
| V60.2 | (Z59.5) | Extreme Poverty |
| V60.2 | (Z59.6) | Low Income |
| V60.2 | (Z59.7) | Insufficient Social Insurance or Welfare Support |
| V60.9 | (Z59.9) | Unspecified Housing or Economic Problem |

Other Problems Related to the Social Environment

| | | |
|---|---|---|
| V62.89 | (Z60.0) | Phase of Life Problem |
| V60.3 | (Z60.2) | Problem Related to Living Alone |
| V62.4 | (Z60.3) | Acculturation Difficulty |
| V62.4 | (Z60.4) | Social Exclusion or Rejection |
| V62.4 | (Z60.5) | Target of (Perceived) Adverse Discrimination or Persecution |
| V62.9 | (Z60.9) | Unspecified Problem Related to Social Environment |

Problems Related to Crime or Interaction With the Legal System

| | | |
|---|---|---|
| V62.89 | (Z65.4) | Victim of Crime |
| V62.5 | (Z65.0) | Conviction in Civil or Criminal Proceedings Without Imprisonment |
| V62.5 | (Z65.1) | Imprisonment or Other Incarceration |
| V62.5 | (Z65.2) | Problems Related to Release From Prison |
| V62.5 | (Z65.3) | Problems Related to Other Legal Circumstances |

Other Health Service Encounters for Counseling and Medical Advice

| | | |
|---|---|---|
| V65.49 | (Z70.9) | Sex Counseling |
| V65.40 | (Z71.9) | Other Counseling or Consultation |

Problems Related to Other Psychosocial, Personal. And Environmental Circumstances

| | | |
|---|---|---|
| V62.89 | (Z65.8) | Religious or Spiritual Problem |
| V61.7 | (Z64.0) | Problems Related to Unwanted Pregnancy |
| V61.5 | (Z64.1) | Problems Related to Multiparity |
| V62.89 | (Z64.4) | Discord With Social Service Provider, Including Probation Officer, Case Manager, or Social Services Worker |
| V62.89 | (Z65.4) | Victim of Terrorism or Torture |
| V62.22 | (Z65.5) | Exposure to Disaster, War, or Other Hostilities |
| V62.89 | (Z65.8) | Other Problem Related to Psychosocial Circumstances |
| V62.9 | (Z65.9) | Unspecified Problem Related to Unspecified Psychosocial Circumstances |

Other Circumstances of Personal History

| | | |
|---|---|---|
| V15.49 | (Z91.49) | Other Personal History of Psychological Trauma |
| V15.59 | (Z91.5) | Personal History of Self-Harm |
| V62.22 | (Z91.89) | Personal History of Military Deployment |
| V15.89 | (Z91.89) | Other Personal Risk Factors |
| V69.9 | (Z72.9) | Problem Related to Lifestyle |
| V71.01 | (Z72.811) | Adult Antisocial Behavior |
| V71.02 | (Z72.810) | Child or Adolescent Antisocial Behavior |

Problems Related to Access to Medical and Other Health Care

| | | |
|---|---|---|
| V63.9 | (Z75.3) | Unavailability or Inaccessibility of Health Care Facilities |
| V63.8 | (Z75.4) | Unavailability or Inaccessibility of Other Helping Agencies |

Nonadherence to Medical Treatment

| | | |
|---|---|---|
| V15.81 | (Z91.19) | Nonadherence to Medical Treatment |
| 278.00 | (E66.9) | Overweight or Obesity |
| V65.2 | (Z76.5) | Malingering |
| V40.31 | (Z91.83) | Wandering Associated With a Mental Disorder |
| V62.89 | (R41.83) | Borderline Intellectual Functioning |

# Glossary

## A

**Abasis**   The inability to walk   37

**Abnormal behavior**   Behavior that is culturally inappropriate, is accompanied by subjective distress, and involves a psychological impairment (inability to cope with life's demands)   3

**Abstinence violation effect**   The tendency of an abstainer to conclude that relapse indicates the failure of treatment   345

**Acute**   Type of condition that begins or progresses rapidly, and that tends to end quickly   419

**Addiction**   Chronic pattern of habitual maladaptive behavior, often experienced as compulsive and uncontrollable, that tends to provide immediate gratification   319

**Affective flattening**   Lack of range of emotions   252

**Agnosia**   Failure to recognize familiar objects or people   423

**Agonist**   Chemical that can substitute for other substance at receptor sites   341

**Agreeableness**   Personality factor associated with a tendency to be caring, helpful, and cooperative   191

**Alogia**   Impoverished speech which conveys little information   249

**Amenorrhea**   Absence of menstruation in a woman of reproductive age   392

**Amnestic disorders**   Disorders in which the ability to learn and recall new information is impaired, without impaired consciousness or cognitive deficits   430

**Amniocentesis**   Taking a sample of amniotic fluid to conduct genetic tests on a fetus   359

**Analgesic**   A drug that reduces pain   319

**Androgen insensitivity syndrome**   Condition in which a genetically male fetus is insensitive to the effects of androgen and develops genitalia resembling a female   240

**Anesthesia**   A lack of ordinary sensation in which the body surface becomes insensitive to touch, pain, or heat   37

**Anhedonia**   Loss of interest or pleasure in all aspects of life   252

**Antagonist**   Chemicals that blocks receptor sites for another substance   341

**Anterograde amnesia**   Loss of ability to form new memories   430

**Anxiety**   A sense of worry, concern, or apprehension   140

**Aphasia**   A language disturbance involving impairment in understanding or expressing language   422

**Aphonia**   Inability to make speech sounds, without apparent physical basis   171

**Apraxia**   Impaired ability to execute motor activities although motor functions are intact   422

**Asphyxiophilia**   Intentional deprivation of oxygen to increase intensity of sexual arousal or orgasm   234

**Attribution model of depression**   View that depression is caused by a pessimistic attribution style that emphasizes internal, stable, and global factors to explain personal problems   300

**Automatic thoughts**   Covert self-statements, often pessimistic and negative, that occur readily and may contribute to depression   299

**Autonomic nervous system**   Portion of the nervous system that controls the functioning of many internal bodily processes such as heart rate, digestive processes, and so on   114

**Autosuggestion**   A process that is similar to self-hypnosis   38

**Autosuggestion**   Influencing one's own attitudes or behavior; self-hypnosis   172

**Avolition**   Inability to initiate and complete goal-directed activities   255

**Axon**   Part of the neuron that carries neural impulses to other cells   71

## B

**Behaviorism**   An approach to understanding behavior that emphasizes the relation between observable behavior and specifiable environmental events (or stimuli)   57

**Bereavement**   A normal reaction of grief and sadness in response to the death of a loved one   124

**Bibliotherapy**   The use of selected written materials that may have particular life significance as an adjunct in psychotherapy   210

**Big Five**   Dimensional model of personality that emphasizes the mixture of five main factors: openness to experience, conscientiousness, extroversion, agreeableness, and neuroticism   190

**Binge eating**   Eating much larger amounts of food than normal within a given time   394

**Delirium**   Rapidly developing change in consciousness and reduced attention                     418

**Delusion**   False belief that is firmly held, contrary to the consensus of other people                     249

**Dementia**   Global development of multiple cognitive deficits in memory, speech, and executive functioning   421

**Demonolgy**   The belief that possession by demons or spirits explains abnormal behavior          26

**Dendrites**   Branching fibers of a neuron that receive input from other neurons                     71

**Dependence**   A persistent pattern of drug use involving either tolerance, withdrawal, or inability to cut down dosage                     144

**Depressants**   Drugs that depress the CNS and produce drowsiness, and sedation                     339

**Diagnostic reliability** Consistency and agreement between clinicians in use of a diagnostic label                     9, 93

**Diagnostic validity**   The extent to which a diagnosis measures what it purports to measure          93

**Diathesis-stress model**   A model of mental disorders that proposes disorders develop when an individual with a diathesis (predisposition) experiences significant psychological stress                     124

**Discrimination**   Narrowing the range of controlling stimuli for a response                     41

**Discriminative stimulus**   A stimulus that serves as a signal that a certain response will lead to a reinforcer                     60

**Displacement**   Defense mechanism in which the person shifts a reaction from original target person or situation to some other person or situation (e.g., anger displacement from boss to family)          52

**Dissociative identity disorder**   Rare dissociative reaction in which relatively separate and distinctive personalities develop within the same person                     30

**Disturbances in executive function**   Involve impairments in the ability to plan and execute actions                     423

**Dopamine hypothesis of schizophrenia**   Proposed that the disorder was caused by excessive dopamine activity in the brain (Hence, DA-blocking drugs like Thorazine were useful).          75, 264

**Double-blind design**   Type of experimental design in which both subjects and personnel are kept blind with respect to whether a subject is in the experimental or control group   16

**Down syndrome**   A condition associated with mental retardation caused by trisomy of chromosome 21          360

**Dualism**   The belief that mind and body are separate and follow different laws                     33

**Durham rule**   Legal guideline that insanity concerns the extent to which the criminal act was a product of mental disorder          444

**Dyssomnias**   Sleep disorders that are concerned with abnormal sleep amount, quality, or timing          398

### E
-----

**Echolalia**   Repetition of words or phrases spoken by another person                     249

**Echopraxia**   Repetitively imitating the movements of others          251, 290

**Ego**   In Freudian theory, that part of the mind that mediates between id impulses and external reality          52

**Electroconvulsive therapy, or ECT**   Therapeutic induction of convulsive seizures by applying electrical current to the head; found to have some effectiveness with severe depressions          74, 302

**Electroencephalogram (EEG)**   A record of electrical activity of the brain in terms of brain frequencies, measured from the scalp          98

**Encephalitis**   Inflammation of the brain                     361, 415

**Endophenotypes**   Observable traits that can serve as biomarkers for a disorder                     265

**Epidemiological research**   Often involves the study of the incidence of a disorder in a population          11

**Exorcism**   The practice of expelling demons from a body that they possess                     26

**Experimental group**   Group on which manipulation of interest is performed in an experimental design                     15

**Experimental method**   Research method in which conditions are manipulated in order to test the effects of manipulations on various measures                     15

**Exposure and response prevention (ERP)**   Prolonged exposure to fear- or anxiety-producing stimulus or situation while escape, or the compulsive act, is prevented   156

**Exteroceptive**   Relating to external, environmental stimuli          143

**Extinction**   Repeated presentation of the conditioned stimulus without the unconditioned stimulus with the frequency and strength of conditioned responses tending to decrease, eventually to zero          41

**Extroversion**   Personality factor associated with the tendency to be outgoing or socially gregarious          190

## F

**Factor analysis** Mathematical technique to analyze a matrix of correlations to reduce dimensions and identify factors that may simplify the relationships 190

**Fainting** Loss of consciousness, slowing of heart rate, and drop in blood pressure often associated with acute fear states 140

**Fear** A sense of dread, terror, or fright 140

**Fetal alcohol syndrome** Constellation of fetal abnormalities resulting from maternal alcohol use during pregnancy 335

**Fixations** In Freudian theory, refers to an unusual investment of libidinal energy at a certain psychosexual stage 53

**Flashbacks** Re-experiencing some of the symptoms of intoxication in the absence of recent ingestion 338

**Flooding** Therapeutic technique in which the person is made to confront the stimuli that arouse anxiety until the anxiety extinguishes 131

**Fragile X syndrome** Condition in which the tip of the X chromosome is at risk of separation 359

**Fraternal or dizygotic (DZ) twins** Twins that result from the simultaneous fertilization of two separate ova with such a pair having the same degree of genetic similarity as any two non-twin siblings born to the same parents 69

**Free association** Basic procedure in psychoanalysis in which the patient is asked to say, without censorship, whatever comes to mind 55

**Functional MRI (fMRI)** Imaging technique that uses magnetic fields to detect changes in blood flow, producing a measure of brain activity 106

## G

**Gambler's fallacy** The inaccurate belief that past losses alter the future likelihood of a win 349

**General adaptation syndrome (GAS)** A generalized model of physical stress response that includes the alarm stage, the resistance stage, and (if stress continues) the exhaustion stage 113

**Generalization** Responding similarly to similar stimuli 41

**Generalized amnesia** Complete loss of memory for one's life history 177

**General paresis** Severe disorder characterized by various mental symptoms as well as bodily paralyses and caused by a syphilitic infection of the brain 34

**Genes** Units of hereditary information carried in a chromosome by DNA 66

**Genotype** Total set of inherited characteristics determined by a person's genetic makeup 66

**Glove or sleeve anesthesias** When the insensitive area of the hand or arm corresponded with that which would be covered by a glove or sleeve 38

## H

**Habit reversal therapy (HRT)** Therapy that involves awareness training and engagement in a response that is incompatible with the compulsion 159

**Habituation** Lessening of a response as a function of repeated presentations of the eliciting stimulus 131

**Hallucinations** Sensations or perceptions in the absence of an external source 250

**Hallucinogens** Drugs that produce marked changes in perception 338

**Hemianesthesia** The condition of the whole of one side of the body becoming insensitive 37

**Homeostasis** State of equilibrium or balance in a dynamic system 116

**Humanistic approach** Emphasis on viewing people as whole human beings rather than analyzing them in an impersonal fashion 77

**Hypnosis** A trancelike state induced through suggestion in cooperative subjects 36

**Hysteria** A condition that includes emotional arousal and physical symptoms that seem to have no organic basis 35

## I

**Iatrogenesis** The inadvertent and avoidable induction of a condition or disorder by a therapist during the treatment process 178

**Id** In Freudian theory, that part of the mind from which instinctual impulses originate 52

**Ideas of reference** False interpretation of events in terms of special meaning for the self 196

**Identical or monozygotic (MZ) twins** Twins resulting from the splitting of a single fertilized ovum who have exactly the same genetic makeup 69

**Illusions** The incorrect perceptions of sensory stimuli 250

**Institutionalization** The tendency for residents of an institution to become less able to function in the outside world the longer they remain within the institution 450

**Interobserver reliability** The extent to which different observers (or raters) agree on the way they categorize or in some way quantify a given observation   12

**Interoceptive** Relating to internal, physiological stimuli   143

**Intoxication** A reversible problematic change in behavior and cognition following ingestion of a substance   322

**Intrapsychic** Refers to unobservable mental events such as ideas, wishes, and unconscious conflicts   52

**Introjection** In psychoanalytic theory, part of the process of identification, whereby a person incorporates or internalizes the characteristics of others   297

**In vivo exposure** Exposure to the actual feared stimulus, rather than an imagined or symbolic stimulus   149

**IQ** Intelligence quotient, a standard score indicating intellectual functioning as compared to others in the population   356

**Irresistible impulse rule** Legal guideline that insanity concerns a person's inability to resist committing the crime   443

**Isolation** Defense mechanism in which a person separates emotional from intellectual content, or otherwise separates experiences that would be anxiety arousing if permitted to occur together   52

### K

**Kegel exercises** Exercises to tense and release vaginal muscles   228

### L

**La belle indifférence** The condition of hysterical patients appearing calm and indeed quite cheerful, instead of being worried or depressed about their physical symptoms   38, 171

**Learned helplessness** The theory that depression is caused by a lack of connection between responses and their outcomes (i.e., a lack of control over events)   299

**Libido** Psychoanalytic concept referring to sexual instincts   53

**Localized amnesia** Failure to recall events during a circumscribed period of time   177

**Lunatics** Those whose mental problems were traceable to the phases of the moon   34

### M

**Magnetic resonance imaging (MRI)** Imaging technique using variations in magnetic fields to produce 3-dimensional images of the brain and other organs with better resolution than the CT scans   106

**Malarial fever therapy** A treatment for general paresis that involved infecting the patient with malaria to cause a high fever   35

**Malingering** The intentional faking of a physical or psychological symptom   165

**Masochism** Preferences for obtaining sexual gratification by experiencing pain inflicted on oneself   234

**McNaughton rule** Legal guideline that insanity concerns an individual's inability to distinguish right from wrong in committing the crime   443

**Melancholia** Particularly deep level of depression characterized by absence of interest or pleasure in all things, changes in sleep, changes in weight, and/or excessive guilt   285

**Meningitis** Inflammation of the meninges, the protective covering of the brain and spinal cord   361

**Mental status examination** Brief interview and observation method to provide an overview of a person's general level of psychological functioning   100

**Mesmerism** Closely related to the phenomenon of hypnosis; derived from the techniques of Anton Mesmer   36

**Mirror neurons** Neurons in primate brains that discharge when a movement is executed, as well as when the movement is observed in others   172

**Modeling** Teaching a behavior by performing the behavior and having the learner imitate it   64

**Monoamine hypothesis** Hypothesis that depression is caused by a deficiency of certain monoamine neurotransmitters in the brain   294

**Munchausen syndrome** Earlier terminology for the mental disorder in which symptoms are intentionally feigned, for no apparent reason   166

**Mutism** Refusal to speak   251

### N

**Naming fallacy** The incorrect assumption that by applying a label or name to something, we have in some sense explained it   7

**Narcotics** Opiate drugs that produce stupor and pain relief   339

**Negative reinforcement**   The contingent removal of an unpleasant stimulus, which strengthens subsequent responding   60

**Neglect syndrome**   A spatial disorder involving inattention to the left visual field due to damage to the right parietal lobe of the brain   416

**Neurons**   Individual nerve cells   71

**Neurosis**   Anxiety-driven condition that results when id impulses threaten to overwhelm the ego   247

**Neuroticism**   Personality factor associated with the tendency to experience negative emotions   190

**Neurotransmitters**   Chemical substances released into the synapse that enable transmission of impulses from one neuron to another   72

**Night eating syndrome**   Eating pattern in which individuals consume more than half of their daily calories in late-night binges   397

## O

**Obsessions**   Intrusive thoughts that are difficult to stop or control   152

**Oedipal conflict**   In Freudian theory, the erotic attachment to the opposite-sex parent, involving feelings of competition and hostility toward the same-sex parent, and fears of retaliation (castration anxiety in boys) from the same-sex parent   51

**Openness to experience**   Personality factor associated with a tendency to show imaginativeness, independence, and preference for variety   190

**Operant conditioning**   Type of learning in which the consequences of a response control the response's future probability   41

**Organic view**   Belief that abnormal behavior is caused primarily by biological factors   33

## P

**Panic attack**   Rapidly developing sense of intense fear and anxiety   140

**Paradigm**   A model or framework from which to view a phenomenon   24

**Paranoia**   Unfounded, irrational, or exaggerated suspicion or mistrust of others   4

**Parasomnias**   Sleep disorders that are concerned with abnormal events or behaviors involving the sleep cycle or sleep-wake transitions   398

**Parasympathetic nervous system**   Division on the autonomic nervous system primarily involved in conservation of energy, such as increasing digestive processes   115

**Paruresis**   Inability to urinate in a public restroom   176

**Pavlovian conditioning**   Learning process whereby a formerly neutral stimulus comes to elicit a response as a result of pairing with an unconditioned stimulus   41

**Performance anxiety**   Fear of not being able to perform sexually, which in turn hinders sexual performance, and may be central to the development of sexual dysfunctions   219

**Personality**   The stable and enduring pattern of relating to oneself and to the world   189

**Personality inventory**   A self-report questionnaire in which brief responses to a collection of test items are used to assess personal characteristics or behaviors across various personality dimensions   102, 190

**Phenotypes**   Observed characteristics that result from interaction between genotype and environmental influences   68

**Phenylketonuria (PKU)**   Rare single-gene recessive metabolic disorder that results in intellectual disability   70, 359

**Phobia**   Strong, irrational fear of some specific object, animal, or situation   54

**Phototherapy**   Use of board-spectrum light to treat seasonal depression   305

**Phrenologists**   Those who attempted to describe personality by feeling the bumps on a person's skull   190

**Placebo effect**   When an expectation of improvements is sufficient to cause improvement   15

**Plethysmographic assessment**   Assessment of sexual arousal by measurement of genital blood flow   233

**Polysomnography**   Using a polygraph to make a continuous record during sleep of multiple physiological variables (such as breathing, heart rate, EEG, and muscle contractions)   398

**Positive reinforcement**   The contingent presentation of a pleasant result, which strengthens subsequent responding   60

**Positron emission tomography (PET)**   Imaging technique that measures metabolic activity (such as glucose utilization) as an indication of the functioning of the brain or other organs   106

**Prematurity**   Preterm delivery and low birth weight, may be associated with multiple impairments in behavioral, cognitive, sensory, and CNS functioning   361

**Preparedness**   Biologically-based tendency to form associations between certain stimuli more readily than others   148

**Primary reinforcers**   Events, usually biological in nature, which almost always provide reinforcement, such as eating when hungry (Primary reinforcers do not acquire their reinforcing properties through learning.)   59

**Privileged communication** Information disclosed to a therapist that cannot be legally revealed without the written consent of the patient     451

**Progressive relaxation** The systematic tensing and relaxing of specific muscle groups     122

**Projection** Defense mechanism in which the person disowns some impulse and attributes it to another person     52

**Projective tests** Tests in which the person is presented with ambiguous stimulus materials and asked to respond in some way, based on the assumption that persons project characteristics of their own intrapsychic processes onto their responses     101

**Pseudocyesis** False belief of being pregnant, accompanied by reported pregnancy symptoms as well as some objective signs of pregnancy     176

**Psychoactive** Altering mood, perception, or brain function     319

**Psychogenic** Originating from psychological factors     169

**Psychological tests** Highly standardized procedures for obtaining samples of behavior     100

**Psychoneuroimmunology** The study of the neural effects of psychological events on the immune system     121

**Psychopath** Antisocial personality, involving characteristics such as lack of empathy or concern for others, frequent rule violations, impulsivity, and superficial charm     199

**Psychosis** Severe psychological disturbance involving personality disorganization and loss of contact with reality     247

**Psychosurgery** Procedure that attempts to treat abnormal behavior by surgical intervention on the brain     74

**Psychoticism** Personality factor associated with the tendency to show aggressiveness and interpersonal hostility     190

**Punishers** Types of consequences that weaken or suppress the behaviors that produce them     59

**Purging** A compensatory activity intended to reverse the effects of eating, usually involving self-induced vomiting or use of laxatives     392

## R
------

**Random sampling** Selecting subjects by chance from some larger population     11

**Reaction formation** Defense mechanism in which a person behaves in a way directly opposite from some underlying impulse     51

**Refractory period** Period following orgasm in males during which further sexual arousal and orgasm are not possible     218

**Regression** In Freudian theory, refers to a return to some earlier state of psychosexual development in the face of some current frustration     53

**Reinforcement** Consequence that strengthens the future probability of a response that produces it     59

**Relapse** Re-occurrence of symptoms after a period of improvement     144

**Reliability** The extent to which a measure consistently yields the same results on repeated trials     11

**REM sleep** Sleep phase that involves rapid eye movements, often associated with vivid dreaming     401

**Repression** Defense mechanism in which the anxiety-arousing memory or impulse is prevented from becoming conscious     51

**Resistance** In psychoanalysis the phenomenon in which patients unconsciously resist gaining insight into unconscious motives and conflicts     55

**Retrograde amnesia** Inability to recall events that occurred before the onset of the amnesia     430

**Reversal design** This experimental design is one in which new reinforcement contingencies are instated for a period of time, followed by reinstatement of the old reinforcement contingencies, and finally the installment of the original, new contingencies. Sometimes a fourth reversal is included, the purpose of which is to show that the new contingencies are causing any observed changes in behavior.     62

**Rule-governed behavior** Behavior that is controlled by the verbal description of a contingency rather than the contingency itself   349

## S
-----

**Sadism** Preference for obtaining sexual gratification by inflicting pain on one's partner     235

**Sanity** The mental ability to distinguish right from wrong, and to form the intent to commit an act such as a crime     442

**Savant syndrome** Exceptional ability in a narrow area     371

**Selective amnesia** Loss of memory for some but not all events during a particular period of time   177

**Sexomnia** Sexual activities during sleep, without conscious awareness     405

**Significant difference** A difference unlikely to have occurred by chance and therefore reflecting a real effect     15

## V

## W

# Bibliography

## A

Abbot-Shim, M., Lambert, R., & McCarty, F. (2003). A comparison of school readiness outcomes for children randomly assigned to a Head Start program and the program's wait list. *Journal of Education for Students Placed at Risk, 8,* 191–214.

Abi-Dargham, A. (2004). Do we still believe in the dopamine hypothesis? New data bring new evidence. *International Journal of Neuropharmacology, 7* (Suppl. 1), 51–55.

Abrahamsen, D. (1979, July). Unmasking 'Son of Sam's' demons. *New York Times Magazine.*

Abrahamson, L. Y., Seligman, M. E., & Teasdale, J. D. (1997). Learned helplessness in humans: Critique and reformulation. *Journal of Abnormal Psychology, 65,* 44–52.

Abramowitz, J. S. (1997). Effectiveness of psychological and pharmacological treatment for obsessive-compulsive disorder: A quantitative review. *Journal of Consulting and Clinical Psychology, 65,* 44–52.

Abramowitz, J. S., Foa, E. B., & Franklin, M. E. (2003). Exposure and ritual prevention for obsessive-compulsive disorder: Effects of intensive versus twice-weekly sessions. *Journal of Consulting and Clinical Psychology, 71,* 394–398.

Adamis, D., Treloar, A., Martin, F. C., & MacDonald, A. J. (2007). A brief review of the history of delirium as a mental disorder. *History of Psychiatry, 18,* 459–469.

Ader, R., & Cohen, N. (1975). Behaviorally conditioned immunosuppression. *Psychosomatic Medicine, 37,* 333–340.

Ader, R., Cohen, N., & Bovbjerg, D. (1982). Conditioned suppression of humoral immunity in the rat. *Journal of Comparative and Physiological Psychology, 96,* 517–521.

Akiskal, H. S., & McKinney, W. T. (1975). Overview of recent research on depression. *Archives of General Psychiatry, 32,* 285–304.

Aldrich, M. S. (1992). Narcolepsy. *Neurology, 42,* 34–43.

Allen, M. C. (2008). Prematurity. In P. J. Accardo, *Capute and Accardo's neurodevelopmental disabilities in infancy and childhood: Vol 1: Neurodevelopmental diagnosis and treatment* (pp. 199–226). Baltimore, MD: Paul H Brookes Publishing.

Allen, P., Aleman, A., & McGuire, P. K. (2007). Inner speech models of auditory verbal hallucinations: Evidence from behavioral and neuroimaging studies. *International Review of Psychiatry, 19,* 409–417.

Allison, K. C., Grilo, C. M., Masheb, R. M., & Stunkard, A. J. (2005). Binge eating disorder and night eating syndrome: A comparative study of disordered eating. *Journal of Consulting and Clinical Psychology, 73,* 1107–1115.

Alpert, H. R., Connolly, G. N., & Biene, L. (2013). A prospective cohort study challenging the effectiveness of population-based medical intervention for smoking cessation. *Tobacco Control, 22,* 32–37. doi:10.1136/tobaccocontrol-2011-050129

American Law Institute. (1962). *Model penal code: Proposed official draft.* Philadelphia, PA: Author.

American Psychiatric Association. (1952). *Diagnostic and statistical manual of mental disorders.* Washington, DC: American Psychiatric Association.

American Psychiatric Association. (1968). *Diagnostic and statistical manual of mental disorders* (2nd ed.). Washington, DC: American Psychiatric Association.

American Psychiatric Association. (1980). *Diagnostic and statistical manual of mental disorders, Third Edition.* Washington, DC: American Psychiatric Association.

American Psychiatric Association. (1983, December). *American Psychiatric Association Statement on the Insanity Defense.* National Criminal Justice Reference Service. Washington, DC: Congressional Sales Office GPO.

American Psychiatric Association. (1994). *Diagnostic and statistical manual of mental disorders* (4th ed.). Washington, DC: American Psychiatric Association.

American Psychiatric Association. (2000). *Diagnostic and statistical manual of mental disorders, Fourth Edition, Text Revision* (Fourth Edition, text revised ed.). Washington, DC: American Psychiatric Association.

American Psychiatric Association. (2012, December). *DSM-5 development fact sheet.* Retrieved March 29, 2013, from APA *DSM-5:* http://www.dsm5.org/Pages/Default. aspx

American Psychiatric Association. (2013). *Diagnostic and statistical manual for mental disorders, Fifth Edition.* Arlington, VA: American Psychiatric Association.

American Psychological Association. (2002). *Ethical principles of psychologists and code of conduct.* Washington, DC: Author.

American Psychological Association. (2006, September). *Report of the working group on psychotropic medications for children and adolescents: Psychopharmacological, psychosocial, and combined interventions for childhood disorders: Evidence based, contextual factors, and future directions.* Retrieved 2013, from http://www.apa.org/ pi/families/resources/child-medications. pdf

American Psychological Association. (2011). Practice guidelines regarding psychologists' involvement in pharmacological issues. *American Psychologist, 66,* 835–849. doi:10.1037/ a0025890

Amnesty International. (2004, March 5). *"Stop violence against women".* Retrieved August 14, 2008, from Amnesty International: http://www.amnestyusa.org/violence-against-women/stop-violence-against-women-svaw/page.do?id=1108417&n1=3 &n2=39&n3=1101

Angst, F., Stassen, H. H., Clayton, P. J., & Angst, J. (2002). Morality of patients with mood disorders: Follow-up over 34–38 years. *Journal of Affective Disorders, 68,* 167–181.

Anisman, H., Prakash, P., Merali, Z., & Poulter, M. O. (2007). Corticotropin releasing hormone receptor alterations elicited by acute and chronic unpredictable stressor challenges in stressor-susceptible and resilient strains of mice. *Behavioural Brain Research, 181,* 180–190.

Anthony, M. M., Brown, T. A., & Barlow, D. H. (1997). Heterogeneity among specific phobia types in *DSM-IV. Behaviour Research and Therapy, 35,* 1089–1100.

Antoni, M. H., Cruess, D. G., Cruess, S., Lutgendorf, A., Kumar, M., & Ironson, G. (2000). Cognitive-behavioral stress management intervention effects on anxiety, 24-hour urinary norepinephrine output, and T-cyto-toxic/suppressor cells over time among symptomatic HIV-infected gay men. *Journal of Consulting and Clinical Psychology, 68,* 31–45.

Antonio, M. H., & Lutgendorf, S. (2007). Psychosocial factors and disease progression in cancer. *Current Directions in Psychological Science, 16,* 42–46.

Antonuccio, D. O., Danton, W. G., & McClanahan, T. M. (2003). Psychology in the prescription era: Building a firewall between marketing and science. *American Psychologist, 58,* 1028–1043.

Applebaum, P. S. (1988). The right to refuse treatment with antipsychotic medications: Retrospect and prospect. *American Journal of Psychiatry, 145,* 413–419.

Archibald, H. C., & Tuddenham, R. D. (1965). Persistent stress reaction after combat. *Archives of General Psychiatry, 12,* 475–481.

Ardolf, B. R., Denney, R. L., & Houston, C. M. (2007). Base rates of negative response bias and malingered neurocognitive dysfunction among criminal defendants referred for neuropsychological evaluation. *The Clinical Neuropsychologist, 21*, 899–916. doi:10.1080/13825580600966391

Armstrong, D. D. (2005). Neuropathology of Rett Syndrome. *Journal of Child Neurology, 20*, 747–753.

Asarnow, R. F., Steffy, R. A., & MacCrimmon, D. J. (1977). An attentional assessment of foster children at risk for schizophrenia. *Journal of Abnormal Psychology, 86*, 267–275.

Avery, D., & Winokur, G. (1977). The efficacy of electroconvulsive therapy and antidepressants in depression. *Biological Psychiatry, 12*, 507–523.

Azevedo, F. C., Carvalho, L. R., Grinberg, L. T., Ferretti, R. E., Leite, R. E., Filho, W. J., ... Herculano-Houzel, S. (2009). Equal numbers of neuronal and nonneuronal cells make the human brain an isometrically scaled-up primate brain. *Journal of Comparative Neurology, 513*, 532–541. doi:10.1002/cne.21974

Azmitia, E. C., & Nixon, R. (2008). Dystrophic serotonergic axons in neurodegenerative diseases. *Brain Research, 1217*, 185–194.

Azrin, N. H. (1976). Improvements in the community-reinforcement approach to alcoholism. *Behavioral Research and Therapy, 14*, 339–348.

## B

Bach, P., & Hayes, S. C. (2002). The use of acceptance and commitment therapy to prevent rehospitalization of psychotic patients: A randomized controlled trial. *Journal of Consulting and Clinical Psychology, 70*, 1129–1139.

Bacopoulos, N. C., Spokes, E. G., Bird, E. D., & Roth, R. H. (1979). Antipsychotic drug action in schizophrenic patients: Effect on cortical dopamine metabolism after long-term treatment. *Science, 205*, 1404–1407.

Baechler, J. (1979). *Suicides.* New York, NY: Basic Books.

Baggaley, M. (2008). Sexual dysfunction in schizophrenia: Focus on recent evidence. *Human Psychopharmacology: Clinical and Experimental, 23*, 201–209.

Bailly, L. (2005). Stimulant medication for the treatment of attention-deficit hyperactivity disorder: evidence-b(i)ased practice? *Psychiatric Bulletin, 29*, 284–287.

Balachandra, K., & Swaminath, S. (2002). Fire fetishism in a female arsonist? *Canadian Journal of Psychiatry, 47*, 487–488.

Ballanger, J. C., Davidson, J., Lecrubier, Y., & Nutt, D. J. (2000). Consensus statement on posttraumatic stress disorder from the International Consensus on Depression

and Anxiety. *Journal of Clinical Psychiatry, 61*, 60–66.

Bandura, A. (1977). *Social learning theory.* Englewood Cliffs, NJ: Prentice-Hall.

Banks, S., & Dinges, D. F. (2007). Behavioral and physiological consequences of sleep restrictions. *Journal of Clinical Sleep Medicine, 3*, 519–528.

Banner, L. L., & Anderson, R. U. (2007). Integrated sildenafil and cognitive behavior sex therapy for psychogenic erectile dysfunction: A pilot study. *Journal of Sexual Medical, 4*, 1117–1125.

Bansky, A. J., Coeyfaux, R. R., Samie, M. K., & Cleary, P. D. (1993). Hypochondriacal patients' belief about good health. *American Journal of Psychiatry, 150*, 1085–1089.

Barch, D. M. (2005). The cognitive neuroscience of schizophrenia. *Annual Review of Clinical Psychology, 1*, 321–353. doi:10.1146/annurev.clinpsy.1.102803.143959

Barkley, R. A., Cook, E. H., Diamond, A., Zametkin, A., Thaper, A., Teeter, A., ... et al. (2002). International consensus statement on ADHD. *Clinical Child and Family Psychology Review, 5*, 89–111.

Barlow, D. H. (2002). *Anxiety and its disorders: The nature and treatment of anxiety and panic* (2 ed.). New York, NY: Guilford.

Barlow, D. H., Gorman, J. M., & Sjear, K. (2000). Cognitive-behavioral therapy, imipramine, or their combination for Panic Disorder: A randomized controlled trial. *Journal of the American Medical Association, 283*, 2529–2536.

Barlow, D. H., Raffa, S. D., & Cohen, E. M. (2002). Psychosocial treatments for panic disorders, phobias, and generalized anxiety disorders. In P. E. Nathan, & J. M. Gorman, *A guide to treatments that work* (2 ed., pp. 301–335). New York, NY: Oxford Press.

Barnes, G. M., Hoffman, J. H., Welte, J. W., Farrell, M. P., & Dintcheff, B. A. (2006). Effects of parental monitoring and peer deviance on substance use and delinquency. *Journal of Marriage and Family, 68*, 1084–1104.

Barrett, P. M., Duffy, A. L., Dadds, M. M., & Rapee, R. M. (2001). Cognitive-behavioral treatment of anxiety disorders in children: Long-term (6-year) follow-up. *Journal of Consulting and Clinical Psychology, 69*, 135–141.

Bateson, G., Jackson, D. D., Haley, J., & Weakland, J. (1956). Toward a theory of schizophrenia. *Behavioral Science, 1*, 251–264.

Bazelon, D. (1974). Psychiatrists and the adversary process. *Scientific American, 230*, 18–23.

BBC News. (2011 24-July). *'Breivik manifesto' details chilling attack.* Retrieved 2013 19-May from BBC News Europe: http://www.bbc.co.uk/news/world-europe-14267007

Beck, A. T. (1976). *Cognitive therapy and emotional disorders.* New York, NY: International Universities Press.

Beck, A. T., & Emery, T. (1985). *Anxiety disorders and phobias.* New York, NY: Basic Books.

Beck, A. T., Ward, C. H., Mendelson, M., Mock, J. E., & Erbaugh, J. K. (1962). Reliability of psychiatric diagnoses II: A study of consistency of clinical judgments and ratings. *American Journal of Psychiatry, 119*, 351–357.

Beggington, P., & Kuipers, L. (1994). The predictive utility of expressed emotion in schizophrenia: An aggregate analysis. *Psychological Medicine, 24*, 707–718.

Benazzi, F. (2003). Diagnosis of bipolar II disorders: A comparison of structured versus semistructured interviews. *Progress in Neuro-Psychopharmacology & Biological Psychiatry, 27*, 985–991.

Benbadis, S. R., & Allen Hauser, W. (2000). An estimate of the prevalence of psychogenic non-epileptic seizures. *Seizure: The Journal of the British Epilepsy Association, 9*, 280–281.

Bendetti, F., Sforzini, L., Columbo, C., Marrei, C., & Smeraldi, E. (1998). Low-dose clozapine in acute and continuation treatment of severe borderline personality disorder. *Journal of Clinical Psychiatry, 59*, 103–107.

Benedict, R. (1934). Anthropology and the abnormal. *Journal of General Psychology, 10*, 59–82.

Bergler, E. (1957). *The psychology of gambling.* New York, NY: Hill and Wang.

Bernstein, D. P., & Useda, J. D. (2007). Paranoid personality disorder. In W. O'Donohue, K. A. Fowler, & S. O. Lilienfeld, *Personality disorders: Toward the DSM-V* (pp. 41–62). Thousand Oaks, CA: Sage Publications, Inc.

Bettelheim, B. (1967). *The empty fortress.* New York, NY: Free Press.

Bijou, S. W., & Ghezzi, P. (1999). The behavioral interference theory of autistic behavior in young children. In P. M. Ghezzi, W. L. Williams, & J. E. Carr, *Autism: Behavior analytic perspectives* (pp. 33–34). Reno, NV: Context Press.

Binswagner, L. (1999). Being in the world. *Biological Sciences, 11*, 222–236.

Blanco, C., Okuda, M., Wright, C., Hasin, D. S., Grant, B. F., Liu, S., & Olfson, M. (2008). Mental health of college students and their non-college-attending peers. *Archives of General Psychiatry, 65*, 1429–1437.

Blazer, D. G., & van Nieuwenhuizen, A. O. (2012). Evidence for the diagnostic criteria of delirium. *Current Opinion in Psychiatry, 25*, 239–243.

Blennow, K., de Leon, M. J., & Zetterberg, H. (2006). Alzheimer's Disease. *Lancet, 368*, 387–403.

Bleuler, E. (1950). *Dementia praecox or the group of schizophrenias.* New York, NY: International University Press.

Blier, P., Szabo, S. T., Haddjeri, N., & Dong, J. (2000). Orbitofrontal cortex-basal ganglia system in OCD. *International Journal of Neuropsychopharmacology, 3*, 1–14.

Bloch, M. H., Londeros-Weisenberger, A., Dombrowski, P., Kelmendi, B., Wenger, R., Nudel, J., ... Coric, V. (2007). Systematic review: Pharmacological and behavioral treatment for trichotillomania. *Biological Psychiatry, 62*, 839–846.

Bloch, M. R., Elliott, M., Thompson, H., & Koran, L. M. (2001). Fluoxetine in pathologic skin-picking: Open-label and double-blind results. *Psychosomatics, 42*, 314–319.

Bloodstein, O. (1949). Conditions under which stuttering is reduced or absent: A review of the literature. *Journal of Speech and Hearing Disorders*, 295–302.

Bloodstein, O. (1975). Stuttering as tension and fragmentation. In J. Eisenson, *Stuttering: A second symposium*. New York, NY: Harper & Row.

Bogaert, A. F., Bezeau, S., Kuban, M., & Blanchard, R. (1997). Pedophilia, sexual orientation, and birth order. *Journal of Abnormal Psychology, 106*, 331–335.

Bonanno, G. A. (2006). The illusion of repressed memory. *Behavioral and Brain Science, 29*, 515–516.

Bond, D. D. (1952). *The love and fear of flying*. New York, NY: International University Press.

Bonnie, R. J. (2004). The American Psychiatric Association's resource document on mental retardation and capital sentencing: Implementing *Atkins v. Virginia. The Journal of the American Academy of Psychiatry and the Law, 32*, 304–308.

Borkeovec, T. E., & Ruscio, A. M. (2001). Psychotherapy for generalized anxiety disorders. *Journal of Clinical Psychiatry, 62*, 37–42.

Bouchard, T. P., Malykhin, N., Martin, W. R., Hanstock, C. C., Emery, D. J., Fisher, N. J., & Camicioli, R. M. (2008). Age and dementia-associated atrophy predominates in the hippocampal head and amygdala in Parkinson's disease. *Neurobiology of Aging, 29*, 1027–1039.

Boudet, C., Bocca, M. L., Chabot, B., Delamillieure, P., Brazo, P., Denise, P., & Dollfus, S. (2005). Are eye movement abnormalities indicators of genetic vulnerability to schizophrenia? *European Psychiatry, 20*, 339–345.

Bourchard, T. J., Lykken, D. T., McGue, M., Segal, N. L., & Tellegan, A. (1990). Sources of human psychological differences: The Minnesota study of twins reared apart. *Science, 250*, 223–228.

Bourne, R. S., Tahir, T. A., Borthwick, M., & Sampson, E. L. (2008). Drug treatment of delirium: Past, present, and future. *Journal of Psychosomatic Research, 65*, 273–282.

Bouton, M. E., Mineka, S., & Barlow, D. H. (2001). A modern learning perspective on the etiology of panic disorders. *Psychological Review, 108*, 4–32.

Bowen, M. (1978). *Family therapy in clinical practice*. New York, NY: Jason Aronson.

Bozzuto, J. C. (1975). Cinematic neurosis following *The Exorcist. Journal of Nervous and Mental Disease, 161*, 43–48.

Bregman, E. (1934). An attempt to modify the emotional attitudes of infants by the conditioned response technique. *Journal of Genetic Psychology, 45*, 169–196.

Brenner, M. (1973). *Mental illness and the economy*. Cambridge, MA: Harvard University Press.

Brody, M. L., Walsh, B. T., & Devlin, M. J. (1994). Binge eating disorder: Reliability and validity of a new diagnostic category. *Journal of Consulting and Clinical Psychology, 62*, 381–386.

Broome, M. R., Woolley, J. B., Tabraham, P., Johns, L. C., Bramon, E., Murray, G. K., ... Murray, R. M. (2005). What causes the onset of psychosis? *Schizophrenia Research, 79*, 23–24.

Brown, A. S., Schaefer, C. A., Wyatt, R. J., Goetz, R., Begg, M. D., Gorman, J. M., & Susser, E. S. (2000). Maternal exposure to respiratory infections and adult schizophrenia spectrum disorders: A prospective birth cohort study. *Schizophrenia Bulletin, 26*, 287–295.

Brown, G. W. (1959). Experiences of discharged chronic schizophrenic mental hospital patients in various types of living groups. *Milbank Memorial Fund Quarterly, 37*, 105–131.

Brown, N., Goulding, E. H., & Fabro, S. (1979). Ethanol embryotoxicity: Direct effects on mammalian embryos in vitro. *Science, 206*, 573–575.

Brown, T. A., Di Nardo, P. A., Lehman, C. L., & Campbell, L. A. (2001). Reliability of *DSM-IV* anxiety and mood disorders: Implications for the classification of emotional disorders. *Journal of Abnormal Psychology, 110*, 49–58.

Buchsbaum, M. S. (1977). Psychophysiology and schizophrenia. *Schizophrenia Bulletin, 3*, 7–14.

Budney, A. J., Moore, B. A., Rocha, H. L., & Higgins, S. T. (2006). Clinical trial of abstinence-based vouchers and cognitive-behavioral therapy for cannabis dependence. *Journal of Consulting and Clinical Psychology, 74*, 307–316.

Buka, S. I., Cannon, T. D., Torrey, E. F., Yolken, R. H., et al. (2008). Maternal exposure to herpes simplex virus and risk of psychosis among adult offspring. *Biological Psychology, 63*, 809–815.

Bulik, C. M., Thornton, L., Pinheiro, A. P., Plotnicov, K., Klump, K. L., Brandt, H., ... et al. (2008). Suicide attempts in anorexia nervosa. *Pscyhosomatic Medicine, 70*, 373–383.

Bunney, W. E., Murphy, D. L., Goodwin, F. K., & Borge, G. F. (1972). The "switch process" in manic-depressive illness. *Archives of General Psychiatry, 27*, 295–303.

Burnette, M. M., Koehn, K. A., Kenyon-Jump, R., Hutton, K., & Stark, C. (1991). Control of genital herpes recurrences using progressive muscle relaxation. *Behavior Therapy, 22*, 237–247.

Bustillo, J. R., Lauriello, J., Horan, W. P., & Keith, S. J. (2001). The psychosocial treatment of schizophrenia: An update. *American Journal of Psychiatry, 158*, 163–175.

Butcher, J. N. (2006). *MMPI-2: A practitioner's guide*. Washington, DC: American Psychological Association.

Butzlaff, R. L., & Hooley, J. M. (1998). Expressed emotion and psychiatric relapse. *Archives of General Psychiatry, 55*, 547–552.

Byrne, S. A., Cherniack, M. G., & Petry, N. M. (2013 6-February). Antisocial personality disorder is associated with receipt of physical disability benefits in substance abuse treatment patients. *Drug and Alcohol Dependence*. doi:10.1016/j.drugalcdep.2013.01.004

## C

Cameron, N. (1947). *The psychology of behavior disorders*. Boston, NY: Houghton Mifflin.

Campbell, A. (1999). Staying alive: Evolution, culture, and women's intrasexual aggression. *Behavioral and Brain Sciences, 22*, 203–252.

Campbell, D., Sanderson, R. E., & Laverty, S. G. (1964). Characteristics of a conditioned response in human subjects during extinction trial. *Journal of Abnormal and Social Psychology, 68*, 627–639.

Cannon, M., Jones, P. B., & Murray, R. M. (2002). Obstetric complications and schizophrenia: Historical and meta-analytic review. *American Journal of Psychiatry, 159*, 1080–1092.

Cantor, J. M., Blanchard, R., Christensen, B. K., Dickey, R., Klassen, P. E., Beckstead, A. L., ... Kuban, M. E. (2004). Intelligence, memory, and handedness in pedophilia. *Neuropsychology, 18*, 3–14.

Cantor, J. M., Blanchard, R., Robichaud, L. K., & Christensen, B. K. (2005). Quantitative reanalysis of aggregate data on IQ in sexual offenders. *Psychological Bulletin, 131*, 555–568.

Cantor-Graae, E., & Selten, J. (2005). Schizophrenia and migration: A meta-anlaysis and review. *American Journal of Psychiatry, 16*, 12–24.

Cantwell, D. P., Baker, L., & Rutter, M. (1978). Family factors. In M. Rutter, & E. Schopler, *Autism: A reappraisal of concepts and treatment*. New York, NY: Plenum Press.

Carey, J. T., & Mandel, J. (1968). A San Francisco "speed" scene. *Journal of Health and Social Behavior, 9*, 164–174.

Carlen, P. L., Wortzman, G., Holgate, R. C., Wilkinson, D. A., & Rankin, J. G. (1978). Reversible cerebral atrophy in recently abstinent chronic alcoholics measured by computed tomography scans. *Science, 200*, 1076–1078.

Caron, C. (2011, November 30). *Therapist 'brainwashed' woman into believing she was in Satanic Cult, attorney says.* Retrieved April 16, 2013, from ABC News: http://abcnews.go.com/US/therapist-accused-implanting-satanic-memories/story?id=15043529#.UW24rcqto3U

Cartwright, R. (2004). Sleepwalking violence: A sleep disorder, a legal dilemma, and a psychological challenge. *American Journal of Psychiatry, 161*, 1149–1158.

Caselli, R. J., Beach, T. G., Yaari, R., & Reiman, E. M. (2006). Alzheimer's disease a century later. *Journal of Clinical Psychiatry, 67*, 1784–1800.

Caspi, A., Sugden, K., Moffitt, T., Taylor, A., Craig, I. W., Harrington, H., … Martin, J. (2003). Influence of life stress on depression: Polymorphism in the 5-HTT gene. *Science, 301*, 386–389.

Cassells, C., Paterson, B., Dowding, D., & Morrison, R. (2005). Long- and short-term risk factors in the prediction of inpatient suicide: A review of the literature. *Crisis: The Journal of Crisis Intervention and Suicide Prevention, 26*, 53–63.

Cassels, C. (2013 24-May). *TMS for resistant depression: Long-term results are in.* Retrieved 2013 26-May from Medscape News: Psychiatry & Mental Health: http://www.medscape.com/viewarticle/804736

Castiglioni, A. (1946). *Adventures of the mind.* New York, NY: Knopf.

Cattell, R. B., & Stice, G. F. (1957). *Handbook for the 16 personality factor questionnaire.* Champaign, IL: Institute for Personality and Ability Testing.

Cautela, J. R., & Kearney, A. (1993). *The covert conditioning handbook.* Grove, CA: Brooks/Cole.

CBS News. (2013 14-January). *U.S. military suicides exceed combat deaths.* Retrieved 2013 22-June from CBS News: http://www.cbsnews.com/8301-201_162-57563857/u.s-military-suicides-exceed-combat-deaths/

CDC. (2011 21-March). *Tobacco-related mortality.* Retrieved 2013 23-June from Centers for Disease Control and Prevention home: http://www.cdc.gov/tobacco/data_statistics/fact_sheets/health_effects/tobacco_related_mortality/

Chamberlain, S. R., Menzies, L., Sahakian, B. J., & Fineberg, N. A. (2007). Lifting the veil on trichotillomania. *American Journal of Psychiatry, 164*, 568–574.

Chambless, D. L., Baker, M. J., Baucom, D. H., Beutler, L. E., Calhoun, K. S., & Crits-Christoph, P. (1998). Update on empirically validated therapies, II. *The Clinical Psychologists, 51*, 3–16.

Chen, E., & Miller, G. E. (2007). Stress and inflammation in exacerbation of asthma. *Brain, Behavior, and Immunity, 21*, 993–999.

Chenneville, T. (2000). HIV, confidentiality, and duty to protect: A decision making model. *Professional Psychology: Research and Practice, 31*, 661–670.

Chodoff, P. (1963). Late effects of the concentration camp syndrome. *Archives of General Psychiatry, 8*, 323–333.

Chouinard, G. (2004). Issues in the clinical use of benzodiazepines: potency, withdrawal, and rebound. *Journal of Clinical Psychiatry, 65*, 7-12.

Christensen, R. C. (2004). Olanzapine augmentation of fluoxetine in the treatment of pathological skin picking. *Canadian Journal of Psychiatry, 49*, 788–789.

Clark, D. A., Beck, A. T., & Alford, B. A. (1999). *Scientific foundations of cognitive theory and therapy of depression.* New York, NY: Wiley.

Clark, M. E., Gironda, R. J., & Young, R. W. (2003). Detection of back random responding: Effectiveness of MMPI–2 and personality assessment inventory validity indices. *Psychological Assessment, 15*, 223–234. doi:10.1037/1040-3590.15.2.223

Cleckley, H. (1976). *The mask of sanity* (5 ed.). St Louis, IL: Mosby.

Cleghorn, J. M., Franco, S., Szechtman, B., Kaplan, R. D., Szechtman, H., Brown, G. M., … Garnett, E. S. (1992). Toward a brain map of auditory hallucinations. *American Journal of Psychiatry, 149*, 1062–1069.

Clifasefi, S. L., Bernstein, D. M., Mantonakis, A., & Loftus, E. (2013). "Queasy does it": False alcohol beliefs and memories may lead to diminished alcohol preferences. *Acta Psychologica (Amst), 143*, 14–19. doi:10.1016/j.actpsy.2013.01.017

Coccar, E. F., & Danehy, M. (2006). Intermittent explosive disorder. In E. Hollander, & D. J. Stein (Eds.), *Clinical manual of impulse-control disorders* (pp. 19–37). Arlington, VA: American Psychiatric Publishing.

Coccaro, E. F., Kavoussi, R. J., Berman, M. E., & Lish, J. D. (2006). Intermittent explosive disorder-revised: Development, reliability, and validity of research criteria. *Comprehensive Psychiatry, 39*, 388–376.

Cochran, S. D., Sullivan, J. G., & Mays, V. M. (2003). Prevalence of mental disorders, psychological distress, and mental services use among lesbian, gay, and bisexual adults in the United States. *Journal of Consulting and Clinical Psychology, 71*, 53–61.

Coghill, D. (2005). Attention-deficit hyperactivity disorder: Should we believe the mass media or peer-reviewed literature? *Psychiatric Bulletin, 29*, 288–291.

Cohen, B. L., Barboglio, P., & Gousse, A. (2008). The impact of lower urinary tract symptoms and urinary incontinence on female sexual dysfunction using a validated instrument. *Journal of Sexual Medicine, 5*, 1418–1423.

Cohen, S., Doyle, W. J., & Skoner, D. P. (1999). Psychological stress, cytokine production, and severity of upper respiratory illness. *Psychosomatic Medicine, 61*, 175–180.

Cook, C. R., & Blacher, J. (2007). Evidence-based psychosocial treatments for tic disorders. *Clinical Psychology: Science and Practice, 14*, 252–267.

Cooke, D. J., & Michie, C. (2001). Refining the construct of psychopath: Towards a hierarchical model. *Psychological Assessment, 13*, 171–188.

Cooke, J. R., & Ancoli-Israel, S. (2006). Sleep and its disorders in older adults. *Psychiatric Clinics of North America, 29*, 1077–1093.

Coolidge, F. L., Thede, L. L., & Young, S. E. (2002). The heritability of gender identity disorder in a child and adolescent twin sample. *Behavior Genetics, 32*, 251–257.

Coons, P. M., & Milstein, V. (1992). Psychogenic amnesia: A clinical investigation of 25 cases. *Dissociation: Progress in the Dissociative Disorders, 5*, 73–79.

Coons, P. M., Bowman, E. S., & Milstein, V. (1988). Multiple personality disorder: A clinical investigation of 50 cases. *Journal of Nervous and Mental Disease, 176*, 519–527.

Coons, P. M., Milstein, V., & Marley, C. (1982). EEG studies of two multiple personalities and a control. *Archives of General Psychiatry, 39*, 823–825.

Cooper, A. J., Sandhu, S., Losztyn, S., & Cernovsky, Z. (1992). A double-blind placebo controlled trail of medroxyprogesterone acetate and cyproterone acetate with seven pedophiles. *Canadian Journal of Psychiatry, 37*, 687–693.

Cornell, D. G., & Hawk, G. L. (1989). Clinical presentation of malingerers diagnosed by experienced forensic psychologists. *Law and Human Behavior, 13*, 375–383.

Cororve, M. B., & Gleaves, D. H. (2001). Body dysmorphic disorder: A review of conceptualizations, assessment, and treatment strategies. *Clinical Psychology Review, 21*, 949–970.

Cottraux, J. (2005). Recent developments in research and treatment for social phobia (social anxiety disorder). *Current Opinion in Psychiatry, 18*, 51–54.

Couturier, J. L. (2005). Efficacy of rapid-rate repetitive transcranial magnetic stimulation in the treatment of depression: A systematic review and meta-analysis. *Journal of Psychiatry & Neuroscience, 30*, 83–90.

Coyne, J. C. (1976). Depression and the response of others. *Journal of Abnormal Psychology, 85*, 186–193.

Craighead, W. E., Hart, A. B., Craighead, L. W., & Ilardi, S. S. (2002). Psychosocial treatments for Major Depressive Disorders. In P. E. Nathan, & J. M. Gorman, *A guide to treatments that work* (2nd ed., pp. 245–261). New York, NY: Oxford University Press.

Craighead, W. E., Miklwitz, D. J., Fank, E., & Vajk, F. C. (2002). Psychosocial treatments for bipolar disorders. In P. E. Nathan, & J. M. Gorman, *A guide to treatments that work* (2 ed., pp. 263–275). New York, NY: Oxford University Press.

Crits-Christoph, P., & Barber, I. P. (2002). Psychosocial treatments for personality disorders. In P. E. Nathan, & J. M. Gorman, *A guide to treatments that works* (2 ed., pp. 611–623). New York, NY: Oxford University Press.

Cromwell, R. L. (1993). Searching for the origins of schizophrenia. *Psychological Science, 4*, 276–279.

Cuijpers, P., Van Straten, A., & Warmerdam, L. (2005). Behavioral activation treatments of depression: A meta-analysis. *Clinic of North America, 28*, 469–480.

## D
------

Daban, C., Vieta, E., Mackin, P., & Young, A. (2005). Hypothalamic-pituitary-adrenal axis and bipolar disorders. *Psychiatric Clinic of North America, 28*, 469–480.

Dahl, A. A. (1993). The personality disorders: A critical review of family, twin, and adoption studies. *Journal of Personality Disorders, Suppl 1*, 86–99.

Dahlstrom, W. G., Welsh, G. S., & Dahlstrom, L. E. (1975). *An MMPI handbook, Vol. II: Research applications*. Minneapolis, MN: University of Minnesota Press.

Dahmen, N., Becht, J., Engel, A., Thommes, M., & Tonn, P. (2008). Prevalence of eating disorders and eating attacks in narcolepsy. *Neuropsychiatric Disease and Treatment, 4*, 257–261.

Darwin, C. (1873/1955). *The expression of emotions in man and animals*. New York, NY: Philosophical Library.

Dauvilliers, Y., Arnulf, I., & Mignot, E. (2007). Narcolepsy with cataplexy. *The Lancet, 369*, 499–511. doi:10.1016/S0140-6736(07)60237-2

Davidson, P. R., & Parker, K. H. (2001). Eye Movement Desensitization and Reprocessing (EMDR): A meta-analysis. *Journal of Consulting and Clinical Psychology, 69*, 69–87.

Davidson, R. J., Pizzagalli, D., Nitschke, J. B., & Putnam, K. (2002). Depression: Perspectives from affective neuroscience. *Annual Review of Psychology, 53*, 545–574.

Davidson, R. T. (2004). Use of benzodiazapines in Social Anxiety Disorders, Generalized Anxiety Disorder, and Posttraumatic Stress Disorder. *Journal of Clinical Psychiatry, 65*, 29–33.

Davies, G., Wellham, J., Chant, D., Torrey, E. F., & McGrath, J. (2003). A systematic review and meta-analysis of northern hemisphere season of birth studies in schizophrenia. *Schizophrenia Bulletin, 29*, 587–593.

Davis, A. S. (2008). Children with Down syndrome: Implications for assessment and intervention in the school. *School Psychology Quarterly, 23*, 271–281.

Davis, J. O., Phelps, J. A., & Bracha, H. S. (1995). Prenatal development of monozygotic twins and concordance for schizophrenia. *Schizophrenia Bulletin, 21*, 357–366.

Davis, W., & Smith, S. (1979). Role of conditioned reinforcers in the initiation, maintenance, and extinction of drug-seeking behavior. *Pavlovian Journal of Biological Sciences, 11*, 222–236.

Dawson, G., Rogers, S., Munson, J., Smith, M., Winter, J., Greenson, J., & Varley, J. (2010). Randomized, controlled trial of an early intervention for toddlers with autism: The Early Start Denver Model. *Pediatrics, 125*, 17–23.

Dell, P. E. (1998). Axis II pathology in outpatients with dissociative identity disorders. *Journal of Nervous and Mental Disease, 186*, 352–356.

Dell'Osso, B., Altamura, A. C., Allen, A., Marazziti, D., & Hollander, E. (2006). Epidemiologic and clinical updates on impulse control disorders: A critical review. *European Archives of Psychiatry and Clinical Neuroscience, 256*, 464–475.

DeMeyer, M. K., Pontius, W., Norton, J. A., Baron, S., Allen, J., & Steele, R. (1972). Parental practices and innate activity in normal, autistic, and brain-damaged infants. *Journal of Autism and Childhood Schizophrenia, 2*, 49–66.

Despert, J. L. (1951). Some considerations relating to the genesis of autistic behavior in children. *American Journal of Orthopsychiatry, 21*, 335–350.

Dimidjian, S., Hollon, S. D., Dobson, K. S., Schmaling, K. B., Kohlenberg, R. J., Addis, M. E., ... McGlinchey, J. B. (2006). Randomized trial of behavioral activation, cognitive therapy, and antidepressant medication in the acute treatment of adults with major depression. *Journal of Consulting and Clinical Psychology, 74*, 658–670.

Dimidjian, S., Martell, C. R., Addis, M. E., & Herman-Dunn, R. (2008). Behavioral activation for depression. In D. H. Barlow, *Clinical handbook of psychological disorders: A step-by-step treatment manual* (4 ed., pp. 328–364). New York: Guildford Press.

Dobson, K. S., Hollon, S. D., Dimidjian, s., Schmaling, K. B., Kohlenberg, R. J., Gallop, R. J., ... et al. (2008). Randomized trial of behavioral activation, cognitive therapy, and antidepressant medication in the prevention of relapse and recurrence in major depression. *Journal of Consulting and Clinical Psychology, 76*, 468–477.

Donahoe, J. W. (1999). Edward L. Thorndike: The selection connectionist. *Journal of the Experimental Analysis of Behavior, 72*, 451–454.

Dorsey, M. F., Iwata, B. A., Ong, P., & McSween, T. E. (1980). Treatment of self-injurious behavior using a water mist: Initial response suppression and generalization. *Journal of Applied Behavior Analysis, 13*, 343–353.

dosReis, S., Johnson, E., Steinwachs, D., Rohde, D., Skinner, E. A., Fahey, M., & Lehman, A. F. (2008). Antipsychotic treatment patterns and hospitalizations among adults with schizophrenia. *Schizophrenia Research, 101*, 304–311.

Dougherty, D. D., Rauch, S. L., & Jenike, M. A. (2002). Pharmacological treatments for obsessive-compulsive disorders. In P. E. Nathan, & J. M. Gorman, *A guide to treatments that work* (pp. 387–410). New York, NY: Oxford Press.

Duberstein, P. R., & Conwell, Y. (1997). Personality disorders and completed suicide: A methodological and conceptual review. *Clinical Psychology: Science and Practice, 4*, 359–376.

Dupont, R. L., & Katon, R. N. (1971). Development of a heroin-addiction treatment program: Effect on urban crime. *Journal of the American Medical Association, 216*, 1320–1324.

Durand, V. M., & Mindell, J. A. (1999). Behavioral intervention for childhood sleep terrors. *Behavior Therapy, 30*, 705–715.

## E
------

Earls, C. M., & Castonguay, L. G. (1989). The evaluation of olfactory aversion for a bisexual pedophile with a single-case multiple-baseline design. *Behavior Therapy, 20*, 137–146.

Ekers, D., Richards D., & Gilbody, S. (2007). A meta-analysis of randomized trials of behavioural treatment in depression. *Psychological Medicine, 38*, 611–623.

Elliott, L., & Brantley, C. (1997). *Sex on campus: The naked truth about the real sex lives of college students*. New York, NY: Random House.

Ellis, A. (1962). *Reason and emotion in psychotherapy*. New York, NY: Lyle Stuart.

Erhardt, A. A. (1973). Maternalism in fetal hormonal and related syndromes. In J. Zubin, & J. Money, *Contemporary sexual*

**484**

behavior: Critical issues in the 1970s. Baltimore, MD: Johns Hopkins Press.

Erman, M. K. (2006). Selected sleep disorders: Restless legs syndrome and periodic limb movement disorder, sleep apnea syndrome, and narcolepsy. *Psychiatric Clinics of North America, 29,* 947–967.

Ernst, T., Chang, L., Leonido-Yee, M., & Speck, O. (2000). Evidence for long-term neurotoxicity associated with a methamphetamine abuse: A 1H MRS study. *Neurology, 54,* 1344–1349.

Evans, J. G., Wilock, G., & Birks, J. (2004). Evidence-based pharmacotherapy of Alzheimer's disease. *International Journal of Neuropsychopharmacology, 7,* 351–369.

Even, C., Schroder, C. M., Friedman, S., & Rouillon, F. (2008). Efficacy of light therapy in nonseasonal depression: A systematic review. *Journal of Affective Disorders, 108,* 11–23.

Exner, J. E. (1993). The Rorschach: A comprehensive system. *Basic Foundations, Vol 1.*

Exton, M. S., Gierse, C., Meier, B. M., Xie, Y., Frede, S., Goeble, M. U., ... Schedlowski, M. (2002). Behaviorally conditioned immunosuppression in the rat is regulated via noradrenaline and B-adrenoceptors. *Journal of Neuroimmunology, 131,* 21–30.

Eysenck, H. J., & Eysneck, S. B. (1969). *Eysenck personality inventory (revised manual).* San Diego, CA: Educational and Industrial Testing Service.

## F

Fagan, P. J., Wise, T. N., Schmidt, C. W., & Berlin, F. S. (2002). Pedophilia. *Journal of the American Medical Association, 288,* 2458–2465.

Fairburn, C. G., & Harrison, P. J. (2003). Eating disorders. *Lancet, 361,* 407–416.

Fallon, B. A. (2004). Pharmacotherapy of somatoform disorders. *Journal of Psychosomatic Research, 56,* 455–460.

Fallon, B. A. (2004). Pharmacotherapy of somatoform disorders. *Journal of Psychosomatic Research, 56,* 455–460.

Farlow, M. R., & Cummings, J. (2008). A modern hypothis: The distinct pathologies of dementia associated with Parkinson's disease versus Alzheimer's disease. *Dementia and Geriatric Cognitive Disorders, 25,* 301–308.

Farmer, E. M., Compton, S. N., Burns, J. B., & Robertson, E. (2002). Review of the evidence base for treatment of childhood psychopathology: Externalizing disorders. *Journal of Consulting and Clinical Psychology, 70,* 1267–1302.

Fava, M., & Rankin, M. (2002). Sexual functioning and SSRIs. *Journal of Clinical Psychiatry, 63,* 13–16.

Fenichel, O. (1945). *The psychoanalytic theory of neurosis.* New York, NY: Norton.

Fester, C. B. (1973). A functional analysis of depression. *American Psychologist, 28,* 857–870.

Finkelstein, J. J., Cannon, T. D., Gur, R. E., Gur, R. C., & Moberg, P. (1997). Attentional dysfunctions in neuroleptic-naive and neuroleptic-withdrawn schizophrenic patients and their siblings. *Journal of Abnormal Psychology, 106,* 203–212.

Finklehor, D., & Jones, L. (2006). Why have child maltreatment and child victimization declined? *Journal of Social Issues, 62,* 685–716.

Finney, J. W., & Moos, R. H. (2002). Psychosocial treatments for alcohol use disorders. In P. E. Nathan, & J. M. Gorman, *A guide to treatments that work* (2nd ed., pp. 157–168). New York, NY: Oxford University Press.

Fishbain, D. A., Culter, R. B., Rosomoff, H. L., Rosomoff, R., & Steele, R. (1998). Do antidepressants have an analgesic effect in psychogenic pain disorder? A meta-analysis. *Psychosomatic Medicine, 60,* 503–509.

Foa, E. B., Zinbarg, R., & Rothbaum, B. O. (1992). Uncontrollability and unpredictability in post-traumatic stress disorder: An animal model. *Psychological Bulletin, 112,* 218–258.

Ford, C. V. (1983). *The somatizing disorder: Illness is a way of life.* New York, NY: Elsevier Biomedical.

Forman, E. M., Herbert, J. D., Moitra, E., Yeomas, P. D., & Geller, P. A. (2007). A randomized controlled effectiveness trial of acceptance and commitment therapy and cognitive therapy for anxiety and depression. *Behavior Modification, 31,* 772–799.

Forrest, M. S., & Hokanson, J. E. (1975). Depression and autonomic arousal reduction accompanying self-punitive behavior. *Journal of Abnormal Psychology, 84,* 346–357.

Fossati, A., Barratt, E. S., Borroni, S., Villa, D., Grazioli, F., & Vaffei, C. (2007). Impulsivity, aggressiveness, and the *DSM-IV* personality disorders. *Psychiatry Research, 149,* 157–167.

Fountoulakis, K. N., Grunze, H., Panagoitidis, P., & Kaprinis, G. (2008). Treatment of bipolar depression: An update. *Journal of Affective Disorders, 109,* 21–34.

Fowles, D. C. (1993). Electrodermal activity and antisocial behavior: Empirical findings and theoretical issues. In J. C. Roy, E. Boucsein, D. Fowles, & J. Gruzelier, *Progress in electrodermal research* (pp. 223–237). London: Plenem Press.

Fox, J. H., Ramsey, R. G., Huckman, M. S., & Proske, A. E. (1976). Cerebral ventriculare enlargement. Chronical Alcoholics examined by computerized tomography.

*Journal of the American Medical Association, 236,* 365.

Foxx, R. M., & Rubinoff, A. (1979). Behavioral treatment of caffeinism: Reducing excessive coffee drinking. *Journal of Applied Behavior Analysis, 12,* 335–344. doi:10.1901/jaba.1979.12-335

France, C. M., Lysaker, P. H., & Robinson, R. P. (2007). The "chemical imbalance" explanation for depression: Origins, lay endorsement, and clinical implications. *Professional Psychology: Research and Practice, 38,* 411–420.

Frances, A. (2013, March 20). *Where have all the normals gone?* Retrieved March 31, 2013, from The Huffington Post: http://www.huffingtonpost.com/allen-frances/jon-ronson-ted-talk_b_2978686.html

Frank, E., Salchner, P., Aldag, J. M., Salome, N., Singewald, N., Landgraf, R., & Wigger, A. (2006). Genetic predisposition to anxiety-related behavior determines coping style, neuroendocrine responses, and neuronal activation during social defeat. *Behavioral Neuroscience, 120,* 60–71.

Frankl, V. E. (1969). *The will to meaning.* Ontario, Canada: Don Mills.

Franklin, M. E., Abramowitz, J. S., Bux, D. A., Zoellner, L. A., & Feeney, N. C. (2002). Cognitive-behavioral therapy with and without medication in the treatment of obsessive-compulsive disorder. *Professional Psychology: Research and Practice, 33,* 162–168.

Franklin, T. B., Russig H, H., Weiss, I. C., Gräff, J., Linder, N., Michalon, A., ... Mansuy, I. M. (2010). Epigenetic transmission of the impact of early stress across generations. *Biological Psychiatry, 68,* 408–415.

Freedman, B., & Chapman, L. J. (1973). Early subjective experience in schizophrenic episodes. *Journal of Abnormal Psychology, 82,* 46–54.

Freud, S. (1909/1908). *The standard edition of the complete works of Sigumnd Freud* (Vol. 10). London: Hogarth Press.

Freud, S. (1948). *Charcot. In Collected Papers* (Vol. 1). London: Hogworth Press.

Freyberger, H., & Schneider, W. (1994). Diagnosis and classification of factitious disorder with operational diagnostic systems. *Psychotherapy and psychosomatics, 62,* 27–29.

Froehlich, T. E., Lanphear, B. P., Auinger, P., Hornung, R., Epstein, J. N., Braun, J., & Kahn, R. S. (2009). Association of tobacco and lead exposures with attention-deficit/hyperactivity disorder. *Pediatrics, 214,* 1054–1063.

Fuchs, C. Z., & Rehm, L. P. (1977). A self-control behavior therapy program for depression. *Journal of Consulting and Clinical Psychology, 45,* 206–215.

Furman, L. M. (2008). Attention-Deficit Hyperactivity Disorder (ADHD): Does new research support old concepts? *Journal of Child Neurology, 23,* 775–784.

# G

Gaither, G. A., Rosenkranz, R. R., & Plaud, J. J. (1998). Sexual Disorders. In J. J. Plaud, & G. H. Eifert, *From behavior theory to behavior therapy* (pp. 152–171). Needham Heights, MA, Ally & Bacon.

Garber, H., & Herber, R. (1978). *The efficacy of early intervention with family rehabilitation.* Paper presented at Conference on Prevention of Retarded Development in Psychosocially Disadvantaged Children, University of Wisconsin, Madison. Retrieved July 1978.

Garrett, W. T., Brashear, H. R., Cail, W. S., Lovell, M. A., Clayton, M. T., & Harrison, M. B. (1998). Severe circumscribed cortical atrophy in Huntington's disease. *Neurology, 51,* 638–639.

Gaudiano, B. A., & Zimmerman, M. (2013). Prevalence of attenuated psychotic symptoms and their relationship with *DSM-IV* diagnoses in a general psychiatric outpatient clinic. *Journal of Clinical Psychiatry, 74,* 149–155. doi:10.4088/JCP.12m07788

Gerard, D. L., & Houston, L. G. (1953). Family setting and the social ecology of schizophrenia. *Psychiatric Quarterly, 27,* 90–101.

Gijs, L., & Gooren, L. (1996). Hormonal and psychopharmacological interventions in the treatment of paraphilias: An update. *Journal of Sex Research, 33,* 273–290.

Gloaguen, V., Cottraux, J., Cucherat, M., & Blackburn, I. M. (1998). A meta-analysis of the effects of cognitive therapy in depressed patients. *Journal of Affective Disorders, 49,* 59–72.

Gloster, A. T., Wittchen, H., Einsle, F., Lang, T., Helbig-Lang, S., Fydrich, T., ... Arolt, V. (2011). Psychological treatment for panic disorder with agoraphobia: A randomized controlled trial to examine the role of therapist-guided exposure in situ in CBT. . *Journal of Consulting and Clinical Psychology, 79,* 406–420. doi:10.1037/a0023584

Goddard, A. W., Mason, G. F., Rothman, D. L., Behar, K. L., Petroff, O., & Krystal, J. H. (2004). Family psychopathology and magnitude of reductions in occipital cortex GABA levels in panic disorders. *Neuropsychopharmacology, 29,* 639–640.

Goff, D. C., & Coyle, J. T. (2001). The emerging role of glutamate in the pathophysiology and treatment of schizophrenia. *American Journal of Psychiatry, 158,* 1367–1377. doi:10.1176/appi.ajp.158.9.1367

Gold, J. M., & Thaker, G. K. (2002). Current progress in schizophrenia research. Cognitive phenotypes of schizophrenia:

Attention. *Journal of Nervous and Mental Disease, 190,* 638–639.

Goldberg, D. (2006). The aetiology of depression. *Psychological Medicine, 36,* 1341–1347.

Goldberg, E. M., & Morrison, S. L. (1963). Schizophrenia and social class. *British Journal of Psychiatry, 109,* 785–802.

Goldberg, J. F., & Harrow, M. (2004). Consistency of remission and outcome in bipolar and unipolar mood disorders: A 10-year prospective follow-up. *Journal of Affective Disorders, 81,* 123–131.

Goldberg, S. R., Spealman, R. D., & Goldberg, D. M. (1981). Persistent behavior at high rates maintained by intravenous self-administration of nicotine. *Science, 214,* 573–575.

Goldblatt, M., & Munitz, H. (1976). Behavioral treatment of hysterical leg paralysis. *Journal of Behavior Therapy and Experimental Psychiatry, 7,* 259–263.

Goldney, R. D. (2003). Deinstitutionalization and suicide. *Crisis: The Journal of Crisis Intervention and Suicide Prevention, 24,* 39–40.

Goldstein, T. R., Bridge, J. A., & Brent, D. A. (2008). Sleep disturbance preceding completed suicide in adolescents. *Journal of Consulting and Clinical Psychology, 76,* 84–91.

Gooding, D. C., Tallent, K. A., & Matts, C. W. (2007). Rates of avoidant, schizzoptypal, schizoid, and paranoid personality disorders in psychometric high-risk groups at 5-year follow-up. *Schizophrenia Research, 94,* 373–374.

Goodman, W. (1974, March 17). The constitution vs. the snakepit. *The New York Times Magazine.*

Goodwin, D. W. (1979). Alcoholism and heredity. *Archives of Genreal Psychiatry, 36,* 57–61.

Goodwin, D. W., Schulsinger, F., Hermansen, L., Guze, S. B., & Winokur, G. (1973). Alcohol problems in adoptees raised apart from alcoholic biological parents. *Archives of Genreal Psychiatry, 28,* 238–243.

Goodwin, D. W., Schulsinger, F., Knop, J., Mednick, s., & Guze, S. B. (1977). Alcoholism and depression in adopted-out daughters of alcoholics. *Archives of Genreal Psychiatry, 34,* 751–754.

Goodwin, F. K., & Athanasios, P. Z. (1979). Lithium in the treatment of mania. *Archives of Genreal Psychiatry, 36,* 840–844.

Gorman, J. M. (2003). Treating generalized anxiety disorders. *Journal of Clinical Psychiatry, 64,* 24–29.

Gotlib, I. H., & Hamilton, J. P. (2008). Neuroimaging and depression: Current status and unresolved issues. *Current Directions in Psychological Science, 17,* 159–163.

Gottesman, I. I. (1991). *Schizophernia genesis: The origins of madness.* New York, NY: Freeman.

Gottesman, I., & Shields, J. (1972). *Schizophrenia and gentics: A twin vantage point.* New York, NY: Academic Press.

Gould, S. J. (1981). *The mismeasure of man.* New York, NY: W. W. Norton & Co.

Granic, I., & Patterson, G. R. (2006). Toward a comprehensive model of antisocial development: A dynamic systems approach. *Psychological Review, 113,* 101–131.

Grant, J. E. (2005). Clinical characteristics and pscyhiatric comorbidity in males with exhibitionism. *Journal of Clinical Psychiatry, 66,* 1367–1371.

Grant, J. E. (2006). Kleptomania. In E. Hollander, & D. J. Stein (Eds.), *Clinical manual of impulse-control disorders* (pp. 175–201). Arlington, VA: American Psychiatric Publishing.

Grant, J. E., Odlaug, B. L., & Potenza, M. N. (2007). Addicted to hair pulling? How an alternative model of trichotillomania may improve treatment outcome. *Harvard Review of Psychiatry, 15,* 80–85.

Graue, L. O., Berry, D. T., Clark, J. A., Sollman, M. J., Cardi, M., Hopkins, J., & Werline, D. (2007). Identification of feigned mental retardation using the new generation of malingering detection instruments: Preliminary findings. *The Clinical Neuropsychologist, 21,* 929–942. doi:10.1080/13854040600932137

Greenhill, L. L., & Ford, R. E. (2002). Childhood attention-deficit hyperactivity disorder: Pharmacological treatments. In P. E. Nathan, & J. M. Gorman, *A guide to treatments that work* (2 ed., pp. 25–55). New York, NY: Oxford University Press.

Greicius, M. D., Geschwind, M. D., & Miller, B. L. (2002). Presenile dementia syndromes: An update on taxonomy and diagnosis. *Journal of Neurology, Neurosurgery, & Psychiarty, 72,* 691–700.

Grilo, C. M., Hrabosky, J. I., White, M. A., Allison, K. C., Stunkard, A. J., & Masheb, R. M. (2008). Overvaluation of shape and weight in binge eating disorder and overweight controls: Refinement of a diagnostic construct. *Journal of Abnormal Psychology, 117,* 414–419.

Grilo, C. M., Masheb, R. M., & Wilson, G. T. (2006). Rapid response to treatment for binge eating disorder. *Journal of Consulting and Clinical Psychology, 74,* 602–613.

Grilo, C. M., Sanislow, C. A., Shea, M. T., Skodol, A. E., Stout, R. L., Gunderson, J. G., et al. (2005). Two-year prospective naturalistic study of remission from Major Depressive Disorder as a function of personality disorder comorbidity. *Journal of Consulting and Clinical Psychology, 73,* 78–85.

Grinspoon, L., Dwalt, J. R., & Shader, R. (1968). Psychotherapy and pharmacotherapy in chronic schizophrenia. *American Journal of Psychiatry, 124,* 1645–1652.

Grossman, R. (2004). Pharmacotherapy of personality disorders. In J. J. Magnavita, *Handbook of personality disorders: Theory and practice* (pp. 331–355). Hoboken, NJ: John Wiley & Sons.

Gull, W. (1888). Anorexia nervosa. *Lancet, 1*, 516–517.

Gündel, H., Valet, M., Song, C., Huber, D., Zimmer, C., Sprenger, T., & Tolle, T. R. (2008). Altered cerebral response to noxious heat stimulation in patients with somatoform pain disorder. *Pain, 137*, 413–421.

## H

Haberstick, B. C., Timberlake, D., Smolen, A., Sakai, J. T., Hopfer, C. J., Corley, R. P., . . . et al. (2007). Between- and within-family association test of the dopamine receptor D2 TaqIA polymorphism and alcohol abuse and dependence in a general population sample of adults. *Journal of Studies on Alcohol and Drugs, 68*, 362–370.

Hadley, S. J., Kim, S., Priday, L., & Hollander, E. (2006). Pharmacologic treatment of body dysmorphic disorder. *Primary Psychiatry, 13*, 61–69.

Hammelstein, P., Pietrowsky, R., Merbach, M., & Brahler, E. (2005). Psychogenic urinary retention ("Paruresis"): Diagnosis and epidemiology in representative male samples. *Psychotherapy and Psychosomatics, 74*, 308–314.

Handen, B. L., Johnson, C. R., & Lubetsky, M. (2004). Efficacy of methylphenidate among children with autism and symptoms of attention-deficit hyperactivity disorder. *Journal of Autism and Developmental Disorders, 30*, 245–255.

Hare, R. D. (1965a). Temporal gradient of fear arousal in psychopaths. *Journal of Abnormal Psychology, 70*, 442–445.

Hare, R. D. (1965b). Acquisitions and generalization of a conditioned-fear response in psychopathic and nonpsychopathic criminals. *Journal of Psychology, 59*, 367–370.

Harris, M. (1989). *Our kind: Who we are, where we came from, & where we are going.* New York, NY: Harper Perennial.

Harrison, K., & Cantor, J. (1997). The relationship between meida consumption and eating disorders. *Journal of Communication, 47*, 40–67.

Harvey, D. M., Yasar, S., Heishman, S. J., Panlilio, L. V., Henningfield, J. E., & Goldberg, S. R. (2004). Nicotine serves as an effective reinforcer of intravenous drug-taking behavior in human cigarette smokers. *Psychopharmacology, 175*, 134–142.

Hasin, D. S., Stinson, F. S., Ogburn, E., & Grant, B. F. (2007). Prevalence, correlations, disability, and comorbidity of *DSM-IV* alcohol abuse and dependence in the United States: Results from the National Epidemiological Survey on Alcohol and Related Conditions. *Archives of General Psychiatry, 64*, 830–842.

Hathway, S. R., & McKinley, J. C. (1943). *Manual for the Minnesota multiphasic personality inventory.* New York, NY: Psychological Corporation.

Hawton, K., Clements, a., Sakarovitch, C., Simkin, S., & Deeks, J. J. (2001). Suicide in doctors: A study of risk according to gender, seniority and specialty in medical practitioners in England and Wales 1979-1995. *Journal of Epidemiology & Community Health, 55*, 296–300.

Hayes, S. C. (2004). Acceptance and commitment therapy, relation frame theory, and the third wave of behavior therapy. *Behavior Therapy, 35*, 639–666.

Hayes, S. C., & Heiby, E. M. (1996). Psychology's drug problem: Do we need a fix or should we just say no? *American Psychologist, 51*, 198–206.

Hayes, S. C., & Wolf, M. R. (1984). Cues, consequences and therapeutic talk: Effects of social context and coping statements on pain. *Behaviour Research and Therapy, 22*, 385–392.

Hayes, S. C., Bissett, R. T., Korn, Z., Zettle, R. D., Rosenfarb, I. S., Cooper, L. D., & Grundt, A. M. (1999). The impact of acceptance versus control rationales on pain tolerance. *Psychological Record, 49*, 33–47.

Hayes, S. C., Brownell, K. D., & Barlow, D. H. (1978). The use of self-administered covert sensitization in the treatment of exhibitionism and sadism. *Behavior Therapy, 9*, 283–289.

Haynes, S. G., Feinleib, M., & Kannel, W. B. (1980). The relationship of psychosocial factors to coronary heart disease in the Framing Study: III. Eight years incidence in coronary heart disease. *American Journal of Epidemiology, 3*, 37–85.

Healey, D. M., Miller, C. J., Castelli, K. L., Marks, D. J., & Halperin, J. M. (2008). The impact of impairment criteria on rates of ADHD diagnoses in preschoolers. *Journal of Abnormal Child Psychology, 36*, 771–778.

Heber, R., & Garber, H. (1980). Prevention of cultural-familial retardation. In A. Jeger, & R. Slotnick (Eds.), *Community mental health: A behavior ecological perspective.* New York, NY: Plenum.

Hegarty, J. D., Baldessarini, R. J., Tohen, M., Waternaus, C., & Oepen, G. (1994). One hundred years of schizophrenia: A meta-analysis of the outcome literature. *American Journal of Psychiatry, 151*, 1409–1416.

Heiby, E. M., DeLeon, P. H., & Anderson, T. (2004). A debate on prescrition privliges for psychologists. *Professional Psychology: Research and Practice, 35*, 336–344.

Heilbrun, A. B. (1960). Perception of maternal childrearing attitudes in schizophrenia. *Journal of Consulting Psychology, 24*, 169–173.

Helmes, E., & Reddon, J. R. (1993). A perspective on development in assessing psychopathology: A critical review of the MMPI and MMPI-2. *Psychological Bulletin, 113*, 453–471.

Hendriks, G. J., Keijsers, G. P., Kampman, M., Hoogduin, C. A., & Oude Voshaar, R. C. (2012). Predictors of outcome of pharmacological and psychological treatment of late-life panic disorder with agoraphobia. *International Journal Of Geriatric Psychiatry, 146*–150.

Herbert, W. (1993). States ponder notion of criminal insanity. *APA Monitor*, 8–9. Retrieved April 1979.

Herveck, D. C., Hser, Y., & Teruyan, C. (2008). Empirically supported substance abuse treatment approaches: A survey of treatment providers perspectives and practices. *Addictive Behaviors, 33*, 699–712.

Heston, L. L. (1966). Psychiatric disorders in foster-home reared children of schizophrenic mothers. *British Journal of Psychiatry, 112*, 819–825.

Heyman, G. M. (2009). *Addiction: A disorder of choice.* Cambridge, MA: Harvard University Press.

Higgins, S. T., Budney, A. J., Bickel, W. K., Hughes, J. R., Foerg, F., & Badger, G. (1993). Acheiving cocaine abstinence with a behavioral approach. *American Journal of Psychiatry, 150*, 763–769.

Hinshaw, S. P., Klein, R. G., & Abikoff, H. B. (2002). Childhood attention-deficit hyperactivity disorder: Nonpharmacological treatments and their combination with medication. In P. E. Nathan, & J. M. Gorman, *A guide to treatments that work* (2nd ed., pp. 3–23). New York, NY: Oxford University Press.

Hoek, H. W. (2006). Incidence, prevalence, and mortality of anorexia nervosa and other eating disorders: Services research and outcomes. *Current Opinion in Psychiatry, 19*, 389–394.

Hogarty, G. E., & Ulrich, R. F. (1977). Temporal effects of drug and placebo in delaying relapse in schizophrenic outpatients. *Archives of General Psychiatry, 34*, 297–301.

Hogarty, G. E., Flesher, S., Ulrich, R., Carter, M., Greenwald, D., Pogue-Geile, M., ... Zoretich, R. (2004). Cognitive enhancement therapy for schizophrenia: Effects of a 2-year randomized trial on cognition and behavior. *Archives of General Psychiatry, 61*, 866–876.

Hogervorst, E., Bandelow, S., Combrinck, M., Irani, S., & Smith, A. D. (2003). The validity and reliability of 6 sets of clinical criteria to classify Alzheimer's disease and vascular dementia in cases confirmed postmortem: Added value of a decision tree approach. *Dementia and Geriatric Cognitive Disorders, 16*, 170–180.

Hollander, E., & Wong, C. M. (1995). Obsessive-compulsive spectrum disorders. *Journal of Clinical Psychiatry, 56*, 3–6.

Hollander, E., Tracy, K. A., Swann, A. C., Coccaro, E. F., McElroy, S. L., Wozniak, P., ... Nemeroff, C. B. (2003). Divalproex in the treatment of impulsive aggression: Efficacy in Cluster B personality disorders. *Neuropsychopharmacology, 28*, 1186–1197.

Hollis, J. F., Connett, L. E., Stevens, V. J., & Greenlick, M. R. (1990). Stressful life events, Type A behavior, and the prediction of cardiovascular and total mortality over six years. *Journal of Behavioral Medicine, 13*, 263–280.

Holmes, T. H., & Rahe, R. H. (1967). The social readjustment rating scale. *Journal of Psychosomatic Research, 11*, 213–218.

Holzman, P. S., & Levy, D. L. (1977). Smooth pursuit eye movements and functional psychoses: A review. *Schizophrenia Bulletin, 3*, 15–27.

Honda, H., Shimizu, Y., & Rutter, M. (2005). No effect of MMR withdrawal on the incidence of autism: A total population study. *Journal of Child Psychology and Psychiatry, 46*, 572–579.

Hotchner, A. E. (1966). *Papa Hemingway: A personal memoir.* New York, NY: Random House.

Howard, J. S., Sparkman, C. R., Cohen, H. G., Green, G., & Stanislaw, H. (2005). A comparison of intensive behavior analytic and eclectic treatments for young children with autism. *Research in Developmental Disabilities, 26*, 359–383.

Howell, H. B., Castle, D., & Yonkers, K. A. (2006). Anxiety disorders in women. In D. Castle, J. Kulkarin, & K. Abel, *Mood and anxiety disorders in women* (pp. 59–74). New York, NY: Cambridge University Press.

Hrabosky, J. I., Masheb, R. M., White, M. A., & Grilo, C. M. (2009). Overvaluation of shape and weight in binge eating disorders. *Journal of Consulting and Clinical Psychology, 75*, 175–180.

Hudson, J. I., Hiripi, E., Pope, H. G., & Kessler, R. C. (2007). The prevalence and correlates of eating disorders in the National Comorbidity Survey Replication. *Biological Psychiatry*(61), 348–358. doi:10.1016/j.biopsych.2006.03.040

Hughes, J. R. (1986). Genetics of smoking: A review. *Behavior Therapy, 17*, 335–345.

Hughes, J. R., Pickens, R. W., Spring, W., & Keenan, R. M. (1985). Instructions control whether nicotine will serve as a reinforcer. *Journal of Pharmacology and Experimental Therapeutics, 235*, 106–112.

Hume, W. I. (1973). Physiological measures in twins. In G. Claridge, S. Canter, & S. E. Hume (Eds.), *Personality differences and biological variations: A study of twins.* Oxford: Pergamon.

Humphreys, K. L., Eng, T., & Lee, S. S. (2013, May 29). Stimulant medication and substance use outcomes: A meta-analysis. *JAMA Psychiatry, 70*, 740–749. doi:10.1001/jamapsychiatry.2013.1273"

## I

Ikeda, M., Ishikawa, T., & Tanabe, H. (2004). Epidemiology of frontotemporal lobar degeneration. *Dementia and Geriatric Cognitive Disorders, 17*, 265–268.

Ilgen, M. A., Bohnert, A. S., Ignacio, R. V., McCarthy, J. F., Valenstein, M. M., Kim, H. M., & Blow, F. C. (2010). Psychiatric diagnoses and risk of suicide in veterans. *Archives of General Psychiatry, 67*, 1152–1158.

Ioannidis, J. P. (2011). Excess significance bias in the literature on brain volume abnormalities. *Archives of General Psychiatry, 68*, 773–780. doi:10.1001/archgenpsychiatry.2011.28

Itil, T. M. (1977). Qualitative and quantitative EEG findings in schizophrenia. *Schizophrenia Bulletin, 3*, 61–79.

## J

Jacob, T. (1975). Family interaction in disturbed and normal families: A methodological and substantive review. *Psychological Bulletin, 82*, 33–65.

Janca, A. (2005). Rethinking somatoform disorders. *Current Opinion in Psychiatry, 18*, 65–71.

Jaycox, L. A., Zoellner, L., & Foa, E. B. (2002). Cognitive-behavioral therapy for PTSD in rape survivors. *Journal of Clinical Psychology/In Session, 58*, 891–906.

Jellenek, E. (1960). *The disease concept of alcoholism.* Highland Park, NJ: Hillhouse.

Jenkins, J. H., & Karno, M. (1992). The meaning of expressed emotion: Theoretical issues raised by cross-cultural research. *American Journal of Psychiatry, 149*, 9–21.

Jensen, P. S., Arnold, E., Swanson, J. M., Vitiello, B., Abikoff, H. B., Greenhill, L. L., ... et al. (2007). 3-year-follow-up on the NIMH MTA Study. *Journal of the American Academy of Child & Adolescent Psychiatry, 46*, 989–1002.

Jessop, D. S., Richards, L. J., & Harbuz, M. S. (2004). Effects of stress on inflammatory autoimmune disease: Destructive or protective? *The International Journal on the Biology of Stress, 7*, 216–266.

Jin, H., Shih, P. B., Golshan, S., Mudaliar, S., Henry, R., Glorioso, D. K., ... Jeste, D. V. (2013). Comparison of longer-term safety and effectiveness of atypical antipsychotics in patients over age 40: A trial using equipoise-stratified randomization. *Journal of Clinical Psychiatry, 74*, 10–18. doi:10.4088/JCP.12m08001

Johnson, K. R., & Layng, T. J. (1992). Breaking the structuralist barrier: Literacy and numeracy with fluency. *American Psychologist, 47*, 1475–1490.

Johnson, W. (1959). *The onset of stuttering.* Minneapolis, MN: University of Minnesota Press.

Jones, M. C. (1924). The elimintation of children's fears. *Journal of Experimental Psychology, 7*, 382–390.

Jung, H. H., Kim, C. H., Chang, J. H., Park, Y. G., Chung, S. S., & Chang, J. W. (2006). Bilateral anterior cingulotomy for refractory obsessive-compulsive disorder: Long-term follow-up results. *Stereotactic and Functional Neurosurgery, 84*, 184–189.

## K

Kabot, S., Masi, W., & Segal, M. (2003). Advances in the diagnosis and treatment of autism spectrum disorders. *Professional Psychology: Research and Practice, 34*, 26–33.

Kagan, J. (2007). A trio of concerns. *Perspectives on Psychological Sciences, 2*, 361–376.

Kahng, S., Iwata, B. A., & Lewin, A. B. (2002). Behavioral treatment of self-injury, 1964 to 2000. *American Journal on Mental Retardation, 107*, 212–221.

Kandel, D. B., Kessler, R. C., & Margulies, R. Z. (1978). Antecedents of adolescents initiation into stages of drug use: A developmental analysis. *Journal of Youth and Adolescence, 7*, 13–40.

Kanner, L. (1943). Autistic disturbances of affective contact. *Nervous Child, 2*, 217–250.

Kantor, R. E., Wallner, J. M., & Winder, C. L. (1953). Process and reactive schizophrenia. *Journal of Consulting and Clinical Psychology, 17*, 157–162.

Kaplan, J. R., Adam, M. R., Clarkson, T. B., Manuck, S. B., & Shively, C. A. (1991). Social behavior and gender in biomedical investigations using monkeys: Studies in artherogenesis. *Laboratory Animal Science, 41*, 1–9.

Kaplan, M. S., McFarland, B. H., Huguet, N., & Newsom, J. T. (2007). Physical illness, functional limitations, and suicide risks: A population-based study. *American Journal of Orthopsychiatry, 77*, 56–60.

Kaufman, I. C., & Rosenblum, L. A. (1967). The reaction to separation in infant monkeys: Anaclitic depression and conservation-withdrawl. *Psychomatic Medicine, 29*, 648–675.

Kazdin, A. E. (1998). Psychosocial treatments for conduct disorder in children. In P. E. Nathan, & J. M. Gorman, *A guide to treatments that work* (pp. 65–89). New York, NY: Oxford University Press.

**488**

Keck, P. E., & McElroy, S. L. (2002). Pharmacological treatments for bipolar disorders. In P. E. Nathan, & J. M. Gorman, *A guide to treatments that work* (2 ed., pp. 277–299). New York, NY: Oxford University Press.

Keller, A., Castellanos, F. X., Vaituzis, A. C., Jeffries, N. O., Giedd, J. N., & Rapoport, J. L. (2003). Progressive loss of cerebellar volume in childhood-onset schizophrenia. *American Journal of Psychiatry, 160,* 128–133. doi:10.1176/appi.ajp.160.1.128

Keller, M. B., Klein, D. N., Hirschfield, R. M., Kocis, J. H., McCullough, J. P., & Miller, I. (1995). Results of the *DSM-IV* mood disorders field trail. *American Journal of Psychiatry, 152,* 843–849.

Kendler, K. S., Gatz, M., Gardner, C. O., & Pederson, G. (2006). A Swedish national twin study of lifetime major depression. *American Journal of Psychiatry, 163,* 109–114.

Kendler, K. S., Neale, M. C., Kessler, R. C., Heath, A. C., & Eaves, L. J. (1992). The genetic epidemiology of phobia in women: the interrelationship of agoraphobia, social phobia, situational phobia, and simple phobia. *Archives of General Psychiatry, 49,* 273–281.

Kessel, J. (1962). *The road back, a report on Alcoholics Anonymous.* New York, NY: Knopf.

Kessler, R. C., Berglund, P., Demler, O., Jin, R., Merikangas, K. R., & Walters, E. E. (2005, June). Lifetime prevalence and age-of-onset distributions of *DSM-IV* disorders in the National Comorbidity Survey Replication. *Archives of General Psychiatry, 62*(6), 593–602.

Kessler, R. C., Chiu, W. T., Demler, O., Merikangas, K. R., & Walters, E. E. (2005). Prevalence, severity, and combordity of 12-months *DSM-IV* disorders in the National Comorbidity Survey Replication. *Archives of General Psychiatry, 62*(6), 617–627. Retrieved June 2005

Kessler, R. C., Chiu, W. T., Demler, O., Merikangas, K. R., & Walters, E. E. (2005, June). Prevalence, severity, and comorbidity of 12-month *DSM-IV* disorders in the National Comorbidity Survey Replication. *Archives of General Psychiatry, 62*(6), 617–627.

Kessler, R. C., Coccaro, E. F., Fava, M., Jaeger, S., Jin, R., & Walters, E. (2006). The prevalence and correlates of *DSM-IV* intermittent explosive disorder in the National Comobidity Survey Replication. *Archives of General Psychiatry, 63,* 669–678.

Kessler, R. C., Galea, S., Gruber, M. J., Sampson, N. A., Ursano, R. J., & Wessely, S. (2008). Trends in mental illness and suicidality after Hurricane Katrina. *Molecular Psychiatry, 13,* 374–384.

Kessler, R. C., Sonnega, A., Bromet, E., Hughes, M., & Nelson, C. B. (1995). Posttraumatic stress disorder in the National Comorbidity Survey. *Archives of General Psychiatry, 52,* 1048–1060.

Kety, S. S., Rosenthal, D., Wender, P. H., & Schulsinger, F. (1976). Studies based on a total sample of adopted individuals and their relatives: Why they were necessary, what they demonstrated and failed to demonstrate. *Schizophrenia Bulletin, 2,* 413–428.

Kiev, A. (1969). Transcultural psychiatry: Research problems in perspectives. In C. S. Plog, & R. B. Edgerton (Eds.), *Changing perspectives in mental illness* (pp. 106–126). New York, NY: Holt, Rinehart and Winston.

Kinsey, A. C., Pomeroy, W. B., & Martin, C. E. (1948). *Sexual behavior in the human male.* Philadelphia, PA: Saunders.

Kinsey, A. C., Pomeroy, W. B., Martin, C. E., & Gebhard, P. H. (1953). *Sexual behavior in the human female.* Philadelphia, PA: Sauders.

Kirkpatrick, B., Bunchana, R. W., Ross, D. E., & Carpenter, W. T. (2001). A separate disease within the syndrome of schizophrenia. *Archives of General Psychiatry, 58,* 165–171.

Kirsch, I., Moore, T. J., Scoboria, A., & Nicholls, S. S. (2002, July 15). The emperor's new drugs: An analysis of antidepressant medication data submitted to the U.S. Food and Drug Administration. *Prevention & Treatment, 5*(1). doi:10.1037/15223765.5.1.523a

Kläning, U. (1999). Greater occurrence of schizophrenia in dizygotic but not monozygotic twins: Register-based study. *British Journal of Psychiatry, 175,* 407–409.

Kleber, H. (1990). The nosology of abuse and dependence. *Journal of Psychiatric Research, 24,* 57–64.

Klin, A., Lang, J., Cicchetti, D. V., & Volkmar, F. R. (2000). Brief report: Interrater reliability of clinical diagnosis and *DSM-IV* criteria for autistic disorder: Results of the *DSM-IV* Autism Field Trial. *Journal of Autism and Developmental Disorders,* 163–167.

Klomek, A. B., Sourander, A., Kumpulainen, K., Piha, J., Tamminen, T., Molianen, I., ... Gould, M. S. (2008). Childhood bullying as a risk for later depression and suicidal ideation among Finnish males. *Journal of Affective Disorders, 109,* 47–55.

Knapp, K., Romeo, R., Mogg, A., Eranti, S., Pluck, G., Purvis, R., ... et al. (2008). Cost-effectiveness of transcranial magnetic stimulation vs. electroconvulsive therapy for severe depression: A multi-centre randomized controlled trial. *Journal of Affective Disorders, 109,* 273–285.

Koenigsberg, H. W., Woo-Ming, A. M., Siever, L. J., & Siever, L. J. (2002). Psychopharmacological treatments for personality disorders. In P. E. Nathan, & J. M. Gorman, *A guide to treatments that work* (2 ed., pp. 625–641). New York, NY: Oxford University Press.

Koluchova, I. (1976). A report on the further development of twins after severe and prolonged deprivation. In A. M. Clarke, & A. D. Clarke (Eds.), *Early experience: Myth and evidence* (pp. 56–66). New York, NY: The Free Press.

Kopelowicz, A., Liberman, R. P., & Zarate, R. (2002). Psychosocial treatments for schizophrenia. In P. E. Nathan, & J. M. Gorman, *A guide to treatments that work* (pp. 201–228). New York, NY: Oxford University Press.

Koran, L. M., Abujaoude, E., Large, M. D., & Serpe, R. T. (2008). The prevalence of body dysmorphic disorder in the United States adult population. *CNS Spectrums, 13,* 316–322.

Kraemer, H. C., Kupfer, D. J., Clarke, D. E., Narrow, W. E., & Regier, D. A. (2012). *DSM-5*: How reliable is reliable enough? *American Journal of Psychiatry, 169,* 13–15. doi:10.1176/appi.ajp.2011.11010050

Kroenke, K. (2007). Efficacy of treatment for somatoform disorders: A review of randomized controlled trials. *Psychosomatic Medicine, 69,* 881–888.

Kroenke, K., & Swindle, R. (2000). Cognitive-behavioral therapy for somatization and symptoms syndromes: A critical review of controlled clinical trials. *Psychotherapy and Psychosomatics, 69,* 205–215.

Kryzhanovskaya, L., & Canterbury, R. (2001). Suicidal behavior in patients with adjustment disorders. *The Journal of Crisis Intervention and Suicide Prevention, 22,* 125–131.

Kuhn, T. S. (1970). *The structure of scientific revolutions* (2nd ed.). Chicago, IL: University of Chicago Press.

Kuriansky, J. B., Deming, W. E., & Gurland, B. J. (1974). On trends in the diagnosis of schizophrenia. *American Journal of Psychiatry, 131,* 402–408.

Kutlesic, V., Williamson, D. A., Gleaves, D. H., Barbin, J. M., & Murphy-Eberenz, K. P. (1998). Interview for the Diagnosis of Eating Disorders-IV: Application to *DSM-IV* diagnostic criteria. *Psychological Assessment, 10,* 41–48.

## L

La Greca, A. M., Silverman, W. K., Vernberg, E. M., & Prinstein, M. J. (1996). Symptoms of posttraumatic stress in children after Hurricane Andrew: A prospective study. *Journal of Consulting and Clinical Psychology, 64,* 712–723.

Lader, M. H., & Wing, L. (1966). Physiological measures, sedative drugs, and morbid anxiety. *Maudsley Monograph, No. 14.*

Ladwig, K. H., Marten-Mittag, B., Erazo, N., & Gundel, H. (2001). Identifying somatization disorder in a population-based examination survey, psychosocial burden and gender differences. *Psychosomatics, 42*, 511–518.

Laing, R. D., & Esterson, A. (1971). *Sanity, madness, and the family.* New York, NY: Basic Books.

Lal, H., Miksic, S., Drawbaugh, R., Numan, R., & Smith, N. (1976). Alleviation of narcotic withdrawal syndrome by conditional stimuli. *Pavlovian Journal of Biological Science, 11*, 251–262.

Lam, D. H., Hayward, P., Watkins, E. R., Wright, K., & Sham, P. (2005). Relapse prevention in patients with bipolar disorder: Cognitive therapy outcome after 2 years. *American Journal of Psychiatry, 162*, 324–329.

Lane, C. (2012, June 20). *Arguing Over DSM-5: The British psychological society has serious concerns about the manual.* Retrieved March 28, 2013, from *Psychology Today:* http://www.psychologytoday.com/blog/side-effects/201206/arguing-over-dsm-5-the-british-psychological-society-has-serious-concerns-a

Lane, K. L., Thompson, A., Reske, C. L., Gable, L. M., & Barton-Arwood, S. (2006). Reducing skin picking via competing activities. *Journal of Applied Behavior Analysis, 39*, 459–462. doi:10.1901/jaba.2006.62-05

Lange, R. T., Sullivan, K. A., & Scott, A. (2010). Comparison of MMPI-2 and PAI validity indicators to detect feigned depression and PTSD symptom reporting. *Psychiatry Research, 176*, 229–235. doi:10.1016/j.psychres.2009.03.004

Lanning, K. (1992). *Child sex rings: A behavioral analysis for criminal justice professionals handling cases of child sexual exploitation.* National Center for the Analysis of Violent Crime, Federal Bureau of Investigation, FBI Academy Quantico, Behavioral Science Unit, Virginia.

Larkin, M., Wood, R., & Griffiths, M. (2006). Towards addiction as relationship. *Addiction Research & Therapy, 14*, 207–221.

Larrabee, G. J. (2004). Diagnosis of mild head injury. In J. H. Richer, *Differential diagnosis in adult neuropsychological assessment* (pp. 243–275). New York, NY: Springer Publishing Co.

LaTorre, R. A. (1980). Devaluation of the human love object: Heterosexual rejection as a possible antecedent to fetishism. *Journal of Abnormal Psychology, 89*, 295–298.

Laurema, H. (1993). Nocturnal limb movements in conversion paralysis. *Journal of Nervous and Mental Disease, 181*, 707–708.

Laurila, J. V., Laakkonen, M., Laurila, J. V., Timo, S. E., & Reijo, T. S. (2008). Predisposing and precipitating factors for delirium in a frail geriatric population. *Journal of Psychosomatic Research, 65*, 249–254.

Layon, R. I. (1978). Behavioral approaches to stuttering. In M. Hersen, R. M. Eisler, & P. M. Miller, *Progress in behavior modification.* New York, NY: Academic Press.

Lee, Y. T., & Tsai, S. J. (2010). The mirror neuron system may play a role in the pathogenesis of mass hysteria. *Medical Hypotheses, 74*, 244–245.

Lejoyeux, M., McLoughlin, M., & Ades, J. (206). Pyromania. In E. Hollander, & D. J. Stein (Eds.), *Clinical manual of impulse-control disorders* (pp. 229–250). Arlington, VA: American Psychiatric Publishing.

Lemoine, P., Nir, T., Laudon, M., & Zisapel, N. (2007). Prolonged-release melatonin improves sleep quality and morning alertness in insomnia patients aged 55 years and older and has no withdrawl effects. *Journal of Sleep Research, 16*, 372–380.

Lendon, C. L., Ashall, F., & Goate, A. M. (1997). Exploring the etiology of Alzheimer disease using molecular genetics. *Journal of the American Medical Association, 277*, 825–831.

Lenox, R. H., & Hahn, C. (2000). Overview of the mechanism of action of lithium in the brian: Fifty-five update. *Journal of Clinical Psychiatry, 61*(Suppl. 9), 5–15.

Lenzenweger, M. F., & O'Driscoll, G. A. (2006). Smooth pursuit eye movement and schizotypy in the community. *Journal of Abnormal Psychology, 115*, 779–786.

Lenzenweger, M. F., Lane, M. C., Loranger, A. W., & Kessler, R. C. (2007). *DSM-IV* personality disorders in the national comorbidity survey replication. *Biological Psychiatry, 62*, 553–564.

Leopold, R. L., & Dillon, H. (1963). Psychoanatomy of a disaster: A longterm study of post-traumatic neuroses in survivors of a marine explosion. *American Journal of Psychiatry, 119*, 913–921.

Leor, J., Poole, W. K., & Kloner, R. A. (1996). Sudden cardiac death triggered by an earthquake. *New England Journal of Medicine, 334*, 413–419.

Letnoff, E. J., Williams, T. R., & Sidhu, K. S. (2002). Hysterical paralysis: A report of three cases and a review of the literature. *Spine, 27*, 441–445.

Lettieri, C. J., & Williams, S. G. (2011 8-December). *Sleep-related violence: What every clinician should know.* Retrieved 2013 26-May from Medscape News: Psychiatry and Mental Health: http://www.medscape.com/viewarticle/754852_1

LeVay, S., & Valente, S. M. (2006). *Human sexuality* (2nd ed.). Sutherland, MA: Sinauer Associates.

Levenson, J. C., Wallace, M. L., Fournier, J. C., Rucci, P., & Frank, E. (2012). The role of personality pathology in depression treatment outcome with psychotherapy and pharmacotherapy. *Journal of Consulting and Clinical Psychology, 80*, 719–729. doi:10.1037/a0029396

Levitt, E. E., Moser, C., & Jamison, K. V. (1994). The prevalence and some attributes of females in the sadomasochistic subculture: A second report. *Archives of Sexual Behavior, 23*, 465–474.

Lewinsohn, P. (1974). A behavioral approach to depression. In R. J. Friedman, & M. M. Katz, *The psychology of depression.* Washington, DC: V. H. Winston & Sons.

Lewinsohn, P. M., Holm-Denoma, J. M., Small, J. W., Seeley, J. R., & Joiner, T. E. (2008). Separation anxiety disorder in childhood as a risk factor for future mental illness. *Journal of the American Academy of Child & Adolescent Psychiatry, 47*, 548–555.

Lidz, T., Fleck, S., & Cornelison, A. (1965). *Schizophrenia and the family.* New York, NY: International University Press.

Lieb, R., Meinlschmidt, G., & Araya, R. (2007). Epidemiology of the association between somatoform disorders and anxiety and depressive disorders: An update. *Psychosomatic Medicine, 69*, 860–863.

Lieberman, D. Z., Peele, R., & Razavi, M. (2008). Combinations of *DSM-IV-TR* criteria for bipolar disorders. *Psychopathology, 41*, 35–38.

Lilienfeld, S. O. (2007). Psychological treatments that cause harm. *Perspectives on Psychological Science, 2*, 53–70.

Lilienfeld, S. O., Lynn, S. J., Kirsch, I., Chaves, J. F., Sarbin, T. R., Ganaway, G. K., & Powell, R. A. (1999). Dissociative identity disorder and the Sociocognitive Model: Recalling the lessons of the past. *Psychological Bulletin, 125*, 507–523.

Linehan, M. M., Schmidt III, H., Dimeff, L. A., Craft, J. C., Kanter, J., & Comtois, K. A. (1999). Dialetical behavior therapy for patients with borderline personality disorder and drug dependence. *The American Journal on Addiction, 8*, 279–292.

Lisanby, S. H. (2007). Electroconvulsive therapy for depression. *The New England Journal of Medicine, 357*, 1939–1945.

Lobitz, W. C., & LoPiccolo, J. (1972). New methods in the behavioral treatment of sexual dysfunction. *Journal of Behavior Therapy and Experimental Psychiatry, 3*, 265–271.

Loef, M., & Walach, H. (2013). Midlife obesity and dementia: Meta-analysis and adjusted forecast of dementia prevalence in the United States and China. *Obesity, 21*, E51–E55.

Loftus, E. F. (1997, September). Creating false memories. *Scientific American*, 70–75.

Logsdon, R. G., McCurry, S. M., & Teri, L. (2007). Evidence-based psychological treatments for disruptive behaviors in individuals with dementia. *Psychology and Aging, 22*, 28–36.

Looper, K. J., & Kirmayer, L. J. (2002). Behavioral medicine approaches to somatoform disorders. *Journal of Consulting and Clinical Psychology, 70*, 810–827.

Lovaas, O. I. (1987). Behavioral treatment and normal educational and intellectual functioning in young autistic children. *Journal of Consulting and Clinical Psychology, 55*, 3–9.

Lovaas, O. I., Koegel, R. L., & Schreibman, L. (1979). Stimulus overselectivity in autism: A review of research. *Psychological Bulletin, 86*, 1236–1254.

Lowry, F. (2013 1-May). *Childhood infection linked to schizophrenia*. Retrieved 2013 25-May from Medscape News: Psychiatry & Mental Health: http://www.medscape.com/viewarticle/803421

Luari, A. R. (1982). *Language and cognition*. New York, NY: Wiley.

Lucas, A. R., Beard, C. M., O'Fallon, W. M., & Kurland, L. T. (1991). 50-year trends in the incidence of anorexia nervosa in Rochester, Minnesota: A population-based study. *American Journal of Psychiatry, 148*, 917–922.

Lunde, D. T. (1975). *Murder and madness*. Stanford, CA: Stanford University Press.

Lykken, D. T. (1957). A study of anxiety in the sociopathic personality. *Journal of Abnormal and Social Psychology, 55*, 6–10.

Lyons, C. A. (1991). Stimulus control-application: Smoking. In W. Ishaq, *Human behavior in today's world* (pp. 217–230). New York, NY: Praeger.

Lyons, C. A. (2002). Pathological gambling, impulse control, and the addictions. *Association for Behavior Analysis*. Toronto, Canada: Paper presented in J. Weatherly (Chair), Experimental and conceptual advances in the study of gambling behavior.

Lyons, C. A. (2006). What can gambling tell us about addiction? In P. M. Ghezzi, C. A. Lyons, M. R. Dixon, & G. R. Wilson (Eds.), *Gambling: Behavior theory, research, and application* (pp. 9–18). Reno, NV: Context Press.

## M

Maher, B. A., McKean, K., & McLaughlin, B. (1966). Studies in psychotic language. In Stone P., *The general inquirer: A computer approach to content analysis*. Cambridge, MA: Massachusetts Institution of Technology.

Mahrer, A. R. (1978). *Experiencing: A humanistic theory of psychology and psychiatry*. New York, NY: Brunner/Mazel.

Malbos, E., Rapee, R. M., & Kavakli, M. (2013). A controlled study of agoraphobia and the independent effect of virtual reality exposure therapy. *Australian and New Zealand Journal of Psychiatry , 47*, 160–168. doi:10.1177/0004867412453626

Maldonado, J. R., Butler, L. D., & Spiegel, D. (2002). Treatments for dissociative disorders. In P. E. Nathan, & J. M. Gorman, *A guide to treatments that work* (2 ed., pp. 463–496). New York, NY: Oxford University Press.

Maletzky, B. M. (2002). The paraphilias: Research and treatment. In P. E. Nathan, & J. M. Gorman, *A guide to treatments that work* (2nd ed., pp. 525–557). New York, NY: Oxford University Press.

Mann, M. (1968). *New primer on alcoholism* (2 ed.). New York, NY: Holt, Rinehart and Winston.

Mantere, O., Suomien, K., Valtone, H. M., Arvilommi, P., Leppamaki, S., Melartin, T., & Isometsa, E. (2008). Differences in outcome of *DSM-IV* bipolar I and II disorders. *Bipolar Disorders, 10*, 413–425.

Marangell, L. B., Martinez, M., Jurdi, R. A., & Zboyan, H. (2007). Neurostimulation therapies in depression: A review of new modalities. *Acta Psychiatrica Scandinavica, 116*, 174–181.

Mark, J. C. (1953). The attitudes of the mothers of male schizophrenics toward child behavior. *Journal of Abnormal and Social Psychology, 48*, 185–189.

Marlatt, G. A., & Gordon, J. R. (1980). Determinants of relapse: Implications for the maintenance of behavior change. In P. Davidson, & M. Davidson (Eds.), *Behavioral medicine: Changing health lifestyles* (pp. 410–452). Elmsford, NY: Pergamon.

Marlatt, G. A., Demming, B., & Reid, J. B. (1973). Loss-of-control drinking in alcoholics: An experimental analogue. *Journal of Abnormal Psychology, 81*, 233–241.

Martin, A., Rauh, E., Fichter, M., & Rief, W. (2007). A one-session treatment for patients suffering from medically unexplained symptoms in primary care: A randomized clinical trial. *Psychosomatics: Journal of Consultation Liaison Psychiatry, 48*, 294–303.

Masters, W. H., & Johnson, V. E. (1966). *Human sexual response*. Boston, MA: Little Brown.

Masters, W. H., & Johnson, V. E. (1970). *Human sexual inadequacy*. Boston, MA: Little Brown.

Masters, W. H., Johnson, V. E., & Kolodny, R. C. (1992). *Human sexuality* (4th ed.). New York, NY: Harper Collins Publishers, Inc.

Mataix-Cols, D., Frost, R. O., Pertusa, A., Clark, L. A., Saxena, S., Leckman, J. F., ... Wilhelm, S. (2010). Hoarding disorder: A new diagnosis for the *DSM-V*? *Depression and Anxiety, 27*, 556–572. doi:10.1002/da.20693

Matson, J. L., & LoVullo, S. V. (2008). A review of behavioral treatments for self-injurious behaviors of persons with autism spectrum disorders. *Behavior Modification, 32*, 61–76.

Maurer, D. W., & Vogel, V. H. (1954). *Narcotics and narcotics addiction*. Springfield, IL: Charles C. Thomas.

May, R. (1967). *Psychology and the human dilemma*. New York, NY: Nostrand.

Mazzocco, M. M., Freund, L. S., Baumgardner, T. L., Forman, L., & Reiss, A. L. (1995). Neuropsychological and psychosocial effects of the FMR-1 full mutation: Case report of monozygotic twins discordant for the fragile X syndrome. *Neuropsychology, 9*, 470–480.

Mazzoni, G. A., Loftus, E. F., & Kirsch, I. (2001). Changing beliefs about implausible autobiographical events: A little plausibility goes a long way. *Journal of Experimental Psychology: Applied, 7*, 51–59.

McArthur, J. C. (2004). HIV dementia: An evolving disease. *Journal of Neuroimmunology, 157*, 3–10.

McCabe, M. P. (2005). The role of performance anxiety in the development and maintenance of sexual dysfunction in men and women. *International Journal of Stress Management, 12*, 379–388.

McCord, W., & McCord, J. (1964). *The psychopath: An essay on the criminal mind*. New York, NY: Van Nostrand Reinhold.

McCord, W., Porta, J., & McCord, J. (1962). The familial genesis of psychoses. *Psychiatry, 25*, 60–71.

McCrae, R. R., & Costa, P. T. (1987). Validation of the five-factor model of personality across instruments and observers. *Journal of Personality and Social Psychology, 52*, 81–90.

McGuire, R. J., Carlisle, J. M., & Young, B. G. (1965). Sexual deviations as conditioned behavior: A hypothesis. *Behaviour Research and Therapy, 2*, 185–190.

McKinley, R. A. (1963). *Perceived parental attributed of schizophrenics as a function of premorbid adjustment*. Unpublished doctoral dissertation, IA: University of Iowa.

McLean, P. D., Whittal, M. L., Thordarson, D. S., Taylor, S., Sochting, I., Koch, W. J., ... Anderson, K. W. (2001). Cognitive versus behavioral therapy in the group treatment of obsessive-compulsive disorder. *Journal of Consulting and Clinical Psychology, 69*, 205–214.

McNally, R. J., Bryant, R. A., & Ehlers, A. (2003). Does early psychological intervention promote recovery from posttraumatic stress? *Psychological Science in the Public Interest, 4*, 45–79.

McNeil, T. F., Cantor-Graae, E., & Ismail, B. (2000). Obstetric complications and congenital malformation in schizophrenia. *Brain Research Reviews, 31*, 116–178.

Meehl, P. E. (1962). Schizotaxia, schizotypy, schizophrenia. *American Psychologist, 17*, 827–838.

Meier, M. H., Caspi, A., Ambler, A., Harrington, H., Houts, R., Keefe, R. S., ... Moffitt, T. E. (2012). Persistent cannabis users show neuropsychological decline from childhood to midlife. *Proceedings of the National Academy of Sciences, 109*, E2657–E2664. doi:10.1073/pnas.1206820109

Melnik, T., & Abdo, C. N. (2005). Psychogenic erectile dysfunction: Comparative study of three therapeutic approaches. *Journal of Sex & Marital Therapy, 31*, 243–255.

Merikangas, K. R., Akiskal, H. S., Angst, J., Greenberg, P. E., Hirschfeld, R. M.,

Petukhova, M., & Kessler, R. C. (2007). Lifetime and 12-month prevalence of bipolar spectrum disorder in the National Comorbidity Survey replication. *Archives of General Psychiatry, 64*, 543–552.

Messias, E., Kirkpatrick, B., Bromet, E., Ros, D., Buchanan, R. w., Carpenter, W. T., & Tek, C. (2004). Summer birth and deficit schizophrenia: A pooled analysis from 6 countries. *Archives of General Psychiatry, 61*, 985–989.

Meston, C. M., Rellini, A. H., & Telch, M. J. (2008). Short- and long-term effects of ginkgo biloba extract on sexual dysfunction in women. *Archives of Sexual Behavior, 37*, 530–547.

Meyer, R. G., & Deitsch, S. (1996). *The clinician's handbook: Integrated diagnostics, assessment, and intervention in adult and adolescent psychopathology* (4 ed.). Needham Heights, MA: Allyn and Bacon.

Meyer, R. G., & Deitsch, S. (1996). *The clinician's handbook: Integrated diagnostics, assessment, and intervention in adults an adolescent psychopathology* (4 ed.). Needham Heights, MA: Allyn and Bacon.

Mikkelsen, E. J. (2001). Enuresis and encopresis: Ten years of progress. *Journal of the American Academy of Child & Adolescent Psychiatry, 40*, 1146–1158.

Mileno, M. D., Barnowski, C., Fiore, T., Gormley, J., Rich, J. D., Emgushov, R., & Carpenter, C. C. (2001). Factitious HIV syndrome in young women. *The AIDS Reader, 11*, 263–268.

Miller, J. N., & Ozonoff, S. (2000). The external validity of Asperger disorder: Lack of evidence from the domain of neuropsychology. *Journal of Abnormal Psychology, 109*, 227–238.

Miller, L. K. (1999). The Savant Syndrome: Intellectual impairment and exceptional skill. *Psychological Bulletin, 125*, 31–46.

Miller, W. R., & Rollnick, S. (1991). *Motivational interviewing: Preparing people to change addictive behavior.* New York, NY: Guildford Press.

Miller, W. R., & Wilbourne, P. L. (2002). Mesa Grande: A methodological analysis of clinical trials of treatment for alcohol use disorders. *Addiction, 97*, 265–277.

Mindham, R. H., Scadding, J. G., & Cawley, R. H. (1992). Diagnoses are not diseases. *British Journal of Psychiatry, 161*, 686–691. doi:10.1192/bjp.161.5.686

Minek, S., & Zinbarg, R. (2006). A contemporary learning theory perspective on the etiology of anxiety disorders: It's not what you thought it was. *American Psychologist, 61*, 10–26.

Mineka, S., & Sutton, J. (2006). Contemporary learning theory perspectives on the etiology of fears and phobias. In M. G. Craske, D. Hermans, & D. Vansteenwegen, *Fear and learning: From basic processes to clinical implications* (pp. 75–97).

Washington, DC: American Psychological Association.

Mineka, S., Davidson, M., Cook, M., & Keir, R. (1984). Observational conditioning of snake fear in rhesus monkeys. *Journal of Abnormal Psychology, 93*, 355–372.

Mintz, N. L., & Schwartz, D. T. (1971). Ecological factors in the incidence of schizophrenic and manic-depressive psychoses. In N. L. Corah, & E. N. Gale, *The origins of abnormal behavior.* Reading, MA: Addison-Wesley.

Mithoefer, M. C., Wagner, M. T., Mithoefer, A. T., Jerome, I., & Doblin, R. (2010). The safety and efficacy of the +/-3,4-methylenedioxymethamphetamine-assisted psychotherapy in subjects with chronic, treatment-resistant posttraumatic stress disorder: The first randomized controlled pilot study. *Journal of psychopharmacology.* doi:10.1177/0269881110378371

Modesto-Lowe, V., & Van Kirk, J. (2002). Clinical uses of Naltrexone: A review of the evidence. *Experimental and Clinical Psychopharmacology, 10*, 213–227.

Moene, F. C., Spinhoven, P., Hoogduin, K. A., & Duck, R. V. (2002). A randomized controlled clinical trial on the additional effect of hypnosis in a comprehensive treatment programme for in-patients with conversion disorder of the motor type. *Psychotherapy and Psychosomatics, 71*, 66–76.

Moene, F. C., Spinhoven, P., Hoogduin, K. A., & Dyck, R. V. (2003). A randomized controlled clinical trial of a hypnosis-based treatment for patients with conversion disorder, motor type. *International Journal of Clinical and Experimental Hypnosis, 51*, 29–50.

Mokdad, A. H., Marks, J. S., Stroup, D. F., & Gerberding, J. L. (2004). Actual causes of death in the United States, 2000. *Journal of the American Medical Association, 291*, 1238–1245.

Monahan, J. (1992). Mental disorder and violent behavior: Perceptions and evidence. *American Psychologist, 47*, 511–512.

Monahan, J., & Steadman, H. J. (1996). Violent storms and violent people: How meteorology can inform risk communication in mental health law. *American Psychologist, 51*, 931–938.

Monroe, S. M., & Harkness, K. L. (2005). Life stress, the "kindling" hypothesis, and the recurrence of depression: Considerations from a life stress perspective. *Psychological Review, 112*, 417–445.

Montgomery-Downs, H. E., Crabtree, V. M., Capdevila, O. S., & Gozal, D. (2007). Infant feeding methods and childhood sleep-disordered breathing. *Pediatrics, 120*, 1030–1035.

Moore, D. (2001). *The dependent gene: The fallacy of "nature vs. nurture".* New York, NY: W. H. Freeman.

Mormede, P., Dantzer, R., Michaud, B., Kelley, K. W., & Moal, M. L. (1988). Influence of stressor predictability and behavioral control on lymphocyte reactivity, antibody responses and neuroendocrine activation in rats. *Physiology & Behavior, 43*, 577–583. doi:10.1016/0031-9384(88)90211-9

Morrison, J., Winokur, G., Crowe, R., & Clancy, J. (1973). The Iowa 500: The first follow-up. *Archives of General Psychiatry, 29*, 678–682.

Morrison, J., Winokur, G., Crowe, R., & Clancy, J. (1973). The Iowa 500: The first follow-up. *Archives of General Psychiatry, 29*, 678–682.

Mosher, L. R., & Menn, A. (1978). Community residential treatment for schizophrenia: Two year follow-up data. *Hospital and Community Psychiatry, 29*, 715–723.

Mowrer, O. H. (1950). *Leaning theory and personality dynamics.* New York, NY: Ronald.

Mucha, T. F., & Reinhardt, R. F. (1970). Conversion reactions in student aviators. *American Journal of Psychiatry, 127*, 493–497.

Mueser, K. T., & Berenbaum, H. (1990). Psychodynamic treatment of schizophrenia. Is there a future? *Psychological Medicine, 20*, 253–262.

Müller, T., Mannel, M., Murck, H., & Rahlf, V. (2004). Treatment of somatoform disorders with St. Johns' Wort: A randomized, double-blind and placebo-controlled trial. *Psychosomatic Medicine, 66*, 538–547.

Murphy, H. B. (1968). Cultural factors in the genesis of schizophrenia. In D. Rosenthal, & S. S. Kety, *The transmission of schizophrenia* (pp. 132–153). New York, NY: Pergamon.

Murphy, H., Wittkower, E. D., Fried, J., & Ellenberger, H. (1963). A cross-cultural survey of schizophrenic symptomatology. *International Journal of Social Psychiatry, 9*, 237–249.

Murphy, J. M. (1964). Psychotherapeutic aspect of Shamanism on St. Lawrence Island, Alaska. In A. Kiev (Ed.), *Magic, faith, and healing* (pp. 53–84). New York, NY: Freeman Press, Macmillan.

Murrie, D. C., & Wilson, J. I. (2005). Clinician variation in rates of legal sanity opinions: Implications for self-monitoring. *Professional Psychology: Research and Practice, 36*, 519–524.


## N
- - - - - -

Nemeroff, C. B., & Schatzberg, A. F. (2002). Pharmacological treatments for unipolar depression. In P. E. Nathan, & J. M. Gorman, *A guide to treatments that work* (pp. 229–243). New York, NY: Oxford University Press.

Nestler, E. J., & Aghajanian, G. K. (1997). Molecular and cellular basis of addiction. *Science, 278*, 58–63.

Newcorn, J. H., & Strain, J. J. (1992). Adjustment disorder in children and adolescents. *Journal of the American Academy of Children & Adolescent Psychiatry, 31,* 318–326.

Neziroglu, R., Roberts, m., & Yaryura-Tobias, J. A. (2004). A behavioral model for body dysmorphic disorder. *Psychiatric Annals, 34,* 915–920.

Nishino, S., Ripley, B., Overeem, S., Lammers, G. J., & Mignot, E. (2000). Hypocretin (orexin) deficiency in human narcolepsy. *The Lancet, 355,* 39–40.

Nock, M. K., & Kessler, R. C. (2006). Prevalence of and risk factors for suicide attempts versus suicide gestures: Analysis of the National Comorbidity Survey. *Journal of Abnormal Psychology, 115,* 616–623.

Noyes, R., Holt, C. S., Happel, R. L., Kathol, R. G., & Yagla, S. J. (1997). A family study of hypochondriasis. *Journal of Nervous and Mental Disease, 185,* 223–232.

## O

Obler, M. (1973). Systematic desensitization in sexual disorders. *Journal of Behavior Therapy and Experimental Psychiatry, 4,* 93–101.

O'Brien, C. P., & McKay, J. R. (2002). Pharmacological treatments for substance use disorders. In P. E. Nathan, & J. M. Gorman, *A guide to treatments that work* (pp. 125–156). New York, NY: Oxford University Press.

Odeh, M. S., Zeiss, R. A., & Huss, M. T. (2006). Cues they use: Clinicians' endorsement of risk cues in predictions of dangerousness. *Behavioral Sciences & the Law, 24,* 93–101.

Ogden, J. A. (2005). *Fractured minds: A case-study approach to clinical neuropsychology* (2 ed.). New York, NY: Oxford University Press.

Ohayon, M. M., & Okun, M. L. (2006). Occurrence of sleep disorders in the families of narcoleptic patients. *Neurology, 67,* 703–705.

Okazaki, S., & Sue, S. (1995). Cultural considerations in psychological assessment of Asian Americans. In J. N. Butcher, *Clinical personality assessment: Practical approaches* (pp. 107–119). New York, NY: Oxford University Press.

Okie, A. (2010). A flood of opioids, a rising tide of deaths. *New England Journal of Medicine, 363,* 1081–1083.

O'Malley, G., Leonard, M., Meagher, D., & O'Keeffe, S. T. (2008). The delirium experience: A review. *A Journal of Psychosomatic Research, 65,* 223–228.

Ost, L. G., & Hugdahl, K. (1981). Acquisition of phobias and anxiety response patterns in clinical patients. *Behavior Research & Therapy, 19,* 439–447.

Ouj, U. (2009). Pseudocyesis in a rural southeast Nigerian community. *Journal of Obstetrics and Gynecology Research, 34,* 660–665.

Overmier, J. B., & Seligman, M. E. (1967). Effects of inescapable shock upon subsequent escape and avoidance learning. *Journal of Comparative and Physiological Psychology, 63,* 23–33.

## P

Páez-Blarrina, M., Luciano, C., Gutierrez-Martinez, O., Valdivia, S., Ortega, J., & Rodriquez-Valverde, M. (2008). The role of values with personal examples in altering the functions of pain: Comparison between acceptance-based and cognitive-control-based. *Behaviour Research and Therapy, 46,* 84–97.

Pagnin, D., de Queiroz, V., Pini, S., & Cassano, G. B. (2004). Efficacy of ECT in depression: A meta-analytic review. *Journal of ECT, 20,* 13–20.

Pagnin, D., de Queiroz, V., Pini, S., & Cassano, G. B. (2008). Efficacy of ECT in depression: A meta-analytic review. *Focus, 6,* 155–162.

Pallanti, A., & Rossi, N. B. (2006). Pathological gambling. In E. Hollander, & D. J. Stein (Eds.), *Clinical manual of impulse-control disorders* (pp. 251–289). Arlington, VA: American Psychiatric Publishing.

Pallanti, A., Rossi, N. B., & Hollander, E. (2006). Pathological gambling. In E. Hollander, & D. J. Stein (Eds.), *Clinical manual of impulse-control disorder* (pp. 251–289). Arlington, VA: American Psychiatric Publishing.

Palmer, B. W., Heaton, R. K., Paulsem, J., Kuck, J., Braff, D., Harris, M. J., ... Jeste, D. V. (1997). Is it possible to be schizophrenic yet neuropsychologically normal? *Neuropsychology, 11,* 437–446.

Pandi-Perumal, S. R., Srinivasan, V., Spence, D. W., & Cardinali, D. P. (2007). Roles of the melatonin system in the control of sleep: Therapeutic implications. *CNS Drugs, 21,* 995–1018.

Paris, J. (1999). Borderline personality disorder. In T. Millon, P. H. Blaney, & R. D. Davis, *Oxford textbook of psychopathology* (pp. 628–652). New York, NY: Oxford University Press.

Parry-Jones, W. L., Santer-Westrate, H. C., & Crawley, R. C. (1970). Behaviour therapy in a case of hysterical blindness. *Behaviour Research and Therapy, 8,* 79–85.

Paul, G. L., & Lentz, R. J. (1977). *Psychosocial treatment of chronic mental patients: Milieu versus social learning programs.* Cambridge, MA: Harvard University Press.

Paulose-Ram, R., Safran, M. A., Jonas, B. S., Gu, Q., & Orwig, D. (2007). Trends in psychotropic medication use among U.S. adults. *Pharmacoepidemiology and Drug Safety, 16*(5), 560–570.

Pavolv, I. P. (1928). *Lectures on conditioned reflexes.* New York, NY: International Publishers.

Paykel, E. S., Prusoff, B. A., & Myers, J. K. (1975). Suicide attempts and recent life events. *Archives of General Psychiatry, 32,* 327–331.

Payne, J. L., Potash, J. B., & DePaulo, J. R. (2005). Recent finding on the genetic basis of bipolar disorder. *Psychiatric Clinics of North America, 28,* 481–498.

Pedersen, M. G., Mortensen, P. B., Norgaard-Pedersen, B., & Postolache, T. T. (2012). Toxoplasma Gondi infection and self-directed violence in mothers. *Archives of General Psychiatry, 69,* 1123–1130. doi:10.1001/archgenpsychiatry.2012.668

Pederson, C. B., & Mortensen, P. B. (2001). Evidence of a dose-response relationship between urbanicity during upbringing and schizpohrenia risk. *Archives of Genral Psychiatry, 58,* 1039–1046.

Peele, S. (2007). Addiction as disease: Policy, epidemiology, and treatment consequences of a bad idea. In J. Henningfield, P. Santora, & W. Bickel, *Addition treatment: Science and policy for the twenty-first century* (pp. 153–164). Baltimore, MD: Johns Hopkins University Press.

Perez-Cruet, J. (1976). Conditioning of striatal dopamine metabolism with methadone, morphine or bulbocapnine as an unconditioned stimulus. *Pavlovian Journal of Biological Science, 11,* 237–250.

Perrone, M. (2011 30-November). *Inspector highlights psych drug use among elderly.* Retrieved 2013 26-May from Yahoo News: http://news.yahoo.com/inspector-highlights-psych-drug-among-elderly-190217832.html;_ylc=X3oDMTNud m1qYW01BF9TAzIxNDU4NjgyNzUEYWN 0A21haWxfY2IEY3QDYQRpbnRsA 3VzBGxhbmcDZW4tVVMEcGtnAzJm MzVmM2VmLTU0ZmQtMzMzNC 1hZjRjLTgxOTk2MGExZjg4OARzZWMD bWl0X3NoYXJlBHNsawNtYWl

Peterson, M. J., & Benca, R. M. (2006). Sleep in mood disorders. *Psychiatric Clinics of North America, 29,* 1009–1032.

Petry, N. M., & Roll, J. M. (2006). Cognitive-behavioral treatments for pathological gambling. In P. M. Ghezzi, C. A. Lyons, M. R. Dixon, & G. Wilson (Eds.), *Gambling: Behavior theory, research, and application* (pp. 249–260). Reno, NV: Context Press.

Petty, J., & Oliver, C. (2005). Self-injurious behaviour in individuals with intellectual disabilities. *Current Opinion in Psychiatry, 18,* 484–489.

Phelps, J. A., Davis, J. O., & Schartz, K. M. (1997). Nature, nurture, and twin research strategies. *Current Directions in Psychological Science, 6,* 117–121.

Phillips, K. A., & Hollander, E. (2008). Treating body dysmorphic disorder with medication: Evidence, misconceptions, and a suggested approach. *Body Image, 5,* 13–27.

Phillips, L. (1953). Case history data and prognosis in schizophrenia. *Journal of Nervous and Mental Disease, 117,* 515–525.

Piacentini, J., & Langley, A. K. (2004). Cognitive-behavioral therapy for children who have obsessive-compulsive disorder. *Journal of Clinical Psychology/In Session, 60,* 1181–1194.

Piacentini, J., Woods, D. W., Scahill, L., Wilhelm, S., Peterson, A. L., Chang, S., & Walkup, J. T. (2010). Behavior therapy for children with Tourette disorder: A randomized controlled trial. *Journal of the American Medical Association, 303,* 1929–1937.

Pidsosny, I. C., & Virani, A. (2006). Pediatric psychopharmacology update: Psychostimulants and tics—past, present, and future. *Journal of the Canadian Academy of Child and Adolescent Psychiatry, 15,* 84–86.

Pignotti, M., & Mercer, J. (2007). Holding therapy and dyadic developmental psychotherapy are not supported and acceptable social work interventions: A systematic research synthesis revisited. *Research on Social Work Practice, 17,* 513–519.

Pilver, C. E., Libby, D. J., & Hoff, R. A. (2013). Premenstrual dysphoric disorder as a correlate of suicidal ideation, plans, and attempts among a nationally representative sample. *Social Psychiatry and Psychiatric Epidemiology, 48,* 437–446. doi:10.1007/s00127-012-0548-z

Pionek Stone, B., Kratochwill, T. R., Sladeczek, I., & Serlin, R. C. (2002). Treatment of selective mutism: A best-evidence synthesis. *School Psychology Quarterly, 17,* 168–190.

Pirkola, S., Sohlman, B., Helia, H., & Wahlbeck, K. (2007). Reductions in postdischarge suicide after deinstitutionalization and decentralization: A nationwide register study in Finland. *Psychiatric Services, 58,* 221–226.

Plante, D. T., & Winkelman, J. W. (2006). Parasomnias. *Psychiatric Clinics of North America, 29,* 969–987.

Plomin, R., & Kovas, Y. (2005). Generalist genes and learning disabilities. *Psychological Bulletin, 131,* 592–617.

Polansky, N. A., Borgman, R. D., & De Saix, C. (1972). *Roots of futility.* San Francisco, CA: Jossey-Bass.

Pollin, W., & Stabenau, J. R. (1968). Biological, psychological, and historical differences in a series of monozygotic twins discordant for schizophrenia. In D. Rosenthal, & S. S. Kety (Eds.), *The transmission of schizophrenia* (pp. 317–332). New York, NY: Pergamon.

Porter, J. C., & Ghezzi, P. M. (2006). Theories of pathological gambling. In P. M. Ghezi, C. A. Lyons, M. R. Dixon, & G. Wilson (Eds.), *Gambling: Behavior theory, research, and application* (pp. 19–43). Reno, NV: Context Press.

Post, R. M., Fink, E., Carpenter, W. T., & Goodwin, F. K. (1975). Cerebrospinal fluid amine metabolites in acute schizophrenia. *Archives of General Psychiatry, 32,* 1063–1069.

Potash, J. B., & DePaulo, J. R. (2000). Searching high and low: A review of the genetics of bipolar disorder. *Bipolar Disorders, 2,* 8–26.

Power, K., Simpson, R., Swanson, V., & Wallace, I. (1990). A controlled comparison of cognitive-behavior therapy, diazepam, and placebo, alone or in combination, for the treatment of generalized anxiety disorder. *Journal of Anxiety Disorders, 4,* 267–292.

Prescott, C. A., & Kendler, K. S. (1999). Genetic and environmental contribution to alcohol abuse and dependence in a population-based sample of male twins. *American Journal of Psychiatry, 156,* 34–40.

Prestia, A., Caroli, A., van der Flier, W. M., Ossenkoppele, R., Van Berckel, B., Barkhof, F., … Frisoni, G. B. (2013). Prediction of dementia in MCI patients based on core diagnostic markers for Alzheimer disease. *Neurology, 80,* 1048–1056.

Prien, R. J. (1979). Lithium in the prophylactic treatment of affective disorders. *Archives of General Psychiatry, 36,* 847–848.

Pronko, N. H. (1989). *From Al to Zeitgeist: A philosophical guide for the skeptical psychologists.* New York, NY: Greenwood Press.

Putnam, F. W. (1984). The psychophysiolgical investigation of multiple personality disorder: A review. *Psychiatric Clinics of North America, 7,* 31–39.

## Q

Quay, H. C. (1977). Psychopathic behavior: Reflections on its nature, origins, and treatment. In F. Weizman, & I. Izgiris, *The structuring of experience.* New York, NY: Plenum.

## R

Rachlin, H. (1991). *Introduction to modern behaviorism* (3rd ed.). New York, NY: W. H. Freeman and Company.

Rachman, S. (1966). Sexual fetishism: An experimental analogue. *Psychological Record, 16,* 293–295.

Rachman, S. (1977). The conditioning theory of fear acquisition: A critical examination. *Behavior Research and Therapy, 15,* 375–387.

Radtke, K. M., Ruf, M., Ruf, M., Gunter, H. M., Dohrmann, K., Schauer, M., … Elbert, T. (2011). Transgenerational impact of intimate partner violence on methylation in the promoter of the glucocorticoid receptor. *Translational Psychiatry, 1,* e21. doi:10.1038/tp.2011.21

Ragland, D. R., & Brand, R. J. (1988). Type A behavior and mortality from coronary heart disease. *New England Journal of Medicine, 318,* 65–69.

Rapoport, J. L., Buchsbaum, M., & Weingartner, H. (1980). Dextroamphetamine: Its cognitive and behavioral effects in normal and hyperactive boys and normal men. *Archives of General Psychiatry, 37,* 933–943.

Read, J., Van Os, J., Morrison, A. P., & Ross, C. A. (2005). Childhood trauma, psychosis, and schizophrenia: A literature review with theoretical and clinical implications. *Acta Psychiatrica Scandinavica, 112,* 330–350.

Regier, D. A., Narrow, W. E., Clarke, D. E., Kraemer, H. C., Kuramoto, J., Kuhl, E. A., & Kupfer, D. J. (2013). *DSM-5* field trials in the United States and Canada, part II: Test-retest reliability of selected categorical diagnoses. *American Journal of Psychiatry, 170,* 59–70. doi:10.1176/appi.ajp.2012.12070999

Regier, D. A., Narrow, W. E., Kuhl, E. A., & Kupfer, D. J. (2009). The conceptual development of *DSM-V. American Journal of Psychiatry, 166,* 645–650.

Reif, W., & Rojas, G. (2007). Stability of somatoform symptoms: Implications for classification. *Psychosomatic Medicine, 69,* 864–869.

Renard, G. M., Suarez, M. M., Levin, G. M., & Rivarola, M. A. (2005). Sex differences in rats: Effects of chronic stress on sympathetic system and anxiety. *Physiology & Behavior, 85,* 363–369.

Rhule, D. M. (2005). Take care to do no harm: Harmful interventions for youth problem behavior. *Professional Psychology: Research and Practice, 36,* 618–625.

Ricciardelli, L. A., & McCabe, M. P. (2004). A biopsychosocial model of disordered eating and the pursuit of muscularity in adolescent boys. *Psychological Bulletin, 130,* 179–2005.

Rice, T. (2003). Believe it or not: Religious and other paranormal beliefs in the United States. *Journal for the Scientific Study of Religion, 42,* 95–106.

Ricks, D., & Nameche, G. (1966). Symbiosis, sacrifice and schizophrenia. *Mental Hygiene, 50,* 541–551.

Rind, B., Tromovitch, P., & Bauserman, R. (1998). A meta-analytic examination of assumed properties of child sexual abuse using college samples. *Psychological Bulletin, 124,* 22–53.

Risch, N., Herrell, R., Lehner, T., Liang, K., Eaves, L., Hoh, J., & Merikangas, K. R. (2009). Interaction between the serotonin transporter gene (5-HTTLPR), stressful life events, and risk of depression: A meta-analysis. *Journal of the American Medical Association, 301,* 2462–2471.

Rivas-Vazquez, R. A., Blais, M. A., Rey, G. J., & Rivas-Vazques, A. A. (2000). Sexual dysfunction associated with antidepressant treatment. *Professional Psychology: Research and Practice, 31*, 641–651.

Robins, L. N. (1978). *The interaction of setting a predisposition in explaining novel behavior: Drug initiations before, in, and after Vietnam.* Washington, DC: Hemisphere.

Robins, L. N., Helzer, J. E., & Davis, D. H. (1975). Narcotic use in Southeast Asia and afterward: A interaction study of 898 Vietnam returnees. *Archives of General Psychiatry, 32*, 955–961.

Roelofs, K., Hoogduin, K. A., Keijsers, G. P., Naring, G. W., Moene, F. C., & Sandijck, P. (2002). Hypnotic susceptibility in patients with conversion disorder. *Journal of Abnormal Psychology, 111*, 309–395.

Rofé, Y. (2008). Does repression exist? Memory, pathogenic, unconscious and clinical evidence. *Review of General Psychology, 12*, 63–85.

Rogers, C. R. (1961). *On becoming a person.* Boston, MA: Houghton Mifflin.

Rogers, M. P., Reich, P., Strom, T. B., & Carpenter, C. B. (1976). Behaviorally conditioned immunosuppression: Replication of a recent study. *Psychosomatic Medicine, 38*, 447–451.

Rohan, K. J., Roecklein, K. A., Lacy, T. J., & Vacek, P. M. (2009). Winter depression recurrence one year after cognitive-behavioral therapy, light therapy, or combination treatment. *Behavior Therapy, 40*, 225–238.

Rollin, H. R. (2000). Psychiatry in 2000: A bird's eye view. *Psychiatric Bulletin, 24*, 11–15.

Rosen, G. (1968). *Madness in society.* Chicago, IL: University of Chicago Press.

Rosenfeld, D. S., & Elhajjar, A. J. (1998). Sleepsex: A variant of sleepwalking. *Archives of Sexual Behavior, 27*, 269–278.

Rosenhan, D. L. (1973). On being sane in insane places. *Science, 179*, 250–258.

Rosenthal, D., Wender, P. H., Kety, S. S., Schulsinger, F., Weiner, J., & Rieder, R. (1975). Parent-child relationships and psychopathological disorder in the child. *Archives of General Psychiatry, 32*, 466–476.

Rosenthal, R. J. (1992). Pathological gambling. *Psychiatric Annals, 22*, 72–78.

Rowland, D. L. (2007). Will medical solutions to sexual problems make sexological care and science obsolete? *Journal of Sex & Marital Therapy, 33*, 385–397.

Rowland, D., & Burek, M. (2007). Trends in research on premature ejaculation over the past 25 years. *Journal of Sexual Medicine, 4*, 1454–1461.

Roy-Burne, P. P., & Cowley, D. S. (2002). Pharmacological treatments for panic disorder, generalized anxiety disorder, specific phobia, and social anxiety disorder. In P. E. Nathan, & J. M. Gorman, *A guide to treatments that work* (2 ed., pp.

337–365). New York, NY: Oxford University Press.

Roy-Burne, P. P., Craske, M. G., & Stein, M. B. (2006). Panic Disorder. *Lancet, 368*, 1023–1032.

Russell, C. J., & Keel, P. K. (2002). Homosexuality as a specific risk factor for eating disorders in men. *International Journal of Eating Disorders, 31*, 300–306.

Rutter, M. J. (1997). Nature-nuture integration: The example of antisocial behavior. *American Psychologists, 52*, 390–398.

Ryder, A. G., Costa, P. T., & Bagby, R. M. (2007). Evaluation of the SCID-II personality disorder traits for *DSM-IV*: Coherence, relations with general personality traits, and functional impairment. *Journal of Personality Disorders, 21*, 626–637.

Ryder, A. G., Costa, P. T., & Bagby, R. M. (2007). Evaluation of the SCID-II personality disorder traits for *DSM-IV*: Coherence, relations with general personality traits, and functional impairment. *Journal of Personality Disorders, 21*, 626–637.

## S
- - - - -
Sadek, J. R., Johnson, S. A., White, D. A., Salmon, D. P., Taylor, K. I., DeLaPena, J. H., ... et al. (2004). Retrograde amnesia in dementia: Comparison of HIV-associated dementia, Alzheimer's disease, and Huntington's disease. *Neuropsychology, 18*, 692–699.

Salbach-Andre, H., Lenz, K., Simmendinger, N., Klinkowski, N., Lehmkuhl, U., & Pfeiffer, E. (2008). Psychiatric comorbidities among female adolescents with anorexia nervosa. *Child Psychiatry & Human Development, 39*, 261–272.

Salekin, R. T. (2002). Psychopathy and therapeutic pessimism: Clinical lore or clinical reality? *Clinical Psychology Review, 22*, 79–112.

Sánchez, H. G. (2001). Risk factor model for suicide assessment and intervention. *Professional Psychology: Research and Practice, 32*, 351–358.

Sar, V., Akyuz, G., & Dooan, O. (2007). Prevalence of dissociative disorders among women in the general population. *Psychiatry Research, 149*, 169–176.

Sartorius, N., Kaelber, C. T., Cooper, J. E., Roper, M. T., Rae, D. S., Gulbiant, W., ... Regier, D. A. (1993). Progress toward achieving a common language in psychiatry: Results from the field trial of the clinical guidelines accompanying the WHO classification of mental and behavioral disorders in ICD-10. *Archives of General Psychiatry, 50*, 115–124.

Sartouris, N., Kaelber, C. T., Cooper, J. E., Roper, M. T., Rae, D. S., Gulginat, W., ... Regier, D. A. (1993). Progress toward achieving a common language in psychiatry: Results from the filed trial of the clinical

guidelines accompanying the WHO classification of mental and behavioral disorders in ICD-10. *Archives of General Psychiatry, 50*, 115–124.

Sarwer, D. B., & Durlak, J. A. (1997). A field trail of the effectiveness of behavioral treatment for sexual dysfunctions. *Journal of Sex & Marital Therapy, 23*, 87–97.

Sateia, M. J., & Nowell, P. D. (2004). Insomnia. *Lancet, 364*, 1959–1973.

Scaglione, C., Vignatelli, L., Plazzi, G., Marchese, R., Nerotti, A., Rizzo, G., ... et al. (2004). REM sleep behaviour disorders in Parkinson's disease: A questionnaire-based study. *Neurological Sciences, 25*, 316–321.

Schenck, C. H., Amulf, I., & Mahowald, M. W. (2007). Sleep and sex: What can go wrong? A review of literature on sleep related disorders and abnormal sexual behaviors and experiences. *Sleep: Journal of Sleep and Sleep Disorders Research, 30*, 683–702.

Schmauk, F. J. (1970). Punishment, arousal, and avoidance learning. *Journal of Abnormal Psychology, 76*, 325–335.

Schneiderman, N., Ironson, G., & Siegal, S. D. (2005). Stress and health: Psychological, behavioral, and biological determinates. *Annual Review of Clinical Psychology, 1*, 607–628.

Schramm, E., Hohagen, F., Grasshoff, U., Riemann, D., Hajak, G., Weep, H., & Berger, M. (1993). Test-retest reliability and validity of the structured interview for sleep disorders according to *DSM-III-R. American Journal of Psychiatry, 150*, 867–872.

Schreier, A., Wolke, D., Thomas, K., Horwood, J., Hollis, C., Gunnell, D., & Harrison, g. (2009). Prospective study of peer victimization in childhood and psychotic symptoms in a nonclinical population at age 12 years. *Archives of General Psychiatry, 66*, 527–536.

Schwarte, A. R. (2008). Fragile X syndrome. *School Psychology Quarterly, 23*, 290–300.

Schwartz, R. P., Jaffe, J. H., Highfield, D. A., Callaman, J. M., & O'Grady, K. E. (2007). A randomized controlled trial of interim methadone maintenance: 10-month follow-up. *Drug and Alcohol Dependence, 86*, 30–36.

Segal, N. L. (2006). Two monozygotic twin pairs discordant for female-to-male transsexualism. *Archives of Sexual Behavior, 35*, 347–358.

Segerstrom, S. C., & Miller, G. E. (2004). Psychological stress and the human immune system: A meta-analytic study of 30 years of inquiry. *Psychological Bulletin, 130*, 601–630.

Segraves, R. T. (2003). Pharmacologic management of sexual dysfunction: Benefits and limitations. *CNS Spectrums, 8*, 225–229.

Segraves, R. T., & Althof, S. (2002). Psychotherapy and pharmacotherapy for sexual dysfunctions. In P. E. Nathan, & J. M.

Gorman, *A guide to treatments that work* (2 ed., pp. 497–524). New York, NY: Oxford University Press.

Selfe, L. (1977). *Nadia: A case of extraordinary drawing ability in an autistic child.* New York, NY: Academic Press.

Seligman, M. E., Rashid, T., & Parks, A. C. (2006). Positive psychotherapy. *American Psychologist, 61*, 774–778.

Seligman, M. E., Steen, T. A., Park, N., & Peterson, C. (2005). Positive psychology progress: Empirical validation of interventions. *American Psychologist, 60*, 410–421. doi:DOI: 10.1037/0003-066X.60.5.410

Seligman, M. P. (1968). Chronic fear produced by unpredictable electric shock. *Journal of Comparative and Physiological Psychology, 66*, 402–411.

Seligman, M. P. (1975). *Helplessness: On depression, development, and death.* San Francisco, CA: W. H. Freeman.

Seligman, M., & Hager, J. (Eds.). (1972). *Biological boundaries of learning.* New York, NY: Appleton.

Selye, H. (1956). *The stress of life.* New York, NY: McGraw-Hill.

Seto, M. C., Cantor, J. M., & Blanchard, R. (2006). Child pornography offenses are a valid diagnostic indicator of pedophilia. *Journal of Abnormal Psychology, 115*, 610–615.

Shakow, D. (1961). Segmental set: A theory of the formal psychological deficit in schizophrenia. *Archives of General Psychiatry, 6*, 1–17.

Shandera, A. L., Berry, D. T., Clark, J. A., Schipper, L. J., Graue, L. O., & Harp, J. P. (2010). Detection of malingered mental retardation. *Psychological Assessment, 22*, 50–56. doi:10.1037/a0016585

Shapiro, F. (1995). *Eye movement desensitization and reprocessing.* New York, NY: Guilford.

Sheehan, J. G. (1975). Conflict theory and avoidance-reduction therapy. In J. Eisenson, *Stuttering: A second symposium* (pp. 97–198). New York, NY: Harper & Row.

Sheets, E., & Craighead, W. E. (2007). Toward an empirically based classification of personality pathology. *Clinical Psychology: Science and Practice, 14*, 77–93.

Sheitman, B. B., Kinon, B. J., Ridgway, B. A., & Lieberman, J. A. (1998). Pharmacological treatments of schizophrenia. In P. E. Nathan, & J. M. Gorman, *A guide to treatments that work* (pp. 167–189). New York, NY: Oxford University Press.

Shen, X., & Millet, L. (2012). *Suicide in Oregon: Trends and risk factors.* Oregon Health Authority. Portland, OR: 2012 Report. From http://public.health.oregon.gov/DiseasesConditions/InjuryFatalityData/Pages/nvdrs.aspx

Shneidman, E. S. (1955). Acute paranoid schizophrenia in a veteran. In A. Burton, & R. E. Harris, *Clinical studies of personality.* New York, NY: Harper & Row.

Sieber, W. J., Rodin, J., Larson, L., Ortega, S., Cummings, N., Levy, S., ... Herberman, R. (1992). Modulation of human natural killer cell activity by exposure to uncontrollable stress. *Brain, Behavior, and Immunity, 6*, 141–156.

Siegal, S. (1999). Drug anticipation and drug addiction: The 1998 H. David Archibald Lecture. *Addiction, 94*, 1113–1124.

Siegal, S., Hinson, R. E., Krank, M. D., & McCully, J. (1982). Heroin "over-dose" death: Contribution of drug-associated environmental cues. *Science, 216*, 436–437.

Siever, L. J., & Davis, K. L. (2004). The pathophysiology of schizophrenia disorders: Perspectives from the spectrum. *American Journal of Psychiatry, 161*, 398–413.

Siever, M. D. (1994). Sexual orientation and gender as factors in socioculturally acquired vulnerability to body dissatisfaction and eating disorders. *Journal of Consulting and Clinical Psychology, 62*, 252–260.

Simeon, D., & Knutelska, M. (2005). An open trial of naltrexone in the treatment of depersonalization disorder. *Journal of Clinical Psychopharmacology, 25*, 267–270.

Simeon, D., Knutelska, M., Nelson, D., & Guralnik, O. (2003). Feeling unreal: A depersonalization disorder update of 117 cases. *Journal of Clinical Psychiatry, 64*, 990–997.

Simon, G. E. (2002). Management of somatoform and factitious disorders. In P. E. Nathan, & J. M. Gorman, *A guide to treatments that work* (2 ed., pp. 447–461). New York, NY: Oxford University Press.

Simpson, S. G., McMahon, F. J., McInnis, M. G., MacKinnon, D. F., Edwin, D., Folstein, S. E., & DePaulo, J. R. (2002). Diagnostic reliability of bipolar II disorders. *Archives of General Psychiatry, 59*, 736–740.

Skinner, B. F. (1938). *The behavior of organisms.* New York, NY: Appleton.

Skinner, B. F. (1953). *Science and human behavior.* New York, NY: Macmillan.

Skinner, B. F. (1981). Selection by consequences. *Science, 213*, 501–504.

Skinner, B. F. (1987). A humanist alternative to A.A.'s Twelve Steps: A human centered approach to conquering alcoholism. *The Humanist, 47*, 5. Retrieved July/August 1987.

Slaikeu, K. A. (1990). *Crisis intervention: A handbook for practice and research* (2nd ed.). Boston, NY: Ally and Bacon.

Slater, E. (1961). The thirty-five Maudsley lecture: "Hysteria 311." *Journal of Mental Science, 107*, 359–381.

Smart, R. G., & Fejer, D. (1972). Drug use among adolescents and their parents: Closing the generation gap in mood modification. *Journal of Abnormal Psychology, 79*, 153–160.

Smith, J. E., Meyers, R. J., & Delaney, H. D. (1998). The community reinforcement approach with homeless alcohol-dependent individuals. *Journal of Consulting and Clinical Psychology, 66*, 541–548.

Smith, R. C., Gardiner, J. C., Lyles, J. S., Sirbu, C., Dwamean, F. C., Hodges, A., & Collins, C. (2005). Exploration of *DSM-IV* criteria in primary care patients with medically unexplained symptoms. *Psychosomatic Medicine, 67*, 123–129.

Smoller, J. W., Craddock, N., Kendler, K., Lee, P. H., Neale, B. M., Nurnberger, J. I., ... Sullivan, P. F. (2013). Identification of risk loci with shared effects on five major psychiatric disorders: A genome-wide analysis. *Lancet, 381*, 1371–1379. doi:10.1016/S0140-6736(12)62129-1

Snyder, S. H. (1974). *Madness and the brain.* New York, NY: McGraw-Hill.

Sobell, M. B., & Sobell, L. C. (1973). Individualized behavior therapy for alcoholics. *Behavior Therapy, 4*, 49–72.

Sobell, M. B., & Sobell, L. C. (1995). Controlled drinking after 25 years: How important was the great debate. *Addiction, 90*, 1145–1153.

Sohn, M., & Bosinski, H. (2007). Gender identity disorders: Diagnostic and surgical aspects. *Journal of Sexual Medicine, 4*, 1193–1208.

Sotile, W. M., & Kilmann, P. R. (1977). Treatments of psychogenic female sexual dysfunctions. *Psychological Bulletin, 84*, 619–633.

Spangler, D. L. (1999). Cognitive-behavioral therapy for bulimia nervosa: An illustration. *Journal of Clinical Psychology/ In Session, 55*, 699–713.

Spanos, N. K. (1994). Multiple identity enactments and multiple personality disorder: A sociocognitive perspective. *Psychological Bulletin, 116*, 143–165.

Spanos, N. K., Weekes, J. R., & Bertrand, L. D. (1985). Multiple personality: A social psychological perspective. *Journal of Abnormal Psychology, 94*, 362–376.

Spitz, R. A. (1946). Anaclitic depression. *The Psychoanalytic Study of the Child, 2*, 313–342.

Spitzer, C., Barnow, S., Gau, K., Freyberger, H. J., & Grabe, H. J. (2008). Childhood maltreatment in patients with somatization disorder. *Australian and New Zealand Journal of Psychiatry, 42*, 335–341.

Spitzer, R. L., Williams, J. B., Gibbson, M., & First, M. B. (1990). *Structured clinical interview for DSM-III-R (SCID).* Washington, DC: American Psychiatric Association.

Srole, L., Langer, T. S., Michael, S. T., Opler, M. K., & Rennie, T. C. (1962). *Mental health in the metropolis: Midtown Manhattan study* (Vol. 1). New York, NY: McGraw-Hill.

Staal, W. G., Pol, H. E., Schnack, H. G., van Haren, N. E., Seifert, M., & Kahn, R. S. (2001). Structural abnormalities in chronic schizophrenia at the extremes of the outcome spectrum. *American Journal of Psychiatry, 158*, 1140–1142.

Starkey, M. L. (1961). *The devil in Massachusetts*. New York, NY: Doubleday.

Starkstein, S. E., & Jorge, R. (2005). Dementia after traumatic brain injury. *International Psychogeriatrics, 17*(Suppl 1), S93–S107.

Stein, D. J., Grant, J. E., Franklin, M. E., Keuthen, N., Lochner, C., Singe, H. S., & Woods, D. W. (2010). Trichotillomania (hair pulling disorder), skin picking disorder, and stereotypic movement disorder: Toward the *DSM-5*. *Depression and Anxiety, 27*, 611–626. doi:10.1002/da.20700

Steiner, M., Dunn, E., & Born, L. (2003). Hormones and mood: From menarche to menopause and beyond. *Journal of Affective Disorders, 74*, 67–83.

Steinhausen, H. (2002). The outcome of anorexia nervosa in the 20th century. *American Journal of Psychiatry, 159*, 1284–1293.

Steketee, G., Frost, R. O., Tolin, D. F., Rasmussen, J., & Brown, T. A. (2010). Waitlist-controlled trial of cognitive behavior therapy for hoarding disorder. *Depression and Anxiety, 27*, 476–484. doi:10.1002/da.20673

Stephens, J. H., O'Connor, G. O., & Wiener, G. (1968). Long-term prognosis in schizophrenia using the Becker-Wittman Scale and the Phillips Scale. *Presented in the 124th Annual Meeting of the American Psychiatric Association*.

Stephens, R. S., Roffman, R. A., & Curtin, L. (2000). Comparison of extended versus brief treatments for marijuana use. *Journal of Consulting and Clinical Psychology, 68*, 898–908.

Stice, E. (2001). A prospective test of the dual-pathway model of bulimic pathology: Mediating effects of dieting and negative affect. *Journal of Abnormal Psychology, 110*, 124–135.

Stolzer, J. M. (2007). The ADHD epidemic in America. *Ethical Human Psychology and Psychiatry, 9*, 109–116.

Strain, J. J., & Newcorn, J. H. (2004). Adjustment Disorders. In R. E. Hales, & S. C. Yudofsky, *Essentials of clinical psychiatry* (2 ed., pp. 527–541). Washington, DC: American Psychiatric Publishing, Inc.

Straneva, P. A., Maixner, W., Light, K. C., Pedersen, C. A., Costello, N. L., & Girdler, S. S. (2007). Menstrual cycle, beta-endorphins, and pain sensitivity in premenstrual dysphoric disorder. *Health Psychology, 26*, 201–213. doi:10.1037/0278-6133.21.4.358

Stravynski, A., Gaudette, G., Lesage, A., Arbel, N., Bounader, J., Lanchance, L., ... Fabian, J. (2007). The treatment of sexually dysfunctional women without partners: A controlled study of three behavioural group approaches. *Clinical Psychology and Psychotherapy, 14*, 211–220.

Striegel-Moore, R. H., & Bulik, C. M. (2007). Risk factors for eating disorders. *American Psychologist, 62*, 181–198.

Substance Abuse and Mental Health Services Administration. (2006). The NSDUH Report. *Department of Health and Human Services, SAMHSA, Office of Applied Studies, 30*. Retrieved 1 September, 2008, from http://oas.samhsa.gov/2k6/raceCigs/raceCigs.htm

Sullivan, H. S. (1953). *The interpersonal theory of psychiatry*. New York, NY: Norton.

Sumathipala, A. (2007). What is the evidence for the efficacy of treatments for somatoform disorders? A critical review of previous intervention studies. *Psychosomatic Medicine, 69*, 889–900.

Sundgot-Borgen, J. (1994). Risk and trigger factors for the development of eating disorders in female elite athletes. *Medicine & Science in Sports & Exercise, 26*, 414–419.

Swain, J. E., Scahill, L., Lombroso, P. L., King, R. A., & Leckman, J. F. (2007). Tourette syndrome and tic disorders: A decade of progress. *Journal of the American Academy of Child & Adolescent Psychiatry, 46*, 947–968.

Swanson, J. M., Elliott, G. R., Greenhill, L. L., Wigal, T., Arnold, L. E., Vitiello, B., ... et al. (2007). Effects of stimulant medication on growth rates across 3 years in the MTA follow-up. *Journal of the American Academy of Child & Adolescent Psychiatry, 46*, 1015–1027.

Symkal, A., & Thorne, F. C. (1951). Etiological studies of psychopathic personality. *Journal of Clinical Psychology, 7*, 299–316.

Symons, F. J., Tapp, J., Wulfsberg, A., Sutton, K. A., Heeth, W. L., & Bodfish, J. W. (2001). Sequential analysis of the effects of naltrexone on the environmental meditation of self-injurious behavior. *Experimental and Clinical Psychopharmacology, 9*, 269–276.

Szasa, T. S. (1960). The myth of mental illness. *American Psychologists, 15*, 113–118.

Szasz, T. (1991). Diagnoses are not diseases. *The Lancet, 338*, 1574–1576. doi:10.1016/0140-6736(91)92387-H


## T

Tandon, R., Keshaven, M. S., & Nasrallah, H. A. (2008). Schizophrenia, "just the facts": What we know in 2008. 2. Epidemiology and etiology. *Schizophrenia Research, 102*, 1–18.

Taylor, N. (1963). *Narcotics: Nature's dangerous gift*. New York: Delta Books.

Teesson, M., Lynskey, M., Manor, B., & Baillie, A. (2002). The structure of cannabis dependence in the community. *Drug and Alcohol Dependence, 68*, 255–262.

Thase, M. E., & Kupfer, D. J. (1996). Recent development in the pharmacotherapy of mood disorders. *Journal of Consulting and Clinical Psychology, 64*, 646–659.

Thomas, A., Bonanni, L., & Onofrj, M. (2007). Symptomatic REM sleep behaviour disorder. *Neurological Sciences, 28*(Suppl 1), S21–S36.

Thorndike, E. L. (1911). *Animal intelligence*. New York, NY: Macmillan.

Timimi, S., & co-signers. (2004). A critique of the international consensus statement on ADHD. *Clinical Child and Family Psychology Review, 7*, 59–61.

Timpano, K., Exner, C., Glaesmer, H., Rief, W., Keshaviah, A., Brahler, E., & Wilhelm, S. (2011). The epidemiology of the proposed *DSM-5* hoarding disorder: Exploration of the acquisition specifier, associated features, and distress. *Journal of Clinical Psychiatry, 72*, 780–786.

Toce-Gerstein, M., Gerstein, D. R., & Volberg, R. A. (2003). A hierarchy of gambling disorders in the community. *Addiction, 98*, 1661–1672.

Torrey, E. F. (2002). Studies of individuals with schizophrenia never treated with antipsychotic mediations: A review. *Schizophrenia Research, 58*, 101–115.

Torrey, E. F., Bowler, A. E., Taylor, E. H., & Gottesman, I. I. (1994). *Schizophrenia and manic-depressive disorder: The biological roots of mental illness as revealed by the landmark study of identical twins*. New York, NY: Basic Books.

Trueblood, W., & Schmidt, M. (1993). Malingering and other validity considerations in the neuropsychological evaluation of mild head injury. *Journal of Clinical and Experimental Neuropsychology, 15*, 579–590.

Turner, E. H., Matthews, A. M., Linardatos, E., Tell, R. A., & Rosenthal, R. (2008). Selective publication of antidepressant trials and its influence on apparent efficacy. *New England Journal of Medicine, 358*, 252–260.

Turner, R. J., & Wagondfeld, M. O. (1967). Occupational mobility and schizophrenia. *American Sociological Reviews, 32*, 104–113.

Tyrer, P., & Baldwin, D. (2006). Generalized anxiety disorder. *Lancet, 368*, 2156–2166.

Tyrer, P., Oliver-Africano, P. C., Ahmed, Z., Bouras, N., Cooray, S., Deb, S., ... Hare, M. (2008). Risperidone, haloperidol, and placebo in the treatment of aggressive challenging behaviour in patients with intellectual disability: A randomised controlled trial. *Lancet, 371*, 57–63.

Tyson, A. S. (2006, December Wednesday 20). Repeat Iraq tours raise risks of PTSD, Army finds. *Washington Post*.


## U

U.S. Department of Health and Human Services. (1988). *The health consequences of smoking: Nicotine addiction. A report of the Surgeon General (DHHS Publication No. (CDC) 88-*

*8406).* Washington, DC: U.S. Government Printing Office.

U.S. Department of Health, Education, and Welfare. (1979). *Smoking and health: A report of the surgeon general (DHEW Publication No, (PHS) 79-500066).* Washington, DC: U.S. Government Printing Office.

## V

Valenstein, E. S. (1998). *Blaming the brain: The truth about drugs and mental health.* New York, NY: Free Press.

Valliant, P. M., Hawkins, T. J., & Pottier, D. C. (1998). Comparison of psychopathic and general offenders in cognitive behavioral therapy. *Psychological Reports, 82,* 753–754.

van der Gaag, M., Nieman, D. H., Rietdijk, J., Dragt, S., Ising, H. K., Klaassen, R. M., ... Linszen, D. H. (2012). Cognitive behavioral therapy for subjects at ultrahigh risk for developing psychosis: A randomized controlled clinical trial. *Schizophrenia Bulletin, 38,* 1180–1188.

van Pragg, H. M. (2005). Mood and anxiety disorders: A diagnostic pleonasm? In E. Griez, D. Faravelli, D. Nutt, & J. Zohar, *Mood disorders: Clinical management and research issues* (pp. 491–502). New York, NY: Wiley.

Velakoulis, D., Wood, S. J., McGorry, P. D., Yung, A., Phillips, L., Smith, D., ... Pantelis, C. (2006). Hippocampal and amygdala volumes according to psychosis stage and diagnosis: A magnetic resonance imaging study of chronic schizophrenia, first-episode psychosis, and ultra–high risk individuals. *Archives of General Psychiatry, 63,* 139–149. doi:10.1001/archpsyc.63.2.139

Verheul, R., & Widiger, T. A. (2004). A meta-analysis of the prevalence and usage of the personality disorder not otherwise specified (PDNOS) diagnosis. *Journal of Personality Disorders, 18,* 309–319.

Vgontz, A. N., & Kales, A. (1999). Sleep and its disorders. *Annual Review of Medicine, 50,* 387–400.

Visintainer, M. A., Volpicelli, J. R., & Seligman, M. E. (1982). Tumor rejection in rats after inescapable or escapable shock. *Science, 216,* 437–439.

Vogle, E. H., Castro, M. E., Solar, P. A., & Soto, F. A. (2007). Enhancement of Pavlovian conditioned immunosuppression in rats. *Acta Neurobiologiae Experimentalis, 67,* 71–81.

Vogler, R. E., Weissbach, T. A., & Compton, J. V. (1977). Learning techniques for alcohol abuse. *Behavior Research and Therapy, 15,* 31–38.

Volker, M. A., & Lopata, C. (2008). Autism: A review of biological bases, assessment, and intervention. *School Psychology Quarterly, 23,* 258–270.

## W

Wagaman, J. R., Miltenberger, R. G., & Arndorfer, R. E. (1993). Analysis of a simplified treatment for stuttering in children. *Journal of Applied Behavior Analysis, 26,* 53–61.

Waldinger, M. D. (2007). Premature ejaculation. *Primary Psychiatry, 14,* 58–64.

Walker, E., Downey, G., & Caspi, A. (1991). Twin studies of psychopathology: Why do the concordance rates vary? *Schizophrenia Research, 5,* 211–221. doi:10.1016/0920-9964(91)90079-7

Walsh, T., McClellan, J. M., McCarthy, S. E., Addington, A. M., Pierce, S. B., & Cooper, G. M. (2008, March 27). Rare structural variants disrupt multiple genes in neurodevelopment pathways in schizophrenia. *Science.* doi:10.1126/science.115174

Walters, G. D. (2002). The heritability of alcohol abuse and dependence: A meta-analysis of behavior genetic research. *American Journal of Drug & Alcohol Abuse, 28,* 557–584.

Warheit, G. J., Holzer, C. E., & Arey, S. A. (1975). Race and mental illness: An epidemiological update. *Journal of Health and Social Behavior, 16,* 243–256.

Waring, M., & Ricks, D. (1965). Family patterns of children who become adult schizophrenics. *Journal of Nervous and Mental Disease, 140,* 351–364.

Watson, J. B. (1913). Psychology as the behaviorist views it. *Psychological Review, 20,* 158–177.

Watson, J. B., & Rayner, R. (1920). Conditioned emotional reactions. *Journal of Experimental Psychology, 3,* 1-14.

Weatherly, J. N., & Dixon, M. R. (2007). Toward an integrative behavioral model of gambling. *Analysis of Gambling Behavior, 1,* 4–18.

Webster-Stratton, C., & Hammond, M. (1997). Treating children with early-onset conduct problems: A comparison of child and parent training interventions. *Journal of Consulting and Clinical Psychology, 65,* 93–109.

Wedding, D., Kohout, J., Megel, M. B., Ohlemiller, M., Ulion, M., Cook, K., ... Braddock, S. (2007). Psychologists' knowledge and attitudes about fetal alcohol spectrum disorders, and alcohol use during pregnancy. *Professional Psychology: Research and Practice, 38,* 208–213.

Wedner, P. H. (1963). Dementia praecox: The development of the concept. *American Journal of Psychiatry, 119,* 1143–1151.

Weich, S., Sloggett, A., & Glyn, L. (1998). Social roles and gender differences in the prevalence of common mental disorders. *British Journal of Psychiatry, 173,* 489–493.

Weiss, G., Kruger, E., Danielson, V., & Elman, M. (1974). Long-term methylphenidate treatment of hyperkinetic children. *Psychopharmacology Bulletin, 10,* 34–35.

Weiss, J. M. (1970). Somatic effects of predictable and unpredictable shock. *Psychosomatic Medicine, 32,* 397–408.

Weiss, J. M. (1971). Effects of coping behavior in different warning signal conditions on stress pathology in rats. *Journal of Comparative and Physiological Psychology, 77,* 1–13.

Weissman, M. M., & Myers, J. K. (1978). Rates and risks of depressive symptoms in a United States urban community. *Acta Psychiartrica Scandinavica, 57,* 219–231.

Weissman, M. M., & Myers, J. K. (1978). Rates and risks of depressive symptoms in a United States urban community. *Acta Psychiatrica Scandinavica, 57,* 219–231.

Wells, M. C., Glickauf-Hughes, C., & Buzzell, V. (1990). Treating obsessive-compulsive personalities in psychodynamic/interpersonal group therapy. *Psychotherapy: Theory, Research, Practice, Training, 27,* 366.

Wender, P. H., Rosenthal, D., Rainer, J. D., Greenhill, L., & Sarlin, B. (1977). Schizophrenics' adopting parents. *Archives of General Psychiatry, 34,* 777–785.

Western, D., Shelder, J., Durrett, C., Glass, S., & Martens, A. (2003). Personality diagnoses in adolescence: *DSMV-IV* Axis II diagnoses and an empirically derived alternative. *American Journal of Psychiatry, 160,* 952–966.

Whitfield, C., Dube, S., Felitti, V., & Anda, R. (2005). Adverse childhood experiences and hallucinations. *Child Abuse & Neglect, 29,* 797–810.

Wicksell, R. K., Melin, L., Lekander, M., & Olsson, G. L. (2009). Evaluating the effectiveness of exposure and acceptance strategies to improve functioning and quality of life in longstanding pediatric pain—a randomized controlled trial. *Pain, 141,* 248–257.

Widiger, T. A. (2007). Alternatives to *DSM-IV*: Axis II. In W. O'Donohue, K. A. Fowler, & S. O. Lilienfeld, *Personality disorders: Toward the DSM-V* (pp. 21–40). Thousand Oaks, CA: Sage Publications, Inc.

Widiger, T. A., Costa Jr, P. T., & McCrae, R. R. (2002). A proposal for Axis II: Diagnosing personality disorders using the five-factor model. In P. T. Costa, & T. A. Widiger, *Personality disorders and the five-factor model of personality* (2nd ed., pp. 431–456). Washington, DC: American Psychological Association.

Willerman, L., & Cohen, D. B. (1990). *Psychopathology.* New York: McGraw-Hill.

Williams, B. (2001). Two-factor theory has strong empirical evidence of validity. *Journal of the Experimental Analysis of Behavior, 75,* 362–365.

Williams, J., Hadjistavropoulos, T., & Sharpe, D. (2006). A meta-analysis of psychological treatments for body dysmorphic disorders. *Behaviour Research Therapy, 44,* 99–11.

Williams, R. B., & Schneiderman, N. (2002). Resolved: Psychosocial interventions can improve clinical outcomes in organic disease (Pro). *Psychosomatic Medicine, 64*, 552–557.

Wilson, E. J., MacLeod, C., Mathews, A., & Rutherford, E. M. (2006). The causal role of interpretive bias in anxiety reactivity. *Journal of Abnormal Psychology, 115*, 103–111.

Wilson, G. T., & Fairburn, C. G. (2002). Treatment for eating disorders. In P. E. Nathan & J. M. Gorman, *A guide to treatments that work* (2 ed., pp. 559–592). New York, NY: Oxford University Press.

Wilson, G. T., Grilo, C. M., & Vitousek, K. M. (2007). Psychological treatments of eating disorders. *American Psychologist, 62*, 199–216.

Wilson, G. T., Nathan, P. E., O'Leary, K. D., & Clark, L. A. (1996). *Abnormal psychology: integrating perspectives*. Boston: Allyn & Bacon.

Wingate, M. E. (1976). *Stuttering: Theory and treatment*. New York, NY: Wiley.

Winick, B. J. (1995). Ambiguities of the legal meaning and significance of mental illness. *Psychology, Public Policy, and Law, 1*, 534–611.

Winokur, G., Reich, T., Rimmer, J., & Pitts, E. N. (1970). Alcoholism III: Diagnosis and familial psychiatric illness in 259 alcoholic probands. *Archives of General Psychiatry, 23*, 104–111.

Winsberg, M., Cassic, K. S., & Koran, L. M. (1999). Hoarding in obsessive-compulsive disorder: A report of 20 cases. *Journal of Clinical Psychiatry, 60*, 591–597. doi: 10.4088/JCP.v60n0905

Wisman, E. M. (2012). The role of large pedigrees in an era of high-throughput. *Human Genetics, 131*, 1555–1563. doi:10.1007/s00439-012-1190-2

Witkin, M. J., Atay, J., & Manderscheid, R. W. (1996). Trends in state and county mental hospitals in the U.S. from 1970 to 1922. *Psychiatric Services, 47*, 1079–1081.

Wolf, M., & Bowers, P. G. (1999). The double-deficit hypothesis for the developmental dyslexias. *Journal of Educational Psychology, 91*, 415–438.

Wolff, P. (1972). Ethnic differences in alcohol sensitivity. *Science, 125*, 449–451.

Wolfs, C. A., Dirksen, C. D., Severens, J. L., & Verhey, F. R. (2006). The added value of a multidisciplinary approach in diagnosing dementia: A review. *International Journal of Geriatric Psychiatry, 21*, 223–232.

Wolpe, J. (1958). *Psychotherapy by reciprocal inhibition*. Stanford, CA: Stanford University Press.

Wolpe, J. (1973). *The practice of behavior therapy*. New York, NY: Pergamon.

Wolpe, J., & Rachman, S. (1960). Psychoanalytic "evidence": A critique based on Freud's case of Little Hans. *Journal of Nervous and Mental Disease, 131*, 135–147.

Wood, J. M., Nezworski, M. T., Garb, H. N., & Lilienfeld, S. O. (2001). Problems with the norms of the comprehensive system for the Rorschach; Methodological and conceptual considerations. *Clinical Psychology: Science and Practice, 8*, 397–402.

Woo-Ming, A., & Siever, L. J. (1998). Psychopharmacological treatment of personality disorders. In P. E. Nathan, & J. M. Gorman (Eds.), *A guide to treatments that work* (pp. 554–567). New York, NY: Oxford University Press.

World Health Organization. (2004). Global status report on alcohol. *Geneva: Department of Mental Health and Substance Abuse*. Retrieved 2008 1-September from www.who.int/substance_abuse/publications/global_status_report_2004_overview.pdf

Wortman, C. B., & Dintzer, L. (1978). Is an attributional analysis of the learned helplessness phenomenon viable? A critique of the Abramson-Seligman-Teasdale reformulation. *Journal of Abnormal Psychology, 87*, 75–90.

Wynne, L. C., Singer, M. T., & Toohey, M. L. (1976). Communication of the adoptive parents of schizophrenics. In J. Jorstad, & J. Ugelstad, *Schizophrenia 75: Psychotherapy, family studies research: Proceedings of the fifth international symposium on the psychotherapy of schizophrenia*. Oslo, Norway: Lie & Co.

## Y

Yalom, I. D., Green, R., & Fisk, N. (1973). Prenatal exposure to female hormones. *Archives of General Psychiatry, 28*, 554–560.

Yan, L. L., Liu, K., Matthews, K. A., Daviglus, M. L., Ferguson, T. F., & Kiefe, C. I. (2003). Psychosocial risk factors and risk of hypertension: The coronary artery risk development in young adults (CAR-DIA) study. *Journal od the American Medical Association, 290*, 2138–2148.

Yehaud, R., Marshall, R., Penkower, A., & Wong, C. M. (2002). Pharmacological treatments for posttraumatic stress disorder. In P. E. Nathan, & J. M. Gorman, *A guide to treatments that work* (2 ed., pp. 441–445). New York, NY: Oxford Press.

Yirmiya, N., Erel, O., Shaked, M., & Solomonica-Levi, D. (1998). Meta-analyses comparing theory of mind abilities of individuals with autism, individuals with mental retardation, and normally developing individuals. *Psychological Bulletin, 124*, 283–307.

## Z

Zahn, T. P. (1977). Autonomic nervous system characteristics possibly related to a genetic predisposition to schizophrenia. *Schizophrenia Bulletin, 3*, 49–60.

Ziegler, D. K., & Schlemmer, R. B. (1994). Familial psychogenic blindness and headache: A case study. *Journal of Clinical Psychiatry, 55*, 114–117.

Zigler, E. (1967). Familial mental retardation: A continuing dilemma. *Science, 155*, 292–298.

Zilberstein, K. (2006). Clarifying core characteristics of attachment disorders: A review of current research and theory. *American Journal of Orthopsychiatry, 76*, 55–64.

Zilboorg, G., & Henry, G. W. (1941). *A history of medical psychology*. New York, NY: Norton.

Zimmerman, M., Rothschild, L., & Chelminski, I. (2005). The prevalence of *DSM-IV* personality disorders in psychiatric outpatients. *American Journal of Psychiatry, 162*, 1911–1918.

Zubin, J., & Spring, B. (1977). Vulnerability: A new view of schizophrenia. *Journal of Abnormal Psychology, 86*, 103–126.

Zubin, J., Eron, L. D., & Schumer, F. (1965). *An experimental approach to projective techniques*. New York, NY: Wiley.

Zweig, S. (1932). *Mental healers: Franz Anton Mesmer, Mary Baker Eddy, Sigmund Freud*. New York, NY: Frederick Unger.

# Name Index

# Subject Index